MIKE WORSMAN

THE HAPPIEST

people, places and ideas on earth

First published in Australia in 2023 by TOBIN & FINCH

Copyright © Michael Peter Worsman, 2023

All rights reserved. No part of this book may be reproduced in any form or by any means, electronic or mechanical, including photocopying, recording or by any information or retrieval, without prior permission in writing from the publisher. Under the Australian Copyright Act 1968 (the Act), a maximum of one chapter or 10 per cent of the book, whichever is the greater, may be photocopied by any educational institution for its educational purposes provided that the education institution (or the body that administers it) has given a remuneration notice to Copyright Agency Limited (CAL) under the Act.

A CIP catalogue record for this title is available from the National Library of Australia.

Mike Worsman
The Happiest

ISBN 978-0-6456927-0-9

Please note: Some names and details have been changed or omitted from this book for security and personal reasons.

For more information, opportunities or orders visit
www.thehappiest.com

Author: Mike Worsman
Editor: Andrew Tobin
Cover images by Mike Worsman, with thanks to all those beautiful people who graciously let me capture their image and stories.
Cover design by Mike Worsman.
Text design by Albany Wong and Mike Worsman.

A few words from the author

One question I've always asked myself is: what would I regret most if I died tomorrow?

When I pondered this on the eve of my 30th birthday, in August 2016, I had just one clear and resounding answer screaming at me: not sharing all those astonishing stories and insights I'd come across that had let me become my happiest self.

Two weeks later I started to write this book, which documents the happiest (and unhappiest) people, places and ideas on earth - or at least those I've encountered, as I've journeyed across six continents and more than 75 countries seeking answers to life's most important questions.

Contents

1	THE PAIN AND THE EXPLODING PLANE	1
2	MY SISTER AND THE SECURITY GUARD	29
3	THE BIKER, THE BEAST AND THE WOODEN MAN WHO CAME TO LIFE	75
4	CANCER, CAR ACCIDENTS AND THE MOTHER WHO LOST EIGHT CHILDREN	127
5	MY GRAN AND THE RICKSHAW DRIVER	173
6	THE LION, THE CROCODILE AND THE MAASAI	209
7	JEDI TRUMP AND THE ICELANDIC TOILET	255
8	GROSS NATIONAL HAPPINESS AND THE RICE WINE HANGOVER	309
9	A MAN UP A MOUNTAIN AND THE IDEA THAT PUT HIM THERE	367
10	MY BROTHER AND THE TALIBAN	423
11	MR SMITH AND THE GIRL WITH THE BIG BUM	455
12	THE PRIME MINISTER AND THE SEX SLAVE	489

1

THE PAIN AND THE EXPLODING PLANE

"Wake up, wake up, wake up." It was a whisper but delivered in a frantic tone, a hoarse yelling meant for my ears only and emphasized by the incessant tapping on my leg to help maintain the rhythm. Doubly annoying.

"Uuuuuuuh," I growled, my eyes and mouth both unwilling and unable to open, stuck together with the stickiness of sleep.

Andy (my mate) then started slapping my shoulder, which soon turned into a sort of rough shake of my whole body. He meant to rouse me no matter what and, finally, he won.

"What?" I barked, louder than I intended, as I drifted between sweet sleep and an uncomfortable awakeness. "Seriously, Mike, wake up. The engine just blew up and is on fire," he said, still using a forceful indoor voice – obviously designed to ensure his sick joke didn't startle anyone else. "Shut up," I mumbled angrily, having had enough. "You're not even funny."

A minute or two later, with the hitting, the shaking and the words becoming ever more aggressive, I finally caved and opened my tired eyes. Immediately, I could tell something wasn't right from the number of people praying, but as I peered out the window to my left I couldn't see anything, just black. Was it night already? I thought. Then it moved, intermittent spots of sunlight between the black revealed the thick plume of smoke gushing from the engine of our plane.

My heart hurt. Was it shock? A sign I was about to die? The pain in my chest grew stronger and sharper. Was I having a heart attack? The pain crept down my body into my stomach, and as the plane shook things only got worse. Trying to relieve the tension in my torso, I was slowly twisting my head to the right when I noticed the young girl sitting next to me. About 15 and travelling on her own, her face was a picture of fear. As I turned to comfort her, the pilots spoke in Spanish and she began to cry. The English translation of the message followed and it wasn't hard to work out what had driven her to tears. We were about two hours east of Auckland, New Zealand, 11,000 metres above the Pacific Ocean with smoke gushing from one engine and we'd just been told we would need to remain at this altitude dumping fuel for the next couple of hours (so that the plane would be light enough for us to attempt an emergency landing back in Auckland).

Engine failure isn't what you want when you're flying over the world's largest ocean. Every time I look out the window at the black mass of smoke and fuel they're dumping, my stomach seizes in crippling pain. I wrote in my journal at the time.

No one turned off the in-flight monitors showing the flight path and location of the plane. This made the circles we were doing all the more ridiculous and terrifying, particularly since we could see so clearly the mountain range we still needed to fly over.

Turning my attention back to the girl next to me – who had boarded the flight in Auckland, not Sydney, as Andy and I had – we began by asking her in some sort of weird Spanish-English accent where she had been. She looked at us blankly so we turned to our trusty Spanish phrase book. "Dónde has estado," we finally managed to say, and we eventually discovered through a series of pointing at Spanish words that she'd been visiting relatives in New Zealand, I think. Between the turbulence, tears and awkward TV screen that continued to remind us we were flying in circles like an eagle searching for prey (or was it a bird in a death spiral?), we worked out that this young woman was from Sao Paulo, Brazil, and this fateful journey was her first solo adventure. Being from Brazil, not Buenos Aires (the destination of our flight), we also came to realise that Spanish was her second language, after Portuguese.

The safety of all those around me is all I care about and I think something like this not only makes your heart stop, but also makes your mind melt a little, as you run through the events of your life and what you had wanted to achieve. I continued to scribble in my journal to distract myself – or was I penning my last words?

THE PAIN AND THE EXPLODING PLANE

While it wasn't all that funny given our circumstance, Andy and I shared a rather cautious, tentative laugh as we recalled what we had seen and said when we first boarded the plane in Sydney. After taking our seats we were thoroughly entertained by a toilet door in front of us that was flapping about, refusing to shut, despite the best efforts of one of the flight attendants. Growing increasingly impatient and angry with the door, the flight attendant called her colleague over, who once again tried all the normal methods for closing such a door. But she too failed. The two women raised their voices in frustration as they bashed and kicked the door, jamming their knees into it, willing it to shut. It reminded me of an odd wrestling match – women vs door – and you could tell who was winning. As the commotion got louder, and another two stewardesses came to help, I sensed passengers were beginning to feel uncomfortable.

"Well, I hope their engines work better than their doors," I had said to Andy, as we chuckled at their futile efforts to maintain a sense of order and calmness when faced with a naughty, misbehaving toilet door. It really was an uncomfortable feeling, not because they couldn't shut the door, but because of their complete lack of awareness for how their frustration and anxiety might be making passengers feel.

Of course, recounting this now that we were sitting there terrified, the incident suddenly seemed more prophetic than funny. And unfortunately, the manner of the cabin staff remained one of the most frightening elements of the entire experience. They appeared almost totally out of control, unable to answer how long it would take to dump enough fuel for the plane to land safely, and completely incapable of consoling themselves, let alone anyone else.

Meanwhile, the girl next to us had found a few more words in the phrase book, and we learned that she, like most people, thought Australia was a place of crazy animals that can kill you. She also told us that while Sao Paulo was her home, she dreamed of exploring many lands and cultures in her life.

"Now I am scared," she said in broken English. "I am scared to fly. Or maybe we will die today, so perhaps my dream is lost either way," she told us, miming the plane falling to the ground, as she began to cry once more.

I cannot imagine what this girl must be feeling, all alone, facing that which we all dread — unexpected death — I only hope she takes some comfort in our interaction.

While we'd been trying to distract ourselves, there was little escaping the fact that every second could be our last. The high emotion of the moment was draining. Sweat dripped from my face, in defiance of the icy air conditioning. Of course, I knew from discussions with a close friend 'Barbs' (Justin Barbaro), who was a pilot, and from watching the odd air crash investigation show, that these planes can fly on three engines, or even two, but it was the sparks and flames and complete loss of decorum by the cabin staff that was impossible to block out. What did they know that we didn't? Why weren't we circling off the coast closer to Auckland just in case something happened? Do we try to contact loved ones? Would anyone ever recover my journal if I wrote a last message in it? Will it hurt if and when we die? Why aren't they telling us anything and reassuring us that we'll be OK? Why me, why us?

The questions remained on repeat, with me unable to provide any easy answers.

We'd now been dumping fuel for an hour and a half, though, to those praying and in tears, time stood still. During one of the first broadcasts from the flight deck the pilot told us it would "take the time necessary to ensure the aircraft was at the correct weight for landing." What did that mean? Surely they could calculate how long it would take to get the plane back to a safe weight to land? Then again, the toilet door was still flapping around, so maybe not.

At precisely one hour and 53 minutes after the explosion, the pilots made another announcement: "In a few minutes we will begin our descent into Auckland."

As we approached New Zealand, the plane began to turn sharply. Was this it? Is that all there is? The plane tilted downwards, to the right, forcing me to think that maybe it was. What was happening? People began to pray even louder, heads and fingers all crunched together in their laps rocking back and forward. "Please, please, please," you could hear the sounds of divine persuasion drift through the cabin.

We were no longer flying in a straight line towards Auckland. "Why? Where are we going?" people asked the crew, who were as helpful in their silence as they had been throughout the journey.

As we neared our destination, and the pilots began extending our wings downwards to help slow our descent, the plane began to shake violently. Then, suddenly, a number of those passengers closest to the windows started pointing at something. What was it? Could they see land? Lights? Fire? The airport? From where we sat all we could see was black. That, and people praying, louder now than ever.

The wait was excruciating.

This may be my last sentence – so much love to all – live life to the fullest and find peace within yourself and the world to achieve happiness. Oh turbulence now, great!

As the plane began to make its final few turns and approach into the airport, you could sense something wasn't quite right. Unlike those with window seats, we thankfully could not see the flashing lights of the fire trucks and ambulances that were waiting for us. The plane cracked and screeched in pain as if it were trying its best to stay together. The pilots let the wings down further. Then the usual 'pop' as the landing gear opened turned into an enormous 'clunk' of metallic sounds as the plane dipped to the left – towards the damaged engine. Passengers screamed, and that really scared me.

The terror built, and built, and built, as we were tossed and turned like a paper airplane in the wind.

I looked across to check on the young girl, whose cheeks were glistening with tears. I floated between shutting my eyes and praying for peace and love, to opening my eyes and checking I was still alive.

"Pluys braish for lungin," said the pilot in his uniquely broken English.

People's heads were in their knees, many still clasping them together in prayer. The plane groaned, like a buffalo being grounded by a pride of lions that continue clawing and biting at its neck, awaiting its stillness and surrender to the feast. Then suddenly the plane felt like it turned sideways, towards the wing with the damaged engine. We couldn't be far from hitting …

Land was meant to be our saviour, but instead the tarmac had thrown the plane ferociously towards the left, like a five hundred tonne car travelling at three hundred kilometres an hour with two flat tires on one side. I feared we were about to crash off the runway when suddenly we swerved back to the right. People screamed, while others yelled prayers. The plane whined as the brakes were applied more heavily, the enormous aircraft still snaking down the runway, side to side, back and forth, as sirens and lights blazed outside. The noise of the waning aircraft was deafening as it shrieked in pain.

Then, something happened I'll never forget.

We stopped. "We're safe!" someone yelled, as passengers erupted and cheered ecstatically. "We're alive," said the lady behind us, as she shook her friend's face in her hands. Many clenched their hands tightly together and looked up to thank god for protecting them. Peering around in a bizarre sort of euphoric bewilderment I noticed hugs, high fives and children cuddled in the laps of their parents, while directly in front of me there was a young couple who had dropped to their knees, sobbing hysterically. I honestly have no idea how long it was, but in the time it took us to taxi to the terminal there was a feeling in that plane that we all need to find a way of replicating – minus the need for a near death, exploding plane experience. For in those few short moments it was possible to taste the unwavering joy everyone felt to be breathing. To be alive. To be loved. And to be connected to those human beings around them.

With the lights and sirens wailing towards us, closer and closer, it was as if people suddenly woke up, or maybe it was more a case of going back to sleep, to their former selves. Instead of hugging strangers, as many had been seconds earlier, people turned to fighting each other to get off the plane, or for spots on the next flight out. I know this, because, embarrassingly, I was one of them. Caught up in the chaos, unable to free myself from my survival instincts, or focus on anything past the end of my nose, I grabbed my bags and got ready to run for it. That was, until something shifted in me. Suddenly, I began to see myself and my actions from another perspective, from a distance, as I understood that my survival was no longer under threat. Snapping out of this destructive mind-set meant I could reconnect with what was around me, the people, the girl next to me, I could help her, give her a smile and shut my eyes and be grateful. None of this is possible when we are trapped in a survivalist mind-set. No doubt if I didn't snap out of it, I could have ended up harming others, even myself, as I pursued a selfish 'me, me, me' way of looking at a challenge that was actually faced by 229 people trapped in a burning bullet.

Safely back in the terminal building, it was now 10:45pm and Andy and I sat against a dusty wall awaiting our instructions. We wallowed in the silence as we let that feeling sink in – you know the 'holy shit, what just happened, how am I still alive' feeling? Yeah that one. As we grabbed our phones and prepared to call our loved ones, we looked at each other with a cheeky, relieved smile that was filled with a deep appreciation for the heartbeat that still echoed loudly in our chests. As Andy got through to his parents on the phone and began describing the horrors we'd just been through something dawned on me – I almost died. **I almost died**. I ALMOST DIED!!!!

Sitting there on that chilly tiled floor, I couldn't easily escape my thoughts. Why am I still alive? I wondered. Why not let me die? Thousands die so needlessly every day, why not me? Was there something I was meant to do? Did some higher power want me here? I'd often talked to my mum, even as a young boy, about this inexplicable sense that I was meant to do 'something big', that I needed to help people in some way, but I'd never known how – or even why I'd felt this. Was it ego, did I just want to feel good, or was it my purpose, was 'god' communicating with me?

While those few minutes of contemplation helped me feel more at peace with what had just happened, the next four weeks were the opposite, as god or the universe sent death after me, like some terrifying reminder to remain awake and ever vigilant of these questions and my purpose.

The snake that connected me

After a three-day long fight with Aerolineas management – who were refusing to re-book us on a flight that would get us to Peru in time for our group tour – we finally arrived. Albeit, a day late. Sitting in a local Peruvian bar debriefing over a beer and barbecue chicken, Andy and I contemplated whether things could get any worse. "Well, I guess there's death," he said.

After meeting our guide, aptly named Elvis – he was quite the character – we spent the first day of our fortnight-long expedition mountain biking around Miraflores, a small beachside district of Lima, the capital of Peru. The ride began atop an incredibly precarious, sheer gravel road that snaked down the side of a mountain. What made this path even more serpentine were the cast iron scales that were actually rooftops of shanty homes occupied by squatters, who had taken the only chance they had to own land, by claiming their own piece of the near vertical mountain face. Such was the precarious nature of the hilly terrain, that the locals believed the government would never seek to repossess the land, which, once it had been occupied for more than 10 years, 'officially' belonged to the families inhabiting it.

Their view, though dangerous, was spectacular, with stunning cliff faces, beaches and an enormous glistening cross that stood about halfway up the tallest mountain in the area, Morro Solar. We learned that this larger than life symbol of Christ had actually been constructed out of salvaged metal from a major terrorist bombing during the civil war in the 1970s and 1980s. Locals, mostly Catholic, told us it was a reminder that **even out of the darkest of days good can be born.**

After drinking in the dazzling view, we made our way past a number of disheveled dogs, emaciated children and dangerously fragile huts – built from wood harvested from local trees, a couple of rusty nails (no screws) and pieces of leaky, worn-through steel roofing. These rustic ghettos were a stark contrast to the enormous mansions and hotels that made up the majority of Miraflores, which is one of Peru's more lavish areas. What was wrong with these people, I thought, how could they just ignore this hideous inequality? It was right on their doorstep.

As we boarded our nice, cushy flight to Lake Titicaca the following day, I remember feeling odd. Not unhappy, not ill, more like a child who just found out Santa isn't real. This was one of the first and certainly most telling times I remember feeling a really awkward discomfort with the relative luxury and wealth I enjoyed. Why should the place where we're born so define our fate? Were these people any less deserving? Was it luck? Was I responsible for this? Where was god? Where was humanity? Was the brotherhood and sisterhood of humans a thing? Were we connected? Was that why I felt as I did? I'd like to say I had an easy answer – something that would make you feel happier – but the questioning, the injustice of my entitlement, and of the brutal inequality we're all a part of, is something that haunts me to this day. If anything, the more I've seen, the more overtly sick it has made me.

Navigating through the sheer cliffs and mountains of the Andes on a small local plane was breathtaking, for all the right and wrong reasons. While we heard that there had been record rainfall and widespread flooding that may endanger our chances of doing the Machu Picchu climb, I was shocked at just what this looked like. Flying through Cusco – where you base yourself to do the climb – on our way to Lake Titicaca, you could see rivers swollen to the point of swamping homes, and entire mountain sides that had collapsed into valleys, smothering any life that got in its way.

> *You can literally see the power of the Earth from up here, as you gaze at the mountains and imagine how they formed from enormous plates crashing into each other. You can see evidence of this everywhere, with ridges jutting out from mountain tops and long plates poking out the sides of them. You can even feel it in the turbulence we're experiencing. It is exhilarating and scary ... we're now coming into land and giant pools of water are scattered everywhere, making patterns throughout the landscape. The town is badly flooded, roads have been eroded and homes no longer exist. How unfair. If these people live in the valleys they face flooding, and if they live on the mountains they could disappear in a landslide. The sheer power of water is evident throughout the Andes, as huge crevices and gorges weave a pattern worth marveling at, leading to a place we would likely be dead without, the Amazon. And again, I am reminded of the idea behind the cross of Morro Solar, that good can come from even the darkest events.*

Touching down in Juliaca, 3825 metres above sea level, we were promptly ushered past a welcoming party of small-statured men playing guitar, and onto a bus that would take us to Puno, the largest town on Lake Titicaca. When we reached Puno, we were met by a taxi stand of makeshift three-wheeler bikes, each with a seat for the cyclist at the back and bright orange and gold cloth bench seat for two at the front, covered by a colourful stripy shade cloth. This was a common mode of transport, despite the steep terrain, chaotic and narrow cobble-stone roads and tiny men riding the machines. Now, at the time Andy and I probably weighed around 140 kilograms together, so we weren't exactly light, but not huge either. As a four foot ten man with legs no wider than the wheels jumped on the bike and told us to hold on, I wasn't sure if he'd be able to get us moving. After packing our bags in tight, he didn't just get us moving, we were flying – in and out of traffic, people, chickens, wheelbarrows and goodness knows what else, before suddenly coming to a stop in a random laneway.

The man was sweating profusely. Had we broken him? He looked white, like a pint-sized ghost with a cheeky smile. We offered him some water and he pointed at his seat. "You go," he said, as he laughed with his friends, or strangers, or whoever those people were standing in the street with him. It probably wasn't legal, smart or safe, but as a cyclist who fancied himself as a climber back home in Australia, I couldn't help but take him up on the challenge. After a few close calls with pedestrians, cars, ox carts and directions – "which way is izquierda", left, right, who knows maybe just point – we finally made it to the port, which technically should have been mostly downhill, but in this town, every road seemed to be uphill, or maybe it was just the lack of oxygen, or the fact that our rider's thin little legs were now intimidating me. Who knows, but it had me smiling, I mean really crazy happy, that 'in the moment' kind of joy you can't plan for, because if I knew I'd be doing this, part of the fun would be gone before we even began. As I stepped off the bike and the locals began cackling to themselves, I was reminded of the awe that can be found in the humblest and oldest of human activities – such as connecting with a stranger.

While I sat there wonderfully bewildered with what had just happened, the best thing was we hadn't even arrived. I guess that's why they say happiness is a journey not a destination.

A night in high hell

Out onto the lake we floated. It was going to be a two-hour journey to Amantani Island, but we were to stop along the way at a few of the famous floating reed islands. As we motored out past hordes of people collecting totora reeds – piling them up high on their small wooden boats until they almost sank – it was obvious these things were not only important, but freely available. So what was the big deal? Why was everyone hoarding these long green reeds? I wondered, as our boat passed out into more open water, toward a tiny caramel coloured mass floating in the distance.

As we pulled up next to what was actually a football-field sized mass of dried-out hay coloured reeds, it felt as if we were arriving on some strange movie set or cartoon world. Houses, boats, tables, chairs, lookout towers and a myriad of odd objects – literally everything – was made out of these totora reeds. What really stood out though, despite their

San Juan de Miraflores slum near Lima, Peru. Photo by Jordan Adkins.

Morro Solar.

A river bursting its banks winds through a village in the Andes Mountains.

A badly flooded town near Cusco.

Flood waters tore through homes and buildings.

A displaced persons camp for those who lost their home in the floods.

Collecting totora reeds.

Our ride. That's Andy on the right and me.

A hard day's work.

The toilet I frequented.

A floating reed island.

Missionaries on Amantani Island.

A village elder (left) and a mother and her baby sitting on a floating reed island.

Tsosidad, our mum, bringing me food when I was sick.

Me, sitting in Tsosidad's kitchen feeling terrible.

miniature almost 'umpa lumpa' size, were the people. The outlandishly colourful and smiley women were dressed in dazzling, fluorescent skirts and jackets that would make the Mardi Gras seem dull.

The islands themselves were made entirely from the dense roots and stems these plants develop. In fact, the 2-5 metre thick mass of reeds, which was anchored to the lake floor 17 metres below, actually grew thicker every few months as the local Uros or Uru people renewed the top layer, not only for aesthetics, but to maintain its buoyancy.

> *The most intriguing part of all this for me is the innovator who saw the reeds and thought let's make an island and live in the middle of the lake. How resourceful humans are when we see nature for what it is – a gift that offers all we need.*

But their obsession with the totora reeds didn't end with living on them and in them, the plant also made up at least 50% of the Uros' diet and is the basis for most of their medicine. Often the totora reeds are wrapped around a body part in pain to absorb the hurt, while if it is hot outside, they split the reed open and place it on their forehead to cool down. The white fibrous base is even used to help ease hangovers! Was there anything this plant couldn't do? The simple answer was no, because as we found out, anything that wasn't immediately provided to the Uros by the plant could be traded for in exchange for their totora products. Most commonly this included quinoa, grains, but also the latest technologies and tickets to events.

What I realised pretty quickly was there wasn't much that the Uros needed to go right in order to survive and be happy, as they used the reeds – which were everywhere – for housing, trading and eating, and they simply padded out their diet with fish that they caught or products they bartered for.

After leaving the floating reed islands, I was curious (as I always am) to learn about the Uros belief system or religion, so I asked our guide.

"It is a bit complicated really, since Christianity arrived," he replied. "Mostly they follow Mucha Mama or Mother Earth and Apus the mountain spirits. Their life is one connected deeply to the mountains, the water, the sun and each other, so that is why you will notice they are so peaceful and friendly. They don't need or ask for much, as they know the gods they worship – the sun, water, mountain and Earth – have given them everything. But then there are some who believe in Jesus too, but

I think mostly they just combine the belief systems somehow. Though we have seen some more strict versions of Christianity now appearing here too, which is, well…" He pauses. "Concerning," he whispers, so as to avoid being heard by others who may take offence.

With a sore bum and jaw wide open we finally arrived at what looked like a Hobbit village from Lord of the Rings. Our host family – Tsosidad (our mum), Fransisco (our dad) and their son, Christian – led us to their home, which was a speck of red among a mountain of green, with potato crops, lime trees and local leafy green herbs spattered across the hillside village.

Wow! Amantani Island is beautiful beyond my wildest imaginings. The people live in tranquility, at one with the environment and those around them. The tiny huts carved into the mountain (with doors not even up to my neck) are nearly as stunning as the view they look out on. If only we could emulate what they do here.

A few minutes later, gazing from our balcony, I was shocked by what I saw.

I've just seen the most startling of things. Two hours by boat from the nearest port, and there are two Mormons or Jehovah's Witnesses going door to door, but why? What do they need to change about this loving, authentic culture? Surely if god exists, then he does so very strongly in these people – they are one with all things in god's realm – so why must someone come and tell them they're wrong to believe in the beauty and spirit of the sun, the water and the mountains? Are they not god's creations? Should they not be worshipped? Why can't people accept and appreciate the diversity of all belief systems!? Grrrr so mad.

Within an hour of arriving on the Island – which wasn't floating, just to be clear – we'd been invited to play in a 'visitors vs locals' soccer game. For me, and a few of the other young Aussies on our trip, this was a dream come true. The simple joy and connection of sharing a common love with the locals was unforgettable. Their flamboyant and amazing skills made it a pleasure to watch and be a part of. Surprisingly though, it wasn't a one way street, as they struggled to penetrate our more structured, orderly defence, that eventually saw us win, just. After the match the locals were so fascinated by our style of play that they sat with us and asked us how football (soccer) is taught in Australia. I guess you always admire what's different, what you don't have. So while we

THE PAIN AND THE EXPLODING PLANE

loved their passion and natural flare for the game, they were interested in our more schooled approach.

At about 2am the next morning, I awoke in a pool of sweat, desperately needing to vomit. I was unable to open my eyes because my head was screaming in pain. The miniature huts, which were built on stilts, made it that bit more interesting to try to navigate to the outside toilet, which was about 30 metres away up a hill. As I squatted over the toilet, emptying my body (from both ends) of the potato and beans we'd consumed earlier, the freezing air rushed through the many layers I had protecting me. The icy breeze did little to stop what felt like a cascade of fluid dripping from every pore on my body. I didn't want to wake anyone, so I sat there for about an hour as vomit dripped from me. The odd spurt forced me to roll over and make sure I aimed it in the drop toilet. Unsurprisingly, it stank like shit.

The pain in my head grew worse, the dizziness so bad it was unsafe for me to try to walk back to my room. There was also the sub-zero temperature combined with my roasting body, which made everything more difficult to understand. What was wrong with me? As a guy, you're not meant to cause a fuss, especially not us Aussies, we're meant to be known for wrestling crocodiles, adventuring through the desert and eating our national emblem – the kangaroo. We're not meant to be the needy type, so I continued suffering in silence.

After trying to fall asleep outside the toilet, but failing because it felt like someone was trying to squeeze my brain from inside my skull, I started crawling back to our room. I crawled through a potato patch, past the kitchen and ascended the stairs, on my knees, making sure not to bang my head on the many low hanging beams and doorways. Back in my bed under four or five thick blankets, I began sweating even more. My body was now in some form of shock, unable to deal with the agony that throbbed and stirred in my head. Should I wake someone? I wondered. Just as I contemplated it, the urge to vomit forced me to scurry back to the toilet, nearly falling down the stairs as I vomited in my mouth. Unfortunately, despite my best efforts to clean up after my last episode, the toilet still smelt foul, both vomit and shit seemed to surround me as my head once again lay just centimetres above the old porcelain toilet seat that separated me from the stinking pit below.

Once again, I lay in the bitter breeze, trying to focus on the wonder and awe of this place, rather than the sensation of needles that seemed to be stabbing into my brain. I had an idea by now that this was altitude related, as I'd been looking at the symptoms earlier that day, which included headache, fatigue, stomach illness, dizziness, and sleep disturbance. I had ticked all the boxes, though strangely, had not felt short of breath while running or cycling and really hadn't sensed anything out of the ordinary until now. What really plagued me was a fear of something worse. I knew altitude sickness could kill you, and the way my head felt I feared I may have one of the severe symptoms – cerebral edema (swelling of the brain) – which would explain the headache that had not responded to Western medication I had taken, as well as my inability to walk normally, the increased nausea, fever and the fact I could barely open my eyes.

As I sat there outside a toilet, up a hill, on an island, in the middle of a lake that was three hours by boat and bus away from the nearest hospital, I knew once more that **my life was no longer in my hands**. Even if I suddenly needed medical attention, chances are I'd likely be flown back to Lima for treatment, which was another hour by plane at least. Plus, it was the middle of the night, everyone was asleep and I really didn't want to abandon our trip. So I lay there in silence, listening to the animals – mostly donkeys – and to the thoughts that still echoed in my head from our near death journey to get there. For the first time in my life I also imagined the children, and the men and women I'd seen in the slums of Lima and Puno, and while it didn't take away the pain, it did put it in perspective, and probably distracted me for a moment.

Unfortunately for me, there were at least two more toilet expeditions to go. Each time, I'd invariably head back to our room thinking I was OK, before needing again to crawl 30 metres back down the stairs, around the kitchen, through the garden and into the toilet.

Then, I saw something I wondered briefly if I might ever see again – the sun rose over the dewy grass and potato fields, making them shine, much to the displeasure of my eyes, which felt like they were popping out somewhere in front of my skull. I didn't want to startle the local family, who'd been so kind and accommodating to us, so I wandered back from the toilet and sat on the steps, just in case I needed to run and vomit some more.

Tsosidad was the first to rise, and as soon as she saw my face she ran to wake her son, who could speak a little English. I mimed and explained the feeling in my head and the fact I'd been very ill and he ran to wake his father, who he said could help, I think. I told them I'd tried taking the medicine we had brought with us and they laughed. "No, no, no, not help if high up," said Christian. "Come."

Soon I was sitting in their kitchen, with various members of the community coming in and out, examining me as if I was their own child. They were concerned, and to be honest, so was I. Sitting on a wooden bench inside that smoky, blackened clay hut, I made a deal to do what was needed and wanted of me by 'the world', so long as it kept me alive. Fransisco returned with a small basket of natural remedies – limes, reeds, roots, herbs and more – and asked me to take off my many tops. Sweat continued to pour from my body, despite the bone-chilling temperature. He gestured for me to put my head in my hands and lean forward. Then he began rubbing limes on my back as he said, "It's OK. It's OK. You OK." There were at least four or five people outside at any one time, so I knew I wasn't going to die alone as I had thought I might earlier, hunched over the toilet seat.

The entire kitchen smelt of lime. I remember my skin all the way down my bum and legs felt sticky with the juice. Better to smell that, than what I was smelling a few hours earlier, I thought. While physiologically, the lime and natural herbs they'd rubbed on my back and head hadn't done much to help the pain, something about their demeanour and kindness found its way inside me, and made me feel at peace. The pain remained, but it was bearable so long as they were there. I vomited again, another two times, but the lime smell made everything that bit more pleasant.

Andy sat beside me, feeling sorry for me, as he knew how much I'd finally been enjoying our trip. Of course he chuckled a bit at the colour of my skin, my limey back and the fact that local families continued bringing me food despite my inability to even hold down water or open my eyes.

I sat there half asleep at the table, with a delicious pancake and soup in front of me, for at least an hour or so, as we waited for our tour guide to wake up and help us work out what I should do. I'd made it this far, so I felt I was past the worst of it, and really, all I needed was to find a way to retain some water, as I'd lost a lot of fluid. The pain I was in was now rivalled, if not overtaken, by a more general yet severe ache and weakness throughout my body.

Two people carried me in a chair down the hill towards our boat and our guide, Elvis, who had just awoken. I remained in a state of delirium, unable to properly thank our family, or even understand where I was. I'm pretty sure someone said I'd feel better once we were back in Puno, because it was a hundred or so metres lower than the house we'd stayed in up the hill. The boat trip was hell, each bump like a right hook to the face and jab to the abdomen. I'm pretty sure I faded in and out of consciousness, eventually waking up back in Puno with one thought – 'I'm alive and I'm breathing,' though still exhausted and in pain.

While logic and common sense told me to get a checkup at the hospital or sleep, something drew me to do the opposite – to explore the streets of Puno with Andy. Barely able to open my eyes, it was obvious from the stench of piss and shit (not mine, thankfully), that we'd soon walked into a poorer area of town. A mix of rubbish, fish stalls and homeless people littered the dark and narrow sidewalks. Then, from nowhere a train track emerged, along with a few hundred people and a bustling marketplace of shoes, clothing, spare bike parts and fresh produce. A curious bunch of children began following us, laughing and pointing, probably because I looked like a dead man walking. Amid the pain that echoed in my head came an idea – if I wanted to find my purpose and reason for being, I needed to start doing more stuff. **For good or bad, I just needed to start acting on the hundreds of little thoughts that had rushed through my head for so many years.** Keen to trial this, I grabbed a few of the kids who were running around the rubbish and filthy glass-ridden area barefoot, and took them to a little man in a puffy black coat who was huddled over a pile of shoes. I gestured for the kids to try a pair on, and gave the confused stall holder a generous amount of money to cover the cost, before walking off to find Andy in the fading light.

Well I'm better somehow, after finally sleeping last night. I wonder how those kids feet are feeling in their new shoes? Hopefully they're as relieved as me.

I'm in a bus taking us from Puno to Cusco and the scenery is so big and wild it is bewildering to imagine how anyone inhabits this area. The signs of the torrential rain are getting worse and worse as we drive through a valley that houses a major river for the region, which has swallowed entire homes and villages. The destruction is epic – made obvious by the fields of tents many local people are now calling home. What pains me most is that all of these people are victims of a mother nature unhappy with human activity ravaging the planet.

And yet, these people did nothing to deserve this, while the perpetrators — the big polluters changing the atmosphere — largely go unpunished.

Arriving in Cusco, Elvis rushed to an emergency meeting to discuss our Machu Picchu hike, which was meant to begin the next day. This was the primary reason we'd come to South America and was to be the highlight of our Peruvian tour.

"Hey guys, the path to Machu Picchu is expected to be closed for up to a week, so we will not be doing the Incan trail," said a strangely sombre Elvis on his return. He told us that the day before, a number of people had been killed on the path, including a guide he knew who had tackled a tourist out of the way of a falling rock only to be crushed by it himself. It was sobering. Hundreds of groups were now stuck up the mountain, forced to wait it out until the landslides stopped and they could return safely. Once again, I seemed to have narrowly escaped tragedy.

Was it the knife, the robbery or the shooting?

Touching down in Rio de Janeiro for Carnival — the biggest party in the world — things were completely mental from the word go, as we met our friends Will and Elise, and discovered it was going to be more than 45 degrees Celsius over the coming week, which was less than ideal given the hostel we booked didn't have air conditioning. The next few days are a bit of a blur of beaches, beers and a bustling culture of impoverished people rich with a spirit that shook me to my core.

> *Every footpath is littered with street vendors and at any traffic light there may be up to 20 people trying to sell you something — anything. There is less of a sense of joy and happiness here than in Peru. It is heartbreaking to see the shells of former people lying in streets of rubbish, the stench of urine an overwhelming reminder of the daily battle these people face to stay alive. Wherever we travel I feel a constant guilt in the luck I've been afforded, just because I was born in Australia. I could be any one of these people.*
>
> *A life of simplicity and off-loading any excess money through travelling and helping others is a dream I hope I can embrace and inspire in others. I find it so boring and meaningless to think of just going through life as we are expected to in the West — by the numbers — as if this predetermined route is right for me. I guess I just believe everyone should be free to chase that inner voice, however*

crazy it might make you feel, and wherever it might take you, because that's where happiness is. As I look to the future, I find it hard to imagine staying steady in a career and feel more and more like taking risks. Seeing the world and living without much stuff is my calling. We only have one life, after all.

A few days later we decided to do a walking tour of a 'favela' – a typically low-income area with extremely high density, informal housing that is often run and managed by drug lords, not the government. About 11 million people, or 6% of Brazil's population, live in favelas, which often host nightly dance parties for all classes of society that rake in up to $150 million USD per month in some areas (mostly through the sale of drugs), according to Brazilian media. You felt all this might just be true when our local guide told us not to make eye contact with anyone or look at anything unless she pointed it out. The seemingly random web of peculiar and thin alleyways of shops, sewage drains and doors everywhere was both charming and confronting.

Charming because it resembled a kind of bizarre close-knit community that you could see as hordes of children ran past and around us, curious as to what we were doing there – we did seem to be the only foreigners. This warm interconnectedness was also evident when we were invited up onto a rooftop of one of the houses, where two boys were flying kites, competing against another group of kite-flying kids close by. Groups of parents also gathered, and squabbled in local lounges and the few open areas that attracted sunlight.

I'd be lying, though, if I didn't say that the energy and mood of this place was also a little confronting, especially as our guide informed us that during Carnival, many of these children will be expected to go out at night and pick-pocket tourists, or worse. Furthermore, she explained that people often go missing quite easily in favelas due to rival gangs competing for their piece of the drug pie.

Having descended through the favela, which at the top enjoyed an incredible view of Sugarloaf Mountain, our guide crossed the road to find us a taxi, but just as she did a man yelled at us. "Come play. You must come in." The guy was standing in front of what was clearly the main party venue and bar in the area, holding a pool cue in a way that didn't really allow us to say no. After searching madly to see where our guide had disappeared to, we slowly walked over. We knew we shouldn't have gone in, but it was too late.

The man spoke in a very loud, forceful way and seemed to know just enough English to be intimidating. He insisted we play pool, and make a bet on it. It wasn't really a question, so we agreed, and proceeded to play. Those who weren't immediately hitting the ball looked nervously around for that safe and familiar face of our guide. She was nowhere. Was this a set up? I remember thinking. Probably. I guess that's why they tell you not to carry too much money on you in Rio, because it was about to belong to someone else. As the game became close, we didn't know whether we were allowed to win or not. I imagine the tattooed, skin headed man didn't expect to be beaten. Would he lose his marbles if we won? Would we be dishonouring him? Or had I just watched too many gangster movies?

"Quick get in your cab guys," said a familiar voice. "Sorry, we have to run," we told the man. "Next time," we yelled, as we scurried out of the bar waving politely at him with one hand while pointing at our taxi with the other. "But we have not finished, we must continue, you cannot walk away now," he screamed, as my heart pounded and my mind told me to expect gunshots. Then, before we knew it, we were safe once more, in the back of the cab. As our guide said "Thanks for coming," she did so with an inquisitive look on her face, clearly related to how we'd got to playing pool with that man. Who knows what we'd escaped, but it was time to boogie. The world's largest street party – of more than a million people – awaited.

Returning to our hostel and enjoying a few drinks with the myriad of people staying there, we soon realised we were all headed to the same place, so we decided to walk together. Now ordinarily I hadn't been taking more than $50 or my little point-and-shoot camera with me, but given this was my last hurrah before going home, and I'd just backed up all my photos on a hard-drive, I decided to be daring, and place my remaining money and camera down the front of my underpants. This was slightly revealing given I was only wearing board shorts and no T-shirt due to the heat, but hey, it was my only option.

Walking for about a kilometre through the colourful, crowded and noisy streets of Rio in full flight, I noticed a group of boys staring at one of the girls we were walking with, who had drifted off by herself. I slowly approached her and put my arm around her as I whispered: "Just pretend we're together, as there's a strange group of guys following you." She was quite attractive, with short brown hair and a model-like figure, so it wasn't hard to see why she'd attracted unwanted attention. The only problem was, some of the local guys were often a bit too insistent with getting what they wanted.

The group of about 15 young guys continued following us into the heart of the street party, which was packed tighter than the proverbial can of sardines. All you could feel was other people's sweat rubbing up against your own. Still, as we journeyed deeper into the pile of sardines, they continued tailing us, slowly getting closer. And closer. And closer. I held the girl close to me. But the group of young men pushed her away, and then, somewhat unexpectedly, surrounded me. "Knife, knife, knife," they said in a loud whisper, so as to sound threatening but remain unnoticed. A few of them held me still, not that I was resisting. I even put my hands up to show my compliance. The blade of the knife was firmly held between my spine and kidneys. A few of them tried talking in some form of Portuguese-English, but I couldn't understand them. "English. Only English," I said. Most grabbed at my solitary back pocket, which was obvious (due to not having a T-shirt on) and bulging with change. Their hands poked, slipped and slopped around, as they attacked like a frenzy of seagulls who'd found a few chips in my pants.

It must have taken less than 20 seconds, and they were gone. Disappearing into the night, to find their next victim. They were professional and efficient, but they hadn't got the $150 or camera down the front of my pants, and no one had been hurt, so really it was win-win-win. I got to donate some money to Rio's poor, I got a bum massage and I got a good story to tell. In fact, probably the best part of the story came when I asked my friends why they didn't come and help me – because I could see they looked over while it was happening. Will replied: "We just thought you were making friends with a few of the locals."

That night as I fell asleep in the communal area of the hostel on a beanbag – because our dorm room was too hot – I saw just how different things could have turned out for me, as a guy I'd talked to earlier that night stumbled through the door. Limping and wincing in pain, the hippie looking European with a blond undercut turned around, pointing at his back. I gasped. "What the fuck!" Blood and what looked like surgical glue oozed from a wound that was barely being held together by 20 plus staples dotted up his back like a snake. "What happened?" I asked.

He told me he'd ventured out on his own and saw a young woman getting mugged, so he tried to help her. The next thing he knew he was on the ground being kicked and punched, before someone stabbed him as he tried to free himself. A sad innocence crept into his voice as he explained that he was actually just trying to avoid another scenario he'd witnessed earlier in the night.

Just a few hours before the stabbing he said he'd been leaving a block party when he saw a foreign woman catch a young boy pick-pocketing her. When the boy eventually escaped her grasp, the woman called out to police who were close by. Seconds later the eight-year-old child was shot dead by police, the ladies change-purse in his hand.

I knew stories like this were common, and age was no barrier to being killed in a place like Brazil, where crime was seen as black and white. The police undoubtedly had to send a message that would make attacking tourists (or anybody) unthinkable, but was lethal force the only way? Did killing a kid change anything? Did it make these people any less desperate? To have seen these very same children just the day before in that favela, and to have watched them flying kites and running around playing tag, made this story a tough pill to swallow. It's the 21st Century, how can this be happening? I thought. But I guess time is irrelevant, and saying 'in this day and age' has a different meaning in different communities across the world.

Sitting on that beanbag silently stewing over the sheer struggle some are forced to face while others simply drift through life, was difficult. Why? How is this acceptable? How could the world be so cruel to some, while others are given everything only to squander it away? How is one human being afforded these things, while another is not? Is there a responsibility on those who are given such opportunities to make the most of them? Should there be? These thoughts played on repeat. Unable to sleep, I was besieged by the images of so many children I'd seen walking and living on the streets. The intense silence and darkness of the hostel lobby was, in those moments, life changing.

The more I think about my own death, the closer I feel I am to finding my true self. To be connected to and aware of our eventual end is both terrifying and freeing. Does nothing matter, or does everything matter? What will people say at my funeral? That I made money and had a nice house? Or something more?

Death had indeed haunted me in the most enlightening of ways in

South America, and yet it hadn't claimed me. Why? I wondered. Was I meant to be here?

Boarding the plane home, I found myself internalising a thought that would forever change me. **'If the world wanted you dead, you'd be dead, you have no say, no control'**, I repeated over and over in my head, as I gave myself to 'the will of the world'.

Back in Australia, some time after my South American adventure, I was at my parents' home recounting some of these stories when we heard that a massive 8.8 magnitude earthquake had hit Santiago, Chile, killing hundreds and toppling thousands of buildings across the country, many of which I had explored just weeks earlier.

My mum snickered, not at the news report, but at what she was about to say: "Trust me, someone or something wanted you here, else you wouldn't have been born the way you were." While it wasn't news to me to hear that I was an accident (a freakish one at that), the near death experiences of the past month or so made me more curious than ever to learn about the exact nature of my birth.

Where did I come from?

I probably first started asking questions about my existence when I was 12. At the time I wasn't all that happy, and who knows, maybe I needed to think I had a reason for being. Nine years on (just after that trip) and my purpose for wanting to understand the details surrounding my birth hadn't really changed all that much. I don't think I was any happier and I still had more questions than answers.

Thankfully my parents were, and still remain, incredibly open people – almost to a fault – so they sat me down and told me: "You weren't exactly meant to be born, but we're glad you were."

Eight years before I was born, in August 1978, dad and mum met in rather bizarre, but romantic, fashion. They were both working at the same school, with mum teaching a year six and seven class, while dad had a grade two class that included my oldest sister Cindy – from mum's first marriage. There was a ski camp for the older kids and dad was the only male teacher who knew how to ski, so he was roped into the trip – though not exactly kicking and screaming, as he's always loved the snow. Oddly, due to the school being in a fairly low socio-economic area there were a number of additional friends and family invited on the camp to help make up the numbers. This included mum's mum Moreen (my gran), Cindy (or Cin as I've always called her) and Pete, Cin's dad.

As mum and dad recounted this story more recently, there was the usual mix of pragmatism and dry English humour that surrounded our family. "We exchanged a few looks throughout the trip," said mum. "Then on the bus ride home we sat together and chatted the whole way. The relationship grew pretty quickly," she continued before dad chimed in. "Yeah, we were basically married by the time we stepped off the bus, or at least your mum thought so," laughed dad, who's never been shy to poke fun at a situation, especially those involving mum's intense and sudden emotional connections she forms. Mum went on to explain that while dad was ready to settle down, she wanted to head off and travel.

"I'd been married and tied down for much of my adult life to that point, so I had an urge to be free and explore while I could, so while our relationship grew stronger and we lived together for a while, I was putting in place the plans I needed to travel," said mum. "This included moving into my friend Andrew Tobin's granny flat, where I didn't have to pay rent, so I could save as much as I could during 1979 for my trip the following year." (Just as a side note, the very same Andrew Tobin is today the voice in almost all our videos for The Happiest and A Million Smiles, and was also the working editor of this book).

In May 1980 mum headed off to travel the world and explore her place in it, while dad moved back in with his parents briefly – to save – before buying a unit close by.

With nine-year-old Cin by her side, mum bravely bunny-hopped from Port Moresby, through Indonesia, Malaysia, Singapore and Thailand, before journeying on to Nepal, Delhi and Greece, which is where Cin caught a plane home to her father. "I then travelled to Japan where I reconnected with a man I'd met in Port Moresby. He was an Israeli man, a photographer and travel agent who was wandering the world writing a book as he went. He had the type of mind that thirsted for new experiences and could learn anything instantly. He spoke seven languages fluently. We spent about a month in Japan before going our separate ways, but he would have a lasting impact on my life," recalled mum. "I arrived home in January 1981, and already Paul (my dad) had left for Samoa, where he and a few teacher friends were offered work with one of the local schools."

"We weren't particularly thrilled with the way they whacked their students, or what they seemed to be teaching so out of the seven of us who went, only one decided to stay," said dad. "My friend Frank and I spent a few months making our way through American Samoa, Hawaii and LA, before heading up the coast to Seattle, which is where I fell in love. There was just something about Seattle, it was alive, you could see how bands like Nirvana and Pearl Jam came out of there, and we were only 20 minutes from the best snow I'd ever seen. I also met a girl there, but after three months, I eventually decided it was time to move on. To return to England, to the town I grew up in, in Yorkshire."

After spending a few weeks exploring Europe, dad arrived home in August 1981 to find mum heavily pregnant. "Times were different then," said dad, referencing the hippie era he'd grown up in. "It didn't bother me that mum was pregnant, the only difficulty was with your grandma and grandad, so we kept it hidden for a while."

My sister Bek (Rebekah) was born on 17 October 1981. For the next couple of years mum and dad lived separately. Mum was on maternity leave, but owned a house in a trendy inner city suburb called Goodwood, in Adelaide, South Australia, where she lived with Cin and Bek. Dad on the other hand had built a house in the Adelaide Hills, 25 minutes drive from the city in a place called Bridgewater – which was a beautiful, leafy pocket of heaven – the perfect escape. Sounding like a loved up teenager, mum told me how her and dad were a bit more than a casual fling over this period, and could enjoy deep conversations about most things, typically seeing eye to eye on those core beliefs that had made them kind of like "slightly more mainstream hippies" during the '60s, '70s and, well, they still are.

"Then there was another little gift we didn't expect," said mum. "In January 1983 we found out that your brother was on his way, and this time your dad was the father." It was hard not to think it, so I asked mum bluntly: "Were you practicing birth control?" To which they both just laughed, and said: "Yes, but not very well, obviously." Mum then chimed in with a coy 'I'm about to be funny' look on her face. "We were using the rhythm method, but obviously we weren't very good at keeping a beat." They both laughed, as they explained that while it was unexpected, my older brother was not an unwelcome addition to their lives, which were about to get much closer.

"Almost immediately your dad moved in with me, and after keeping

Gran and Poppa (mum's parents) with Bek, Kane, mum and me.

Mum and dad on their wedding day.　　Me and my mummy.　　Bek taking me for a ride.

My sister Cin and me with our dog, Josh.

Grandad Peter and Grandma Sheila (dad's parents) with Kane, Bek and me.

Me sitting under the old apple tree at our Blackwood home trying to eat a fallen piece of fruit.

Mum holding me just after my birth.

Bek in the dark all this time, we knew we needed to tell your grandma and grandad [on dad's side] about her," said mum. "As dad does, you know, he plainly and simply told them that I was pregnant with his child, and that he had committed to living with me, and that there was another little girl, Bek, who he would become the father of now, too."

The situation was no doubt a little challenging for dad's parents to understand. They had always been slightly more traditional in their thinking. But if there's one thing they've both always known how to do, it was love their grandchildren. "We've always loved Bek, from the minute we saw her, we adored her," said grandma. "She's always been our granddaughter just the same. We just didn't like the lies, and of course your grandad and I wondered why we hadn't seen your mother for so long, because we knew Paul was with her. We knew something was out of place. I think when we found everything out it was a relief really, because at least things could go back to normal, and Bekka was a beautiful little thing by that time. So full of life."

As both mum and dad continued to recount this adventurous period of their life, you could see the qualities in them I've always admired. Dad is Captain Compromise and ever the pragmatist, always willing to bend and shift if it will help resolve a situation and keep things moving forward. It is a gift that stems from his unwavering kindness – a trait he no doubt inherited in part from his father. Mum, on the other hand, is like wildfire, outwardly passionate and a true believer in both spirituality and learning, as well as right and wrong, black and white – an odd mix at times. She was and still is, a typical teacher, hard and uncompromising. Traits, too, that came from her parents and a far harsher upbringing.

"In July 1983, your brother Kane was born," continued dad. "And then a bit over a year later we got married. That year I'd actually been the stay at home dad, because mum wanted to go back to work at the start of 1984. That also meant I could continue doing up the house, which was a good thing." Mum cut in, "But you know your dad, he thought he'd start looking for a job after the wedding, thinking it would take him a few months, but as usual he got the first thing he applied for, which was just up the road at Cornes Toyota, selling cars."

"I knew I was pretty good at sales, so I figured why not earn as much money as possible in the seven or eight hours I'm at work, and at that time the car trade was the place to be," said dad, once again showcasing his very practical train of thought.

The following year mum dropped back to teaching part time, as the two began looking for a house that could be theirs, rather than Goodwood, which mum had bought and they now shared. "Thankfully dad's title as Toyota Salesman of the Year in 1985 – his first year on the job – meant we had a few extra dollars in the bank, and we'd finally found a place we loved, up in the hills at Blackwood on a nice sized block that would give the kids some space to play."

Then at Christmas 1985 mum said she knew something wasn't right. "I'm pregnant, I know it," she recalled saying to my dad at the time. "I always knew when I was pregnant, only this time I panicked."

The reason for the panic was because mum had a 'Copper 7' IUD (Intrauterine Device) in place, which was a small T shaped birth control device inserted into the uterus to prevent pregnancy. It was supposed to be fool-proof, or more than 99% effective as they say. But still, as mum underwent a pregnancy test it confirmed what she already knew, she was expecting.

"I'd never been scared before with the other kids, but this time I was petrified. I immediately went to see my doctor. I knew there were severe risks and complications. 'What's going to happen?' I asked. The doctor told me there was around a 50% chance of spontaneous abortion up until 20 weeks. And given they couldn't get the IUD out, the chances were even higher," said mum. "Looking at this thing in scans was terrifying, it was a gory copper device shaped like a Y or a T so it had three really sharp ends that could pierce the sack where the baby was housed. I was so frightened."

Statistically speaking IUD pregnancies present many risks, especially if the IUD can't be removed early. The first major concern is a 160% greater chance of having an ectopic pregnancy – where the fertilised egg embeds in the fallopian tubes rather than the uterus. Ectopic pregnancies are typically aborted as they often kill the mother. The second is that the rate of miscarriage is around 50% with an IUD in situ, more than two-fold higher than usual. In fact, in a recent study around 16% of women with an IUD miscarried after 12 weeks of pregnancy, compared to just 1% of regular women. Finally, 56% of women with IUDs had a premature baby, while only around 21% of those without a device deliver early. All in all my chances of being born healthy weren't great. The only thing that saved my mum from the terror of this reality, was ignorance.

THE PAIN AND THE EXPLODING PLANE

"I think back in those days they didn't know quite as much, which was probably a good thing, it meant there were less statistics to be scared of. I was basically told that if I got to 20 weeks I would likely be safe, so that was our focus. Be careful, be calm, nothing strenuous, because there was this sharp metal thing right next to my baby," said mum. "And then at 20 weeks we had a scan and it showed the device had lodged relatively safely in my uterus, and you were alive and well."

One hundred and forty days later mum was lying on the dining room floor of their Blackwood home screaming in pain. "I honestly couldn't believe how fat I was with you. I was huge. Much bigger than the other kids. It was alarming. Maybe it was your big head," she laughed. "I just wanted you out, I'd never been afraid of birth before you came along, so I just wanted it over and done with."

After eight hours of pain and suffering, mum defied the odds to give birth to a healthy child. Me. And so my journey began.

While at the time I probably didn't fully appreciate nor understand either of these periods of my life – my birth or those near death moments in South America – both have stayed with me and both continue to shape the lens through which I see the world. For the happiest people I know begin by being thankful for the breath in their lungs.

It's one thing to be alive,

it's another to know who's alive in there.

'Gill Hicks' by Tony Kearney.

2

MY SISTER AND THE SECURITY GUARD

On Thursday 7 July 2005, a 19-year-old violent extremist detonated a bomb, suiciding himself and intentionally killing and maiming as many people as he could. I was standing just one person from him in the rush-hour-packed Tube carriage.

In the time it takes to draw a breath, we were plunged into a darkness so immense it was almost tangible; what I imagine wading through tar might be like. Minutes earlier we were just a bunch of commuters who had followed Tube etiquette: no direct eye contact and absolutely no conversation. But as the smoky darkness lifted, we began reaching out. We even started helping each other. We were calling out our names, a little bit like a roll call, waiting for responses.

I'm Gill. I'm here. I'm alive. OK. I'm Alison. Here. Alive. OK. I'm Richard. Here. Alive. OK. I didn't know Alison, but I listened for her check-ins every few minutes. To be honest I had no idea who Richard was either, but it mattered to me that he survived.

All I shared with them was my first name. They didn't know that I was the head of a department at the Design Council. They didn't know that I published architecture and design journals, that I was a Fellow of the Royal Society of Arts or that I wore black, drank gin and watched TED talks. To them, I was just Gill. And I wasn't ready for all of that to end.

I was so determined to survive that I used my scarf to tie tourniquets around the tops of my legs, and I just shut everything and everyone out, to focus, to listen to myself, to be guided by instinct alone. I lowered my breathing rate. I elevated my thighs. I held myself upright and I fought the urge to close my eyes.

I held on for almost an hour, an hour to contemplate the whole of my life up until that point. Perhaps I should have done more. Perhaps I could have lived more, seen more. Maybe I should have gone running, dancing, taken up yoga. But my priority, and my focus, was always my work. I lived to work. Who I was on my business card mattered to me. But it didn't matter down in that tunnel.

By the time I felt that first touch from one of my rescuers, I was unable to speak, unable to say even a small word, like "Gill." I surrendered my body to them. I had done all I possibly could, and now my life was in their hands.

Days later, when I woke and laid eyes on my hospital ID tag, I finally understood just who I was – and who humanity was too. It read: 'One unknown estimated female.' One unknown estimated female. Those four words were my gift.

What they told me was very clear – my status, my name, that title on my business card I'd worked so hard to get – it didn't matter anymore. To those rescuers who kept me alive in the minutes, hours and weeks following the 2005 London Bombings, I was simply a human being and that's all that mattered. Who I was or wasn't made no difference to the extraordinary lengths that they were prepared to go to to save my life, to save as many 'unknowns' as they could, often putting their own lives at risk to do so. To them, it didn't matter if I was rich or poor, the colour of my skin, whether I was male or female, my sexual orientation, who I voted for, whether I was educated, if I had a faith or no faith at all. Nothing mattered, I was simply a precious human life.

When I first heard Gill Hicks share her story of surviving the 2005 London Bombings, I was brought to tears, not because she lost her legs or had a bunch of strangers pull her from the 'tar' that encased her. No. What made me say 'OMFG' over and over in my mind was the realisation that this – surviving a major terror event – is what it seemed to take for the average human being trapped in the matrix of this modern, materialistic life to escape, and let her light shine.

MY SISTER AND THE SECURITY GUARD

Surely there had to be an easier way to wake people up to their true nature – who they were without their business card? The question rattled around in my brain over and over, until I finally decided to ask Gill to catch up for a coffee and shed a little light on how she'd finally come to accept herself as she was, and what, if anything, I and others might be able to learn from her torturous journey.

"My frustration is that I now know what we're capable of if we unmask ourselves and say to the world 'here I am, this is me'. So, for me it's about how can I do that, and how can humanity do that. When are we reaching our potential and why does it have to take a tragic event for me to have learned this!?" exclaimed Gill.

To understand why it took a terrorist attack to discover her true potential, I asked Gill about her formative years, where she had come from and what her dreams had been. She said her life was always about two things: the title on her business card, and the idea that anything that involved change was absolutely exciting.

"The new was always better," said Gill. "The old was passé, and the present was dull and boring, so anything that represented the new, the change, the journey, was the exciting place to be, to search for and look towards. I guess for me it was how do I break the status quo? How do I break the boredom of everything being rather safe and predictable?" she said with great irony, given her position today.

This obsession with seeking happiness anywhere, except for where she stood, soon saw a 19-year-old Gill making the brave decision to pack her suitcase and leave the safe confines of Adelaide, headed for London.

"I didn't have a plan, all I thought was, I want a change, and change is the greatest thing and it's nothing to fear," she chuckles, acknowledging her past naivety.

With just 40 pounds in her purse, Gill boarded the plane to London full of cheerful assumptions. Dressed immaculately from head to toe, she felt she was a shoe-in to meet someone on the plane who would offer her a fantastic job the moment she landed. She'd even asked the cabin crew if the airport staff searched through every single bag, because she'd folded everything meticulously, thinking she would get a job the moment she landed, so would need a fresh change of clothes, and didn't want security creasing her outfits. Gill recalled a cabin crew member simply shook her head and said, "You've never travelled before, have you?"

"So I arrived in London, having not landed a job on the plane, and I stood on the middle of Westminster Bridge, and looked out at this mass of buildings and people, and I thought, 'What is this actually representing to me? What is this opportunity, and what is holding me back from all the wonders that this place can offer me?' And I realised, the only person between me and what I wanted to achieve was me, standing there with 40 pounds in my purse."

At such a tender age, Gill said she was all of a sudden forced to become her own mentor, her own motivator, her own leader, and once she realised she herself was in control, her plan became simple: follow her instincts.

"It was a completely extraordinary time, and when I left Adelaide, I said to my friends: 'I need to find out who I am'. Of course, I understand now that we can all find out who we are without travelling to the other side of the world, but I didn't know that then. And I think just putting myself in the midst of tremendous change did help me discover who I was, because I'd never been challenged. So challenge and change was a fantastic thing for my early character," she said.

After years of working from the ground up, Gill said her first job application in London involved walking in to the largest publishing group in Europe and saying, "I'm Gill Hicks and I'm fantastic at basically anything, and I could work here. To which the receptionist said, 'I'll just get Sophie down for you.' So Sophie came down and she said hello, and I said, 'Hi, I'm Gill Hicks and I'm really great at stuff and I can work here.' To which Sophie replied, 'I don't think so. Leave your CV on the desk.'"

"Anyway, I managed to keep Sophie engaged long enough to convince her that if I could come in every day for three months without being paid, at the end of that three months she would wonder what she ever did without me. And it worked, I got the job," said Gill, with a sheepish smirk on her face.

Over the coming months Gill said she finally found her forte, and it was in architecture and design. Her career suddenly had a purpose and focus, and she quickly climbed the corporate ladder, landing a number of incredible positions that saw her working with successful teams that put in bids for places like Glasgow, when Glasgow won the City of Culture Award in 1990.

"I was absolutely intoxicated by my work," she said. "Everything I did, how I defined myself, was through my business card. Every social event I went to was work related. Every driving ambition I had was to achieve a greater standing of who I was on a business card. And I was good at it; I mean, I'd gone from a very young person with 40 pounds in her purse, to now being part of a design team that was successful in winning the Olympic bid for London in 2012. The problem was, I'd actually lost sight of what I was trying to do with my life."

"I was the first person in at the office at 7:30 every morning, and I was always the last to leave at 10:30 every night. I had a beautiful relationship with the security staff, and I thought that was special," she laughed, reflecting on the emptiness of chasing success only to realise that it meant everyone liked her, but herself. "I let 10 years of my life evaporate in the pursuit of a title, and to this day, it really gets to me, because I wish I could transport myself back and talk to my younger self to say 'there's a whole lot of life to live,'" Gill said, as her eyes began to glisten with regret.

"My saving grace, as it was, was what happened when my expectations of tomorrow were broken. When what I thought tomorrow would bring, which was going to work, enjoying a gin and watching a few TED talks, was blown to bits, literally."

Gill said she'd often pondered whether there is greater happiness in living a life completely free of challenges, where one's expectations and trajectory in life remain fairly constant, or whether life is more full of joy when we're faced with adversity, because somehow it forces us to decide who we really are and what we're really capable of. To me, I felt Gill was the perfect case study to answer her own question, for she had undoubtedly seen and known both sides of this debate, so I asked her plainly – "well, which has made you happier?"

"Hmmmm," she paused. "Facing my own imminent death, in fact being dead for 30 minutes, absolutely changed my understanding of life," said Gill. "There's never been an easy way for me to share this, but I feel it's imperative I do – as we sat in complete darkness in what remained of the train carriage, death came to me as the most beautiful female voice. She said to me, 'Gill, close your eyes, come with me. You've lost both your legs, you don't want to live like that, come with me'. At the time I had no idea that I'd lost both my legs – I guess my mind was capable of blocking that out, which is proof of how far adversity can push us."

"As I was thinking of how beautiful it would be to go with this voice, an opposing voice came into my field. I called it 'the voice of life', and it was male, and it was angry, and it said, 'Actually Gill, how dare you? How dare you? There's so much you can do, legs or no legs. But you know what? It's up to you.'"

This "voice of life" was a little bit standoffish in a way, recalled Gill, who said it felt as though she was letting it down by being seduced by the idea of death.

"Once I chose to live, something extraordinary happened," said Gill. "I felt no pain and absolutely went into the most amazing instinctive trance, where I tourniqueted the tops of my legs so they stopped bleeding. I then spoke to the other survivors and I said, 'I'm so sorry, I need to not talk any longer because I just need to stem the bleeding and to stare at my watch and wait'. It's crazy to think I was completely conscious throughout the whole process, and I'll never forget the moment that I saw that first glimpse of a light, that was, to me, signaling rescue."

At that moment Gill said she simply surrendered her body to them, "to whoever they were" she laughed, having since become close friends with a number of her rescuers. In fact, on the tenth anniversary of the 7/7 attacks, Gill said she was overwhelmed by the response she got when she went to each of the people involved in her survival to show her gratitude and say "thank you."

"I pretty much got the same reaction each and every time," said Gill. "And that was, 'I was just doing my job'. Something about that really got to me. 'I was just doing my job,' they repeated, one after the other, after the other. Over the years it's made me think about, well then, what is our job? Do we have a responsibility to each other? Is that our primary job? Also, I can guarantee if you are ever in a situation where something dreadful happens, the person next to you will be the person who's your closest lifeline. So is it also our job to at least acknowledge the person who we see next to us every day? I don't know, it's something I've continuously pondered. Finally, there was another quality in all of these rescuers – they never gave up. Now bear in mind, I was 'one unknown estimated female'. I'd lost 75% of my blood, I had no vital signs, no legs and was for all intents and purposes, dead. But still they never gave up, and perhaps that too should be part of our job – to give others hope."

Gill said it was that very idea of her rescuers never giving up hope, coupled with the realisation that she was saved simply because she was human, that inspired her in 2007 to launch a charity called Making A Difference (MAD) For Peace, which is all about finding and celebrating our common humanity. Something she hopes can bridge the hateful divides that cause all forms of violent extremism.

"Something I realised following that morning was the danger of ignorance and blind judgement. For unbeknownst to me, the bomber in our Tube carriage and his three accomplices had wrongly judged and labeled me and all the people they killed and wounded that day as 'the enemy,'" she explained. "That really struck me as a horrid example of how dangerous it can be to assume we know anything about anyone based on where they live, how they look or their beliefs. Because perhaps if they had asked us if we supported the war in Iraq, the war in Afghanistan or the blatant Islamophobia that made them feel hated, many of us might have said 'no', and some might have even added, 'we are sorry, how can we help?'"

Cherishing diversity and appreciating our common humanity within this increasingly integrated world – where we instinctively judge and divide according to our 'tribe' – is one of our biggest challenges if we are to find peace or happiness. For when we move beyond making assumptions based on appearances and begin conversing with one another, the world becomes smaller and more connected. Something Gill is now dedicated to achieving through MAD For Peace.

"I think a good example of this was MAD's first major public engagement project, WALKTALK, which was devised to encourage people of all ages and from all walks of life – who might otherwise never have the opportunity to meet – to come together and walk and, most importantly, talk about their beliefs and focus on everything we have in common," said Gill.

Having held so many titles in the past 12 years, from *head curator* at the Design Council to *enemy*, to *one unknown estimated female*, then *patient*, followed by *victim, survivor, peace activist, speaker*, and finally *wife and mother*, Gill said she is acutely aware of what it takes to redefine who we are if we're not happy with our title.

"What's been very interesting for me, is the transformational bit – the bit that comes between each title – because I definitely know now what I thought I knew as a 19-year-old, which is that **I own my life, because I get to decide in every single moment how I react and how I respond**, and life is simply a bunch of little moments pieced together," she said. "That has been revelatory for me, because even a thought is a moment, and that's where peace and happiness begins or ends, in our mind. But the great thing is we can train our brains, just as I had to do to learn to walk again. Similarly, if you think you're chasing the wrong things, like a job title, or you look at certain people and put them in that box labeled 'enemy' as happened to me, if you can recognize those thoughts, and if you want to make a change, then you need to say, 'OK, change that, change that because I'm owning this, I get to choose how I react and how I respond'. And then those unhappy or destructive thoughts just disappear."

Of course, Gill said the process takes some time to master, because like going to the gym to get bigger muscles, creating new pathways or ways of thinking in your mind takes practice in order to reinforce those new corridors of thought. This process is something scientists call neural plasticity, which basically means our brains are like putty that we can mould and change, which is kind of awesome, because it means that with enough practice we can think and therefore do and be whatever we want. Because as Gill pointed out, "what I think I do."

"What this all tells us is that you are the only person who is able to make a difference in every area of your life," said Gill. "That's not to say that others won't impact on certain areas of your life, so as they say, choose your friends wisely."

Having experienced such a long period of incapacitation herself – being waited on hand and (missing) foot in hospital – Gill said the right team is important, not only for our happiness, as we are social beings, but also because they can assist you with reinforcing the neural pathways that let you be your best self. Gill said, trying not to laugh, that for her, that was her "bastard of a physiotherapist during rehab", a guy called Matt, who didn't exactly follow the text books.

"He was slightly unconventional in his methods," laughed Gill. "What Matt would do is come up behind me and push me over. Now, of course, other patients who were amputees would see this and think 'I don't want him'. But this is what defined my rehab and gave me the mind I have today. He threw me in the deep end, in order to teach and bend and stretch my mind until I learned a new skill. So Matt would come and push me over, and I'd say 'Matt, really? Must you do that?' After doing this a few times I said, 'Oh, I get it, you're teaching me how to fall'. And he said, 'No, Gill, I'm teaching you how to get back up.'"

"That changed everything for me. It changed absolutely everything, learning how to get back up has been the key, I think, to my entire life and certainly to my happiness, because I'm proof, bad things are going to happen — whether it's physical abuse or the media putting bad thoughts in your head — it is how we let them affect us that defines us."

One concept Gill said, that has helped to bring her a greater sense of peace and acceptance, despite all the hate and divisiveness we see in mainstream media, is the knowledge that the two elements that divide us — perception and truth — aren't even real.

"Some of us may see a nine, some of us may see a six, depending on which angle you're looking at it. I could argue on my life that what I see is a nine. My opponent could argue on their life that what they see is a six. And when we both turn our heads the other way, we're both shocked that we're both right," explained Gill, while speaking at a conference called *newday* which I was also presenting at. "This idea has led me to talk about the notion that perhaps there are many versions of a truth. For a truth is only our perception of what we think and believe something to be. And it's absolutely incredible when I'm working with people who are adamant that their beliefs are fixed, and to get them to come to a different space, a less black and white understanding, and to see their mind move; what that does to their own sense of peace and happiness is mesmerizing."

"I think this is part of the overall ideology we all need to hold if we are ever going to find a way through violent extremism, to a happier, more peaceful existence."

In all she has been through — sitting in that tar and dying for 30 minutes, only to be born again as a nameless, legless being — Gill said the greatest lesson she learnt was choice. That if you are not happy, and you are stuck in a job that you don't like, then it is up to you to change it, and to live a life that you choose, because **only you know you, so only you can be you.**

"It's interesting isn't it, because when we're born we don't really get to choose to be alive. It's fascinating that when you do get to choose, how life takes on a whole new depth and breadth and meaning, because I am here due to a choice I made and that is to show up, to participate, to give back and to honour this incredible gift."

"And I must say, it's also appreciating just how fragile it all is, so I don't expect anything anymore. I respect the fragility that is our life. And I've even chosen to never take painkillers, because in changing the way I'm viewing life, I've accepted that actually it's about the full spectrum.

To be able to feel pain, to be able to know disappointment, so that when those moments of extreme joy, absolute wins and happiness come, I know they're part of a balance. Because to know that full spectrum, for me, is what I call being alive."

In closing, Gill put to me a number of questions I have since pondered, and hope to answer throughout this book: "Do we actually have everything we need? Do we have every single tool we need within us to get to where we need to be? To solve the problems we need to solve? How much quiet, self-time do we allow where we just listen to our souls? That's been one of the most extraordinary things for me, to stop the noise and to listen to my body as it tells me it's time to sit down or it's time to get active. It's absolutely extraordinary to think of what we already have in-built, if only we'd stop to notice it," she said, before slowly getting up from her seat, carefully balancing on her prosthetic legs and giving me a hug.

While finding and being your truest self doesn't have to involve the excruciating agony of having your legs blown off, it is often an endeavour met with pain. This is nothing new. Two hundred thousand years of fight or flight evolution has taught us to be scared of 'the other' – people we see as unlike ourselves. You only need to look at the burning of witches, the abandonment of disabled children who were thought to be cursed, or the fact that we in Australia stole an entire generation of Aboriginal children in order to try to breed out their race. What our unconscious, instinctive, survivalist-based nature (something discussed at length in Chapter 6) does is judge, rather than ask questions, because up until the last few thousand years people rarely had to encounter strangers regularly, unless they were attempting to kill them. Previously, we typically lived in small-scale societies without the ability to travel or communicate widely, which meant if we saw someone different approaching, we often shot first and asked questions later. Back then, there were few reasons to try to understand, let alone respect and admire, those people who were different, as they were probably just trying to hurt us and take our stuff. The issue is, the human mind is lagging in its adaptation to our current situation: the reality that very few people are out to get us, to steal our bread or crops, because these days the vast majority have enough to survive. When we come to recognise and amend this weakness in our ever-evolving consciousness, I think astonishing and unique people, like

...l joins Muslim, Jewish and Christian leaders to walk from Kings Cross to Tavistock Square to celebrate unity on the 10th ...niversary of the 7/7 attacks. Image by Kristian Buus/British Future.

...l speaking at *newday*, the conference where we first met. ...age by Cath Leo Photos.

Gill with one of her rescuers PC Andy Maxwell on the 10th anniversary of the attacks. Image by Stefan Rousseau.

...l in Trafalgar Square on the final stretch of a 430 kilometre walk for peace she did in 2008. Image by Caroline Eluyemi.

My sister Bek in her late teens.

my sister (who taught me to be me), will be able to thrive, free from the emotional torment of being constantly judged as weird or different.

My sister, my hero

The pain of not fitting in isn't the only minefield we must cross if we are to find and be our happiest selves. The highly sophisticated consumer driven world, in front of us at every turn, is perhaps the greatest test we must overcome. As it stands, those in charge (the 1%) want us to believe that the only way we will be happy is if we have a decent education (as if university in and of itself will make us a better person), a good job (which is measured financially and in terms of status), a nice house (the bigger the better), a dog, 2.4 kids, and of course, plenty of 'likes' on our Facebook posts. The epitome I guess, would be somewhere between the Queen and the Kardashians. It's not to say that this sort of life or these things won't make us happy, they might, but not if they trap you in a job you don't like, so you can pay for a house and family you never see.

While millions are undeniably being misled by this *one size fits all* approach, and plenty seem to be seeking answers in the wrong places, that burning question of *who am I?* never leaves us. It is our birthright. The ideal curse for a curiously conscious being. **For in discovering your 'who', you will see the universe, and the universe will see you.**

So how do we actually find our truest self? I think there are just two things we need to do: *be awake* and *be looking*. Regrettably, these are behaviours most of us have come to avoid. Because, of course, it's much easier to follow, simply doing whatever is seen as 'cool' or 'normal', rather than being your crazy, weird, whacky and irreplaceable self. Not only do the marketing executives of the world want you to feel this way – unpopular if you don't own whatever they're selling – they also need you to feel that who you are is inadequate, because if *you* were enough, *you* wouldn't need to fill your life with so many things, and they'd be out of a job. As my sister puts it, "when your soul is fed by all the ingredients that make you you, it will be less hungry to consume those shiny objects we're told will make us whole, but which leave us starving." As it stands, we are told to look outside ourselves for pretty much everything – education, entertainment, companionship, even in answering our innermost questions. But is 'who we are' really something that other people or things can help us determine? To me, the curiosity to discover *who* we are is usually ignited as a teenager, and as my sister is living proof, sometimes it never disappears.

As a child, the younger of my two sisters, Bek, was a fervent exerciser of her mind and body. She loved nothing more than challenging herself, and openly enjoyed the process of growing new parts of herself, like when she worked for weeks and weeks to learn how to whistle or read, or climb the highest tree around.

"There was revelation in each new goal attained, like a secret truth revealed," said Bek. "The books I devoured were not just stories, they added depth to my very being; new ideas were new realms of existence, and I think I drove everyone around me a bit crazy with all my questioning, because I could never get enough. The abundance of play and imagination that filled my early world (thanks to our parents' ardent efforts), and the ecstatic joy that accompanied it, has been something I have never been willing to let go of, and it has poured itself into my adult life."

To this day Bek remains obsessed with colour, cartoons, music, comic books, painting and all things that are an expression of what she calls "the pure state of being that a happy child experiences as a daily occurrence." While Bek doesn't belong to any specific religion, she does describes herself as a 'believer' and a deeply spiritual person, who takes ideas from a range of ancient and modern texts.

Interestingly, Bek never met her biological father, whom mum described as "worldly and thirsty for knowledge, but full of ego." I've often wondered just how much of his DNA Bek inherited; especially given the only dad she knew was my brother's and mine. Physically of course, she never quite looked like us (with darker, curlier hair, and different skin tone and facial features). She also had a slightly different way of seeing the world, she always had an added intensity, as if she felt emotions more deeply – more joy, but also more pain. Bek's 'differences', though noticeable, were always irrelevant to me and our family; to us, she was a sister, daughter, niece, cousin and granddaughter just the same. The problem was, in treating her 'the same as everybody else', we may have in fact been harming her, as she was different, and sometimes we need to be vigilant of that and adapt our behavior to accommodate those differences. I don't know if it was her tomboyish nature, different look or lack of conviction in herself (something every child finds difficult), but Bek suffered at the hands of a society that didn't have a box for her to fit in.

"Most of my school life was fraught with peril," said Bek, when I asked how those early years had shaped her life. "I loved it and had a joyful and very social time up until grade 3, after which it was just misery. I was a tomboy when I was young, and after grade 2 copped no end of insults at school about it, to the point where going to school made me feel sick. I was constantly called a boy and I hated it, because all I was doing was following my instincts, and doing the activities I liked. All of a sudden though, all this distortion of identity was heaped upon me, and it seriously messed with my mind, leaving me with soooooooo much anxiety. It was truly awful."

While there were more bad days than good during this time, Bek said some of her fonder memories revolved around running, as she was always an exceptional long distance athlete, and also excelled in a game called 'the shuttle run'.

"The shuttle run (or beep test) was played with classmates and involved running between two lines about 20 metres apart and making it to the line opposite you before a siren on a recorded tape sounded. The time between sirens got shorter and shorter as your pace got faster, until it was a flat out sprint. Those who couldn't keep up, were out. Whenever I played, it always came down to me and a boy called Daniel. We were both so determined," she said. "What I came to revere about these challenges was the point you always reached where, in order to keep going, you had to actually move beyond the body, which wanted to break, and the mind, which screamed to stop, and move through pure will and spirit alone, where overcoming yourself becomes the real goal."

I have often said my sister could have played for Australia in just about any women's sport. She was frequently one of the best baseballers, cricketers or runners, even when compared to the boys. Sadly though, her incredible talents on the field were not seen as a positive, but purely as something that made her 'different', and some kids just couldn't suppress those powerful evolutionary instincts that left them feeling threatened, because their brains couldn't compute who she was. She could throw further, run faster and punch harder than most boys, and I don't think I can ever remember Bek wearing a dress or having long hair. Somehow this just didn't sit well with other kids, who'd been groomed by society, and evolution, to see difference and feel the need to prove their superiority. But when Bek didn't bend and shift and change herself to suit the wants of the popular kids, they felt endangered, so they began bullying and excluding her. 'If people can't fit in they need to get out,' we seem to believe. But this isn't confined to the schoolyard, it's also why the left and right of politics is creeping further and further apart – because neither is willing to listen, without judgement, to the other. Both would simply prefer to stick their head in the sand and think they're right, because that feeds our sense of superiority. The thing is, if we honestly stop and think about how boring the world would be if we were all the same, and then instil that philosophy in our kids, perhaps we might see a few less children feeling the way my sister did.

"As I entered my pre-teens I still loved the learning, but I couldn't deal with the social aspect of school at all. I even struggled to stay involved in sport during this period," said Bek. "I went from being extremely gregarious to being more and more determined to live in my own head where things were better and not fraught with the danger of being hurt by others."

Needless to say, this distance between herself and others was the very thing that prompted Bek to become even more different. Suddenly, she spent lots of time in the library, reading by herself instead of talking to people on the sports field. Her sense of isolation only increased with the years, as she unknowingly developed a silent mood-altering condition that would go on to nearly kill her – and me.

"I met few friends with whom I resonated, and I grew increasingly bored with school curriculums and educational power structures, to the point where in year 9, I misbehaved simply because I felt there was nothing better to do," said Bek. "The school eventually asked me to leave, so I never completed year 9 and never did year 10 at all."

After six months of working at Hungry Jacks (Burger King), Bek eventually returned to school, and went on to complete year 11 and 12 over three years at Marden Senior Secondary College, where she achieved a graduating score of 96.6 out of 100. In fact, she even received six bonus points for the mix of subjects and school she graduated from, so in effect she got 102.6 out of 100, which meant she could go on to study anything she wanted at university. Not bad for a year 9 drop out, right!? But unfortunately, this did little to mend the wounds Bek developed through her early years.

"The hurt and separateness engendered in me during my time at school is something I am only now really getting over as a 35-year-old. It's true those old wounds cut deep," admitted Bek. "My distrust of people made it very easy for me to shy away from a career that would engage me socially, like practicing law or being a teacher, and into one that engaged my mind and spirit fully, but in a very limited social sphere."

"I'm not sad about my choice, but I am sad that it has taken so much of my life for me to feel confident in basic interaction, just because I had a really bad time at school."

A year after she finished school – at which time my mum, dad, brother and I were living in a rural town called Gin Gin, in Queensland, Australia – I remember being woken by a phone call late one night. I heard whispers as mum answered, and a sort of terror grew in her voice. A few hours later when I got up, I learned that Bek was in hospital; she hadn't been able to eat or drink for a week and had experienced a serious heart problem.

I don't remember mum talking about any ongoing sickness (though Bek has since told me she'd been ill for weeks), so immediately I assumed it must have been the result of some form of accident or something. I was beside myself. The only thing that had stopped me from killing myself in those bleak years living in mum and dad's 'dream community' – an eco-village called Kookaburra Park – was the thought of, and interaction with, my sister and my best friend, Sam. These were dark days for me indeed (year 8 and 9), as I began to find it more and more difficult to connect with my friends, who had no interest in politics or the arts as I did, and who (in part thanks to my brother, who gave them some pot) turned to recreational drugs to escape the mundane feeling that comes with being a teenager living in a small country town. Having seen what marijuana had done to my brother (an addict), I was unwilling to give in to smoking weed (or anything else), and slowly I became less 'cool', because all I wanted to do was drink alcohol, which was 'so yesterday'. My love life was also pretty tumultuous during this time, with the parents of 'the love of my life' not letting her see me because they assumed I was a low-life like my brother.

Unlike my sister, who said "I always had a secret world I could escape to, filled with so much beauty and wisdom from old scriptures and writings that were like a form of armor to protect me from the harshness of humanity," I had nothing. I'd always been a people person with plenty of close friends and family, but all of that was back in Adelaide, the very city where my sister lay dying in a hospital bed.

When my mum told me about Bek's condition, I just assumed we'd all be flying back to be with her, but given neither mum nor dad were working much at the time (they'd been building their dream home), they said we didn't have the money, so only mum was going back. I was in hysterics. One of my favourite pastimes during those years was swearing at my parents and I didn't disappoint on this occasion, hurling whatever emotional abuse I could at them, to try to get them to see my pain, my hurt and most of all, my love for Bek.

"She's my sister, she's your fucking daughter, how the fuck can you sit here while she's laying in a hospital bed, are you fucking mad? Please, please just let me go. You know what she means to me, if I had the money to pay for it I would, please don't be stingy idiots."

Devastatingly for me, they were not tuned into my wavelength – largely due to the fact they were too busy chasing their own utopian fantasy of living in an eco-village of like-minded people, which was just part of trying to find who they were – and my pain went unheard.

That night I nearly ended it. With a knife to my wrist, I began to push down hesitantly, curious to see how much I would bleed. The pain – both physical and mental – spurred me on. I didn't want to feel this way anymore. 'It would be so easy, no one would care, my parents obviously didn't love or understand me,' I thought – but then I noticed a photo of my sister next to my bed and it made me freeze. What if she survives? I wondered. And I'm gone? I knew and appreciated at that point the trials my sister had been through, and for some years she had been my greatest source of inspiration, not only because she returned to school and aced her final tests, but also because, as she explained, she re-found some semblance of love and enthusiasm for life through those teachers she encountered.

"Probably the most life-changing time happened when I went back to finish school. There, some of the most dedicated and intelligent teachers I have ever met showed me just how sublime learning can be, and I came to a new sense of being through the sheer joy of intellectual pursuit. It enraptured me – Classics, English, Chemistry, F.Scott Fitzgerald, *Apocalypse Now*, Eliot's *Wasteland*, Greek mythology, Buddhism and the Beats and quantum physics ... and on and on, I couldn't get enough. I spent hours hassling teachers, mad for information, as I felt I was finding myself in the work, finally encountering ideas like my own, full of spirit and idealism. And the teachers loved it, they fed me so much extra material and sent me home often with their own books. The intellectual freedom I had and the recognition I received at this school boosted my confidence immensely, and gave validity to the trains of thought about *right action* and *right purpose* I had been developing in my time away from school. It was all a very wholesome affair and of immense value to my mind and personality at the time; it bridged me back into the world," said Bek, as a contented and thankful grin etched itself on her face.

With a pool of blood collecting in one hand and tears streaming down my face like lonely rivers divided by a nosey mountain range, I knew then I couldn't abandon hope of re-finding my own semblance of love and enthusiasm. I also couldn't leave Bek, because in that moment I finally understood her agony. I sensed what it was to feel completely alone in who I was. I guess somehow it didn't seem fair for me to go and leave her even more alone, so I put the knife down and cleaned my sheets so mum and dad would never know.

After a few painstaking weeks of soul searching, prayers and having no idea what was going on with my sister, we finally got some kind-of-good news. Our GP in Adelaide (who was a family friend) noticed a few irregularities in her hormone levels and ran some tests that led to a diagnosis of hyperthyroidism, which basically meant that her thyroid – the little thing in your neck that regulates your hormones and metabolism – was out of control. Doctors concluded that a 'thyroid storm' – a huge burst of hormones – had caused her severe sickness and heart abnormality. Far beyond this one episode however, the diagnosis also helped us all to make sense of Bek's severe ups and downs as a teenager, as it was thought she'd had the illness for a long time, though undiagnosed.

Despite so much pain, so much distraction and even this medical condition, Bek always remained resolute in her commitment to seeking the truth of her spirit. It's how she suggests she was able to overcome so many problems in her life, including this near-death experience.

"These were my first lessons in spiritual transcendence, whereby I came to understand what power is strongest in man, that, like Plato says, while body and mind pull the chariot of each individual being, it is spirit that drives, that holds sway. **The power to keep going in life, against all adversity, physical and mental, comes from spirit**," said Bek, who as you might gather, has never lacked spirit. "This was something I understood from a very young age. It was my secret to coping and living in a world that set me apart, and it gave me an incredible inner strength, and from feeling this strength I decided I would feed the spirit most in my life, before body and mind."

"This is a choice I have never regretted!" she exclaimed. "My spirit and the truths revealed through it have kept me from falling apart during the hardest times in my life. It has been my company in times of abject loneliness, my compass when deciding on a career and my most proud achievement, for it has helped me live humbly and happily in a culture intent on always screaming for 'MORE!'"

In 2002, when Bek began her double-degree in Law and Arts, majoring in Classics (a blend of philosophy and history), at the University of Adelaide, she said she was eager to become a lawyer, simply to help people, "to right wrongs and deliver justice to the needy."

"By the time I finished my degree in 2007, I had absolutely no faith in the Western legal system to be able to deliver justice to people. Our law does not seek justice, it seeks to apply precedent and unfair notions of equality. It overcharges for its services, obfuscates through language and is highly antagonistic and adversarial, making argument more important than getting to the truth (as in an Inquisitorial system). And because of the prestige and lucre involved, it does, in my opinion, attract too much of the wrong sort of person," said Bek, distressed by her own words. "During my whole time at Law School, I never once heard a student talk about a case with any sense of pathos and real concern about the fact that most people who come to the law are facing, or have had, a horrendous experience in life. If we fail to take into account the emotional turmoil engendered by these experiences, how are we to deliver true justice?"

At any rate, Bek said she didn't seem to see eye to eye with anyone, making no friends, and slowly the righteousness with which she had approached her chosen career began to "seem like a joke." The thing about being true to yourself, according to Bek, is it means you can't just have noble intentions, you need to act on and be willing to sacrifice for them. For instance, when she graduated from university, Bek was offered the opportunity to write law books, for good money, from anywhere in the world. The problem was, she was never very good at speaking or abiding falsehoods, and she knew that this work would have required her to abandon who she was. That's why she said "no," happily turning down her first and only chance to work in law, to instead pursue another dream of playing music, which she has done ever since.

"It's not easy to say no to money and notoriety, but I coped by always feeling that I had a purpose removed from most (as we all do), and a way of seeing things that was all my own (as we all do). What made me fearful was not isolation, but the inadequacy of *others'* sense of purpose, for as Eric Hoffer says 'What monstrosities would walk the streets were some people's faces as unfinished as their minds'. I think this idea made jumping into music easy, because like most art forms, music's capacity for the speaking of absolute truth, the fertilisation of personal growth and freeing of the mind is unbridled," said Bek, as she began tapping on her chair like a drum. "When you play music and your whole spirit lifts you up, you stand as one with God, as one act of creation mirrors another. I have never experienced anything that makes me feel as holy and humble as bashing on my drums, it feels like existing in pure truth, and there is nowhere else I would rather be."

The most difficult thing Bek has done in her life (and that anyone might do), is choose truth above all things, truth as a state of being, as an epistemological premise. It has been difficult, not because the seeking was hard – for being and doing 'you' is a form of "ecstasy" she said – but the basic separation from people it has caused, has been horrendous.

"It's an excruciating thing, to see clearly the mystery in the world and the meaning in the stars and to be all alone with your knowledge. Knowledge that should move mountains but has no eyes of expression in our culture," she explained.

For the best part of a decade I have felt that a big part of 'being me' or fulfilling my own purpose has been to heal the wounds etched deep into Bek's heart (and others like her), for it is those who have seen and known the immense lightness and darkness that comes with chasing who you are that can inspire others to do the same (think Mandela, Gandhi, Martin Luther King – being true to themselves was not easy, but through their own struggle they inspired millions to do the same).

"It is important to undergo that journey of self-discovery no matter the pain it causes you, because we all have a personal overcoming to work through as part of our lives – a darkness to confront, a question to answer or quest to undertake, and only through the doing of these tasks will we fulfil our true nature and achieve our purpose in life – the two essentials to a sustained happiness," explained Bek, who, in my opinion, enjoys a very deep form of happiness, which is distinctly different from those who have a lot of fun getting drunk, going clubbing and having sex with strangers. The funny thing is, Bek said, having fun often helps us to escape or forget who we are, while finding happiness comes from having the courage to face and to be who we are. "If we never spend time learning who we are and striving to be the best we can, how can we expect the necessary collisions, confrontations and joys that will bring us to a full vision of what we need to be truly happy?"

As a truth seeker and a truth speaker, Bek said she believes others can find happiness by first learning to control their minds and their desires, and through observation of the processes of the mind – learning to be keenly aware of those experiences that help grow us as people, and those that stifle our dreams.

"People must learn to have the strength to choose that which is best for them and will make them into the fullest version of themselves, even if it is very difficult," she said. "This process of the refinement of choice is made much easier if one continually spends time alone in a quiet space getting to know the nature of their inner dialogue, analysing what wants and desires drive them, and considering these drives in relation to who they really want to be."

"Self-knowledge and self-satisfaction go hand in hand," claimed Bek, who went on to explain that **what we want and what we need are often two very different things** that lead to two very different paths of learning. "But we will never know which will bring us most happiness, unless we really know who we are."

The freedom to find and be who we are is a privilege few are afforded easily. Whether that's due to having domineering parents who insist you become a doctor, engineer or lawyer, or whether it's because you lack access to resources or time due to being trapped in poverty or the wrong environment – there will inevitably be barriers you encounter within your family, community and culture. Being part of a white, middle-class Australian family with two well-educated parents who grew up in Christian households, but who have adopted more rounded spiritual beliefs now, my sister and I never had to worry about cultural or environmental factors impacting our ability to be ourselves. Fortunately too, due to my parent's growing up during the hippie era of the 60s, which was characterised by its free thinking, anti-establishment and non judgemental ways, I think there was little pressure to be any particular thing. No career was seen as better or worse. So long as we were happy, that was all that mattered, and that allowed us to dream, both wild and big.

While the mental shackles of fitting in were never applied to us as kids by our family, my parent's journey to free themselves from 'the expectations of others' was hugely painful, for both them, and us.

When I was 12, my parents were in the midst of a mid-life crisis, rediscovering who they were. Three years earlier, in 1996, we'd experienced three deaths in our family, which set off a chain reaction that continues to shape our family today. My mum's father, my poppa, died from throat cancer. My mum's grandma, my nanna, died of old age. And perhaps most notably, my dad's brother, Uncle Robert – who died on the very same day as my nanna – died of a rare form of cancer. In fact, my parents were attending a meeting at my brother's school that morning – because he had been suspended – when mum got a call about my nanna and then dad got a call telling him it would be his brother's last day, so to come now and say goodbye.

The prolonged, yet premature nature of my uncle's death made it tough for anyone to accept. He suffered from a soft tissue sarcoma, which manifested first in his lower back, before spreading through his body and eventually into his brain. Robert was a tremendous athlete in his youth, and his death was a stark reminder of the fragile state of our being, even if things seem fine on the outside.

At the time of his brother's death, my dad was working 50 plus hours a week managing car yards and advising rich men on how they could make even more money. This, of course, had its perks. It allowed us to live a comfortable, upper middle-class existence. But just as we never saw the cancer growing in my uncle, so too an illness was festering in my father and he needed freeing from it.

"You'd never believe it, but one of my bosses actually gave me grief for visiting Robert when he was sick. I'd never taken a sick day in 15 years and was still selling more cars than anyone, but still this guy pushed me to believe I was doing something wrong," said dad, during one of many chats we had for this book. "It was like he wanted me to feel guilty for being with my family during that time. It wasn't the only reason, but it definitely hastened my decision to leave that car yard and probably paved the way for me to get out of the car industry and any money grabbing business. Looking back, it was a good thing, but it was tough at the time."

They often say things need to get worse before they can get better, and my uncle's death was exactly that. The pain and emptiness were catalysts. Reasons to rethink and reflect. Suddenly, life seemed short. Suddenly time mattered more than money and love mattered more than possessions.

Within a few short months my parents made a series of incredibly brave decisions that changed everything. Dad quit his job. Then, they sold our massive two-story house, which had its own accompanying tennis court and pine forest. Both decisions had very obvious tangible ramifications – dad was unemployed and we didn't have a house. But it was the final less-tangible instrument they added to their symphony of change that would transform the tone of our family forever.

They had committed to chasing a long-held dream of living in a sustainable community with others seeking a more connected existence. At the time I didn't know they'd ever held such beliefs, and it all seemed like chasing fairies to me. Nevertheless, to find and explore where and how this might look, my parents decided to buy a camper trailer, boat and 4-wheel drive and head out on the open road in search of utopia, or at least, their version of it.

It was a hopelessly romantic notion. A decision that boldly illustrated what we were always taught as children – to be bold enough to pursue our wildest dreams. The only problem was, my parents had arguably become so infatuated with their own salvation, they had forgotten how this journey might impact us kids.

At the time, Bek was finishing her last couple of years of high school and decided she needed to stay in Adelaide, so my oldest sister Cin took her in while we were away.

On 4 February 1999, mum, dad, my brother Kane and I pulled out of our driveway in a white Landcruiser with a tin boat on the roof, towing a pop-up Jayco camper trailer that we'd call home for the next six months while we were travelling around Australia. While there was an abundance of fabulous towns and communities we visited during the trip, the one that housed the most fairies in my parent's opinion was the very place my brother and I detested most. It was an eco-village just outside a small rural town that was known as 'the toilet town' because it was located on the main highway and was a popular place to stop and excrete waste – at one of a whopping nine public toilets. But this isn't what made it a shitty place to live. It was also highly racist (a xenophobic politician by the name of Pauline Hanson was popular in this area), it was relatively poor (and seemed to house a lot of dejected individuals as a result) and it was a haven for growing and selling marijuana (and carried all the problems that come with this).

In the bubble that was this eco-village, my parents began to explore their true nature, who they really were; and while it arguably meant neglecting their role as parents at times, I wouldn't change anything. All the pain was worth it, because as Bek said, their own suffering and the resulting mid-life crisis was proof of what we as human beings must all try to avoid.

"The indirect lesson our parents taught us was the painful reality of losing sight of who they were, the trauma of sacrifice for others taken too far, to the point of self-negation. Our dad was a teacher when he first met mum, but as our family grew, he decided to seek out a more lucrative job, and joined the used-car trade. He spent many years in this business, and as I watched him with my child's eyes, I saw him slowly crumble inside. In his infinite generosity and love for his family he worked too hard, was away from us too much, and never had enough time to himself, to even feel well rested, let alone achieve any of his own personal dreams," said Bek. "It broke my heart the more I sensed what was happening within him."

I think the sadness of watching our parent's inner turmoil play out only strengthened Bek's (and my) belief that one's personal sense of purpose and mission can be easily subsumed by the demands of family, to the point of negative self-nullification, if left unchecked. This is probably why we both hold a similar, yet uncommon position, when it comes to how we think about our 'need' to procreate.

"I decided I would seek self-fulfilment before all other goals in life," said Bek. "Then, if I chose to be a parent, I'd have a full and happy self to give my child."

I know some people say that having children has helped them to discover who they are, and of course that might be so, but the pressure certain cultures place on young men and women to have kids is often a huge distraction (to add to the already long list of distractions we've discussed) that doesn't allow individuals to discover their true nature. The problem is, if we don't take the time to understand *who* we are, and if we aren't willing to make the sacrifices necessary to stick by that, then inevitably we end up doing what others tell us is right, which is chasing a career, wealth and lots of shiny things. Something that, when practiced by my parents, only added to Bek's sense of isolation and misery.

"What was a challenge was the absence of my parents from my sphere as a healing, mentoring force. The trouble I had with mum and dad always being at work – because they constantly wanted more – was that it made me feel so isolated, on top of me already being self-isolating and not having any real friends. I just felt so weird growing up like this. I can't even begin to tell you how dark isolation can make the mind. How terrifying it is to feel that, day after day, amongst thousands of people, and then to feel it at home too. To feel like there is nowhere to hide except deeper in your mind, and so you shut yourself off and get real hard on the outside, to protect yourself from feeling the pain. Yeah, it was bad."

Frighteningly, materialism and technology – both of which require us to be individualistic and disconnected from the people right in front of us – is driving thousands of children to feel this same way. In fact, Childline UK, a charity that offers free counseling services, said it carried out more than 4000 counselling sessions over a one year period (1 April 2016 – 31 March 2017), for kids suffering from isolation, with many feeling their parents and friends had no time for them.

"I think we in the adult world are addicted to being busy, and that our children and young people are suffering as a result," said Founder and President of Childline UK, Dame Esther Rantze. In a shocking sign of the times, the charity reported speaking to children as young as six, while a staggering 73% of calls about being lonely came from young girls (like my sister).

Of course, there's little chance of either parents or children being very happy if the other is not. Whether it's kids complaining about loneliness and neglect, or parents complaining about being underappreciated and overworked, the two issues can be solved with one magic bullet – pursuing your truth.

"In seeking out *who* we are, most will inescapably come to understand the heart of our human condition, which is that we are all missing parts of ourselves," said Bek. "If we can accept and perceive that we need help from others in order to fill in those gaps, then perhaps we might have reason to see beyond those material objects and technology, to that which can make us whole – love and connection."

I think my own worldly experience (which stands in contrast to my sister's more solitary, scholarly existence) has shown me that when we feel, understand and see ourselves, we can in turn feel, understand and see others more fully, and vice versa. For instance, when I first came across poverty in South America, suddenly I understood my privilege and responsibility as a fellow human being (something which has massively shaped who I am). Similarly, by perceiving my own weaknesses and vulnerabilities, I began to share more empathy for those around me, who were also struggling with their own challenges in life. The thing about finding and pursuing our true nature said Bek, is that it's not only a core building block of our own happiness, it's also a critical part of establishing a more flourishing society.

"We can create a happier world by having the courage to be the best version of who we are. As Nelson Mandela said, 'You are a child of God, your playing small doesn't help save the world'. We must all learn that sacrifice today is part of building a better tomorrow, and not be fearful, but hopeful, for 'as we are liberated from our fear, our presence automatically liberates others' (Mandela, again), and one act of kindness reverberates around the world. That's why love *has* to be the vehicle of this change, sacrifice for any other end is only seeking death, not renewing life."

From bullied super-kid, turned high school drop-out, to becoming a law graduate that now plays music in the forest in Tasmania, the thing I've always respected most about Bek, and why she's been one of the most pivotal figures in my life (and happiness), is that she is unreservedly herself. Though I, and in recent years she, will admit there are flaws to taking this idea too far.

"Most people struggle to be themselves, but I was probably always too much myself," said Bek, whose life showed me that there must be a balance between fitting in and believing that you are so different that it leads you to imagine you are all alone – as my sister did. Coupled with a painful childhood that taught her not to see or trust the good in people, Bek's beautiful and unparalleled mind was left imprisoned, as the divide between her and others grew, and grew. What I detested most, was that this restricted her ability to express and share her incredible truth, knowledge and wisdom with the world. While I think this tended to make me unhappier and more upset than it did her, I'm adamant from our recent discussions that it didn't allow Bek to be her absolute happiest either, because as she explained recently, the solitude left her trapped in her own mind, halfway across the circle of life, with all the answers and happiness in the world, but few to share either with.

To me, she'd come to the same point as Christopher McCandless, the American traveller made famous by the book and film *Into The Wild*, which follows McCandless's journey through the backwoods of Alaska, where he found truth and joyous meaning, but notoriously wrote "Happiness is only real when shared" just before his unexpected death in the wilderness.

With my sister thankfully alive and well and affording me the privilege of bringing her story to life, I had just one final question: "where can we find happiness?" To which she sharply replied, "love," before continuing to share a few of her more recent revelations.

"I am learning to swim. Our whole life is a great river of being, and I am learning to swim, not to float or struggle, not to be hard like the river rock or tossed like the floating branches, but to swim – fluidly, elegantly, dancing in the water around all obstacles. In essence, I am learning to let go," said Bek. "Through a great movement of love and recognition that is so much a part of my whole life coming together this last year, I have realised that **one of the final steps on my path to happiness is simply letting go of everything I have held onto so tightly**, and being kind; no more, no less, because shared love is our only path to divinity."

"Quite simply, I realised that love is the end of my truth, and I must testify to its strength as my greatest teacher. I am practicing this reality every day at work (she chose to work at a small community supermarket part-time between playing music, because she wanted to re-engage with humanity) and at home – I am expanding my field, and I often get amazing reactions from people at work, which tells me I'm on the right track. I realised the other day, as I lay in bed musing on my answers to some of these questions, that for the first time in my adult life I am actually seeking happiness as an end in itself, and it is making me feel amazing, infinite, beyond anything I have ever known, like a child's heart with the strength of mind of an adult, like a holy circle re-closing, the knowledge that love is the end, and the way. What a blessing at the end

Tickling Bek in the garden at my house.

of so much trial, so much weight and adversity, for the final greatest step to simply be release..."

I'd often wondered what drew me to my sister and other 'pure beings' (those living out their true nature) so much over the years, but in Varanasi, India – said to be the holiest place on earth (at least for Hindus) – I found an answer, in this little journal entry I made while sitting on the banks on the Ganges River:

> *It seems like no matter what drives you, there is a need to feed our inner being – whether you want to call it a soul, god, consciousness, spirit, heart or life force – this hungry beast craves new undertakings, knowledge and diversity. That's why we are born different. This is why they say variety is the spice of life. For in our mishmash, that inner being is made rich, filled to the point of feeling whole or complete, which is the defining feature of the happiest people I've met.*

Be your own Passenger

This journal entry may have been *my* answer, but did others see what I saw? Who do *you* admire? Do they feed your inner being? If so, how? I mean, when I think about who we tend to idolise, it is the rock stars, sports people, noble activists and actors that have risked everything to chase their dream – to be *who* they are. But is that what we see in them, or is it the money, popularity and freakish talent? Which part of them do we most want to emulate? Do fans of Ed Sheeran think only about his raw music ability and consummate fame, or is it his humble vulnerability and story that attracts them? Do they see the fact that he was homeless for two and a half years and understand that this was a sacrifice he made in order to pursue his truest self – the musician we now know? I wonder if people know how badly he was bullied as a kid, simply because he wasn't like everybody else?

"I was a weird kid when I was little. I wore big glasses, had hearing problems, had a stutter and I had ginger hair," said Sheeran, in an article in the *Daily Mail*.

When he was asked about running into some of those same people who had picked on him as a child, Sheeran shared a confronting truth. "When I went home and went to the pub and saw the people who used to be dicks at school, it's kind of depressing. They not only haven't done anything, but they don't know that there is anything out there," he said. "They are so stuck in their little world. So I feel sad for them – they are kind of being bullied by life." As fellow musician, Frank Zappa says, "If you end up with a boring miserable life because you listened to your mom, your dad, your teacher, your priest, or some guy on television telling you how to do your shit, then you deserve it."

When I sat down and spoke with one of Sheeran's friends, Mike Rosenberg, or as he is more commonly known Passenger, in February 2012, he was still busking on the streets, doing what he loved – writing and playing music. With his hit song *Let Her Go* (released in July 2012, just after we spoke) selling more than 10 million copies and having more than 2.5 billion views on YouTube, it's fair to say his life has since changed. But how did he get to where he is today, and what role did his stern commitment to being himself play in that?

Passenger unofficially began when Rosenberg was roughly 17, and he announced to his parents that he was dropping out of school to chase his dream.

"I quit school just because I wasn't doing anything, I wasn't motivated, and I just wanted to play music," said Rosenberg, who I met and filmed in a park in Adelaide, in front of an Adelaide Fringe Festival tent he was due to play in later that night. "Much to my mum's horror, I left school and then got various awful, terrible jobs, and did music in pubs and stuff. I was singing and writing a lot by this point, which put mum's nerves to rest, because she could see I was serious about it."

Born on 17 May 1984, and 27 at the time I interviewed him, Rosenberg admits, "it was pretty grim" in the early days, until he met a more experienced friend who specialized in soundtrack composing called Andrew Phillips, who he partnered with to form /*Passenger.* – and yes, they initially had the slash and the dot in the name.

"Andrew was a bit older than me, but we started working together, and over four or five years made our first album and put a band together," said Rosenberg. "It was great, they were a really lovely bunch of guys, and I think we did some really cool stuff. But there were a few things that we just didn't get right, that just didn't sit right with me."

In an interview with *Rolling Stone* in December 2013, Rosenberg said he felt the album they put out in 2007 called *Wicked Man's Rest* compromised their vision in order to please other people. "I was a lot younger then and didn't have such a strong vision for what I wanted it to be," he told *Rolling Stone*. "A lot of the eccentricity and what made it great had been kind of ironed out. As a result, it didn't really please anyone – it wasn't cool enough for the cool kids and it wasn't poppy enough for the pop kids."

In 2009 the original four-piece band that was /*Pa*ssenger. broke up, and Rosenberg took his solo act to the streets of Europe, before landing a supporting gig for Lior (an Australian singer/songwriter) in October of that year, in Australia. Staying in hostels and carrying his knapsack, a bag full of CDs and guitar with him everywhere, he said the decision to go it alone was one of the toughest of his life.

"Going solo was pretty hard because I was only young when the band thing was going on and so to all of a sudden not having that support system was quite difficult," said Rosenberg during our interview. "At the same time though it was very freeing, because suddenly there wasn't any conflict or ego, apart from my enormous one [he laughs]. I just did my own thing, and it's worked better, I think people have understood my music better with just a guitar and vocal on stage. It seems to be a simpler message," said Rosenberg, who spent his early years writing songs and posting albums on Facebook, hoping for a few likes.

"That period taught me to just be and do, I didn't expect anything," he said. "Because, you know, busking's so up and down from one day to the next. One day you can sell 100 CDs and it feels like you're really progressing, but then there are other days where you get shouted at by a tramp and it starts to rain and no one stops to listen, and you just think at the age of 27 what are you doing? Shouldn't you be doing something proper? So, it's kind of up and down."

Passenger's ability to dance to the beat of his own drum – to be himself – was a major learning curve he said, as he came to realise something he'd always known – that everyone has their own road and way of doing things.

"I think busking for a lot of musicians would be ridiculous and a horrible idea," said Rosenberg, during our chat in the park. "I've been busking since I was 11 or 12, instead of getting a paper round, because it was better paid, and I played *Wonderwall* really badly. So, yeah, I've always done it and I guess in the last three or four years it's become a serious way of life for me. And, yeah, since going solo, I just haven't looked back. It's just been travelling and busking and playing."

"I love it man, I think again it kind of goes with that honesty. No smoke machines or bullshit around your music, it's just you on the street singing your songs and if people want to listen they can, and it's free, and there's no obligation. And if they don't, then they can go and grab a sandwich or whatever, you know what I mean? I think that's really nice. It just seems to hit people, they're not expecting it, they're off to Subway and suddenly it's, 'Oh, I actually quite like that.'"

What struck me right from the start about Passenger's music (and his character) was the rawness with which he expressed himself. When I asked him about the personal nature of the stories behind his music, and how he finds the process of expressing such deep feelings, he said it gets easier with time.

"It's pretty difficult to be so open as you're starting to write songs, but I think with the singer/songwriter genre it's actually necessary to be vulnerable and open and honest," said Passenger, who was accompanied by his good mate, fellow musician and manager at the time, Stu Larsen, who sat next to me listening. "I don't know man ... I think the idea of a great song is just writing something usually pretty simple, like harnessing a simple idea and putting it to music. And connecting with people."

When I followed this up by asking him "what's your favourite song that you've written?" his distinctly dry English-Australian humour made me laugh.

"They're all crap, mate. They're all bloody rubbish, I hate them all," he laughed. "No, I don't have a favourite. I write an awful lot, and I've got to the stage now where I'm not too precious about songs, or even albums. There was a time where I'd make an album and then I'd just feel dreadful for months, and think 'oh God, it's just crap and I hate it, and I wish I'd put this song on'. I was talking to a mate of mine a while ago and he was just like, 'Yeah, it's fine. But you're going to make a record every year for the next 30 years or whatever, so don't worry about it, it's a document of where you're at, at the time', so yeah that's a nice place to be because you can just take the pressure off yourself a bit."

Of course, this happy-go-lucky approach to writing and recording music probably isn't the mind-set of most major record labels – who thrive on professionalism and are driven by profit – and as such, Passenger said he'd always been reluctant to join them.

"Over the past few years I've had a couple of offers. I just ... I think you've got to make a decision as a musician about why you're in it, and what you want from it. Like if it's fame and huge amounts of money, then yeah, being with a major label is the way to do it. They've got huge clout with the radios, they kind of decide who makes it and who doesn't in some ways," he confesses. "But, yeah man, you have to draw the line somewhere and you either choose creative control, freedom to pick your own artwork, and the songs that you put on the record, and how you dress, and how you shave your beard, and all this kind of stuff. Or, you go the other route where ... it's maybe easier in some ways but, I don't know man. I just decided that I wanted to look back on my career and be proud of the stuff that I did, and that's the most important thing."

As fate (and having the right friends) would have it, Passenger's 'road' took an unexpected turn when Ed Sheeran asked him to tour with him in late 2012 and 2013. That, coupled with the unexpected support of a guy who heard his song *Let Her Go* in a café in the Netherlands, and immediately asked to pitch it to radio stations (this guy's job). Within three weeks Rosenberg had his first number one hit. Since then, Passenger has become one of the most recognized names in music, topping the charts in more than 30 countries. Despite such a sudden rise to the top though, Passenger says his life and goals have remained the same.

"Some people expect me to have changed overnight because of one big song," he said in a 2014 interview with David Smyth from the *Evening Standard*. "But if the past 10 years don't keep me humble, nothing will. It's not much good being a really famous arsehole," said Rosenberg, who admitted his good mate sitting next to me during our 2012 interview was a big part of what kept him humble and focused on the small stuff.

"Actually, I'm travelling with a guy called Stu Larsen at the moment, and have been for the last year or so. And we play a lot of gigs together and whatever," said Passenger, who gazed across at Stu with a sort of hardened blokeish smirk as if to say, yes I appreciate you, but I'm not about to kiss your arse. "He's really inspiring in the way that it's never ever about getting songs on radio, or promoting himself like it is for most musicians. They're all ... and me included, so driven to get their music to as many people as possible, and blah blah blah, charging around. And Stu is very much about the journey, and legitimately about that. It's just a great force to have constantly, because it reminds you of actually what's brilliant about what we do. Which is **travelling around, meeting people, and playing music, they're the three brilliant things. Not the idea of fame or fortune or these pots of gold that never actually materialise.**"

A 2014 survey – which asked British children "what do you want to be?" – found 41% of kids just want to be "rich" or "famous" and they don't care what passion or profession gets them there. The study of more than 1300 five-to-ten-year-olds did not ask parents to give their children a list of answers to choose from, but rather asked the child to think for themselves. And the results were shocking!

Perhaps reflecting the influence of celebrity lifestyles and reality television, being "rich" was the most frequently mentioned answer, with 22% of children expressing this desire, followed by being "famous" at 19%. Parents were also told to ask their children whether they thought money could buy happiness – 75% of the youngsters said "yes". When their children were asked how much money they thought would be a comfortable amount to earn per year as an adult, the most common answer was "£1 million" per year (around $1.35 million USD).

The desire for fame and fortune came ahead of professions involving helping the public, such as "police officer" which was the most popular profession at 16%, followed closely by "zoo keeper" at 14%, "fire fighter" at 13% and doctor at 10%.

The UK study was closely backed by another a few years earlier in 2009 that compared the career goals of today's pre-teens with those from 25 years earlier. Not surprisingly they were very, very different:

Kids' Career Goals Today	Kids' Career Goals 25 Years Ago
Sports star: 12%	Teacher: 15%
Pop star: 11%	Finance: 9%
Actor: 11%	Medicine: 7%
Astronaut: 9%	Scientist: 6%
Lawyer: 9%	Vet: 6%
Emergency services: 7%	Lawyer: 6%
Medicine: 6%	Sports star: 5%
Chef: 5%	Astronaut: 4%
Teacher: 4%	Beautician/hairdresser: 4%
Vet: 3%	Archaeologist: 3%

A number of parallel studies have shown that British kids aren't alone in their want for fame above all else. Three different reports, with one going back to 2007, illustrate that the days of kids wanting to grow up to be scientists, shop owners or teachers, is over. Now they want to be actors, singers, sports stars or YouTubers.

This trend towards fame was first noticed in 2007 by psychologist Yalda T. Uhls who completed a study with Dr. Patricia Greenfield at the UCLA campus of the Children's Digital Media Center in Los Angeles. The study, which was published in *Cyberpsychology*, found that in 2007, "fame was the number one value communicated to preteens on popular TV. Interestingly enough, community feeling (to be part of a group) ranked number 11 in 2007, while in every other year it came in at number one or number two."

"These days, it's easy to see the phenomenal success of teenagers who achieved fame, such as Justin Bieber, or infamy, such as Rebecca Black," writes Uhls. "Kids, already focused on popularity and status, crave the virtual audience that they see bringing so much attention to others." The problem, or at least one of them, says Uhls, is that children today naively think that fame comes easily, without a connection to talent or hard work.

Passenger, of course, is proof that fame *is* about hard work, talent and persistence. While there's a real chance that fame doesn't pan out for 99.9% of the kids seeking it, even those who get there, Passenger said, need to be prepared for disappointment if they don't take stock of the small wins along the way, by being present and loving what they do.

"There are all these milestones when you're just starting out," said Rosenberg. "You think, 'Oh, I'd love to play Glastonbury, or I'd love to sign a record deal … all of those things', and actually when you do those things, you're playing Glastonbury, it's pissing down, you're hungover, no one's listening, and it's rubbish. Meanwhile, a pub gig in front of 30 people is life changing. It's always the things you think will blow your mind that are generally pretty average. And the silliest, smallest moments with two or three people can actually be the turning points."

Rosenberg's quick wit, child-like antics, and ability not to take himself too seriously were such a clear part of who he was, that after finishing our interview I suggested he might like to climb a tree close by and play a few songs up there for us to use as overlay vision and music to accompany our videoed conversation (which you can find on thehappiest.com). A few minutes later, Passenger was perched on an ancient overhanging branch of a tree doing what we all should be able to do best – being himself.

But what if you don't have Passenger's voice or brazen charm? How do you see who you are as being enough, when there are some who clearly seem to be more? I mean, sure, we all have a talent, but not every talent is going to lead to glowing accolades and stardom, right? So what do we do if that's the case? Wallow in self-pity? You could. But once you're done crying you might like to consider this: we all have a ripple, however big or small, so no matter who you think you are, **who you are matters to someone** (most likely many people). And the truth is, that no other version of you, no matter how perfect it seems, will ever bring you or those around you any happiness, unless it is your truest self.

Meeting the Happiest Man Alive

Someone who absolutely embodied this sentiment was the man we coined *The Happiest Man Alive* – a remarkably unremarkable guy – who was about as far from being a celebrity or sporting prodigy as you might get, but that's the point, it is not only who he is, but also who he isn't, that makes his story so damn awesome!

Travelling through a small town, 80 kilometres south of Colombo, Sri Lanka, my girlfriend Sash (now my wife), her father and I were preparing to stop at a famous bakery called New Monis. "They have the best cookies in Lanka," said Sash, who was always proud to show off her homeland (having moved to Australia as a 16-year-old). As we rounded a long bend, an old man seemed to be dancing out on the road. Nearing his position, it seemed as if he was directing traffic, whistling, saluting and smiling at every car that passed. Then he looked at us. He lowered his head so he could peer directly through the windscreen, and gestured for us to enter the business he stood in front of. As chance would have it, we were in fact headed there anyway, and my father-in-law Sunil began indicating. The security guard, or parking attendant, or whoever he was couldn't believe his luck, and he let out a belting whistle that echoed through the buildings and cars, as he walked out in front of traffic, to stop the cars, so that we could easily pull into one of the car parks in front of the shop. He'd 'got us' I think he thought, his charm and charisma had wooed us to stop. I imagine if I'd seen him and we hadn't have been stopping there I would have wanted to go back, so I guess his assumption was half true.

interviewing Passenger, who was as funny as he was relaxed. The bare feet say it all.

Passenger climbing the tree.

Stu Larsen and me filming Passenger singing up the tree.

Stu Larson, Ed Sheeran and Passenger doing a sound-check
Photo by Ron Ibarra.

The Happiest Man Alive.

MY SISTER AND THE SECURITY GUARD

As he danced over to open our doors and greet Sunil you might have thought he was a young Billy Elliot, but in all honesty as we saw his ripe, sweaty face a little closer, he looked more like my Grandma's age. Who was this guy? I wondered.

Sitting and eating our cookies, my eyes were fixated on just one thing – the security guy. I'd noticed that most shops in Sri Lanka had one of these people dressed in brown pants, or a skirt for women, and a mustard coloured shirt with a small official looking badge and a brown tie (but without any weapon whatsoever). "Who are they?" I asked Sash and her father. "They're basically security guards, but they probably had more of a role during the war, in checking bags for weapons and bombs and things, but now they are more like the people who help with parking or welcoming guests. The best ones are kind of a jack of all trades," explained Sunil.

I don't know exactly how long we sat there, eating what ended up being very average cookies in my opinion, but this bloke literally seemed like the happiest person I'd ever seen. It was funny, because he didn't appear to have any reason at all to be so smiley, but you couldn't bloody stop him. As we left the bakery, I had a feeling that he needed to be the subject of my first ever video for A Million Smiles (the organisation I'd just launched a few months earlier, to capture and share stories about happiness – more on that next chapter). I could see Sunil's confusion when I relayed my desire to stop for a quick interview if the security guard was working when we drove back past in a few days time. "I know it's a bit odd," I said. "To make a film about a random security guard. But there's just something about this guy." So I crossed my fingers and hoped that our paths would meet again.

Three days later, amidst the blistering waves of heat bouncing off the road, I noticed a familiar movement, as a man jumped out on the road with one arm in the air, his hand flapping about directing a car, while his other hand was perched just above his lip. Then with two fingers resting on his lips that piercing whistle sounded – our man was working! Woohoo! I said in my mind. But Sunil insisted we hurry, so Sash and I ran and asked him if he was interested in being in a video. As you might have guessed by the fact that I'm now writing about him, he said "yes."

With no time to lose, we got stuck in. "What is your name and how old are you?" I asked him, through my trusty translator, Sash, who was a bit rusty in deciphering some of the longer, more sophisticated Sinhalese words he was using.

"My name is Welipanna Vithanage Sugathapala," he said. "But people mostly call me WV Sugathapala, and I'm 60 years old," he continued. 'Christ!' I thought. 'How does a bloke at that age stand on his feet all day in the boiling humidity of a place like this?'

As it turned out I was wrong, it wasn't just all day, as Sugathapala explained that his shifts can vary, but mostly involve waking before dawn and working late into the night. This wasn't so that he could get ahead, or buy a new car, these long hours simply gave him the means (and only just) to feed his wife and three children. His tattered hat, broken flip-flops and rusty old push-bike were all signs, to me, that this guy was dirt poor, and there was probably very little about his life most might envy, except, of course, for the way he chose to live it.

"Always smiles! That is how I spend my time," he smiled. "It is like an exercise for my body, it cleans my blood. Every day I make those people who come here happy, and it makes me happy, and that is my happiness in this world."

But this wasn't always the case. In fact, about 10 years before our interview, Sugathapala was made redundant from a more prestigious and high paying job with Asian Cotton Mills, which he held from 1990 to 2005. Losing his job not only coincided with, but was in fact the result of, the massive 2004 Boxing Day earthquake that triggered a giant tsunami which killed thousands across South-East Asia and Sri Lanka, including several of Sugathapala's closest friends and family. Damage to the cotton mill and surrounding infrastructure from the tsunami left this dedicated husband, father and breadwinner destitute and with nowhere to go.

"There were days I was nearly unable to feed or shelter my family," he said, as he took out a number of photos of him, his wife and children, to show us. With Sri Lanka reeling from one of the worst natural disasters in its history, the prospect of finding a job was not an easy one. But after months of searching, he landed a position at a private security firm and was assigned New Monis Bakery, something he said he never really planned for.

"This wasn't my dream from the beginning," he said. "I was in another job, but when I came here, I was automatically very happy. From the day I got here."

Rather than dwell on what might have been – that higher paying job or those dreams he had for himself and his family – Sugathapala chose to do the only thing he could – be happy in *who* he was, *where* he was. Instead of becoming spitefully fixated on the past, or forever wishing for a different future, this humble Buddhist chose to concentrate his mind on the present, where he went about re-defining the most mundane of jobs. In his own way, and by following his own child-like heart, Sugathapala illustrated that the role of security guard could be about something more than just keeping people or a business safe. "It could also be about human connection and sharing happiness," he said.

What every child blindly striving for fame must remember is that by tapping into the force that comes from living consistently with our identity, this lowly security guard, who only attended school up until grade 8, has change the world.

Since releasing his video – called *The Happiest Man Alive* – more than 27 million people have witnessed Sugathapala's incredibly simple, yet powerful message and story (which you can see on thehappiest.com). In the first 48 hours post-launch, not only was his story shared on the hugely popular international news website UpWorthy among others, it was also featured on mainstream TV, radio and in newspapers in Sri Lanka. It wasn't long before Sugathapala was being swamped by fans wanting selfies, and a few weeks into the mayhem a national radio program even decided to host their breakfast show at the bakery, which included a 'quick money grab' where Sugathapala was placed in a large transparent plastic hexagon, and told he had to catch the money that was being blown around by a big fan.

Yep, crazy! And it didn't end there. Over the next few months the then 61-year-old received a host of local and national awards from a number of community groups, Sri Lankan security services, his local temple and even the media. But I think the thing that gave me the biggest grin was when one of Sash's friends, who worked for the United Nations in Sri Lanka, said she saw the video at work. I of course assumed she meant people were sharing it around via email, and I thought 'cool'. But actually, as it turned out, Sugathapala's attitude toward his career and life was being used as part of the UN's official staff training day, as an example of how to remain motivated, and how to get the most out of yourself and your work. Not bad for a bakery security guard who never finished high school, right!?

And that's the thing. I think what made Sugathapala such a hit (and still does) is that he clearly prioritises **being a man of value, rather than being a man of success**, something Albert Einstein said was at the heart of a good life. With years to ponder my answer, I can firmly say that what I loved most about Sugathapala was his unrivalled ability to see beyond what he was not, or what he didn't have – such as a popular talent or skill, like music or sport – and to instead imagine and chase the best version of himself, despite, as he says, facing a plethora of issues every day.

"We all have problems, you can see my life is not perfect, but there is no use dwelling on those problems," he said, standing uncomfortably in the scalding heat, completely unaware (as were we) that millions would one day hear these words. "You see, we live for a very short time, we have come to this life for a sort of stop-over. So there is no use in holding anger, vengeance and jealousy with anyone in this stop-over. Be happy with everyone, smile, have fun and die that way. That is what I tell the world. That is all you can do."

Despite his relative fame in Sri Lanka – which led to a few endorsement deals and ads he filmed with local companies – Sugathapala is still working at New Monis Bakery as a security guard. When my family and I visited him in January 2017, he said he was content to see out his days there, sharing what happiness he can with anyone that passes by.

False Evidence Appearing Real

A common and often overlooked challenge that Sugathapala, Passenger, Gill and Bek have all had to overcome in order to become their truest self, is fear. Because whether you're a 60-year-old dancing and whistling in the street or a musician or activist sharing uncomfortable truths, there will inherently be those who disagree with what you say, what you do and even who you are. So how do you stop that fear of being 'different' from crippling you and putting you back in your place? Well, there is a guy I know. His name is *The Fearless Human*, and he's got the whole 'being an awesome individual who politely doesn't give a shit about the haters' down pat.

The Fearless Human was actually one of the first stories I wrote and filmed for a news organisation I founded in 2011 called Our World Today

People coming to get a selfie or photo of Sugathapala after our video went viral.

Sugathapala doing his actual job.

The 'quick money grab' machine.

Sugathapala doing his thing with the radio show. That's his wife to the right of shot.

Sugathapala showing us a photo of him and his family.

My parents and me with Sugathapala years after we first met, in front of a sign New Monis had made to promote our video.

Dancing Tommy.

(again more on that next chapter). The man behind *The Fearless Human* title was a guy by the name of Thomas Franklin, AKA Dancing Tommy.

Travelling around Australia in search of inspiring stories, I came to a small seaside town called Byron Bay, which is one of the most beautiful and picturesque spots on the east coast of Australia. Wanting to find a story that was out of the ordinary (something or someone I couldn't google), I went to the local pub and asked the barwoman who she thought I should interview if I could only speak to one person in town. Without hesitation she said, "Oh I know the guy, his name is Tommy, let me call him and see if he is free to come down, you'll love him."

Twenty five minutes later I felt a tap on one shoulder. I turned around just in time to see someone ducking behind my other shoulder, so I spun the other way and found a giant set of pearly white teeth surrounded by a wild, woolly beard and the most out-there eyebrows you've ever seen. Each strand was like a little copper wire jutting out centimetres from his face in a kind of hysteria of directions. Befitting of his enigmatic brows, was the black beret that sat atop his head, unsubtly accompanied by a yellow parachute jacket and a pair of bright purple tights with huge white high-top shoes and matching purple socks – this guy was clearly unperturbed by social norms, and I loved it! You could just feel this pure form of energy radiating from him. And you just knew he had been through the wringer and come out the other side as a glimmer of hope for us all.

As we sat and chatted at the pub I offered to buy him a beer, but he declined. An Aussie guy saying "no" to a beer! Who was this man? We soon ventured back to the house of two Byron Bay filmmakers, who were mates of Tommy's, and who were happy to lend me a hand by letting me use some of the videos they'd shot with Tommy, as well as loan me some of their lighting equipment for the interview (which you can watch on thehappiest.com). With two stalls and a camera in place, Tommy, who was probably six foot two or three, but seemed like a mystical giant of a man, lumbered over and bent down to take a seat. We didn't know it at the time, but we were about to change each other's lives forever. "So what do you do? Who is Thomas Franklin?" I asked.

"I'm in the business of making people smile," he said, gleaming with a giant grin. "Because I didn't know how to smile when I was younger and people helped me to smile. Strangers came into my world and helped me to have a genuine smile, and to pass that forward, it's beautiful."

"Once upon a time I was a really, really unhappy person and I guess we all struggle with finding happiness," continued Tommy. "I was heavily addicted to drugs and alcohol. And there was a moment in my life where my family didn't trust me and my friends didn't want to know me."

One of the hardest things to cope with, said Tommy, was seeing the pain he was causing his mother, who was constantly bereft, disappointed that like most addicts, her son was slowly killing himself with his poisons. Never quite stopping for long enough to see who he could be without the drugs, Tommy simply went on trying to escape, because being "numb" to the world was his only way of coping.

"It was just temporary relief from the pressures of modern day living," explained Tommy. "But then one day, riding my bicycle, I got hit by a car, went 15 metres through the air and broke my collar bone and fractured three ribs. My whole back was a scab from sliding on the road. I bounced like a beach ball. It was the only day of the year that I had my helmet on [he paused, taking a deep breath]."

"It's an absolute miracle that I'm still breathing," he said in a sombre tone.

Laying in a hospital bed writhing in pain, Tommy finally hit rock bottom (something a lot of psychologists say is essential in order for an addict to change their behaviour). Whether it was the time he was given in hospital to sober up and look at himself, or the realisation that what had happened to him was "a miracle", this near tragedy woke Tommy up big time!

"I just remember looking up to the stars and being so thankful for the breath in my lungs and realising that something had to change. I needed to find a new me," he said.

The next few months were torture, said Tommy, as he found himself trapped in-between what he'd always known and the great abyss of the unknown. "Fighting so hard to go against the grain from everything that I knew and everything that I'd done for so long, and being rejected and shunned for that. Like walking away from friends that just wanted to party hard – and that's all I wanted to do – but I knew I couldn't do it anymore because I'd be homeless or dead," conceded Tommy.

"What changed me was actually seeing the light at the end of the tunnel, the light that signalled the end of life and me saying 'no, not yet', and physically and mentally turning around and facing that really huge mountain that you think you can't climb over, that was the beginning of the me you see today," said Tommy, who was noticeably emotional. "Then getting to the top of that mountain and looking and seeing all the green grass, and realising that the grass is greener – that was my salvation. That's when I knew I'd won."

The road hasn't been an easy one, admitted Tommy. To go from a life absent of any real thought or responsibility, and to have to find a new reason to get up every morning that didn't involve getting high with friends. "Just having to find joy in the simple things of life, was one of the hardest things," said Tommy. "I guess in a sense, that's how I started dancing."

I've often thought how I might describe Tommy's dancing in words (you're probably better off visiting thehappiest.com to see our video), because he doesn't exactly have a recognised style, other than to say he releases the inner child that lives within us all. When I first wrote about him, I said, "He is innocence and freedom personified, like a newborn, he is pure energy, completely void of judgement or ridicule." I think, as you watch his arms flailing, head bobbling, butt jiggling and legs flapping, he stirs in you a sense of permission, that you can be anything, even yourself. But what does Tommy get from his dancing? "Why do you do it?" I asked.

"When I dance, I'm never happier. It's a therapy for me. Some people will be at work and they'll be like, 'Ah, I want to go for a surf'. Or, 'I want to go down to the pub, or go have a beer'. Or some people, 'I want to go for a skate'. But for me, I just want to go for a dance. Like when I am really frustrated or I've had a really hard week, I just cannot wait to hit the dance floor," said Tommy, who has been free of drugs and alcohol ever since his accident.

At the time I first interviewed Tommy, he held a number of different jobs, including MC at the local quiz night at the pub, dancing in the odd music video and, despite not having any formal dancing training, he was also teaching dance classes in Byron Bay – something that he said left him feeling more ecstatic than any drug ever had.

"It makes me really like the happiest I could be, because I'm sharing what I've been given. I've been given this liberty and this joy that's completely transformed my whole life and I can share it with people. People are seeing it and they're going, 'Wow'. And they're just smiling. I even had some random guy came up to me the other night and he said, 'Man, you're putting smiles on the faces of Byron Bay.'"

But the reality of Tommy's beautiful and daring individuality, and how his gift was seen by some, nearly made me cry. As I returned to Adelaide to edit the video I'd shot with him in Byron Bay, I began searching for videos that strangers had filmed and posted on YouTube of Tommy dancing. A whopping eight people had posted videos of him dressed in a yellow suit, dancing through Byron Bay in the rain, and predominantly the comments were positive. But a number of other clips weren't so flattering; with numerous videos including audio suggesting (incorrectly) that he was on drugs. One teenager saying, "I want what he's on," while another commented, saying "Drugs. DO NOT USE THEM KIDS!" The caption on another video was "Hippy guy at Byron Bay, Australia loving life and dancing on his own :) obviously tripping..." Then there were the ever-predictable "weirdo," "crazy guy" and "loose goose" comments, one person even writing "what a fucking dead beat." Of course, if any of these people had ever met Tommy, or asked him about why he danced, they might have seen that all he was doing was expressing who he was, his true nature, and that definitely didn't require drugs.

"I like to really express myself," said Tommy, "which can be a difficult thing in society today, because people like to put up their walls, they like to judge or have fears in letting people know how they feel, or being vulnerable. I think that's why people are drawn to me, because **I just do what I want.**"

Given where he is today, "probably" is a bit of an understatement. Shortly after we made our first video with Tommy (which went pretty viral), we sent a link to a popular news program in Australia called *The Project*. Our hope was that we (my own news organisation, Our World Today) would partner with *The Project* and produce more positive stories for them free of charge – because as you'll hear more in the next chapter, we wanted to show that good news could sell just as well as the fear mongering stuff we see plastered across our TV screens every night. Obviously, they didn't like the idea (or saw us as a threat) because they never got back to us. Thankfully though, they did start copying a number of the stories we featured, including our piece on Dancing Tommy, which saw them film and release their own story called Byron Bay's Dancing Man just a few months after we did. This national media coverage was the beginning of a sharp rise to fame that arguably peaked when Tommy tried out for *Australia's Got Talent* in 2013. As I watched his audition I wondered nervously whether the judges would 'get him' and be willing to openly support his eccentric style. When the audience, including a number of judges, gave him a standing ovation, I nearly cried with joy. The response was incredible, and the sweat that thrashed from his beard became widely known as "salty rain." As one of the judges, Australian singer-songwriter and dancer, Timomatic, said, "Oh Tommy, I am riding your wave brother. I actually couldn't help myself, I felt I had to get up and dance and I feel like that's what you do when you dance, you get people up and people don't have control, and that's a beautiful gift that you have."

Tommy's audition video went on to receive more than four million views online, as he became one of the show's most popular contestants, breezing through the semi-finals, before very nearly taking out the grand-final (I think the problem was a lot of people that loved him simply weren't the type to vote on such a show). While he didn't win, this exposure well and truly put Tommy on the map, and ever since he's been travelling the world, dancing, doing corporate workshops, shooting film clips and advertising campaigns, and promoting and performing at the biggest music festivals across the globe.

But none of this would have been possible, said Tommy, if it hadn't been for a man who taught him that "FEAR is False Evidence Appearing Real", something he said spoke volumes to him, and has since defined his life.

"Stepping through the 'false evidence appearing real' has been very freeing, and realising that fear is just such a pushover when you see it for what it truly is – when you understand that it is pretty much a figment of our imagination, then you will see that whatever it is that you want to do, you can do," said Tommy, when we interviewed him in Adelaide a few months after I met him in Byron Bay (this video is also on thehappiest.com). "Because fear shouldn't stop you from being you, but fear does stop us from doing the things we want to do, that we desire to do."

"You can't live your life dictated by fear," he said, as a mischievous smile grew across his face, "but that's not going to stop some people from trying," Tommy remarked, alluding to an alarming story that unravelled when we flew him to Adelaide to speak at the launch party for Our World Today (as well as to film a follow up story).

Waiting in Brisbane airport for his flight with a lot of time to kill, Tommy decided to whack on his headphones and have a little dance.

A while later, just before his flight was being boarded, airline staff approached Tommy and said, "Excuse me sir, some of the passengers are a bit concerned that you've been using illicit drugs and you could endanger their safety, so we may not be able to let you on the plane."

"This got me really worried and concerned," said Tommy. "That just because I chose to enjoy myself by having a little dance, a little jiggy, that people thought that I was a madman, or on illicit drugs, and that I was going to hurt people."

"See kids, kids can kick and scream and tantrum and yell and somersault and back flip, and do whatever they want, and people are like, 'Oh, it's just kids. They can do whatever they want'. But the second an adult chooses to let their hair down in a respectful way, just shaking it out, you know, people look so badly upon that. And that's so sad," said Tommy, with a rare frown on his face. "People have the right to express themselves, and I chose to do that, and it threatened my chances of flying to Adelaide."

"It just made me think about society and how they view things that are different. We're very scared of things that are different, and everyone's different. No one's the same, and we should be very accepting of that."

"But how do we do that?" I asked. "How do we foster acceptance, so that everyone has the opportunity to become their happiest and truest self?"

"One of my philosophies is talk to people as if they were already your friend. And smile. People don't smile at people anymore. Everyone walks through the streets with their head down."

"It's OK to look at people, not necessarily stare, but just acknowledge people. Just acknowledging them, saying 'hello', or 'excuse me', or give them a nod, or give them a grin. It's just common courtesy, and then with that connection we're gonna feel closer and less fearful of each other, because suddenly you know that the guy with the big beard who dances at the beach, or in the airport, isn't so different to you," he laughed, before sharing a soft, blissful nod, as if saying *yeah*. "I know it's tough to hold onto the kind, warm culture, with all of today's 9 to 5 dog eat dog kinda pressure, but just don't forget, you need to open your arms to have a hug," he said as he opens his arms. "Being open, being willing to be yourself and to share yourself. As hard as that may be sometimes, there's this good thing about humanity where some people see vulnerability and they don't take advantage of it. And then the next time you see them they're even dropping their guard, and suddenly we allow that safe and loving space for everyone to be who they truly are."

What's clear to me from the thousands of people I've met, interviewed and observed in my travels is that the happiest individuals are those who are living out their true nature – who they were born to be. Further to this, I think the happiest societies and communities are those that have moved beyond those divisive and judgemental evolutionary habits, and learned to accept and celebrate 'difference'. The problem is, that just as you are reading this, billions of people are being told the exact opposite – that fitting in and being popular is what matters – because, of course, these are the pivotal ingredients to becoming rich and famous, which seems to be what many are unhappily chasing. I think seeing through the façade, and all those false messages that constantly bombard us – telling us that you'll be happy if… you do what I say, or you own what I'm selling – is the first step in freeing your mind from the shackles of a one size fits all or outwardly focused approach to happiness. Because we all know, deep down, that **listening to our inner voice is the only thing that will fulfil our inner being and make us whole**. So whether you listen to Chinese philosopher Lao Tzu who said, "Care about what other people think and you will always be their prisoner," or Nirvana frontman Kurt Cobain who wrote, "Wanting to be someone else is a waste of who you are," the message is simple: you were born an original, don't die a copy, because you will have wasted that precious energy that lives inside of *you*, and only *you*.

If you haven't already, I think the best place to start is to actually stop (for an hour, or a day, or a week) and listen to your inner voice – because that is the common element that led to Gill, Bek, Passenger, Sugathapala and Tommy to finding and being their happiest selves.

Once we discover who we are,
then it's about understanding why we are.

A young Afghan girl, by Abdulhai Darya.

3

THE BIKER, THE BEAST AND THE WOODEN MAN WHO CAME TO LIFE

Like a lot of ridiculous and exciting stories, this one began in a bar, with two guys drinking a beer. Yes, I was one of them, and the other was a guy I'd met at university three years prior – Chris Campbell. Just a few months before our catch up I'd returned from that horror trip to South America, and Chris, having seen some of my photos on Facebook, was curious to learn more about the continent that had so nearly broken me. At the time, Chris was dating a gorgeous Colombian girl, Marcela, so was keen to travel to her notorious (thanks to Pablo Escobar) homeland, as well as explore the effervescent and untamed culture and expanse that is South America. As you might imagine, I didn't want to leave the poor guy petrified by my experience, so I suggested we might need a beer or two to help digest and soften a couple of the tales I had to share. Given what good mates we were (and how much we drank together) during the three months we studied together, he suggested we head to The Coopers Alehouse – a local Adelaide watering hole.

Just to get you up to speed, the subject Chris and I studied together at university was a practical film and television component that involved us (film students) teaming up with journalism students to produce a nightly news broadcast for the World Police and Fire Games, which were held in Adelaide from 16-25 March 2007 (kind of like an Olympic games for emergency service personnel). The TV news bulletins were being created by a team of around 50 UniSA students and were airing at the Games Village every night. Our primary assignment (making kickass videos of the 8000 athletes competing) involved us working long hours and partying even longer ones, as we decided to film and sample the nightlife of the games. For us, it was a heaven sent opportunity to throw ourselves into a world we were desperate to enter – the media – and we had a great time finding out what was required to be a newshound. Immediately we realised that no matter how long we spent chasing a story, we spent even longer editing our work ready for broadcast.

The most exciting episode we filmed for the games was arguably covering the paintball wars between the American and Australian teams. The Australians (mostly Customs Officers) were there to share in the fun, while the Americans were hardened, trained professionals. The result was a colourful massacre with the well-drilled Americans (who'd won national tournaments in the US) coming out in impressive formation, with highly practiced shooting skills. It couldn't have been more than about 45 seconds and every Australian was splattered with paint from head to toe while not one American wore even a flesh wound. Yep, I thought at the time, the Americans are really good at war. It was fun to watch the bewildered Australians react like fish in a barrel as the super smooth Americans hunted them down in a ridiculously one-sided encounter. But of course, that would have made for a slightly boring news broadcast, so we made it look like the pathetic Australians (who we filmed practicing impressively before the actual match-up) were in fact a little more competitive than they were.

Pulling my first ever uni-related all-nighter to edit the story – which I could have edited either to glorify the Americans or vilify the Australians (who I could have made to look incapable of protecting our borders) – I suddenly understood the sort of power that you have when you're in charge of choosing what goes into, and just as importantly, what is omitted, from a news story.

Sipping on a beer three years later, Chris (24) and I (23) regaled each other with everything we'd done in our time apart. I'd got a job as a journalist with WIN TV, working in a regional area called the Riverland, before taking on a role with the Royal Adelaide Hospital in Marketing and Public Relations. Chris, meanwhile, had landed a job as a TV news editor with Channel 9 and the ABC, before winning a position with the Darwin Detention Centre helping refugees. His time at the detention centre coincided with the eruption of the 'refugee problem' in the Australian psyche – which was fuelled by fear mongering news headings such as *Illegal Boat People Arrive In Droves*. What newsrooms, of course, failed to mention was that refugees have a lawful right to enter a country for the purposes of seeking asylum, regardless of how they arrive or whether they hold valid travel or identity documents. These rights were put in place to avoid situations like the holocaust or Rwandan genocide from becoming even bloodier.

As the beers evaporated and the conversation got rowdier and more honest there arose a theme to our mutual talk-fest. We had both been desperate to crack the media business and win jobs in this highly competitive industry and we'd both succeeded, but in doing so we were both dissatisfied with what we found. There were many incidents that accumulated to sour my view of an industry I had loved from afar since I was a kid, but two episodes in particular stand out…

The first was a run in with management over an interview with a prominent independent politician called Nick Xenephon. Nick enjoyed a high profile in our shared home state of South Australia, and I found him to be a thoroughly agreeable individual. He understood the importance of the media to someone such as himself who didn't have a major political party to fall back on, and he was always only too happy to accommodate requests, even unusual ones, so long as he was getting his face and message out there.

At the time, the Riverland was in the throes of the worst drought in decades. The landscape was littered with fields of dead orange trees. The unreported story in the area was the number of suicides among farming families, as generations of growers watched everything they'd built disappear before their very eyes.

Nick was campaigning in the Riverland as part of his first ever bid for a federal Senate seat, hoping to 'level-up' his State-based political clout. I'd been fortunate enough to land an interview with Nick where I was going to ask him about the climate-induced pain of the region, and when and how he would lobby the government to respond, if he was elected? Then, on the morning of my interview, a nothing story broke in Adelaide that really was little more than gossip, but because I was the only TV correspondent in the Riverland I became the designated reporter and was sent a series of questions I had to ask Nick on behalf of all the major news services across Australia. I didn't like the story, and I didn't like the questions, because both distracted from the important issues I wanted to raise with Nick. Unfortunately, I wasn't given an option. I was just four months out of uni after all.

The 'story' that had got everyone in a tizz was that Nick had apparently 'forced' a colleague who owed him some money to go to an

ATM, withdraw the cash and give it to him. That was it, and what should have been a petty, private squabble was deemed to be an Australia-wide scoop. Anyway, I asked Nick the questions I wanted to about the drought, before apologizing, telling him I didn't want to ask these questions but I was being forced to do so, and went ahead and grilled him about 'the scandal'. It was a horrible experience that to me undermined my job – which, as I was taught in university, was: to educate the public about events and issues and how they affect their lives. How did a politician asking someone to repay a debt constitute as 'an issue that affected the public', I wondered, as I fought not to include any part of his personal squabble in the story I presented that evening. I knew he was running for public office, and as such 'everything was on the table', but there were thousands of farmers in the grips of a drought that saw many committing suicide and all that the mainstream Australian media seemed interested in was seeing if Nick would 'bleed and break' like most politicians do under the weight of media scrutiny.

A few weeks later, after taking some time to reflect on my very short career to that point, I turned away from the industry I so badly wanted to be a part of, because I simply couldn't be proud of the level of honesty, transparency or blatant negativity that underpinned at least 70 to 80% of the stories I was made to cover. As I handed in my resignation, I felt a darkness leave me – the weight and expectation that I would *do or* say *anything* if it was popular (and loosely seen as being in the public interest). The repercussion of this impassioned choice to quit 'my dream job out of university' was that I was forced to head back to Adelaide where I once again took up stacking shelves at Foodland, the supermarket I worked at during university (funnily enough, this job actually paid more than being a TV reporter). All in all, my journalistic adventure lasted five months and taught me one thing – I didn't want to be a mainstream journalist.

While I knew being in front of the camera wasn't for me, I thought I'd take up an opportunity to do an internship at Channel 9 as a news cameraman (while stacking shelves in my spare time). The experience bolstered what I already knew – the problem with the whole industry is what goes on behind closed doors, as news directors, editors and chiefs of staff decide whether to present people as gods or devils, depending on what will sell best or what their bosses – like Rupert Murdoch – tell them to do. This is, of course, most often based on what politicians or agendas will further their business interests and maximize their profits.

My second encounter with the belly of the media-beast was from a slightly different perspective. Between 2008 and late-2012, I worked in the public relations department of the Royal Adelaide Hospital, where I wrote press releases and talked to the media to try and generate good news stories about all the life saving work of our dedicated staff and researchers. The problem was, 'good news' was often a tough sell, whereas if a doctor or nurse ever made a mistake it was front-page news.

On Sunday 29 January 2012, the well-known bad boy biker, Vince Focarelli, was targeted for assassination by a fellow biker group. Four bullets hit him but failed to kill him. His step-son, Giovanni, however, wasn't so lucky and was killed in the attack. Vince was rushed to the Royal Adelaide Hospital for treatment and following him was a horde of reporters forced to camp outside the hospital as part of a ghoulish death-watch. I was in my office in the hospital fielding reporter's questions about Vince's condition when suddenly all hell broke loose. Before the general manager of the hospital had even finished filling us in, police, bomb squad personnel and robots were scurrying down the halls of the hospital and the alarm went out to evacuate or bunker down, depending on where you were. I'm not sure why, but I chose to ignore the kerfuffle. It certainly wasn't a case of bravado, but rather a weariness with all the over-reaction. What we'd been told was that a man had dropped off a parcel at reception and asked for it to be delivered to Vince, before running away. As the GM of the hospital, a quirky little English woman, said, "It was probably a friend dropping off a box of chocolates." But still, the drill to clear out and lock down proceeded, and the media loved it. Flashing lights, the bomb squad decked out with a robot to retrieve the package and a supposed murder plot was enough to well and truly get the media frothing at the mouth with extravagant theories about who, how and what was trying to kill Focarelli.

As it turned out the general manager had been correct – it was a friend dropping off a box of chocolates, and the reason he had 'run away' was because he was double-parked, as parks were particularly difficult to score around the hospital. Anyway, the prospect of a 'bomb' being delivered to 'notorious gangster' Vince Focarelli was widely reported, but there was no follow-up report of the 'bomb' being a box of chocolates. I had even spoken to a number of journalists, alerting them to the amusing misunderstanding and the fact we had never been under any threat of being bombed. Ironically, but not surprisingly the only thing louder than the unexploded bomb was the silence from the media on the subject (partly because the truth was revealed just after their story deadline of 5pm).

So that was the mood of the men and women of the fifth estate, suspicious and hungry for blood. In fact, just the next morning when the media called for an update on Vince and I told them that he'd improved overnight and was now stable and, in all probability, was going to be fine, there was an audible sigh from a number of reporters. "Excuse me?" I snarled. "I've just told you a person is going to live and you're disappointed? You should be fucking ashamed of yourself!" I slammed down the telephone. No, this wasn't a world I wanted to be a part of. And I should clarify, it wasn't just when bikers 'inconveniently lived' that I heard this familiar sigh, it was a common occurrence whenever a tragic event turned out to be less fatal or critical than first thought, because of course the heading 'everybody is OK' isn't going to sell as many newspapers as '3 Critical, 1 Dead After Stabbing/Crash/Shooting etc', therefore my 'good news' was their 'bad news' – ruining their story.

Chris listened patiently before recounting some of the horror stories coming out of the Darwin Detention Centre, and the public and media's growing hostility towards people escaping whatever it was these refugees were running away from – persecution, poverty, war and imminent death.

"Refugees need to be treated better, politicians need to be more humane and the media needs to change," said Chris, encapsulating my thoughts exactly. But what could two young idealists do to change the media landscape? Well, we could have carried on drinking, got smashed, gone home, woken with terrible hangovers and forgotten all about what we'd discussed. In fact, that would have been the most natural sequence given the privilege and ease of our lives. But instead, we stayed and talked and sipped on a few more beers and drew in our minds the blueprint of a battle plan.

Into the belly of the beast

It sounded so simple, so achievable when we both agreed: "We need to start our own news organisation." I don't know if Chris said it or

I did, but the important thing was we held a shared vision. I think the resounding notion that led to this crucial mission was this: before we can create something, we must first be able to imagine it – from the chair you're sitting on, to women's rights or the end of Apartheid – someone first had to imagine those things, before they could become reality. Similarly, if humanity is ever to create the world so many dream of – of peace, prosperity, equality, unity, and kindness – then we need to be able to imagine it, but the never-ending barrage of negative, fear-inducing news makes this very, very hard. Instead of news 'reflecting society back onto itself', as one of our uni lecturers had taught us, we were only ever exposed to the very worst of humanity – murder, war, crime, terror, domestic violence, scandal, inequality, riots, conflict, corruption and car crashes, just to name a few. How can this possibly inspire anything but more of the same? And the worst part is, this is not the truth – across the globe, crime and murder rates are ever decreasing, diseases are being defeated each year, technology is liberating millions and deaths in armed conflict are at an all-time low. The fact is, the vast majority of us spend our days working to make this world a better place. From Gill Hicks and Dancing Tommy, to the six most generous countries on Earth who together donate roughly 410 billion dollars to charity each year. Or take the 86% of Australians who have gone out of their way to help a stranger in need, or the 30% who do this every month.

Perhaps, we thought, if more people could see and be surrounded by a more 'positive' view of humanity, it might inspire a more positive reality, just as one of Oprah Winfrey's favourite books, *The Secret*, had illustrated – if you think positive, you create positive and if you think negative, that is the energy you get.

We knew we had a mountain (or three) to climb before even thinking about bringing this bold idea to life, so we began formulating our thoughts, and caught up with a few friends and colleagues who worked in the field. As I recalled one of Chris's journalist buddies, Wilson, saying: "it's funny, they (TV news services) spend all their time making you want to cut your wrists, and then at the end they put that fluffy little happy story just so you don't go through with it." Another of his friends, Peter Run, who was a prolific writer and professor of politics who had fled South Sudan said: "When you live in a place without free press, you realise the power of the media. It frames how a society thinks and therefore acts. If they tell you that your country is doomed you will believe it, if they tell you a politician is corrupt you will believe it and if they show you the worst of humanity, you will believe that everyone is like that."

It didn't take us long to see that our dream was something people were hungry for. But how was it going to work? What would it look like? Where would we operate? And why would people change their age-old evolutionary habit of being drawn to those things we feel threatened by? We knew we needed to answer a whole gamut of questions, not least of which was "how do we fund this?" With just one chance to get it right, Chris and I drew up a schedule that would give us 14 months to: create a business plan that involved hundreds of conversations and thousands of pieces of research, while at the same time exploring a name and branding for the organisation; then start talking to sponsors, writers, photographers, business managers, editors, videographers, and so on, before finally launching a demo website that would allow us to further attract sponsors, media and hype for the main event, which was to be the launch of a fully fledged online news organisation on 1 August 2011. That first meeting at the pub was in late February 2010.

During this extended period of planning and set up, Chris was working part-time for the ABC as a TV news editor, as well as casually with the Australian Refugee Association on a number of education and mentoring projects. I was still at the hospital, working in marketing and PR, but, to be honest, my mind was mostly elsewhere, because as anyone who knows me will tell you – once I have an objective in sight (and Chris was the same), it's all or nothing.

And we were up to our necks in it.

I remember the waves of ups and downs as people kissed our feet and offered their help, before telling us we were "doomed to fail."

What defined this most tumultuous and hectic period and kept us on track and efficiently swimming through the stinking, overcrowded swamp of tasks that confronted us was our WIP (Work in Progress) document. It was literally (OK, maybe metaphorically) the best thing we ever did. What it did was take this huge 'unrealistic and impossible' dream and break it up into tiny parts. Each week we'd catch up and go through the work we both needed to achieve during the next seven days, as well as adding things to our longer-term plans. Then, the following week we'd come and tick off what we'd done (normally it was everything) ,which allowed us to feel the cogs turning, to remain connected (we knew what the other was doing) and it kept us working efficiently, professionally and to a deadline. As we'd wade through the to do list, what it also did was force us to recognize our strengths and weaknesses, as we split tasks accordingly.

Chris was always the more likeable, friendlier face and the softer spoken of the two of us. I often called him 'the good cop'. He was the dreamer (the eagle first, and worker bee or 'buffalo' second, according to various personality tests), meticulous in how things looked, and had a natural charm that made people want to be near him. In contrast (though we had a lot of similarities too), I was the more intense, outwardly passionate and often outspoken and brutally honest type. I was the 'bad cop'. I was the doer (the worker bee/buffalo first and eagle second), scrupulous with how things sounded and read (I was the editor), and I would inspire people through my attitude and obvious commitment to the dream. It should be said that there was a lot of overlap, and technically we both had a broad range of skills that made things easy – we could write, design, photograph, had an eye and mind for marketing, and we could both film and edit videos. But I think what we realised very early on was that our single greatest strength wasn't a skill, it was actually that we were super 'normal' guys that people could relate to. The only difference was, we had a giant dream – a world where peace reigned and kindness was king. And we were chasing it!

For the next six months all we did was absorb – like sponges. We asked and researched and learned how and what we needed to do next to take this euphoria we were living and turn it into something real and meaningful. Undoubtedly, it was in this time of deep reflection and endless questioning that I found my *'why'* – which was to share stories that could inspire a better world. I think what helped me discover my *why* at such a young age (and may help you find yours) were two things: I looked at what I was good at (storytelling) and asked myself where that overlapped with what I felt was the greatest need in the world (which was to change the media).

Some of the research that went on to influence my *why*, as well as guide and justify what we were doing, included a study by McCrindle Research Institute which found that 95% of Australians agreed that the media reports more negative than positive news (I'm not sure what the other 5% were watching). The study also saw 93% of people admitting that this made them feel as though there is more evil in the world than good. It came as no surprise then that researchers found only 31% of people believed that there were more acts of kindness in the world than acts of terror. What Mark McCrindle, the author of this study and a book he published as a result of his findings called *The Power of Good*, said was: "The perception of worsening violence and less kindness is largely based on crime coverage in daily media reports, and is refuted by solid research." In fact, **for every act of road rage, violence or abuse in Australia, there are 38 acts of kindness towards strangers.** But where was this being shown, we wondered? As Rich Noyes, a media researcher suggested, it wasn't. In fact, his 2005 study found that the percentage of 'positive' news stories was just 15% while 'negative' stories made up a whopping 85% of what we see on our TV screens and in our newspapers. A more recent study in 2014 (after we launched) found that just 1 in 17 news stories was positive, so roughly 6%, while 94% were negative.

But that's because negative news sells, right? Well maybe, but according to McCrindle, 93% of Australians said they "wanted to hear more positive news stories." And as US psychologists and neuroscientists discovered by scanning people's brains and monitoring their emails and social media posts: good news spreads the fastest. "When you share a story with your friends and peers, you care a lot more about how they react. You don't want them to think of you as a Debbie Downer," says Jonah Berger, an Assistant Professor of Marketing and Social Psychologists at the University of Pennsylvania. Studying the *New York Times*' website to see which articles were shared the most, what Berger discovered was that scientific, exciting, and funny articles were shared much more than devastating or negative stories.

This was all music to our ears. Maybe we've got a chance at making something of this, we thought. But the flipside was, psychologists, neuroscientists and our own instinct told us we were competing with 200 thousand years of evolution – which had made us seek out news of dramatic, negative events. This is because, as *Psychology Today* writer Ray Williams puts it: "Our brains evolved in a hunter-gatherer environment where anything novel or dramatic had to be attended to immediately for survival. So while we no longer defend ourselves against sabre-toothed tigers, our brains have not caught up." This near-obsession with 'what could go wrong or what could be threatening' is unquestionably in-built and planted deep in our subconscious. To the extent that we had tens of people tell us outright: "that's what the news is, everything that goes wrong in a day ... but good luck changing that!"

What Chris and I felt we needed to better understand was – what does hearing good or bad news actually do to us? How does it affect our brain or our body? What behaviours does it promote or prevent? Hmmmm... Where do I begin?

Let's look at children. An Australian study we looked at found that 44% of children aged 8-16 felt it was important to keep up to date with the news, however, more than half of those surveyed said that news makes them often or sometimes feel afraid (57%), or angry (56%), while 71% said it made them feel sad or upset. Research by the American Academy of Child and Adolescent Psychiatry (AACAP) also found that children and adolescents are prone to imitate what they see and hear in the news, a kind of contagion effect described as 'copy cat syndrome'. "Chronic and persistent exposure to such violence can lead to fear, desensitization (numbing), and in some children, an increase in aggressive and violent behaviours," writes AACAP. The problem is, with most news services constantly distorting the truth, children are often falsely coming to the conclusion that violence is "a normal part of life."

A study we often quoted showed that in Philadelphia, the number of crimes dropped by 20% over a specific period, while the incidence of crime reporting in traditional media increased by 600% over that same period. Given AACAP says crime makes up around 30% of all news reports, it is little wonder a range of experts and reports intimate that children are more prone to violence, bullying, anxiety and fear, if they watch the news.

As adults, it doesn't get much better either. To comprehend the damage permeated by a news cycle defined by the phrase "if it bleeds it leads," we must first understand how our adult brain works and what we need in order to feel OK, let alone be happy. It's fair to say that the first thing Chris and I became through this process was 'pretend professors of positive psychology', which is the science of happiness. The 3:1 ratio was probably our first major concern. For as leading scholar and researcher, Dr. Barbara Fredrickson had shown, people needed to experience positive emotions in a 3-to-1 ratio to negative emotions in order to feel good about life. For example, if you're working as a receptionist and you have 4 people come past your desk and three are kind and polite but one is not, you'll feel the world is OK, but if that is reversed and three are impolite and rude and just one is kind, you'll feel as though life sucks and people are pricks. When we think about the necessary ratio of 3 positive experiences for every 1 negative experience – which we need to feel OK or happy – and then stack that up against the current 1:17 ratio of positive versus negative news stories we are showered with, there is no way that watching a news bulletin can make you feel anything but depressed, fearful and pessimistic.

The next thing we wanted to know was what were the positive ramifications that might come from launching a more balanced news organisation? The first study we stumbled across was by Harvard Medical School, which found that happiness is more infectious than the flu. Their research confirmed that within a social network, happiness spreads among people up to three degrees removed from one another. That means when you feel happy, a friend of a friend of a friend has a slightly higher likelihood of feeling happy too. To us this provided further justification for seeing happiness, like health, as a collective responsibility that we the public, and the media, must be a part of fostering. Because, as we discovered next, through a conversation with neuroscientist Marco Iacoboni from University of California in Los Angeles, we all have these things in our brain called 'mirror neurons'. These neurons are activated both when we perform a certain action – such as smiling or picking up a cup – and when we observe someone else performing that same action (it's why when someone picks up a drink for a sip, we feel the need to copy them). Speaking with Iacoboni, he said that if we're wired to automatically internalise the movements and mental states of others, then "we should be more careful about what we watch." "This is a tricky argument, of course, because it forces us to reconsider our long-cherished ideas about free will and may potentially have repercussions on free speech," he said. "But there is convincing behavioural evidence linking what we see people doing in the media to what we see people doing in reality."

With science all but confirming that 'what we see we become', we also went about investigating what sorts of stories could have the greatest social impact for good. What we arrived at were those tales of selfless souls, giving all that they are and all that they have to others. The 'founder' of positive psychology himself, Martin Seligman, irrefutably proved that altruism – a selfless concern for the welfare of others (which may include volunteering or donating money to charity) – actually boosts your immune system and triggers the same pleasure systems in the brain as food and sex... so stop masturbating and go help someone in need! Haha.

Admittedly, we knew it wasn't the job of journalists to make people happy, but what we wanted to understand was the power of our (and mainstream media's) words and imagery. While this is just a fraction of what we dug up, the vast number of scientifically-based concepts we digested during this period would go on to reshape our minds, creating and reinforcing new pathways to a more resilient and happier state of being – something we'd both call on in the months and years ahead.

With our official launch imminent and on track for 1 August 2011, Chris and I held a '100 days to go party' to get people excited, on board and introduce them to Our World Today, the organisation that wanted to 'do the impossible – change the way the media operates'. By this stage we'd found a major sponsor in UniSA, who housed the largest journalism school in the State (where we'd both studied), as well as a few local businesses who were willing to literally give us money based solely on an idea and our word – something that gave us so much energy at the time.

A few months out, Chris and I were in the midst of an all-out charm offensive, sharing our passion and vision with universities, philanthropists and businesses across Australia. The days were long, and the coping mechanisms for living off four hours sleep were often pretty seedy. We were by no means regular drinkers, but when we had a big win (or if it was a Friday afternoon and we didn't have any meetings), we celebrated with our ever-growing team of writers, marketers, business developers, designers, videographers and so on. We knew that the bonds we formed through these collegial activities were a huge draw card for our 60-odd 'staff' – none of whom were paid a cent, including us. In fact, in order to dedicate myself more wholly to Our World Today, I decided to sell my house (which I'd only just bought a year earlier) and wound back my hours (and pay) by going part-time at the hospital. The process also left Chris and I perpetually single, because we were forever preoccupied, and nothing could compete with the rush of what we were doing (not even love). Funny as it might sound to some, the 'sacrifices' that I made, at no point felt like a burden to me. Quite the opposite. With each giant leap or risk, I felt my soul becoming more whole, and happier, as if I was filling in some of those holes that I'd dug whilst chasing a more shallow, selfish sense of purpose.

Through finding my *why*, I think I was finally able to understand and accept my 'who' (as can often be the case, for our *who* and *why* are very much interlinked). What this did, just as it had with Sugathapala, Passenger and so many others, is it allowed me (and Chris) to create something from nothing. A new energy for the world – our true form – a mission concocted just for us.

Forty-eight hours out from our launch we got a phone call that would haunt anyone. "The website is still having a few problems," said our developer, who was a distant friend doing us a favour, because he believed in what we were doing. For the next 72 hours we didn't sleep. From testing the website and writing and editing stories, to uploading videos, printing and distributing promotional materials and creating hundreds of custom design files in Photoshop to stop some of the website glitches, it's fair to say we were tapped into some higher power that turned us into frantic little Energizer bunnies.

Seeing the sunrise and set from our office – which was basically a few desks and computers at the back of an art gallery in the city – was confronting. Would we be doing this forever? I wondered. But the pure mayhem was also liberating, we were doing and being *us*, and it was a rush I have not felt since.

Then, on Monday 1st August 2011 at 7:06am, with the click of a button, Our World Today (OWT) was born. At 9am with all the bugs fixed, we sent off a flurry of emails, social media posts and personal text messages to our biggest supporters, letting them know "we are live!"

With endless reassurances that the website couldn't possibly crash, we continued our assault, ensuring the thousands of people we'd met and spoken to in the months leading up to the launch knew it was go time – that it was time to act on all those kind words of support they'd lent us.

Then, at 9:37am, with the click of a button, Our World Today and our dreams came crashing down – 'page not available' – read the screen that should have contained our homepage. "Holy shit!" I yelled to Chris, who was sitting right next to me. "The website has crashed." We immediately called with our developer to let him know what had happened. Like us though, he had also pulled an all-nighter, only he was now asleep. We asked another friend who understood websites better than we did to see

Chris and me.

Minutes after we went live.

Our inaugural (Adelaide-based) team of volunteers, at our launch party.

Our *BBQ to Boardroom* photo by Benjamin Liew.

Chris and me doing a radio interview.

Speaking at TEDx Adelaide.

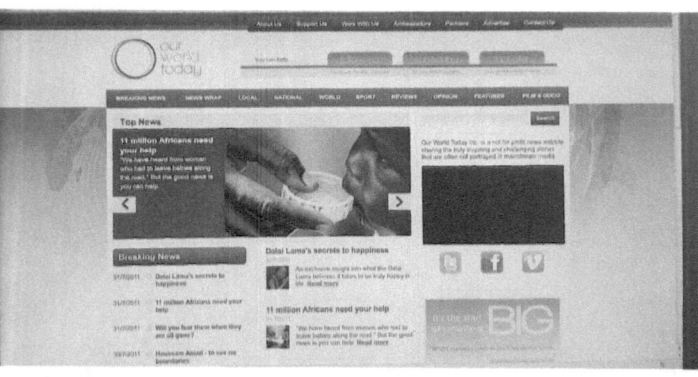
Our website.

Our 'Happy' event with our two co-hosts Jo (left) and Pippa (right).

Meeting Dr Hakim Young and Kathy Kelly.

Today Tonight filming their story on us in our 'art-gallery-office'.

what he could do. By the time he'd logged onto our back-end, we'd got a hold of Adam (our developer), who repeated my words, "Holy shit! The website has crashed," he said. "Well duh," I felt like saying. But I bit my tongue as he had been a hero throughout the process and didn't deserve my sudden anger. "This is impossible," he said. "To cause the site to crash you'd need more than 30,000 people on the site all at once, all clicking on multiple stories and videos." "Wow!" Chris and I said in tandem as we turned to one another with eyebrows raised. I guess there was an upside to this dilemma – but we still needed it fixed and soon, because who knows how many people were sitting there frustrated, and who knows how many may never return if this is their first experience. With a bit of shuffling around of websites on his servers, Adam had us back up and running within about 45 minutes, though it felt more like five hours. I should note that at the time *The Advertiser*, the largest news website in South Australia, had between 25,000 and 60,000 users per day, so 30,000 all at once was huge.

We re-sent a number of messages and emails, slightly proud of what we'd achieved, that said: "Hey guys, as you may have noticed our website just crashed due to having too much traffic – who said good news can't sell!!! – but don't worry we're back online now, so please enjoy the remarkable stories on offer and thanks again for your support, Chris and Mike." Things mostly ran smoothly from that time on, with only the odd glitch to worry about. On the Friday of that week (the 5th August), the day after my birthday, we held a massive launch party with around 300 people, including Dancing Tommy, local politicians and business people, a Master Chef contestant, our sponsors, a well-known band and of course, most importantly, our team of believers, who'd helped us bring this enormous vision to life.

On 26th September, shortly after our launch, a PR agency we hired to get the word out landed us a story on a show called *Today Tonight* – a national news and current affairs show. My own PR knowledge and instinct would have been to decline the opportunity because *Today Tonight* were not the most reputable news show on TV. Unfortunately though, ego and a lack of interest from other media (who understandably didn't want to promote a rival) got the better of us, and we accepted the offer.

Automatically when I saw they'd sent a journalist by the name of Frank Pangallo, a guy I'd often refused to let any of our doctors at the hospital talk to, I knew we'd need to be on our A-game. We needed to be tight and not miss a word – and thankfully following the interview I felt we'd nailed it (shirking his repeated attempts to rattle us). Still, as our story aired on TV, it was a stark reminder of why we were doing what we were doing. Frank turned our story into a farce (as much as he could), making it sound as if we were just two young naive kids with no understanding of the 'mighty media industry'.

Setbacks like this interview were tough because we were constantly giving it our all, baring our souls daily, but we knew we must rise above the doubters – what we were doing was too important to give up on – and most of the time such days simply made us work even harder. It's difficult to explain the chaos and pressure we were under. Picture managing a daily news organisation with a team of 150 volunteers from 15 countries (and time zones), who required coordination and direction from me (the editor), and who wouldn't have had a website or business to write for if not for Chris, who did a lot of the non-content related work, such as building relationships and organising events.

The weight on our shoulders grew by the day, as things got serious, with new sponsors, new writers and far more epic stories being released with each passing week. The momentum was palpable – like being crowd surfed by thousands of strangers who dreamed as we did – of a world united by extraordinary feats that our website fed them, rather than divided by the angst and division their TV sets forced down their throat.

We were convinced that Our World Today was an idea whose time had come. And it soon saw us giving a TEDx talk, speaking at a Pecha Kucha night and various other public events, as well as being invited to cover a range of significant stories, which saw our journalists interviewing Zac Efron, Taylor Schilling, our then Prime Minister Kevin Rudd, our then State Premiere Jay Weatherill, Nick Vujicic, Passenger, Tom Green, Dr Hakim Young, various Olympians and even the now 70-year-old Tibetan Buddhist monk Matthieu Ricard, who has been called 'the world's happiest man'. We spoke to soldiers on the ground in Afghanistan about their experiences – good and bad – from coping with the threat of IEDs and seeing their mates being killed, to the locals they met, the schools they were building and the young girls who were finally free to attend them. Unlike mainstream media, we felt the war was about much more than the body count of 'soldiers' versus 'terrorists', and we maintained that the public had a right to know why our soldiers were dying and where our billions of dollars of tax-payer money was going. We had a Chinese man who'd worked in an iPhone factory put together an exposé on the many injustices that go into making Apple's beautiful devices, and we followed the money trail behind the wild over-prescription of antidepressants. Our World Today did and went where other media would not (usually because they were too afraid of losing advertising revenue if they made Apple or other multinationals look bad).

Despite being labelled a 'good news' website, what we did in reality was try to show people that there is something to be learned from every disaster, tragedy or war – a silver lining – and this is what provided the meaning and positive balance we were after (which was not evident in mainstream news). For example, when Amy Winehouse died, the traditional media covered every aspect of her excesses and her poor choices, highlighting her failures, rather than her triumphs, while Our World Today was one of the only news outlets in the world that highlighted the millions of dollars she had donated to street children so they could avoid making the same mistakes she did, and be spared the pain she endured. While both approaches to the news can be easily justified, only one has an inspirational message, only one has the ability to create a better world.

"The media is about scaring people into submission, but we are about empowering them into action," I said in an interview we did for a book called *BBQ to Boardroom*. "We don't make the news, but we as the media can choose to report only what makes a difference to people's lives," I continued. "For instance, how does it help anyone to know that a motorist was killed in a single-car accident in a remote location? All that does is make everyone a bit more scared. Whereas if the motorist's mother made a statement that her son was killed because of excessive alcohol or because of sleep deprivation as a way of warning others of the danger of driving under such conditions, then it could inspire people to abide by her warnings and we would run such a story."

The problem, as Chris described it in his interview for the same book, was that there was no balance, no hope, no sense of empowerment, "everything is about 'how can we scare them enough to get a reaction, to keep them coming back to us for more,'" he said. "But by feeding into people's fears, the media promotes that fear as a normal state. It's a vicious cycle, with the media telling you to be afraid, very afraid, then, reporting that people are afraid, very afraid," explains Chris. "The bad news for society is that fear inhibits positive thought and positive action, impeding our evolution towards a better world."

For all of these reasons and more, we always saw Our World Today as much more than a mere news website. We knew we needed to be a beacon for change: a place where other media outlets could come to find and copy 'alternative but popular' stories (like Dancing Tommy), where young journalists could be trained to think differently about 'what constituted a news story', and a platform that proved once and for all that 'good news sells', because at the end of the day money is what makes the media world go round (for without it no one has a job).

In early 2012 (less than 6 months in), it was this very thing – money – that was starting to take its toll on us. Chris (who was working as a university tutor in filmmaking) and I (who was still at the hospital 'partly-part-time') were struggling to keep Our World Today afloat without using huge amounts of our own money (every cent in our bank account). Yep, the reality of 'launching a non-profit start-up' was tough, but this was just the beginning. We'd massively outgrown our tiny office and couldn't recruit more staff unless we had more space, so we asked our landlord and good friend Mr Z (Zoran), who owned the restaurant next door and managed a number of buildings in the area, if we could take the space upstairs from the art gallery (a giant open area), which was only being used for one month a year by the Adelaide Film Festival as a ticketing office. Being an avid fan of all we were doing, and as an absolutely fabulous and warm human being we still love dearly to this day, Mr Z said "yes!"

This was great news, but in reality, it only generated an even bigger issue: where was the money going to come from to fit out the new space and buy more equipment? By that time, I had surrendered to, and firmly believed in, 'faith' – that if we are on the right path, all we need will come to us, and if it doesn't then it wasn't meant to be. I know a lot of people pay lip service to this idea, but I wonder how many truly practice it? (More on that in later chapters).

What happened next didn't exactly help us financially – I decided to take leave without pay from my work – but the decision was necessary, as it allowed me to dedicate all of my time to growing our team, business and making this thing financially and managerially sustainable. Part of our strategy for growing our team and business meant taking the more expensive but much larger office space upstairs and simply crossing our fingers that a way to pay for it would present itself. Within days of moving into the new office, Chris had managed to win a government grant that gave us six reconditioned computers for our budding team, and a number of career talks we'd given at various universities were bearing fruit, with new marketing, video and journalism students jumping on board to volunteer and fill the seats in front of those computers. But we still didn't have enough furniture, and the office was a bit derelict and lacked the colour and inspiration we wanted to represent.

Understanding that growing our audience (and revenue) was just as central to our sustainability as growing our team, we launched a number of marketing initiatives, including a video series called 'The Gift Of Giving' (which you can view via thehappiest.com), a major movie fundraiser where we screened the film *Happy* (after meeting the director Roko Belic) and monthly events in our office (where we somewhat 'illegally' sold alcohol and food). In December 2011, we also made a bold decision to dedicate a large percentage of our resources to creating an online TV series covering the Adelaide Fringe Festival (a major arts and comedy festival that ran from 24 February to 18 March 2012). We felt it was a great opportunity to meet a lot of famous faces, who would have large social media followings, and who might be willing to support our cause or at the very least share the story we filmed with them (which would put us in front of a new audience).

What we produced (largely thanks to Chris) was exceptional! (See the 4-part series via thehappiest.com) Fringe Festival management and directors were blown away, and in the years since they have emulated what we created with *Fringe TV* by producing their own online series. Part of our longer-term thought pattern was actually exactly that: we hoped to partner with the Fringe Festival who would pay us (not some film company as they ended up doing) to create *Fringe TV* in future years. We also felt that special 'products' such as *Fringe TV* might only be available to members in the years ahead. What eventuated from this experiment was far from that which we'd imagined – the four weekly-episodes we produced were as professional, entertaining and funny as we could have possibly hoped for – but like so much of what we'd done to that point, people simply didn't get behind it in the way they'd promised, and we needed.

Life was tough! But as we'd always done, we persisted. We dug deep, because we knew that this dream was why we were here. It was our purpose, and the universe drew us to do whatever was necessary to keep the Our World Today heart beating.

For me, that meant taking on the role of Senior A-Grade Football Coach at Murrayville (a small rural town 250km from Adelaide). Having broken five bones in my back playing for the same team in the previous year, I felt this was a dangerous but incredible opportunity, and the dollars involved were too good to say no to. Plus, it was clear to me that this was the end result of my leap of faith to sell my house and take leave without pay in order to continue pursuing my *why* without restraint. On 5 April 2012, with a $6000 down payment in hand (despite not yet taking to the footy field), Chris and I went about re-painting and dramatically remodeling our office space with a new film studio, chill space, whiteboard-walls, putting green and custom-made boardroom table that doubled as a table tennis table. Finally, our base of operations reflected the rest of Our World Today, which was modern, shiny, positive and always beautiful to look at (largely thanks to our two designers Jeff and Carol). The space we had created was everything we'd dreamed of, and with it came a giant party, new volunteers (with a more formal roster structure), and plenty of new sponsors, partners and people stepping up to the plate – because what we'd created was a hub where people wanted to be (and be seen).

Somewhere in between the chaos and severe lack of sleep, Chris and I had even managed to snag ourselves a couple of beautiful girls who we'd both go on to marry. For me, the first I heard of Sash (in October 2011) was when I was editing a story one of our journalists had written about her pending trip to the UN climate talks in South Africa. For Chris, our need to print some T-shirts for the business (in June 2011) gave him an excuse to reconnect with a girl who'd stolen his heart during a trip to Cambodia in late 2010. While he knew Sophea (his now wife) didn't print T-shirts herself, he felt she might know someone who did, given she was an avid seamstress. In the months ahead, the only thing Sophea stitched up was Chris' heart, and in December 2011 he made the voyage to Cambodia to 'see if his feelings were real'. Returning with a newfound spring in his step, I remember Chris telling me, "When I landed and our eyes met, and then as we walked through the airport, it was as if we'd known each other forever – everything was just so comfortable – our hands were just drawn together."

Over the next twelve months their relationship, and the future of

Our World Today was torn in two, as a number of problems, including absurd visa issues with Sophea, eventually led Chris and I down different paths.

Till death do us part

Shortly after the one year anniversary of Our World Today, Chris and I went through a process of again being sponges, absorbing a year's worth of data and learning and formulating a plan to move forward more effectively. Around this same time we were asked to hold a prestigious 'In Business' event at our stunning new office. We also found a possible third wheel (Evan) to help drive and manage OWT alongside Chris and myself. Evan was exactly what we needed (he was our 'bear', to Chris' 'eagle', and my 'buffalo', when it comes to leadership/personality styles).

As the three of us sat down to pour over more than 1600 stories, which had been viewed by 180,000 people in that first year, what we realised was clear – things had to change. Since that initial burst in popularity, which extended across 3-4 months, things had plateaued, no matter what we'd tried (including *Fringe TV*, *The Gift of Giving*, new partners, more sponsors, a better office, bigger events). Nothing had got us the hits we had in those first few weeks or months. Crunching the numbers – next to a timeline of what marketing, how many writers and what types of stories we were publishing at the time – there were a few revelations that were about to shake the core of our organisation.

Firstly, of the top 10 most popular stories that year I'd written seven of them. The problem was, twelve months in I was so busy holding down the role of editor, director, chief of staff, speaker, recruiter, photographer, filmmaker, university liaison and assistant event planner that I'd abandoned the very thing I was best at and the thing I loved most, which was storytelling. The next giant data-slap in the face was this: our breaking 'up to the minute' stories weren't selling – it seemed that people were not coming to us for their daily news (they clearly didn't see us like the BBC or Aljazeera). Rather, what they were drawn to when they landed on our website were those investigative, in depth, inspiring feature stories, like Dancing Tommy or the iPhone exposé. Finally, the inconsistency across the board shone both anecdotally and statistically. The quality of our writing (pre-editing), marketing, events, videography...

it was all far too up and down, because as Chris and I had discussed, too many of our volunteers lacked the commitment or the skills to uphold the standard we expected, unless we held their hand.

The next step, we knew, was critical, and would set the tone for our eventual rise or fall.

A week later we sacked everyone. Well, kind of. We drew up a new business structure and job descriptions for each position and began advertising – putting the ball back in the court of our volunteers. It was a tough call to make, to downsize from what was a pool of around 150 volunteers at that point, to a dedicated team of 25 staff/volunteers who would hold far greater responsibilities. We of course knew most of the individuals who we wanted to stay, and we asked them to apply for certain roles, but we were also terribly curious to see who we'd weed out. The thing is, we knew that if OWT was going to get better, so too everyone had to get better, including Chris and me. A huge part of that was going to come from inviting Evan on board officially as a third co-director and our new chief of staff. Together with training up another editor, Anna (one of our most committed and talented writers), we knew this would give me the freedom to write more and find new partnerships to grow OWT's audience and revenue.

While the new business structure was designed to get all our puzzle pieces in order, it was our new model for how we would create and distribute content that was really going to bring these pieces together in an enthralling way that would hopefully deliver meaning, recognition and a renewed point of difference to OWT. The new concept was that we would select a weekly theme (aligned with current global events), such as body image, poverty, refugees, mental health or terrorism, and we'd investigate that issue from every possible angle, through 10-15 inspiring and in-depth feature stories that would be released across the week. Instantly, the signs were good, our viewership was up and attracting new sponsors was a breeze, with the theme giving us a distinct advantage and making certain businesses an easy target: for instance, during the week on 'poverty', we had an Australian charity working in international development take up our offer to advertise with us exclusively for that week.

Had we finally cracked it? We wondered. Not counting our chickens just yet.

The quality of the content under this new model, I honestly felt, was fantastic! It asked all the right questions and poked all the right pressure points to affect change and once and for all show our media colleagues that there was another 'more ethical and still lucrative' way to do things. It's probably worth pointing out that at this point (late 2012), no one had really cracked a financially sustainable model for online news. With the world moving online, newspaper and TV revenues were plummeting, and the damage of this digital leap was being felt by thousands of staff being laid off right across the media landscape. Even the likes of The New York Times and CNN were forced to scamper to work out how the hell you make money, sharing news online. Facing the same question, we felt lucky in a way, because we still weren't paying anyone (thus, no one to lay off), and despite the fact that we hadn't yet reached our lofty goals, we got a prodigious amount of happiness from every moment of every day, because what were chasing was something far grander than money or prestige.

I think one thing I failed to realise at the time is that it was actually through this experience of being so inundated by good and bad emotions and infinite wins and loses every single day, that my mind was able to become such a sieve for collecting happiness. Reflecting on just how OWT altered and reshaped my brain while writing this chapter, I have no doubt that it was dealing with the tireless daily challenges and disappointments that allows me to this day, to so easily be able to dismiss bad things and let negative events pass quickly over me. I simply didn't have the mental time, will or energy to be anything but optimistic and positive during that period, as the alternative would have crushed me to a pulp.

Another thing too, that I didn't see coming, was the eventual outcome of an article I sat down to write on 1 October 2012, as part of our week themed 'mental health'. I'd interviewed our state Minister for Mental Health, John Hill, about what the government could and was doing to curb the alarming rise in anxiety and depression. In researching this piece, there were two statistics that shocked me and shook me to my core: the first was that **loneliness had just become the leading cause of depression in the Western world, amidst a global population of 7.5 billion;** and the second was a TED talk by Ron Gutman, which stated that most adults (roughly 70%) smile less than 20 times a day, while the vast majority of kids smile around 400 times a day.

Standing at a busy intersection in the city, just minutes after I'd finished writing this article, I nearly burst into tears. Chatting to a friend next to me, the great void and disconnect between people who were standing right in front of us, just inches apart, was unmistakable. Hundreds of souls, isolated by technology, busily looking at their phones, not daring to lift their head to say hi or simply smile at the person next to them. There was no acknowledgment at all, by anyone, that in that moment they were sharing this space, this life, with other social and emotional beings that they were innately connected to. I remember turning to my friend and saying, "This is fucked, there is something so wrong here. I was wondering how in a world of 7.5 billion people so many could feel lonely, but when you see how we behave, how distracted we are by everything that doesn't matter, it is so glaringly obvious. I'm going to do something about this, I'm going to inspire the world to smile at one another again."

From this observation and a subsequent month of intense self-exploration, unfolded a concept to capture a million smiles (and the stories behind those smiles) from around the world, with the hope I might bring some happiness back into people's lives. It would be my own little adventure, an escape from the pressures of OWT, and a chance to do what I loved – photograph and write about people. Within weeks I'd developed the concept, built a website and booked a three month trip to visit Vietnam, Cambodia, Myanmar, India and Sri Lanka, to look at what inspired some of the world's most impoverished people to smile. Thankfully, Evan's addition as director, and his ability to write and edit well, had provided me with the reassurance that he could cover for me while I made this first trip for what I called A Million Smiles. Of course, I was still writing my weekly story, assisting with editing and sending hundreds of emails every few days (when I had Wi-Fi) to ensure OWT remained alive and well in my physical absence.

By the time I returned from this expedition in January, Chris, Evan and I had acknowledged that Our World Today was in a state of stagnation, and this new structure, new content model and even a new state-of-the-art website (which was donated at a cost of $100,000 by the company that built it) hadn't saved us. In fact, the overpromise of "a lavish new site that could do everything we'd ever wanted," which turned into a mess of ongoing bugs and glitches, very nearly broke me. My patience, commitment and faith teetered on a knife's edge – it was as if everything that I loved was being eaten by the world and shat out as a stinking gooey mess.

And that mess only got worse.

Not only was our readership idle and Chris's visa battle (to get Sophea to Australia) raging, but then without warning, our biggest fan at UniSA, who was responsible for them being our largest sponsor, left his job as the head of the School of Communication, and with him went three quarters of their funding commitment. When our second biggest donor went out of business all together, all in the same month, we knew change was on the menu. The money itself wasn't the real bother (thanks to my ongoing footy contract), but it was a catalyst for thought – thought that led us to an exciting new place.

Stripping back the layers that Our World Today had left us wearing, we again asked ourselves the two questions anyone trying to find their passion should ask: What makes us happy? And what does the world need? At the intersection where these questions meet, you will find your reason for being, and if you follow that you will find true happiness. As we already knew, that intersection for us wasn't too far from where we stood and what we were already doing – sharing stories to inspire a better world – but these questions did lead us to dramatically re-evaluate *how* we'd do that. No longer would we pander to conventional news models or cater stories to fill the gap in mainstream media. We were going to do what we wanted, how we wanted – and we were going to get back to that joy and exhilaration we experienced in the lead up to launching Our World Today.

So on 30 January 2013, nearly three years after that fateful catch up over a beer, Chris and I said goodbye to Our World Today. The final sentence of our last ever email seems as relevant today as it was back then: "Remember, with every click of your mouse you choose the media that confronts us daily, as ultimately each click makes money and tells a business what you want. So, click on horror headings and that's what you'll get, or alternatively, click on awe inspiring stories and choose to see more of that world."

With a shaken spirit, but renewed spring in our step, we welcomed our next adventure. This time Evan drew up the business plan, while Chris and I did what we do best – created and built – though it's fair to say things were a little different and much slower this time around. This largely coincided with Chris landing a full time job in February 2013, so he could 'support' Sophea to get an Australian visa (this also saw them get engaged, buy property in Cambodia and pay a lawyer to coordinate their visa application). With Chris also choosing to go back to university to do a Master's degree in Sustainability (among other things), Evan and I had wondered whether to steam ahead on our own, leaving Chris (who seemed distracted) out of it. But something inside me was bound to Chris, and I refused to let go of that (for better or for worse, till death do us part – haha – people often said we resembled a married couple). In the months ahead, I was offered a part-time role with the Leaders Institute of South Australia, which sounded stimulating, and Evan headed back to uni to finish his Graduate Diploma of Legal Practice (GDLP), which would allow him to practice as a lawyer.

Happily chasing our own paths, what we'd achieved together by September 2013 was quite remarkable: a new brand and website called *Life Sauce*, ready to roll out! Our vision was to inspire people to be their best, by seeing others who were. In essence, we were getting back to our roots – to those human stories (like Dancing Tommy and a lot of tales in this book) that sing to the heart and enrich the souls of those who read or watch them. *Life Sauce* was to be a monthly magazine published online (with a best-of edition printed annually). Stories would be released regularly on social media, and we would work harder to partner with other news organisations to get our stories out there, which would be far easier as we'd no longer be seen as 'competition' for daily news broadcasters. The best part of this model – it would allow us to enjoy the ride (something we'd unwittingly been pulled away from at times throughout the course of OWT).

With our 'i's dotted and our 't's crossed, the three of us nervously held this newfound dream in our hands, ready to let it loose, to let it fly and turn our wildest imaginings into reality. That was, until it dawned on me that somewhere between March and October (though part of me knew it all along), I'd become the only one who was left holding onto the dream with the same energy with which it was conceived. By the time Chris sent us both an email on 28 October 2013 that read, "No more visa application docs. No more court. No more YSP. No more TAFE. Uni is almost done and I am 1/2 way through my thesis," the idea was dead. Evan's mind had moved onto visualising life as a lawyer or a fictional writer, and I hadn't been willing to wait for another platform to share inspiring stories, so that's what A Million Smiles had become, and I'd had instant and resounding success, with Sugathapala's story 'The Happiest Man Alive' reaching more people than all of Our World Today's stories combined.

The thing I came to realise about dreaming with others – or connecting multiple '*whys*' – is it relies on impeccable timing and finding the same wavelength; two elements Chris and I shared for the best part of three years. While it was beyond sad to let go of all that we'd created, I knew I wasn't abandoning my *why* (just fulfilling it through A Million Smiles) and ultimately I'd found the one thing we all crave – true friendship. To this day, Chris remains my best mate and is a soul that still resonates with my own *why*. That itch too, to create together, has never ceased either, and I have little doubt we'll join forces again one day, for **the energy amassed when dreamers collaborate toward a common cause is unparalleled – to me it is god's truest form, our ultimate challenge**. The difficulty is, overcoming those obstacles and sacrifices we must make in order to live a life connected with that greater pool of energy that is our *why*.

While our decision to pack up shop left hundreds stunned enough to finally pledge their financial support to us (by becoming monthly subscribers), it was a case of too little too late, and the success of A Million Smiles' second and third feature videos, both of which went viral, had reaffirmed to me that I was on the right path – I was fulfilling my *why* – sharing stories to inspire a better world. And they were…

Hasith, much more than a story

Hearing gunshots outside his house in the slums of Colombo, Sri Lanka, a 25-year-old man named Hasith went outside to check his younger siblings weren't playing in the streets. As he stepped out on to the street he was struck by a stray bullet (the result of warring gangs), which entered his right shoulder, before clipping (and burning) his spinal cord and becoming lodged next to his vertebrae.

He was immediately paralysed from the chest down. For six months, Hasith lay unconscious in hospital, as his family was told to expect the worst. Paralysed from the shoulder blades down and suffering horrible bedsores, there may have seemed little worth fighting for, but after 182 days this gentle but determined giant awoke. With no memory of anything, even his mother's name, Hasith would soon learn the extent of his problems, as simple tasks such as eating, drinking, talking and even going to the toilet would need to be etched into his memory once more.

When I met Hasith he was 31 years old and had been lying on his bed unable to move for the best part of six years – that's 2200 days. Something about this guy – his genuine hurt and the kindness of he and his mother – made this horrid occurrence that much more tragic. Not only was he the eldest son, one month away from heading for a job in Kuwait (aimed at lifting his family out of poverty) at the time he was shot, but even after this terrible accident, he continued to help his poverty-stricken neighbours and friends fix up old computers for free, something he was extremely proficient at. This guy was the definition of caring – but also trapped. At the time he hadn't left his bed in weeks and had absolutely no plans or idea of how he'd ever escape this heart-wrenching existence. "It is hopeless," his mother told us in tears. But if life has taught me anything it is that nothing is hopeless. Nothing. Not while love and passion reign. Not while there is purpose coursing through our veins.

The early success of our videos in Sri Lanka led me to post Hasith's story on A Million Smiles' Facebook page, with a request for help (particularly from any doctors who might re-look over his case, which had been examined through the stretched public health system). Within days we'd found and Skyped a leading surgeon in Sri Lanka, who after conducting scans was adamant that he could remove the bullet for free – because he was a kind man and liked A Million Smiles. We'd also raised $2300 to help with Hasith's rehabilitation costs ($1300 was my own money). Then, on 12 April 2013, after years of 'hopelessness', a Sri Lankan doctor by the name of Suneth Rajawasan arranged for a local surgeon Dr Himashi Kularatne to remove the bullet that was said to be part of what was preventing Hasith from walking again.

A week later, scans confirmed that the surgery had gone well and it was time to start rehab! The thought that Hasith and his family may finally be free of this shocking burden was gripping. Anxious for news about how he was progressing, I called Hasith two days into what was meant to be 'an intensive three month course of therapy'. When he turned around and said he wasn't in therapy, and that he needed more money 'for rehabilitation' – nearly immediately after I'd given him that $2300 – I was shocked. He'd always been such a humble and grateful

Hasith.

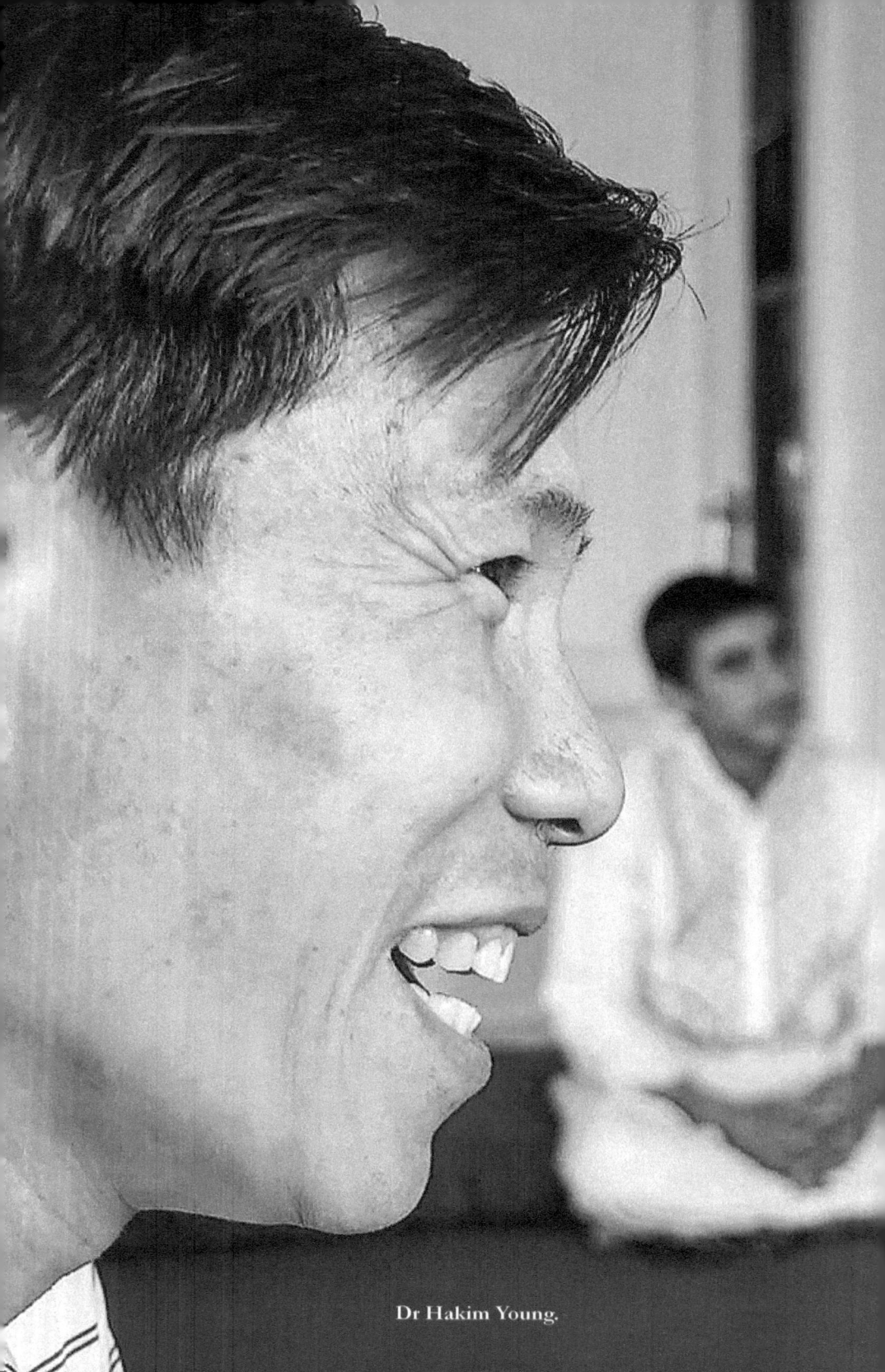

Dr Hakim Young.

guy. "Where did all the other money go?" I asked. Following a number of confusing conversations that my wife painfully translated over Skype, Hasith finally admitted that the donated money was used to pay back some bad loans his family had taken out in order to remain in their house. I wasn't furious, as most around me were, but I felt sadly betrayed. We'd often queried if they needed extra cash – because we were happy to help with more than just his injury – but they'd never mentioned these dangerous debts with loan sharks. While it was clear that this was because they were embarrassed by their inability to manage finances or life, their excuses did little to mend the fine threads of trust we'd built. "Why didn't you tell us Hasith?" I pleaded in tears during our final call. "We would have just given you more money over a longer period of time to pay back the loans and get you the rehab you needed. But now, you've made it impossible to trust you, and that is so so so sad. It breaks my heart," I said. "I'm so sorry, but we can't help you anymore."

While Hasith's story didn't end well (he remained paralyzed and bed-bound until his death in late-2018), this experience felt as if god had grabbed my beating heart from my body and held it up to my eyes, as if to remind me I was on the right path.

No longer was I just writing stories to inspire a better world, this newfound sense of freedom to express my deepest purpose and self through A Million Smiles had allowed me to become part of the story – a brushstroke in the lives of those I met. From trading in love, friendship and stories of hope, to gifting money, goods and a listening ear to those who needed it, I went from astute observer and recorder of good deeds, to someone preoccupied with carrying them out.

It was during these first couple of years of A Million Smiles that my best and happiest self began oozing from every pore of my body, seeping out of me uncontrollably, expressing itself through those photos I was capturing and those videos and stories I was sharing, which have since reached more than 120 million people from every country on Earth. It was as if I was finally living by those words I'd written to myself during a difficult period of Grade 12, when I felt I was trapped in a system of education that wasn't allowing me to set the sort of goals and commitments I wanted to, because I guess most of my desires weren't tangible things, as you can see here in this journal entry I wrote at the time:

Why do I persist in that which has claimed so many and left so many empty.
I must find it, it is within me. While the system is outside me.
I must not let it consume me as I felt it was tonight.
I must explore, and wonder if I consider schooling at all.
It dazzles me as to why I bother.
Has it created depth to my life, or is it really so important to be the 'norm'?

I believe I have these thoughts not for me, but to share with those I know who might also have them.
I will be the greatest person on Earth, because I will be me...
I will create that which has not been done before.
I will be life for those who need it, as a heart machine is for the dying.
I will bring help to those who need it.
I will create light in this darkened world.
Hope, I will create for the hopeless.
I will make my life a light and display it to the world.
My arms will be my mind's servants and I will bring god to those who wish to find it.

Like most thoughts, these words eventually passed. Fading into my subconscious somewhere. In fact, when I finished Grade 12 I really just wanted to be was a masseuse, because it would allow me to pursue my love of painting – which I felt was my calling back then. Unfortunately, my parents wouldn't give or loan me the $2000 for the massage course I so badly wanted to do (because they "simply didn't have it," they said) and I was forced to apply for university. I knew I'd have the grades to do almost anything I wanted, but the problem was nothing called me, so I applied for five completely different courses – Psychology, Physiotherapy, Journalism, Marine Biology and Teaching – and felt I'd let the universe decide. As fate would have it, I got into Journalism and sub-majored in filmmaking!

As you know, my paid work since graduating from my degree has included working as a journalist on TV, in PR for Adelaide's largest hospital and in marketing and social media for the Leaders Institute of South Australia. Arguably however, the most defining moment of my 'paid career' occurred during my time with OWT, when the Business and Marketing Manager of the Heart Foundation in South Australia, Darrin Johnson, asked me to produce "a video that was a little different and more positive than their usual go-to marketing materials," for their annual gala fundraiser. This was something Chris and I had become well known for through Our World Today. The resulting video followed the story of a husband and father of two, Scott Mosen (now a close friend), who had a massive heart attack at just 28 years old while playing touch football. The astonishing tale and images of Scott playing gleefully with his children caused a well of tears, according to Darrin, but what made it such a defining moment (for them and me) was that the firm message of hope – that together, we as human beings can do anything if we unite toward a common cause – seemed to work in engaging people to give more than the typical self-orientated fear-based stories they'd shared previously. This uniquely emotive, yet positive and deeply human form of storytelling is what I have since become well known for in the industry – and thankfully it is a style that has become popular with online audiences.

Much in line with OWT and A Million Smiles, I've chosen to use my career as a filmmaker, writer and social media/marketing consultant to create and share inspiring stories for a huge number of charities, NGOs and the odd government or commercial project that interests me. Since opting to go it alone – quitting my job with the Leaders Institute to launch my own business called Give Media in late 2013 – I have been lucky enough to be able to spend roughly 20-30% of my time 'making money' (doing something I really, really like), which has meant I've been able to focus 70-80% of my life on A Million Smiles/The Happiest (something I really, really love). Of course, there are exceptions to both these statements. I have absolutely loved some of my paid work, such as filming a number of moving stories in the largest refugee camp on Earth (more than my unpaid work at times). There are also boring tasks, challenging interactions and countless let downs associated with establishing any organisation, let alone one you care about, like A Million Smiles/The Happiest. The resounding pain and indescribable happiness of your work and your *why* being so entwined is just part and parcel of everything feeling more personal and heart-wrenching – because it actually matters to you.

For instance, when I travelled to Afghanistan in August 2015 to visit Dr Hakim Young, a man I'd first met and interviewed as part of OWT, I was terrifyingly excited. That year Afghanistan was the deadliest place on Earth for foreigners (journalists particularly), but in my mind I knew it was where I needed to be. The universe was pulling me there, and much to my mum's displeasure, that's how I did life; **I'd listen to that inner voice, no matter where it told me to go**. "Don't go Mike. Don't go, please," pleaded mum, who'd never been afraid for me before. "If the world wanted me dead it would do it regardless of me being in Afghanistan or Australia," I replied. "I would be more scared of being hurt if I refused to follow my heart. Every ounce of my being is calling me to make this trip, so don't stress, I'll be fine, it's only a bit over a week." The trepidation on my mum's face was unmistakable and frightening – I'd never seen her like this, ever. If I'm being honest, it was enough to make me a tad nervous, but two weeks later I was off to fulfil my end of the promise I made to Hakim, to come and visit him and the Afghan Peace Volunteers (APVs), with whom he worked.

What Hakim showed me – who he was and all he'd created – was phenomenal. He was and remains my greatest hero. Not because he is rich, famous, good looking or owns a nice house or car, but because he is so humbly and so beautifully following and fulfilling his *why*, no matter what. And I think ultimately, that's what every hero, whether real (Malala, Martin Luther King) or in comic books (Batman, Superwoman) has in common – they sacrifice what they need in order to be who they truly are and live out their purpose.

The ins and outs of this hair-raising trip and life in Afghanistan were tough, but the far harsher and more heart-wrenching reality came when I returned home and discovered that A Million Smiles followers seemed completely uninterested in anything I did or captured while I was in Afghanistan. To me, it was a giant slap in the face that felt entirely personal, because the universe had screamed at me to go there and do this work, but to this day, the photos and videos I produced while in Afghanistan have been some of our least popular, despite being my favourite and arguably our most important. I guess what this, and countless other painful 'let downs' have taught me, is that persistence and remaining true to your *why* is all you can control – the outcome and how that passion manifests, can vary so drastically from one day to the next that it is simply not worth worrying about.

"It's all a journey," Hakim said to me one day as we sat on a Persian rug eating lunch (a vegetable soup with local Afghan bread) with about five to six Afghan youth who lived in the communal house where I stayed during my time in Kabul. "It is so difficult to accept sometimes – that we can't control the outcome – especially when you are trying to work towards peace, because it should be a common goal. But all we can do is what we feel is right in our heart at that time, and hope that those actions we take edge our dream that little bit closer to becoming a reality."

To edge my dream – of sharing my hero's story with the world – that bit closer to becoming a reality, I spent a number of weeks (in the lead up to writing this) tirelessly interviewing Hakim about every facet of his life, emailing and Skyping him, in addition to analysing the numerous interviews we conducted in Afghanistan. What I discovered was confronting, not for Hakim, but for me. His words both tore at and galvanised different parts of my being – making me more whole and contented.

The wooden man

On 24 March 1969, a mother was being frantically wheeled into the delivery room of Kadang Kerbau Hospital in Singapore when her son suddenly popped out.

Born to a lower working-class family, Teck Young Wee (or Hakim as I was first introduced to him in 2010) lived on the 13th floor of one of the oldest 16-storey government housing blocks in Singapore.

"For the most part, as a working class family in the fast-developing Singapore, life was easy. We never went hungry and I didn't feel I lacked anything. Even the tears I shed whenever my mother would drop me at kindergarten went away when I was told emotions weren't for sharing. I just shut myself off, thinking, like many misguided people, that emotions were a sign of weakness."

While the strict, formal, materialistic quest for perfection played a large part in Singapore's post-war boom, the ramifications of building a society around such stringent rules and expectations was evident in one of my favourite tales from Hakim's childhood.

"Kindergarten was an enjoyable time during which I adopted a daily routine. Once, for my homework (yes, homework for kindergarten kids!), I had written a Chinese character and was completely dissatisfied with how the strokes of my pen looked on the page. I tried erasing the faulty part of the character, and made a hole in the paper. I cried. My mother suggested that instead of creating the hole, I could have persuaded myself to be content with my own handwriting."

Seeing Hakim surrounded by the defective mess of Afghanistan, which has been ravaged by war for nearly two decades, and observing his contented and gracious attitude towards it all, it's nearly impossible to imagine his younger-self kicking and screaming with dissatisfaction at an imperfectly drawn Chinese character. To me, it is a reminder that there is more than just one form of oppression. There are the glaringly obvious regimes we hear about in the news, such as the Taliban, who unsubtly force their neighbours and communities to obey their strict brand of Islamic law or suffer the brutal consequences. But equally dangerous to human happiness are the highly sophisticated social, economic and political regimes that subtly force us to chase the false idea that we must become 'the perfect person' (the smartest, richest, best looking and so on) or suffer the shame of not achieving such standards (just as Hakim felt even as a kindergarten student). For Hakim, Singapore's clinical and regimented social and education systems were – so far as his happiness was concerned – just as stifling as his life in Afghanistan.

When I first met Hakim in 2010, it was his skill at public speaking that drew me to him. He and fellow peace activist and friend Kathy Kelly delivered a public seminar in Adelaide about the war and their peace efforts in Afghanistan, which I covered as part of Our World Today. After spending a bit of time together, outside of our formal interview, something about Hakim warmed my soul, and it was then and there that I made a promise to visit him in Afghanistan and get to know the faces of the people he spoke of so fondly.

Five years later, as I wandered through Kabul airport, terrified by the number of helicopter gunships and abundance of men holding machine guns, I remember seeing two things that jolted me out of my fear-coma. The first was a garden of sunflowers, which were Sash's and my favourite flower and a kind of good luck symbol. The second was the beaming smile of Hakim, who was much thinner than I remembered. Accompanied by two other Afghan youths, the four of us quickly made our way through a large car park and past three security checkpoints, before jumping into an old white car that looked like a taxi (though they seemed to know the driver). I assumed we weren't in a rush, so why did it seem like I was being smuggled out of the airport? As we exited the tiny road lined with armed guards, a giant roundabout filled with cars, buses, vans and trucks confronted us. Traffic was barely moving. But our driver persisted in joining the squeeze of vehicles carefully maneuvering through the chaos. Then, in his classically nonchalant way, Hakim turned to me and told me something that suddenly reminded me of where I was – a war zone.

"A few weeks ago we had a big suicide attack just over there, that's why there's lots of added security," he said, before I butted in. "Really! How did it happen? Who were they targeting?" I'm sure my voice had a quiver of terror in it by this stage. "It was just a Talib in a car who found a way through checkpoints. I don't think they had a specific target, but it was so near the airport that they may have assumed they'd kill some foreigners, but it was only locals who died in the bombing."

What had I done? I remember thinking, as my eyes began frantically looking out for single men driving vehicles that looked like they could house a bomb. Shit, there was a lot of them! As my stomach filled with the most torturous blend of pain and dread, and my head screamed the words 'I hate this place. I just want to go home', I very nearly asked them to turn around and put me on a plane home. The drive seemed to last forever, so many cars to torment me. What on earth was I going to do? This was not me. I was captain calm, forever the optimist, with a mind strong enough to endure anything. Right!? I'd coped with worse, hadn't I? Maybe. But this was new. I'd never felt the terror or panic of war, the discomfort of knowing you could easily die at any moment.

'This is why you're here,' I told myself over and over. 'This is the injustice you are here to cover.'

It's probably fair to say I didn't sleep much that first night. But as the morning call to prayer echoed across the small vegetable patch that greeted me as I sat up from my thin mattress and looked outside, the weight of fear began to lift (not much, but slightly). I tried to block out the negativity in my mind and focus on my mission, which was to capture and share the often untold stories of everyday Afghan people, and to see what their experiences might teach the rest of us about happiness.

As Hakim and the youth debated whether or not I looked Afghan enough to walk through the streets safely, I shared with them what now seemed like an ironic and funny story. I had decided to grow my beard in the lead up to the trip in order to hide my white skin and fit in to what I assumed would be a largely bearded male community. As I looked around however, and noticed I was the only bearded male, I soon learned that those stereotypes of Afghanistan being full of rough looking men with beards was not true, and especially not in Kabul, where most were clean shaven. After some debate and testing within the APV community (many of whom thought I was local), they decided I looked northern-Afghani, and with the addition of a scarf from that region would be safe to walk the streets. As safe as anyone could be, at least.

There were still a few rules I needed to abide by, which Hakim felt had kept their international guests safe over the years. These were: not speaking when we were close to strangers (as it was a dead give away that I wasn't local), we'd also take different routes each day when we walked the roughly one kilometre from the APV house to their community centre and office, and I needed to largely keep my head down and look serious, said Hakim, who laughed at the notion. "That's just how most Afghans are, so to blend in, that's what we need to do," he said. "But don't worry, you can smile and laugh and talk when we're inside or alone."

Wearing a loose pair of grey pants and an old maroon T-shirt I took my first step out of the relative security of our house and onto the fairly neat but dusty street outside. Hakim and I walked briskly past the checkpoint at the end of our road (which was a small bunker and hut held by Afghan military) and through the back streets of Kabul, trying to take the quietest route, so he could continue sharing his story.

Piece by piece, with every step, my fear unknowingly began to subside. Before long, I felt composed enough to begin asking Hakim how and why he'd become a doctor in the first place?

Unsurprising to me by now, Hakim took his time as he pondered his response. "In retrospect, 18 was too young to have chosen a life passion," he said, as we walked along a street filled with old, rusty cars being attended to by a horde of mechanics (some children), all eager for business. "So, my motivations for being a doctor weren't fully mature, adult motivations. At 18, I wanted to be a doctor because it was a profession that would put me in touch with people and provide opportunities for me to be of some service and help. I couldn't imagine working with machines, and 'good students with good grades chose to study medicine' was the prevailing wisdom of the time."

"While I no longer subscribe to that elitist worldview, at that moment I chose to tow the line of societal expectation," he admits. "I was lucky, in that doctoring turned out to be one of my passions. But what if it did not? What if it merely became a dispassionate route to earn good money, or for me to appear to be like a good student or person?"

"Well?" I asked him.

"I think schooling and employment should be made more and more egalitarian, so students can better figure out what they are really passionate about instead of unthinkingly falling into the elitist social structures. The belief is that doctors contribute significantly to society, and while many do, that is also true of garbage men, social workers, agriculturalists, nurses, teachers and homemakers."

While his schooling and home life had given him a grounding in values, service, relationships and the unique perspective of having less than those around him, it was in fact his first few experiences of doctoring that would allow Hakim to see his *why* in a new light.

"Between 1993 and 1999 I worked in a range of government hospitals and clinics and was often confronted by death, so a man dying of cancer was nothing new, except on this occasion," said Hakim, before pausing as if to tantalise my story-buds that little bit more. "I've forgotten the guy's name, but not his message and not what happened."

"I was a medical officer on night duty in a government hospital in Singapore and a patient in his thirties, who had cancer and whom I had been taking care of, had asked to see me. He gestured to me to bring him a pen and paper. The cancer had spread to his throat and vocal cords, and after extensive surgery he had a tracheostomy tube and had lost his voice. After a few minutes, he passed his hand-written message to me, a doctor he didn't know personally. The gist of his message was this: *Dear doctor, you are young and I'm sure you have a promising and bright future ahead of you. But tonight, I felt a need to give you a message regarding an important lesson I've learned in my life. I am very rich and have enough wealth for my family and even for their future families. But, all this wealth is not useful to me now. I'm dying. So, I know you may want to spend your energies building a good career as a doctor, but please remember this patient of yours and his message. At the end of your life, you will not regret not having worked another hour to earn more money. You will regret not having spent another hour with your family and friends. Relationships are everything.* The patient died peacefully a few days later," recalls Hakim, as goose bumps spread across my arms.

Some years later, in June 2002 – after hearing and feeling this message time and again – the then 33-year-old Hakim gave up his cushy life working in a Singaporean medical practice to head to Quetta, Pakistan, to work for a local NGO who was helping to educate and care for Afghan refugees fleeing the US-led war. "Quetta was the 'wild, wild East', where there were laws that weren't enforced or followed, and where goods, weapons and humans were liberally smuggled and 'traded'. The varied, multi-genealogy and life-seasoned Afghan faces fascinated and endeared themselves to me, and as I looked around in pain as dust covered my eyes, I realised that I was a long way from the carefully manicured façade of Singapore."

The dust, Hakim laughs, was in fact one of many things in Quetta that helped him to see life more clearly. Another he recalls, was a boy called Najib, who was a 12-year-old Pashtun orphan who collected trash for a living. In the time period after the U.S./NATO forces launched Operation Enduring Freedom on 7 October 2001, in retaliation to the September 11 attacks (which were executed by 19 extremists, *none* of whom were Afghans), Najib's parents were killed, and he fled to Quetta in Pakistan with his grandma, as refugees.

"Pashtuns had been painted by mainstream media as wild fighters who made up a majority of the Taliban," said Hakim, with a soft sombre voice he reserved for significant moments of his story. "But Najib disproved this stereotype in every way, sealing my scepticism about all forms of propaganda and demonisation of 'the other.'"

"It became a psychosocial agony for me to think that the 'war on terror' was targeting 'fighting-age males' who were only a few years older than Najib. The harshness of Najib's orphaned refugee life also highlighted the ineffectiveness of war in curbing extremism – after all here was a boy with a loving home and family, which had been ripped out from under him by an unnecessary conflict that had left him vulnerable and far more susceptible to the likes of the Taliban than he had been previously."

"Then there was his daily labour for food – searching the streets for rubbish he could resell – which awakened me to the unfairness and inequalities of today's corporatised, financialised and militarised global socio-economic system, and my complicity in it."

Out of this newfound sense of pessimism and cynicism for the world, grew an unlikely thing – hope – which Hakim says was the result of a profound revelation that mutual kindness and friendship reaches far beyond cultural or age barriers, and has the ability to bring lasting peace and happiness to those who chase it.

"When Najib made the decision to befriend me, rather than me befriending him, all of those walls and inhibitions I had came crashing down. After a while, in the afternoons, when he was collecting his trash, he would come by and say hi and share fruit for a few moments with me."

"It made me think about my own worldview, my whole understanding of poverty, why children have to suffer because of the decisions of adults who are often totally unknown to them. I mean, what was it about Najib that made him deserve that kind of difficult, tough life?" questions Hakim. "Did me being born in another country really make me more deserving of a better life? What if any one of us had been born in Afghanistan, how might we hope people would treat us?" Hakim paused momentarily, wiping a solitary tear from his eye. "Not like this. Not without love."

"Despite all this though, despite the obscene hand he had been dealt, I saw a resilience in Najib that motivated me, that captured me."

Then, one day Hakim invited Najib and his grandmother to share Pakistani mangoes, "which are particularly sweet when they're in season" he says, very nearly salivating at the thought. Realising that Najib's hands were grimy and black from collecting trash, Hakim felt that the least he could do was try to clean them before he shared the mangoes.

"When his hands had been cleaned, I, like most foreigners, unthinkingly asked Najib to smile for a photo," recalls Hakim. "From behind me, the grandmother got very angry and through an interpreter said, 'Why are you asking Najib to smile? Najib has no reason to smile and until you can find a reason for him it's unfair for you to ask him to smile.'"

"This got me thinking really hard about what it means to live in different situations where we have to survive. Maybe we are trapped like Najib was. And whether there was anything I could do to give more reasons for people like Najib to smile," said Hakim in an inquisitive sombre tone, as if still questioning his ability to help kids like Najib to smile.

"This experience was to stay with me, guiding me and motivating me when I eventually began a website to blog about the Afghan Peace Volunteers in 2009, calling it *Our Journey to Smile*. I last saw Najib when he came to say goodbye to me, sometime in late 2003, explaining to me that his life there was too difficult and that he and his grandma were leaving Quetta for Iran. I regret not offering some way for him to go to school, learn a skill or run a small business in Quetta. Najib reinforced in me the value that being with and **encouraging even just one fellow**

human being is worthwhile, and life-affirming. For this is what he had done for me."

After working in Quetta for two and a half years, Hakim took on a role with an international NGO as a public health specialist stationed in Bamiyan province (a mountainous area west-north-west of Kabul), where he'd travel hours into the most remote villages to interview and teach locals about basic healthcare measures.

Amidst the hundreds of discussions he had about ill health and the systemic failures of a corrupted Afghan-American government, Hakim said there was always one desire and need that locals expressed above all others – peace.

"With almost every Afghan I befriended, I witnessed first-hand the psychosocial, environmental, economic and mental devastation of war," said Hakim. "Once, when I was on the way back to my village home, I jokingly asked a young Afghan boy if he was afraid of wolves. Winter was closing in, and locals have many stories of wolves descending from the mountains to prey on animals. He replied, 'I'm more afraid of war than wolves, because without peace, it is impossible to live'. I began to consider peace-building and non-violence, including what I view to be its natural requisite, the abolition of war, as a human responsibility and passion."

After a number of years living with and alongside youth who'd lost brothers, sisters, friends and parents at the hands of the Taliban and the U.S./NATO forces, it dawned on Hakim that something needed to change – both within himself and others. On a Saturday afternoon in October 2009 Hakim joined a number of local youths who held a tent vigil at the Bamiyan Peace Park, to deliver their message of reconciliation to then US President Barack Obama. The culmination of months of meetings and actions among youths in the area, this tent vigil was the birth of the Afghan Peace Volunteers (APVs), who operated out of Bamiyan until mid-2011, when they (Hakim and numerous other members) made the bold decision to move to the capital, Kabul.

Awakening of the wooden man

"I used to be described by my closer friends as being a 'wooden' person, and by that, my friends were referring to me as being too serious and too focused on tasks, work and objectives. I was also wary of 'over-emotional' persons, buying into the erroneous belief that feelings are 'illogical' and not helpful to those who wish to be strong, successful people. Then, my inner emotional world turned upside-down through discovering a wide gamut of human emotions in the course of my work among Afghans, including the experience of sorrow, grief, anger, trauma, gratitude, communalism and simple joys in the midst of poverty."

While the nature, setting and clientele of his work changed dramatically as he transitioned from medical doctor to humanitarian peace-builder, Hakim says he remains committed to curing the internal mental suffering that causes so much of our poor physical health.

"I still see myself as a doctor, trying to rid myself and others of the diseases of 'keeping up appearances', apathy, uncaringness, addiction to materialism, exploitation of others and of nature, excessive preoccupation with self, violence, militarism and war," he explains. "This 'doctoring' is not the job of one person, but the job of communities, which I have had the privilege of participating in, with the Afghan Peace Volunteers community.

"As my life, work and passions have evolved, my status as a human being has become my primary identity. A job title or description, and the artificial social status that comes with it, has become unimportant to me. For me, **it's more meaningful to follow a life of passion than to 'fit into' a life profession**."

Since 2009, Hakim's passion (or *why*) has been building peace, relationships and hope in Afghanistan and abroad. He began his work as a social entrepreneur, dispensing small business loans and setting up a tailoring workshop. At the same time, he volunteered alongside local youth as they registered the Afghan Peace Volunteers as a legitimate organisation and established the Borderfree Nonviolence Community Centre (their base of operations in Kabul since 2011). For more than a decade, Hakim and the APVs have worked tirelessly to advocate for peace and expand their programs, including feeding, clothing and teaching thousands of Afghan street kids and their families.

"I don't have any official off-days but on the Afghan off-day of Friday, I spend a large part of it with the 100 street kids who attend morning and afternoon sessions at the Borderfree Street Kids School, where about 12 volunteer teachers create a safe and caring space for the kids to learn."

What stunned me, and cannot be overstated, is that after attending the Borderfree Street Kids School for just twelve months, these street kids, who are attending classes just one day a week (and are at times largely illiterate when they join), are scoring higher on literacy and numeracy tests than the average Afghan child who attends school five days a week. It's amazing what a little TLC can do!

"We are all responsible for contributing to the restoration and healing of relationships with nature and the human family. To me, I hope that the APVs can be a tiny example of how a small group of people in a war zone and one of the least developed countries in the world can persevere in trying to build nonviolent individual and societal relationships, and alternative behaviours to the current status quo, including pursuing the seemingly impossible vision of abolishing war."

As if on cue, one of the sounds of what Hakim is trying to get rid of, a bird of war, hovered overhead and drowned out our talk of peace. My own heightened-senses dreaded the pounding of helicopter blades every time I heard them, for some small part of me wondered if I was about to be the 'unavoidable' collateral or casualty of a mission gone wrong (just as thousands of innocent men, women and children have been over the years since the war began).

"It's a common sound," said Hakim calmly, as I waited for the whirring and the vibrations to leave us to our imagining.

"It's so common that I honestly don't notice the helicopters flying by nowadays, though this one is quite low, but still not as low as they sometimes go. They sometimes fly so near us that the windows and doors rattle and vibrate and picture frames fall," he said, as we both poked our heads out the window to look up at the helicopter. "It's frightening what we can get used to," he added.

It was a good time to bring up a particular question that had been nagging at me. Why did Hakim abandon the serene life of a well-rewarded doctor for a seemingly risky existence in a war zone?

"There's more to life than just being a doctor or earning enough money to have what is perceived as a comfortable life. There has to be much more to life than that. I think we all understand it, and I understood it even as a kid. So, I'm not unique. I think, if every one of us would be quiet and understand what would make us fulfilled human beings, satisfied with what we're doing in life, and finding meaning in what we do, then it wouldn't be difficult to give up the so-called 'career' or 'success' in order to experience life in its fullness."

From the bustling streets of Singapore to a remote rural village in Bamiyan Province, Afghanistan, the previously career-focused city-slicker said it was in having *less* – in being still, being in nature and being able to find the time to think – that he found *more*.

"There in Bamiyan I began to learn many things, including what it means to be a truly happy person," said Hakim, as he shut his eyes peacefully. "Don't get me wrong, I was happy with my medical practice in Singapore. I laughed and I smiled quite a lot. But I think many people intuitively know that the happiness, in places like Singapore, is not exactly what happiness is. The happiness people in the developed world look for is just a semblance of the real happiness that we long for, because you see, we don't get happier when we have more things, more stuff around us – taller buildings, fancier cars, and there are always long queues for the latest iPhone. That's not happiness to me anymore."

"I know people everywhere understand this, so I want to encourage both myself and others to just go for it," Hakim urges. "Put down your gadgets and seek out the things that matter, that you love. That's my life now, and I'm privileged to be able to taste a bit of the happiness that I long for here in Afghanistan."

While he laughed riotously saying that not everyone needs to pack-up and move to a war-zone, I was still left wondering: 'why Afghanistan?' How was it that he'd failed to find the happiness he longed for in Singapore? I mean, it has the third highest GDP per capita in the world at $87,855, while Afghanistan was ranked 168 at $1919 per person, per annum. Singaporeans also had a life expectancy that was 22.6 years greater than that of the average Afghani who was only expected to reach 60.5 years of age. With its lawlessness, poverty and impending doom of continuous wars that have lasted 40 years, what did Afghanistan offer that Singapore did not?

"Physically, Singapore would be considered a physical 'heaven,'" said Hakim. "But the wealthy city-island state is emotionally cold. True happiness, I learned very quickly in Afghanistan, comes from engaging with people. For me, it comes from my Afghan friends. But it is something we experience all our lives and everywhere in the world. On days when you and I are able to connect with another person on a deeper level and recognise our shared wishes and difficulties, and then be able to tell one another that we care, that you are valuable, that your pain and suffering is not just something you have to know on your own, that is happiness. However, one may choose to be unhappy or to suffer temporarily for the happiness of others, or for a cause."

Such a sentiment and belief is, most definitely, something I could connect with, for since connecting to my *why* and living that life, I have rarely felt sad as an individual (despite my sacrifices). That's not to say I'm not unhappy at some of those things I see and hear about our world, but ever since I made that decision to dedicate every ounce of energy, money and time I had to sharing those stories that could inspire a happier and more peaceful humanity, I've felt deeply satisfied with my life. If I were to find out I was dying in a year, there's little I'd change about my life (except I'd hurry up and finish writing this book).

As Hakim and I sat there pondering our conversation, what I came to realise was that having our happiness so deeply connected to our *why* was undoubtedly a blessing, because no one could take that away from us, which made it such a lasting source of joy. Don't get me wrong, it can be tough too, because when you are so passionate about something, those people and things that seem to be working against that dream hurt you, but that's something you need to let go of, for as Hakim says; **"there will always be pain so long as you care about something, but that doesn't mean we should aim to live a life where we don't care about anything, for that would be the saddest life of all."**

How this looked for me in Afghanistan was as follows: I cared so much about re-humanising Afghanistan in the eyes of the world, through those stories I was capturing, that I knew we might need to travel out of Kabul in order to gather more interesting footage. While the prospect of leaving the house was tough enough to cope with, the thought of heading out of Kabul and spending unnecessary time on the roads was numbing. The fear literally brought my mind to its knees. But as I looked around at those innocent and friendly faces that confronted me, I knew that I must get over myself, and my fear, and realise that in order to honour and fulfil my *why*, I needed to forget about the people and things that were working against me – such as my fear of death at the hands of the Taliban or US-led forces. What helped me do this was remembering that in a few days, when I left, these people would remain here, so what was I complaining about?

Sitting in silence as I collected my thoughts and packed my filming equipment, I felt that little voice inside telling me that it was going to be OK. I'd long trusted my gut to keep me safe – which it had so far.

Minutes later we jumped in a car belonging to one of a small list of drivers the APVs trusted, and slowly headed to Lake Qargha (pronounced car-ga), which was around 30km from our home in Kabul. Traffic was shocking, and as we crawled through the streets, past marketplaces, I played my terrifying game – spot the lone male driver and guess which one had a bomb on board. I knew that this game went against the compassion, logic and very reason I was in Afghanistan – which was to show the world that most Afghans are good-natured, well-intentioned people – but I couldn't help myself. Fear had crippled the rational part of my mind, and I guess looking back, my survival is really the best proof that the vast majority of Afghans are only interested in peace. But that wasn't going to stop me from freaking out a few more times before the day was out.

With my GoPro in hand, ever so slightly poked out the car window, Hakim suddenly grabbed my arm and said, "Put it away, it's not safe here, I don't want the guards to see you." Unbeknownst to me, we were passing a military base, which Hakim said had confiscated cameras and harassed people who'd filmed near it in the past. My heart raced, as I noticed the heavily armed personnel I'd been unknowingly filming. The problem was, I couldn't see the largely camouflaged guards on the tiny GoPro screen that I'd been focusing on.

As we headed to another part of Kabul and climbed up through the dry, arid hillside, the number of children picking up rubbish became alarming. The only ones who weren't seemed to be those selling candy-floss by the roadside – a local treat that Hakim said people bought on their way to the lake. What people, I wondered quietly? We seemed to be the only ones on the road.

Then appeared a site that to me epitomised the absolute sadness I felt for the countless families that called this country home – a beautifully stunning blue lake, set against a gorgeous sandy-brown backdrop of hills, surrounded by small villas, cafes, horses, shops and even a local theme park. But all of it seemed abandoned and empty, minus a handful of kids collecting trash.

"This place used to be full every night, it was the heartbeat of Kabul, where families would come to have fun, eat and be entertained. But even this place was attacked on several occasions, by gunmen and suicide bombers," said Hakim, as we stepped down from the car and were met by the horridly ironic image of children collecting rubbish in front of an empty theme park.

For the next hour or so as I filmed Hakim 'doing his thing', I saw his words and his philosophies come to life. The first thing he did was crouch down to the eye level of a small group of dust-covered children who each had a stick with a half torn bag on the end of it, which housed useful trash they'd later try to sell. You could see Hakim's heart ache and rile in discomfort as he spoke to the children and learned that these kids had travelled all the way from Jalalabad – a 118km journey along what is considered one of the deadliest roads on Earth – to be here. "They're telling me that the fighting is too bad in their district now, and that it is so hot their crops will not grow, so they have come here to try to survive for some time," relayed Hakim, who spoke in Dari with the kids.

When he asked their ages and whether they were attending school, you could see his joy at learning that most were getting an education, but were sent out to collect trash each day after school to help support their impoverished families. "This young boy just told me that he sometimes walks all the way from his village down the mountain to the lake, just to find rubbish that he can sell. "How much does he earn?" I asked Hakim, who then translated my question. "He doesn't know exactly, because his parents negotiate the price for the trash he collects, but in my experience, it is normally one or two dollars a day," said Hakim

As we neared the shore of the lake, a group of young men appeared on horseback, like a scene out of a movie. The dust exploded from the hooves of the graceful black beasts as they tore back and forth along the dusty beach. Abdulhai, one of Hakim's friends, suddenly jumped on one of the giant black horses that was being offered up for a ride by one of the local youth. With the best English out of those living in the APV house, which I called home, Abdulhai had become one of my closest friends and teachers. As a prodigious photographer, who could tap into the battered and bruised but irrepressible heart of Afghanistan with every click (as you can see from his images throughout this chapter), I stood silently in awe, as I wondered just how Abdulhai had maintained such a gorgeously gentle soul? What came as a shock to me, was that Abdulhai, his older sister and brother actually had every reason to be filled with hate and vengeance. Their father had been killed by the Taliban, who had also forced them to flee their home. But instead of demanding 'an

akim with Najib and his grandmother, in the photo he describes king for.

A child stands atop a roof in front of a building that is rife with the signs of war.

s hard to imagine a peaceful or happy country thout an empowered female population.

I wonder how these two girls feel about their future?

akim speaking to kids who were collecting rubbish at Lake argha. Notice the theme park to the right in the distance.

Abdulhai about to set off on a horse at Lake Qargha. The top four images on this page are by Abdulhai.

'Flying kites' by Abdulhai Darya.

Hundreds of people sell services and products in the street. Most are lucky to earn $1 a day.

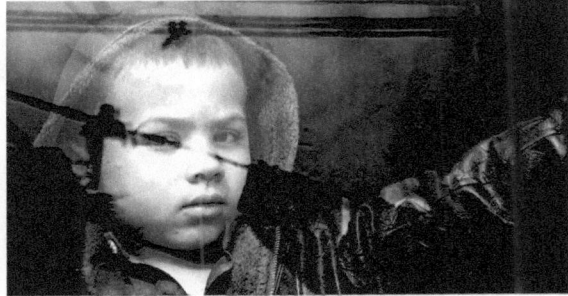

A child peers out from his window.

A child helping his grandfather.

Toboggan!

Children simply want to be free and safe to play.

A child peers out from behind the perceived safety of the gate to his home.

This old man has no reason to smile, but still he does.

These are the children we risk killing in war. All images on this page are by Abdulhai.

Some of the families from one of the IDP camps where the APVs help.

Me (centre back) and my Afghan friends. Yep, I'm the only guy with a beard!

APVs protesting on the streets.

"We want peace!"

APVs giving winter quilts to the needy.

Zarghuna (centre) and APVs saying #Enough! to war and the greed that fuels it.

eye for an eye', the trio had become walking, talking examples of what is required to end the war – love and forgiveness. Because as Abdulhai explained, "only those things can mend the wounds of our past."

As Abdulhai off and took flight, hurtling towards us at breakneck speed with a boundless freedom and unimaginable faith in the horse, I began crying, and it wouldn't stop. I was furiously sad. **"Why can't we stop this? How on Earth have we let our leaders design a system that requires us to go to war for the sake of an economy? What is the purpose of prosperity or money if it means we've got to kill?"** I shrieked out across the water, in a rage of passion. "He's amazing, but this sucks. Sorry," I said to Hakim, as we both marvelled at Abdulhai's ability to maneuver the horse with such effortless precision and ease. "How can people live like this? Without the freedom to do what they love, when they want?" I asked aloud, upset at everything that surrounded me – the kids with rucksacks of rubbish, the abandoned lake and theme park, even the fleeting joy on Abdulhai's face, which would soon disappear, but was a symbol of what we should all be aspiring to protect.

While I've often felt sad leaving people who are suffering to simply suffer more, this was much worse than normal, and as we walked back to the car and waved goodbye to the kids and youths we'd befriended, I wept profusely. With tears still clouding my eyes, the truth of my pain was that this was unquestionably the worst situation I'd seen anywhere in the world, and that's why it hurt to feel as if I was abandoning these people. At the risk of repeating myself, caring sucks sometimes. But what I knew I needed to do was use that pain as a motivator, to try to do the impossible – end the war – because I knew that it was an enormous privilege to be afforded the opportunity to come and see this, so I bloody well needed to make the most of it. In that vein, I'm here to tell you (and anyone who will listen) that **fighting for peace is not working**, and we need to demand that our politicians open up a new dialogue. Because, let's face it, the 'war on terror' has failed – it has only created more terrorists and generations of damage. In Afghanistan, the situation is essentially back to what it was before the war began (perhaps worse), with around 100 needless deaths per week, resulting from the various conflicts and attacks across the country.

A reminder of the terror faced by Afghans everyday confronted me as we descended back past the candy-floss stands down through a long valley that stretched out in front of us. Staring out the front window, dissecting what I'd just witnessed and been a part of, I noticed a helicopter approaching the small town we were about to pass through. This was nothing new. Like the locals, I'd nearly become used to the sights and sounds of war, but something was off about what was happening up ahead of us. The helicopter had stopped and was hovering close to the outskirts of the village, about 500 metres ahead of us slightly to our right. Traffic had slowed. Why, I wondered? People appeared to be running, as a traffic officer stopped cars to let people cross the road. I was confused, was this normal? Were people running frantically, or just scampering home. In my head it was all out chaos.

Then, two orange flares were fired from the helicopter.

We'd come to a near standstill and were now just a couple of hundred metres from where the bird of war was circling its prey. I'd seen enough movies to know that the military use flares to signal or mark a location, often for bombing. I had tried to remain silent, as our car windows were down (because it was hot and there was no air-conditioning) and I didn't want pedestrians to hear me speaking English. I whispered to Hakim, "Can you see that? What is going on?" He looked up to the right. "Hmmmm, it is probably just warning some people or alerting them of something." "Of what though, of what?!!!" I felt like yelling. I tried to slow my heart rate a little by shutting my eyes, but that just made things worse. My imagination was not in a good place. Why would a helicopter shoot off flares? I wondered, over and over. But all I could think of was, a drone or a fighter jet was about to lay waste to the village – the village we were about to drive through. "Is this normal?" I asked softly. "Sort of," replied Hakim. People outside seemed to be looking up at the helicopter too, which was now directly to our right, about 70 metres away. Just as we passed, the helicopter rose into the sky. Was this it? Was it getting out the way so that something else could drop a bomb? Why did it need to shoot flares?

I decided to shut my eyes and think (or pray as most would say) about all that was – my life, what I'd just seen, whether this was my time – then I immediately opened my eyes with a renewed peace, for I knew I was where I needed to be (dead or alive). As I turned around to look at where the helicopter had been I saw nothing, even the smoke from the flares had subsided. "Thank you!" I said to who ever was listening inside my head.

Some days later, from the safety of Delhi Airport on my way home,

I tried to Google 'why helicopters shoot flares', and found a few possible answers, including as a defense measure if they feel someone may be firing an infra-red homing missile from the ground. The other reason was as I'd thought, to alert someone or mark an area. It may have also have just been a military exercise. Whatever it was, to me personally, it didn't matter. What mattered was that **34 million human beings (in Afghanistan alone) were being forced to live like this every day – in constant fear – not knowing if or when or where they would be safe, or if or when or where they would be killed.**

While I knew and could see that Hakim and the other members of the APV community weren't frightened like I was, I wondered how they dealt with it, and what that might teach me, and us, about coping with difficult situations. During breakfast on my fifth morning (the day after our trip to the lake), I found myself alone with Hakim, so I asked about the big scary elephant in the room that clouded my mind every night – how do you cope with the relentless fear of being killed?

"I keep fear at bay by acting passionately, and refusing to be paralysed, and by writing, and even using that anxiety and horror to propel my work, for it is at the centre of why I am here after all. Because no one should have to live this way."

This line, like any good Taylor Swift song, was stuck on repeat in my head for days – no one should have to live this way! No one should have to live this way! No one should have to live this way!!!

There has never been a truer or more poignant line spoken.

I mean, seeing what this struggle for power (between the US, Russia, China, Islam and Christianity) was doing to the people of Afghanistan made me want to curl up into a ball and die (so god knows what it was doing to those forced to live it every day). Personally, I struggled to feel OK at any point during my trip. I cried most days, barely slept and yet in the middle of all this hurt and angst I felt the most abundant tenderness and affection with every stranger I met. I could see why Hakim had felt that his happiness and survival were so entwined with those relationships he held. But I wanted to find out more. I wanted to know how he handled and viewed the inherent happiness and pain that comes from human connection.

"We can't be happy alone – or at least I don't think I can be, maybe some people can – but that means we're going to suffer and be hurt sometimes, because we're all imperfect and we'll all leave this world someday," says Hakim with a rare sadness on his face. "If we can't be happy alone, then maybe it's better to connect with other people's happiness and suffering," he said, as he began to get emotional.

"When speaking on this, I often get teary," he paused. "Because when I was in Singapore, as a teenager, I stopped crying and when I came to this part of the world I learned to cry again. But it's not a crying prompted by sadness but a crying that identifies with people because they are not having an easy time. I can easily go back to Singapore and have quite a comfortable time and then I don't have to deal with this pain, but that wouldn't make me happy."

As someone who was suffering deeply from all I'd seen in Afghanistan, as well as the guilt and emptiness that came from knowing I'd be going home to my relatively luxurious life in Australia in a few days, I asked Hakim what I or other ordinary folk abroad could do to help the happiness of all Afghans?

"We can wake up and look at the compassion that is present within each and every one of us and say, I want to live simpler. I don't need another physical object or material object to make me happy, because I know it doesn't, and to do something different instead of going to buy another thing. Connect with someone nearby, someone you might see as 'different', and say 'I want to do this', not only for the other person, because we are truly happy when we do something for someone else, but also for ourselves. Because it is human connection and compassion that can end conflict and prevent wars," says Hakim vehemently. "We can live with a lot less in the developed world. I know for sure Singaporeans can live with a lot less. We're always saying this about ourselves, that we complain a lot. That we have everything and yet we're still complaining. We know deep down that we cannot be happy from wanting more and more of those things. We know it. But we need to act on it out of compassion, because our greed is also what feeds the war and inequality here, and everywhere."

Being a species that, according to science, is hard-wired to be empathetic – to care for others, whether we like it or not – it would appear that what Hakim is saying and asking for – the abolition of the fear and greed that feeds war, and the formation of love and equal relationships that brings peace – will make us all happier.

"Whichever way you look at it, **I think that if enough people** pursue that happiness they long for, and they find their passion, it will start a revolution that will bring the change we all seek."

As with every interview I've ever done, I asked Hakim if there was anything else he wanted to add? Any last words he felt I or others might find happiness in? He sat there in silence for a few minutes. A nervous anticipation built between us, before he closed his eyes for a moment, and began to speak.

"Well, I'm sitting in the centre that the Afghan Peace Volunteers have built and created and established. It's called The Border Free Nonviolence Community Centre, and it is the first centre in Afghanistan that intentionally teaches and promotes nonviolence. We had a phrase at its opening last year that read: *Love can open every border, it can break every border.* The borders in our minds, in our hearts. The borders that separate us, the borders that make us fear one another, the borders that make us wage war against one another, those borders can go away if we spend a little more time on loving other people."

My eyes welled with tears. It was so simple.

As I hugged, waved and said goodbye to 20 or 30 of the Afghan Peace Volunteers I'd met, I felt compelled to say something. So I made a promise: "I will share your stories (such as Hakim's, which can be viewed on thehappiest.com), I will tell the world about your love and your want for peace, because nobody should have to live the way you are. It's not right. And I hate that I am leaving you."

Out of nowhere, having seen the tears in my eyes, Abdulhai's older sister Zarghuna (who was typically shy and reserved, but whom I got along well with as she wanted to be a journalist) replied in her soft sombre tone. "It's OK, you don't have to worry about us, we are used to it," she said. "Yes, but that's the thing, no one should have to get used to this," I responded instantly.

As we made our way back to the airport through the hellish traffic I played one last game of 'spot the bomber', before passing through three security checkpoints outside the airport terminal, and then two more inside the terminal, before one final full body and bag check as we walked up the steps leading up to the plane. Taking off next to a plethora of highly advanced state-of-the-art military helicopters and planes, which stood in such callous contrast to the image of children collecting rubbish in their rucksacks, I couldn't help but repeat that line over and over — no one should have to live like this. *No one should have to live like this.* NO ONE SHOULD HAVE TO LIVE LIKE THIS!

So, what do we do about it? The only thing we can do — start a revolution. A revolution that will be built on more and more people chasing the happiness they long for — the happiness that comes from finding and pursuing your *why*. As acclaimed thinker Brené Brown says, "Don't ask what the world needs. Ask what makes you come alive, and go do it. Because what the world needs is people who have come alive."

Discovering your *why*...

Here are a few questions and frameworks I've used over the years to ensure I remain on track, living out my *why* each and every day.

1. Ask yourself: What does success look like to me? And how do I want to be remembered? Be honest. Make an extensive list. Now, see if the words surrounding each question are the same, similar or drastically different. I guarantee you that if the words surrounding these two questions are close to the same, you'll be happy every day of your life.
2. Look at where your innate skills, passions and talents intersect with the greatest needs of the world. That is where you will find your purpose and be happiest working.
3. Think about what you would do if you were given just two years to live. Would you quit your job? Why? Where would you spend your time? Think long and hard, and then ask yourself why you're not doing or living that way right now? Because we never know how long we actually have left.
4. Last but not least, if you are yet to find your *why*, but seriously want to, don't lock yourself into debt. Chasing dreams requires freedom and flexibility and that's often stifled by the need to earn a certain amount to pay back loans.

Our who and our why may feed us,

but it's gratitude that makes us whole.

4

CANCER, CAR ACCIDENTS AND THE MOTHER WHO LOST EIGHT CHILDREN

Journal entry 5.9.2015: Today I got back from Afghanistan. I flew into Sydney for some filming work, and found myself on a train sitting across from a young family that nearly broke me. All were on their phones completely neglecting the reality in front of them, when all of a sudden one of the children began kicking and screaming for attention from her mother. The young girl was trying to use a voice-activated program on her iPad, but the train was too loud and it wouldn't register her voice. She persisted and the tears and screams got louder. "It's not fucking working, mummy," yelled the ten-or-so-year-old girl. "I can't deal with this," screamed the mother in return. The screeching of voices, mostly related to the mother's inability to pay attention to her daughter, was deafening, and yet it helped me hear what was important. I'd been gifted this incredibly humbling world perspective that made it easy to be grateful for the fact I was on a train, which was not likely to be bombed (as in Kabul), and I needed to be grateful for that no matter how ungrateful those around me were.

I want to start with a brief history lesson that's rarely told and even more rarely remembered, but has the potential to set us free from much of our needless suffering... There was a time when everything was worse, much worse, than it is today. And when I say everything, I do mean everything. In fact, as Rutger Bregman, author of *Utopia for Realists*, puts it, "For roughly 99% of the world's history, 99% of humanity was poor, hungry, dirty, afraid, stupid, sick, and ugly." Did you know that as recently as 1820, 84% of the world's population lived in extreme poverty? By 1981 that percentage had dropped to 44%, and now, in 2018, it has fallen further to about 10%. If this trend continues, poverty (and its ensuing issues) should be all but eradicated in the coming decades, allowing every human to enjoy abundance. But will we be any happier?

What do we need to be deeply satisfied? To feel fulfilled with our bit in this world? To be grateful? Can we ever have enough? Can we have too much? What does that look like? When does our want for more inhibit our happiness? And how the hell can we learn to *appreciate* what we have when everything and everyone is telling us to **be more, buy more, earn more and do more?**

I guess what we need to ask ourselves is: is it really *their* fault? Should we be blaming *others* for our dissatisfaction? Or could the answer lie within us? Is there something in our DNA that leaves us forever wanting more? Well, yeah, sort of, there is this strange psychological phenomenon known as the *hedonic treadmill*, which impacts every single one of us to a varying degree. In theory, it goes like this: in 1971, two guys by the name of Brickman and Campbell found that when a person makes *more* money or becomes *more* famous, their expectations and desires rise in tandem, which results in no permanent gain in happiness. In fact, nothing that you focus on (good or bad) will make as much difference as you think to your happiness according to their paper *Hedonic Relativism and Planning the Good Society*. Good and bad fortunes may temporarily affect how happy a person is, but most people will end up back at their 'normal' level of happiness.

I know what you're thinking – why have I written this book then – if it's impossible to change our level of happiness? Well that's because it's not. Far from it. It's just that we need to look at things a little differently. According to renowned psychologist and author Edward Diener, **happiness is largely about the relativity of our circumstances, not the circumstances themselves.**

"Automatic habituation (an innate human trait) is adaptive, because it allows constant stimuli [your beautiful spouse or big house] to fade into the background. Thus, resources remain available to deal with novel stimuli [your slowing computer or a promotion opportunity], which are most likely to require immediate attention. The happiness system is thus hypothesized to reflect changes in circumstances rather than the overall desirability of the circumstances themselves," writes Diener in his book *The Science of Well-Being*.

This idea that happiness is defined by our change in circumstances, rather than the circumstances themselves, was further illustrated in a 1996 study by geneticist David Lykken and psychologist Auke Tellegen. The two Minnesota professors – who compared the well-being levels of thousands of pairs of identical and non-identical twins – either raised together or apart – found that 50% of your happiness is determined by your genes, while just 10% is determined by the circumstances in which you live and 40% of your happiness is the result of your actions, attitude or optimism, and the way you handle situations.

What this means is that your daily reality is actually relatively unimportant. Where you live, what you have, how much you earn – it matters little. How else might we explain the fact that we are wealthier and more connected than ever, yet more of us are depressed and lonely than at any point in human history? Such sad statistics are proof that more is not always more, or that more is not always better, and that **it is how we think about and view our reality that really matters** – is the glass half empty or half full? What about those who can't afford any glassware? Did you think about them? How might they handle seeing their neighbour's nice new crystal Champagne flutes filled to the brim with a delectable Moet and Chandon?

Welcome to what I perceive to be the greatest barrier to happiness in the developed world and one of the most pivotal challenges of the 21st century – *appreciation* and *gratitude*.

Personally, being grateful hasn't always been a strong suit for me – not for the first decade or two of my life anyhow. Growing up, we were upper-middle class and enjoyed most of the perceived essentials for a happy life – a good school, nice clothes, lots of toys, the odd holiday and typically, after a bit of nagging, the latest sports equipment. But, there were always richer kids, or smaller families that could spend more on their children, so I still never felt like we were spoilt. I mean I knew we were lucky, because I was a documentary addict and had seen the way millions of other children lived. But the problem was, remembering that 'luck' when the latest football boots or Derwent pencils were released. Because like most people, I wanted more. The latest. The best. All the time.

And in all honesty, there's nothing wrong with that… well, sort of.

This endless ambition we hold isn't in and of itself a bad thing – after all, we'd either be extinct or still sitting in a cave somewhere waiting to go hunting without it. The problem is, when we let our endless pursuit of growth or progress overwhelm and block our pursuit of happiness.

What's often misunderstood is that we can have both – happiness and progress (though arguably they're the same thing if happiness is our goal?), but for that, we first have to understand what's keeping us on the hedonic treadmill: forever ungrateful and unappreciative of everyone and everything around us.

This isn't me preaching or telling you how to live – this is decades of scientific experiments conducted upon hundreds of thousands of people speaking for itself. Because some things just don't make people happy, no matter how much they might think or want those things to. As researcher and writer, Richard Eckersley puts it, "One of the most important and growing costs of the modern way of life is 'cultural fraud' – the promotion of images and ideals of 'the good life' that serve the economy but do not meet psychological needs, nor reflect social realities."

Endless studies have proven beyond a doubt that it is not the hedonic treadmill that is broken, but the goals we're all striving to achieve. Because fortunately (or unfortunately for some), beauty, money, weather, education, status and children have next to no effect on our happiness, well-being, and life satisfaction. What's more, a growing number of longitudinal studies that have tracked people over the course of their lives have found that as their circumstances have changed – they've received promotions at work, built a bigger house and upgraded their car – their happiness has remained mostly unchanged. Reinforcing the notion that these things are just a distraction to the true fulfilment we all seek.

What does this mean? What can you do? Well you could ignore it. Ignorance may give you some bliss for a while. But what the following stories are proof of is that **the successful pursuit of happiness requires a departure from the business-as-usual approach to life**. That getting married, buying a house, and having kids isn't necessarily enough. That seeking wealth and fame is a dead-end. And escaping the rat-race means intentionally pursuing counter-intuitive life strategies.

For me, that's been about finding out *who* I am and *why* I am, and sacrificing whatever I need to pursue that journey. The thing is, if I didn't appreciate my freedom and immense privilege, I would have never been able to quit my job, sell my house and invest every cent I have into those so-called 'pipe dreams'. Perhaps too, if I'd never seen the devastating injustices of racism, poverty, war and greed across the world, I may have given up by now. And certainly, if I wasn't grateful for all I've seen and experienced (the good, the bad and the ugly), there's no way I would have written this book, or found my happiest self.

Mr Everything

My first real lesson in appreciation and gratitude was delivered by one of my closest high school friends – Tom Bunning.

It was impossible not to love Tom. He was everything you wanted a friend to be. He was big (if ever we needed protection), handsome, friendly, clever, generous and worldly beyond his years. He was everything I wanted to be – a world traveller and an intrepid adventurer. In the days before I had travelled at all, Tom, thanks to his mother's work as a globe-trotting agricultural economist focusing on third world economies, was totally at ease with the concept of 'other', an idea I was desperate to explore.

Part of a journal entry from 3.10.2006: He was impossible not to love. A big cuddly bear and best friend to so many, he lived a life few dare dream of. From travelling the globe and meeting world-leaders with his mum, to holding a share portfolio in High School, there would be few stupid enough to say there was anything Tom couldn't do.

Tom and I were classmates at Unley High School in South Australia, when he announced to anyone who would listen (and we all did) that he was going to Bond University – on a scholarship! That was even before he applied for one, but guess what? He applied and he did get that damn scholarship, so off he went to Queensland and our relationship during those first couple of years of university was forced to settle for his occasional visit back to Adelaide. Still, if he wasn't my very best friend, he was certainly in the top three.

One September evening in 2006, Tom was on one of his visits to Adelaide and he was staying with me in my rental in Hyde Park (a nice suburb close to the city). Tom wanted to go out partying, but I decided to spend the evening with my girlfriend at her house in nearby Unley, about one and a half kilometres away – both houses were just off King William Road.

At six o'clock the next morning I was woken by a call from Andy (the mate I would join on the burning plane a few years later). I was groggy from lack of sleep, but even in my disorientated state, I could tell Andy was deeply distressed. "It's Tom," he said in a croaky whisper, "he's fucked." "What happened?" was all I could muster in response. I don't remember too much else of the conversation except that Tom was in hospital, in the ICU (Intensive Care Unit) and I needed to get there NOW. I think what distressed me most was Andy's sense of desperation and hopelessness. Andy was a young man made for a crisis. He was unflappable and always so serene, so for someone like him to have been hurled into the black pit, something bad must have happened to Tom. I probably broke several road rules on the way to the hospital. Early Sunday morning traffic in Adelaide was far from gridlock, but there were still too many cars and traffic lights on the road for me. The drive from Unley to the Royal Adelaide Hospital was normally an easy 12-minute saunter, but I did it in eight.

When I got there I didn't know where the ICU was (I wasn't working there yet). I'd never had reason to visit it and it's a place, I've been told since, where people go to die. I asked whoever looked faintly medical and finally found the ICU waiting room. Ever since I'd got the call, I was consumed by conflicting emotions. First was my very real fear that Andy was right and Tom was destined for a hideously premature death (he was only 19), but a close second was my crushing sense of guilt. Tom had asked me to go out with him and I knew (even if I had no basis for thinking it) that if I had been with Tom, whatever happened to him wouldn't have happened because I would have stopped it from happening. Instead, I had chosen a night of carnal pleasure seeking over my role as my best friend's protector. All these years later, I still feel traces of those guilt pangs, and so many times I have wished I'd gone through the sliding door that led to a night of celebrating with my friend.

I wasn't Tom's only friend (far from it), and the ICU waiting room was filled with people like me who loved him. His mum was living in Timor-Leste at the time, and Tom was on the way back to Bond Uni via Adelaide after visiting her, so here were a bunch of friends, a replacement family, all sharing the pain. There was no talking among us. A few nods and grunts of recognition but nothing that could even leave a fingerprint on the sombre mood. Medical people came and used medical terms to describe his condition, but the overriding message we heard was that Tom was going to die. A phrase I do remember was "His brain is swelling and we can't stop it." Even with my limited medical knowledge, I knew that was not good news. The other message I took away from those first couple of hours in the waiting room was that even if by some miracle Tom survived, he would not be the Tom we knew.

We had been warned, but nothing, and I mean absolutely nothing, prepared us for what I would see when I was finally ushered into the room where Tom lay (only two people could go in at a time). Tom? That wasn't Tom. It was some sort of alien life form with an unnaturally large head and a vile, broken body stuffed with tubes to cater for the comings and goings of whatever it was that needed removing or injecting into this life-form we were tricked into believing was our big cuddly friend.

'Breathe, just breathe', I said to myself, and when I did and when my racing mind and grieving soul calmed, I began to see the faint outlines of a young man that I once knew. When you see someone you love in a condition so wretched, your responses are to either run away or move forwards in a gesture of support. I moved forward and stroked his hand, seemingly the only part of his body I could touch without fear of causing him more damage. Not surprisingly, Tom was in an induced coma.

Turns out he was hit by a car on King William Road, walking from another friend Tom Langley's house to mine. It seems there was some sort of altercation with some other guy and Tom ended up standing on the road. Whoever that guy was, he ran away when the car hit Tom. Some witnesses said they could see Tom standing in the road and there was another guy there, and the car just drove straight into Tom without trying to swerve or slow down or anything. The police didn't do much to find out what happened. They finally interviewed the other witnesses three months later, after I did a CrimeStoppers interview for local TV, and after that we found out roughly what had happened. Sure Tom had been out partying that night, but he was no more than a social drinker, who welcomed the loosening power of alcohol, because at heart he was a shy man.

After a week or so in the ICU and just as things seemed on the up, Tom suffered another setback. I was at university when I got the call. I remember distinctly what class I was in, where I was sitting and the feeling of wetness on my cheeks as I ran to my car. For the second time in a week, I was told my friend would die.

Tom's brain had continued swelling all week and all the drugs to control it hadn't done the job. Over the weekend, the pressure in his brain was so high that the oxygen to a large part of his brain was cut off. He sort of had a long slow stroke, while he was in ICU. On Monday morning, when all the consultants and specialists were back in the hospital, they took him into surgery and did a full bifrontal craniectomy – removing all the bone across his forehead – to reduce the pressure. While the procedure was successful, Tom was given slim to no chance of survival, as doctors warned sternly of what his life might be like even if he did wake up.

I remember standing there watching Tom's mum (who'd arrived back from Timor-Leste the day after the accident) massage his hands, at times gripping tightly as if to urge him awake. Her only son, lifeless before her, but he would not be without love while his heart still beat.

Those who knew Tom knew of his stubbornness, so despite few signs of life, we remained standing forever by his side in hope.

Weeks passed. Progress was slow, as a grim reality set in. Would he ever wake? When the swelling subsided, it was time to see if Tom was still in there. The drugs were stopped and machines turned off.

All the monitors went haywire. So the drugs and machines were quickly reinstated.

Another week later they tried again. There was no response.

It didn't look good. Until…

With a rather gaunt, slim face and thin layer of skin separating the front of his brain from the world, his left hand twitched.

Journal entry 24.09.2006: I saw signs of life in Tom today and I cried. Tears of relief, tears of fear, as I asked myself a truly scary question – just how 'alive' is he?

Initial reports were not great, as doctors began to assess the full extent of his head injuries.

The most shocking part to me was the revelation that more than a third of Tom's brain was classified as 'dead'. I tried to imagine how I would cope after losing so much of my brain, and I simply couldn't. What it did give me was the gift of appreciation that I didn't have to endure what my dear friend was battling. It was as if he was fighting for all of us crowded around his bed in the ICU.

I was always afraid that every visit would be the last time I would see Tom alive, so I often stayed as long as I was allowed, and returned as soon as I could to sit with my friend and bear witness to his journey.

The blow he suffered was primarily to his head and he had several closed fractures in his skull and at the back of his nose, but the rest of his body didn't escape unscathed. He had a punctured lung and cuts and abrasions up and down his body. Later on in ICU, he got pneumonia, a terrible pseudomonas drug-resistant infection and had procedures like a bronchoscopy and a tracheotomy. When I first saw him, it was his swollen head that was positively scary – but now, with a millimetre of stretched skin separating me from the front of his brain, I needed to get used to sitting and talking to him without being mesmerised by his uncomfortable new look. The brain, fighting to save itself and its host body, was bulging way beyond where it would normally be confined by his skull – the skin covering his forehead was protruding from its normal resting place. Slowly the swollen brain began to subside and slowly, very slowly, Tom began to return. His skull, incidentally, was stored in the morgue, where just about everyone associated with Tom's care feared the rest of him would soon end up.

For three months, Tom lived without his skull, wearing instead a helmet in case he fell or bumped his exposed head on something hard. And fall he did. I only found out later of the duplicity involved in Tom's treatment. When he was likely to have visitors, Tom was presented as a resting patient supported by the best medical expertise any society could afford, but when there were no visitors, or when it was time to sleep, Tom was tied to his bed. Tom had no movement in his right side, but his right hand, along with his left, was tethered to the bed. Now I'm sure the rationale would be that it was done to protect him from himself, but it was something Tom found incredibly frustrating given he couldn't talk, he didn't know where he was, he didn't know why he was there and what was being done to him.

One night in ICU, after his mum left, and they tied him to the bed, Tom must have been left on his own for a really long time and become really stressed – even though in ICU he was supposed to have a nurse with him 24/7 – because one of the other nurses told Tom's mum the next day that they found him on the floor, one arm still tied to the bed.

Somehow, even though he could hardly move, Tom had wrestled one of his hands free, struggled down the bed – there were railings on each side – and been on the floor for who knows how long. He must have been in a massive panic. All alone and tied to a bed. Not knowing what was going on.

This particular torment escalated when they moved Tom to the ward the next day. That evening, after all his visitors had departed, his mother Anne returned from a short break, and was horrified by what she saw. The nurse was dressing Tom in a special shirt which had ties all over it, so they could tie him to the bed (kind of like a strait-jacket). Tom was fully conscious by this stage. Anne recalls that Tom was looking at her in bewilderment. Anne demanded the nurse remove the shirt. She then had to sign a declaration saying she was accepting responsibility for any injury Tom might suffer as a result of not being tied down. To make sure the nurses did not tie Tom to the bed again, Tom's mum stayed in the room every night, 'sleeping' on chairs, until they agreed not to tie him to the bed.

I know Tom's story means so much to me because of the love I had for him, but it has also enriched my life to the extent that I believe his story of survival and perseverance is one that should adorn great monuments.

Journal entry 18.10.2006: Undoubtedly, in my eyes, Tom's greatest skill is his ability to understand the struggles of humanity and communicate compassionately to find resolutions. I'd always seen him as a future Prime Minister or UN Delegate.

What I learned from Tom's trials and tribulations, and what I continue to learn from his resilience and quality of character, is to be grateful for the small stuff, the tiny stuff, the stuff you think is so insignificant it never crosses your mind – things like being able to move, think, laugh, have sex, laugh while having sex, cook, talk, clean and ultimately be who I want to be and make my own decisions. For Tom, all of these things were taken away following the accident and months in hospital, where he had to learn everything again (and he's not alone, one billion people or 15% of the world's population live with some form of disability).

What still sends a chill up my spine every time I look at Tom are those tiny little victories we learned to celebrate together, no matter how small. Victories like the word "Geordie" or the seemingly nonsensical

CANCER, CAR ACCIDENTS AND THE MOTHER WHO LOST EIGHT CHILDREN

"slocol mocol." They were the first words Tom uttered after the accident. Geordie was the name of his late, beloved first pet, a beautiful and devoted red heeler, and Tom used the word "Geordie" as his reply to everything. Slocol mocol was a bit more difficult to decipher and it took Rachel, a friend and regular visitor to the ICU, to crack the code. She worked out what Tom was trying to say by following his eyes when he spoke the phrase and noticed they were being drawn to a vending machine with its distinctive logo advertising everyone's favourite soft drink, Coca Cola! Throughout this part of his recovery, Tom recalled years later, he thought he was making perfect sense and having in-depth conversations with those around him, when in fact all they heard were garbled sounds. And even before there were sounds emanating from his hurt head, he remembers watching the nurses chat away, and trying to join in, but being unable to produce any sounds. Either no one had explained to him what had happened or he was unable to comprehend the explanation offered. There's also a slight chance he simply couldn't remember anything he was told, as his short-term memory was severely impaired after the car caused his brain to rebound violently against his skull.

While conversation was a challenge in those early months – and still can be – physical interaction with this former gifted athlete was more enjoyable. We used a nerf ball to encourage Tom to move and react and the first time he caught a nerf ball thrown at him was a moment of genuine joy. Another win, we thought, as we revelled at Tom's refusal to surrender and the strength he displayed in his recovery.

So after four weeks in ICU, Tom was now in a regular ward. With his brain settling down and the swelling all but gone – which exposed the massive crater where the skull from his forehead should be – we all rejoiced. It might not sound like much, but this was a colossal victory – a sign that he may well live to tell his tale. It was there in Ward R3 that my interest in photography played a small part in helping the restoration of Tom's memory, by showing him all the pictures I had of our earlier exploits and adventures with our mates. I remember fondly those cheeky smiles as we told Tom of the super-man he once was. As we did this, we promised ourselves that he would again live to be that man. Of course, at this stage, we still didn't know whether Tom would ever walk, talk coherently, read, write, remember, taste, smell and even feel the wide range of emotions his journey would no doubt evoke.

To paint a picture of Tom's brain at this point, you need to imagine a city or town that's just had a third of its roads destroyed by a flood (of blood). Everything's a mess. How do people (or neural messages in his case) get around or through the mess? Can the roads be rebuilt, which footpaths were too damaged to traverse? Or is the only way to go around the destruction to rebuild completely? Maybe. But how do you rebuild what's broken? After all, this was no road, it was a brain. Doctor's (as they had done all along) remained pessimistically unsure, but we (and no doubt Tom) held onto hope that what can be unmade, can be remade.

Just recently I saw a 4 Corners episode where the reporter visited the Syrian city of Raqqa shortly after it had been liberated from three years of ISIS rule. It seemed as if almost every building in this once beautiful city had been bombed but there, among this incredible destruction, were ragged inhabitants beginning to rebuild. It was, I thought at the time, an apt metaphor for the battle to revive Tom's mind.

Further recovery saw Tom rewarded with a shift to Hampstead Rehabilitation Centre in Northfield, where brain injury patients are accommodated during their rehabilitation. It was a fairly uninspiring (old and daggy), but relaxed space, and whenever I visited Tom we would head straight for the pool-room for a game on the green velvet. The activity was supposed to be good for promoting hand-eye coordination and Tom and I always enjoyed ourselves crouched over the table of coloured balls.

An aside. There were several other brain injured patients at the facility, but one who always interacted with us was a youngish man who would come up to the table, irrespective of the state of the game, and use his hands to fling around the balls. At first, it was slightly bewildering and annoying, but once we'd worked out that it was his 'thing' and his way of becoming involved in our game and in connecting with his fellow human beings, I looked forward to his interruptions almost as if it was his turn. This patient was known for his violent tendencies and was always shadowed by a security guard whose job it was to keep him in check.

Uncanny violence is an unfortunate but common by-product of brain injuries, but thankfully Tom's placid pre-crash nature remained. Every time I visited Tom and observed other patients, most of whom seemed worse off and weren't recovering at the rate he was, I felt so grateful that Mr B (as I called him) was still who he was – a stubborn, spirited bastard not willing to give up on anything.

A lot of the patients there couldn't talk due to their injuries, and another patient that Tom struck up a relationship with was a fellow mute mate who he regularly challenged to a game of chess. Here was clear evidence that part of their brains were functioning perfectly well and what had failed them was their working memory and communication channels. Tom was and still is a very impressive chess player. I love my chess and Tom and I have really good battles when we go to war over a chess board. However, unfortunately for my ego, he normally wins (even without a third of his brain).

As parts of Tom's brain began coming back to life, like a computer rebooting after a major system-wide malfunction, doctors began to get a clearer picture of what would, what may and what would not recover. They officially diagnosed Tom with aphasia, a condition where the communication channels in the brain are disrupted. The disruptions affect how information is received and processed and how a person responds. Some years later, we were given a strategy to try to help us understand part of what it's like to live with aphasia, which went like this. We were told to sit with a group of people or even just one person and have a conversation. We could listen to everything being said, and we could think about what we wanted to say, but before we could speak we had to count to 30. Try that and you'll see for yourself how it can disrupt the natural flow of conversation, where most people speak before thinking, never mind delaying their speech with a forced count of 30. By the time you work out what they're saying, and have the words organised to say something, the conversation has moved on; it's a different topic altogether now so you just stay silent. That, we were told, was what Tom was experiencing. This was incredibly frustrating for Tom and still is 13 years later, especially for a guy who had been an avid overachiever (and a renowned debater and public speaker). A guy who got the English prize and the Maths prize when we finished school and now couldn't talk properly, read, write or understand what we were saying.

But it wasn't only Tom's brain that had been smashed and broken, his body too had been battered and lay idle for six weeks before entering Hampstead. His entire right side still had few signs of feeling or life, courtesy of the damage to his head. I remember seeing Tom's cumbersome 6 foot 2 inch frame holding on tightly to the parallel bars that were there to help him walk again. I remember the stress balls, ropes, stretch bands and endless physiotherapists who pushed him to nearly kill himself in order to improve just a fraction. But above all of this, I remember those moments that my friend would look at me with a defiant smile as if to say 'did you just see that!?' Seeing the enormous lengths this guy had gone to, just to be alive, let alone learn to crawl, swim, kick, catch, and walk again, you couldn't help but smile with him, as the seeds of appreciation planted themselves firmly in my gut.

> *Journal entry 7.10.2006: I'm so glad I left Uni early today, as I was there to see Tom take his first steps unassisted. I imagine he must have felt like Neil Armstrong taking those first few 'impossible' steps on the moon… Boy we take a lot for granted.*

One of the rituals Tom found really frustrating at Hampstead was lining up for his daily supply of medication, but he still managed to find a humorous takeaway, as he explained to me years later.

"The problem was," he began, "because of the frequent turnover of staff, they never really got to know us and every day someone different would be doing the medications at mealtime. To get your medication, you had to say your name. But, of course, I couldn't say my name. So when the nurse wheeled the medication trolley up to me I just sat there. The nurse would then read out each name on the list of patients. When I heard my name I waved my hands around, and I got my medication. It was a daily frustration. I had a job to do, say my name and get my medication, and I couldn't do it. This happened every day. And every day I got more and more desperate to say my name."

"So every night, after everyone left, I worked at saying my name. I sat there in my room, on my own, practising saying my name, 'Tom'. I worked really hard at it every night I was in Hampstead, but it never happened. The first time I managed to say my name was the day after I left Hampstead! Boy, was I mad. Thrilled at finally being able to say my name, but frustrated that I never got to say it all those months when getting my medication!"

Four months, one day, seven hours and 42 minutes after that first phone call alerting me to Tom's condition, this larger than life character who I'd grown even closer to through this misfortune, walked out of Hampstead and waved goodbye to the doubters.

As the years passed by, the speech therapists, neurologists, brain scans, physiotherapists, psychiatrists and a plethora of drugs, had seemingly done their job. Half a decade after those first words and steps post-accident, Tom had rebuilt much of his former self. And technology helped too – developments in speech to text and text to speech were a massive boost for Tom that allowed him to communicate.

His intelligence was still there, albeit masked by his communication difficulties. He even began to dream a dream all but a few deemed impossible – to return to university. His drive and ambition to do good and help others also remained intact, and saw him become actively involved in the aphasia community, becoming the first person with aphasia to be elected President of the Talkback Association for Aphasia Society of South Australia. Tom too, continues to exercise his love for politics, by remaining actively involved in the Labor party, being an extra set of hands or feet on the ground during election times (personally, I still think he'd make a great MP or more). And his love of travel and being part of the world is definitely still there. Since his accident Tom has travelled to countries like Vietnam, Myanmar, Laos, Hong Kong, New Caledonia, France, England, Russia and Japan, sometimes with his mother's work, but mostly on his own, and he has many more travel plans to come.

Everything Tom did, and everything Tom embodied, made me grateful to call him a friend. With every 'can't' he's overcome, every 'glass ceiling' he's smashed, he's made me a better person, more aware of my complete and utter privilege, and more grateful for how easy my life was, and is. Without the sense of appreciation I gained from watching my friend go through hell, and without Tom's 'can do' attitude compelling me to push myself, who knows, perhaps I'd still be sitting in an office at the Royal Adelaide Hospital unhappily dwelling on what might have been.

As French writer and philosopher Voltaire said, "Appreciation is a wonderful thing: It makes what is excellent in others belong to us as well." While much of Tom's brilliance and fight had already rubbed off on me, he wasn't done teaching me how to remove the 'im' from impossible. In fact, in July 2012, after arduous negotiation with Adelaide University regarding his specific needs, he re-enrolled in university and studied a subject called The Ethics of War and Peace, which he passed! Finding the intense English requirements of university difficult to cope with, Tom decided to transfer into an IT and programming course at

Australia's leading vocational education and training provider, TAFE. He also began to dabble in some mathematics, exploring the possibility of doing a maths degree. Tom also started going to the local library for some quiet time, and one day was surprised to find that he could memorise long lists of numbers, like all the numbers that go on forever after the decimal point in pi. And yes, when I test him on it and he gets it right (which he always does), he gives me the exact same smile he did in the hospital whenever he was proud of one of his long list of achievements.

Tom and his mum kept researching all the possible therapies for recovery after brain injury, including stem cell technology, which he's still waiting to progress to a point that may be able to help him. His mum knew about neuroplasticity from the Canadian neuropsychiatrist Dr Norman Doidge. His first book, The Brain That Changes Itself, was a NY best seller and that book gave us all hope for Tom's future. Doidge's second book, The Brain's Way of Healing, came out in 2015 and Anne and Tom went to the packed out Adelaide Town Hall to hear him on his book tour. The therapy that stood out, according to Tom's mum, was Chapter 4 on cold laser (now called photobiomodulation). They thought they would have to go to Toronto for the therapy, but after some research, they found the only cold laser clinic in the whole of Australia was five minutes from where Tom lives. In December 2015 Tom started a three-week intensive laser therapy program. On Christmas Eve he said the alphabet. The first time in 9 years. He still does cold laser therapy, but he bought some of the lasers and does it himself, at home. The change since the lasers has been a miracle.

One of the more daring decisions Tom made after the lasers came in January 2016, was that he decided to stop taking the surplus of drugs he'd been prescribed ever since the accident. This wasn't some whimsical choice. As with everything Tom did, he'd thoroughly researched the desired effects and side effects of each drug online, as well as consulting with a doctor, and felt it was time to see how his body would go without all the substances in his system. It didn't take long to notice a difference. I remember his elation as he said, "my brain is awakening now, I can feel it." And he wasn't wrong. His speech improved out of sight. He was even able to read a little, write a little and focus his mind on any given task – such as losing weight (something he'd long wanted to do). With the pills that were making him fat now gone, and a new exercise regime and diet in place, Tom lost 30kg over the next three and a bit months.

Like a wild animal escaping its captors, Tom's mind was roaming, running, jumping, and soaring – the new pathways created during even a single conversation were tangible, as if all the street-lights had been turned on at once.

Today, Tom lives independently in a central Adelaide townhouse that he bought and redesigned to suit his needs. While he's endured further setbacks, including a botched effort by surgeons to fix his mis-shapen forehead from when they re-inserted his skull, and a number of seizures that led to him being diagnosed with epilepsy, Tom remains resilient. He is a living breathing example of one of my favourite quotes by John F. Kennedy, who said "As we express our gratitude, we must never forget that the highest appreciation is not to utter words, but to live by them."

So, to my dear, dear friend who taught me my first and abiding lessons in gratitude, I am eternally grateful. No matter what my circumstances, I am first of all grateful for the air in my lungs and from there, grateful for every opportunity, every experience, every challenge, every victory, every moment of joy that life has thrown my way, and our way. Thank you, Tom Bunning.

Journal entry 18.11.2006: Tom may be unable to read, write or even speak, but the world will hear his voice.

End of the island state

One of the most difficult things to do is change a habit. It's tough – but not as tough as holding onto those toxic behaviours we know are doing us harm. For me, one of those things was complaining and feeling hard done by. You know how it goes: why did my parents leave me to fend for myself during university, how come I didn't get that job, why don't I look like that, and when will I get my lucky break? Everyone else has it so much easier and better than I do… Why? Why me? You suck god!

What Tom's experience taught me was to pipe down, shut up and be thankful. I mean who was I to complain? My skull was in one piece, my lungs hadn't collapsed, my brain wasn't bleeding and I could walk, talk and read to my heart's content. What this, and numerous trips exploring some of the poorest countries and communities on Earth did for me, was free me from the mental shackles of thinking of myself as an island, disconnected from the pain and suffering of others. It let me see my ego for what it was – selfish and nearly entirely useless when it comes to finding happiness. From this grounding in compassion and putting myself in others' shoes, the seeds of appreciation grew. And caring became my life and career. From interviewing and sharing stories about the poor, the malnourished and the starving, to rape victims, war victims and victims of domestic violence; from quadriplegics, terminal cancer patients and the blind, to the elderly, the downtrodden and the forgotten – it was through remembering my place, my good fortune and our innate connection to the suffering of others that those seeds of appreciation grew into prodigious trees, adding goodness to everything I did or felt. Because to me **that's what *gratitude* and *appreciation* does – it makes a good thing better and a crap thing bearable.**

It teaches us to stop and find the positive.

I think if there was one talent I've learnt that makes me happier than anything else, it would be that – finding and holding onto what can make me better, and letting go of all that's going to drag me down.

But that's not possible without accepting what is, and finding the positive in the vast ups and downs by recognising that pain and suffering are necessary parts of life – of being whole – for without such emotions we'd have no reference from which to understand love and happiness. We'd probably learn a whole lot slower too, as it is most often anguish and sorrow that leads us to growth and progression. Just look at our exponential evolution in morality in the past 100 years. It's seen women given the vote, the environment given a voice, the end of colonisation (for the most part), legalised racism defeated in the United States and South Africa, an apology for stealing Aboriginal children in Australia and a 67% reduction in global poverty levels. Yes, there are still grave injustices occurring. Yes, more needs to be done, but if we don't stop and take stock of how far we've come, I can guarantee, we'll never be happy. It's also hugely draining on one's energy to dwell in the darkened negative space, and that's not good for anyone – certainly not the cause you want to fight for. To me, it's about remaining optimistic but not naïve, positively passionate rather than angry, and forever grateful for the privilege that lets me do this work of caring for others.

Me and Tom.

Padhmini and Nethmi.

CANCER, CAR ACCIDENTS AND THE MOTHER WHO LOST EIGHT CHILDREN

The wave of suffering connects us all

A great reminder of the importance of gratitude came when I visited Sri Lanka in late 2012. Nearly eight years earlier, a 9.3 magnitude earthquake (the third largest ever recorded) in the Indian Ocean triggered a series of devastating tsunamis, killing 300,000 people across 14 countries, including 35,000 in Sri Lanka. Visiting some of the worst hit areas nearly a decade later, I didn't know precisely what I would find, but I was curious to see what I and others might learn about happiness (and sadness) from those who lost everything in what was one of the deadliest natural disasters in recorded history.

My first observation generated in me a sense of shock and total emotional exhaustion at the scale of this thing. Against the backdrop of a deceptively calm and serene ocean, I walked through the rubble of huts, homes and businesses that used to line the shores of Sri Lanka's southern coastline. There were old clothes, toys, shoes, curtains and children's flip-flops strewn everywhere. All of it had clearly remained eerily untouched, like a living memorial and stark reminder of the sudden violence with which the water had come and taken people from the land. Photographing the ruins of former lives, I met a local mother Priyana who stood there mourning – as it was close to the anniversary date of 26 December.

"You can't imagine it," said the woman, through an interpreter I'd taken with me. "The wave was taller than any of these homes, more powerful than the steel and cement that we were told would keep us safe [she begins to sob]. The worst part is that my daughter is still out there, somewhere, without her Amma [mother] to hold her hand. We never found her body, she was just there and then she was gone. That is a mother's torture." I stopped the interview to hold her as she wept. Some minutes later she continued, "You know it was hard to go on. To breathe, or speak or do anything but sit and cry. But then my neighbour had lost her two sons and her husband, and had no means of rebuilding her life. She was waiting for help to come. So my husband, son and I turned to her and offered her shelter with us – in what was left of our home."

"We had lost a lot, but others had lost everything. It doesn't make it right, or easy, but it made us feel less alone, our cries were not the only ones heard in our village," said Priyana, who was 43 years old and now living in one of many new settlements built by Red Cross following the disaster. Curious to visit one of these post-tsunami constructed towns, I asked Priyana if she knew where I could find one. She pointed to a small road that led up a hill close by. "People don't trust the ocean now, so we go to live in the highland," she said, before hugging me goodbye.

Walking curiously towards the area I was directed to go to, I noticed a young girl inquisitively peeking out of the front door of her home. My interpreter told me that this was one of the houses Priyana had alluded to, so we walked to the entrance and knocked. Wearing a purple sarong and pink T-shirt, the mother of the house, Dammika Padhmini, invited us in for a tea. Immediately I noticed that their TV stand and hall tables were lined with photos of a large family, several children, and yet, just one girl greeted us. 'Oh no,' I thought, swallowing deeply as horror overcame me. It was all I could think about as I sipped on my tea – where was everyone?

The agony of waiting for answers was short-lived, as Padhmini took her old plastic chair and sat it in their doorway, unravelling her story.

"We never knew this thing 'tsunami', it meant nothing to us, but when we began to hear screams that is when we saw the water coming to us. It was not like a wave, it was a wall of water. So in our home in Peraliya (their former village), my husband and I climbed onto a coconut tree, with three of our four children. The fourth child, our 7-year-old girl, was studying in school at that time," recalled Padhmini, who was clearly finding it tough to think about. "As the water surged beneath our feet, horror filled my heart. Death was in my brain. We didn't know if our other daughter was safe. We were just hanging onto what we could. My husband cuddled our two-year-old baby, while I helped our 13-year-old daughter hang on. Our 18-year-old son was perched just next to us – he was the best climber."

When the body of water (which reached as far as 3 kilometres inland) receded, fishermen scurried to grab fish that had been left along the shore line, as others climbed down from trees and rooftops to gather their things or find missing loved ones. Padhmini said she was eager to make sure her other daughter was safe, so she sent her older son and daughter to find her. Before they had a chance to return, a second gigantic surge of water rushed towards Padhmini, her husband and their youngest child. Panic set in. There was no time to get back to the coconut tree they'd sought refuge in previously.

CANCER, CAR ACCIDENTS AND THE MOTHER WHO LOST EIGHT CHILDREN

"The water hit us like a bomb blast. It was immense. I was swept into the water before managing to hang onto some debris and then a tree. I could see my husband, he was about 20 metres from me holding our toddler in his arms. He was in a bad place, water rushing around him as he strode through the debris and water. Then, he tripped and fell. His grip of the fabric covering our child loosened, and then tore," she pauses, breathing quickly and in tears. "The fast currents came and took the baby under. My husband's hands searched for her, he dived under, groping wildly, his eyes searched, as did mine, but our baby was nowhere to be found."

"With gashes from the debris, my husband and I waited, writhing in pain, for our other children to return. But they never came home."

All four of Padhmini's children died that day.

In Sri Lanka alone, the Tsunami had left 900,000 people homeless – including Padhmini and her husband – and yet, she never once spoke of this. Because it simply didn't matter.

"Our children were gone," she said with a disarming calmness, as if her long and painful journey was finally over. "You appreciate how meaningless a home or objects are when you lose what truly matters. And I was 37, so we knew we may never get the chance to be parents again, because I was too old."

For years Padhmini and her husband tried and failed to conceive. The blessing ceremonies, natural remedies and prayers to get pregnant fell on deaf ears.

"We will be alone. It was hopeless," she recalls. "Here in Sri Lanka, if we have no children we have no life, no way to survive when we are old. That is the responsibility of our children, just as we looked after our parents before us. So we had a fear we would die young and unhappily, because we had nothing, no one," she pauses with a sigh. "No hope."

Then who was this girl dancing behind us throughout the interview? Why had she come and sat on Padhmini's lap so lovingly, I wondered? Was she a grandchild? A neighbour or niece perhaps? She interrupted my confused thoughts. "Then, with all hope lost, three years after our life was crushed by that water, I became sick. I thought, what now? But then I felt something familiar, it was not a normal illness. I went to the doctor and they confirmed it, I was pregnant. I couldn't believe it!"

Not only had she become pregnant at the age of 40, but the good news freed Padhmini from her self-imposed exile – which was born out of her terrible pain. Within days of 'emerging', Padhmini said she heard a number of stories about the grave loses other families had faced. One woman in particular stood out, she said, "because she had lost eight children, and like me, was too old to have any more."

"I'd been so tied up with my own pain, reliving that day over and over, that I'd forgotten about those around me. That there were others suffering, most just as much as my husband and I. It was an awakening. Eight children, can you imagine," tears welled in her eyes. "I'd never been more grateful. Our dream had come true – to have a child – and the stories had freed me from some of my pain. It taught me to appreciate that *my* life and *my* sorrow was not all that existed."

"When Nethmi was born she forced me to focus on the now. To appreciate what was in front of me – the dream I had dreamed for so long, of having a child. And Nethmi is just complete, she is everything," says Padhmini, as Nethmi runs towards her, eager to listen to what her mother has to say about her. "If we fail to see the goodness in this moment, we cannot be happy. I was not happy. I was living in the past. Hoping somehow for another future. But I was not living. Because I was not present."

As Nethmi asked me to chase her outside (sensing the end of our interview), I couldn't help but think about our need to let go of our hurt and our fears in order to be met by peace – the state from which all forms of appreciation are born. For behind appreciation is acceptance and an acknowledgment that no one and nothing is 'out to get us', there are simply good and bad people and good and bad days, and each of us will encounter plenty of each. The only question is, how will we choose to see them. Is suffering a cruel but inevitable human flaw designed to hurt us? What if we didn't feel emotions? What if life was free of pain? How about joy, love and serenity? Would life still be worth living? How would we learn? Without the horrors of our human condition continually punching us in the face, how might we learn to overcome? How might we grow, evolve and progress towards a better state of being?

To me, the key to seeing all people and days as good or positive is to appreciate that for whatever reason they have happened (whether you believe in fate, karma, coincidence or simply that all things are connected through cause and effect), you cannot change what has been. It is done. You can only decide whether you want to see some good, some purpose, some meaning in it. Whether you want to be grateful for some, all or none of whatever amazing or nasty thing just happened. Because as science suggests, it is not our circumstances that most impact upon our happiness, but the way we react to their ever-changing state.

The Lady of the Lake

Someone who taught me this, though she arguably wasn't all that happy herself, was Sam Ath (pronounced Some-At), a 43-year-old Cambodian woman who in all likelihood is dead.

When I went to visit the Choeung Ek Killing Fields just outside of Phnom Penh, Cambodia in late-2012, the last thing I expected to find was children laughing. But from behind a fence that enclosed the site where 8895 bodies were exhumed following the brutal and bloody Khmer Rouge regime, a group of young kids ran and jumped down a hill into the water, which lay on the other side of the mesh divide. Noticing my interest in their activities – I was taking some photos – the children ran to the fence and waved ecstatically, sharing what few English words they knew with me. "Hello Mister, how are you?" they said, laughing hysterically as they jumped up and down. Behind the screaming kids, were a few older children standing next to a decrepit hut, perched on stilts above the side of the lake. One girl in particular caught my eye. She wore both deep pain and unbounding happiness on her face, as if trapped somewhere between life and death. While the other kids displayed the same immense joy that she did, their smiles were not pushing through any obvious barriers – they were just kids – but this girl was something else. Wearing a black T-shirt with a fluorescent green animated baby on it, pink and orange cartoon three-quarter-pants and holding some sort of toy in her hand she stopped, and looked at me, deep into my soul (in a way few could). She raised her middle and index fingers, making the V for peace, before skipping off with her friends. Who was she? I had to know.

Walking back through the killing fields with my driver, who was also my interpreter, I asked him why there were just a few isolated grubby huts by the lakeside and who lived in them. It was an unfamiliar sight, to see a house by itself in Cambodia, as people typically lived in close-knit villages with groups of adjoining homes. My interpreter, who owned a bright pink tuk-tuk and called himself Bob, said that the people living by themselves have mostly been pushed out of their community. "No one wants to live alone, it is just for those people who cannot live anywhere else, like in their village," said Bob.

As we left the deathly quiet killing fields and made our way down a narrow, windy, tree-lined road to the area I'd seen the children run to, I heard a familiar "hello mister!" As I turned to the market stall the words had echoed from, two young girls flapped their arms about frantically, with a smile beaming ear to ear. It was the girl I'd been looking for, and her friend, though this time there was a more wow'ish enthusiasm to their delight at seeing this strange, white man venturing into a place that was clearly not on any tourist map. With a single yell (alerting their friends to my arrival), tens of children streamed up from the banks of the lake where they'd been hiding out in boats or playing with the local goats and cows. Counting "1…2…3…GO" then running as the kids chased after me down a thin dirt path towards what was apparently this girl's house, it was hard not to notice just how far off the beaten track I was being taken. Who deserves to live all the way out here? I thought, no matter what they've supposedly done.

Nearing a wooden, thatched hut precariously suspended out across a swampy inlet from Lake Boeng Choeung Aek, which bordered the killing field, a slightly hunched and tattered-looking lady emerged from under the timber structure. A select few of the kids greeted her with a chuckle and "hello", while others remained silent and kept their distance. Bob said that she was the owner of the house, and that the young girl I'd befriended also lived here. "How do they know each other?" I asked Bob to translate. "Is this girl her daughter?" The woman – who was missing her four front teeth at the top and who had a smile that resembled an old broken Greek temple worn away by hundreds of years of weather – looked at me with dread. What had I done, I wondered? She looked down, being careful not to make eye contact as she said, "We both have HIV." The world stopped for a moment. "Fuuuuuck," I said under my breath. That was not what I was expecting. "So, is she your daughter?" I asked once more, assuming my question had been misunderstood the first time. "No!" said Sam Ath.

"One day I noticed Sompec (the girl) just sitting by herself, and when she explained that she had been abandoned I knew I must help," Sam Ath continued. "No child should be left without love. So while my community had already rejected me, because I had HIV, I knew that I could do something to change her fate, so I invited her into my home. **What little I had was now hers too.**"

"Over time I became like a mother to her, and we have grown stronger together, so I hope we have many more years on this Earth," says Sam Ath as she hugs Sompec, who is clearly overcome by her adopted-mother's words.

"People, they are afraid of us. They think we are cursed because of our disease," she continues. "So we are forced to live like this, because even some people think they will get HIV from being close to us."

For those of you jumping up and down with outrage and thinking "how could people still be so ignorant in the 21st century?" it's important to remember that between 1975 and 1979 Cambodia effectively lost an entire generation of its most educated people – its teachers, doctors, writers and philosophers – were all targeted and exterminated by the Khmer Rouge regime, which altogether wiped out roughly 25% of Cambodia's population (1.2 to 2.8 million people). Today, the effects of this intellectual extermination are unfortunately felt by those like Sompec and Sam Ath, who are the victims of an uneducated society.

None of this, of course, justifies or makes their situation right, but I think **when we see the whole of a picture it becomes easier to forgive, let go of hate, and discern the good we might take from such a situation** – like the simple appreciation that you're alive, have likely never had to face this, or the fact that we can all play a part in stopping this from ever happening again.

Donning a T-shirt that read *Tough As Nails* (though I doubt she knew what it meant, as she didn't speak a word of English) Sam Ath's determination to see beyond her potentially crippling circumstances and to react to her ever-changing state in a way that gave her meaning and connection, was at the heart of what little happiness she enjoyed.

"After the Khmer Rouge I had no land, nothing, because my parents died and their land was taken by the regime. Then I got HIV from a man who mistreated me, and now I am just trying to stay alive, and be good to the people like me, who are forgotten."

There was seemingly nothing in Sam Ath or Sompec's life to be grateful for, and yet, that very thing – life – was something both appreciated, because they knew millions of Cambodians had it stolen away just a few decades earlier. This didn't mean they were happy people, for the most part they were not, but what stood out was their resilience (they were *tough as nails*) and their ability to find the tiny wins, the miniscule details of each day worth appreciating, worth holding onto. Things such as offering me (a bizarre foreigner with a whole bunch of cameras) a cup of tea and their last biscuit, when they may have no idea where their next meal is coming from. In such cultures it would be rude to say no, so I sat with her and listened, and told her that one day the world would hear her story and be moved by it. Well, I guess this is that day – when her suffering and her ability to see beyond her own selfish needs might inspire you to **see what you have and be grateful for it**. To understand that it is not your circumstances that determine your happiness, but how you react when they change (for better or for worse).

The boy with one leg

Not long after I left Cambodia, I found myself sitting on a remote beach in western Myanmar called Chaung-tha. Sipping on a beer, perusing the images and stories I'd captured in Cambodia, a soccer ball suddenly came flying past my nose.

Three boys quickly followed it, scurrying to get to it first. As the laughter and mayhem passed and I went back to focussing on my screen, something I'd seen suddenly registered. That boy was missing a leg! Yep, as I looked at a dozen or so kids running back and forth along the beach, there was one boy with a giant wooden crutch on his left side, instead of a leg. This kid was nuts – running, diving, being knocked down; he even used his wooden apparatus to steal the ball, get himself up off the sand and generally seemed determined not to let his 'disability' get in the way of his abilities. Wow! My computer faded into the background as I became transfixed on this boy. Yes, his friends took advantage of him having just one leg (what young boys wouldn't?). And yes, his constant face planting into the sand was hilarious. But he seemed entirely unfazed. Committed to do and be himself – in the most awesome way possible. When the game paused for a break, I called the bartender and asked him to invite the boy over and help me speak to him.

"Hello!" I said. "Hello mister," replied the young boy, chuckling at his attempt to speak English. The cheeky go-getter quickly explained (through my trusty translator) that his name was Sein Myint Aung and

Choeung Ek Killing Fields.

The girl I came to know as Sompec.

The path to Sam Ath's house.

Sam Ath and Sompec's house.

Filming an interview with Sam Ath, as local kids watch on.

Giving Sam Ath a big hug after hearing her story.

Each seemed grateful they had a hand to hold.

Sam Ath (left) and Sompec.

he was 9-years-old and in grade 3 at school. "What happened to your leg," I asked.

"When I was a baby I was born in the slums over there [he points down the beach] and I had a bad deformity to my leg. It was rare. Nobody knew what to do. The doctors said there was nothing my mum could do, because we had no money to travel to see some people who knew about this disease, so they cut off my left leg when I was just a few months old," he said with a defiant smile plastered across his face. "So how does a child in Myanmar be so happy with just one leg?" I ask him naively.

"Well, if I concentrate on what I don't have then I only have one leg, but if I focus on what I do have then I have one awesome leg and a piece of wood, and that's all I need to be happy," laughed Sein, as he ran off to fetch a stray ball from the game which had just restarted. I was tempted to interrogate this wise young man further, but I felt that this single line was a perfect representation of all I could see before me – of his ability to stretch the realms of possibility – so instead of calling him back over, I decided to go play.

Watching on in near-horror as we joined in the game of beach soccer, Sein's every kick, dive and header was mind bending; as his seemingly enormous physical limitations were met by an even greater mental will to overcome them. As if he hadn't yet proven himself to be able enough, Sein ran off indicating he'd be back soon. Minutes later he returned riding a bike, using his one leg and crutch to push the pedals. "How on Earth did he even contemplate riding a bike, let alone figure out how to do it?" I said aloud, as the interpreter asked Sein.

"Other people were riding, so I wanted to do the same. I just had to look at what I had and imagine a way that I could get on and off, that was the hardest part, because I don't have two feet to put down to balance like my friends. I also have to have one hand on the crutch, so I only have one hand to direct me too, which is hard in the sand," said Sein, as he sat there on his bike leaning on his crutch, which held him up. "The bike was hard, I fell a lot, I still do. But I can't let my deformity stop me. I just have to tell my mind to keep going."

Sein's ability to conquer his physical limits, and use his mind to imagine and create completely new realities (where you can ride a bike with one leg), is evolution in progress. By stretching my spirit and now yours, he pushes the human race forward, by letting us **believe in the**

impossible and by showing us what can be achieved when we focus on what we have, rather than what we long to have.

Seven years on, I think what what Sein taught me was that even our greatest curse can be a blessing. When the world tears us apart, perhaps it is god's way of suggesting or challenging us to put ourselves back together in a more beautiful way. Certainly for Sein, and for me too, that saying "our scars make us beautiful" is utterly true. And science agrees.

Experiencing hardship is actually good for you

A study of 14,986 adults conducted by researchers from the University of British Columbia and Universitat Pompeu Fabra Barcelona found that people who have pulled through hard times are happier in the long-run.

The 2013 study suggests that some of the most painful experiences in life – divorce and death of a loved one – may come with an eventual upside, by promoting the ability to appreciate life's small pleasures. Individuals were asked to indicate whether they had experienced these events and, if so, to specify whether they felt they had emotionally dealt with the negative event or if they were still struggling with it. They then presented the adults with six positive scenarios, which included going on a hike or looking at a waterfall, to see if and how their past traumas disrupted their enjoyment of present pleasures. The study, which was published in the *Social Psychological and Personality Science Journal*, found that people who have previously dealt with pain are more able to enjoy momentary pleasures.

"Individuals who had dealt with more adversity in the past reported an elevated capacity for savouring," the researchers wrote.

Such research seems to support the maxim: "what doesn't kill you makes you stronger", an idea that is supported by psychologist Lowri Dowthwaite who argues that our hardships are key to our happiness.

"Research shows that experiencing adversity can actually be good for us, depending on how we respond to it," writes Dowthwaite in an article for *The Conversation*. "Tolerating distress can make us more resilient and lead us to take action in our lives, such as changing jobs or overcoming hardship."

"In studies of people facing trauma, many describe their experience as a catalyst for profound change and transformation, leading to a phenomenon known as 'post-traumatic growth'. Often when people have faced difficulty, illness or loss, they describe their lives as happier and more meaningful as a result. Unlike feeling happy, which is a transient state, leading a happier life is about individual growth through finding meaning. It is about accepting our humanity with all its ups and downs, enjoying the positive emotions, and harnessing painful feelings in order to reach our full potential."

It sounds odd, but countless studies have shown that roughly **50% of people who struggle with adversity emerge from the event saying that their lives have in some way improved**.

Welcoming hardship may go against all our evolutionary instincts, which tell us that a safe, comfortable and easy existence is what we should pursue, and yet, evidence suggests we must learn to appreciate the full array of life's ever changing circumstances – good and bad – if we are to discover our happiest state.

You might as well choose happiness

Someone who might be considered an expert in this field – who has not only been given lemons, but had those lemons squeezed in her eyes by a seemingly cruel and vengeful god – is Natalia (Nat) Dewiyani.

On 25 May 2015 Nat (now a dear friend) was diagnosed with a very rare form of cancer called Ewing's Sarcoma. If you haven't heard of it, don't worry, most haven't, not even those in the medical fraternity. With such limited information available, Nat took to the world wide web, where she soon discovered that by invading her, the cancer had taken an even rarer route. It turns out Ewing's usually affects children and very young adults under the age of 20. It affects boys more frequently than girls and usually manifests in people of Caucasian descent, rather than of African or Asian origin. When she was diagnosed, Nat was 38, was (and still is) a woman and is an ethnic Chinese! To miss out on the three significant markers but still be diagnosed is beyond all understanding – it's like drawing the short straw from a bucket of spoons – it would be reasonable to expect her to be constantly sobbing and bemoaning the unfairness of it all.

Strangely though, when I met Nat, I was greeted by one of the biggest laughs you are likely to hear... anywhere! A laugh that is repeated often as she finds the humour in almost every exchange. You'd expect a recounting of her cancer journey to be filled with sombre reflection, but every obstacle she encountered and every setback she suffered is a source of great meaning and unbridled amusement to her and she rewards you with that raucous, infectious laugh and you find yourself laughing along at episodes that would make many people curl up in horror.

Oh, and these conversations are not for the squeamish!

Nat was first alerted to a 'problem' by spotting (specks of blood) in her underwear and went along to get it checked out. There was a lump 'down there', but it was dismissed as 'probably a cyst', so she was given antibiotics, sent home and asked to come back if it didn't go away. Unfortunately, the 'cyst' grew, and Nat returned to her GP, who was puzzled. "I have never seen anything like this before," explained her GP, who immediately wrote a referral letter to the emergency department at the Royal Women's Hospital in Melbourne and asked Nat to go there ASAP. Sitting uncomfortably in emergency with her mysterious lump, Nat's imagination wreaked havoc. 'What could it be? What does 'I've never seen anything like this before' mean,' she worried. At last, someone called out her name. The doctor introduced herself and asked Nat to change into a hospital gown. This was the first of many undignifying moments Nat was to face in her journey, as she stripped naked, before being poked and prodded in all manner of places. Being a fairly healthy person, all of this came as a particular shock. "I hadn't been to a GP, let alone a hospital in some time," she recalls.

Still, as her doctor continued to examine the lump things got worse. When it comes to phrases you don't want to hear your doctor utter "this is interesting, I've never seen anything like this before, let me call my colleague," is high on that list. "When multiple doctors marched in taking turns to check out this oddity in your most private of spaces – and none of them could name it – you start imagining the worst. And I think they did too," says Nat.

"Without delay I was wheeled into the operating theatre and had the walnut sized lump removed under general anaesthetic," she continues. After removing the mass, Nat was sent home and told, "Don't worry, it's not cancer." After two weeks, Nat was called back in for what she thought was a routine follow up on her surgery. Sitting there, smiling sheepishly at her surgeon, Nat didn't anticipate what she heard next, "there's no

Nat.

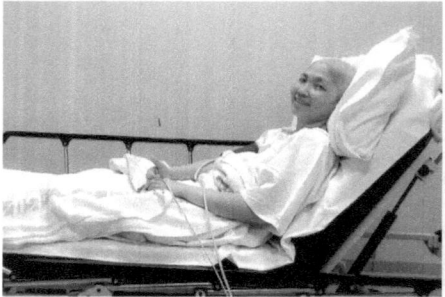
Nat prepares for the fight.

Nat with her mum.

Finding new ways to have fun.

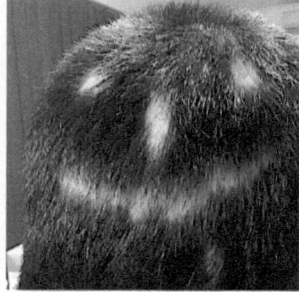
The smiley face Nat made in her hair as it was falling out.

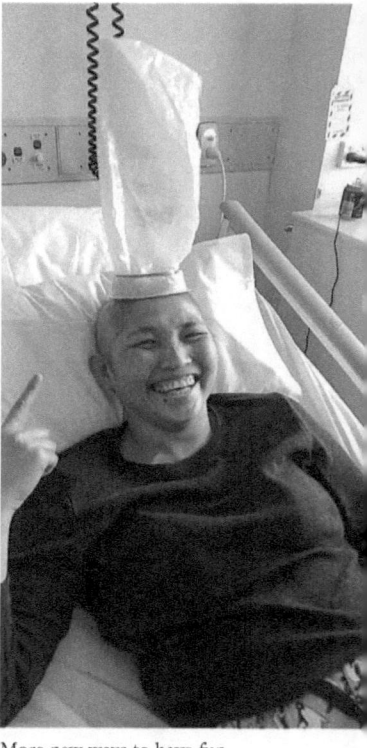

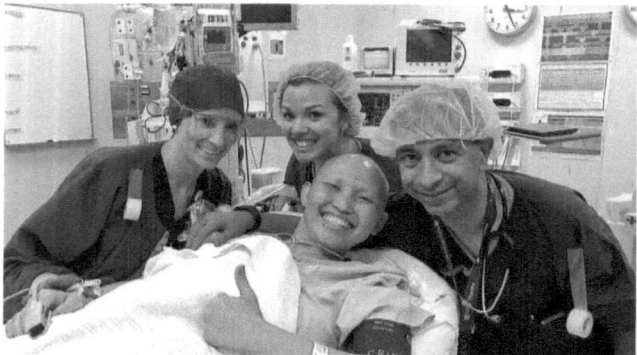
Nat with some of her care team in ICU.

More new ways to have fun.

I joined Nat for one of her free hugs events.

Nat and her partner Kim on the way to a major check-up.

easy way to say this... **it is cancer** and we have organised for you to see specialist team at Peter MacCallum Cancer Centre in a few days. We will call you." While Nat's surgeon had given this particular demon a name – Ewing's Sarcoma – she refused to write it down for her, because she didn't want Nat to google it. "Please wait for the specialist appointment to find out more," she pleaded. But Nat, being human, couldn't resist. When her curiosity led her to type "Wing Sarcoma" (as this is how she'd heard it) into Google and it came up with Ewing's Sarcoma, it wasn't happy reading. "Instantly, I could see why my surgeon didn't want me to go searching," she says. "The prognosis was not good." As she sat there reading, Nat says she was forced to come to terms with the very real possibility of an early death.

"Early on I wished it wasn't cancer. I begged that I'd wake up and it would all have been a dream," says Nat, sitting at the rooftop cafe of the Peter MacCallum Cancer Centre, where we caught up for our first ever 'official' interview (we'd normally met and chatted as friends with an ice cream in one hand). "I don't think anyone will ever be prepared to hear the word 'cancer', because the next word that inevitably enters your mind is 'death'. So it was hard. Kind of numbing. As if gravity stopped and everything was floating to a new spot. Then you process the necessary questions – will I die, when, who do I need to make peace with and so on – and then you wake up to a new reality, where the buildings and the people remain mostly familiar, but death is right there in front of you."

Curious to understand how Nat went from 'scared newcomer' to the founder of an organisation called Laughter with Cancer, I was just about to ask the question 'how did you cope with your diagnosis?' when something distracted her. "Come. There is my friend Tara, you must meet her." Approaching a table where a woman in her late 30s was sitting with an older couple (that I later discovered were her parents), I honestly felt uncomfortable. This woman looked sick. Like really sick. And who was I to be saying hello, anyway? I was just another stranger that didn't know anything about what she was going through. It was the first time I ever felt guilty that I didn't have cancer. I don't know if it was intentional of Nat or not (I had whined about having a bad day), but as I walked back to our table to let Nat and Tara speak in private, this huge weight of expectation was lifted from me. Nothing mattered anymore. The writer's block I was suffering, the fact I was struggling to find enough paid work – it was no longer important – this woman and the life Nat lived (helping people to cope with cancer) had given me the jolt of appreciation I needed. Learning later that Tara was a mother of two and had just undergone three days of chemo to treat a tumour in her lungs that had just tripled in size, I suddenly became even more thankful that I was sitting on a roof, in the sun, talking to my dear and inspiring friend Nat about her epic adventure with cancer.

"Going back to your question of how did I cope with the diagnosis, I guess I was just grateful for the strength I'd gained in overcoming all of life's challenges up to that point. Like being from a conservative culture, and coming out as gay, there's nothing that can prepare you for that. Feeling as if you're somehow 'wrong' or 'not good enough' or 'disappointing' others by simply being yourself, how do you retrain your mind to cope with that?" asks Nat, before answering her own question. "Well, for two weeks I couldn't, I actually stopped smiling entirely," continues Nat, who today only stops smiling to chew food (and barely even then). "It was in those darkest hours, in my deepest despair, that I found solace, and grew the strength to deal with what was unknowingly to come."

"As I laid there curled up in a ball on the floor one day, the pain of coming out encasing me, something compelled me to surrender, and in that moment of surrender, I felt this blanket of love cover me. Every time I tell this story I get goose-bumps," she laughed, as she looked down at her arms, which were covered by those peculiar little bumps of mysterious energy. "I'd never felt that kind of love before. To feel and to be loved, regardless of my flaws, healed me. I think love has more power than we'll ever realise. Certainly understanding what unconditional love is, changed me. It taught me that love is not something you earn because you have done something or have become someone. It also showed me where my journey needed to begin – with love. So that's when I promised myself, if I can get through this [coming out], I want to use this experience to help others to get through their darkness too."

"I think everyone has this fear of 'am I good enough?' But what this experience and feeling taught me was that **you can just be you, in all your differences and flaws, and still be loved**. And this is the foundation for why I can love others without judgment, because I have experienced a divine love free from judgment."

Finding love for herself, Nat says, was the foundation for appreciating life. But what turned this IT worker of 13 years into someone who could cope with that most life changing of six letter words: cancer?

"By the time I heard that word 'cancer', I'd come a long way. My father's sudden death in 2012 – which took just nine days to go from 'a non-threatening rash' into 'a fatal heart complication' – reminded me that life is short, and all of a sudden I thought 'what do I really want to do with my life?'" she said. "I always loved people and had long desired to study psychology, but my dad, who was typical of most Indonesian fathers, was concerned that it may not give me the best future. So, I ended up studying IT at Melbourne University. I guess his passing served as a reminder to do what I loved before it was too late – so I became a life coach."

Sitting before the completely awesome, effervescent, rambunctious, crazy, quirky and cute bubbling body of energy that is Nat today, it is literally impossible to imagine her in IT – working with machines, rather than people. The first video I ever saw of her was actually a time-lapse of her hugging 438 people in Federation Square in Melbourne. And this is just one of several hugging challenges the outlandish Asian has completed. But still I was curious, how had the c-word not crushed the innocence and beauty in her, as it did so many?

"What probably played the biggest part in freeing me from that typical fear response, was the fact that I'd had three weeks to process and make peace with 'the worst' when I first noticed the bleeding and the lump down there. My balls," she says, laughing and pointing at her crotch. "Cancer to me was not the thing I was most afraid of, I was far more scared of losing who I was, and becoming dark and jaded by this thing growing inside me," Nat continues. "If you can't find the positive, you will suffer – a lot. I believed that then, but I know that now. Once you are diagnosed with cancer, you don't have time to delay accepting what it is – because treatment begins immediately – but still, some people never make peace with cancer, and that's what I want to amend."

"I want people to have faith in themselves, that even if you don't know how you'll get through it, you will find a way. You are stronger and more in touch with yourself than you know. And if you change your mind-set you will have a better experience dealing with cancer. Guaranteed!"

"I said to myself right from the start: I can make it a curse or a blessing. I don't have the choice of what happened to me. But I have the choice of how my life will be. If I saw cancer as a curse I know I wouldn't be speaking to you right now," recalls Nat in a rare sombre tone. "So for me it all began by surrendering myself to the reality in front of me – **I had cancer – but that wasn't all I had, that wasn't all I was**. I was determined that I was going to smile every single day for the rest of my life, however long or short it might be, and even if I only smiled once a day. Ultimately, I knew that in the battle between being in heaven or in hell I would end up wherever I believed I was, so I chose a heavenly playground."

Time to tackle the devil…

Nat's chemotherapy program (which started on 17 June 2015) was both relentless and brutal, and included 10 months of treatment made up of 14 cycles, each three weeks apart. The trouble with chemotherapy, of course, is that it not only kills cancer cells but a whole lot of other, essential cells as well. So while Nat's mind was flexing its might, the chemo seeping through her veins was causing her body to collapse. Sixteen days after her first treatment, she had lost all her hair. Ninety-six days in, she ended up being rushed to the ICU, where she spent two days being bounced from hospital to hospital as her condition worsened. When her blood pressure reached 40 over 60 and an infection took hold, it looked like cancer might have the last laugh."

"It was pretty scary," says Nat. "But it was also quite freeing. I remember when my hair started to drop, I got one of my friends to make a bald smiley face at the back of my head by pulling out two eyes and a smile worth of hair. It was one of the funniest days of my life," she giggles uncontrollably.

"Cancer pushes you to let go. Because everything is stripped away. Your job. Your health. Your identity – like losing your hair. Your freedom of being able to do what you want. Your pleasures – I couldn't taste food anymore. And even your need for money disappears, because your future feels limited. It is as if you've lost everything," she laughs. "But at times you need to lose everything, before you can find yourself. This is when I learned what being grateful truly means, because **it is when you have nothing that you realise and see that the little, tiny, itty-bitty things are what matters**, not those big material ambitions society tells us to chase."

Bald, wearing a hospital gown and waiting for death's inviting whisper – the only thing that would make the pain go away – Nat had two profound revelations that both stirred and soothed my soul upon hearing them. The first was this: "If you want to know if something matters to you or not, imagine taking it into the hospital and asking whether it would make you feel better or not. So your successful career, bring that to the hospital, and does it make you feel better or not? Or your big house (OK maybe you can't take that), or your nice car, take that and see if it makes you smile. Because when you're lying helplessly in hospital, unable to walk, or eat, not even the most delicious food can make you better because it all tastes like shit. And if you can't walk, you can't even get to the car so that's utterly useless," she laughs. "The second message was to take it one breath at a time, live in the present and love every moment, because the future can so easily be stripped away."

"This is when I stopped wanting to be 'better' all the time. People in my profession often like to say they'll coach their clients to 'be their best selves', and I think this is something I hear a lot in general too," I interrupt to admit to Nat that I use the term quite a bit and she laughs, shaking her finger as if I was a mischievous child. "But when I laid there begging whoever was in my mind not to let me die, I guess I came to understand that just being myself was enough. There is no best self, nor worst self, just yourself. And that's what I vowed to be *if* I survived."

And there was a big if – a number of them in fact. During radiation therapy (which followed her chemotherapy) Nat suffered a horrific third degree burn (yes, in her down there region). The worst part of the whole experience was going to the toilet, a task she describes as being like pouring boiling wax on your genitals and bum. Then, on 6 December 2015, Nat's depleted immune system once again fell victim to a serious infection and she was rushed to the ICU, before spending four weeks in hospital recovering. The open wounds from her burns had likely allowed the infection in, and she was on life support drugs for three days – three more days to semi-consciously contemplate her very premature death.

While the sense of battling something as humbling and horrid as cancer was in many ways liberating, the side effects of the war were debilitating, and not just for her. "People often forget the carer, so I want to acknowledge Kim, my girlfriend, and the parallel struggle she faced to find strength to endure the pain of [most likely] losing me," says Nat. "Mum found no pleasure in my suffering either. She was far away in Jogjakarta, Indonesia and was being forced to relive a nightmare she had endured a few years earlier when my younger brother received a one in 10 million diagnosis of a condition that resulted in his nervous system shutting down (Opsoclonus Myoclonus). Don't forget, Mum had also lost my dad just nine days after being admitted to hospital with a 'non-threatening rash'. That time frame played on my mind too, and forced me to confront the very real possibility that I could well be dead tomorrow, so how am I going to fill in today?"

Her answer – was to help others. That's right. She was dying, but with what might have been her last few breaths, she decided to use her gift of a positive and resilient mind to serve those around her who were facing a similar journey. This is where Laughter with Cancer was truly born. Where it went was from a Facebook page documenting her story, to a living, breathing philosophy and movement to redefine the way we think about and engage with cancer.

"Cancer was a blessing for me. I am grateful for it, because it was a catalyst for change. A change I didn't see coming. A change that's seen me become a servant to something greater – and that's humanity," she says.

Since defeating Ewing's Sarcoma in early 2016, Nat has channeled the experience into a career defining move that has seen her become an inspirational life coach and in-demand public speaker. "Happiness is my core topic," says Nat, before adding, "you can never underestimate the transformative power of choosing happiness."

As a corporate speaker, Nat discusses the power of utilising happiness and humanity in the workplace in order to overcome destructive business norms such as burn-out, stress, anxiety and fear. As a life coach she works with clients to find happiness, meaning and purpose, while releasing them from misplaced fear and limitations.

"One of the more frightening trends that is becoming more and more common is something I call 'social media envy,'" she says. "Our newsfeeds are there all the time, showing us places we'd rather be, people we'd rather be and things we don't have," she sighs despondently. "Think about what this creates – no matter how successful you are – because everyone struggles with these questions of 'am I enough?' or 'is what I have enough?' And, it is even easier to compare yourself now, visually it is right in front of you, all the time and if you don't have the toolkits to let go of it, the comparison can really wreak havoc in your mind."

Have you ever wondered why we think this way? Why we love to compare so much? Well, it's actually a phenomenon scientist's call social comparison theory and it's an innate tendency that appears in primates. Even when we are reasonably happy with what we have, we become discontented once we compare ourselves to someone who has something better.

I heard of this experiment during a TED talk given by primatologist Frans de Waal that brilliantly lays bare the tendency of discontent. In an experiment carried out by de Waal's team, two capuchin monkeys are placed in separate cages and are taught to hand stones to a researcher outside the cage in exchange for a reward. The first monkey completes the task successfully and is rewarded with a cucumber, which the monkey relishes. When monkey number two succeeds at the same task it is rewarded with a grape, which it too relishes. The problem is, both monkeys can observe each other, and in monkey world it appears that grapes are much more highly valued than cucumbers, something the researchers knew. When they repeat the task of asking monkey number one for the rock, and offer it a cucumber in exchange, the monkey takes a small nibble of the food before it becomes agitated at seeing its friend next door still eating its grape. Monkey number one then proceeds to throw the 'not good enough' reward back at the researcher. When the second monkey is again rewarded with a grape, for performing the same task of passing a rock, the first monkey goes bananas and starts screeching and rattling the cage. On the third attempt, when the procedure is again repeated, the first monkey goes ape (pun intended) and immediately throws the cucumber back at the researcher before trying to reach outside the cage and bang on the counter where the cucumber and grapes are sitting. While de Waal didn't indicate whether the experiment went any further, I suspect if it did it ended with the monkey murdering the researcher. What this simple study illustrates rather graphically (see the video on thehappiest.com), was that by rewarding a competitor 'unfairly' you can create enormous dissatisfaction in a primate despite rewarding them with a trophy (a cucumber) which they were once happy to receive.

For the most part, there is no harm in looking at your neighbour and wishing you had his nice new roof or swimming pool – it's been the foundation of our evolution – learning from others in order to survive more easily. But, when we add social media into the mix with social comparison theory, we ultimately set ourselves up for failure on a massive scale.

A study by Science Direct (which used women and Facebook as

its control) let female participants spend 10 minutes browsing their Facebook accounts, a magazine website and an appearance-neutral control website before asking them to rate their mood, body dissatisfaction and appearance discrepancies. The results? Researchers found that Facebook usage had put the vast majority of women in a more negative mood where they began making more appearance comparisons, giving them a greater desire to change their face, hair and skin.

"How can you ever feel like you're enough when you compare your 'behind-the-scenes' with everyone else's highlight reel," says Nat, an avid Facebook user herself. "To look at all those perfectly manicured online personas and see them as anything but that – a façade, fake – will spell death for what gratitude you might naturally hold. And without gratitude, I know, I can tell you, life is an empty vessel devoid of happiness."

When we surf social media, we're not only annihilating our sense of appreciation for what we have and who we are, we're also often so busy continuously scrolling – curious about what we're missing out on and what everyone else is doing – that we're neglecting to be grateful for those things and people right in front of us, including ourselves and our life – which is happening right now – offline. How many dinners have you been at where half your mates are preoccupied with their phones? And how many times have you found your conscious-mind telling your instinctive-mind off for reaching in your pocket and filming the concert or waterfall instead of simply watching and appreciating it?

All this anxiety and ungracious self-loathing is because, like it or not, we're addicted. In fact, the University of Chicago found that social media is more addictive than cigarettes, and harder to abstain from than alcohol.

How do we manage this? What can we do to overcome the inherent negatives associated with social media? It's hard to imagine us running out onto the streets and smashing our smartphones. And we're a while away from creating a world that's good enough (and equal enough) for everybody to feel peacefully content. So what do we do? How do we create a modern mind for the modern world? "The harder things got for me, the more grateful I knew I needed to become in order to maintain my happiness," says Nat. "Because gratitude opens the door to inner peace. Knowing that you are enough, even if you have cancer. When something bad happens, we lose our job, our health and we think something is missing, we can't live, but if you have that sense of gratitude, no matter what life throws at you then you will always feel whole. I always say, 'If you can be grateful with nothing, you have everything, but if you cannot be grateful, even if you have everything, all you have is nothing.'"

Of course, when it comes to social media it can be hard to find people worse off, because it's all become a giant competition to be the best. But if you look around, real life is full of mediocrity and people suffering far more than you. "There was actually a lady who was a mother of four, Julia Watson," recalls Nat with a glint of sadness in her eyes. "She was terminal. And she gave me a lot of perspective and strength. Even in her last days she was fighting to live. She would have given anything for another few minutes, and that made me so grateful for the time I had. Because it was obvious from watching Julia and so many friends pass, that **when your time is up, that's all you want – more time.**"

Just as Nat herself was getting used to the thought that she might have a little more time, the unthinkable happened, and she was diagnosed with cancer – again! In May 2016, a year after her Ewing's Sarcoma diagnosis, doctors found a nasty melanoma on Nat's back. It was Groundhog Day. Deja vu of the worst sort, said Nat. But, as always, she found something to be grateful for. "They caught it early and said it hadn't spread, which was so fortunate. All I have now is a big scar on my back as a reminder!" While it will still be a few years before she's given the all clear from this latest, unwelcome visitor, she's not letting that slow her down.

"I live one day at a time and have managed to simplify my prerequisite for happiness – if I'm breathing, I'm happy!" she says. Nevertheless, Nat is managing to cram into each day what many people might achieve in a lifetime of hard slog. I think, probably, because she knows all too well that 'time is precious'. Since her diagnosis on 25th May 2015, Nat has made and posted a daily video blog on her Laughter with Cancer Facebook page, to inspire others to see, feel and learn from her horridly happy journey with cancer. The captivating series of more than 1000 clips is a priceless resource for those battling cancer (and for those not), and is one of a number of free offerings she's gifted to the world. Another is this: as an unashamed hugger of anyone and everyone she encounters, one day a friend of Nat's commented that if she had a dollar for every hug she handed out she would be a rich woman, indeed. Enthralled by the concept (and excuse to hug more people), Nat launched Hugs for Change and raised $5000USD to build a kitchen and classroom for the slum children of Colombia! Her ambition is to hug a million people and use the money raised to do good wherever in the world good is needed – "and isn't that everywhere?" she asks rhetorically. And I begin to understand why she regards this journey as the most fun and fruitful adventure of her life.

But the question still remains: how many others will she convince to think this way? Will she ever fulfill her mission to change the way people see cancer – to be a word devoid of crippling fear? The staggering thing is, by the age of 85, roughly one in two of us will have been diagnosed with some form of cancer in our lives. Each year, 12.7 million people discover they have cancer and 7.6 million people die from the disease. However, evidence shows that 30 – 40% of these deaths can be prevented (by a balanced diet, healthy weight, exercise and limiting alcohol intake), and one-third can be cured through early diagnosis and treatment.

What do all these numbers really mean? Well, one – if you don't have cancer you should be bloody grateful, two – if you do have cancer, you're not alone, and three – if you appreciate life then be or get healthy to give yourself the greatest chance of avoiding cancer. But if you can't evade cancer's overbearing arms, then embrace it, and get ready for one hell of a ride.

"Things will happen that you won't expect – and the world will shock you in the best of ways. For instance, when I couldn't work and my finite finances were drying up, a group of friends went on a fundraising drive to help me out, and when chemo robbed me of my hair, 10 friends shaved their heads in a show of support! It was beautiful!" My eyes welled. "Why can't we do this anyway?" I sighed. **"Why do we wait for tragedy to be grateful for our friends, family and to focus on those things that matter, like giving?"** Nat interrupted my outburst. "It's hard you know, we've become creatures of comfort, so we tend to sit back and watch until something really forces us to stand up, take stock and act."

So do we need things like cancer then? To wake us up? What would the world look like without suffering? If there was no poverty, war, disability or tsunamis? Would it be better? Would we be happier? Or would we be fat, lazy slobs, with no reason to get out of bed?

"It's tough to tell someone to be grateful for trauma and suffering – just as it is hard to ask them to be appreciative of their breath. I mean for most, breathing is something so seemingly insignificant and in the background. But I think that's where it all begins," says Nat, who I imagine standing on a podium shouting this to an audience of millions one day.

Early in January 2018 I was being 'naughty' and scrolling through my Facebook feed when I saw a post from Nat. It was one of those sad yet oh so beautiful messages that you know is going to make you cry before finishing. So that's exactly what I did. The introduction from Nat read: A powerful message to start your day. Remembering Holly (Butcher) with her moving message she left behind. This story is close to home as we battle the same cancer, Ewing Sarcoma. My deepest love and condolences for Holly's family on her recent passing.

Nat then posted Holly's last message and I reproduce Holly's words here in their entirety because … well read it and you'll know why:

A bit of life advice from Hol:

It's a strange thing to realise and accept your mortality at 26 years young. It's just one of those things you ignore. The days tick by and you just expect they will keep on coming; Until the unexpected happens. I always imagined myself growing old, wrinkled and grey- most likely caused by the beautiful family (lots of kiddies) I planned on building with the love of my life. I want that so bad it hurts.

That's the thing about life; It is fragile, precious and unpredictable and each day is a gift, not a given right.

I'm 27 now. I don't want to go. I love my life. I am happy. I owe that to my loved ones. But the control is out of my hands.

I haven't started this 'note before I die' so that death is feared – I like the fact that we are mostly ignorant to its inevitability. Except when I want to talk about it and it is treated like a 'taboo' topic that will never happen to any of us. That's been a bit tough. I just want people to stop worrying so much about the small, meaningless stresses in life and try to remember that we all have the same fate after it all so do what you can to make your time feel worthy and great, minus the bullshit.

I have dropped lots of my thoughts below as I have had a lot of time to ponder life these last few months. Of course, it's the middle of the night when these random things pop in my head most!

Those times you are whinging about ridiculous things (something I have noticed so much these past few months), just think about someone who is really facing a problem. Be grateful for your minor issue and get over it. It's OK to acknowledge that something is annoying but try not to carry on about it and negatively affect other people's days.

Once you do that, get out there and take a freaking big breath of that fresh Aussie air deep in your lungs, look at how blue the sky is and how green the trees are; It is so beautiful. Think how lucky you are to be able to do just that – breathe.

You might have got caught in bad traffic today, or had a bad sleep because your beautiful babies kept you awake, or your hairdresser cut your hair too short. Your new fake nails might have got a chip, your boobs are too small, or you have cellulite on your arse and your belly is wobbling.

Let all that shit go. I swear you will not be thinking of those things when it is your turn to go. It is all SO insignificant when you look at life as a whole. I'm watching my body waste away right before my eyes with nothing I can do about it and all I wish for now is that I could have just one more birthday or Christmas with my family, or just one more day with my partner and dog. Just one more.

I hear people complaining about how terrible work is or about how hard it is to exercise – be grateful you are physically able to. Work and exercise may seem like such trivial things ... until your body doesn't allow you to do either of them.

I tried to live a healthy life, in fact, that was probably my major passion. Appreciate your good health and functioning body – even if it isn't your ideal size. Look after it and embrace how amazing it is. Move it and nourish it with fresh food. Don't obsess over it.

Remember there are more aspects to good health than the physical body ... work just as hard on finding your mental, emotional and spiritual happiness too. That way you might realise just how insignificant and unimportant having this stupidly portrayed perfect social media body really is. While on this topic, delete any account that pops up on your news feeds that gives you any sense of feeling shit about yourself. Friend or not. Be ruthless for your own well-being.

Be grateful for each day you don't have pain and even the days where you are unwell with man flu, a sore back or a sprained ankle, accept it is shit but be thankful it isn't life threatening and will go away.

Whinge less, people! And help each other more.

Give, give, give. It is true that you gain more happiness doing things for others than doing them for yourself. I wish I did this more. Since I have been sick, I have met the most incredibly giving and kind people and been the receiver of the most thoughtful and loving words and support from my family, friends and strangers; More than I could ever give in return. I will never forget this and will be forever grateful to all of these people.

It is a weird thing having money to spend at the end. When you're dying. It's not a time you go out and buy material things that you usually would, like a new dress. It makes you think how silly it is that we think it is worth spending so much money on new clothes and 'things' in our lives.

Buy your friend something kind instead of another dress, beauty product or jewellery for that next wedding. 1. No-one cares if you wear the same thing twice 2. It feels good. Take them out for a meal, or better yet, cook them a meal. Shout their coffee. Give or buy them a plant, a massage or a candle and tell them you love them when you give it to them.

Value other people's time. Don't keep them waiting because you are shit at being on time. Get ready earlier if you are one of those people and appreciate that your friends want to share their time with you, not sit by themselves, waiting on a mate. You will gain respect too! Amen sister.

This year, our family agreed to do no presents and despite the tree looking rather sad and empty (I nearly cracked Christmas Eve!), it was so nice because people didn't have the pressure of shopping and the effort went into writing a nice card for each other. Plus imagine my family trying to buy me a present knowing they would probably end up with it themselves ... strange! It might seem lame but those cards mean more to me than any impulse purchase could. Mind you, it was also easier to do in our house because we had no little kiddies there. Anyway, moral of the story- presents are not needed for a meaningful Christmas. Moving on.

Use your money on experiences. Or at least don't miss out on experiences because you spent all your money on material shit.

Put in the effort to do that day trip to the beach you keep putting off. Dip your feet in the water and dig your toes in the sand. Wet your face with salt water.

Get amongst nature.

Try just enjoying and being in moments rather than capturing them through the screen of your phone. Life isn't meant to be lived through a screen nor is it about getting the perfect photo. Enjoy the bloody moment, people! Stop trying to capture it for everyone else.

Random rhetorical question. Are those several hours you spend doing your hair and make up each day or to go out for one night really worth it? I've never understood this about females (confused face).

Get up early sometimes and listen to the birds while you watch the beautiful colours the sun makes as it rises.

Listen to music. Really listen. Music is therapy. Old is best.

Cuddle your dog. Far out, I will miss that.

Talk to your friends. Put down your phone. Are they doing OK?

Travel if it's your desire, don't if it's not.

Work to live, don't live to work.

Seriously, do what makes your heart feel happy.

Eat the cake. Zero guilt.

Say no to things you really don't want to do.

Don't feel pressured to do what other people might think is a fulfilling life. You might want a mediocre life and that is so OK.

CANCER, CAR ACCIDENTS AND THE MOTHER WHO LOST EIGHT CHILDREN

Tell your loved ones you love them every time you get the chance and love them with everything you have.

Also, remember if something is making you miserable, you do have the power to change it – in work or love or whatever it may be. Have the guts to change. You don't know how much time you've got on this earth so don't waste it being miserable. I know that is said all the time but it couldn't be more true.

Anyway, that's just this one young gal's life advice. Take it or leave it, I don't mind!

Oh and one last thing, if you can, do a good deed for humanity (and myself) and start regularly donating blood. It will make you feel good with the added bonus of saving lives. I feel like it is something that is so overlooked considering every donation can save 3 lives! That is a massive impact each person can have and the process really is so simple.

Blood donation (more bags than I could keep up with counting) helped keep me alive for an extra year – a year I will be forever grateful that I got to spend it here on earth with my family, friends and dog. A year I had some of the greatest times of my life.

'Til we meet again.

Hol xoxo

I never met or even knew of Holly, but the honesty and vulnerability of her message resonated with me. So thank you Holly and farewell, I hope you know that your final words were not wasted.

Before you race out and take up smoking in the hope of getting cancer, I guess I'd better inform you that trauma and adversity aren't the only paths to deep gratitude and the happiness it yields. Those of us who can harness the stories you've just read, and who can use those lessons housed within them to stimulate and reinforce the gratitude pathways in our mind, will also come to know the intense bliss of appreciation. From Tom, Nat and Sam Ath, to the mothers of Sri Lanka and the boy with one leg, what these people did for me was show me that our happiest state comes from being present, appreciating every moment, not sweating the small stuff, seeing that there are others suffering too (often worse) and understanding that what you have and who you are is enough. So **stop thinking that you need to do it all and be it all**. Start by switching off from social media (even just a little), and when you are logged in remember that those posts in front of you are somebody's highlights reel – not their 24/7 reality! As Nat's friend Julia Watson pleaded: "Do this for me. Find what makes you shine (and you probably already know what it is), and start making steps towards it. They can just be baby steps, but make them. Plant the seed. DO IT NOW. You don't need perspective the way I got it – and believe me, you don't want it. Do it while you still have all the innocence of someone who has a lot of years in front of you. Because, by the law of averages, some of you haven't – you just don't know it yet … I've got a hunger. Haven't you? Don't die with your light inside you."

Sitting in a local cafe for some time wondering how to end this chapter I felt a buzz in my pocket. It was a dear (but new) friend I had filmed as part of my paid work* emailing me to invite me to his wife's funeral (I couldn't stop crying, tears literally fell onto the keyboard as I typed this very line). What's my point, you ask? I think when all is said and done; gratitude should be a daily ritual, because we're all dying.

*Their story can be seen in Chapter 11.

From a foundation of gratitude,

rise the hands of the giver.

5

MY GRAN AND THE RICKSHAW DRIVER

Journal entry 25.12.12, in Sri Lanka: In the dark of night, I do not worry about those I cannot see, but those I can. The homeless here are plenty. Sleeping rough in doorways and stairwells that line one of Colombo's busiest streets – Galle Road.

And they're just the ones I've laid eyes on.

But we can't let them lay eyes on us if we are to succeed in our mission.

A rare streetlight threatens to give us (Sash and I) away. We duck behind a parked car. Anonymity is crucial. We see our first 'recipient' in the distance. He's surrounded by several more. We are two people armed with an idea and the tools we need to execute it.

We carefully creep up beside a young, scraggly, gaunt homeless man who lies on an old cardboard box that barely covers the length of his short body. His clothing is stained, torn and smells of fecal matter. His pillow, perhaps ironically is an empty bottle of booze. Was this a sign? Was he an alcoholic? Should that matter? My wife quietly places a package by his side.

We repeat this process a dozen or so times, making sure we're neither seen nor heard by our recipients.

Then we approach our final recipient – a family of four we've passed by and spoken to a number of times. The mother, father and their two boys (who you can read more about in chapter 11) sleep at the end of Sash's Grandpa's street (Rohini Road) outside a local tailor which is about 30 metres from Galle Road. In the dead of night we snigger a little as the father's snoring echoes through the still quiet street. I place our final parcel beside the mother, who cuddles her two children tightly to her chest.

We'd done it. What a rush! More than 20 people — most of whom, unremarkably, feel shunned and forgotten by society — will wake up tomorrow to find a package containing food, sanitary goods and toys (for those with kids). The best thing is they'll have no idea who's done it. It's especially important that they don't feel it's just another rich white guy (or poor white guy as the case may be). The anonymity means everyone and everything will (hopefully) look that much brighter, even if only for a minute or a day — because clearly someone loves and cares for them.

As we wandered home the hint of peace (as if this is how the world is meant to be and feel) overcame me, and I cried, for two reasons I think. One: I'd found my calling (my happiest state) — giving — and it had set me free. My pain and worries largely disappeared in my pursuit of helping others to solve some of their problems. And, two: Twenty people (the number we helped) was a drop in the ocean — and our little bit of love wasn't a long term solution to their needless misery. How could there still be such disparity in this world? What more could I do? I'd literally given my last cent to the man who'd been shot in the spine (from chapter 3), so I was stuck. Helplessly unable to help the helpless. But why was the world so cruel? How come god hadn't made me rich? Was it my unwillingness to exploit people — like most wealthy folk? Or my inability to horde money while others suffered — again, a common trait of the super rich? Either way, I was poor and confused — a strange mix. I guess the sea of emotion had swept me onto the rocks, where I was being pounded by feelings of elation and frustration. Generally all at once.

This was the first time I'd ever experienced the joy of undertaking what I call 'Selfless Santa' — an activity I've come to relish whenever I have the chance (though I must come up with a better name). The person that taught me to look to such acts for a sense of arcane joy was not the richest, nor most devout or righteous woman I've known. In fact, she was probably more likely to be seen or heard erupting into raucous laughter at the latest neighbourhood gossip or sex scandal than she was to be reciting a psalm. All her mischievous revelling aside though, this woman was a saint. She was the most ordinary superhuman — god-like and kind, but entirely self-effacing. There is no shrine that celebrates her life — just a gravestone — and yet this woman reshaped hearts at a rate attune to a prophet. How do I know all this you may be wondering? This woman was my Gran – Moreen Malcolm Trevena Irvin.

The Old Owl

Gran was, and remains, the most generous person I've met. She was also one of the wisest too. That's why we'd call her 'Grannikens the Old Owl'. Well one of the reasons at least: she also had a pointy nose and ears, wide flat cheeks and a box shaped face, which was quite owl-like; and then of course there was her colossal collection of owl statues and ornaments hidden throughout her house, which, at last count (in 1998) totaled 324.

When I interviewed Gran in October 2013, (unknowingly) just five months before her fairly unexpected death, she laughed at the notion that her story might be called 'The Old Owl'.

"Oh, 'The Old Owl!'" she scoffed with a grin. "Well I guess that's me. But I've lost a lot of me feathers! I know when I'm having a shower in the morning, I've lost a lot of my feathers," she hoots wildly, throwing back her arms, as her false teeth just about fall from her mouth because she's laughing so much. Yep, that's my Gran – no muzzle and giving whatever she can to make people happy – even if it is a dirty joke.

What I didn't know about Gran, and failed to realise until this quite formal discussion, was a lot. I knew that she'd suffered dearly for much of her life, and I'd seen her remarkable transformation into this cheery old lady who became a role model of kindness, crudeness (in humour) and giving in our family. But I was oblivious to where it had all come from – her motivation to change – and where she had come from in those earliest of years. Those were things, together with so much else I was about to find out.

Born on 8 November 1926, Gran was a child of the Great Depression. She grew up penniless and in perilous circumstances that were tough on everyone. Let alone a young girl (pre-women's rights). The other defining characteristic of Gran's early years (because things could have turned out very differently otherwise) is that she was given up for adoption at just six-weeks-old by her unmarried mother Florence 'Flo' LeRay. At the time single mothers were deemed 'immoral' and their children as 'a drain on resources'. This archaic belief saw thousands of children throughout the 19th and early 20th century forcibly removed from their mothers at birth. Unaware of any of this for some years – her adoption, or that it was part of a systemic plot against 'un-holy' single mums – Gran said she simply revelled in the blessing of having parents who loved her in the way Bert and Rita Trevena did.

"Like everyone in those days, I grew up with nothing. But I used to look at mum and dad and think they were just wonderful. I was so blessed [she pauses for some time]. Perhaps you don't understand that, [she pauses again] about truly blessed," she sits there silently, before chuckling softly under her breath. "Funny."

Gran says her parents were known as "good Christian people," she laughs to herself, before explaining that the term "bad Christian people" never seemed to be used for the naughty followers she met at Sunday school every week. "I guess God is good was the mantra," she laughs, before pausing in silence and taking a breath. "To me my parents were good people – full stop! They were just lovely. I loved them to bits. There wasn't a bad bone between them," she sighs, clearly bemoaning so many years without them. "We laughed a lot, some nights we never stopped. We used to sit around the table, dad would wag his leg after he'd had a couple of drinks [Gran shakes her leg riotously, mimicking her dad] and mum would sing along as she stood by the stove. Oooooooh [she moans] they were just delightful."

And they were generous too.

During the great depression, Gran's father ran three or four cows, and did a milk round that meant waking up at 2am every day to ensure his family could eat. This also included Gran's grandmother (Rita's mum) who lived with them, because Bert was the only reliable earner in the family (remembering that unemployment in Australia hovered between 25 and 30% for much of the early 1930s).

Typifying the generosity of Gran's father was the story of how he sold his first house. Living in a tiny one-bedroom place in Payneham (an Adelaide suburb), Bert and Rita knew they needed a bigger home in order for their adoption bid to move forward. So despite the looming economic crisis, Bert made a handshake deal with a friend for him to buy their Payneham house (for 135 pounds), and let him pay it back slowly over time (like a mortgage, but without the legal contract or guarantee).

"Dad was never a greedy man, and he was a trusting man, which is needed if you are to be generous. You can't think lowly of others;

Gran's six kids. (Left to right) Steve, mum, baby Leigh, Jason, David and Matt.

Mum, Gran and me on the day of Gran's 80th birthday.

Gran around the time of her wedding.

Gran and Poppa's wedding day.

Gran as a child with her adopted mum and dad (below).

Gran laughing with one of her best friends, Sheila Anderson, who was one of my fondest mentors as a teenager.

Gran cracking up during our interview for this book.

Gran and 'the ladies' at the Thrift Shop I used to help at.

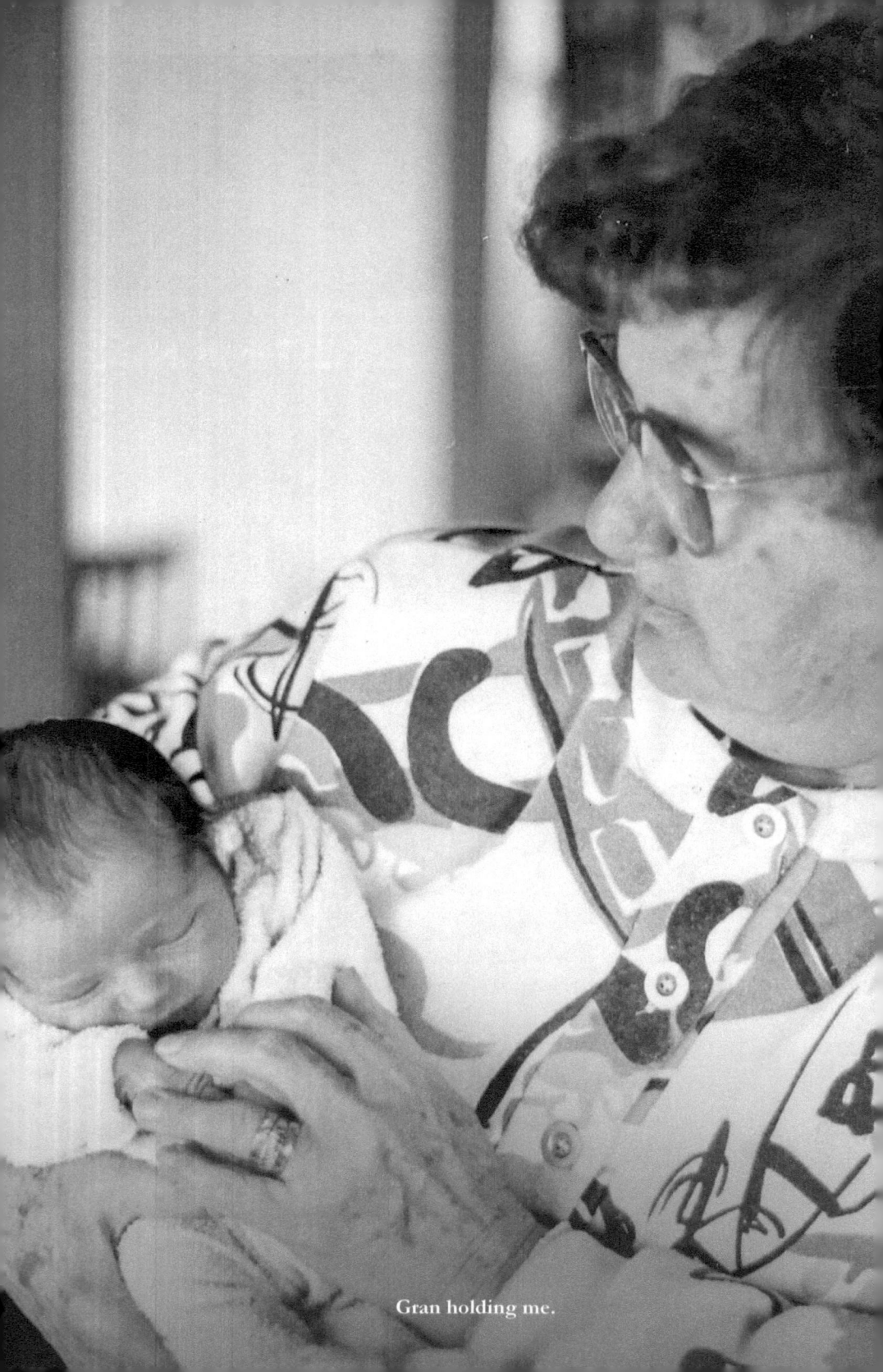
Gran holding me.

you must see them as you see yourself. Only then might we give truly, without guilt or selfish undertones," said Gran, before continuing. "And that friend, Uncle Elvidge, he walked to our home in Glen Osmond [about five kilometres] every week to pay the mortgage and hand dad the money. It was such a joy for dad to see him so often and to know he was helping a friend. And in return, he was a blessed man, dad was. Much loved and admired – not just by me."

Without these regular payments from her uncle, Gran's parents would have defaulted on their own mortgage, and this is where the real degree of generosity came to bear. Money is one thing. But to have a generous nature. To see giving as a noble endeavor – that is something altogether different.

"My family said there were the *givingtons* and the *grabingtons*," recalls Gran, who admits to seeing plenty of both during those financially scarce years.

When Gran finally found out she was adopted at the age of 16, the news nearly broke her (and her parents). Who, what, when, why, she wondered, as the fear of having an unknown black hole within her life took hold. Frantic for answers, Gran began the hunt, praying that her birth mother was out there somewhere, alive and well. As it turns out, she was. But the fairy-tale didn't quite play out as she'd imagined. My own mum (who met Gran's biological mum a number of times) described her as a dirty old fat slob who was mean, uneducated and had a chin covered with whiskers. Needless to say, Gran's anxiety died down immediately after their reunion. The thought of being anything but adopted suddenly made Gran quiver. As an ironic aside, Gran's birth Mum actually ended up adopting two children; after she and the man she married found out they were sterile.

Fortunately (or unfortunately, Gran might laugh) she and her husband, Roy Tapscott Irvin (my Poppa), certainly didn't suffer the same fate. Marrying in 1947, their first handful of years of wedded life bore two children (first my uncle Jason in 1949, then my mum in 1952). It was around this same time that Gran's life took a nosedive, as her mum died abruptly of what could only be described as 'grief'. When Gran's Auntie Ruby (her mum's dearest sister) was diagnosed with cancer, she drank a bottle of turps and killed herself. Hearing the news, but being unable to attend her sister's funeral (due to a peculiar communication problem between family members), Gran's mum Rita was left in emotional ruin and died shortly after. Besieged by the loss of his beloved wife, Gran's father then contracted bowel cancer. After a long and tiresome battle with the beast, Gran's treasured role model and rock was gone. Bert's death occurred just weeks after Gran gave birth to her third child, my uncle David, on 10 December 1955.

Life had taken a sad turn. Gran described it as a "hollow" period. But for a moment, some years at least, there was calm. Well, sort of. I guess calm is a relative term. And in relative terms it was about to be demolished, with the birth of three more boys: Matt (in 1958) who was born deprived of oxygen and suffering a mild form of brain damage as a result; then Steve (in 1960) who had a severe kidney disease; and finally Leigh (in 1964) who literally screamed all night, from the moment he was put to sleep, until the moment he was held again. Life was horrid. "We would have done anything for calm. It was a nightmare," said my mum, who sat in on my interview with Gran, and chimed in from time to time to fill in any blanks. "I don't know how she coped," my mum continued. "Your Gran juggled constant dysfunction and turmoil [mum pauses], I couldn't imagine being her." But Gran was never one to complain. In fact, when I asked her what's made her life interesting, she responded with "the fact that I had six children and I didn't even try. They just popped out." When I tried to fish for a more serious answer, asking her to describe the impact of having kids on her life, she responded as only Gran could. "The impact… hmmmm… well my feet didn't touch the ground half the time," she hoots once more, referring to … well I'll leave you to think about that.

As a highly skilled carpenter (and brilliant baker on the side), my Poppa was quite the catch, except for one sad but simple truth that slowly became more and more evident to my Gran. "He just had no concept of what a woman liked or needed," she sighs. "But neither did a lot of men back then. They just wanted to own you. Silly fools [she laughs]. I guess that's one thing that has changed probably in the last 60 or 70 years – you don't tell a woman what to do today! Just look at your mum," says Gran, who gazes in my mum's direction trying to incite a reaction. In spite of his flaws (and chauvinistic social norms), Poppa was a good man says Gran. "Silly old Billy he was. But I loved him. Whatever love is, I loved him. Nobody else."

Despite the callous emotional abuse (mostly when he was drunk) and the very odd case of sexual abuse (driven by the belief that he owned her), Poppa's misguided heart never stemmed Gran's love. Not for him. Not for her children. Not for anyone. It's why her most touching response (in my opinion) was her answer to the question: How do you still have so much love for everyone?

"Why shouldn't I?" She paused for some moments. "That's what I can give. It's all I could give at times," she says, with an inflection befitting of her (irrationally) low sense of self worth. "So that's what I did." Admittedly, Gran's life isn't one you'd choose from a line-up, but when the jokes stopped (mostly) and the veil was lifted, out came a wisdom only hardship can birth.

"Living in a time where there wasn't much money, you never had it, people never had stuff. There was no higher purchase [credit]. Higher purchase came in much later, so my parents had nothing unless they paid cash for it. That was it!"

It may seem impossible to imagine a world without credit. But **what are the repercussions of all that debt?** Has putting everything on plastic made us less generous? Can we even afford to give when the average credit card debt per person in Australia is $3300USD, while in America it is around $5800USD? The funny thing is, in Australia this only accounts for 1.9% of our household debt. The total sum that we Aussies owe the banks is $2,000,000,000,000 (two trillion dollars), which equates to roughly $250,000 per household, $20,000 of which is considered 'bad debt' (the type that can't make you money, so anything that's not a home loan or investment). In the US, total household debt rose to an all-time high of $13.15 trillion at year-end 2017, according to the Federal Reserve Bank.

When I told my Gran a few of these facts and figures, she shook her head. "Bad debt… that makes it sound like there is good debt," she hoots aloud, "haha," before looking up in disbelief.

You might call her old-school or think her out of touch, but if you consider the harm that debt puts us in – it traps us in careers we don't like, it is one of the leading causes of divorce and has been linked to anxiety, depression, high blood pressure and lowering your immune system – my Gran might just have a point. If nothing else, what her story is, is a timely reminder that not so long ago, being in debt wasn't normal and owning a credit card wasn't a necessity of life. What! Why? I hear you screaming. How did people get the things they wanted? The simple answer is, they didn't. Instead – and I know this might sound strange to those growing up in a time and land of plenty – but they lived with less.

"What did that teach folks back in those days about life?" I asked.

"Restraint. Yeah. Not to live beyond their means," she nods, before pausing thoughtfully. "Because so many people today live beyond their means. It's why people can't be happy. Because they are not free. Back when we were kids, you never had any sort of debt, people couldn't afford it, because there's always a bit of interest. That little bit of interest. And what does the interest do? Just adds and adds to the bills," says Gran, as she moves her fingers higher and higher as if building a castle. While Gran's generation wasn't exactly free – because they had no money and a distinct lack of opportunity – she says there are no excuses today. **"There is no reason not to spend time with friends and family, not to travel, not to be yourself, not to give,"** she says, alluding to all the things that made her profusely happy in her later years.

"There is enough today. People have enough. But I think youngsters are very greedy. They lock themselves into debt, and throw away the key. It's like a prison, they can't escape it. And they wonder why they're not happy [she rolls her eyes]."

Now, Gran's not one to say that we don't need money to be happy, quite the opposite. In fact, her own joy for life only came to pass when she was let off of Poppa's financial leash. When she was "no longer in debt to the man of the house," she chuckles, imitating a deep manly voice. Gran's first and only paid job was at the War Veterans Home in Myrtle Bank. She'd always held a strong affinity for those who served, as she had cousins and friends go off to war. "The only thing that saved your Poppa from serving was actually poor eyesight," she says. "Instead he helped to build warplanes at Parafield Airport."

Gran's job at the War Vet's Home was essentially as a waitress. A loud and chirpy people-lover who was so generous in giving herself to others, I could just imagine her running around the dining room setting tables, and giving an extra scooping of dessert to the men who were doing it extra-tough. Mum said Gran would often come home talking about the old boys who couldn't walk, as they were her favourite, because they gave her an excuse to get out from behind the counter (where the able bodied men came to be served) and have a chin wag with the fellas.

"I just loved it. The work. The women. The chatter. The old soldier boys. And I was rich! I got 9 pounds a week. 'Woopidoo' I thought."

MY GRAN AND THE RICKSHAW DRIVER

Gran's first paycheck came in May of 1971, and unsurprisingly, she spent it on buying the baby furniture my mum so desperately needed for my eldest sister Cin, who was born on 5 June. While she didn't earn much, this was the first time in her entire life (as a 45-year-old) that she held money in her hands that was hers, and wow did she know how to use it! Gran immediately opened a secret bank account that was to be used to do all those things she'd only ever dreamed of, like supporting and (when she could afford to) spoiling her growing nest of grandkids in a way she could never do for her own children. There were always a few lollies, biscuits and red Split ice creams (yum!) for us at the weekly Sunday roasts she and Poppa held. Though my favourite treat was always Gran's pan-fried cheese sandwiches. Yes, the taste was superb, but it wasn't the food that made me smile (and kept me coming back for more), it was the joy with which she cooked it – with which she gave it, and us, her all. She'd start by slowly lathering the bread in butter and placing the cheese and gherkins inside, before her customary throw of the sandwich into a blisteringly hot pan, so it would sizzle and smoke. Tossing the sandwich up and down in the pan – making sure sparks flew from the gas stove. She'd then beat and bash the bread with a spatula – because that was what made it good! – before giving it one or two final flips and cutting it into quarters. It probably only cost her 30 cents to make one, but each and every experience was priceless, and I loved nothing more than rollerblading to her house after school for 'the usual'.

Another of Gran's treasured traits that she passed down the line was her ability to sacrifice today for a better tomorrow. She was never one to concern herself too much with the future – she knew happiness didn't exist there – but Gran would often do this thing where she'd grow these little gems of goodness, so that in the years to come, the whole world would sparkle. For instance, when each of her six grandchildren were born (I was the youngest), Gran opened up a bank account and would deposit $2 a week in them (a good bit of money back then). The idea was that we couldn't access the account until we were 18, at which time that $2 here and there had grown to a few thousand, and could support us in whatever dream it was we were chasing at the time. And that was the most selfless part – she never told us how to spend the money she gave us. There were no strings. No judgment. Just love. Because that's why she gave – she loved us – purely and unconditionally. To give for any other reason, she would say, "was pointless", it was "empty."

What fascinated me most about Gran's meticulous savings habits – a task she undertook for us all – was that it was never driven by a desire to rid us of the economic troubles she had faced (she knew too well the benefits of such adversity), she did it simply because she was a givington – and nothing made her happier. She also loathed the evil that was born from the grabingtons of the world. And that's how she saw things – how she viewed people – if you gave more than you got then she was a fan, if you didn't… well… she'd politely dislike you.

She might sound ruthless, but to Gran there was no excuse not to be generous, because to her, **giving was not a financial transaction, but a personal one** – being generous of herself, her time and her money was, she knew, what transformed lives. Even as a child Gran understood this, because her parents proved it to her every day. And now it was her turn.

From her weekly $2 donation, to buying us board games, books, computers and cars, Gran's financial and material gifts were just a small part of her cherished legacy. The other, more revered side of her generosity, was her ability to feed the spirit of those she cared for, by humbly crafting scenarios that might make a person more whole. For instance, when I was about 7, Gran went out of her way to let me visit her at work in the War Veteran's Home, where I got to meet and hear stories from the old diggers. Albeit, most of the words probably drifted over my head because I was a child, but still it made me feel special – as if I was part of another world. When she retired from the War Vet's and took up a position volunteering at the Julia Farr Centre Thrift Shop (close to my school), there was one day of the week I looked forward to more than any other – Tuesdays. I'd run, cycle or skate the 500 or so metres from school down to the thrift shop, where I'd demand to be put to work by Gran. She'd promptly have me marking prices, counting stock or tidying the store, before I'd look over her shoulder as she counted the sales for the day at 4pm sharp. If she hit a certain mark (normally $300) I'd get to take home one thing I wanted from the store. More often than not – even if the day's sales didn't hit the mark – she'd throw in the money for the little toy or knick-knack I wanted. Oh how I miss those days! The funny thing is, I couldn't tell you one thing she ever bought me from the thrift shop, but I can vividly remember her stories, the sound she and her friends made as they laughed and gossiped, and of course, the huge thrill they all got from giving back to the Julia Farr Centre, which was a 'home for the incurables' – or in slightly more politically correct terms – a hospital and accommodation for people living with acutely debilitating conditions.

When my nanna (Poppa's mum) died in March 1995, she left half of her estate ($45,000) to my Poppa. When he too died later that year in August (after a tiresome battle with throat cancer), Gran subsequently inherited the $45,000. Coupled with the fact that she was still living in the house she grew up in with Bert and Rita (which was now worth a pretty penny), Gran's generosity became even more frenetic as she metamorphosed into the woman she was born to be – Mrs Givington.

The thing I was probably too young to comprehend or appreciate during this awakening of sorts, was that Gran rarely splashed out on herself. From a cruise on the QE2 – where she paid for her best friend to come with her, to buying Bek a car and lending me the money to buy my first laptop (without which it's unlikely I would be the filmmaker or writer I am today), Gran's ability to see beyond the self was and remained at the centre of her happiness. When her youngest son (my uncle Leigh) died in a freak mining accident in 1999, where a one-tonne rock fell on him as he walked through the mine next to a colleague, Gran inherited a further $200,000. Immediately and without a single thought of 'me' or 'I', she gave $20,000 to each of her five remaining children, keeping just half to redistribute as and when she wished – which of course was widely and often.

One of the fondest and proudest contributions Gran made, I know, was taking on my sister Bek during her darkest days. Living in Gran's front room (in 1997, when she wasn't attending school) and then again in a caravan in Gran's backyard when she returned to complete year 11 and 12 at an adult re-entry college, Bek says that Gran's magic was not in any one thing she did, but rather in her whole spiritual undercurrent. "She was the fulfillment of all I had come to read and know of pure love – the love we all want. Free from strings, judgment, or any sense of expectation. Gran took me and encased me in a love so rich and dependable. She'd rarely enter into deep conversations about philosophical idealism, which is what I spent a lot of time thinking about, but she didn't need to, because she was living it. I was never hungry, cold, alone or without a hug. She would pick me up from my late classes [that finished at 9pm] and drive me home without even a whisper of it being a chore. Most of the time she'd even insist on stopping to get me a beer, which I'd drink as we sat in her kitchen, usually watching the late night movie on SBS. Gran didn't give – she *was* giving. She was it. The definition. The embodiment. Her entire being was orientated towards others. She was the crystallization of that sort of suffering and pressure that forms diamonds. She was the most ordinary superhuman, a heavenly commoner. The type of person you as a writer and I as a musician write about because she was ancient wisdom incarnate."

In 2005 Gran was pushed into selling the family home she'd lived in for 79 years by my financially focused uncle who felt she would be 'better off' downsizing her home and reinvesting her assets elsewhere. Just to fill in a bit of the detail – uncle David (mum's only reliable brother) undoubtedly believed this decision was in the best interest of my Gran (who he loved dearly) for two reasons: one, her house had become too big and old to manage easily; and two, she lived a long way from him, which was an issue given he was her primary carer and she wasn't getting any younger. Subdividing and selling her enormous property in Fullarton (a wealthy suburb) and moving her into a smaller newer home around the corner from him (in suburb where house prices were on the rise), I remember feeling as though something was a bit off. Gran loved where she lived – all her friends (79 years of them) were just minutes away and this move isolated her from all of them (as her new residence was across the other side of the city). I love my uncle sincerely (and he's become a generous man in recent times, volunteering in an elephant orphanage in Thailand and supporting his children and grandchildren, just as Gran did), so it is tough to write this (because he has changed a lot since this) but at the time I remember thinking "you bastard, she doesn't care about making money, she's 79 and just wants to be close to her friends."

Lonely, but with a sea of cash to her name (around $300,000), the time Gran might have spent with friends soon became occupied by helping others. It could be anyone – family, friends, strangers, her cat Muffy – it didn't matter, it was like a gambling addiction, only in reverse. She'd bet on the fact that giving you that money or assistance would make you happy, and if it did, she'd get the greatest return of all – happiness. Her success rate must have been at least 95%. Largely, I think, because she wouldn't give blindly. She knew that money couldn't change a person's heart – that if a person had bad intentions, giving them money would wind up with that money being used for bad – so she was careful... well, sort of. I think her most common phrase was still "why not."

I remember asking for that computer (which my parents said they couldn't afford), and when I told her how much I needed it and what it would mean to me, she said "why not, the money is just sitting there, so if you need it you just tell me, and you can have it." I wasn't one to take advantage, so I borrowed the money as a loan and had paid more than half of it back when she told me "that's enough." If only she knew how much that meant to me (my eyes still get cloudy thinking about it).

But my family and I weren't the only ones that benefited from Gran's generosity. For the best part of a decade she volunteered at the Royal Adelaide Hospital as a beloved Lavender Lady – helping to keep lonely patients who didn't have any visitors company, as well as doing laundry and assisting with the needs of palliative care patients. It was actually while volunteering in this role that Gran contracted a horrid case of the shingles (a painful blistery rash), which right up until she died, plagued her dreadfully. Even still, there were no regrets, no complaints, no wishing she hadn't given her time to the hospital. Because if Gran had to suffer in order to take away another's pain, she would. Because that's who she was.

A givington.

And that's why she was happy.

Becoming a givington

As Anne Frank famously wrote in her diary "no one has ever become poor by giving", for it is in enriching the lives of others that we ourselves become wealthy. This is because true wealth is not acquired through worldly possessions, but by leading a fulfilling life. And there is – according to science and the laws of being human – nothing more fulfilling than knowing you have made a palpable difference in the lives of other people. It's lucky I guess – because chances are **without the givingtons, we'd all be dead**.

Empathy and generosity are the two primary drivers that have allowed our inherently social species to survive and thrive. Without this instinctive quality telling us to take care of one another by sharing resources, love and knowledge, we would've gone extinct a long time ago. Generosity is therefore, in part, a survival instinct.

But there's a little more to it than that too.

Giving doesn't just ensure life; it makes it worthwhile. As Winston Churchill aptly stated: "We make a living by what we get. We make a life by what we give." Indeed, it is through giving that we provide connection and meaning to both our own lives and the lives of others. That's why it makes us so goddamn happy!

Think about it. When was the last time that squandering your cash on more material 'stuff' actually filled that deep-seated emotional void? I mean, what would make you happier – buying a pair of hideously expensive shoes, or seeing the look of surprise, elation or gratitude when you treat a friend or stranger to something they've longed to do? Would you feel better buying a tub of ice-cream and devouring it alone or sharing it with others? Alone right!? Then you get it all. But seriously (my ice-cream addiction aside), if we want to be a happier species, we all need to start by overcoming the 'me me me' of social media and the 'more more more' of TV advertising, and then, trust in what science is telling us about all the shit that's going on inside of you.

The problem with this, as I see it, is twofold: one, scientists are inherently boring, uncool and love jargon; and two, when David Beckham tells us to buy H&M clothing (and he looks so happy doing it) or when Oprah tweets about buying a Microsoft Surface (and who doesn't want to be like Oprah), all logic and reason disappear, and we see those material things as an emotional decision. Maybe a new pair of jeans *will* make me happier, we think. But of course, in the long term they don't. And we're back at square one – searching for an excuse, a reason, not to do that awkward and confronting thing of looking inside ourselves for the solution. The tough thing is, we crave an instant fix for our woes, and hate to take on that huge responsibility for feeling like crap. How could it be my fault? We think. I'm doing everything society asks of me – I'm even wearing H&M, but why don't I look as happy or hot as Beckham does in that ad? Well, unfortunately this modern, materialistic, egocentric, pop-culture society is actually the heart of the problem. So you're going to need to stop, rethink and reset – turn yourself off and on again. This may take time, sometimes a lot of time. But it will be worth it. Freeing ourselves from this inherently selfish wants-based society, and surrendering to the overwhelming science of it all, will make you happier.

In fact, in recent times, research has shown us – irrefutably – that giving makes us far happier than receiving. Thus, in a way, we are actually being both selfish and selfless by giving to others. Numerous studies have shown that giving money to others or to charity is one of the best ways to boost your emotional and physical health, because it is guaranteed to make you happier, instantly.

Michael Norton, a professor at Harvard Business School, conducted one such study. Along with his colleagues, Norton questioned 632 Americans about their level of income and what they spent their money on. They were also asked to rate their own happiness. Norton and his colleagues found that, regardless of income, those who spent money on others were decidedly happier than those who spent more on just themselves.

But it's not just financial generosity that gets our happy hormones pumping; the same chemicals are also present when we give ourselves and our time to others. New research by sociologists Christian Smith and Hilary Davidson as part of their *'Science of Generosity Initiative'* actually shows that Americans who describe themselves as 'very happy' volunteer an average of 5.8 hours per month, while those who are 'unhappy' give just 0.6 hours.

While the catalysts that drive us to give are many and complex, according to Paul Zak, a professor at Claremont Graduate University, the 'moral molecule' that makes us generous, is clear. The neuroactive hormone Oxytocin has long been associated with empathy, trust and an ability to connect socially. To me, the fact that we've got this hormone charging through us and connecting us to the emotional needs of others, is yet another indication that generosity is part of our DNA. Certainly it must be a major element of any happy human genome. The embodiment of this idea is something I found in the most unlikely of places... The most unlikely of people. A lady aptly named Happy, who was dirt poor, but created infinite riches for those in need.

Guerrilla giving

High up in the mountains of Uganda, my chin felt as if it were dragging in the stiff gravel as I ambled along the side of a precarious, winding road, ogling at the sheer miracle of this planet. 'Wow! Just WOW!!!' I thought. But then, all of a sudden my eyes re-focussed, and a horrific numbness grew. As I looked out through the endless valleys in the distance, you couldn't mistake the signs of civilisation's most shocking war – our one-sided war upon nature. The beautiful patterns formed by terraced fields of maize, beans and cassava stood like soldiers in military formation. Waiting nervously in front of their sophisticated might was a towering wall of untamed organisms that was the jungle – an entity that takes our garbage – carbon dioxide – and turns it into the essential ingredient for life – oxygen. Despite this though, our war on nature (driven largely by greed) is butchering Uganda's forests (and many others), at an average rate of 3.3% per year since 1990. (Globally, there's around 7 billion trees cut down annually.)

Having meandered along on foot for some time, soaking in and capturing the front lines of this war, Sash and I – exhausted by what we'd seen – jumped back in our waiting car for the final stint of the journey. Crossing into the dark and obscure world of Bwindi Impenetrable Forest – home to half the world's population of critically endangered mountain gorillas – there was no mistaking Mother Nature's generosity in my eyes. From the trees full of monkeys laughing and playing together, to the stunning flowers and cool dense air pouring from the moist wet trees, nature's gifts were abundantly clear. And are capable of being an unbridled source of happiness. Don't get me wrong, nature takes too. The difference is that it does so in balance. Human beings on the other hand... well... we seem to have forgotten that when we take without giving (or replacing), we end up with missing pieces – holes or gaps – either within our world, ourselves or those from whom we pillage.

Someone trying to mend a few of these holes, was Happy, who worked as a Sherpa carrying bags for tourists during their gorilla trekking (the activity Sash and I were there to do). The odd thing was, we didn't find her on our trek, or in the forest, but rather when we stopped at a local shop and asked two beautifully, bubbly ladies 'who in their village we should talk to about happiness'.

The women quickly called over their friend who took us to the other side of the tiny mountaintop town – close to where we were staying – to a few buildings crowded with kids. Curious, at who we were and why we were making funny faces at them, the children began emerging from what seemed like every crack, crevice and corner of the tiny hut (see photos). Some made faces back, while others laughed and a few brave souls came to say hello. Then, all of a sudden everyone froze and looked up the path we'd just descended. It was Happy, and as her name suggested, she had a giant smile ear-to-ear, beaming with a raw, high spirited form of love. She felt warm and we hadn't even touched. Her dreadlocks and casual clothes gave her a candid charm, while the response from the kids told you everything you needed to know about her.

"Two years ago we were seeing a lot of children losing their parents to HIV Aids," said Happy, during an interview we conducted the following day. "Most of these children were staying in the villages with their grandparents, but of course some of those grand-guardians were dying too [of old-age], so I decided to collect all of those children who'd lost everything and give them a place to call home. You know, somewhere to belong, to come together, to get an education and to become a good human being, filled with love."

Previously, nearly all of these children (there were around 140 in her care when we met) were lying, cheating and stealing to survive – damaging crops and causing unrest in the community as they ran amok. But Happy's dream wasn't just to help house, feed and educate orphans, she also wanted to assist disabled children to find a way to do something more than merely survive.

"At least they are now changed – the orphans and the disabled children who have come to us – because our love for them has allowed them to develop a heart of also liking themselves. This is the biggest transformation we hope for. It is more important than the education or shelter we can give them, because if you can love yourself, you will be happy," she explains.

The thing you need to realise about Happy is, she was poor, dirt poor. She had no reason at all to be so generous. She'd been mostly self-educated, lugged people's bags for a living, and lived so far from the spotlight it wasn't funny. But in her meekness she found everything. Purpose. Meaning. Her happiest state.

"To me, it's important to give even if you don't have. Because if you share the little you have with your friends and your family, you will make them happy. And that will make you happy," she says. "Or if you give to people that don't have, and you share your love, knowledge or experiences with that person, you will be satisfied. Fulfilled, you know."

"I smile everyday, because I am just happy to still be alive and looking after my fellow orphans, although I cannot give all of them so much clothing or a good place to sleep, I'm trying my very best to see that they can be happy, as I am."

While Happy isn't what we in the West would term an orphan – her dad passed away some years ago, but her mum is still alive – she clearly feels an affinity with those who've lost something significant, and hopes her love can fill those gaps they're left with. What's difficult to comprehend about Happy's attitude, and what cannot be overstated, is that she literally comes from nothing. She is the absolute epitome of a village girl. Humble and unremarkable. But that's also what makes her so extraordinary.

"I've grown up here. I was born here and have been in this village all my 30 years, so I know everybody around, and in our family there are seven children and my father had two wives, but still, even though we lived in poverty, my parents had a heart for helping. When we were little, actually one of our rooms in that tiny house was for those orphans from the streets to stay with us," says Happy. "But this is why I know I am one of the lucky ones who must give back, because I had a home, some clothes, some schooling. Those orphans we cared for had nothing. And still I have no money, not much stuff, but I think God is now using me, so I am a lucky lady, to help these orphans to become somebody in the future. A teacher. A doctor. You never know, because love can transform people – our school motto is actually 'Let Love Change Me' so yeah, that's what we hope for."

In the three days we spent with Happy and the kids, there was one girl in particular who caught my eye repeatedly. Perhaps because she had only one eye herself. What had happened? I wondered. And how and why was it that she wouldn't stop smiling? Was it her dusty and disheveled lacy green dress? Her shaved head? Her missing eye? Could it have been her old and tattered purple plastic necklace? Or was it her lack of shoes – something all the kids went without? What made her so goddamn enthusiastic and happy?

As I asked Happy about the lively young girl, I quickly discovered it wasn't her past. Just four months earlier, Imatriat lost both her parents in a horror car crash coming up the same dreadfully unsafe road we navigated to get to the mountaintop village. The head on collision had also crushed her right eyeball, which had to be forcibly removed by surgeons. In spite of all this though, as Happy said, "she's still attending class and she's so clever and loves music, dance and drama. But what we're so happy to see is that she's having a smiling face all the time."

It seems almost unbelievable that an 11-year-old in Imatriat's position could be OK with life. But as Happy explains, part of the education and thinking of her teachers – all of whom are orphans and volunteer their time – is that it is not what we don't have and can't give that defines us, but what we do have and do give.

No matter how small that gift might be.

"We don't need many things to be happy, but the little you have, you should be happy with it. You should be content, because only then can you give. And that is what we see getting in the way of the happiness for those people who have a lot of things. Like some of the people who I carry bags for. They have this expensive stuff, but they are missing it, they have no smile," Happy laughs. "They have their cars, they have their nice houses, but they don't have a smiling face, so they should learn from these orphans. Because their smiles come – not from giving things, they don't have things – but from giving something we all have in us, you and me, everyone, and that is love. That is what drives them. What makes us all happy."

Selfishness and greed – I think we all know – are not the answer, and yet we, the privileged, persist with certain assumptions that have trapped us into such mind-sets. We either blame people for their disadvantage, believing such communities have done this to themselves, or we rattle off excuses like 'I can't afford it' or 'one day when I'm retired'. What Happy, her band of 15 orphan teachers and their 140 odd kids proved to me, was that love is the greatest gift we can all give, and it doesn't cost a cent. It's also available right now – everywhere. **All it takes is one act to get the cycle started**.

Take for instance Happy's village. Most would live on less than $2 a day. When this pint-sized dreamer in her mid-20s told her community that she was going to do something to help the orphans and kids living with a disability, she was largely dismissed. But the moment she opened the doors to the tiny, crowded hut that initially doubled as a school and shelter for the kids, the skeptics turned into believers. And surprisingly – given their circumstances – the hundreds of families living in nearby villages began dropping off fruits, vegetables, clothing, medicines and building materials to help the kids.

"It makes me happy, because even the people from the community contribute now, they donate. Someone might bring a tonne or two of beans. Another might bring some cabbages, so they do support us, even though they don't have much. They do charity work and help us because that is how they want to be – happy."

And happy they were. I'd actually go so far as to say that Nkuringo township, which housed the orphanage, was one of the happiest places I've visited. Not only were the people generous – taking time out from anything they were doing to give you a smile – but the entire place was a throwback to a time when things seemed a lot less complicated. Where adults cackled and sang on porches and children ran barefoot along the rough dirt roads, pushing and shoving as they chased a makeshift sphere of plastic dressed as a soccer ball. As numerous locals remarked, "we're on top of the world", and, well, yep, they were – not just in terms of their altitude either.

"Our way of life is not broken. Yes, we are poor. But we feel whole, so we see no need to develop like the West," Happy reassures me. "We feel that if we have a problem, like we have not enough clothes or food, then, because we are close to one another, you know, connected, we will be OK. There will be someone there to give us what we need. And that is how we are happy. It's just the culture. Everyone is happy because they know happiness is the way... and **happiness comes from just appreciating what you have and then from sharing that with others.**"

Venturing into the fields and homes surrounding Nkuringo, it was obvious that these cheery, rural people were living just as their ancestors had thousands of years ago. This wasn't because they had to – they knew how the West lived – they simply rejected our perceived superiority. And why wouldn't they? With million dollar views in every direction and a revered role as protectors of the critically endangered mountain gorillas, they were a connected and purpose-led people. Both of these elements, Happy says, lead to and come from prioritising generosity.

"I hope that people can see what we're doing, and see that even when we give a little, because that is all we can offer, then we receive much back. The hand which gives, receives. And conversely, if you don't give then you will remain without." "Without what," I ask her. "Without everything. You are empty, no love, no friends, no kindness. Because when you give, that is when you get more of those things, that is what these children have taught me."

Don't think for a moment that Nkuringo is some fantasy-land void of conflict or problems. It's not. You need only look at why these orphans exist to see the flipside of their idealistic and isolated existence. Most deaths related to HIV occur for two reasons: people either can't access antiretroviral HIV medication due to availability/affordability, or shockingly, the stigma associated with being HIV positive means they don't seek diagnosis or treatment. It probably doesn't help that churches, community leaders and even the President of Uganda have all suggested that gay people, women and 'unsavoury individuals' are responsible for the spread of HIV. Misinformation is rife – one woman even exclaimed to me "HIV is the devil's work, if you got it, you're evil!" Filming a number of stories about HIV prevention projects throughout sub-Saharan Africa (where more than 25 million – two thirds – of all HIV cases exist), lack of education was a common theme. Fuelled by a conservative traditional culture, blind faith and seclusion, things in Nkuringo were no different. That was, until Happy unintentionally stepped in.

It was never Happy's mission to convince her community that HIV wasn't the devil, or that sufferers were not cursed, but through persuading her neighbours to think and see orphans and the disabled as equals, she began to notice a marked difference in the way people approached the whole premise of HIV.

"It's very important to see one another as equal, because if you look at someone with disgust or you laugh that this one doesn't have a leg, or an eye, or has HIV, then the community will not be happy. **There will not be peace or goodness when there is judgment** that some are better and others worse," says Happy, passionately explaining that this is at the core of what they teach their students. "My orphans and the community members who are with us know that being equal is good. These children could not be happy if they were ignored or judged poorly – no one can be. That is why we all have the same blood – all human – because we are all family and should give love and respect to one another accordingly."

The following day, as I found myself face to face with a 420-pound silverback (after trekking hours through dense forest), Happy's observations around the significance of seeing past our differences seemed particularly relevant. Here was a creature that "could snap you in half if it wanted," according to one of our guides (who held a large rifle and machete in hand). So why wasn't it? Yes, they'd been habituated with humans, but these were still wild beasts by all accounts. The fact that we were forced to duck, dive and roll across the forest floor so as to not disturb the gorillas was proof of the fragile calm between the two species.

When one of the baby mountain gorillas – a two year old girl – poked her head out from behind a tree and began approaching us as we sat amongst the vegetation, the tension (and awesomeness) was unmistakable. Like any toddler, this fluffy, black ball of energy was curious – her soulful brown eyes darted between anything and everything that moved. Insects, bugs, birds and other gorillas. But as she edged closer and closer to us (within arm's reach), her mother stood up to check on her – and she was huge! Then came daddy, with his silver backside glistening in one of the few rays of light poking through the dense canopy. The alpha male of the group took a few tired steps towards us (he'd just been napping). We were told to remain still. Very still. Then, all of a sudden he stopped, sat down and pulled a branch down towards him. Phew. He was just hungry. Oblivious to the concern she was causing, the baby gorilla continued poking around our bags, crawling between us, no doubt wondering what these funny looking creatures were doing just sitting around. I'm sure she must have pondered why we weren't eating, sleeping or playing, which were the three most common habits of these stunning primates.

Mesmerized by just how similar they are to us in every way (particularly hairy people like me), I wondered how it was that we'd very nearly wiped these beautiful creatures off the face of the planet. How had we taken, and taken, and taken, to the point where there are just 800 mountain gorillas left in the wild. Photographing their eyes time and time again, I became utterly engrossed in the deeply human pain reflected in them.

What have we done!? I cried inside.

As we left the gorillas behind, and began our long trek back to civilisation, I couldn't help but think about how important the idea of oneness is to giving. Undeniably (in my experience), if we can see enough of ourselves in another, we typically won't hurt them. If we don't, of course, well that's a different story. According to an international team of researchers led by the National Autonomous University (UNAM),

One of roughly 800 mountain gorillas left in the wild.

The curious baby girl, with her mummy behind her.

The front lines of our war on nature.

The first two people we met in Nkuringo Village. Also the women who suggested we talk to Happy.

A boy holding his beloved soccer ball.

A young girl playing on the street with her baby sister.

The woman who took us to go and see Happy.

Kids at the orphanage/school running out of their room to say hi.

"My dream is to be a singer."

Happy (right) with her mum.

The volunteer cook at the orphanage preparing a meal.

Group shot!

More kids curiously peeking out to say hi.

Imatriat and a number of her fellow orphans.

we human beings have caused the extinction of 477 animal species in the past 100 years alone (between 1000 and 10,000 times higher than the natural extinction rate). We've also destroyed about 120,000 square kilometres of natural forests (roughly the size of England) *every year* since the year 2000. For 99.9% of our existence (all but the last couple of hundred years) we have arguably done this out of necessity and without the knowledge or foresight to understand that it may harm us in the future.

Nowadays, of course, there is no excuse. Yes, there are billions of mouths to feed, and millions of homes being built every year, but **what's the use of any of this 'progress' if it costs us our planet?** Of which – I often feel we need reminding – we have only one.

The funny thing is, the Earth won't die – global warming, polluted oceans and the infestations of exotic species won't claim the planet – but it may yet destroy us. Because this ecosystem we all inhabit and rely on for water, oxygen, food and life itself, works in a sustainable, cyclical system of give and take that we seem unwilling to accept or participate in. I get that we like to think or feel as if we are in control of nature, even superior to it – we'll take what we want, right!? But I fear such arrogance could be our undoing. After all, Mother Nature need only sneeze, shake or cry and our insignificance and fragility becomes instantly apparent. We run to the hills, run from our homes, run underground, run to the water, run from the water, we run, and run, and run. But what happens when we stop running? Where do we turn for answers? Some blame god, some accuse governments, some even yell foul at big business, but the truth is, we're all complicit.

Don't get me wrong, there are varying degrees to which each of us is messing up the planet – I carbon offset my flights, I don't drive much, I recycle, I'm vegetarian, I live in a tiny apartment, I pay more for green electricity, I wear the same few clothes most of the time, I even support eco-tourism – but at the end of the day, I'm sure that my carbon and ecological footprint isn't nil. I'm not part of nature's divine cycle – and that's a big problem. Because unlike past extinctions, caused by events like asteroid strikes, volcanic eruptions, and natural climate shifts, our own extinction will almost certainly be caused by us – humans. More specifically, our inability to co-exist with, or partake in, the circle of life. The problem is (thanks to our ego) we seem to believe that this perfect circle is there to serve us, so we've cut the top off (destroying more than

50% of forests), poked a small hole in the bottom of it (destroying half of all marine life in the past 40 years) and have turned the circle into a funnel that feeds our ever growing want for more.

"Indeed, if current rates (of human population growth) were to continue unchecked, population size would be, by 2100, about 27 billion – clearly an unthinkable and unsustainable option," Rodolfo Dirzo, Professor of Environmental Sciences at Stanford University, told Discovery News in relation to an article he published on extinct species.

Dirzo and his colleagues call for "decreasing the per capita human footprint," by developing and implementing carbon-neutral technologies, producing food and goods more efficiently, consuming less and wasting less. I'd also add to that women's empowerment, as the film *2040* suggests.

Haldre Rogers and Josh Tewksbury, authors of another paper in the same publication, believe that, "Animals do matter to people, but on balance, they matter less than food, jobs, energy, money, and development." They continued, "As long as we continue to view animals in ecosystems as irrelevant to these basic demands, animals will lose."

So what, right!? So long as we survive… But that's the awkward thing – if animals and ecosystems disappear, there's a fair chance we'll go with them. Such is our reliance on fish, forests, insects and bees; to pollinate, procreate and provide us with all the food, medicine, materials and oxygen we need to exist; that even a slight glitch in the system could mean catastrophe. The problem as I see it is this: because Mother Nature doesn't take a day off, because she doesn't falter as a provider, we've come to take her boundless generosity for granted. The danger of throwing our environment out of balance, by under-valuing its significance, has recently seen a number of economists and ecologists argue that we should assign an explicit monetary value to the services of our ecosystems. In a seminal paper published in *Nature* in 1997, economist Robert Costanza and his colleagues from the Australian National University, estimated that ecosystem services are annually worth roughly twice the world's economic output. In 2014, that would have meant ecosystems generated more than 156 trillion dollars (that's $156,000,000,000,000) in that year alone. The more instant and obvious economic spinoffs of Nature's abundance are also endless.

For example, in Australia, the Great Barrier Reef generates 64,000 jobs and was valued at $56 billion, according to a 2017 report by

Deloitte Access Economics. In Southeast Asia, the Mekong River Basin, through its fisheries, supports 60 million people, while in Namibia, 73% of visitors are nature-based tourists, who account for 14.2% of that nation's economic growth. Similarly, in Latin America, whale watching alone generates over $275 million dollars a year, while in the United States, shark-watching generates $314 million per year, directly supporting 10,000 jobs. Multiple studies too, have demonstrated that turtles are worth more alive than dead, and yet, their numbers continue to decline. Even if we put our morals and survival aside, and look at Mother Nature as a giant bank, we must ask ourselves: how many times can you rob a bank before it shuts down? What if it can't regenerate the funds being stolen? Or, as seems a likely case through climate change, what happens when the guards start firing back? When the ice caps melt and oceans rise, flooding Miami, Manhattan, Tokyo and Sydney? What will we say once we've gone too far? Will there be anything we can give back? Any way we can say sorry to those future generations set to inherit an uninhabitable planet?

Ultimately, I think happiness comes from recognising and putting into practice a thought that Happy shared with me repeatedly, which is this: **"Once our basic needs are met it is our duty and our calling as social, empathetic creatures to serve others, to say thanks by giving back."** Of course, in this individualistic world we've constructed, which screams for us to have more, do more, and care less, the most generous gift we could all give one another (and future generations) is to simplify what we deem to be our 'basic needs'. I mean, why has the average house size in Australia gone from 100 square metres in the 1950s to 240 square metres today, despite family sizes decreasing? Do we really need all that extra space? Or is giving each child their own bedroom, lounge room and TV adding to the isolation and breakdown within families? After all, to own a bigger home someone's got to pay for it, and usually that means mum and dad working harder and longer hours, which isn't good for anyone's happiness. The second, and arguably more important half of this process, is about having the mental will not to take more than your basic needs, to treat your resources as if they were scarce, and then, to begin giving once you reach that point. "Because if we don't start giving more than we're taking, we may all end up with nothing," concluded Happy.

At the time we visited the orphanage, its 140 inhabitants were sharing two tiny dorms of around 15 metres squared. Forced to squeeze seven or eight children to each bunk bed, Happy was desperately trying to expand, and was in the process of developing a number of new dorms and classrooms for the kids. Clearly hampered by lack of funds – evident in what the children were made to eat each day or the lack of chairs and blackboards in many classrooms – we did what we could to assist, but as is ever the case, it was not enough. So here's a great opportunity to begin putting into practice all that you've read in this chapter and book so far – and help Happy and the kids. With few resources to help her fundraise, such as a website or reliable internet access, Happy simply asked us (if we were to ever publish her story) to simply include her email address. So please, if you've been inspired by her story, send Happy an email via happykyoheirwe@yahoo.com and she'll no doubt update you on how the school is progressing and what their basic needs are at that time, whether money, goods or volunteers. We'd also love to know if you decide to give, so get in touch with us too, via thehappiest.com.

As you might have guessed by now, I've never been poor, but I have pushed myself to go without at times. From giving the last cent in my bank account, to a few random experiments I've undertaken, my purpose for giving to a point of discomfort (other than helping others), has often been about gaining insight into how billions are forced to live daily. Probably the most notable measure I devised and undertook to do this, was when over the course of three months in the lead up to Christmas 2011, I decided to live without money (aside from rent and bills). I also couldn't ask for anything from others; and only if they questioned me, could I tell people what I was doing. Though I was offered money from time to time, I could not take it, nor could I accept something if someone was buying it just for me. For example, that dear friend Zoran, who owned the restaurant next to the Our World Today office, was not allowed to make a meal just for me (though he offered), but I was able to accept food that was left over or may not be used that night. As you might guess, it was tough. I was hungry, a lot, and lost five kilos in the first month alone.

Six weeks into the experiment, I was curious to push things further, so I added a new rule: I could spend money on others, but not myself. I could also now accept gifts, but not if people were doing it because they knew what I was doing – it had to be selfless gesture, not driven by guilt. This was fascinating, and oh so satisfying. Not only because it taught me a lot about human nature (and the inherent goodness in people), but also because of the reactions it aroused in others.

The most memorable incident occurred when all my friends came around for our weekly cards night and we decided to head out for my favourite ice cream. Somehow the boys hadn't seemed to cotton on to what I'd been doing, so when I paid for all seven of their ice creams and then sat there without one they were shocked. "What are you doing?" said Andy (the guy from the plane), "where's your ice cream?" When I explained myself, some laughed and said I was mad or stupid, while others offered to get me an ice cream. Sadly though, it was too late. I explained that I could not accept a gift once I'd revealed my secret. Sitting there, watching my friends devour my most beloved treat, I could see that my decision had made everyone uncomfortable and unhappier than they might have been otherwise. The opposite was of course true of how I felt – I was ecstatic and got such great joy out of giving without want or the ability to receive anything in return. Later that night I couldn't help but wonder which element of what I'd done had made my mates so awkward. Was it that I'd shouted them ice cream? I doubt it. Could it be that they really, really wanted me to have an ice cream? Not likely. What seemed to me to be the problem was that they felt guilty seeing someone right in front of them going without something that they had. So why didn't more of them – why don't more of us – feel the same discomfort when we see or hear stories about the billion-odd people forced to live in a near constant state of starvation? Is it proximity? How they look? That 'they' seem different to 'us'? What drives our apathy when it comes to giving?

To me, there is just one agonising truth, and that is this: we believe we are more deserving than the other person, full stop. Don't get me wrong, I acknowledge the excuses (sometimes I even use them myself), you know the ones – I don't have money, it's too hard, I'm too busy, it's not my fault – but for all that they soften the blow (in our mind), in reality that person's suffering continues, and with it, so does our own. Because when all's said and done, we are highly emotional, empathetic beings who want to be and do good. Looking back, it seems ironic that the man who showed me the alternative to this – what life looks like when we see all as equally deserving – was in fact one of the most down-and-out people I've ever met.

The rickshaw driver who brought me closer to god

I'd long romanticized travelling to India. It seemed such a rich, colourful and deeply spiritual place, rooted in ancient knowledge that was as odd as it was honest. As a child, I remember seeing a Sadhu (a guru/religious man) wrap his penis around a sword and let another man stand on the sword – I think it was meant to indicate that he'd moved beyond a state of suffering (for his penis' sake I hope he was right!). In more recent times, I'd been intrigued by the role dowries play in entrenched poverty, gender rights and violence against women. I was also curious to see for myself the reality of India's so called 'outlawing' of the caste system, and how on Earth a single country could house 370 million people living on less than $1.25USD a day. From the moment I landed – and had a taxi driver attempt to scam me, nearly crashed into a bus, got lost finding my hostel and felt my entire body burning in the 51°C air – I knew India was going to be a place I'd find answers. To what questions, though ... well, I was about to find out.

Delhi's old-fashioned charm wooed me immediately, as labourers hauled sacks of spices, jewelers weighed gold on dusty scales and an endless symphony of car, bike, bus and truck horns blared like the perfect soundtrack to the mayhem of this pulsating metropolis. Eager to experience as much as I could, I decided to join a food tour that would take me through the mystical laneways of Old Delhi. As it turned out, the tour started just a few blocks away, so my tour guide (a man from my hostel) summoned a local rickshaw driver and we jumped into the back of his pedal-powered cart.

Before we'd even really got going I screamed internally. 'Huh!? What are we doing!!!? Why are we turning around? The traffic is going that way, why are we going against it!!!!!!!?' Sensing my terror, my guide reassured me, "this is normal, it's OK." A car mirror then sideswiped our cart and he calmly, but sternly told me to keep my hands inside the cart "AT ALL TIMES!" For the next few minutes I watched in awe as our thin wily driver evaded the frantic waves of oncoming traffic.

Then suddenly, without warning, he stopped.

Cars, bikes, rickshaws, buses and tuk tuks honked and yelled as he graciously stepped down from his seat and stopped the oncoming traffic. What on earth was he doing? I wondered. I asked my guide. He shrugged, "I don't know." Finally, our driver lent down and grabbed something off the road. What was it? I thought. A gold ring? Money? A lotto ticket? What was worth all the fuss? As he turned to face us, I nearly didn't see it – tucked under his arm was a pigeon. Pushing his bike to the side of the road as he cradled the bird, this mysterious man held the pigeon out towards me and pointed at its eyes. I could see that it was blind and had a film covering its eyes. Later on I learned this was a common but terrible condition caused by the extreme heat Delhi had been experiencing. Not satisfied with merely removing the bird from harm's way, this man (who had me spellbound) set about fetching his water bottle and giving the bird a drink, before finding a safe place to leave it.

As this rough, dishevelled, ghost of a man climbed back on his rickshaw and invited us to take our seats, a gentle grin filled his face. Wow! I thought. What had I just witnessed? Who was this man?

Standing in a crowded marketplace having just dismounted our rickshaw, I unwittingly found myself taking our driver's hands and just holding onto them tightly as I looked into his pain-filled eyes and said "thank you for being you." I then awkwardly bowed my head as I asked (through my guide) if he'd be interested in coming by the following day for an interview. Bewildered at first by my request – I don't imagine the Indian newspapers had ever done a story on him – he and my guide deliberated back and forth, until a familiar head wobble (I'd seen a lot in Sri Lanka) told me that I'd get an answer to those questions I'd been pondering about who this man was.

Standing at the reception desk of my hostel the following day, talking with my guide and a few other staff about the 'pigeon man', there was one guy who just couldn't help himself. "He is a bad man," yelled this 20-something year old guy donning a stylish haircut and neat blue shirt "He is a low life, a gutter dweller, an alcoholic, why do you want to speak with him? There are better stories in India you know." "Yes, but there is something about him," I replied politely. "I mean, why would a guy in his position – so poor and so downtrodden – bother stopping to help a defenceless bird? There must be more to him," I intoned. The outburst by the staff member, Vihaan (who I think was a manager), had scared off a few of his colleagues, and unfortunately (but perhaps fatefully) this guy was the only one left to help me translate. When I told Vihaan I was about to invite the rickshaw driver in, so we could speak in the air-conditioned comfort of the hostel, he looked at me like I'd just slept with his girlfriend. Stomping around begrudgingly as I fetched my newfound friend – who was still wearing his dreary purple bandana, stinking old brown shirt (which I suspect used to be white) and torn jeans (not the fashionable type) – I couldn't help but feel as if maybe, just maybe, Vihaan's presence might add an unforeseen angle and depth to this story.

As I opened the door for this nameless figure I was so excited to meet, something visibly threw him. Was it the bitterly cold air of the hostel (remembering it was around 50°C outside)? Could it have been the relative 'luxury' of this somewhat beat up old building? Or was it the malicious contempt oozing from Vihaan's pores? As his solemn and innocuous eyes darted back and forth between the doorway, reception desk, ceiling, Vihaan and me, it was clear that he felt as if he was somewhere he was not meant to be. His body language was borderline unwatchable, and I knew we couldn't continue until the air had been cleared. I tried my hardest to forget those poisonous words Vihaan had spewed earlier, which I think was simply code for 'this guy is an untouchable' (the lowest vehemently despised caste under the caste system) and we don't want him here. Passing him a glass of water and a deep and heartfelt smile, I sat down, shut my eyes and hoped he could feel my love for him. Who knows, I thought, maybe he was just nervous to speak to some random Aussie guy about saving a bird.

"OK, let's get started," I said enthusiastically, with notepad in hand. "What is your name, age and where are you from?" I asked via Vihaan, hoping I could trust him with these simple questions at least.

"I am Saddam Hasan [pronounced Hussein]," he said. Well shit I thought, as I chuckled inside. Saddam seemed utterly oblivious to the infamy that came with his name. "I am 22 years old and my family, we are from a small village in Bihar province, which is [1100km] east of Delhi, near Nepal and Bangladesh."

"So why did you come to Delhi?" I asked.

"I knew how to make the headlights for cars and buses, so I was moving here to work in a factory, and life was good, but then the factory closed down and I had nothing," said Saddam, whose eyes told a much deeper story of pain. "So what happened?" I queried. "Are you happy today?"

As Vihaan relayed my question, I could see from Saddam's face that I'd hit a nerve. He took a few breaths to try to quell the tears, but it was too late, and I ran to get him a tissue, which was greeted with a bitter and shame-filled smile, as if he'd done something wrong. The pain of this poor man's face was bottomless. What on Earth had happened, I wondered, as I waited for him to gather himself.

"My life is not going well. Things are tough. In the factory I was happy, but now I lost my job, I have nothing. [He pauses] I tried to find more work, but for me it is not easy [tears well] and now I am just drinking [he moans aloud] and not someone of value," he said agonisingly, hating every word he uttered. I honestly couldn't handle seeing him like this (there were clearly two men inside this body, waging war against one another), so I changed tact for a moment. "Tell me about where you do find happiness. Why did you save that bird? Clearly you are a good man."

"All people and things are the same for me. That is the truth. If you see that, and be kind to all, that is how a human can be happy," he smiled, even if ever so slightly. "Tell me more," I pleaded. "Tell me more, what are your dreams?" For the first time during our brief interview he looked me in the eye as he said, "I want to save all beings, so they do not suffer."

"My soul is telling me to do this work, so I am happy when I can help others," he continues, with a sudden surge of energy to his voice. "In Islam it is important to be praying and thinking that everyone is the same. All people are common. If we trust in that, then **if I have some food and my poor neighbour does not, then I must help them**, even if I am hungry." My skin tingles, as a brief smile from Saddam causes me to choke back tears. Before I get a chance to ask him anything, his thoughtful look breeds words. "I saw a dog with its neck cut some days ago, so I took him to the Jain [an ancient Indian religion committed to harmlessness] animal hospital to get help. There was also a man on the road some month's back who had been hit by a bus and was partly unconscious and bleeding a lot. He'd been left there, so I put him on my rickshaw and dropped him to the hospital, leaving him with all the rupees I'd made that day, which was only 50 [less than $1]." Seeing Saddam's mood lift as he shared these tales was comforting, but oddly Vihaan seemed unflinching in his disdain for this man. If anything, there seemed to be an additional layer of contempt growing in him. A morbid sort of jealousy that stemmed from my interest in Saddam's extraordinary stories and thoughts – which I don't imagine aligned with what Vihaan felt a foreigner should be impressed by.

With his self-confidence and sense that he was in a safe place at a high point, I re-addressed the elephant in the room. "So what happened? What's led you to this point?"

"When I was small we had a happy life. But then, when I was eight years old my father died," Saddam said, as that well of emotions he'd subdued returned. "I don't know how, but suddenly my uncle and grandfather had taken all the land and money we should have inherited from my father for themselves. They said my mother could not have it, and widows are powerless in India, so what could we do? [Saddam sobs uncontrollably]. My two brothers, younger sister and I were forced to stop school because my mother could not afford it. We got no help when my father died [he riles in pain]; no one was there for us. We were forced to go and beg," he says, choking through the final words before crying irrepressibly in front of me. Holding his shoulder as tears welled in my own eyes, the gravity of his pain reverberated through his violent gulps and pants as his entire body shook.

After a brief interval, Saddam expanded on his move to Delhi as a 14-year-old. "I trained up to work in a factory, but when I was 19 it suddenly closed. At the same time, the girl I loved also left me [he pauses once again as the pain becomes too much], because I could no longer look after us. I had nothing. How could I exist? I wanted to die, but I knew I couldn't leave my mother alone. And my sister also, she was needing a dowry, so she can be happily married, so now I am helping my family to collect enough money for her. This is why our life is tough now, this is why I am forced to be a rickshaw driver."

As Vihaan relays the tragedy of Saddam's life to me, you can see him trying to let go of his preconceived judgement, but something inside him just won't let him. Instead, he downplays Saddam's pain by suggesting "this is common, anyone can tell you this story in India." Perhaps, I thought, but that doesn't make it OK. Writing madly as Saddam gathered his thoughts, I nearly missed one of his most excruciating realisations, as he whispered rather dejectedly to us, "I am broken, but I know I must try to be whole again."

Echoing the pain of my alcoholic brother (who you'll meet in Chapter 10), I decided to ask Saddam more about the specifics of his situation – where he was living, how he survived and what he did with the little money he made. As it turned out, he was given a room at a distant uncle and aunty's house, in exchange for taking and picking up their children from school every day. Outside of this, a twelve to fourteen hour day of rickshaw riding earned him roughly $3USD per day. From this a staggering $1.20 goes to paying the man who rents him the rickshaw, leaving Saddam with just $1.80 to live off – well, sort of. Of the remaining money, nearly half went directly into a fund he'd set aside to support his mum and his sister's dowry, so actually, in reality Saddam was surviving on just a little under $1 a day.

Feeling utterly ashamed of the privilege I enjoyed (merely because I was born in Australia), my pent up thoughts began bubbling to the surface. "This is not OK," I yelled, before taking a deep breath as I looked towards Vihaan. "It may be common, but to accept such inequality is to ignore our humanity." Perhaps not sensing my total disgust at the ungodly culture and beliefs that drive such disparity, Vihaan spoke. "You cannot help these people. They have done this to themselves. He is an alcoholic," said Vihaan.

My blood boiled.

I couldn't look at him, so I shut my eyes and sat in silence. 'You need to help this guy,' screamed my conscience. 'What would Saddam do if the roles were reversed?' I asked myself. With barely enough money to get me to Kolkata, let alone Uganda (my next destination), I looked over at Saddam, who sat there anxiously mute – likely sensing the tension between Vihaan and I. To hell with it, I thought. I might wind up living off $1 a day until I got paid for the work I'd be doing in Uganda, but that little voice inside of me was screaming, 'it will be worth it!!!'.

"What would you do if someone gave you a few hundred dollars?" I suddenly spurted out. Reluctantly, Vihaan translated, and Saddam replied, "I would buy a rickshaw of my own and send the rest of the money to my mother." "OK," I said, before pausing. "I am going to buy him a rickshaw, if he's happy for me to do this?" Vihaan's displeasure and jealousy was overwhelming. "You should not give this man money, he will waste it," said Vihaan; "he does not deserve it." "Perhaps you're right," I said, "but perhaps you're not." He looked at me confused. "Tell me Vihaan, what is lost if he wastes the gift I offer him? Nothing. But if I walk away and deny him this second chance – what then might we lose? How many lives might he touch, given this opportunity? [Vihaan stared blankly in disgust] The one thing I can guarantee is that if I do nothing, nothing will change." "Yes but, why him?" Vihaan pleaded. To which I replied, "Why not?" (Unconsciously echoing my Gran). "He is a hopeless case," replied Vihaan snappily. "He can't be helped."

"With that attitude I'd agree, but when those who can give, do give, then all human suffering will be a thing of the past. So please tell him, that if he'd like to, I will go with him tomorrow and buy him a rickshaw," I said sternly – sick of his negative bullshit. "Please tell him, there are no strings attached. I simply wish to give him an opportunity to express his inconceivable kindness and leave his mark on this world." I'm not exactly sure what was translated, but after a bit of bizarre hesitation, and bewilderment at the prospect of someone wanting to help him, Saddam agreed.

The next morning, I hopped on the back of Saddam's mortgaged rickshaw (where it all began) and we made our way to a road a few districts over, which was meant to be full of rickshaw dealers. Expecting to see rows upon rows of completed rickshaws for sale in large yards (like a car yard), the reality, as I was about to learn, was that nearly all rickshaws were made to order. Ordinarily this would have been fine, but I'd planned on leaving Delhi that night, and the man said there was absolutely no way he could build one in less than 24 hours. Hmmm, I wondered. "I suppose I'll have to stay then," I told the shop owner, who was proficient in English. I guess it was lucky I hadn't yet booked my train to Varanasi.

Waking at dawn, with an incessant need to learn a few words of Hindi so I could express myself to Saddam, I crammed like I'd never crammed before. When he arrived at 8:30am to pick me up, I tried my best to speak to him, but I might as well have been talking gibberish. I quickly ran back into the hostel and asked a few of the staff (not Vihaan) who were unbelievably supportive of what I'd done, and urgently asked them to write him a letter on my behalf. It read:

Dear Saddam,

Firstly, thank you! You have inspired me to be a better person, and for that I will be forever grateful. Your generosity and kindness is a gift that has touched me deeply. I only hope that by returning he favour (in the form of this rickshaw) you are able to share this with more people. Keep being beautiful, keep being you.

Fingers crossed we cross paths again one day.

Your friend from Australia,

Mike :)

Saddam with pigeon in hand.

Saddam showing off his new wheels.

It seemed an inadequate gesture given how he'd impacted my life, but as I passed him the letter (written in Hindi) and an A Million Smiles T-shirt that read 'smile – you know you want to', the smile on his face finally told me that he was at peace being around me. It might not sound like much, but to see Saddam's walls come down and have him let me into his life was world-changing for me. As he said in the most broken of English, **"We are same, you and I."**

That we were. But more needed to be done if he was to get back to a point of loving himself (a situation that would cure his alcoholism). As we repeated the same terrifying journey to the rickshaw dealer, I sat there meditating about Saddam's future – wishing, praying and doing all that I could to give him the energy he'd need in the days, weeks and months ahead.

You might dismiss such a spiritual act and deem it useless – I know I used to – but I guess it is about giving what you can to those who need it, no matter who you are or what you believe in. I knew a rickshaw in and of itself likely would not change this man's life, but if I could convince him that he was as deserving of his own love and kindness as anyone else, then I knew he'd be a different person the next time we met.

With the rickshaw construction taking a little longer than anticipated, Saddam soon pointed me to a local street restaurant for lunch. Insisting that he join me – why should I eat and not he – I could see his trepidation and knew it was something to do with me being white. But why? I pondered quietly, observing the many curious eyes trying to work out why we were seated together. Was it good or bad for him to be seen with me? I guess my problem was I'd grown up in Australia, where no one really cares who you are. After sharing some food and a Coke, we returned to the elderly Indian shop owner who was gleaming from ear to ear – it was done! The next ridiculously crazy, but fun part of instilling the belief that he deserved his love and kindness as much as anyone else, was (I felt) for me to take him for the first ride on his new rickshaw – because I was just as much his servant as he was mine. This romantic idea was of course short-lived, as the reality of Delhi's traffic terrified me, but hey, I tried, and I really didn't want to kill Saddam before he'd had the chance to reveal his true beauty to humanity.

Half an hour later, I experienced one of the happiest moments of my life as I watched Saddam shake hands with the man who'd loaned him a rickshaw all these years and say what I imagined to be – 'I'll take it from here'. I don't know what an extra $1.20USD per day has done for Saddam, but I know it won't be wasted no matter what, because it was a gift of love and love is never wasted. Yep, I'm a softie, but in all honesty, I envisage he's better able to support his mother, sister and one of the most humble, gentle and caring individuals I've ever met – the man himself, Saddam Hassan – to whom I simply say thank you for your generosity!

When it comes to giving, I know certain egos demand that we see ourselves as tiny gods, worthy of deciding who lives and who dies. But for me personally, amidst all I've seen, I think **our happiest state comes from seeing all people as part of one entity – one family – humanity.** To me, if we were meant to live disconnected and solitary lives, why then was empathy so inbuilt into our DNA? And why does loneliness crush us so much? Why were we given the capacity to feel what others feel? Why is it that when one suffers, we are all forced to suffer?

As Scottish philosopher David Hume wrote in 1740: "Your corn is ripe today; mine will be so tomorrow. 'Tis profitable for us both, that I should labour with you today, and that you should aid me tomorrow."

What's apparently obvious (and as such, a great source of frustration to me) is that giving is the one thing that can make us *all* rich, not just financially, but spiritually too. Generosity is literally good for everyone. Not simply because it releases happy hormones, but because it connects us. When we give selflessly, we say to the other, 'I see myself in you and therefore I do not want you to feel pain'. Such acts reaffirm our shared humanity, and are critical in taming our ever-destructive ego, which wants nothing more than for you to believe that you are more deserving and more important. In truth, of course, such beliefs deprive you of that purpose and meaning we all crave, which comes from giving all that we are to the world, and being positively affirmed in the process. Whether you want to listen to science, religion or simply my Gran, there's no denying the unparalleled joy that comes from being a givington.

Looking forward, I not only see the cultivation of more generous individuals and societies (something discussed at greater length in coming chapters) as essential to our proper function and happiness as a species, but in my humble opinion, it will also decide whether we as a species live, die or thrive.

Happiness may be within our control,

but it cannot be forged alone.

So how do we find joy within the human tribe?

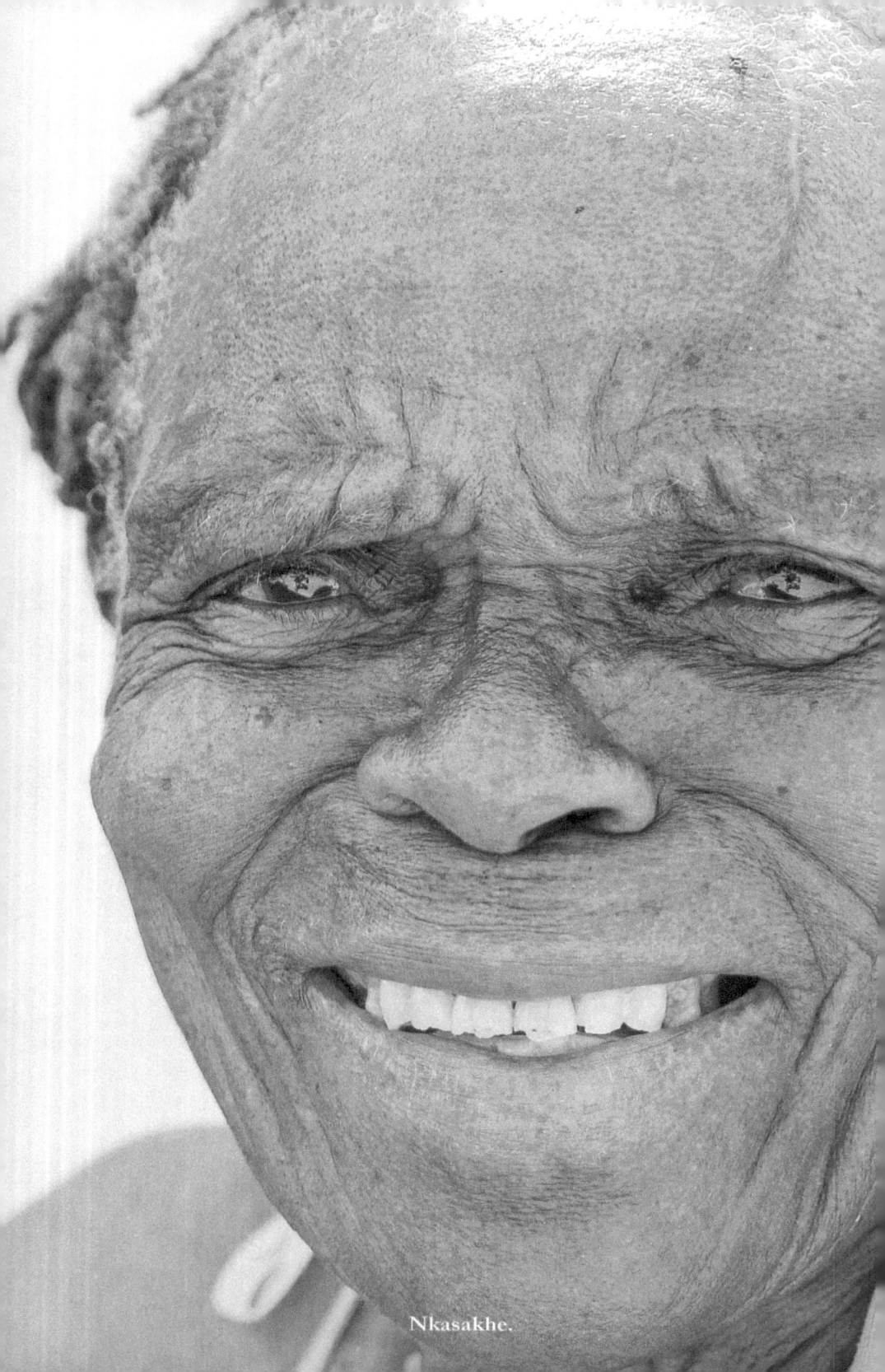
Nkasakhe.

6

THE LION, THE CROCODILE AND THE MAASAI

How are we supposed to live? It is a question that's rattled round my head for months now, and yet, I'm not sure I'm any closer to answering it.

To me, there are two broad terms or definitions or ideas I'd like to explore:

Survivalist-based *human beings: For the best part of 200 thousand years this is how 99.9% of us have existed – perpetually trapped in a state of needing to think about and act to survive.*

Conscious/opportunity-based *human beings: As we've slowly adapted and evolved and added resources to the mix – both physically and mentally – life has become incrementally easier and more full of choice. As our thinking-time and choices have slowly expanded, so too has our consciousness – and it's been a cycle – the more time we've had to explore and think, the more we've learned > the more we learned, the more opportunities we uncovered > the more opportunities we've uncovered, the more resources we've developed to help us free up time to think and explore > on and on we've advanced... gaining ever more opportunity and knowledge, as our circle has widened.*

We can see more than ever. We can be more than ever.

This more conscious/opportunity-based existence has given us the capacity to develop our conscience and create a more considerate and happier society – one where the wants of mind and body are met, leaving our spirit free to explore – and yet, something is missing. The balance is out.

We've expanded the circle, but left no time to explore it.
We've connected the world, but disconnected from each other.

THE HAPPIEST

*We've left the village, and the community that comes with it.
We've freed ourselves, by locking ourselves in debt.*

...And so, the question remains: how are we supposed to live? Are we happier as survivalist-based beings or does true satisfaction come from a more conscious/opportunity- based existence? Is it one or the other, or do we actually need to be a bit of both? Where does our happiest state exist? This journal entry was the amalgamation of musings I had during my three and a half month journey through East Africa in 2016, the land where we *all* began.

At the end of a blisteringly hot, dry and flat 50-kilometre drive from the town of St Lucia in far-eastern South Africa, was a scattering of a few thousand clustered shelters we came to know as Nkundusi Village. Positioned along the banks of Lake St Lucia – the largest estuarine lake in Southern Africa, covering an area of about 350km² – each cluster of mud brick huts typically housed a family of between 10 and 50 individuals. Nkundusi and the entire lake area fell within the greater iSimangaliso Wetland Park (a World Heritage site). Worryingly, as we got closer and closer to what was meant to be a vast swamp, the only place I could see any moisture was in the sweat dripping incessantly into my eyes. The land looked like a burnt, naked body. Blistering, peeling and cracking as the dried out dams and streams and lack of green made it feel as if we were in a desert, rather than a wetland. As we passed countless children grasping at water bottles, sucking any moisture they could from the large yellow containers, the bare and dusty brown haze became uncomfortable to look at. You knew the locals relied on this same parched and barren soil to survive. And you knew they had done nothing to deserve this post-apocalyptic nightmare that confronted them. They had lived in harmony with nature for thousands of years, but in a few short decades *our* impact upon this planet had all but severed their connection and understanding of the weather systems that had kept them safe for millennia.

As we (Sash and I) stepped down from our car with two local guides we'd befriended, every movement caused a puff of dust to spray. As our feet continued to crash into the loose top soil, it was as if we were walking across a bakery floor full of dirty, brown flour. Exploring a small cluster of about nine buildings, a woman emerged from a doorway of a smoke-stained hut that was adorned by a cryptic cow's skull and horns.

As she neared, Nkasakhe, who had grey, slightly balding dreadlocked hair and dark, deeply set eyes invited, my wife and I to sit with her. Over the next hour, we learned that Nkasakhe was a traditional Sangoma healer, responsible for the health and wellbeing of more than a thousand people in her village. The Sangoma fulfil a wide variety of social and political roles in the community, including divination, healing physical, emotional and spiritual illnesses, directing birth or death rituals, finding lost cattle, protecting warriors, counteracting witchcraft, and narrating the history, cosmology, and myths of their tradition. Those called to the sacred role (by the spirits), undergo years of tutelage under the existing Sangoma, who decides when the incumbent is ripe to take on this holy life-time commitment.

My curiosity about her life and her surrounds threw up a thousand questions until, finally, I asked about the happiness of Nkundusi (pronounced Kun-dus-si) residents. "Do you think the people here are happy?" I asked. I wasn't sure if her delayed response was because the question made no sense or because she was giving it very careful consideration, but when she did finally speak, her slow, calming voice belied the panic in her message.

"Happiness," she paused, "is difficult." Then she paused again. As I was trying to take in the profundity of her observation, she continued. "We have been in severe drought for nearly two years and it has dried out our lake. There are just a few pools of water left, and these are our last real sources of water. The problem is, all the crocodiles and hippos that are normally so spread out across the lake are now concentrated in these pools. So sadly, we are finding a lot of women and children are disappearing and being eaten by these animals when they are going to fetch water. And you know, we cannot survive without water, so this is making our life very troublesome."

Troublesome!? Can you imagine the response in any developed city that lost more than one person to a wild animal? It was my turn for a delayed response. "How do the authorities let this happen?" I asked, when I finally found my voice. "And if they won't help, why don't the people here move, even if only temporarily?"

She smiled in that forlorn way I remembered my Gran smiling when I asked her something ridiculous. "We have a saying here 'perseverance is the mother of success'. We have lived here for thousands of years and we will endure. Working together to survive. Sharing and serving one another wherever we can, because while we continue to do good by one another, there will always be hope, and from hope happiness rises."

As we explored some of the indigenous settlements close by, mostly by car with the air conditioning on full blast in a desperate attempt to escape the heat, I had one last question I was dying to ask Nkasakhe: what did happiness mean to her, personally? This time there was no hesitation. "As a Sangoma we believe we are called to serve by a higher spirit, and we are given powers to do so. So to me, my happiest days are when I am able to help people by using the abilities I have."

When our time with Nkasakhe was over, we walked to a point that looked out over the arid lake bed. My gut instinctively tightened with the sense of dread over what I was witnessing. In the distance was a steady flow of colourful dots. The women and children of Nkundusi venturing toward the horizon, and closer to the sparkle of a few ponds that hadn't yet surrendered to the relentless dry. Watching on as the women and children of Nkundusi were forced to play this deadly game of survival evoked a palpable sense of terror within me. The horror of what we might witness if we had binoculars forced an idea loose in my head. In the daze of the days ahead, everything I'd seen and heard in Nkundusi festered into a question that in many ways shaped my journey through East Africa: Are people living this survivalist-based existence happier than those living a more conscious/opportunity-based life?

At a glance, the answer seems obvious, right? How could someone who is constantly worried about their very survival ever find time to be happy? Well maybe it's not about finding time, maybe it's just about being present in the present, and that's what so many of us in more developed countries have forgotten. But, then again, what about the crocodiles and hippos? Surely, one cannot smile if they're constantly facing imminent danger? I mean, if your present is that bad, what good does it do for you to be in the present? And does the ability to think bigger or more long-term really destroy one's happiness, anyway? Is it more or less harmful to my mood if I'm ignorant of the world around me? Does that sea of knowledge available through the internet free my mind to dream and create, or does it clog it with gunk, rendering it unable to ponder a life worth living?

These were just a few of the questions and ideas that bounced around my mind as we journeyed by bus north-west through South Africa to Johannesburg.

When I thought back to what Nkasakhe had said, and how she had described her role as "feeling the Earth, the people and her place in it," I wondered if perhaps the entire premise of that original thought of being either survivalist-based *or* conscious/opportunity-based were even true. Here was a woman who had to fulfil a myriad of social, spiritual and political roles in the community, including curing biological and mystical illnesses and protecting the history, cosmology, and mythology of her culture. Given such a broad and diverse CV, was she conscious/opportunity-based or survivalist-based? To me she was a bit of both. A survivalist-based human being who was incredibly conscious of local customs, nature and worldly energies, but who rarely contemplated more global events or opportunities. I mean, she didn't have a phone or the internet. Speaking of which...

As the bus to Johannesburg bobbled and bumped and day turned to night, and suddenly phone screens lit up just about every face on the bus, I wondered: with all this additional information, knowledge and connectedness we have at our fingertips, have we become any more conscious? Are there, in fact, more opportunities? Well, maybe. Technology has undeniably made us less survivalist-based by allowing us to be more efficient, better planned, and more flexible and able to do things when, where and how we want. But is that actually giving us more time to think about and act in any way we choose, or less? Has the constant need to keep up and remain relevant – by 'checking-in' at the coolest clubs, photographing the most delicious food or posting the best selfie – simply trapped us in another form of that survivalist-based mind-set, where we constantly feel we are in competition (not to survive, but to be popular), rendering us unable to focus on anything else other than how many likes our next post is going to get?

The most frightening part is, the more you dig (ironically, online) the more you come to realise that **smartphones are carving a hole in the human psyche so deep and so vast, there may be no coming back.** And it's terrifying.

Tech-tick-boom!

In her article, *Have Smartphones Destroyed a Generation?* Dr. Jean Twenge, who has been studying generational differences for 25 years, explores just how and why these tiny little devices are killing us and making us ill. While Twenge's analysis focuses on a group she calls iGen, those born between 1995 and 2012, her findings tell a story that should make us all open our eyes and turn off our phones (at least for a while). The avid author, academic and researcher says it was around 2012 that she began to notice abrupt shifts in teen behaviours and emotional states.

"What happened in 2012 to cause such dramatic shifts in behaviour?" she asks. "It was exactly the moment when the proportion of Americans who owned a smartphone surpassed 50%. The advent of the smartphone and its cousin the tablet was followed quickly by hand-wringing about the deleterious effects of 'screen time'. But the impact of these devices has not been fully appreciated, and goes far beyond the usual concerns about curtailed attention spans."

Rates of teen depression and suicide in the US have skyrocketed since 2011, says Twenge, who describes iGen as being on the brink of one of the worst mental-health crises we've ever seen. What's particularly alarming is that much of this deterioration can be traced to their phones.

"The results could not be clearer: Teens who spend more time than average on screen activities are more likely to be unhappy, and those who spend more time than average on non-screen activities are more likely to be happy," writes Twenge. "There's not a single exception. Eighth-graders who spend 10 or more hours a week on social media are 56% more likely to say they're unhappy than those who devote less time to social media."

Having pored over the *Monitoring the Future* survey, which has asked a sample group of American 12th-graders more than 1000 questions every year since 1975, and queried eighth and tenth graders since 1991, Twenge says today's teens surprisingly seem less inclined to chase sex, drugs, a job or any other form of independence, and are more content to sit at home 'studying' in their room. Because, as she points out, "They don't need to leave home to spend time with their friends." The problem is, this thought process is quite literally leaving them either grossly unhappy or dead.

"Eighth-graders who are heavy users of social media increase their risk of depression by 27%, while those who play sports, go to religious services, or even do homework more than the average teen cut their risk significantly," says Twenge. "Teens who spend three hours a day or more on electronic devices are 35% more likely to have a risk factor for suicide, such as making a suicide plan."

While these figures represent the outline of an alarming circle, what's in the middle? What are our smartphones or social media making us do that's causing us to become so depressed and suicidal? To start with, **the number of teens who get together with their friends nearly every day dropped by more than 40% from 2000 to 2015,** with the steepest decline coming in recent years. What's more, just 56% of high-school seniors went out on dates in 2015, while for baby boomers and Gen Xers that number was about 85%. Despite Tinder's best attempts, the decline in dating also tracks with a decline in sexual activity, with the number of sexually active ninth-graders being cut by almost 40% since 1991. But kids aren't only lacking in person-to-person connection, the nature of social media (despite it 'linking' kids day and night) has also led 48% more girls and 27% more boys to say they 'often felt left out' in 2015 than in 2010.

There is one upside. Since 2007, the homicide rate among teens has declined, but as Twenge suggests, that's probably just the result of teens no longer spending as much time together. After all, it's very hard to kill someone without human contact. Sadly, what this actually meant was that in 2011, for the first time in 24 years, the teen suicide rate in America was higher than the teen homicide rate.

A wealthier population and an information economy that rewards higher education more than early work history is also causing more parents than ever to encourage their kids to stay home and study, rather than socialise or get a part-time job. In the late 1970s, 77% of high-school seniors held a job during the school year, while by the mid-2010s, only 55% did. The number of eighth-graders who work for pay has also been cut in half. **The problem is, an easy life doesn't teach us much.** Whether stacking shelves, flipping burgers or working retail, the responsibility and social skills we learn from battling the challenges of any work environment teaches us resilience, compromise and unselfishness, as well as an appreciation that money doesn't grow on trees (as my parents often told me, despite me working from the age of 13).

Ensuring a young person is conscious of the value of hard work is not something we do for our benefit, but because it gives them the dignity of standing on their own two feet, and builds the tools and character to survive and thrive as an adult. Finding that balance between throwing an ill-prepared child headfirst into the real world, and wrapping them in cotton wool, is critical in order to grow a healthy and resilient conscious state of mind from which to navigate modern life.

While our innate social-nature, and in turn our happiness, is clearly under attack from technology, our raw mental capacity is suffering too. In fact, a study published in the *Journal of the Association for Consumer Research (JACR)* suggests a smartphone can affect its user's cognition simply by sitting next to them on a table, or being anywhere in the same room with them.

"If you grow dependent on your smartphone, it becomes a magical device that silently shouts your name at your brain at all times," says prominent technology writer, Robinson Meyer, in an article discussing this study. "In the study, Ward [the lead researcher] and his colleagues examined the performance of more than 500 undergraduates on two different common psychological tests of memory and attention. In the first experiment, some participants were told to set their phones to silent without vibration and either leave them in their bag or put them on their desk. Other participants were asked to leave all their possessions, including their cell phone, outside the testing room," explains Meyer. "In the second experiment, students were asked to leave their phones on their desk, in their bag, or out in the hall, just as in the first experiment. But some students were also asked to power their phone off, regardless of location."

In both experiments, students who left their phones outside the room did best on the test. Adrian Ward, one of the authors of the study and a psychologist at the University of Texas, said that if a phone is out of sight in a bag, even if it's set to silent, even if it's powered off, its mere presence will reduce someone's working memory and problem-solving skills.

But the mental impediments these devices are unknowingly causing us doesn't end there.

If I told you there are just five things a human being needs to survive, would you know what they are? I'll give you the first four for free: oxygen, water, shelter, food and... can you guess? It is something we're being denied daily as the 24/7 buzzingly-busy smartphone culture takes hold. What is it? I think Twenge explained it best with this conversation she had with her students about the fifth essential for survival – sleep. "I asked my undergraduate students at San Diego State University what they do with their phone while they sleep. Their answers were a profile in obsession. Nearly all slept with their phone, putting it under their pillow, on the mattress, or at the very least within arm's reach of the bed. They checked social media right before they went to sleep, and reached for their phone as soon as they woke up in the morning (they had to – all of them used it as their alarm clock). Their phone was the last thing they saw before they went to sleep and the first thing they saw when they woke up. If they woke in the middle of the night, they often ended up looking at their phone. Some used the language of addiction. 'I know I shouldn't, but I just can't help it,' one said about looking at her phone while in bed. Others saw their phone as an extension of their body – or even like a lover: 'Having my phone closer to me while I'm sleeping is a comfort,'" shares Twenge.

Sleep experts believe teens should be getting about nine hours of sleep a night, and say a teen who is getting less than seven hours is severely sleep deprived. As of 2015, 57% more teens were sleep deprived than in 1991, and in just four years from 2012 to 2015, Twenge says 22% more teens failed to get seven hours of sleep.

"Two national surveys show that teens who spend three or more hours a day on electronic devices are 28% more likely to get less than seven hours of sleep than those who spend fewer than three hours, and teens who visit social-media sites every day are 19% more likely to be sleep deprived."

A good night of zzzzzz's has long been underestimated as a necessity for survival, despite a severe lack of sleep being linked to compromised mental capacity, susceptibility to illness, weight gain, high blood pressure, and even anxiety and depression, both of which are gateways to suicide.

Unsurprisingly, the unconscious consequences of this huge techbubble we live in stretch far beyond us as individuals, as the 'virtual world' bends and shapes society's perceptions of what the 'real world' even is. The rapid growth of social media, coupled with our ability to access and share news 24/7 via globalised borderless communication channels, has given rise to a dangerous and often misleading fear of 'the other' – something that is causing great distress and unhappiness. The problems, and the solutions, as I see them, are threefold:

What we're drawn to. Unfortunately, our innate survivalist nature pulls us to search for those things that we believe are a threat to us and our preferred way of life. While we may do this as a protective measure,

200 thousand years of evolution has taught us to be suspicious and wary of those things that are different to us, and sadly for some, being exposed to 'difference' only makes them feel less safe, more in fear and more unhappy. The cycle of dread is only made worse by the fact that we can now easily seek out, reinforce and heighten our terror for any topic we want to find. If, for instance, I was terrified of air travel, I'd be able to find thousands of articles online about plane crashes that would support that panic (and I'd feel justified in my fear). The problem with fear (as you'll see from the Tennessee school story discussed later in this chapter) is it breeds more fear, and this phenomenon has led to bitterly divisive communities being established online (and consequently offline), including a new Nazi party in Germany or KKK and Islamaphobic hate groups in America. As researchers suggest, our brains still react to fear as if we're all still living in imminent danger, which for most, is not the case. Our brains simply haven't caught up with our reality, they say.

How we see things. Thirty milliseconds of exposure to someone's face is all it takes to provide sufficient information for your brain to form an impression of them. As ecologist and author Jared Diamond says, it's only in the last 7,500 years that "people had to learn, for the first time in history, how to encounter strangers regularly without attempting to kill them." Previously, we'd always lived in small-scale societies without the ability to travel or communicate much (languages were mostly tribal and localised). What this meant, is if someone from another tribe approached, there was no diplomacy, it was shoot first, ask questions later. The issue is, again, that our mind has failed to adapt to our current situation, which is that the world is more connected and peaceful than at any point in human history. Unfortunately though, the media won't let us see this. Instead, their obsession with conflict and tragedy heightens our primitive fight or flight response, when in actual fact, if we stop and think, we can probably appreciate that despite our differences in appearance, the vast majority of human beings have similar hopes and dreams, and pose absolutely no threat to us… which leads me to my final point.

Perceptions versus reality. If we want to be happy, we need to stop rushing to judgment, and we need to start questioning and seeing through the misinformation and the financial or political motives that underlie what we see in the media and online. Because sadly, a lot of it has us in a tizz, for no reason at all. Having worked with journalists for a number of years, I can tell you, a lot of it is rubbish, or at the very least heavily skewed towards getting ratings, which editors believe comes from having the most horrifying headlines, not the most truthful. What this misrepresentation does, is alarming! For instance, according to an international survey conducted in late 2014 by Ipsos Mori, Australians believed Muslims made up 18% of the country's population, when in reality it is just 2%. The sad thing is, Americans, Canadians, Belgians and the French had similar overestimations, the French going so far as to say 1 in 3 compatriots were Muslim, when the real figure is 8%. On another hot-button issue – immigration – our perceptions are a little less skewed. Australians believe immigrants make up 35% of the country – higher than the true number, of 28%. Italians and Americans on the other hand, both said immigrants make up 30% of their population, while the reality is just 7% and 13% respectively. Australians also believe a whopping 23% of the population is unemployed, when the data says it's 6%. We also said 15% of teenage girls are getting pregnant, when in reality it's a mere 2%. That figure is 3% among Americans and Britons, but they guessed 24% and 16% respectively.

Now, what we must ask ourselves is: how on Earth does all of this misperception occur if not for dramatic (and in my experience, often intentional) misrepresentation in the media and online? How do we as conscious/opportunity-based beings find the time to question and fact check what we see and read, rather than let our fearful and judgmental survivalist-based mentality take over? Personally, I think it is about being mindful of the fact that, left unchecked, without proper education and proper utilisation, greater awareness and access to information can actually make us unhappier, through subjecting us to our greatest insecurities and fears, 24/7.

While smartphones, the internet and social media aren't evil things designed by the devil to make us unhappy, the addictive, lonely, lazy, 24/7 nature that comes with being 'wired into them' is throwing our lives dramatically out of balance. The challenge for us all is to become and remain aware of how technology is altering our state of mind, and then, to have the mental will to free ourselves from those negative influences, and to form new behaviours. Once we're aware of, and have broken free from, our instinctive survivalist-based way of using technology – which is very ego-centric and making us depressed, anxious and suicidal – the next part of our tech-conscious-awakening is to turn the tide, and to use these incredible tools for good, for happiness. What does that look like exactly?

You might start by switching off from mainstream media and following a more ethical and positive online news source. You could choose to use Facebook as a way to keep in touch with long distance friends, but not as a replacement for those people you could catch up with in person. Perhaps you'll see the internet as a sea of knowledge, full of answers to those questions that plague you, that plague all of us. What's clear is, having all these additional resources to grow our awareness of the world doesn't make us happier or wiser, unless we take the time to think about and appreciate the knowledge at our fingertips. Despite some of the doom and gloom, I think ultimately technology is a good thing, as it has dramatically awakened and accelerated our consciousness. But at the same time, it has also overwhelmed it, being capable of almost grinding it to a standstill. Turn it on? Sure. But when and how do you turn it off? Or when and how does it turn us off?

I mean, look at the unhappiness facing Nkundusi – the catastrophic drought. Technology has been used by scientists to irrefutably prove that human beings, through increased carbon-emissions, have caused the earth's atmosphere to warm, propelling our climate into a state of chaos and unpredictability. However, the 97% of climate scientists who say this are now being drowned out by a sea of noise, created and disseminated by the big polluters via technology (traditional media and online), because their survival as an industry would be threatened if countries were to move away from carbon emitting fuels such as petroleum, coal and gas. So while on the one hand, someone like Nkasakhe might be able to make more sense of the drought facing her village if she had more time to think, explore and utilise technology (like most conscious/opportunity-based beings), there's a fair chance it wouldn't make her any happier. After all, what would she find? That her government and the developed world were ignoring them? That politicians and the super-wealthy were risking her survival in order to maintain profits? Perhaps she might wonder if the people making such decisions were even more survivalist-based than her – utterly unable to see past tomorrow?

But there is always a flipside, a yin and a yang. The enormous benefits of the tech-boom, and the rise of a more conscious/opportunity-based population, who are aware of and helping those in need, was what took us to our next destination – Xai-Xai in Mozambique. The largely impoverished coastal area 200km northeast of the capital Maputo, was home to a fantastically efficient aid project I had been asked to film a story on. My client was The Campaign for Australian Aid, which represented a coalition of organisations that wanted to see the Australian Government doing and giving more to help the world's most vulnerable people.

Give me an egg and I'll give you happiness

One of those people was Miguel Mulungo AKA 'The Chicken Man'. He was a hilarious, bouncy guy I fell in love with immediately. His life up until very recently was entirely survivalist-based. His country was the 7th poorest in the world, with an average GDP per capita of $1228USD per year – a wage Miguel could only dream of achieving. The rural property he called home was a shared parcel of land with six or seven small huts that were occupied by Miguel, his family and a few distant relatives. Oh, and chickens. Lots of chickens. In fact, it was his relationship with these feathery animals that brought us there.

During the 1990s, a team of Australian veterinary experts travelled to Mozambique to produce a local heat-tolerant vaccine for Newscastle disease, which is a highly contagious and lethal avian illness that can wipe out entire chicken populations sporadically and without warning. Since it was first recorded in South Africa in 1945, Newcastle disease has become one of the greatest threats to the livelihoods of rural families living throughout the African continent. For the past 15 years, the Australian government had proudly funded and supported the work of the Kyeema Foundation, which had assisted governments to manufacture and establish sustainable community-based distribution mechanisms for the vaccine across Mozambique and other nations. While community vaccinators are able to charge a small 'fee per bird vaccinated', which covers the cost of the vaccine and keeps the project running sustainably, ongoing financial support for expansion of the project has been a major challenge. In fact, due to huge cuts in Australia's aid budget, funding for expansion of this program was being culled. While it was hoped that the video I was there to create could inspire the government to rethink this decision – by illustrating just how effective this program was at saving lives and alleviating poverty in rural areas – sadly Miguel's story fell on deaf ears, and funding for the project finished in mid-2016. Thankfully, in the year following our filming, Kyeema was able to secure 12 months funding for the project through Europe (EU) Aid, however ongoing financial support for expansion of the vaccination scheme is not yet guaranteed.

Suddenly, the decisions of two supposedly conscious/opportunity-based government institutions thousands of kilometres away, could be the difference between life and death for Miguel, his family and others like them.

It sounds dramatic I know, to think that a bird could determine one's ability to survive, but as Miguel explained, chickens not only provided eggs and meat, which were a major source of food, they were also like a money tree for the poor. As chicken populations grew, rural households had resources (excess eggs or birds), which they could sell or trade for labour, food or anything else they needed. But, if those birds suddenly died, Miguel said that the money tree withered and died too.

"A few years ago my family and I barely had enough to eat, but now thanks to the people who come and give my chickens the Newcastle vaccine, we are able to keep our chicken flock alive and growing. This means we can feed our children three times a day, and can even trade chickens when we need to take them to hospital, or to pay for school fees and books," said Miguel with a huge, beaming smile. "Life is getting better. Happiness is possible now, because we have lots of chickens."

I must confess, I never had chickens on my list of things that could bring a person happiness, but I guess I was wrong. For Miguel, these birds were the difference between being utterly survivalist-based, and having just enough food and financial security to feel safe, which gave him a fraction of time each day to think and act in expansive, more fully-conscious ways. In all I have seen, those who go from no time to think, to even a few minutes a day, seem to have the most dramatic rise in happiness. And researchers agree. A number of international studies suggest there is actually a relatively low annual income threshold (in the US it is $34,000USD while in many developing nations it is around $5000USD) beyond which you don't become happier, despite 'having more'. Observing this phenomenon time and again, and speaking to those involved, I think that greater happiness is actually derived from the sudden sense of peace that comes from being able to stop and think about life, and devise a few plans to ensure one's ongoing future. It might also help that families who break free from poverty typically remember

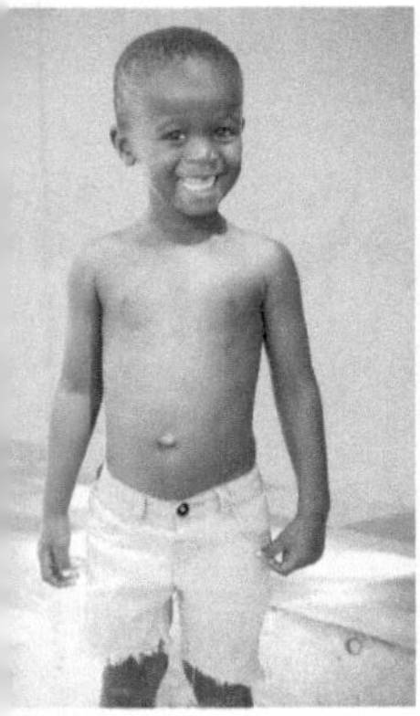

Some of the happiest survivalist-based people I met during my trip through East Africa.

Miguel and his family.

Fishermen, roughly where the boy was found.

(for at least a generation) what it was to have less, so are inherently more grateful for all they have.

"It's amazing! One drop of the vaccine in the chicken's eye and they don't die anymore. My family and I can sit and share stories and help one another and we can even help to feed other people in our village, so they can survive better now too," said Miguel.

What I couldn't see immediately, but felt in the background, was an intersection where a deep sense of happiness existed for both survivalist-based and conscious/opportunity-based beings. Travelling in one direction are those nice and shiny, yet often empty, conscious/opportunity-based beings, whose greatest threat to survival is their own unhappiness (in fact the World Health Organisation says depression will be the leading cause of disease in the developed world by 2020 and we will see one suicide every 20 seconds). Travelling in the other direction are those survivalist-based beings, whose greatest threats to survival are a lack of food, money, access to clean water, sanitation and medical treatment. In fact, **poverty kills more people than heart disease and cancer combined, including 22,000 children every day.** I'm not sure if you see what comes next, but what if we could kill two birds with one stone, or rather, let both birds live and keep the stone? If the greatest threat to conscious/opportunity-based beings is unhappiness, and the greatest threat to survivalist-based beings is a lack of resources, then the stone that will solve both problems is giving.

Science and experience tell us that even the most privileged are made happier by giving, while for those trapped in a survivalist state of being, going from living off $2 a day to $14 a day is the most significant leap when it comes to happiness. I remember thinking at the time, that if this intersection could become more of a roundabout, and people could forget about what car they were or were not driving, and simply connect, co-exist and co-operate at the most basic human level, we may actually see an end to those things that are causing all of us unnecessary suffering. Perhaps then, none of us would need worry about our survival again. Perhaps then, we could all be happy.

If you think I'm a dreamer, you'd be right, but I've also been living in that roundabout for the past decade, so I know it works. The only question is, will you join me? Will you defeat your survivalist mentality? That innate itch, telling you that you forever need more. Will you continue to define success by how much you have? Or will you redefine the term, to mean how much you give? Will you be remembered for your wealth or your generosity? What part will you play in ending needless human suffering? The alternative is a merry-go-round of pain and sadness that feeds on those who are consciously unconscious. Those who look on in silence, blaming survivalist-based beings for their demise. 'Why don't they just make better decisions?' some think. Well, one such place and story that taught me a thing or two about this was Lake Malawi and **The Tale of Unintended Consequences**:

> We were heading back from the drop-toilet up the hill one morning when I began laughing at the way Sash walks with her big butt poking out and her head wobbling side to side waiting for the next distraction. "There's actually something going on down there, people are running towards the lake," said Sash out of the blue.
>
> As we got closer to our room, which overlooked the lake, I noticed a lot of people standing around. Then, suddenly, one by one they started hoping into their thin wooden fishing boats and paddling out onto the lake. Nearing the gathering, I noticed a boy in a purple shirt was in tears – screaming uncontrollably what sounded like 'papa'. We scampered towards the rocky point, where I noticed some canoes huddled together out on the lake, all looking in the same place – about 100 metres from shore.
>
> "What's wrong," I asked, not really expecting an answer given the language barrier. "I can swim, can I help? Has someone fallen in?" It was difficult to get a response in English. "Yes," was all I heard. So I began undressing.
>
> Soon I was running along a dangerous shoreline of rocks, as more onlookers began to gather. Why wasn't anyone jumping in to help? I wondered. I guessed, perhaps, because they couldn't swim. But why were they so calm? Where was the panic? Was I the only one who could feel the urgency? When I finally found the only local who seemed to be dressed in bathers ready to jump in, he asked me, "Can you swim?" "Yes," I almost spat the word in my haste. "OK then, we wait for the snorkel and mask to come and you help me." His quiet and solemn tone said it all. We weren't going to be rescuing anyone, but rather retrieving their corpse.

By this time, I'd told Sash to run and find some more people to help, so she was no longer next to me.

Still, if we were going to be retrieving the body of what I assumed was the young boy's father from the bottom of the lake, it was safer for me to do this than to risk more lives. As a man passed me a pair of blue surgical gloves, I consciously tried to calm myself, as I prepared for my first encounter with the unexpected reality of accidental death. It filled me with a real sense of dread and panic at what we might find, when we reached those canoes out on the water. My first encounter with a corpse was under entirely different circumstances, when I leaned in to kiss goodbye the gentle, resting face of my beloved Gran as she lay there, serene and slathered in mortician's make-up. She'd had a wonderful life and though I was distraught at letting her go, I was at peace with the prospect, largely because of the absolute calmness and acceptance with which my gran approached her death. She knew she was dying and was grateful for the long, mostly-happy life she had lived.

Reflecting the serenity I felt at my gran's deathbed were the picture-postcard surrounds in which I now found myself. The water was still and crystal clear. Colourful fish glided past and the ancient rock formations on the floor of the lake were fascinating, demanding to be admired. Under altered circumstances, this would have been one of our trip's happier memories. But right now, it was no tourist idyll. Sash had raced back with her swimming clothes on, and quickly put on her snorkel and mask and joined me in the water. We both followed the local swimmer. As I peered up and saw the boats, I remembered the young boys tears and panic and I hurt, probably for him, but also for me. So many thoughts raced through me and I remember thinking this was the first time I had gone swimming in medical gloves.

As we got close, my breaths drew shorter as breathing began to hurt. And then, we saw him.

I thought it would be his father. I thought he would be floating or laying on the bottom of the lake. But I was wrong. It was a child. The boy's brother or friend perhaps. And you could see him, even from the surface. It was so life like, he was completely upright, his foot pinned under a rock and his two arms outstretched, reaching towards the surface, with his mouth wide open, as if yelling for the help that never arrived. He was rigid and stiff and yet his body moved with the gentle lapping of the water. It was eerie. So much so that Sash thought he was alive and swam back to shore as fast as she could to fetch more people to help. There were markings on his face that I at first interpreted as skin blemishes, until I realised that was where the fish had nibbled him. He was missing pieces from his eyes, mouth and nostrils. It was not a time for any squeamish reaction as the local man and I devised a plan to recover the body.

We both tried diving down to move the rock or tie something around the boy, so we could pull him up, but it was too deep. Normally, I think I would have been fine, if we had been retrieving an inanimate object such as a rock or a piece of luggage, but given the nature of our task, air refused to fill my lungs for more than a few seconds, and as I dived down time and again I swallowed a troubling amount of water. I felt ill, as if I had a bad fever. I was sweating. The heat in my body was boiling my brain. Still, I tried in earnest to free him. Up and down we went. Until finally, the rope caught around his arm for just long enough that the fishermen in the canoes holding the rope could jolt him free. As his body slowly floated to the surface, you could see he was bloated and had likely been underwater for days.

Rather than hoist the body on board one of the flimsy boats, we floated him back to the shore. I think Sash still believed he was alive, and had found two others who were eager to help. By this time, there were hundreds of locals lining the shore, with a distinct clump bereft and bellowing in pain. You could hear them between every splashing-stroke as we paddled in. It was the family of the nameless boy we'd just exhumed from the lake. The boy, Sash had just realised, was dead.

I quietly exited the water, some distance away from where the body was taken ashore. Sash met me and we cried. The sorrow. The exhaustion. The pain of having water in my lungs. I didn't want to shut any of it out, for in the days ahead I knew we would need to call on every ounce of sadness and suffering to give us the energy to do something about this.

With adrenaline still gushing through our veins, Sash and I immediately began investigating the truth of what had happened, so we could ascertain if or how this boy's death and others like it could be avoided. What we came to learn (after days or probing) was confronting. Firstly, the dead boy had come to the lake to go fishing with his friend (despite not being able to swim) when he suddenly fell from their precarious dugout-canoe and disappeared in the murky water. What was even more shocking to discover perhaps, was that during violent storms, tens or even hundreds of local fishermen were suffering the same fate, because they often opted to stay out on the water during the nasty weather. The dilemma was, they need to catch fish to keep their family alive, and sometimes the storms stirred up the fish into their nets, which made the risk worthwhile.

Of course, the wives and children left without a husband or father would beg to differ, but still, this is the situation facing thousands of families in Malawi, who fish to survive. To the average onlooker this situation seems avoidable – if you see a storm, get back to shore – but what if that meant your family didn't eat that day? Or what if the storm wasn't that bad, or misses your location? Then you've lost time, money and fish to the man that ignored the rough weather, and ultimately his family survives that little better than yours.

On the one hand, you can understand that human beings will do anything to survive, even if it means fishing from impossible-to-balance canoes on a lake filled with dangers, despite not being able to swim. But, if survival is the name of the game, how was it that they were willing to risk that very thing, rather than invest in a life-jacket, swimming lessons or safer boat? Asking around back in Nkhata Bay, it seemed as if the time, knowledge and system to ensure people used the lake safely was simply not something that was prioritised by the people. That's despite a quick Google search confirming it is in fact a widespread problem that kills hundreds every year.

The problem is, as Eldar Shafir, a psychologist at Princeton University and Sendhil Mullainathan, an economist at Harvard, write in their book *Scarcity: Why having too little means so much*, human beings don't make good decisions when they perceive things to be in short supply. While the experience can give rise to our uncanny and innate ability to manage short-term problems, the pair say that's all it allows us to do. "Scarcity consumes you," Shafir and Mullainathan explain. "You're less able to focus on other things that are also important to you ... If you want to understand the poor, imagine yourself with your mind elsewhere. Self-control feels like a challenge. You are distracted and easily perturbed. And this happens every day."

How I came to view the problem was as follows: Imagine you're a decision and you're travelling along a brand new four lane super highway with no traffic and clear signage. There's a fair chance you'll be able to see things clearly and arrive at the right destination without delay. Correct? But what if there's cars, cows, motorbikes, trucks, buses, broken signs, potholes everywhere, people beeping and yelling and a traffic jam (of competing priorities) is making it impossible for you to reach your destination. Chances are you'll wind up hitting a pothole, exiting and getting lost, sitting in traffic or disappearing in the noise. Whichever way you look at it, you (a decision) are either going to be lost, broken, distorted or go nowhere.

This is what happens inside the mind of someone with a "scarcity mentality" says Shafir. In their lack, individuals and families are forced to ask questions like 'what's for dinner?' and 'how will we afford the medicine, school, bus or shelter?', which constantly take up (and jam) three lanes of traffic. Of course, the remaining lane is so badly riddled with the potholes of poverty (such as bad governance and poor infrastructure) that nearly nothing gets through. This is how and why the scarcity mentality (the survivalist-based mind-set) can lead to poor decisions – such as going fishing out on a lake without a life-jacket despite being unable to swim.

During our 67 hour journey by local minivan, plane and bus to Rwanda (via Dar es Salaam in Tanzania), I couldn't stop thinking about whether those who have greater time to think about their surroundings – the more conscious/opportunity-based beings of our world – are in any way better placed to find happiness than those more survivalist-based beings who are more trapped in the now. Is that ability to dream of a bigger, brighter future essential to one's happiness and peace of mind? Or is it, in fact, harmful? Does being in a constant 'state of flow', not worrying about the future and 'what ifs', make someone more content and fulfilled? Is ignorance really bliss? What do survivalist-based beings miss out on, and what do they gain? Does their lack of awareness, or their focus on the day-to-day, really make them less conscious? In what ways do they think differently? What role does instinct play? Are we more conscious when we're simply creatures following our gut trying to survive? Is that our natural state? Or are we evolving into something else?

Since our time immemorial, human beings have walked the earth doing both horrid and great things to survive. In modern times, however, the very idea of living simply to survive is becoming obsolete for much of the world. For while 84% of the world's population lived in extreme poverty in 1820, now that number is less than 10%. With leaps in agriculture, healthcare and technology making life safer and easier than at any point in our history, where do we turn to next? What elements of our survivalist-based selves do we need to hold onto in order to maintain happiness, and which must we shed?

What better place to seek answers than a country and people that very nearly wiped themselves off the map?

We rise together

Standing in stark contrast to the wearisome half-truths that plagued our time in Malawi, was the untainted honesty of Rwanda – known largely for its 1994 genocide (between Hutu and Tutsi ethnic groups) that saw 800,000 people killed in the space of 100 days. Unbeknownst to us, we arrived in the capital, Kigali, during their annual week of mourning (April 7-14). Unlike most war-time slaughters – such as the Gallipoli landing on 25 April 1915, or D-Day on 6 June 1944 – there was no talk of heroes or honour and no sense of triumph in the air during that week. There was only sadness. Deep sadness.

"The cruelty of what human beings, all of us, did to one another in this country must never be forgotten, or we risk repeating it," said one Rwandan radio host. But he wasn't alone. On every radio, and every TV, all you could hear or see was talk of the genocide. When I asked why, I was fascinated to learn that the President of Rwanda, Paul Kagame (the leader of the Tutsi resistance that eventually ended the genocide), had made it mandatory that during the national week of mourning, media outlets only air content relating to the genocide. No music. No pop-culture. No ignoring the problem. No half-truths. Just raw, unadulterated horror.

"Our President has dedicated this week to remembering, because when we forget, that is when genocide can come again and divide us, destroy us," said Christian, the son of the family we AirBnB'd with in Kigali. "Everything must discuss the genocide. As much as it pains us, we must be conscious of our past, in order to find a better way forward. We were a united country before colonialism divided us [into Hutus and Tutsis] and we must get back to that place, that idea of being one and the same. A nation of Rwandans."

During the genocide, Christian and his mother Speciose (both Tutsis) were taken in by their Hutu neighbour, who hid them in his attic along with others. Thousands of Hutu families risked being hacked to death by machete or beaten to death by a club if they were found to be aiding and abetting Tutsis, but still, this was one of the most common means of evading the government-backed Hutu forces if you were in the Tutsi minority. During this extended period of 'kill or be killed', you would think it natural to be absolutely survivalist-based, and yet, it drew out of some a profound and very conscious sense of humanity. Conscious/opportunity-based members of this society provided a lesson more pivotal now than ever before.

"No matter what those seeking power want us to believe, we are all far more similar than we are different," said Christian.

When we understand that — and truly value it — we won't need to fight for our survival. Those who have, will naturally give to those who don't, because when we see ourselves in others, we begin to understand that if we ease another's suffering, in turn we ease our own. What then would we have to war over? If we were all equal, and if we all shared, perhaps we could forget about surviving and start living.

Such a shift in consciousness might sound impossible, but the more Rwandans I met (mostly in Kigali), the more I became convinced that certain policies of President Kagame and his government were doing exactly that. One such practice he re-introduced and prioritised after the genocide was Umuganda, which can be translated as 'coming together in common purpose to achieve an outcome'. Umuganda is held on the last Saturday of each month at 8am and involves families, neighbours, and even former enemies working together to clean and care for their community. It's one reason why Rwanda is known as the cleanest and greenest country in East Africa. Umuganda has even been responsible for the building of new schools, hospitals and hydroelectric plants. This concerted effort to bring Rwandans together once a month is estimated to be worth more than $22 million USD per year to the country's economy. Its true value though, was a little harder to measure. The collective rise in consciousness, away from the survivalist-based mentality that nearly laid waste to this country, was profound, but I soon discovered this changed-mind-set wasn't just the result of this one idea.

In addition to this bold move to get people working together for a common purpose, Kagame and his ministers also introduced a mandatory community service program for all high school graduates. The most awesome and conscious objective: to reconnect students with what it meant to be Rwandan before colonisation, before the Belgian and French forces split the country into Hutu and Tutsi. Before these united people were divided and conquered.

The theoretical component of this program, which steps the youth through the old ways of peace, unity and sharing, is a pertinent precursor for their (minimum) two weeks of compulsory community service. Graduates are able to select a charity or cause they wish to be a part of and often volunteer anywhere up to three months between finishing school and starting university or work. From all we saw and heard, the outcome was a more aware and connected youth. A generation that could envisage a Rwanda without walls or boundaries.

When I bumped into two young boys on their way home from a game of basketball, another somewhat anecdotal yet connected sign of a growing consciousness popped out of their mouths.

"We can be happy, because we know who we want to be, we have a future, a goal – Rwanda is going to be the Switzerland of Africa," said one of the boys. "You know, we are small, landlocked and lacking in natural resources, so we need to think differently. So what do we have? We are smart, we are building infrastructure and technology – like free public Wi-Fi for all – which will allow us to be a high-end business centre delivering next generation services for the region, like the Swiss do," said the other boy.

Clearly these boys had a hefty vision (a further sign of being highly conscious/opportunity-based), but was this a collective belief and dream Rwandans held? Such a notion stands in stark contrast to a society that just a decade earlier found itself trapped and divided in a grotesque war for superiority and survival. Had they done away with this survivalist-based mentality? Had the country been united towards a more conscious, common and connected goal?

When my wife and I were both robbed of our (pretty average and cheap) mobile phones while we scrambled to get on a local bus, I thought twice. But the more Rwandans I met, particularly youth (who were not directly involved in the genocide, but are still forced to deal with it), the more the highly-conscious vision seemed to reverberate.

"We can be a symbol of hope, I think, of what is possible when corruption and division is replaced with a people-centred, unified vision," said a 17-year-old boy who dreamed of being a singer. "We will be Africa's Switzerland," re-iterated a university student named Grace. "Rwanda will be the shining star of East Africa, a symbol of peace and unity," surmised the CEO of a local peace-building NGO we visited.

Unmistakably, mere survival was no longer the priority of these people (not in Kigali at least, which is where we spent most of our time). But how did they make that leap. Thirteen years ago, one in seven Rwandans were murdered – often by those closest to them, including neighbours and even family. In the Genocide Memorial Centre, there were two stories and images I will never forget. Both exemplified just what we're capable of when trapped in a crazed survivalist-based mind-set. The first was the story of a Hutu wife who hacked off her Tutsi husband's penis and head. The second was a 7-year-old girl and her mother, both of whom were raped before being tortured and chopped to bits.

Why not just kill them? I wondered, as my soul ached at reading endless stories like these. If you want to exterminate a race, however wrong that might be, why is there so often a need to inflict additional suffering? If Tutsis were the "rats" and "vermin" of the Earth, as the Hutu propaganda claimed, then why touch them, let alone rape them? Certainly this malicious behaviour went beyond mere survival, or did it? Did the minds of those perpetrators (some of whom were forced to kill or be killed) need to believe the propaganda in order to protect their own minds from short-circuiting or melting in the heat of the madness and hell that confronted them? I mean, if you had any sort of conscious-base within you, seeing these people as utterly inhuman was probably the only coping or survival mechanism to stop you from becoming crazy, depressed or suicidal.

Still, the madness of it all was too much for some. Christian's older sister was one such case. For some days I wondered why our AirBnb family seemed quiet and closed off about the week of mourning.

I was under the impression they'd all survived, though Christian and his mother had been separated from his father, older sister and other relatives. I forget now how it came up, but we came to learn that the older sister had suffered what we in the West would call severe PTSD. And she wasn't alone. So while the killing stopped on 14 August 1994, the deaths continued, including Christian's sister who eventually killed herself. Suicide was commonplace in the months and years following the genocide, because ultimately, I think, we're all a little more conscious than the animalistic-survivalist-monsterous-nature that possessed people and propelled this genocide.

That's why, I think, in 2005, when more than 12,000 traditional 'Gacaca' courts (where ordinary citizens try, convict and set punishments for perpetrators) began hearing cases, a huge wave of suicides ensued. From March to December 2006, authorities reported 69 suspects killed themselves, while another 44 tried to. What this tells me, encouragingly, is that all humans are somewhat innately conscious, but that conscience towards others can be subsumed by circumstance and pressure. If we were here merely to survive or pass forward our DNA, why do we find our animalistic survivalist-based tendencies so hard to live with? Why is it so hard to kill without emotion? What are empathy and guilt here to teach us? Why does harming or killing another so often make us want to kill ourselves? These questions continued on repeat with each beat of my heart.

Umuganda. Mandatory community service for their young. A shared vision for what Rwanda could be. A deep sense of disgust at what they'd done. And the honesty not to shy away from it. It all seemed to play a part in raising the conscience of Rwandans, many of whom, following the genocide, had no doubt been left with a surreal shell-shocked version of a survivalist-based mind-set. While Rwanda remains the 20th poorest country in the world (with an average GDP per capita of just $1905USD), meaning poverty and a scarcity mind-set still prevail in parts, the government (who is accused of being a little authoritarian at times) seems to have provided the people with an uplifting platform from which to make decisions and expand their sense of self. A more conscious and connected state of being. And for the most part, this seems to be breeding a happier and more peaceful society.

As we left Kigali and journeyed along the winding mountain paths, through tea plantations and over the border into Uganda, something changed immediately – the noise. Ugandans were loud. Forever joking and laughing like mad at the simplest of things. If I had a device for measuring 'life', I'm sure it would have been off the charts. Rwanda's quiet and solemn nature may have made Uganda's buzz seem even more obvious, but there was something about this place that was unexpectedly pleasant. Uganda had undoubtedly known its fair share of war and was still the 25th poorest country, which meant many were trapped in a survivalist mind-set, but there was something else at play here. A sort of unwritten and unspoken bubbling band of energy that bound the people together in a cheery-consciousness I only wished I could be a part of. Unfortunately though, we had our own 'date with survival' to contend with before we could enjoy anything about this vivacious country.

Trapped in traffic

When our bus (from Kigali in Rwanda to Kabale in southern Uganda) overshot our stop by a few kilometres, we became stranded in the middle of nowhere with no phone or internet and little understanding of where we were in relation to where we needed to be. I couldn't help but remember a few blogs I'd read that suggested Uganda wasn't exactly safe, and my own survivalist-based mechanisms began to fire. My heart pounded. My mind was absorbed in each and every step or move we made. I constantly kept on top of our escape options. I'd eyed off tools close by I could use to defend us, and I had a few loose bits of change in my pocket I could offer anyone who seemed hostile.

We waited for the longest three minutes of my life, hoping someone might come to us. A lost white guy and brown girl standing by the side of the road had typically drawn a lot of attention in Africa (yes we'd been lost before), but right then and there, nothing. No offers of a ride, no buses slowing down, not even anyone trying to sell us food or knick-knacks.

With limited options, I put my brave face on and walked into the only shop we could find, which was a petrol station of sorts. I pointed at a piece of paper I had that said Lake Bunyonyi, which is where we were headed. "OK, those men are Taxi," said the thin shop-keeper, as he smiled peculiarly from behind the counter. "They take you," he continued, as he pointed towards two seriously scrappy looking men standing by a dirty old car that had absolutely no taxi sign or symbol on it.

My survivalist-based mind told me we had a few hours until nightfall and needed to find our hostel, or else. We fought off just enough of those survival instincts and followed the random men to their white (though the dust made it look brown) early 1990s Toyota. Why did both of them need to come? We wondered nervously as we jumped in the back seat. What could two men do that one could not? One side of me went to the obvious, while my more rational conscious mind tried to calm me by sympathising that the driver must get bored being by himself all day, so he brings a friend.

After five or ten attempts at telling them where we needed to go, we scratched our heads. Had we got the name of the place wrong? "Gorilla Packers, Lake Bunyonyi," we repeated a few more times. But the wheels of the car weren't moving. My mind wondered if it was all a game. A ploy to 'get us'. The men then called friends and repeated the name we gave them.

Who were they talking to? I wondered. What else were they saying that we couldn't understand? Short on patience and sick of standing still, we said, "We need Internet or Wi-Fi." This they understood. "Internet, OK," replied the driver's friend. We knew that if we could get to somewhere with a computer, we could bring up an email with the exact name and address of the place we were staying. Hopefully that might do the trick, we thought, with fingers crossed.

Using some of those survivalist-based trains of thought, when we finally found and arrived at an internet café, we decided it was better for me to go in, while Sash guarded our stuff from a growing group of young boys who were hovering about outside. If she was in the car with the door shut and locked, at least they couldn't touch her, I figured. Though, I'm not sure if I was more worried about them or the men in the car. I remember hating these thoughts, but my mind was in complete fight or flight mode – on maximum alert. With one eye on Sash and one on the computer screen, I searched for the email we needed to print out. Of course, nothing went smoothly, and it felt as if the process took hours, when in actual fact it was probably about ten minutes.

By the time I walked out to the car, there must have been around 50 kids gathered, all up to no good in my mind. Where had that initial charm of Uganda gone? Was this area of the country rougher than the towns we'd stopped at on our bus ride, or had my mind taken me to a darker place, as a means to survive? Where was the love, innocence and positivity that defined most interactions I'd had in Africa?

Distrust and a distinct lack of patience or empathy characterised our car ride, as the men squabbled about which route to take to get to our hostel. Twenty minutes in, I remember wondering why they kept stopping and talking to strangers on the side of the road. "Do you know where we are?" I asked bluntly. Clearly we were lost, but they pretended not to understand English all of a sudden. As time passed, my anger grew. Finally they called a friend, who seemed to give them the directions they needed. Then, out of nowhere, they turned to us and said they wanted more money. They insisted we pay each of them the agreed total for the fare (30,000 Ugandan Shillings or roughly $10), so double what we'd originally said. Just as my mind had begun relaxing, again I was forced into overdrive. Communicating, let alone rationally explaining that only one of them was driving, so why are we paying both of them, was pointless. I bit my tongue and negotiated to pay them a bit more than the agreed total, mostly just to ensure our safety. After all, life and peace of mind are priceless.

About an hour and a half after being dropped by the roadside by the bus, we arrived at our destination. While I'd been so wrapped up in my own survivalist mind-set, I'd hardly taken the time to appreciate... well anything. These strange men, as it turned out, were actually rather lovely, and had severely undercharged us to begin with. I'm also pretty sure that the reason they were spending time driving together was because they were secretly in a relationship (a criminal offence in Uganda). They'd also rather remarkably dealt with the bizarre situation of two lost travellers turning up at a petrol station and asking them for a lift, only to find out that these English-speaking foreigners rather stupidly didn't have a hard copy of their hostel booking. As our hostel manager so poignantly put it, "You were lost and they kept you safe, helped you find an internet cafe and got you here, so that's good." I guess the instinctive dickhead in me just couldn't see that through my survivalist-based mind-set which had created a drama out of nothing.

Sitting there rather embarrassed at what FEAR ('False Evidence Appearing Real', as Tommy put it) had done to me, I remembered a news story that a professor had shared with us at university about a school in Tennessee, USA. The context he gave us was around being mindful of the fear we can propagate as journalists, and even citizens, because panic he said could spread like wildfire, in less than the time it takes us to blink. The story he shared, re-written here by *BBC Focus Magazine's* Daniel Bennett, exemplifies just how powerful and potentially damaging that survivalist-based fight or flight response can be for our mental and physical health:

> In 1998, at a high school in Tennessee, a teacher complained of a pungent "gasoline-like" smell in her classroom. Soon after, she fell ill, reporting symptoms such as nausea, shortness of breath, dizziness and a headache. Almost immediately, several students in her class started to experience similar symptoms and, before long, the rest of the school was stricken.
>
> The building was evacuated as fire fighters, ambulances and police arrived on the scene to tend to the sick. That evening the local emergency room admitted 80 students and 19 staff members; 38 were hospitalised overnight.
>
> But what was the mysterious toxic gas that sparked the outbreak? Several extensive investigations by Government agencies found nothing. Blood tests showed no signs of any harmful compounds. Instead, according to Timothy Jones a local epidemiologist, the fear of being poisoned had spread, fuelling the symptoms experienced by everyone inside.
>
> A report in the New England Journal of Medicine attributed the outbreak to a phenomenon known as 'mass psychogenic illness', which occurs when the fear of infection spreads just as virulently as the disease itself. The students and staff had decided that, based on the behaviour of those around them, there was a real threat they needed to be afraid of.
>
> The 'outbreak' in Tennessee demonstrates that people can be scared – to the point of self-induced sickness – without there actually being any real threat present.

Thankfully, the cracked and darkened lens of fear that we developed during our own survivalist-based experienced, soon disappeared, as we crossed the border into Kenya to visit a community who'd all but overcome the scarcity mentality, despite living in abject financial poverty. What I was keen to learn was: what tools or ideas have allowed them to break free from their survival-based mind-set? How do those struggling to survive adopt a more conscious/opportunity-based approach to life? And does that lead to greater and more lasting happiness?

As fate and irony would have it, a Facebook post I made asking – "Who should we meet or where should we go to learn more about happiness in East Africa?" – ended with us talking to the 'communications manager' (basically the person with the best English/phone/Facebook account) of a traditional Maasai village in southern-Kenya, near Mount Kilimanjaro. The potential for the internet to increase our consciousness and connectivity was about to take full flight, as we were invited to spend a week living in a cow dung hut, learning from one of the longest surviving traditional cultures on earth.

Warriors of conscience

A few hours by bus from Nairobi, we arrived in Kimana. Through the dusty, diesel-ridden air, I remember these flashes of colour that made me smile. I was entering a photographer's dream. There were people pushing carts of corn and meat, while others ran from bus to bus desperately trying to sell whatever foods and crafts they'd made. Among the waves of chaos – like polka-dots against a baron landscape – all I could see were the Maasai. Draped in beads that would make a rainbow seem dull, their tall, dark, thin figures were wrapped in bold shades of mostly-chequered red and blue cloth (called shúkà). It felt as though I'd travelled to some beautiful distant planet out of Star Wars, where colour was the god being worshipped. Was this just a show? I wondered. For the tourists? Wait, we were the only foreigners in sight, I realised, as I gazed around in awe. Dust continued to dry my eyes, but I didn't care. The chaos all around mattered not. To me, time stood still. The exquisite form, shade and texture of each Maasai I saw was so dazzling it didn't even occur to me to get my camera out and capture it. Then suddenly, my glorious nothingness (it felt like I hadn't moved in hours) was interrupted when a giant man in red climbed from a motorbike. "Mr Mike?" he said inquisitively. "Hello," I responded, "you must be Benson, we are so happy to see you… shall we go?"

"No, no, let us sit. We can talk, and we ca-ca-can get something to eat," he said in his slightly stuttered, yet soothing English accent. "It is a long way to our village, so let us rest a ley-a-li-little," he continued, unperturbed by the rush of vehicles around him. "We are in no rush are we?"

It was the first time I'd heard that phrase used during our three months in Africa. Something that was of course the result of most of the Continent being survivalist-based, where people were forever in a state of doing, constantly moving, washing, walking, building, digging, cooking, carrying and cleaning – it was non-stop. Never nothing. No time to stop and think. But there was something different about this guy. As if his heart beat to a different drum. A more pure sound. An ancient tune.

Benson's body, his mind and his spirit all seemed undeniably in sync.

As he secured his bike down and gestured to walk with him, I was mesmerised by his long legs as they moved slowly across the gravel footpath – he even seemed to walk more calmly than others. Methodically. Without a worry in his mind. His lengthy, efficient strides reminded me of an elephant that didn't want to step more than it had to. His elongated frame swayed to the left and we entered a small laneway, crossed behind a few shops and arrived at a restaurant he invited us to sit at. We told him to order his favourite thing, "our shout" we said.

A bottle of Fanta arrived, and Sash and I laughed. Of course, we should have known. Something about watching this man – with facial scarification, two teeth ritually removed and beads dangling from well-stretched earlobes – drinking that familiar fizzy orange refreshment, was so disarming. Almost immediately, he felt more like a brother or a mate than the tribal warrior I'd imagined and could see right in front of me. With every sip he took, and every word he shared, we were drawn closer. He looked alien, but felt like a twin.

"You should know, we have been in drought for a long time," he said. "This is very bad, because we are pastoralists, so we rely on the land, the rain. You will see our people, and our cows, are unable to get enough food right now. But I think you know about this, Australia understands drought don't they?" he inquired knowingly, curious to learn more. "Yes," we replied, "but our farmers have ways of coping most of the time, and sometimes if it is very bad, our government will support them a bit."

"Wow. Yes we are just a small village, living with our animals, just in huts made of cow dung, but we know how others live. We know the news of the West, the bright lights of Hollywood, the celebrities you follow and the damage this climate change is doing not only to us, but elsewhere. We have seen your fires in Australia, and California and Sweden."

How did he know all this? Who was this guy? How was this survivalist-based pastoralist living in the middle of nowhere so damn conscious of everything? How was it I could hear his conscience? His concern for others. Was he in fact survivalist-based, as he looked? I mean, his village was struggling to eat enough, so I guess that suggested they were, but what were we going to find as we dug a little deeper into the culture, rituals, society and beliefs of the Maasai? What had their harsh semi-nomadic life taught them about happiness? And what might the rest of us learn from that?

The painfully slow two-hour car ride to Olasiti Village (Benson's home) provided a number of insights. In between the bumps and bounces over endless potholes and divots, the image of what we were entering became clearer. Each town we passed, every interaction we witnessed, it all told a story of a confused, fragmented people. The Maasai, Benson said, were facing a number of difficult decisions around identity and future proofing their way of life.

"You can see all around us here there are more kinds of developed townships where Maasai are living, sometimes keeping some of the traditional ways, but often just adopting the Western thinking. Like mostly they are getting a job, making a house just for themselves, and buying all the toys and foods that make so much rubbish and pollute our Earth," said Benson, as a young boy on his way home from school stopped to pick up a water bottle among the trash that surrounded him. "There are about 42 ethnic tribes in Kenya, and almost all have done away with their culture and their traditions, basically because of material things. Trying to run with the Western world or trying to have bigger things. I don't know what they're actually looking for," professed Benson, who nearly bashed his head on the roof of the car as we hit a bump.

We pass another field of rubbish with a few tin huts, a couple of power poles and the odd cement brick building with a satellite dish on it. Benson tells me TV is so often seen as kind of "like magic in the eyes of our youth," he says. Looking back at a number of the photos I took as we passed through one of the main towns that fell between Kimana and Olasiti, one thing that struck me as odd was the number of people sitting or standing by themselves, often looking sad. Being alone in a

One of the somewhat trashy 'modern' Maasai towns.

Children search through the rubbish for useful things.

Benson showing us how to pump water.

The women welcoming Sash.

A Maasai man standing next to the tiny doorway to his house.

The fence of acacia bushes surrounding Olasiti Village, and one of the openings which is closed at night.

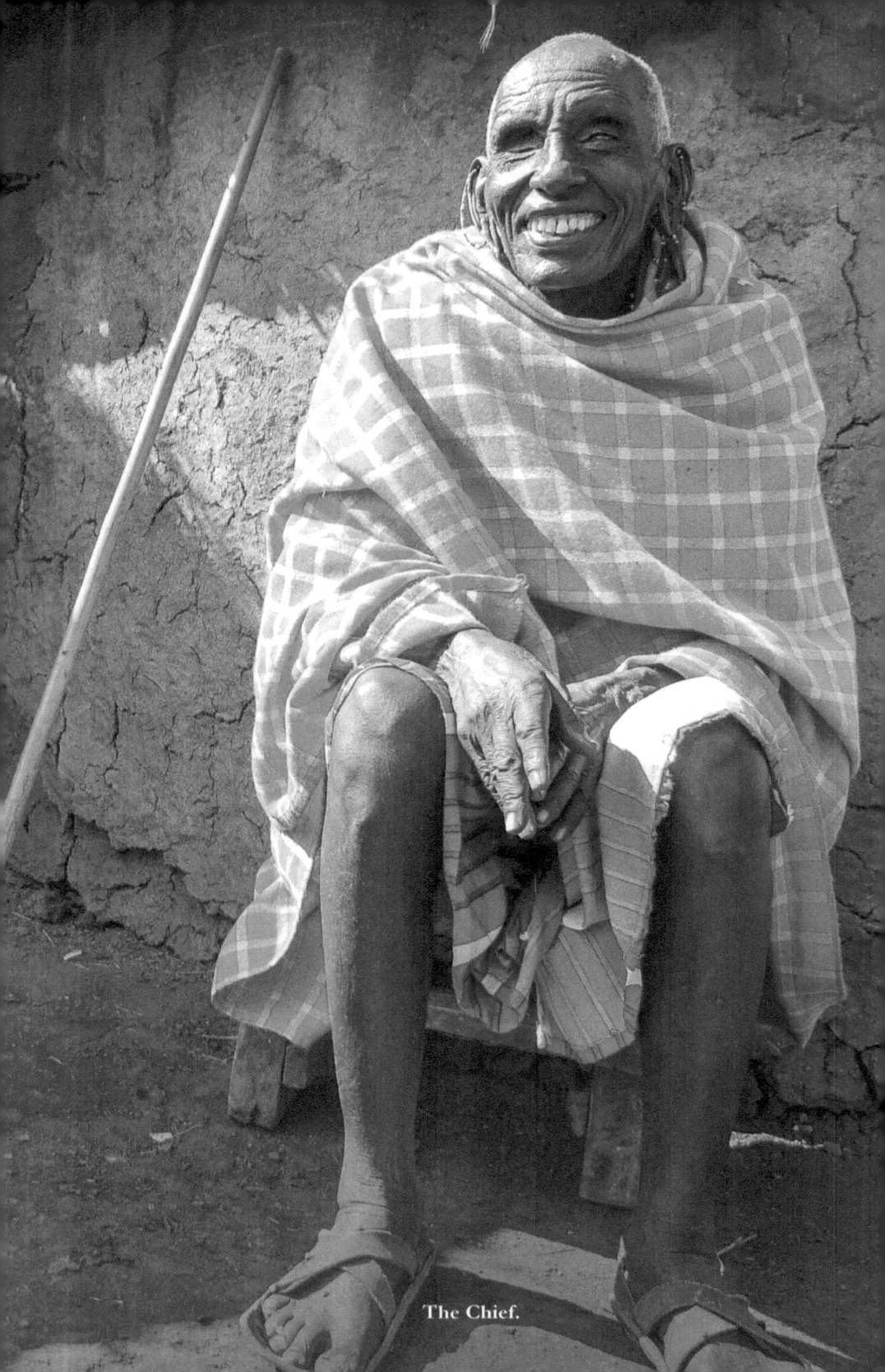
The Chief.

traditional Maasai village (as I was about to learn) was near impossible. Not only did it go against their survival, because many eyes and hands were needed to remain safe in the presence of wild animals, but a huge part of their pastoral existence meant cooperating and sharing in order to ensure they and their animals not only survived, but thrived.

"Something you will see in our village, which has got a total of 496 persons, is that we feel that happiness just comes when we can live together and embrace the spirit of oneness. **If we have our family, our animals are good, we have water, then we are complete.** We believe that we are running along just the same track with other people, with the rich Western cultures, and even globally. Yeah. Ah, we are nearly here, you can see our village there," he said, interrupting his story and pointing towards a circular fence called an enkang, which was built from thorned acacia (a native tree) to keep the hyenas, lions and other dangerous creatures out.

Walking through one of the openings in the fence, we were greeted by a circle of huts made from wood, interwoven and covered in cow dung to make them waterproof. Don't worry, I didn't know cow dung was waterproof either, probably because I'd never needed to know this to survive. The ring of huts were less than shoulder height, packed tightly together (a foot separating each house) and had just one tiny door (despite Maasai people being huge). All of this, Benson said, was "simply part of survival, when you are living among wild animals, such as lions and hyenas." About 6 metres inside the circle of houses was another circle of prickly acacia branches, which housed the tribe's cattle, goats and sheep at night. I guess a bunch of sleeping animals was kind of like the bull's-eye if you were a predator, so it needed the most protection. Patrolling outside the village at night, Benson said, were the warriors. "These are men who know how to kill any range of animals," he chuckled confidently.

"We have survived here for hundreds of years, enduring colonisation by the Germans, then smallpox, the drought of 1897, 1898, then the British occupation, then the slave trade, and plenty of bovine and other disease outbreaks, but now we are facing our biggest threat – Westernisation. Kenyan and Tanzanian governments want us to change. Want us to develop. But why? Are those people with all those things happier than us? Do they survive any better than us?" Benson pondered aloud in frustration, as we walked towards the house of the village elder and Chief.

Benson's awareness and moral sense of right and wrong – his conscience – was off the charts, despite his survivalist roots. What I was curious to discover was – does the village's 97-year-old Chief share the same interconnected wisdom? As I was introduced to Lememe Temuka I bowed my head for him to touch (when greeting anyone in Maasai culture, the younger of the two always bows their head and lets the other touch it). Then, something unexpected. I was told to place my hands palm-up out in front of me. The Chief, who was mostly blind (but in outrageously good health otherwise), grabbed my hands and held them tightly. He then began spitting on them, before Benson gestured for me to wipe the spit on my face, which I did. Thankfully, the drought had made Lememe a little dry in the mouth, so there wasn't too much spit to soak up (haha), but in all honesty, that interaction held significance for me beyond being showered with an old man's bodily fluid. It was proof of how expanded perspectives are capable of broadening consciousness. After all, spitting on someone in Australia would probably get you in a fight, whereas for the Maasai, it was a sign of connection, a benediction. I was able to recognise this, and truly I felt blessed. Here was this guy who'd walked the earth, surviving for 97 years on a diet of milk, ugali (maize-meal mixed with water), cattle's blood and raw meat (on special occasions), and he'd just shared one of his most sought after offerings – his spit – with me. Don't get me wrong, it wasn't on my bucket list before visiting Olasiti, but something about that moment made me so curious to learn more about the Chief. So I asked him what made him happy?

"I am blind, but still I can see what matters. I am alive. I am living with my community. I am loved. Respected. And I know to be true the Maasai proverb that says **'it is impossible to find a man who has everything, but it is possible to find one who enjoys the things he has'**. Just as we also know here in this village, Olasiti, that 'it is better to be poor and live long than to be rich and die young', because to be truly rich we must gain knowledge and wisdom and then share these things we come to understand, and of course this is made easier if we have a long life," he said via Benson, who was proudly translating. "With these types of thoughts, we will be happy."

"He is a very wise Chief," Benson added enthusiastically. "This is why we feel lucky to have him."

OK, so this guy was also quite clearly a bit more than some simple-minded elder wrapped in a red cloth, holding a stick. He too had largely broken free from the survivalist-based mind-set and had found a more radical, conscious and conscience-based lens through which to view the world. But how? What was it about the traditional Maasai lifestyle, culture and traditions that let them escape the mental shackles of poverty and constant need, despite still living in it? Was it the routine? That each day had a blueprint? Could it be their connection to the land? Their communal nature? Was it their Christian beliefs? Sophisticated social structures? What gave them the time and opportunity to build a broader awareness about the world, and to understand their place in it? How had they developed the means by which to think and act in ways of their own choosing, while millions of Africans in similar positions seemed trapped by their survivalist-based nature? How had they found what appeared to be a happier balance?

Yet again, Benson seemed to have the simplest of answers for this innately complex set of ideas.

"We know that nothing stands still, not animals, not nature, not the world, so **we must adapt and be moving constantly, but not in ways that harm us**, not in ways that destroy who we are, our culture, our traditions, our nature. For the Maasai, living like this in traditional villages, we do see the need to 'upgrade' the way we do things, but we do not want to change them entirely," he explains, as we walk towards one of two brick structures that stand outside their village. "This is one of our great achievements. Our water well, because before we had it we were getting water from the swamp, which caused lots of illness and problems for our animals and people. So this is something that does not change our culture or traditions, but is a welcome upgrade. You will see when you taste the water, it is that which comes straight from Mount Kilimanjaro, naturally cooled and fresh," he said with a proud smirk, as he handed me a bottle to try.

To this day it is the best water I have ever tasted, and as someone that loves my drinks icy cold, it was mind-blowing, straight from the Furtwangler Glacier 5800 metres above us. Benson tells me that the glacier is a small remnant of an ice cap that once crowned the summit of the mountain, but due to global warming, 85% of the ice cover has disappeared between October 1912 and June 2011. In fact, scientists predict that the glacier could vanish entirely as early as 2018, but at the latest by 2040. While I was fascinated to learn more about how this might impact them, I wasn't done investigating just what else they'd upgraded, and how it was that these things hadn't changed their way of being. "What is that other building, the bigger one over there?" I asked.

"Well in 1999 to 2001, we started a school under the big acacia tree just over there. I was the founder and teacher. But there were a lot of children to fit under the tree and it was very hot and uncomfortable in summer, so like the well, we worked together with some friends from overseas who had visited us and we embraced that spirit of oneness that defines us, and we built this new school building," he said, as we made our way towards the school, which consisted of three classrooms made of local wood, cement and a galvanized steel roof. "When I was small, just 8 years old, the missionaries came to our village to spread Christianity and formal education. Attending a mission school until grade seven, when the government closed it (because missionaries were taking all the best students from government schools), what this taught me was the significance of having an education. Not just because it made me smarter, but because it taught me to understand and respect my place as a Maasai person in relation to the wider world."

"This is significant," he reiterated. "Because a lot of youth here, they just see the development and technologies and think that our lifestyle is not as good, but when you understand that the Western ideas also have problems, then you can make an informed decision about who you want to be and where you want to live," continued Benson rather somberly, obviously upset about those abandoning their Maasai roots. "So that is why formal education is our biggest and most risky upgrade, because it exposes them to other thoughts, but it also gives them the knowledge to see themselves and explain themselves in relation to everything else. If we can instill this in all our kids, then at the end of the day we will have a formidable community, I think."

The school, Benson explained, was partially funded by the Kenyan Government and partly by communal funds (and a few European friends he'd made). The nature of their education too, was a kind of a fusion between the formal Western system adopted through much of Africa, and a form of natural Maasai wisdom. For the most part, the kids learnt in English, however, it is *what* they learnt that was utterly astounding. Here's what was written on the board of a classroom we randomly entered:

Seeing groups of men or women sitting, chatting or helping one another make jewellery or tools was one of the most common sights in Olasiti.

Kids running to the school.

These two loved the camera and were our best friends by the end of our stay.

The school blackboard, as mentioned.

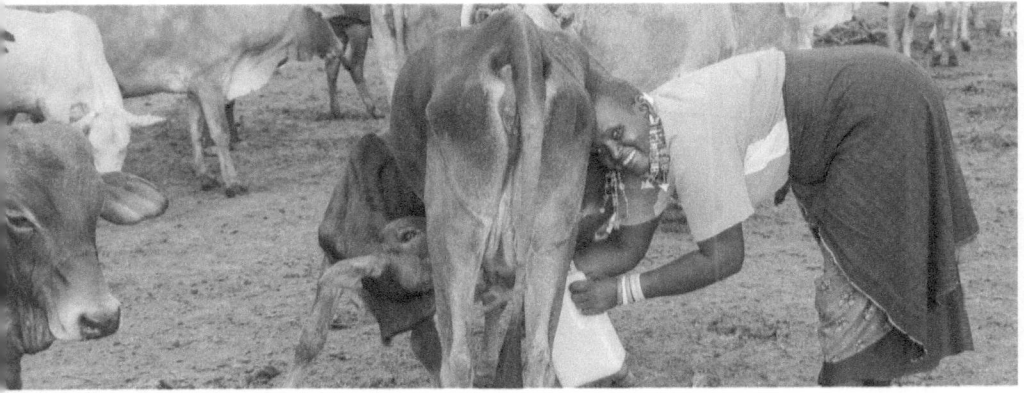

Cows are milked every morning and night by the women.

Children help their mothers with herding and milking the goats.

What a view! An elephant in front of Mt Kilimanjaro.

Sash and Mama Elizabeth laughing because Sash couldn't milk the cow.

How we got around.

One of the other Maasai I interviewed quite a bit.

An Olasiti Maasai woman in all her bling.

As a result of the video we made, Benson was invited to speak at a conference in France.

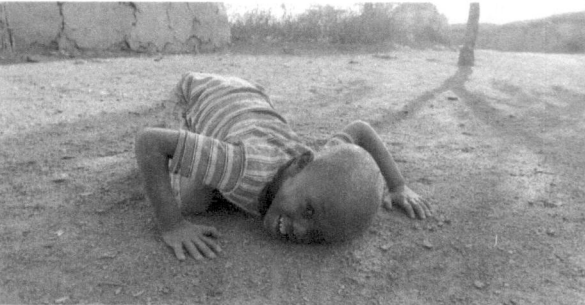
"What are you doing?" I asked. "Listening to the earth," he responded.

THE LION, THE CROCODILE AND THE MAASAI

    War/Insecurity   Ignorance   Laziness
How can we solve the above problems?
Answers: Working hard, irrigation, plant trees, government to provide free education and security, saving for the future, doing volunteer work.
What we require daily is called ___
Write three basic needs ___ ___ ___
Name three difficulties we face in getting daily needs ___ ___ ___

Try to guess what grade were learning this? The answer was grade 3 kids, 8-year-olds! Suddenly you could see that for all the upgrades the Maasai had made to their transportation and communication systems, through the use of motorbikes and mobile phones, what was really being upgraded were their minds and perspectives. The conscious base, from which all their views and decisions were formed and made, was widening. To delve a little deeper into how and why the Maasai culture and lifestyle had supported this, I felt I needed to spend a day simply sitting and observing (and filming), so that I might form a few relevant thoughts or questions to explore. (All of which you can see via the Maasai video on thehappiest.com)

On day two, as I poked my head out of our cow dung hut at 5am and began observing the Maasai way of life I could see that it was highly disciplined and well ordered. Like clockwork. First, the men check outside the village walls to make sure there are no dangerous animals nearby waiting to claim their herds. They then clear the spiky acacia branches that act as a gate overnight, and finally, they steer the cattle and goats out of their circular pen in the middle of the village to an area just beyond the perimeter of the community. Then, it's the women's turn to take over, as they attended to the cows and goats, ensuring they're healthy, before milking them. Kids are typically tasked with managing the baby cows and goats, which often run around making mischief by getting lost or trying to suckle their mother's teat while she is being milked. All this time the men stand guard and explore the area they plan on herding the cattle to for the day, to make sure there are no lions, hyenas, elephants or buffalo close by. Surprisingly, Benson said it is actually buffalo that cause the most deaths around Olasiti. Once the milking is complete, a group of young boys, assisted by a few men, herd the cattle to the predetermined grazing area. Once the cattle are in place, a select group of young boys (who are trained to be pastoralists, rather than attending school) take on the responsibility of shepherding the animals until sunset. Most often there are two to three boys for each sub-herd of cattle, which normally consists of between 10 and 20 animals, owned by a particular family group. While some might argue the validity of not 'formally' educating these kids, or of sending young boys out to oversee cattle in a land of apex predators (I know I did), this is probably the singular most important element of the Maasai lifestyle. Why? Because it allows the adults to do something survivalist-based beings typically cannot – it gives them time to think and act in ways of their own choosing. And this is what makes the Olasiti Maasai community one of the happiest villages I've seen, anywhere. Because over the past few hundred years, the Maasai have spent this time designing a sophisticated social structure that supports their culture and traditions, while breeding and maintaining a lasting sense of peace and happiness.

As I wandered through the village filming, I found a group of men congregating under a tree making a spear, and a team of women sitting together conversing as they pieced together the extraordinary beaded formations they wore from head to toe. What was the significance of this behaviour? Was it intentional? Did it have a meaning? Or were they just sharing chitchat? I decided to break my silent observational state and ask Benson what it was all about.

"Why are the men and women sitting in small groups talking, is this something you do everyday?" I asked.

"Yes, we feel this is of utmost importance to happiness in our village, because as one famous Maasai proverb says 'once we come together and unite as a community, we prosper, but then if we divide, we fall'. So that's just all about bringing the people together, bringing all the minds together, so that we can know when there are problems and we can find a way to live together in harmony, as one," he said, as he and a number of men wrapped a piece of cow skin around a long wooden spear and bony spearhead, fixing them together. "If we can find time to talk together like this every day, then no issue becomes so great, so big. So these meetings are like a daily council gathering where people can voice concerns, ask for help, or just remain connected, so we are moving forward as one community.

"We even talk about how to spend the funds we make, because when we sell products [jewelry and cloth] to tourists who walk through our village or in hotels around Amboseli National Park, which borders our village, just 50% of profits go to the person who made and sold the item, and then 50% goes back to the community. This idea serves many purposes. It came about to save us from fighting each other for sales and money, because even if I don't sell something, at least if one of us can, then we all benefit. It also means there is a unified incentive to working hard, because it assists your family, but also you are benefiting the entire village. That is why you see the women happily working together, sharing tools and ideas for their jewellery," said Benson, as he took me to introduce the women he was talking about. "You see, if each lady was just getting 100% of the profit from what she could make and sell, then perhaps there might be a less friendly feeling, more competition, more greed [he pauses], and greediness cannot go together with happiness, to me they are opposites."

I asked Benson to expand on this in our sit down interview with him the following day. "What did you mean when you said greediness and happiness can't go together? Why do you believe this?" I asked.

"Well, as for us, we don't need much. For us, the only key to happiness or the only thing we need is just health, water, and when you have some education that is good too. But that is all. Life is good now because with just this we can focus on our living together, our partnering, how we collaborate together as families, as friends, and we feel like we are OK, because we are connected and we see that we are moving on well," he explains, and visiting doctors have tended to agree. Despite eating the same few things every day (raw milk, Ugali and occasionally blood), traditional Maasai villages are for the most part a picture of health, with medical professionals reporting that most tribes are disease-free, many had not a single tooth attacked by dental cavities, and echo-cardiogram tests applied to 400 young adult male Maasai found no evidence whatsoever of heart disease, abnormalities or malfunction. Basic and healthy, Benson says the Maasai diet is all about simplicity, convenience and ultimately survival, rather than gluttonous pleasure. He described it as "one of many sacrifices" they have consciously made in order to maintain a humble, worry-free and largely money-free lifestyle.

"I think when people live like this, **when people can admit and abide to live the way we live, free from greed, I just see a happy world.** I just see a world which is free of war, a world which is free of suicide, a world which is full of love. I just see a world with people living together, living with nature and understanding that nature belongs to all human beings. So yes we must use it, but we also have to preserve it, because it must be here for all generations, even those not born yet. With greediness, like eating a lot of meats and fast foods all the time, that does not happen, greed destroys everything and I think if the Western world does not do away with greediness, it will finish you people, it will finish this world and there will be no more generations. So then you will not be happy? Because you will not exist," he says zealously.

"All right. There will be people who might not listen to me, those who might criticise or maybe insult our tribe for our different way of thinking, our different lifestyle, but I want to tell them what I know. I want to let them know that despite living in a cow dung house, despite living with animals, despite not having degrees or diplomas, or even masters like you do, despite all this the Maasai are very important. Because irrespective of all these things, we are still using the same oxygen, we are still human beings, and we are very important people. And we believe we are doing a lot before the eyes of who is watching all of us," he says as he looks and points to the sky. "We see that we are all custodians of this nature, this earth, for our children and grandchildren and so on, and that is how we should be judging our life, by that question: is how we are acting going to make their future better or worse?"

One thing I thought I knew about the Maasai before visiting them, was that in order to become a man you had to kill a lion with nothing but a spear and your bare hands. This was true once, Benson told me, but not any more. In fact, over the past few decades, he said the Maasai began to notice lion numbers disappearing so fast that they abandoned this long-held survivalist-based tradition altogether. The reason I say it was an act of survival was because the killing of lions in such a way not only taught Maasai warriors how to defend themselves and their village from the savage claws of this big cat, but it also proved their superiority over this apex predator for centuries, which made the lions scared of approaching their communities, which ultimately kept them safe. The following day, when Benson took us out on a motorbike safari and the bike ran out of fuel about 20 seconds after he said, "This is the area where we should see lions," the thought that 'they are scared of us' was the only thing that kept Sash and I a little bit calm. Still, as Benson walked off to get fuel, leaving us in complete survival mode, wondering how we'd fend off a lion, it was easy to see why the Maasai had felt this tradition was necessary. I think if I'd killed one before, or at least felt like they were actually scared of me, it would have made the next 10 minutes a whole lot easier. I could only imagine feeling this terror every day of my life, as the Maasai no doubt might without this ritual. Despite this survival-based need, in 2010, the year he was set to partake in the ritual, Benson said a complete ban was placed on killing lions, because elders were scared the animals might become extinct.

"For hundreds of years this had been a Maasai tradition, a rite of passage for a young man, but in recent years our chiefs could see that the destruction of their habitat and illegal poaching by game hunters and farmers was killing lions at an alarming rate. Given we rely on it so much, we have always believed in living in balance with nature, so this important ritual was put to an end, even though it was largely for our own survival that we did it," said Benson. "You see, we were never greedy, we never went out to kill all the lions just for fun or because we could, there was always a purpose and a respect given to them, and that is why we have now become custodians for them."

These days, Olasiti's Maasai warriors are more likely to be seen kissing lions than killing them, with the government employing them as rangers to spearhead anti-poaching conversations and activities. Today, there are fewer than 20,000 lions left in the wild, while in 1880 their number was around 1.2 million.

Another thing I'd read a lot about in relation to the Maasai was female genital mutilation (FGM) or 'cutting' – the agonising, brutal, often fatal practice of mutilating, and often then sewing up a young girl's genitalia in readiness for marriage. Unfortunately for Benson, I'd decided to re-watch the film *Desert Flower* on our plane ride to South Africa, and it had me furiously inquisitive to 'hear the other side', and ask how this practice could ever be part of a happy society? The movie, for those who don't know or can't remember, follows the rise of a goat-herding Somalian girl, Waris Dirie, who, at 13, runs away across the desert to escape a forced marriage, gets to London, is spotted working in McDonald's by a fashion photographer and becomes a supermodel. One scene of the movie in particular troubled me, as Waris is forced into hospital due to problems arising from FGM. When the British doctor asks a Somali translator to tell Waris that he needs to operate immediately because she's been stitched up too tightly in what was clearly a botch up, the Somali man instead asks Waris: "Aren't you ashamed? Showing this white man your body? Our tradition is of no concern to them." The translator then goes on to tell her (in their local language) that she is betraying her parents, her people and her heritage, before saying "Does your mother know what you're about to do? Shame on you!" Having seen Waris Dirie and a fellow South Australian Khadija Gbla (from Sierra Leone) speak on a number of occasions about their own experiences with FGM I was ready as ever to get stuck in. Though, I must say, I did feel as if I was about to start treading on toes I had no right to tread on.

Fully understanding that I might seem hostile, while all he'd been was hospitable, I finally decided to broach the subject with Benson in private, during one of our informal interviews walking through the bush. "Does your village perform FGM?" I asked. "And do you think women in Olasiti can be happy while they are forced to have their genitals mutilated?" I continued, assuming the answer to the first half of my question.

"Actually, we are very proud to have done away with this tradition. FGM stopped in our village 10 to 12 years ago, because we had two girls who died because of the process and many other complications, like very serious bleeding, leading to an unhealthy life for those girls. So now it is banned, completely, and even we are now telling other villages and Maasai peoples to stop this, because it can harm the women," said Benson, in his ever calm and non-defensive or judgemental way. "I think things like this, they can be passed down and never questioned, because we don't stop to think about what it is doing. But we are very happy that together as a community, we came to understand it was damaging our people and some were even not surviving, so we talked about it and put an end to it."

Benson's understated and very matter of fact way of putting things often forced me to pause, think and reflect on what he'd just said, before I could truly soak up the significance of his words and react accordingly. 'Wow!' I felt my mind saying, before the same word came rushing from my mouth, "Wow!"

The ability to change and adapt in order to create healthier, easier and more harmonious living conditions is without doubt the cornerstone of what has given rise to happier, more progressive conscious/opportunity-based societies. The problem is, our innately survivalist-based minds can at times struggle to keep up with the rapid rate of change, brought about by our ever-growing awareness as human beings. This rise in awareness is of course the result of our increasingly globalised world, where knowledge, technology and travel has allowed us to expand our minds, by opening our eyes and hearts to new thoughts, new possibilities.

The thing we tend to overlook, but which is paramount to happiness, is what conditions are necessary in order for an individual or a society to turn an awareness of a 'better way of being', into a reality? How do we go from seeing the change we desire, to being the change we desire? Think about this: if you were frantically busy at work, barely finding enough time to complete your day-to day-tasks, and someone rushed into your office telling you that one or two of your company's policies were out of date, do you think you'd make time to fix them immediately? If you had to decide between performing the tasks that would make your boss happy, therefore bringing you money to keep your mortgage paid, or fixing up some old document, what would you do? In my opinion, the reason we often seem to so blindly repeat the mistakes of our past – such as lying, judging, stealing, polluting, killing and so on – is because we continue to allow ourselves to be trapped in a survivalist-based mind-set even when our life is no longer under threat. This is because somehow we've come to believe that 'being busy' means we are 'successful', that having no time in our day is a sort of status symbol (and who doesn't want that?). Perhaps it makes us feel as though our time is important, that people want us or need us. I mean, when people ask you "how have you been lately?" how often do you find yourself replying "so busy," as if that is a good thing, a mark of your value or success. The second layer to this issue is our survivalist-based definition of success, which typically means having loads of money, power and material possessions. In the past, when resources were scarce and accumulating large amounts of stuff was the only guarantee of survival, it's understandable that we chased these things. But right now, the notion that we need more and more and more stuff to survive, to be 'successful' and happy, is utterly false, and even dangerous. You need only look at the fact that depression and suicide rates among millionaires are greater than those with less material wealth to figure this out.

What exactly does any of this have to do with FGM or the Maasai? Well, it all comes back to the fact that happiness (in my experience) is far more available to conscious/opportunity-based human beings than survivalist-based, but only if you know where and how to look – or rather, where and how to listen. Like the elders of Olasiti doing away with FGM, progressing towards a happier state of being as an individual or a society can only be done when we have time to stop and think and reflect on those choices we have made and are making. To change ingrained cultural behaviours like FGM, or even the idea that 'success = money = success', we must first take the time to understand why and how these things became part of our subconscious, and the way our subconscious forms meaning.

In the case of FGM, its origins are not well known. I had no idea before researching this story, but it is said that a Greek papyrus dated 163 B.C. mentioned the operation being performed on girls in Memphis, Egypt, at the age when they received their dowries, supporting theories that FGM originated as a form of initiation of young women practised as a sign of distinction amongst the aristocracy. Unknown to me, the procedure was also performed by Australia's Aboriginal people, as well as in ancient Rome as a form of birth control, and in the United Kingdom and United States to cure women of a now discarded theory called 'reflex neurosis', whereby doctors believed many disorders like depression and neurasthenia (chronic fatigue) originated in genital inflammation. In some communities today, it is valued as a rite of passage to womanhood or puberty, while others see it as a means of preserving a girl's virginity until her wedding, which is a prerequisite to marriage, and as one writer states, "marriage is vital to a woman's social and economic survival."

As conscious/opportunity-based human beings with an established conscience, we may scoff at this and say 'there's no excuse'. But imagine you are the mother, father, sister or girl at the centre of this barbaric ritual, and your option is either 'undergo something really painful, which could kill you' or 'be shunned by your community, which could kill you'. What do you choose? Well, thankfully you don't have to, and that's the point. When we're able to sit back in relative comfort, we can make better decisions, because we can see the bigger picture, that there are other ways, better ways, maybe even happier ways. Having or finding the time to make the right choice is the one element of a conscious/opportunity-based life that is most essential to being the happiest we can possibly be as human beings. That's why ***time* must be seen as the greatest luxury**, the thing we should all be chasing, because I guarantee, that with enough of it (used wisely), you will be able to find and make those choices that lead you to happiness, just as Olasiti Village had.

While there will be people who disagree with the age and 'arranged' way that some girls are married off, or the practice of polygamy in Maasai culture (among other things), their style of living genuinely seemed to work...

Journal entry 14.5.16, living with the Maasai: With a select number of young boys overseeing the cattle during the day, and the remaining kids attending school, the adults were free to wash, cook, clean, explore business opportunities, make jewelry and tools to use or to sell, and to meet and talk and maintain the peace and harmony of the village. An hour or two before sunset, some of the men are sent out to help herd the animals back in. Again, the cattle are directed towards a patch of land near one of the gates to the village. After repeating the process of milking and looking over their cows, goats and sheep, the women and men slowly move the animals inside, separating the babies and the young, who are housed in a few detached pens to avoid injury from larger cattle during the night. Then, in the piercing red rays of a setting sun, the smell of smoke fills the encircled village. Shockingly, most of the fires were lit inside their huts, which I think is why we'd noticed a few croaky voices, cataracts and generally bloodshot eyes amongst the tribe – but who were we to judge? The dinner menu was: Ugali porridge, with a side of milk. The only time this might change is for a special occasion such as a birthday, wedding or traditional ceremony, where someone sacrifices a goat or sheep, which is shared by the village. Following dinner, family groups often mingle and let their children play, before putting them to bed. The parents might enjoy one final cup of tea (which is basically a dash of tea with lots of milk and sugar) as they have one last chit chat before heading to bed by around 10 or 11pm. This routine simply repeats, over and over and over. Every day, without fail.

Could you do it? Would you be happy living like this? How might you deal with the repetition? What about sleeping on a piece of wood covered with a cow hide, inside a house made of dung, eating nothing but milk, blood and maize meal? Would you survive in a Maasai village? Do you need to? I mean, is this really the only path to happiness? Of course not, but it is one of them, and therefore we must learn from this survivalist-based community of highly-conscious, opportunity-seeking beings, because at the end of the day, Olasiti Village (not necessarily all Maasai) seemed to have found a recipe for a happy, peaceful and sustainable way of life, and to their credit they weren't willing to give it up. Not for TV, not for cars and bricks and mortar. Not even for the Kenyan and Tanzanian governments, who had instituted programs to encourage the Maasai to abandon their traditional way of life. For while they know that their lifestyle isn't without flaws, it is the happiest way they know how to survive, and ultimately, isn't that what we should all be chasing?

What all of this means, and what I took from my time in Africa, was the need to be able to discern the good elements from the bad when it comes to our survivalist and conscious/opportunity based mind-sets, because ultimately, we're all a bit of each. Next, we need to set about adopting and acting on those positive insights (our need to connect, rebuild 'the village' and use our time wisely), while being ever vigilant and limiting of those more negative aspects (our addiction to judgement, phones, being busy or that 'need' for more), which can often creep into our lives. Because at the end of the day, consciousness and the ability to think and act from a broader understanding of our world is undoubtedly an advantage when it comes to happiness, but only if we can construct a mind and lifestyle that can let us cope with and process all the information we're taking in. The central factor in all this is, again, time, or more accurately 'time out' from the pressures of our 24/7 go-go tech-obsessed society. Without this time and a wide-ranging awareness, we risk our competitive, judgemental and fear mongering survivalist state destroying our peace of mind amid a modern reality that is constantly confronting us with new, better and different things. Let us not forget though, the one thing that has never changed – **we need human connection** – without it we are an empty shell; silent, meaningless and unhappy. So put this book down and go talk to someone.

*If time and togetherness are the keys,
then why can't we open the lock?*

Kristen and Scott.

7

JEDI TRUMP AND THE ICELANDIC TOILET

America has long fascinated me. Such power. Such influence. What we watch, wear, drink and eat. How we live. What we think. Who we value. Even where we go to war, and consequently who lives and who dies. The United States of America has and continues to dominate global happenings more than any other country on Earth.

But are they happy? Is the American Dream working?

What can we learn from the culture and politics behind 'the land of the free and the home of the brave'?

And finally, what did Donald Trump's election in 2016 say about the happiness of everyday Americans?

The last of these questions was one that captivated me during Trump's 'highly unlikely' nomination as Republican presidential candidate, and even more so throughout his 'impossible' election to the highest office in the United States, and arguably the world.

An underdog billionaire (a powerful oxymoron) with more schooling in reality TV than politics, Trump's numerous victories to me always made sense. **He had heard the cries of an American people screaming for change. Change long overdue and long ignored by Washington.** He also took advantage of a growing move towards nationalism across the globe. His rhetoric too, was raw, bullish and didn't seem to pander to the wants and wills of endless campaign sponsors who'd been shaping and crafting the words of presidential hopefuls for decades (because ultimately, it was business friends, small donations from everyday Americans and his own deep pockets that made up the bulk of Trump's campaign funds). Then there was his way with social media, which even Kanye West would be proud of. I mean this guy was literally a walking, talking headline (who garnered an estimated $2 billion of free media coverage during his campaign). From his hair, to his pouty lips and complete lack of presidential behaviour, all of it was a sort of giant 'fuck you' to the establishment, and people loved him for it.

"Why wouldn't you?" asked a middle-aged Caucasian man I ran into in Detroit. "We've been poked, prodded, but mostly ignored by Washington for decades, and he is a chance for real change, or at least to be heard." He paused and took a deep breath. "Look around," he continued, "the American dream has been killed off by our politicians, so what harm could this guy do? ... And I say all this as a long standing Democrat."

The idea that 'a growing population of people had been ignored' came up in more conversations than not. It was a sentiment that echoed and reverberated around the country, though clearly "it did not penetrate the self-righteous and all-knowing Democratic party walls," said one Kansas City mother, "because they just thought they had it won, so why did they need to listen to us, or anyone?"

To get to the bottom of the Trump saga and see what we can all learn about happiness from this cultural and political powerhouse, I travelled to the US for the first time in July 2017, and returned twice over the following 12 months.

My first port of call in all this was Salt Lake City, Utah, a place defined by its largely Mormon population who belong to The Church of Jesus Christ of Latter-day Saints (LDS). Within Utah, roughly 60%, or 1.5 million residents, are Mormon, and the family I stayed with were no exception. My hosts Wendell and Mary Wild were actually the parents of a long-time follower of A Million Smiles, Corrie Wild-Kraatz. Seeking to meet with and learn from diverse religious, cultural and political groups during my time in the US, Corrie suggested I might find the LDS community interesting.

As it turns out, 'interesting' was a massive understatement. These people – the LDS community (they prefer LDS to Mormon) – were unlike anything I'd seen or experienced. I wasn't sure if I'd been transported back or forward in time, but the people in this place were kinder and more positive than the 21st century I knew. The buildings, roads and houses were cleaner too, and so were their minds. There were fewer homeless people. Less crime. More trees (this was particularly surprising given it was an arid valley before the LDS settled there). Something about these Latter-day Saints made whatever they touched turn to gold. Was it God's will? Hard work? Or were they indeed saints? I wasn't sure (and I'm still not), but whatever they were doing, it appeared to be working. Salt Lake simply oozed family, community and an unfamiliar happiness. People wanted to be and to do good. Even the Salt Lake City Police Department seemed kinder than most – they hadn't killed anyone since 2015. 'Wow!' I remember thinking, given nearly a thousand people are killed by police in the US every year, but I wasn't entirely surprised. The LDS were gentle, polite and openly expressed their love and friendship for their fellow beings. I'd literally feel my blood warm as they smiled, waved and said "hello" to me. You could tell that these people had at some point been unpretentious farmers, and you just knew they'd shared a common suffering to get them to where they were (namely the *Mormon War* of 1838 and *Utah War* of 1857-58). Without doubt, these were truly connected people, respectfully serving a higher power. And nothing, I mean absolutely nothing (whether you were a local or a stranger), was too much to ask. I think if I ever needed a kidney (god forbid), Salt Lake City would be a good place to find a donor.

Yep, on the surface this place seemed divine – a little slice of heaven, right here on Earth. But my inner sceptic wouldn't shut up. What skeletons were they hiding? Why did their brand of happiness feel so unfamiliar? Was it disingenuous? A sham? Had jealousy poisoned my mind? Or was it that age-old evolutionary trait of fearing what we don't know? Why had I never seen such a town or people before? I had to know, I just had to. So with a belly full of curiosity and questions, Corrie (who was no longer an active LDS member) introduced me to a number of community leaders she felt might shed a light on things.

Driving through the stunning, manicured streets of suburban Salt Lake City, and passing by the perfect lawns, perfect houses and perfect people, I felt as if I was in an ad spruiking the American Dream (or the epitome of 21st Century life). But as with any advertisement, I wondered, could I believe what I was seeing? Was this real? Or really fake?

The American Family

The first couple I met with were businessman and former Mayor of Farmington City in Utah, Scott Harbertson, and his wife Kristen

Frazier-Harbertson, a very proud, stay-at-home mother of 6, and now grandmother of 15.

This was the big, all-American family I'd longed to pick the mind of.

"So how do we create happier people and a happier world?" I asked. There was a pause, as each turned to the other. Surprisingly, it wasn't the former politician who opened proceedings, as Kristen said that a happier world was impossible if we didn't first change the individuals that collectively made it.

"If you see up on the wall [she points to a sign], the three things important in my life are faith, family, and freedom. Personally, I want to be remembered as the grandma that didn't give the best gift, but gave her time. So, family is very important to me. I have been blessed to be a stay-at-home mum. Cause you know **a mother has the ability to shape the world, because she is shaping the souls born into it.**"

While Kristen's answer provided insight into the thinking that gave rise to the strong sense of faith, family and community that defined much of Salt Lake's culture, Scott's response was telling of almost every other observation I'd made around the kind, gentle and polite nature of the LDS community. "What my father taught me was that without obedience, there could be no happiness. Whether that's to me, or to the commandments of God," he said. "It took me a long time, probably until I was in my late teens, before I figured out that was really true, that being obedient, not having to look over my shoulder, because of the lie I told or something bad that I did – that was the only way to find peace and happiness."

Politely digging my nails in to their ideas throughout our nearly two-hour interview, it seemed Kristen and Scott shared two pressure points, two words that they returned to time and again, whenever I pushed them for answers. These were 'family' and 'resilience', and they were most often applied in relation to the decay of a happy American society.

"One of the fundamentals that I feel we have really lost in our modern American culture ... and perhaps across the world, is valuing the family unit," says Scott. "You go back to the time when I was born in the '50s, and there wasn't a lot of wealth, people were just getting by, but I remember as a kid growing up, we were happy. We'd go outside and play, drink water out of the gutter, we even walked two miles to school. Now, every mum feels like she has to drive her kid to school, because she's afraid something's going to happen to them. That's a sad state of affairs."

Rather than seeing this as a by-product of rising inequality – which has led to the desperation, division and fear eating away at the freedoms and innocence of today's children (and parents) – Kristen says the problem is "we've wussified our children, and now their kids are suffering," she says. "They've just got used to such comfort; luxury goods paid for on credit, you know. They don't know how to work at things, how to suffer for a better tomorrow."

The rapid rise of this (supposedly 'youth') culture infatuated with instant, material pleasure, comfort and entertainment, is in part a sign of the affluent times in which we live, but there are a few other things too, that have led to this uncomfortably comfortable situation. The first is that creature comforts and an 'easy life' are precisely what we're told will make us happiest (by the masterful marketing executives who need us to buy their products). 'We deserve them', the advertisements tell us 'because we've worked hard'. That may be true, and let me be clear, there's nothing wrong with seeking comfort – it's a natural survival instinct – but what Kristen, Scott (and I) are asking is: **what is the hidden cost of all that comfort?** Another, slightly more awkward (and telling) question I'd like to pose is, who is leading this desire for comfort? Children? Not from what I've seen. I mean, yeah, kids might want the latest iPhone, candy or basketball shoes, but they're not the ones with the financial control. Parents are. And parents (I saw it all the time working in the ice cream aisle of a supermarket) are cracking at the first sign of emotional discomfort within their child. What's causing this as I see it is threefold: one, our maternal or paternal instincts tell us to do exactly that – to protect our kids, stop them crying and provide them with a better life; two, the guilt of neglecting our children (so we can work more and earn more) is causing many parents to spoil their kids in the only way they can – with stuff – because love and time are a rare luxury for many exhausted and busy mums and dads; and three, humanity has never been so wealthy, which often means saying 'no' is not a matter of affordability, but is about teaching restraint (to yourself and your kid).

The most damaging part of all this comfort seeking is that it's subtly dismantling the family unit, both in the US and across the globe. Largely I think, that's because those creature comforts (the nice house and car) and guilt ridden gifts for the kiddies, require money, lots of money, and that means parents are working more, and spending less time as a family. In fact, right now in the US, in 56% of married families with children under six, both parents work. The only winner in all this is of course is the childcare industry, which has grown from 262,511 facilities in 1987 to 766,401 in 2007, as the number of kids spending at least one day a week in child care has more than doubled to 64.8% (as of 2016). When I queried Scott and Kristen about why they felt the family unit had dissolved, they cited pornography, Satan, addiction to technology, the ease of divorce and this lack of work/home/family structure due to "women wanting careers."

"I'm not saying that there's not a place for them (women) in the workplace, but their number one responsibility should be to raise the kids," says Scott. "And to help them understand what life's all about [he looks at Kristen in acknowledgement that she'd done that]. We don't have that anymore, and so are people happy? [He pauses, as if wondering himself] Yeah, maybe, but I don't think the true happiness that used to be there is there anymore, and that's one of the reasons why – the family unit's shot the pot."

Before all the feminists out there (like me) get up in arms, there is some logic behind what Scott says. I mean physiologically, if a child is breast-feeding, a mother is arguably best positioned to look after them in those early days. Most women too, are inherently more nurturing, which to my mind is the most pivotal quality of any good parent, and essential in raising a happy child. Now, does this mean mums should bear the entire responsibility of raising a child? No. And should women be forced to choose between 'career' and 'child'? No. But do women face discrimination in workplaces because they require time off to give birth and raise children? Yes. The potentially devastating effects of this (for mother and child) are that women are rushing back to the office immediately after their baby is born. In fact, a quarter of American mums are back at work within just 2 weeks of giving birth, while about half are back within 5 weeks and just a quarter take 9 weeks or more. And no, that's not because dad's are suddenly staying home – there has been no great role-swap – lots of kids are simply growing up with absentee parents, in full-time childcare.

Unfortunately, solving this problem isn't as simple as answering a few yes or no questions or quoting a few statistics. In the US in particular, there are a plethora of complex cultural and political issues that make 'a happy family unit' a very difficult thing to achieve.

One of the most substantial barriers to American women (and therefore families) being able to simultaneously raise a child and have a career, is that **the US is one of just a handful of nations in the world that is yet to pass laws supporting paid maternity leave**. As numerous mothers told me, "this is because corporations own this country and our politicians, and for them profit comes before health and happiness."

A more recent cultural change that's dismantling the family unit is the whole 'education generation' thing. Don't get me wrong, a degree, masters or PhD is a good thing, but there are a few hidden costs. One – with 'smart' becoming the new 'fit' under the modern definition of 'survival of the fittest', it's never been more important to succeed in higher education. In most countries outside the US, it's simply about graduating, because the most prestigious colleges are publicly owned, giving everyone the same opportunity to not only survive, but thrive. America's particular brand of capitalism however, means that prestige can and must be bought. Just ask the ten richest people in the US, all of whom attended private Ivy League Universities. As of 2015, this pressure to attend the best colleges has driven roughly 50% of American parents to save for their kids' tuition, again forcing mums and dads to spend more time at work and less time with their families. Two – with 6% of America's population now attending college, compared to just 3% in 1965, there are more young people than ever moving to where the education (and job) opportunities are, which is seeing a big split among rural and small town families in particular. Three – the pressure on children to perform, coupled with ludicrous amounts of homework, means kids are spending more and more time in their room 'studying' (or sneakily chatting on social media and playing video games), and less time sitting and chatting with their parents and siblings.

And that's my next point: I can remember the days (and I'm not that old) when we'd all sit around the dinner table or family TV discussing the news or the latest schoolyard or workplace gossip. These days, either our wealth or willingness to go into greater debt, has seen the average size of a house built in the US increase by 62% since 1973. With family sizes hitting an all-time low, living space per person has more than doubled over this period. And then there's the tech-resources boom, which gave rise in the US to 343 million TVs, 336.8 million active mobile phones and 290 million Internet connections as of 2016. With all this technology, extra space to do our own thing and longer work hours to afford it all, it's a wonder families function at all.

In my own experience (in America and abroad), the happiest families are those that work humbly together to make the most of life's infinite, unpredictable, changing circumstances and opportunities. They do this by supporting one another unconditionally. They're united. Yes, they cry together, but they also celebrate together. The happiest families allow each individual to strive to be their best, while remaining loved and connected by common dreams, beliefs and stories. When a family unit (and I'm not just talking about blood relatives) can prioritise and balance their individual wants and needs, with their capacity to fulfil those wants and needs while remaining supportive, loving, united and connected to their family, then they will find happiness. There are exceptions of course, like if a family is poisoning the mind or strangling the freedom of an individual, then perhaps he or she will need to find a new set of 'relatives' – for a time at least.

When it comes to expanding the family unit and having children, it is worth bearing in mind that this is often a critical and stressful time, which carries the potential to tear families apart. To create the happiest situation for child rearing, plan ahead and save (if you can't get paid parental leave), so that both parents can enjoy the gift of that child. Because otherwise, "what's the point?" says Scott. **Why have a kid if all it means is you end up working all day and night to pay for childcare, a bigger home, a new SUV and gifts for your spouse and child to say sorry for never seeing them?** As American columnist Abigail Van Buren wrote in one of her *Dear Abby* columns, "If you want your children to turn out well, spend twice as much time with them and half as much money."

While the LDS community certainly seems well placed to retain the family ideals of old, for most Americans, I think, the family unit is changing, and in some instances, even being replaced. The old village structure where communities worked and raised children together is next to non-existent in modern-day America. Large multigenerational households that we still see in Asia and parts of Europe are also all but gone. And now too, the nuclear family is dissolving. So, what's replacing it? In one word – individualism.

Individualism is defined as "the habit or principle of being independent and self-reliant" and is "a social theory favouring freedom of action for individuals over collective or state control." In essence individuals are prioritised over the group or groups to which the individual belongs.

This should, of course, come as no surprise; for individualism, with its attendant egoism and selfishness, is simply an inevitable by-product of a culture and political system focused on and obsessed with unrestricted capitalism, which it terms 'the American Dream'. At the centre of this dream lies the notion that, as per the Declaration of Independence, "all men are created equal," and therefore, anyone, "regardless of the fortuitous circumstances of birth or position," should enjoy the same opportunities as the richest or noblest of families – if they work hard enough. What this means in practice is that the status quo easily maintains itself, and poor individuals bear the brunt of the responsibility for their disadvantage.

The American Dream

Sitting there on the Harbertson's lush leather sofa in their enormously spacious two-story home, I wasn't surprised to hear them praising the American Dream and its capitalist roots. And why wouldn't they? Clearly, whatever system they were a part of had been kind to them, and had equipped them with the education and means to thrive. But had it done the same for others? Was everyone, "regardless of the fortuitous circumstances of birth or position," enjoying the opportunities the Harbertsons had? Thinking about a homeless woman I'd just met in downtown Salt Lake City, I couldn't help but feel that her story – of being ruthlessly molested by her parents, before running away from home and school, and marrying a man who ended up beating her to within an inch of her life – did not give her an equal chance in life (see more of her story in chapter 10).

Interestingly, while the Harbertsons often suggested that lazy or entitled individuals, rather than government or corporate policies, were the cause of unemployment, homelessness and other social inequalities, their finger-pointing attitude altered significantly when it came to prisoners.

"At the Davis County Jail, where we volunteer as social workers and educators, we've noticed that inmates, every one of them, comes from a dysfunctional family," says Scott, before Kristen interjects. "They can't help that they are where they're at. That's all that they know, what they saw as kids … mum and dad were in jail, so now they are." In a staggering 70% of cases, Kristen is correct – that's right – seven out of ten US children with a parent in prison are doomed to follow in their footsteps.

"I have to tell you this story I heard about a guy down in the Texas prison system," says Scott animatedly. "When this guy found out that 65% of released prisoners returned to prison within a year, and within five years 95% were back behind bars, he thought, 'this is ridiculous', so he decided to do something about it. He felt one of the things that these men or women (inmates) don't know, is how to run a business, or how to be a good employee, or how to be an entrepreneur, so they decided they were going to teach them," said Scott, relaying the story he'd heard. Under the Texas scheme, when a prisoner had nine months left on their sentence, they were sent to a class that would teach them about running a business. When inmates who had attended these classes returned back into society, an astonishing 16% of them started their own company, while a ridiculous 70% of them got a job, due to the knowledge that they had learned during the program. "I look at that, and I think, why can't other jail systems pick up the same thing, teach these inmates skills to keep them out of prison rather than just off drugs. Why don't they teach them a life skill? Give them something that once they get out, they can say, 'I can do that,'" says Scott, before Kristen yells out an answer to his rhetorical question. "It's a moneymaker is why. These private prisons are worth millions."

She wasn't wrong, just understated. The US prison system actually costs taxpayers $74 billion USD (that's more than the GDP of 133 nations!), of which around 10% goes to private prison companies who pocket roughly $700 million USD in profit annually. With Time Magazine's Lauren-Brooke Eisen and Inimai Chettiar suggesting "approximately 39% of the nationwide prison population (576,000 people) is behind bars with little public safety rationale," the pair concludes the country could "save $20 billion annually" by simply letting these people go or having them complete some community service. To put that in perspective, twenty-billion-dollars is enough to employ 270,000 new police officers,

360,000 probation officers, or 327,000 school teachers, all of which would increase public safety a whole lot more than perpetuating the cycle of disadvantage that leads to most low-level offenders winding up in jail.

Alternatively, when you consider that it costs around $22,000USD a year to keep a low-level drug offender locked up, compared with just $9500 to send them to a state college – where they could learn a skill to better their life and country – it makes you wonder, who is made happier by locking these people up? Is it the politicians, who garner votes promising to be 'tough on crime'? Or the private prison companies that make a fortune imprisoning uneducated and disenfranchised youth? Certainly, both benefit, but I wonder, at the end of the day, does the power and money make them happier, or would living in a more educated, kinder, harmonious, free and equal society have greater effect on their happiness bottom-line?

As I looked across at Kristen and Scott, who were visibly upset by the injustices of their justice system, the answer seemed obvious. But when, where, why and how exactly did this culture of inequity and division come to pass?

At a glance, the Declaration of Independence seemed ordained to protect against such bigotry, as it enshrined the opportunity for everyone to improve their life, no matter who they were. It even went so far as to proclaim: *"We hold these truths to be self-evident, that all men are created equal, that they are endowed by their Creator with certain unalienable Rights, that among these are Life, Liberty and the pursuit of Happiness."*

Of course, at that time 'all men' only meant white property-owners. The Creator (or the rich white men penning the document) did not endow these unalienable rights to women, slaves and people without property. While such injustices were commonplace among most citizens in most countries at the time, what seemed new and revolutionary and radical about America, was the idea that "fidelity and merit" were "the only sources of honour [in the US]," wrote German migrant and author F. W Bogen in his 1851 novel *The German in America*. "The rich stand on the same footing as the poor; the scholar is not a mug above the most humble mechanics; no German ought to be ashamed to pursue any occupation … Above all, there are no princes and corrupt courts representing the so-called divine 'right of birth.'"

"That's what's great about America," Scott tells me, 166 years later. "Whatever you want, you can go for it. You've got the freedom to do what you want to do, no matter who you are." This permission to seek out one's own happiness, free from aristocratic or government controls, must have sounded like a dream to those oppressed, impoverished and marginalised communities fleeing Europe and Asia. But how would these people cope with all that newfound freedom? Would the intense and incessant competition of unbridled capitalism make men or break men? Or, would it do as it was meant to, and lift everyone who wanted to work hard, up and out of the gutter, endowing them with the unalienable right to life, liberty and the pursuit of happiness? Of all the social experiments we've seen, America and its unadulterated brand of capitalism has arguably been one of the most telling when it comes to basic human nature. So, did it work? Has exponential freedom led to a better life for all Americans?

When it was founded on 4 July 1776, America was said to be a land of Benjamin Franklin's 'Poor Richard'... of men and women content to accumulate their modest fortunes a little at a time, year by year by year. "In the early years, Americans' ravenous appetite for land was born of European deprivation confronting New World opportunity," writes Carl N. Deglerin in his book *Out of our past; the forces that shaped modern America*. "Demand, which had been pent up for centuries, suddenly encountered plentiful supply. The settlers' hunger for more and more territory thrust them relentlessly westward, where they could establish farms and ranches that they themselves could own. This was the American Dream in its earliest form, and for the people living the dream, it had an aura of double-edged incredulity. There was disbelief not only at their own good fortune, but also at the backbreaking work required to capitalise on it."

Fortunately or unfortunately, the discovery of gold in California in 1849 brought in a hundred thousand men looking for their fortune overnight – and a few did find it. Thus was born the California Dream of overnight success. Historian H. W. Brands noted that in the years after the Gold Rush, it was the California Dream that spread across the nation: "The new dream was the dream of instant wealth, won in a twinkling by audacity and good luck." With such sudden and extreme wealth growing in the pockets of a few, and a new underclass of 3.9 million former slaves emerging from obscurity – not to mention the rise of the women's suffrage movement – the notion of America remaining a place where "all men were equal" and free from hierarchical or aristocratic controls began fading. By the late 1800s, the gap between the haves and the have-nots widened, fast. This rapid period of industrialisation, expansion, population growth, and, for some, prosperity, really went on to underpin the America we know today. The America that superseded the European powers of old. The America that set in motion the idea that capitalism – an economy unrestrained by government restrictions or high labour costs – could provide the perfect conditions to build gigantic corporations, transportation and communications networks, heavy industries, banks and financial organisations. In essence, there was now proof that a free market economy could create progress, power and money – though those final two elements were largely reserved for the 'deserving few', of course. **The 1%, who today control 43% of America's wealth and enjoy an average net worth of about $8.4 million (70 times the average net worth of the other 99%).**

The innate problem that has led to America's current culture of inequity and division is in fact the very same thing that has seen it thrive – economically speaking – and that is capitalism. Unfortunately, the reason capitalism was, is, and will never be fair, is because this romantic notion that "all men are created equal" is simply not true. We are in fact all insanely different. Just look around. Some are born with all the intellect, wealth and physical advantages you could imagine, while others face disability, disadvantage and a home environment that all but guarantees their low-standing place in this world. For instance 30% of people who are abused in childhood will become abusers themselves, while economically speaking, 62% of Americans raised in the top fifth of incomes stay in the top two-fifths, and 65% born in the bottom fifth stay in the bottom two-fifths. Let's not forget also that 19% of people live with a disability and that seven out of ten kids who've had a parent go to jail will end up there themselves. In free market capitalism, a flourishing economy is idealised to translate directly into a flourishing society, thus eliminating the need for government to make too many laws in regards to either the economy or society. This keeps government 'small', but it also squashes the marginalised in society into the ground, for an economy in and of itself cannot help the disadvantaged, only a human and humanely focused government can do that.

One of the principal barriers I see standing in the way of the socialist reforms that might curb the inequality and division plaguing America and other capitalist nations, is this fallacy of 'hard work'. The idea, which I heard repeatedly, was that *if only* these disadvantaged people worked harder, *if only* they had the right attitude and really wanted a job, then they'd somehow be OK. "That's what's so sad," says Kristen (discussing her husband's factory, which employs a lot of Mexicans, Latinos and Polynesians), "there are no Americans that will do the work." "We've created our own problem, because the government makes it so easy – 92 weeks you can take on unemployment. So we've enabled, we've created this mess." From Kristen's point of view, the only thing that stood in the way of success for many people, was their own attitude – not any disadvantage or personal damage they may have inherited or being subject to in their lives.

Staggeringly, this is the very same woman who said prisoners "can't help where they're at." I do empathise to some extent with Kristen, and agree that in certain circumstances, work ethic can play a role, but for the most part, **the idea of hard work being the great equalizer that can undo centuries of institutional cultural and political disadvantage is nothing but a fairy-tale the rich tell the poor in order to give them something to hope and labour for** – and which they tell themselves as an excuse not to help or not to feel guilty.

The thing I think we've got to remember in all of this is that while we might not be born to equal circumstances, that doesn't mean we can't live under them. To do this, of course, we, through our cultural and political systems, must begin by seeing and treating all people as worthy of help. We must understand that equality between men is the ideal to work towards, not the starting point. The happiest societies I've witnessed are those that embody the maxim of 'treating everyone as you yourself would wish to be treated', and who understand that this does not always mean treating everyone the same. For some people need a bigger hand-up than others. Take for instance my 10-year-old cousin, who has autism. Without an enormously tailored and specialised school, care package and teachers (all of which come at a huge cost to Australian taxpayers), there is no chance he could enjoy a standard of living 'equal' to many other children. Similarly, a new life-saving drug, Spinraza, which is used to treat spinal muscular atrophy – a rare muscle-wasting genetic disorder in children – has just been made available by the Australian government for just $39.50 per script for ordinary patients, or $6.40 for concession patients. Previously Spinraza cost parents $165,000 per script. With some children needing up to seven doses a year, this was simply unaffordable for most families. The whopping $241 million a year investment to subsidise Spinraza via the government's Pharmaceutical Benefits Scheme (PBS) provides substantial help for roughly 150 families living with children suffering from the disease.

In both of these cases, without significant government intervention and support, and the often uneven redistribution of taxpayer money to provide some semblance of equality, these children would be left by the wayside, or worse, dead. Of course, the rich will always be able to afford the best treatment, school and care, but as Gandhi suggests, "the true measure of any society can be found in how it treats its most vulnerable members." And that's why we need unbiased, incorruptible governing bodies: to level the playing field, so that each individual "regardless of the fortuitous circumstances of birth or position" is afforded the opportunity to fly.

"I think that is a key point of being happy in this world," says Scott. "Serving others, not worrying about numero uno all the time." Kristin agrees, nodding profusely, before suggesting God (and His messengers) made it pretty obvious how we were meant to treat one another. "We're to love everyone, right? That's the first two great commandments, 'Love the Lord thy God with all thy heart, might, mind, and strength'. And the second is likened to, 'Love thy neighbour as thyself'. We are to love everyone, and everyone should have their free agency to choose how they want to live," says Kristin.

America's forced marriage of culture/politics to religion has long absorbed and confused me, because, as I was about to hear time and again, loving everyone and treating them as you'd have them treat you, was a Christian obligation, until it seemed, you entered the voting booth. But why was this? Why? … Were Christianity's charitable and egalitarian ideals simply too great a threat to capitalism? Did Americans worry that a Jesus-like leader may implement a more 'socialist' system – a dirty idea to many Americans? Or was it more to do with the horribly polarizing choice voters faced, whereby you could *either* be a 'pro life' Republican or a 'pro equality' Democrat, but unfortunately *not both*? A far less divisive question I found myself asking most Christians across America was: so is Jesus the ultimate leader in your opinion? "Yes, of course," replied Scott (and almost all I asked). Given Kristin and Scott voted for Trump, I was curious to know, did this mean that they felt Trump was most similar in his beliefs and actions to Jesus?

"I don't look at Trump in that way," replied Kristen immediately. "I have to separate it. That is the country, not my religion. So, yes, I pray for the leaders of our country, that they will do good, that they will have good intentions, but I don't put him [Trump] up there with Jesus." "But surely someone like Jesus is who you would like to see leading?" I probed. "Yes, but they don't exist," Kristen interjected. "Don't get me wrong, I'm looking for someone who is, but it is really hard to find someone like that. I don't know if the world or America will ever elect someone who has those values. I think we're past that."

Saddened by such an ignorant, defeatist statement (clearly some countries have elected fabulously compassionate and egalitarian Jesus-like leaders), and perplexed by how they could see their responsibilities as Christians as unrelated to their choice of who to elect to the highest office in the land, I continued questioning. "So should you have a big wall to keep migrants out?" I queried. "Of course we should," said Kristin assertively. Scott looked far less convinced. "We have the right to protect our sovereignty," continued Kristin. "People are welcome to come here, but you do it the right way, through the system. These people who are coming over, and then the government is giving them free healthcare, and food stamps, they haven't done anything, and our government is just enabling them."

Jesus, of course, preached and showed compassion for all – most decidedly the poor, the despised, the outcasts – and hoped that we might learn to do the same (Matt. 4:24-25; 9:9-13). I'm not sure how this policy and instrument of division – the wall – could ever be seen as compassionate. And it didn't even make any real practical sense, because as I'd witnessed and heard, ever since the slave trade ended, it has been illegal or semi-legal migrants from 'south of the border' who have propped up the economy of Middle-America (those living in the heartland of the US – typically the Midwest and South – not on the coasts) by working their arses off for next to no money. Something Scott and Kristin were both direct beneficiaries of.

"I've got a production line," says Scott. "And whenever we put an ad out, that's typically what I get is, a lot of new migrants that come in and apply for that job."

"Of course, they want to come to America for the purposes of having a better life, which I agree with, and I think that's what America gives everybody hope for," continues Scott. "Now, am I all for sending them ('semi-legal' migrants) all back? No, because if we do we're going to be in a mess. The economy is just going to tank. I'm going to lose all my workers, and my production line will disappear. So, we need to figure out a way to make this system fairer, so that they can come to America and fulfill their dreams, and have an opportunity to progress and grow, but not make it so difficult on them to do so."

Scott and Kristin's often conflicting beliefs – such as showing immense compassion for prisoners, but not always migrants, the poor or jobless – was at times mystifying. What it said to me was that adhering to "loving everyone and doing unto others as you'd have them do unto you," was in conflict with something else in their psyche. Coming to understand more about the political and cultural beliefs surrounding the American Dream (throughout my journey and from reading a hell of a lot), the Harbertson's beliefs began to make more sense. What they and many Americans couldn't shake was this capitalist and slightly patriotic notion that the US provided everything a person needed to be able to 'make it', so long as they worked hard enough and didn't allow unnecessary competition (through untapped migration).

Going from being a Republican stronghold in 2012, where Mitt Romney defeated Barrack Obama 72.8% to 24.8%, to a minority state in 2016, where Trump won just 45.5% of the vote (defeating Clinton on 27.5% and independent Mormon-candidate Evan McMullin on 21.5%), I was eager to hear what other views there might be in Utah. Conveniently, my hosts the Wild's had arranged a family dinner with some of their friends from church so I could find out. Corrie's brother and his (boy)friend, who was kept a secret, arrived first, followed by Laura and Aaron Evans, who were a slightly younger version of the all-American Harbertsons – or so it seemed on the surface. As I got digging, the language, manner and alignment of the Evans' LDS beliefs were in fact worlds apart from what I'd heard earlier that day from Kristen, and to a lesser extent Scott.

"I have a brother who's Democrat!" exclaimed Laura. "A total Democrat. And most of my family is more right, but when I'm with him and I hear him talk in more detail about why he feels that way, I find myself agreeing with him. But then, when I get with other more right leaning people and I hear their views I can't help but feel there's elements to both that are good, and both genuinely want what's best for society. I think each has good intentions, but there are a few elements to each that push politicians and the media to portray Democrats and Republicans as two entirely different species."

"I think there will always be differences of opinion and views on the role of government," continues Aaron. "On the liberal [Democrats] side, government should be more active, while on the conservative side, it's more the individual maybe choosing to act through other channels. So for me, it's not about 'should we help', it's 'should we help them this way or should we help them that way.'" Sitting once more in the luxury of a beautiful home – not on the floors of a detention centre on the Mexican border, a waiting room in an abortion clinic or in the gutters of Salt Lake City – I couldn't help but wonder whether these people, the current beneficiaries of the American Dream, had any idea that there were some trapped in an American Nightmare, who'd argue no one was helping them. As if reading my mind, Laura responded in kind.

"It's about perspective too, because you, Mike, have such a unique perspective because you've been able to go to all these communities and see what really a poor person is, whereas here in Utah, most people don't or can't comprehend such things. To them, someone who's poor only has one car, you know. They have a very different perspective and I think that's also what creates the conflict is sometimes people want to judge why someone's poor without understanding their background, or what it is like in their shoes. We often think the underprivileged don't deserve our help because they made bad choices and they need to solve it themselves. Then you have the refugees who we all know did not get themselves into that situation and I think anyone would want to help them, but still it seems we want to judge or blame them."

"So what about Trump's wall then? How does that sit with you as LDS?"

"Not well," screams Laura eagerly. "No. Not well," added Aaron. "It basically says we don't want you here," reiterates Laura. "To be honest with you, I think Trump talks big to get the reactions he wants – the votes – I see it a lot, but most of it is smoke and mirrors."

In my own country of Australia, and I think the US is much the same, politicians need a problem to fix, a cause to rally voters around – unemployment and the economy often being the most common choices. What politicians do next is choose a scapegoat, someone to blame for those problems, who isn't part of their key voting demographic. So the left blames corporations and the rich, and the right blames government bureaucracy and the poor – well, typically at least. The problem is, **pointing fingers in order to garner enough votes, solves nothing**. It helps no one in the society they are meant to be serving. It simply divides us and distracts us from those often more pressing and real concerns to our happiness. In America, for instance, the total unemployment benefits paid between April 2017 and April 2018 were $29.29 billion, according to the US Department of Labor, while the annual health care costs of obesity-related illnesses were a staggering $190.2 billion, or nearly 21% of annual medical spending in the United States, according to a Cornell University study. In addition, obesity is also associated with job absenteeism, costing approximately $4.3 billion per year, while on average an obese employee will cost a business $506 per year in lost productivity. Who is labelled the greater burden on the economy and country though? The unemployed.

Because pointing fingers at obese people during an election campaign and yelling 'we're going to fix this problem' wouldn't get you elected. Not only is weight a touchy topic, but 'obesity' is also bipartisan and indiscriminately affects 37.9% of the population – white, black, rich, poor, dumb, smart – it doesn't matter. Furthermore, with an additional 32.8% of Americans considered 'overweight', that means 70.7% of the population (a large majority ... pardon the pun) may be put out or feel attacked by such a contentious campaign, even though it's designed to help them (and their country). With a 24/7 news cycle and social media landscape that rewards politicians who can articulate their message in less than 140 characters, the ability to discuss, let alone tackle or solve something as complex and taboo as obesity seems impossible, and such ideas are likely sidelined before they ever see the light of day. Instead, politicians war over easier targets, such as the unemployed, despite the fact that obesity impacts the economy, health and happiness of a country far more than 'helping thy neighbour' who doesn't have a job.

The issue at hand – and this is fuelled by that survivalist 'me versus you' instinct – is that we want someone to blame (it can't be our fault), so we look to those who are different to us, marginalised, those we either fear or ridicule. That's why, if there were an official list of popular and easy people to blame for our problems, the unemployed – who are typically thought to be lazy and uneducated – would be fairly near the top. The only group that regularly eclipses them (and I think Trump knew this) are of course migrants and refugees. And why wouldn't politicians want to blame them. They're the perfect target. Not only do they not get to vote, so they can't directly hurt either party regardless of how badly they're treated, but in the modern context they seem a welcome scapegoat for everything that is going wrong in society – because the middle to upper classes, who've blossomed under the current system, don't want to blame *it*, or themselves, for the demise of the country. In America, of course, there has long been a love/hate relationship with migrants. Middle-American farmers and manufacturers love their cheap labour, because it props up the economy and makes some of them stinking rich. And yet, it's these very same people who spew hatred upon migrants for being 'social welfare cheats' or for stealing American jobs' – two ideas that seem to be in constant conflict with one another. The conversation everybody seems to be avoiding (whether knowingly or not), is that the American Dream, which was born from a capitalist petri dish, is actually the problem. Here's why...

In a free-market system where you're given the choice between employing an illegal migrant for $6 an hour, a legal migrant for $10 an hour or an American for $16 an hour, who would you choose? Even if you were a patriot and wanted to support American jobs, you simply couldn't, not if you wanted to stay in business, because if even one or two of your competitors chose to employ migrants, they'd be able to undercut your price by roughly half. Without strict government regulations to dictate and police wages and workplaces (such as what we have in Australia), the flood of migrants crossing the Mexican border will continue – because that's how US businesses have continued to line their pockets post-slavery. If America puts up a wall against migrants, the reality for businesses is that they will likely lose profits by having to pay higher wages.

"To me, the ideal solution isn't to shut them out or to just let them flood in," says Laura. "I think the ideal would be to use the extensive resources we have here in America to strengthen those countries that migrants are coming from, to a point where they don't want to leave. That's the only real solution, a wall would just be a bandaid. A political stunt."

As acclaimed writer George Orwell said, "political language ... is designed to make lies sound truthful." So how do we find the truth – the American reality? Who is hurting the happiness and dreams of everyday Americans? Put simply, it is the corporatocracy (the marriage of business and government), which is led by the soaring elite of American society, the top 0.01% of the country (around 32,500 people) who earn an average annual income of more than $27 million, or roughly 540 times the national average income. What these people have done ever more sophisticatedly over the years, is buy political influence, or become politicians themselves, in order to protect their money and social standing – to the detriment of all of their countrymen. As one of seven Miami fire fighters I spoke to put it, "It's lobbyists. How is that even legal? That I can give money to a political campaign, and in exchange they vote in a certain way that benefits my interest. How is that not bribery? That's like a drug dealer going to a cop and saying, 'Hey, listen. Here's a little money, don't be on this corner at 10 o'clock tomorrow'. It's crazy."

With roughly 57 members of US Congress considered members of the financial elite and a further 250 members of Congress being millionaires, asking politicians to enact changes that would reduce the wealth of the upper classes is an obvious conflict of interests (something congresswoman Alexandria Ocasio-Cortez has all too often pointed out as she works to fight for the working-classes). It's also little wonder that tax cuts for the wealthy are repeatedly enacted while the reverse is so rarely true. **The average wage of the bottom 90% of American workers has actually declined by 9% from $33,526 in 1979 to just $30,438 in 2012** (pre-tax, adjusted for inflation and excluding government payments). Over the same period, the top 10% have seen 76% growth in their earnings.

There were numerous excuses I heard to justify such grossly lopsided statistics and again lay blame on someone else. The most common was the whole 'trickle down economics' theory: 'rich people and organisations need tax cuts because they're the ones who employ people, so if we help them there will be more jobs and less unemployed people taking our taxes and not contributing anything'. Another slightly less common, but interesting idea was: 'we need more rich people in America to pay taxes, so we should be encouraging big business by giving them tax cuts'. The final point I heard in various iterations was: 'if the rich can avoid paying taxes, why shouldn't they, if they're smart enough? I mean the homeless and unemployed take advantage of the system, so why shouldn't the rich?'.

'Don't worry they do,' I felt like saying. In fact, Forbes estimates that US companies are stashing roughly $2-trillion in cash overseas to avoid paying tax on it. That's not really comparable to an unemployed person collecting welfare and food stamps. If those organisations brought this money into the US, it would inject $420 billion into the economy. That's more than enough to foot the health bill for the obese and have enough left over to give the 6.5 million unemployed $30,000 each. OK, it might not be spent like this, but the point is, if these giant corporations were held to account, if they weren't in bed with politicians, and were made to pay their fair share of taxes in America, the economy and the country would be far better off.

"Just as the commandment 'Thou shalt not kill' sets a clear limit in order to safeguard the value of human life," wrote Pope Francis in 2013, "today **we also have to say 'thou shalt not' to an economy of exclusion and inequality**. Such an economy kills. How can it be that it is not a news item when an elderly homeless person dies of exposure, but it is news when the stock market loses two points? This is a case of exclusion. Can we continue to stand by when food is thrown away while people are starving? This is a case of inequality. Today everything comes under the laws of competition and the survival of the fittest, where the powerful feed upon the powerless. As a consequence, masses of people find themselves excluded and marginalised: without work, without possibilities, without any means of escape," the Pope concludes.

Just to paint a tiny picture of this huge problem: there are now 1,542 billionaires across the world, more than ever before. In fact, **the combined wealth of the 64 richest people on Earth is equal to the combined wealth of the bottom 3.5 billion human beings – that's half the world's population!** Unsurprisingly, the US has 42% of the world's millionaires, and 49% of those with more than $50 million in assets. So while America ranks as the 4th wealthiest country when it comes to average wealth per adult – which was $388,585 in 2017 – the reality for most Americans is far grimmer. According to the Credit Suisse Global Wealth report, Americans' median wealth was a mere $55,867 per adult – half have more, half have less – which puts them in 24th place globally, well below Japan, Canada, Australia and much of Western Europe, including Iceland (which sits on top on both measures).

The sort of hyper-inequality on display in America is an unfortunate but inescapable by-product of the competitive nature of capitalism, a point Pope Francis again made during an address in Bolivia in July 2015. "Time, my brothers and sisters, seems to be running out," he said.

"We are not yet tearing one another apart, but we are tearing apart our common home. Today, the scientific community realises what the poor have long told us: harm, perhaps irreversible harm, is being done to the ecosystem. The earth, entire peoples and individual persons are being brutally punished. And behind all this pain, death and destruction there is the stench of what Basil of Caesarea called 'the dung of the devil'. An unfettered pursuit of money rules. The service of the common good is left behind. Once capital becomes an idol and guides people's decisions, once greed for money presides over the entire socio-economic system, it ruins society, it condemns and enslaves men and women, it destroys human fraternity, it sets people against one another and, as we clearly see, it even puts at risk our common home."

While the Pope alludes to the frightening reality that climate change may cause the second great Flood, chances are the rich will survive it. Something the super-wealthy may not be able to survive however, is the growing discontent of the masses. And they know it. In a recent report by UBS, the Swiss bank that prides itself on advising more super-wealthy families than any other bank, Josef Stadler, the lead author, says his billionaire clients are aware of the widening gulf between rich and poor, and fear that hard-pressed people might rise up and take direct action. "We're at an inflection point," he says. "Wealth concentration is as high as in 1905, this is something billionaires are concerned about. The question is, to what extent is that sustainable and at what point will society intervene and strike back?"

This question, I feel, is already starting to be answered. Just look at Wikileaks, Occupy, Black Lives Matter, even Trump's election. While all these things were fuelled by anger and division, there is something they have in common – they all serve as a resounding F-U to the establishment. So I don't think it's about 'at what point' will society intervene and strike back? It is happening right now, and if those people in power – AKA those with lots of money – continue to ride everyday people into the ground, things are only going to get worse. Much worse. Because as former CIA employee and infamous leaker of classified National Security Agency (NSA) documents, Edward Snowden put it, "there's a limit to the amount of incivility and inequality and inhumanity that each individual can tolerate. I crossed that line. And I'm no longer alone."

What happens when enough people join Snowden? When the

everyday American says enough is enough. You can't freeze our wages. You can't force my family to choose between food and healthcare. What happens when home ownership falls out of reach for most? Or when the 45,000 deaths per year attributed to a lack of health insurance become unacceptable? **What happens when people lose faith in their government's ability to serve or protect them?**

In the words of Professor James Davison Hunter, we will see "a class war" born from the "widening gap between members of America's middle class." In such a scenario, of course, there can be no happiness. Just fear, anxiety and hate.

So what's the solution? "Well, I think He taught it," says Aaron. "I think Jesus taught us to love one another, to serve one another, to help the poor and needy, and I think that's a personal responsibility whether you're Christian or not … I think we use labels a lot, we say it's the government's responsibility or it's business or it's whatever, but it's really me. Who am I? Who do I vote for? What does that say about me and my beliefs? My want to do good."

Before I got a chance to ask Aaron to elaborate, I noticed Laura itching to say something. "I really want to know more about you, about Australia, like how did that whole getting rid of guns thing work?" she asked me. "How did it happen?" The shoe, it seemed was suddenly on the other foot, as I became the interviewee. "It works amazingly," I said. "You just about never hear of people being shot in Australia, because there simply aren't any guns, no one owns one, not unless you're a farmer or a biker maybe." Aaron and Laura resembled a deer in headlights. Complete shock! "So nobody is dying from guns?" she gasped. "There may be the odd case," I replied. "But when people are mad in Australia and they want to hurt someone, they're more likely to punch them or at worst maybe use a knife, which physically and emotionally must be a lot tougher than pulling a little trigger from a few metres away." You could see Laura's mind trying to compute what I was saying, as if it were the first time she'd heard such a thought.

"The thing is," I continued. "Even if I wanted to get a gun I honestly wouldn't know how or where I could obtain one legally, or illegally. There's no Walmart selling these crazy automatic guns you have. I think that's probably why we haven't had a mass shooting since our very conservative Prime Minister, John Howard, banned rapid-fire weapons following a massacre in 1996, where a lone gunman killed 35 people in Port Arthur in Tasmania." "OK, wow, did you hear that Aaron, no mass shootings!" says Laura. "So how did they get rid of the guns?" asks Aaron. "And doesn't that mean it is even more dangerous if just a few bad people have guns?" Huh, I thought, before responding to his misguided logic. "No, not at all, because our police have guns, far more than the criminals, so that keeps us all equally safe," I said. "In terms of how we got rid of them, our government just instituted a forced gun buyback scheme, so there was an incentive to lay down your arms and in less than 2 years it got rid of around 600,000 guns." The pair honestly couldn't believe my words – so I told them to Google it to check I wasn't lying.

My own Google search after our interview showed one stunning fact: since 1996, the murder rate in Australia by gunshot fell by 72% from 98 deaths in 1996, to 35 in 2014, despite our population increasing by five million people. It's even helped in gun related suicides, because as I told countless Americans who asked similar questions, it is really hard to kill someone with a gun, including yourself, if you don't have one. In contrast, the US saw 372 mass shootings, 64 school massacres, and a total of 13,285 people killed by firearms in 2015, according to the Gun Violence Archive. **Even after taking into account the difference in population size, the US still sees 1000% more deaths by firearm than Australia.**

Sadly, just as I was finalising this chapter, there came a glaring example of how Australia's more socialist (for the common good) gun laws look next to America's more capitalist (we have the right to own what we want) gun laws. On 9th November 2018, my home city of Melbourne experienced its first terrorist attack, as a crazed man set his car on fire and stabbed three people (killing one) in a crowded mall, before being shot dead by police. At the same time, a lone gunman entered a bar and grill in Thousand Oaks, California and opened fire, killing 12. Two days later, Australian Federal Police foiled an alleged mass shooting when one of the men planning the attack raised a red flag when he went to buy a gun (which he was never sold). Conclusion: regulation of guns will save American lives. A lot of them!

I don't know about you, but all this talk of disadvantage, division and guns had once again made me confused. Several Mormons (and other Christians) had told me this was God's promised land where "the gospel of Jesus Christ could be restored" by establishing a country where freedom, rights and opportunity for all were guaranteed – just as the Declaration of Independence had suggested. So what happened? Where had that belief gone? Had the individualistic nature of capitalism killed off the Christian fundamentals of love, community and working for a common good? What had happened to 'thou shalt not kill' or 'love thy neighbour? Surely owning a gun goes against such commandments? Regardless, my point is this: how on Earth can anyone be happy when they're constantly looking over their shoulder in fear of 'the other side'?

What the LDS community taught me, and what they gave me, was hope and insight. Hope that (particularly amongst their younger members) there is a growing understanding of what love means, and how it relates to the cultural and political decisions they make. The insight I gained was this: religion does foster community and selflessness and is one of very few pillars standing against the culture of greed and individualism propagated by capitalism. BUT, and this is a big but, only when it is taken seriously. Only when these words by LDS leader Joseph Smith are understood and acted upon: "We are to feed the hungry, to clothe the naked, to provide for the widow, to dry up the tear of the orphan, to comfort the afflicted, whether in this church, or in any other, or in no church at all…"

One woman who seemed determined to embody and (unknowingly) propagate the rebellious, self-sacrificing cultural and political views of all those religious leaders we look up to, was Stacy Hill, a local of Kansas City, Missouri; my next stop. When I told my hosts Marcus and Linda that I planned on walking through the backstreets of some poor neighbourhoods to find a few locals to talk to, they looked at me oddly. Explaining to them that this was very important to me (and would happen regardless of their approval), they decided it might be easier and safer for Marcus to drop me off and wait around the corner while I interviewed whoever was willing. After speaking to a 72-year-old black Muslim biker about the bitter divides he'd experienced as a child, "fighting even to be able to drink from the water fountain as whites," it was heartening to see what had arisen when the shackles of inequality were torn down.

"Welcome!" said a woman, as I approached a bunch of people selling random household products on the side of the road. "How can we help you?" she continued. "Some detergent, toilet paper, shampoo, we've got the best prices in town." When I explained that I was actually a writer and filmmaker from Australia interested in learning more about happiness in America, Stacy called over her husband and two friends. "This guy wan'a know what makes us happy," she laughs, showing off her bright gold plated teeth and huge diamanté cross which swayed across her chest with every movement.

A few minutes into our conversation, Stacy's uncanny energy for life began to reveal itself, so I grabbed my camera and hit record (eventually creating a story that you can find on thehappiest.com). What this young black woman from the heartland of America was proof of was the inevitability of change – of progress. She may not have lived through the civil rights movement, as so many I spoke to had, but she was confirmation to me that the suffering so many endured was worth it. Because Stacy was free, and boy was America a better and happier place for it.

"We just love to give back," says Stacy. "And to make sure no one is left behind, is what we're here for." In mid-2016, Stacy met her now-husband Loren, who she described as "a beautiful man that simply couldn't see and therefore reach his potential," because he lacked self-belief.

"What I witnessed next was something that has changed my life," she says. "Because as I began telling Loren just how much I believed in him, and promised I would be there for him, I noticed a complete transformation that made him, and made our relationship, so much better, so much stronger [she looks across to Loren]. Seeing the difference it made having just one person by his side, we decided to start a not for profit organisation that could do this for more people, so we launched 'We Believe In You.'"

In order to fund this enormously bold dream, Stacy uses extreme couponing to buy everyday products at a discount. She then sells these products (via her roadside stall) and uses profits to feed, clothe, support and inspire her community. In their first two years alone, the organisation fed thousands of people via their annual cookout, as well as providing hundreds of toys to underprivileged children. Stacy has also counselled hundreds of families and young people who have been transformed by the rare energy and love that oozes from her.

"They say life is what you make it," says Stacy. "And a happy life I think comes from what you give back, but also what you give up to do that. Like for me, pursuing this full time, meant taking a giant leap of faith. I walked away from my cushy job as a construction inspector for Kansas City, which I had for 18 years. But that's the price of chasin' bigger dreams, you gotta be ok wid da small house, ol' car, long as I can see smiles, and long as I can get from A to B, and I can go to sleep and wake up and be happy, that's what matters."

Growing up poor, and barely escaping poverty before plunging herself into this risky and selfless undertaking, it seemed as if Stacy had found a way of somehow blocking out the survival instincts that often plague such decisions and invariably kill such dreams before they see the light of day. "When you grow up not having everything that you want," she says, "and then you're able to give back to the community and give back to someone who's not able to get it themselves, it's an amazing feeling. Because I was like them, not long ago. We all were at some point. The world ain't been rich like this forever, you feel me. But we gotta rise together, that's the tough bit."

"That's why it's so important to remember the less fortunate, because they deserve what everybody else has. They're human too. Some [she stops for a moment], some tell themselves they ain't, but they are. We all are. That's why I don't want no one to be judged, based on what they have or what they coulda had. Because everybody falls. No one's perfect. That's why *We Believe In You* is all about telling them how you feel, telling them that they're somebody. Letting them know that they're loved just as much as somebody who has everything."

Admittedly it hasn't always been easy, says Stacy, who's consistently ignored the need to please others – those who tell her to focus more on her own successes. The only thing I can say is – thank god she hasn't.

"You know what Mike, the thing is, if we let one man, ten men, decide who we are or how we should live, we'll go nowhere," says Stacy. "I think people, all of us, the next generation, we need to decide what our legacy will be. For me, it's doin' right in the community, because then you ain't worried about who the president is, or what politicians are doing, because even they can't dictate my life … so yeah, don't let no one else stop anything you wanna do. **If it's important, then it's on you to make it happen, and that's what I think lots'a younger people are realising. We can do it. We can make this better.**"

"We can," I whispered, as I drew a long breath and sat in silence. I'm not sure how much time passed, but with the hair on my arms still standing alert like a hungry dog waiting for food, the voice of an elderly lady forced its way into my far-away mind. "What's all these cameras for?" she said. "You must be looking for me," laughed the tiny woman wearing large hoop earrings, a funky black hat and patterned tights. "Have you ever seen a 79-year-old lady do the splits?" Before I'd had a chance to think about the question, down she was, on the ground, arms and legs stretched out like a star. "OK, wow!" I said, still utterly fixated on Stacy's final words. "This woman," the old lady grabbed me and pointed to Stacy. "She is a saint! You won't ever hear no pope speak her name, but we know it. She's doing miracles everyday down here."

Standing there in the street on the outskirts of Kansas City, waiting to be picked up by my hosts, I couldn't help but think I'd just met the happiest person in America. But what gave Stacy, a lower-middle class woman, the right to be so damn satisfied with life?

Was it her oral bling? The giant diamanté cross around her neck? Or the fact that she flat out refused to say Trump's name because "it aint gonna do no good, so why spend time on it." Personally, I'd argue it was all of these things. Stacy had found the 'perfect marriage'. Her culture (that oral bling, which represented her African American heritage) was in perfect harmony with her political views (her refusal to let Trump or Washington distract her from doing good), and of course all of this was very much aligned to her religious beliefs (the cross).

For the first time since landing in America, I felt I'd found someone who was truly at peace. What such a state of being symbolises I think, and the reason why peace – and therefore this marriage of cultural, political and religious ideals – is such an essential building block to our happiness, is because when the warring factions of our heart and mind stop yelling, that is when you know that you are who you are meant to be. I suppose it's like Gandhi said, "Happiness is when what you think, what you say, and what you do are in harmony."

Stewing in my head for nearly a year before writing this chapter, Stacy's words in retrospect were just the beginning. The origins of a thought process that I was about to discover was shared by hundreds of Americans I'd speak to – but particularly the young.

The New American Dream

Travelling across much of Midwest, Northeast and even the South of America, what I began to notice as I reflected on the hundreds of conversations and interviews I was conducting, was that every time I spoke to someone under the age of about 40 (this is not to say it didn't happen with others too), I felt hope. But why? What did young people know that others did not? What did they feel hope in? What did they see it in? What didn't they see it in? And how is that perspective giving rise to a new American Dream?

In Chicago, by the shores of Lake Michigan, I met a man in his early-30s named Aly. Born to a Catholic mother from Mali and Muslim father from Senegal, Aly's early years were defined by a brooding tension between the two families that eventually ended in his parents' divorce. Then, when Aly was just seven his father died, and his mother was forced to flee, fearing her husband's family would try to take custody of Aly and his sister. For the next year, the two siblings lived with relatives in France, while their mother chased a job opportunity in Brazil, which eventually led to a position with the United Nations in New York. "Then I had a sort of 'typical' middle-class existence in the US," says Aly.

What's changed, I think, particularly in the last generation or so – and why I'm sure our happiest days are ahead – is that that term 'typical' now comprises of lots of previously untypical situations. Take mixed-race families for instance. A generation ago, marrying someone who was from a different country, culture or religion was nearly unheard of, with just 3% of marriages in the US in 1960 considered interracial. Today, 16% of marriages are interracial, and few would flinch if they saw white, black, Muslim, Hindu, African, Asian, Christian, Hispanic... whoever it was, together. This contemporary ability to see past these divisive labels is something Nobel Peace Prize winner and former Director General of the International Atomic Energy Agency, Mohamed Mustafa ElBaradei, says is imperative if we're to live in a happier and more peaceful society.

"If I look at young people now, you know, I have hope," says ElBaradei, in an interview with Morgan Freeman during the Netflix series *The Story of Us*. "They are colour-blind, religious-blind, ethnic-blind, [so much so] that they would treat each other as part of the same human family. That is, if somebody dies in Darfur, they will react the same way as if somebody dies in LA." Citing the interconnectivity that's come with technology as a major part of what's allowing us to "talk to each other ... to educate each other" and to "understand each other," ElBaradei says **there's a hope today that's not been possible before**.

The 72-year-old Muslim biker I spoke to in Kansas City.

Stacy standing at her road-side stall.

The 79-year-old lady doing the splits.

Stacy with Loren with two friends who were helping them out.

Aly.

While it could be argued that America (and the world for that matter) is as divided as ever across cultural, religious and political lines, there is considerable unity among the young. Optimism too. And I think that's because this is the most educated generation in history, by a long way. What this means is that young people (and many older people too) are no longer dumbfounded witnesses to the injustices and unhappiness they can see. Instead they are astute and informed onlookers eager not to repeat the mistakes of their predecessors.

"Take the American Dream for instance," says Aly. "To me it has always been to a certain degree an illusion, which is if you make enough money you're going to be happy. That's been coded as, if you get a good education and you work very hard and you're good at what you do, then you will be rewarded with, well…" Aly fails to end his sentence. And that's the troubling bit, what are people being 'rewarded with?' Because statistically speaking, the American reality indicates it's not happiness. In fact, between 1999 and 2016 the Centres for Disease Control (CDC) says America's suicide rate increased by 25% from 29,199 deaths to nearly 45,000. That's more than twice the number of homicides – making it the 10th-leading cause of death in America. Pardon the French but that's got to be a fucking blight on someone or something! So who or what is to blame? During the same period (1999-2016) the US economy grew from $9.3 trillion to $18.57 trillion (despite the GFC). So if it's not money or the 'success' of the country that has and is continuing to cause a record number of people to forfeit their lives each year, what is it? And more importantly, how do we stop this needless suffering?

Combing through hundreds of pages of reports and articles that suggest the answer lies in "better coverage of mental health conditions by health insurers, and reducing access to lethal means (guns and narcotics) amongst susceptible populations," I couldn't help but feel as though that was akin to telling the FBI to focus their energy on being really good at re-attaching someone's limbs after a bomb blast, instead of looking at ways to prevent such extreme acts of violence. I'm not saying that the government and other agencies shouldn't look at the above measures, just that, as Aly further suggested, there are more fundamental issues at play, issues which I believe young people are ever so slowly waking up to.

"First of all it's about admitting that the capitalist American Dream is a complete lie – if happiness is the end game. I mean, I know tonnes of people who have lots of money and they are some of the most unhappy people I know," says Aly, reflecting a sentiment I heard time and again from people right across the country. "But still, that's the vision sold to Americans. I think partly because religion has less and less of a role in people's lives, they really think to themselves, 'OK, let's try materialism.' Like if I have lots and lots of things then maybe I will be happy. Ironically, I think that most of us kind of instinctively know that's bullshit. But there are so many messages that you get bombarded with every day in the media and by your friends, that that's the way to happiness, and most just give in."

"The other path to achieving the American Dream I guess, is you know, there's this concept of the rat-race. Like if you push hard enough and step over enough people's shoulders and you're able to rise to the top, you'll be happy, because you'll have shown that you're number one and you're great and everything."

The problem with structuring a society around this idea – the capitalist pretext of every man for himself – is that for every winner, there will be a loser, or sometimes many. Whether it's underpaid workers, mum and pop investors who are sold a scam or consumers who are forced to pay above market rates, the simple maths of it is: **someone must pay in order for another to get rich.** Just look at the financial crisis of 2007-2008. In the years leading up to the collapse, a group of greedy bankers, aided by a financial sector left unchecked by Washington, were making billions of dollars from dodgy subprime mortgage bonds, not for a moment stopping to think about potential losers. And why would they? Capitalism doesn't teach us to consider others. And yet, as the dominoes of the GFC began to fall they hit all of us, because as Aly suggests, people, towns, states, countries, none of these things exist in isolation anymore.

"We are more connected than ever, you know, digitally, economically, like it or not, and our systems need to reflect that," says Aly. "One of my all time favourite proverbs is a proverb from the Kikuyu tribe from Kenya. It says, *I am only well if you are well.* This sense that your health and your happiness is literally tied to my health and my happiness. Like physically, when you do better, I'm better. But also it means that when you suffer, I suffer." And suffer we all did in the wake of America's housing market collapse. In fact, a study by the University of Oxford published in the British Journal of Psychiatry compared suicide data from before 2007 with the years of the crisis and found there were more than 10,000 "economic suicides" associated with the recession across the US, Canada and Europe, including around 4750 'excess suicide deaths' in America alone.

What's interesting is that suicide rates in many countries, for example Sweden and Austria, remained stable, despite an equal amount of economic turmoil and distress. "If suicides were an unavoidable consequence of economic downturns, this would just be another story about the human toll of the Great Recession," wrote David Stuckler, a senior research leader in sociology at Oxford, and Sanjay Basu, Assistant Professor of Medicine at Stanford. "But it isn't so. Countries that slashed health and social protection budgets, like Greece, Italy and Spain, have seen starkly worse health outcomes than nations like Germany, Iceland and Sweden, which maintained their social safety nets and opted for stimulus over austerity (slashing public-sector government spending)." In their New York Times OpEd, provocatively titled *How Austerity Kills*, Stuckler and Basu suggest countries could prevent repeat suicide increases by offering greater social support for people affected by recession, including government "return to work" programs and psychological interventions.

"Our research suggests that investing $1 in public health programs can yield as much as $3 in economic growth. Public health investment not only saves lives in a recession, but can help spur economic recovery," the pair say. "Second, treat joblessness like the pandemic it is. Unemployment is a leading cause of depression, anxiety, alcoholism and suicidal thinking. Politicians in Finland and Sweden helped prevent depression and suicides during recessions by investing in active labor-market programs that targeted the newly unemployed and helped them find jobs quickly, with net economic benefits."

In conclusion: "these economic suicides are avoidable."

With nearly twice as many Americans dying as a result of the GFC than 9/11, I wondered whether the irrefutable evidence linking 4750 suicides and the financial crash itself back to a lack of socialist policies had sparked any debate over America's capitalist obsession?

"In one word, no," says Aly. "You don't even get permission to think, 'What would the world look like with an alternative form of capitalism?' No, we're taught that this is it, this is all we've got, this is the best we can do. It's just sometimes as much as I love this country I feel bad for US citizens because so much is concealed and hidden away from us, like how well other more socialist countries are doing both economically and in terms of wellbeing. I'm not completely sure whether it's that or it's the fact that it's one of the largest empires in the world, which thinks of itself as superior, but yeah, we're not all that open to change, even under such a weight of evidence."

The thing is, Aly says in pain, "I get it, but it frustrates me to hell, because we are at a crossroads where we need to ask, **do we create a more inclusive, connected, compassionate country, or do we keep increasing the number of people who are disposable?** Because that's what is happening right now, we keep saying 'you're not worth it, you're not worth the time and trouble to take care of.'"

What this neglect by Washington of uneducated, low-income households has caused, according to researchers, is a surge in deaths from drug overdoses, suicides and alcohol poisoning. And nowhere has this been more prevalent than among uneducated whites – those with a high school education or less. The reason this group is most at risk is because 'relative status over time' is a major contributor to depression and suicide, and no status has diminished more than the privileged status of white working-class men.

Despite the fact that the bottom 90% of Americans (of all races and ages) are earning less today than their parents did, it is white middle-aged low income men and women between the ages of 45 and 64 who have experienced the sharpest rise in suicides in the past two decades. What's alarming about this is that suicide numbers within this age group have been stable or falling since the 1950s. So what's caused the sudden anomaly?

While men still remain nearly four times more likely to commit suicide, 55-year-old New York based fashion designer Kate Spade (who hanged herself on 5 June 2018) became part of the fastest growing demographic of suiciding people – white, middle aged women – who saw an 80% increase between 1999 and 2016.

Since the turn of the millennium, there have been just two groups of Americans who have seen a decline in suicide numbers: black men and those aged 75 and older. What this points to, researchers say, is a belief within these communities that their relative status has improved, they have still seen some progress (since World War II or the civil rights movement) even if they remain disadvantaged. The problem, Aly says, is that under the current model of the American Dream, "there is more disadvantage, more 'losers', than ever before."

"Even if you do what this society tells you you need to to win, which is that you get a good education, you work really hard ... you may still find yourself with two low paying service jobs, unable to make ends meet, and that'll make you frustrated. It can feel like you failed, and that can create a tremendous amount of shame and that shame goes one of a few ways – it turns into anxiety or depression or suicide or you cover that shame by scapegoating and blaming others for your downfall. And that's what we're seeing with Trump, that's what got him elected, he says migrants or the Chinese are the problem and people just regurgitate it, like he's a Jedi or something."

"I actually stayed in Upstate New York with mostly poor rural white folks a couple of years ago, and these folks lived mostly in trailer parks and things like that. I actually think that some of the energy around Trump was a lot of these folks who had been abandoned by both parties for many years who didn't feel seen by the political establishment. Even though many of them had actually voted for Obama twice, I think they'd become disillusioned by even his inability to get things done. So I think they kind of just wanted to throw a brick and a wrench into the system and see if it worked."

"I believe that's why Sanders also performed really well in the primaries, because he was different. Anti-establishment. A democratic socialist. And actually I've spoken to a lot of Trump voters after he was elected and many of them were saying, 'Yeah, we possibly would have considered voting for Sanders'. So it was kind of Sanders or Trump, but no one in the 'camp of the forgotten' was interested in voting for Hillary Clinton, because there was such a revulsion around the political establishment and that's exactly what she represented," explains Aly, in a way that made a lot of sense to me.

"I really think it was the unhappiness of a lot of people that allowed Trump to come to fruition," agreed John, a man I met at a Detroit bus stop. To me, Aly and John had explained Trump's impossible triumph. People were literally dying of unhappiness and wanted a change.

You're probably wondering by now where all that talk of youthful hope and optimism has gone, and what on Earth this 'new American Dream' is all about. I guess I felt I needed to paint a picture of the

American reality that confronted me, before I could get onto who or what is going to change it.

Strolling through the backstreets of a rundown Detroit neighbourhood – 'a dangerous place' I was told – death and hope were everywhere. "Excuse me," I said nervously, eager to stop two young black men wearing baggy shorts, hoodies and bandanas. "Can I ask you about life in Detroit?" One of them immediately put his hand in his pocket. 'Oh shit am I about to be shot?' I thought. "This is what Detroit need to be more about," he said as he handed me a CD. "This some-a my music, you feel me. Like when all is crumblin' that's what sustains us, bring us together, is what's real," he says, rather poetically, before his friend intervenes. "We seen a lot right here. Detroit. We been like the biggest city in America one time. Now [he pauses] we like a wasteland, but we comin' up again, rebuildin', cause them big business is gone now. Taken what they could and left. That's how this country works… 'least now we can get on with it," says the shorter of the two men, before his much lankier and more musical friend interrupts, "that's it yo, now we in control, now we gonna make what's right for *people*, not them fat cats."

What these two guys were referring to was Detroit's epic rise and fall. A journey that saw the 'car-city' become the 4th largest in the US with a population of 1.85 million and 296,000 manufacturing jobs, before the gasoline crisis of 1973-74 slowly eroded America's love for big cars. By 2013, following the bankruptcy of its two largest employers Chrysler and General Motors (despite a $17 billion bail out attempt by President Bush), the population fell to just 690,845. Then on 18 July 2013, Detroit officially lost its wrestle with capitalism, as it became the largest city ever to file for bankruptcy.

Exploring the shells of dilapidated factories, houses and an urban landscape that has been likened to New Orleans after Hurricane Katrina – except that Detroit's disaster was man-made and took decades to unfold – I heard a man yell at me from his verandah, before waving at me vigorously with concern. Did he think I was lost? Taking the opportunity to ask him about the plight of Detroit, and what's been done with these empty plots of land, his reply was in line with why I'd come to Detroit. "You can see this green type of movement comin' up all over town. You gonna hear people sayin' nothing goin' on in this city, but we got lots happening, just not the same as we used to," says the man in his 70s, as he gave me directions to a place downtown I might be able to learn more about this 'greening of Detroit' I'd read so much about.

Walking the roughly 10 miles to the city, I once again found myself swamped by conversation, as a dozen or so black youths who looked like the bad guys from every US cop show I'd seen, showed me a glimpse of the future. "We got no beef wid-chew," says a girl in her early twenties. "We got no beef wid no one," she continues, before her boyfriend interrupts, " 'cept maybe dem old white people who still bein' racist," he adds, as both tell me "like, we mostly hang out wid blacks, but that just cause that's what we got here in Detroit, but we love all our friends and stuff of all colours and flavours," they laugh. Keeping in mind that the pain and injustice of being treated like animals (pre-civil rights) is just one generation removed for most younger African American people, these words (which I heard all across the US) were telling. To me, they signalled the inevitable – **we will see an end to (almost all) racism in America and abroad – within the next couple of generations**. What makes me so sure of this is not just the discussions I've had or the observations I've made, it's actually seeing how I (a white) was treated by other communities. The statistics too are pretty hard to ignore.

Before we continue, here's how the following generations are defined:

> **The Silent Generation** were born between 1925 and 1945 and were shaped by the great depression, world war two, numerous civil rights movements and witnessed the emergence of technologies most would come to take for granted.
>
> **Baby Boomers** were born between 1946 and 1964 and came of age during the relative prosperity of the post-war years. While they desired cars and houses, they also launched the environmental and anti-Vietnam movements and rejected the very institutions and values that provided security for them growing up.
>
> **Gen X** was born between 1965 and 1980 and were the first generation of 'latchkey kids' with dual-income families and an increasing divorce rate among their parents. They saw the end of the Cold War, Apartheid and the Berlin Wall, as well as the birth of computers, which all seemed to signal the beginning of a truly global marketplace.

Millenials (Gen Y) were born between 1981 to 2000 and were the first digital natives, spending their time getting degrees, so they could work in front of screens not machines. Climate change, 9/11 and the 'war on terror' ensured this generation would pay for the divisive cultural and political tactics of those traditionalists in power.

Take these findings by Pew Research, an organisation that, for the past two decades, has tracked the answer to the question: 'is racial discrimination still the main reason why many African-Americans can't get ahead today?' When polling began in 2000, just 30% of Silents and Boomers agreed, while 35% of Gen X supported this statement. Fast forward to 2017 and the only group to have reduced their support is the Silent Generation, who fell to 28%. Boomers climbed to 36%, Gen X rose to 40% and Millennials sit on 52% agreement with this statement. Whether you agree or not, what the study indicates is that millennials are a more compassionate and connected generation that is able to understand and put themselves in the shoes of others. Education is of course a huge part of this. We young people have been lucky enough to have movies, teachers, movements (like Black Lives Matter) and the internet feeding us a more accurate picture of America's past and present than previous generations. De-segregation, though it still has a way to go from what I saw, also continues to gain momentum, allowing more and more interaction between African Americans and other communities (an essential catalyst in breaking stereotypes fed to us by media). The most telling of all however, is that **millennials are the most racially diverse generation in American history, at just 60% white, that's compared to 85% white in 1960**. The tipping point for this majority, researchers say, will be sometime after 2040, and by 2060 whites will be just 43% of the US population. "This marks a significant change for a nation that has historically been dominated by a white majority that holds the most power in terms of economy, politics, education, media, and in many other realms of social life. Many believe that the end of the white majority in the US will herald a new era in which systemic and institutional racism no longer reign[s]," says sociologist Dr. Nicki Lisa Cole in her *ThoughtCo* article on 20 August 2018.

"When you connect with someone else and build something that supports your direct community, I think that it helps ten-fold everyone within that space, more than any type of government, or politics, that we have out there. The beauty and power of numbers is such an impactful way of giving power back to the people, and really allowing us to do what helps us," says Steffi Min, the first face I saw as I arrived at a small community garden in the heart of Detroit City. The 20-odd-year-old and a band of colleagues and friends were actually touring the US as part of Future Clear, a New York-based production collective that creates environments and events to act as experiments and testing grounds for the formation of new ways of living and interacting with each other. Standing inside a large open pyramid that housed a giant metal gong in the middle, I was curious to find out more about what this was all about. "How did you get to this point?" I asked.

"Well, quitting my 9 to 5 job was the hardest thing that I ever did," says Steffi. "All that stability I'd craved was suddenly gone. But when I decided to break out of the cycle of the day-to-day, I really was able to open up an entirely new set of experiences, and it allowed me to flow more, create my own schedule and be more present with what I wanted to do. Quitting really allowed me to create the life I wanted to live, and I think, or hope, I'm now the embodiment of my favourite Rumi quote, '*Set your life on fire. Seek those who fan your flame.*'"

It takes a certain amount of privilege I think to turn your back on a regular job, for there is rarely a pot of gold waiting at the end of that rainbow. But as Steffi suggests, all this education and time to think has left millennials with an insatiable appetite to explore our *why* through our vocation, not just make money. "I think millennials are seeking to make a positive connection to ourselves and the earth," she says. "Through the widespread use of technology and access to information, we live within a culture of thin veils. We can see how everyone has and is living and in the case of our baby boomer parents, I guess that focus on settling down and raising a family didn't seem to bring them the sort of fulfilment we're chasing. So there is a sense of reinvention, a breaking away from that culture of tradition, in order to create a strong sense of self through the 'work' that we do."

"And what about Trump?" I asked. "What does his election say about the happiness of Americans?" She pauses, before responding. "A lot of people are seeking change in radical ways," says Steffi. "And I see the attraction of wanting to elect someone who has a completely different political background, with no experience. Because again, **the traditional approach passed down by previous generations has not given us**

the country we desire. This is, sort of, what our entire project is about, travelling through these different states and cities, and really talking to the people about what are their hopes and dreams?" "And what are they saying?" I interjected. "What we're hearing is diverse, which is beautiful, because that's what has let nature thrive for millennia. The challenge is to use that natural yin and yang that's present in all of us to build diverse and strong communities, rather than let it destroy them." "How are we going to do that?" I continued probing. "Right now, on this trip, we're teaching people the basics of meditation, because when we take time to think, to slow down, to stop and internalise, we can approach our next interaction with a presence and calm that's more likely to lead to genuine connection, and that's where everything good comes from."

Putting Steffi's theory to the test, I thanked her for her time and took a moment for myself before approaching a woman who I suspected was in charge of the garden. Immediately, Sue, who was the volunteer coordinator, garden manager and webmaster at *The Greening of Detroit*, reminded me of my mum. Her looks, mannerisms, even her green thumb, it was remarkable. And like my mum, she was proof that hope and the need to find purpose in one's work was not an idea millennials held exclusive rights to.

"I would say I'm quite a happy person," says Sue. "I'm a competitive person, like I was a real sports nut as a kid, so when I got into my corporate lifestyle, I climbed that ladder fast because I'm competitive. Over the years, I was able to step into different roles with more and more responsibility and pay, but that was not my thing. It became very stressful for me, and when I came home every night complaining about my job, after two years I said, 'I've got to get out of here,' and I just quit. My husband and I went on a three week road trip across the country, and I never felt so great in my life. It's been the best decision I ever made, honestly."

Sue's choice to leave her job with Bosch, in order to pursue a life of service to her community through *The Greening of Detroit*, did admittedly cause a certain amount of anxiety where money was concerned, **"but that's the modern American Dream isn't it?"** she asked me curiously. **"To sacrifice the material to find out who you are and chase your passion."** "It certainly sounds like a dream I could buy into," I said. "That's what a lot of the happiest people I've met have in common," I continued. "But why is this the case do you think?" Sue pauses, gently

Sue from the Greening of Detroit.

Dewey. The man with cancer.

Steffi Min from Future Clear.

Krishe. The South African migrant.

The area of Wall Street I interviewed people. Most of whom wished to remain anonymous, ergo there are limited photos of those I spoke to.

The Charging Bull of Wall Street surrounded by tourists.

Thousands of tourists grab the bull's testicles everyday. Lucky boy!

Christiana. The HR Consultant.

Ralph and Nateara.

holding a flower in her palm. "Well," she smiles. "My husband and I really downsized, and we live a minimal lifestyle nowadays, we like to ride bikes, eat what we grow and share what we can with others. In doing this, all those complexities of your complicated, big corporate job go away. He [her husband] actually left his job last year too."

"I know a lot of young people who are doing this and they live a small lifestyle, and I give them such kudos for doing that. It might be the era I grew up in, but I think people don't have to live such a big life. It took me years to figure that out. But now I look at nature, how it works together, how it never takes more than it needs, and that's my goal."

Founded in the 1980s by Elizabeth Gordon Sachs, after Dutch elm disease wiped out 90% of the tree canopy in the city, *The Greening of Detroit* is a compelling reminder that hope sprouts from the darkest of days. "What we're doing is we're transforming yesterday's industrial urban centre into tomorrow's clean, green city," says Sue, referring to the 100,000 trees and enormous urban farming movement that's taken root in Detroit. "What we're seeing, and what studies suggest," says Sue, "is that when you're living among trees and gardens, you're healthier, your community is healthier, there's less crime, your air is better. So that's the major focus of what the greening has been about." With 33,000 empty lots and vacant houses being transformed into urban agricultural spaces that are currently producing 181,436kg or 400,000 pounds of food a year, the greening of Detroit is not just some hobby or a sideline, it is a central part of the city's model for wholesale revitalisation. But Detroit's rebirth is just getting started, with Hantz Farms set to build the world's largest urban farm right in the middle of the city.

A few days later, in the middle of another much bigger city – New York – my own hope and happiness nearly broke. All I wanted was out. I needed home. I needed to sit and weep in my wife's arms, because 'nothing I do will make a difference' I thought, 'no interview, book or film can possibly reach enough of this ever expanding population I could see in front of me, so why bother speaking to anyone about anything?'. To this day I still don't know what caused such a flip in emotions. Was it the severe lack of sleep, due to the cacophony of horns and paper thin walls in my AirBnb; or was it that peculiar feeling of being painfully alone despite being surrounded by 8.6 million people? What finally freed me from this depressive episode were two conversations.

The first was with an amazingly uplifting and resilient couple, Ralph and Nateara, who I met riding a subway to the Bronx. The pair so humbly embodied all that I wished the world could be. The second, was a man named Dewey, who I met at Long Beach. He'd recently finished six months of cancer treatment that left him unable to walk.

What these interactions did, was remind me of why I was doing what I was doing, as well as provide me with a well overdue shot of gratitude. Holding onto this new found energy, I gathered my things and hopped a subway to a place I'd both revered and feared – Wall Street. Exactly what hostilities would greet me, I wondered, as I poked and probed the financial elite about the meaning of life and how we find happiness?

With a flood of Asian tourists all eager to grab the famous *Charging Bull* by its nuts and a swarm of barricades and armed guards 'keeping the peace' around Trump Tower, Wall Street looked more like a Chinese shopping mall than the epicentre of global financial markets. The upside of all this heightened security was that it helped me answer my first question: how was I going to engage with, let alone stop, the decidedly frantic business people I wished to interview. With traffic blocked from entering the section of Wall Street near Trump Tower (a site of huge protests after the election), local workers taking a cigarette break in the middle of the street became prime targets. "Tell me about Wall Street. Tell me about the happiness of people on Wall Street..." I asked Christiana, a trendy 26-year-old woman who seemed in less of a rush than most. "I think it really varies," she says. "I think the younger generation especially is getting a lot better than some of our management, probably. There's definitely a demand for work-life balance... Being a millennial especially, a lot of our bosses came from a different era when it was way, way, way more work intensive. Now I feel like there's sort of a cultural shift... Taking time off is big. Unlimited PTO (paid time off) is a really big thing I'm seeing. A lot of consultants really value that more than they do money a lot of times. So yeah... I think my generation's become a little happier, a little more easy go lucky when it comes to corporate demands."

As a HR Consultant who'd moved to New York from Pennsylvania five years earlier, I was eager to know whether Christiana felt workplaces were becoming happier or not? "Well, we saw a big paradigm shift in the world of work when a lot of our parents went from working on farms or in factories and things like that, where it was just a lot of working to live, and now you're ... [she pauses a moment] well, we're faced with a generation who are 'living to work', not in the bad way that it sounds, but in the way I now see a lot of staff saying 'I know 40 years of my life is going to be spent working, so it needs to be something that is fulfilling and it needs to be in an environment that gives me some balance and freedom too.'"

Well that was easier and friendlier than I thought. So I upped the ante, and picked out two much older, more intimidating guys who were waiting for their lunch – a Gyro (the American equivalent of a falafel roll, these were my favourite). "What makes people happy here?" I asked. "Money," said one, an immaculately dressed stock analyst in his late 40s. "And *how* does that make people happy?" I continued. "It doesn't, but it allows you to rent happiness for a while," he laughed smuggly, referring to hookers, drugs or various other quick fixes. "It lets you escape," said the other man, starting to unwrap his Gyro, "like we are now," they chuckled as they walked off, clearly not wanting to think about the sad reality of their answers. With the taste of blood in my mouth, the hunt was now on. I was desperate to find the biggest, meanest and most pompous looking lion and to have him reveal his soul to me. His truth.

Hiding in plain sight, a group of eight or so men entered my field of vision, as they stood chatting on the vehicle-less road. "So who knows the most about Wall Street?" I asked. "Who's asking," one man in his 60s responded. After giving my spiel, I immediately threw a question out there to all of them. "Who's the happiest guy here?" They all looked at someone else, with the majority eventually pointing to two different guys. "Why him?" I asked. "He's the money man," said a man in a blue checkered suit, with a thick New Yorker accent. "He's like the puppy of Wall Street," interrupts another guy, laughing at his own quick wit. "Everyone loves him and he ain't broken no crimes like The Wolf, you know." The group snicker either with or at the makeshift comedian. "This guy here though," says a man in his 50s pointing to a balding older man "he ain't ever in the office [everyone laughs], so he must be the happiest. Money just falls in his lap. And all you see is pictures of him and his family going to these places you ain't ever heard of. Where was that last one?" he asks the older man, who appears a little shy. "Macedonia," he says quietly. "Is that what makes you happy?" I ask the older man, as a younger guy whistles loudly at the group from the footpath. "Let's go ladies," he yells, and most follow the command. The only one to lag a little is the older man who, once the others are out of ear-shot whispers,

"It's not the money, it's how you spend it that makes you happy. You gotta use it, before it uses you."

"What do you mean…" I asked, but I was too late, the mystery man had already disappeared into a mob of lunch-goers all speeding to get somewhere. The next hour was tough going, no one wanted to talk, until out of the corner of my eye I spotted a young man leaning against a barricade, peacefully listening to music. "Sorry to interrupt," I said. "I'm a writer from Australia curious to learn more about happiness here on Wall Street." Whipping off his headphones in a frenzy, it was clear this guy was preparing to do battle with an idea he'd long wrestled with. "Money is a sickness. Money is a drug," said Hazem, who was forced to go by a different 'more white' name post 9/11, in order to make money. "It is, absolutely. You have people who trade money, you know, they're up and down, up and down. The highs and lows of that, it gets them. That's why people today, young people, they try to make their money real quick and then quit because otherwise you're going to have a heart attack at 40, and nobody wants that."

While it wasn't something I anticipated uncovering on Wall Street, once again I found myself confronted by this notion of using the system (or money) before it used and consumed you. For Hazem, perhaps more than others, there was a very real concern that he'd already lost much of who he was. "I'm in the finance area, and after some ups and downs, I'm doing well, but I'm doing something to please other people, and to please the person that I think I should be, not the person I am. You know what I mean? Like I actually would… [he pauses dramatically, as if his next words could kill or save him, and maybe they might] like I'm thinking about quitting and just becoming a musician because that's what I want to do. I need to. I think I just need to walk out of that office and be like, *I'm free*."

"Cause like, that's the real freedom that we should be chasing in America, and I think we're starting to. [Young] people don't seem as willing to live their life as a means to an end, because we can see that doesn't lead to happiness, we can see that more is not more. And actually by spending time getting more, you're denying what you're naturally good at, and that's what we want, that's what I want [he smiles resolutely], to have my own time back so I can be the person I am and person I want to be."

One person who I think personified this new (or revamped) American

Dream "of marching to the beat of your own drum," as Hazem put it, was Krishe, a real estate agent who worked at 30 Wall Street, right next door to Trump Tower. The South African born migrant, who was on a smoko break when I met her, sounded to me like an early American explorer grateful and excited to see what this new-found-land had in store. "Happiness is a concept to me that I'm going to find. I don't know where it is yet, but I guess New York is a good place to look. Because for my personality – I'm a very ambitious person – this is a place I fit in a little better, which makes me happy. There's no judgement too. There's cultural divides, different beliefs, but people here are free to walk and talk and do their thing. I like New York for that reason," says the 28-year-old, whose dreams I think reflect the 50 million migrants that call America home. "Money is what I'm working towards here, because it will afford me the luxury of doing what I want. I don't want to live hand to mouth. I'm South African, and from a poor family, so I know what it is to live hand to mouth. I don't want to do that anymore. That's my goal. To find happiness is just to find freedom to do whatever it is that you want to do in life." This notion was of course rather similar to what the founding fathers said, except that back then it was only white property owners who were truly free. "So what does the term 'the American Dream' mean to a young migrant today? And what does it have to do with happiness?" I asked.

"You can do anything ... but we all, we get so comfortable in our little niches, in our little groups. Sometimes we're blinded by the people we surround ourselves with because those are the people you grew up with ... If you really want to progress though and you want to find happiness, you're going to have to one, find it on your own, and two, you're going to have to expand. I'm a very open minded person and that's why I will find happiness, I think, whereas being too close minded, you'll never escape your little groove for long enough to find who you really are."

What Christiana, Hazem, Krishe and a number of other Wall Street workers showed me – much to my amazement – was that money was no longer king, and a new queen was rising. Her name: self-actualisation. And she is slowly tearing down the facade of 'wealth equals happiness' and replacing it with a generation obsessed with meaning, passion and discovering who they are. To me, being able to focus on one's purpose, rather than one's survival is the ultimate luxury. Millennials (particularly the privileged) suddenly have the time and knowledge to seek answers to life's greatest question: 'why are we here?'. The decidedly internal nature of this pursuit is one of many reasons why I think younger generations have been labeled narcissistic or self obsessed. Because for good, and for bad, we are. The thing we must all remember, though, is that the happiest people are those who care less about doing their hair or having perfectly pouting lips for a selfie and more about working out who they truly are. They also possess strong family, community and spiritual connections.

It sounds like the opening to a joke, but as I approached a young Jew, Muslim and Christian in Central Park, what they told me was exactly that: true happiness is "tied to the discovery of who we are and the connections we make," said the young Christian girl, "and that's why these two things are the modern American Dream." "That's why listening to people with your heart and not with the ears only is so important," said the 17-year-old Muslim friend, "because that's how we learn about who we are, is through that connection." "Yeah, that's why great conversations I think are the best way to grow yourself," said the Jewish girl, looking fondly at her friends. "To be understood too, helps," the Muslim girl interrupts, "because that gives you peace to be who you are."

"Connection is everything," said a young Dominican girl, Samari, on South Beach, Miami, as if continuing the conversation I'd had just a day earlier in Central Park. "I am living my life happy, worry-free, because I know we're the same," she continued. "There's no difference between me and you, so that means I have peace where maybe some others hold fear." A little further down the beach I met two young guys each reading a book. "We are in a time now where a lot of people our age and younger, some older too, are exposed to all this information, and books and travel and living in new places," said Joel, who moved to America from the Spanish Canary Islands. "When we do this, we start learning, and you realise that you're not 100% right, your family's not 100% right, your country's not 100% right. There's no perfect way of doing things. What I think we're finally gaining from all this dialogue and connectivity of cultures – and technology is speeding this up – is this kind of human global knowledge, like a general mind where we understand one another and see that happiness is doing good for others and getting the same thing back in return, because then you to go to bed and rest well, no one to harm you."

"Problem is," says Robert, who was sitting on the beach with friends listening to music, "they want to tear us apart from each other, because

South Beach, Miami. (Left to right) Billy, Henry, Janique, Robert and Baneesha (or something else that auto-corrected in my phone to 'brash a rich').

Joel (right) with his boyfriend Parker on South Beach.

Samari on South Beach.

Cowboy.

Kermit Ruffin's Treme Mother In Law Lounge.

Michelle Jeong (Pg 304).

J.D. Lenzen (Pg 306).

Bradford Rubleu enjoying a local delicacy, turkey necks.

A 'second line' parade. This quintessential part of New Orleans culture invites people to walk, sing and dance through the streets, backed by a jazz band. What began as a way to celebrate jazz musicians at their funeral, is today a weekly occurrence, held each Sunday, as well as alongside other festivities.

then you're an individual, and you keep consuming to fill that hole your [missing] community leave you with." "You know what they say about shampoo?" says Janique, popping her head over Robert's shoulder. "They say you shouldn't shampoo your hair because it strips you of your natural oils, you feel me? I feel like there's always been a lot of people out there who's trying to shampoo you. They want to strip you away from you. But I feel like happiness is comin' cause now we know, we seen, we ain't different." "You a stranger five minutes ago," interrupts Baneesha, the smallest of the five friends. "But now you ain't see, cause you talkin' to us." "And that's what we gotta do," interrupts Billy, who looks like a friendly black-hulk. "Talk," he says before Robert finishes his sentence. "Even when you ain't agree with someone, talk, and listen, 'cause you asked what makes us happy and for me its progress and solutions, which comes from unity, you know."

This common and well-founded belief that 'connection breeds happiness' is the primary reason that, to me at least, African-Americans seemed like the happiest race in America. But how is it that the most incarcerated and lowest paid members of a society are happier and committing suicide less? From Harlem and the Bronx, to Detroit, LA, Kansas, Miami and New Orleans, the horrible inequality and injustices African-Americans endured as slaves and now (for many) as citizens, is in many ways what's bound them together and given them a sense of community and happiness rarely seen among other groups. This shared suffering, coupled with their village roots and relative poverty (which necessitates them supporting one another more in order for them all to survive better), are all things that have preserved family and community, and curtailed the rise of individualism among black people. While this observation provided me with insight, and in some ways an answer to Scott and Kristen's dilemma of how to bring back the family unit, unfortunately the solution – enduring a shared suffering, relative poverty and coming from a village background – was not practical, nor advisable. So what is? How can America, how can we all, generate that culture of connection and community we crave so badly?

In a dark, out-of-the-way dive bar, with the smell of freshly cooked turkey necks in the air, I found my answer. *Kermit Ruffin's Treme Mother In Law Lounge* in New Orleans was initially a place I was hesitant to enter, and even more hesitant to stay, as I looked around and realised I was the only tourist, and only white person there. Remaining that way for much of the three days I spent at the historic venue, which R&B superstar Usher helped to rebuild after hurricane Katrina, I guess what I realised and what the 82-year-old stalwart of the jazz venue told me, was that the hope of a new American Dream laid in "letting people be who they want to be, and be with who they want to be with."

"I'm from Mississippi; I'm not really from New Orleans," said the former truck driver they referred to only as Cowboy. "Where I'm from, as a kid, black was black and white was white. You was a white man where I come from [he points to my arm] and I was a black man [he points to his arm] and I still is, but I got a different position now, I feel better in this age, all over the country you know, because back in 'em days I was treated like a dog some places. Not right. Not fair."

"So how can people be happy then? Like what should the American Dream be, if happiness is the end goal?" I asked the 82-year-old. "If you misused, you can't be satisfied. You're never happy if you misused, because people make you out to be of a different class. Like when I left my home as a little boy, I felt like I wasn't nobody [his eyes begin to water]. That's the end of that," he said, eager to hide the pain such memories invite. Cowboy remained silent as I grabbed us a beer. "Be treated like you a person like anybody else, that shouldn't be a dream, but that is what satisfies you," he said. "When I found happiness was when people treated me different ... as me. But if things didn't change from when I was a kid, them civil rights, I couldn't do that. So you know, that's when I can be happy, when I'm free, when I'm me," he said rather poetically. "But," he said, before I could get a word in, "I'm not happy like I was, not since my wife died ... My daughter died too, just 37 years old. Just got my son living 59 years now, and four grandkids, I'm happy 'bout them at least."

While it might have been easier to make my point if I stopped at his quote about "when I'm me, I'm happy," the thing I think we need to address is that **people, not things, are important.** "You only know that if you've gone without it," said Cowboy, before his friend, who sat with us during the interview, chimed in. "It's like these rights we got today, if it ain't been for ya Cowboys and these people, we'd never 've had 'em," said 55-year-old Bradford Rubleu, who was the one to really take me under his arm during my time at Kermit Ruffin's. "So is that why African-American people seem happier and more inclusive do you think?" "I s'pose," replied Bradford. "I'm gonna tell you. I don't really have the exact answer for that, but I tell you what, when you ain't gotta watch out for a whole lot of money, you ain't rich, everybody not trying to get what you have, I guess that could give you a small piece of mind. You know, you can just live and be happy. That's all. [He pauses, perhaps thinking back to the question] So ... I guess that sayin' if you worry 'bout what matters, family 'n' community, you ain't gotta concern ya'self wid all da nonsense stuff, like what-choo own."

"That's why we happy here, we got the real feelin', like love, and we embrace the people who come here [he looks at me and opens his arms], cause we know that's what we want if we come to your country and home you know," said Bradford. "So that's my Dream, you know, cause my mother was Cherokee Indian and my dad was Black American, so like they taught us to not be mad against a colour in school, that's what we gotta do. Always embrace everybody the same as you do the people you know. Even if they not from around, you give them that love too, cause that what make us closer. That's how we need a be movin' forward."

I know I've spent a lot of words on why it will be young people that will see and affect the changes we need in order to create a happier America (and world), but I want to be clear when I say that we, the young, will not, and do not, do this alone. We are the privileged heirs of a culture and political system that's served in getting billions out of poverty and hardship, and in uniting some of us, but **what this new dream needs to do is go one step further and let everyone be free to be who they are.** Wasn't that what the Declaration of Independence was talking about anyway? "The right to life, liberty and the pursuit of happiness." And isn't that what every single government should be hoping for – that *all* their citizens are able to thrive as who they are?

To glimpse the future, and see what happens when people are surrounded by a culture and politicians that let them think, do and be themselves, I travelled to San Francisco. A place that's long embraced inclusivity and counterculture. Waiting to interview a local trucker in a pub, I was reminded of just how far this city had come when I heard the phrase, "maybe we should go to a straight bar." But San Fran is not only a hub for gays, goths, artists and Asians, it also happens to be home to the best economy in America, with a GDP per capita of $126,820USD in 2016. Surely, surely, these people must be happy then?

My first insight came via my host, Michelle Jeong, a highly-successful entrepreneur who was born and raised in a very traditional Chinese immigrant family with extremely strict parents. "I grew up in a very Irish neighbourhood, we were one of the very first non-Irish families to move into that little pocket, and a lot of people don't realise how racially divided this city once was, not too long ago," said Michelle, now in her early-40s. "All my friends had red hair and freckles and were named Mora, Shamus and Bernadette. The first dance I learned was an Irish jig, and I went to an all-Irish Catholic school that was just a quarter-mile walk away."

Battling to understand why she had to have black hair, small eyes and learn Mandarin and classical piano, Michelle says her childhood – when compared to that of her two teenage daughters – paints a clear picture of how far this city (and country) has come. "There was a lot of pressure, from both sides, because I was too Chinese for the Irish and too Irish for the Chinese," she said. "At 13, I had suicidal thoughts [she pauses] ... there was a lot of racism, a lot hidden as well as overt... you'd walk by and people would do the whole 'ching-chong Chinaman' thing. They would talk with slanted eyes. They would try to mimic what they thought Chinese people spoke. I really didn't have any of that – I sounded as American as I do now – but you didn't love yourself from that perspective. You wanted to reject everything that you were born with."

"I'm just glad my daughters are living in a different time," said Michelle. And "different" is right. In 1994, a US-wide study found just 29% of the Silent Generation, 31% of boomers and 36% of Gen X believed 'immigrants strengthen the country'. Fast forward to 2017, and 79% of millennials, 66% of Gen X, 56% of Boomers and 47% of Silent's now agree with the sentiment, according to Pew Research.

While San Francisco mostly lived up to the hype of being this happy, futuristic place where 'different' was accepted and even normalised, there was a familiar stench in the air. It was the homeless, or more precisely, what they represented. Massive economic inequality, born out of what actor Jim Carrey calls "capitalism without conscience." Because, despite the top 1% of San Francisco households being progressive, rainbow-loving, tree hugging people (for the most part), they're still earning $3.6 million each, 44 times the average income of the bottom 99%, which stands at $81,094. The top 1%'s share of total income in the region has actually gone from 15.8% in 1989 to 30.8% in 2016, making San Francisco the first ranked city in California for economic inequality, according to the Californian Budget Center. The economic growth has reduced unemployment to 3.4%, a commendable feat, but with 64,000 jobs added in 2015 alone, and only 5000 new homes built that same year, the median house and apartment price has jumped to $1.61 and $1.2 million respectively, making the minimum qualifying income to purchase a property roughly $254,000 a year! As Frederick Kuo, a local journalist writes in Quartz (QZ), "If causal factors leading to housing unaffordability are not resolved over multiple generations, the social stratification will start to resemble countries like Russia, where a small elite control a vast share of the country's total wealth."

The result? "A society where the threat of class warfare would loom large," says Kuo. Not exactly the happy future I'd hoped to find. The major problem is that a society's level of happiness is tied less to how much people have, and more to how much they have comparative to their neighbours. "At the same time, when a system no longer provides opportunities for the majority to partake in wealth building, it not only robs those who are excluded of opportunities, but also of their dignity," concludes Kuo.

I might be shot for saying this (by those who argue a free market and guns are essential freedoms), but the only way to ensure a more even distribution of wealth, and therefore a happier society and future for all Americans (and the world for that matter) is by instituting more equitable government policies designed to level the playing field. Without such measures, suicide, poverty, crime and lack of cohesion will continue to eat away at the fabric of peace and happiness that countless decades of steady economic growth would have otherwise afforded America. The good news is, from my observations, conversations and the statistics I've since found, this seems like an inevitability. There *is* a new American Dream, and it's being driven by the most educated, diverse and liberal generation in history. A 2017 study by Pew Research shows that 57% of millennials have "consistently liberal" or "mostly liberal" views, while just 12% have "consistently conservative" or "mostly conservative" views. 31% had mixed views. When it comes to gay rights, immigration and their willingness to accept more government involvement in income redistribution and universal health care, "young people lean left" says journalist Derek Thompson.

No matter your cultural or political persuasions, what all of this tells me is that for the vast majority of Americans whose needs have been ignored by Washington for decades, help, hope and even happiness is on its way. Because **we millennials have heard the cries and seen the division, tension and unhappiness that 'capitalism without conscience' creates, and we want out.** This doesn't mean tearing down corporations or abandoning capitalism altogether. Rather, it's about using the education, connection and privilege we've been afforded (thanks to those generations before us), and devising a happier way forward for all. Because *I am only well if you are well.*

Prominent San Francisco author and entrepreneur J.D. Lenzen says it's about creating a society where you'd let a stranger use your toilet. "In Iceland I had this experience where I had to use a restroom," said J.D., in an interview Michelle had arranged for me. "I was walking down the street and I was talking to my wife. I said, 'I got to go to the bathroom really bad,' but I'd just left the shopping mall. These two ladies were sitting out in front of their place ... Anyway, this woman overheard me, and she said, 'Come on over,' and she pointed into her house, and then said, 'You go in. You go up the stairs. Circle around and it's the second door.' She didn't follow me. Didn't ask my name. Nothing. I went in there, and I went and used the bathroom, and I almost wanted to cry, because I realised this is how far we've fallen in America. We cannot do this. No one would ever dare to do such a thing. As I walked back past the women, who simply continued their conversation as if this were just a regular normal thing, I nearly ... I almost got teary. They didn't know why. I was blown away." J.D. pauses, and my arms tingle.

"This is true freedom," he concludes.

Iceland isn't only "the happiest country" J.D. says he's travelled to, it also features in the top 3 or 4 happiest nations on Earth in a whole host of different studies and indexes, including the *United Nations World Happiness Report.* As of 2018, America ranked 18th, in this same report. But why? What's stopping America becoming the happiest country on Earth?

Right now, as J.D's toilet story suggests, it's the division, the fear and the inequality that means citizens don't trust one another. What's causing this *is* capitalism, because "once capital becomes an idol," Pope Francis reminds us, "it sets people against one another [and] the service of the common good is left behind."

"Companies we used to own, own us. Governments that used to be voted in, are bought. And our supposedly free press, who could expose all this, are now owned by these very corporations," says Travis Verta, in the hit TV show *Continuum*.

Evaluating what the top ten or so happiest countries have in common, a healthy capitalist marketplace is there. However, the higher up the list you go, what you start noticing are numerous government policies that benefit everybody. Call them socialist, leftist, progressive, call them what you want, but free or subsidised university/college, free universal health care and a robust parental leave scheme is good for everyone! Yes, these things cost money. And yes, the happiest nations are among the highest taxed, but if such measures are proven to make a country happier, shouldn't we adopt them? Distinguished American economist Jeffrey Sachs, who co-authors the UN *World Happiness Report*, says it's a no-brainer. "Happiness is a result of creating strong social foundations," Sachs tells CBS, "and if other nations prioritised 'social trust' and 'healthy lives', they could also find that their citizens become happier and more content."

"They [Norway, Finland, Denmark and Iceland] are happy because these societies are not only prosperous but also have high equality, social trust and honesty of government. They enjoy long, paid vacations, zero out-of-pocket costs of healthcare, zero or low tuition costs and quality public services for all," he tells CNBC. What such equitable socialist policies would do for America, according to Stanford researcher Raj Chetty and his team, is drive innovation, entrepreneurship and jobs. Looking at the number of inventors born in the San Francisco Bay Area between 1980 and 1984, what researchers found was that an estimated 51% of all inventors came from families in the top 20% of income earners, while just 7% came from families in the poorest 20%. Chetty and his colleagues estimate that if all people across race, gender and socioeconomic status were given equal opportunity and help to succeed, the country would have four times as many inventors as it does today – including 760 more inventors born in the Bay Area every year. These kids, whom Chetty calls "Lost Einsteins," are not only the key to a flourishing economy, they may also be the person who cures cancer or takes us to new galaxies. The only thing they need, Chetty says, is a chance.

When capitalism is served with a healthy side of socialism, it forces us to connect, to consider those lost Einsteins, that helpless prisoner, migrant or neighbour; in short, it asks us to serve the common good. Unadulterated capitalism, on the other hand, brings out our very worst survivalist-based instincts. It forces us to compete and judge and ridicule, which only serves to drive distrust and division between strangers, communities, even families.

What my experience in the US taught me about how to build the happiest cultural and political systems was this: *listening is everything*. Being forced to sit and listen and respond only with questions (not judgement or my own self-serving opinions), what I found was that **we all have a lot more in common than those in power (including the media) would have you think**. If, or when, we shut up for long enough to understand this, to see the hope, the solutions in this hope, I'm sure we'll start to build the love, the social trust and the understanding necessary to ensure the masses, not the few, are the beneficiaries of the hard work we all put in. Because that is what all of the happiest societies have in common – a culture and political system hell bent on building and preserving equality.

*If equality is the destination,
where does the road begin?*

8

GROSS NATIONAL HAPPINESS AND THE RICE WINE HANGOVER

What difference does a river make? How about a flag or border? What about an ideology? Standing in Detroit (USA) staring at a Canadian flag that stood at the other side of the Detroit River, I couldn't help but wonder how significant that body of water was. Like, why were the buildings on the Canadian side so much smaller? Were they poorer? Less populated? Does size even matter? Did it make them less happy than their super-sized southern neighbours? Well...? With more questions than answers I decided to jump on a bus and see and hear for myself.

"We're doin' good, yeah," a 20-odd-year-old hipster Barista told me. "Canada is a nice, open, free place, we don't need to lock our doors or worry too much about guns," said the middle-aged mother he was serving. "Yeah I ain't complainin', we ain't perfect, but our government helps us with study and healthcare and stuff. All the basics are right, they're good here," concluded a university student waiting for his cappuccino.

Tired of the somewhat safe, monotonous and predictable nature of the answers I was attracting as I made my way along the main street of Windsor, I decided to stop at a local bar where two older gentlemen, Ken and Gerry, were sitting enjoying a quiet beer. "So what makes a couple of guys like you happy?" I asked rather brashly, trying to fit in. "What's makes me happy?" said Ken, reflecting on my question. "I live in Canada [he nods at Gerry]. We have an open concept. Accept people from the distant shores. Take them for who they are. They come from wherever. Australia [he looks at me], Syria or wherever. Why not open your arms to them? We need more people to pay for our pensions anyway," the pair laughed, as they gestured for me to grab a stall and asked the waitress to pour me a beer. "Integrity. And kindness," continued Gerry. "Be kind to each other. **Have opinions, but don't hate people for their different opinions** ... that's what we strive for here in Canada. You're no better than anybody and nobody's better than you. You could have been born anybody in the world, you could have been born anyone – anywhere too – so don't be too proud. Don't think you're any less or any better than anybody," said Gerry, before Ken interrupted him. "That's the best thing about this place – our little bit of socialism. Seeing everyone as worth something. But you've got to have a balance of socialism [and capitalism]. You can't have just one, you can't have just the other. You've got to be willing to give up a certain percentage of your money and control to make it work though."

And therein lies the problem.

Relinquishing control is terrifying. It goes against every instinct of our survivalist brain. People have literally screamed at me in the street insisting "there is no way someone else knows how to spend my money better than me!" "I get it, and for the most part I agree," I'd typically respond. But at the same time, without cooperation, without trust, without empathy, without government, "the life of man [is] solitary, poor, nasty, brutish, and short," writes acclaimed political philosopher Thomas Hobbes, who went on to say, "the condition of man ... is a condition of war of everyone against everyone." At the time he wrote this (1651), it must be said the world was a wholly different place. Humanity, and particularly those monarchs in power, were in a bitter, brutal fight to secure the resources necessary to rule, because as Hobbes noted, 'subjects' would only remain loyal so long as the 'sovereign' could protect them.

Times have, of course, changed. Governments have replaced monarchs for the most part. More than half of all countries are now considered 'Democratic'. And humans no longer seem so easily convinced that they should spill their blood for the erroneous glory of expanding their nation's borders (again, for the most part). **We have, by all reports (and there are many), entered the most peaceful and prosperous period in recorded human history.** In the past 200 years, homicide rates have fallen by between 50 and 75%. Over the same period, the number of human beings dying before their 5th birthday has radically declined, from 43.3% to 3.91%. Remarkably (and I think this hit home for me given I'm currently 33), overall life expectancy has more than doubled from 30 in the early 1800s, to 72 as of 2016. This is all far less surprising when you consider that a whopping 89% of people lived in extreme poverty in 1820, while today that number is less than 10%. Similarly, in 1800, the percentage of illiterate people was 87.95, while in 2018 it was just 13.75. Global GDP has also grown by a staggering 44,424%, from $336 billion USD in 1800 to $149,603 billion USD in 2014. Tax rates have also steadily increased throughout the 20th century, from less than 10% in the early 1900s to an average of 25.1% across OECD countries as of 2014.

What all this progress has done (in most developed countries) is all but guarantee the protection of citizens, leaving politicians with an entirely new conundrum: what next? Do we persist with this idea that GDP growth will inevitably create a better or happier society? The statistics, the social angst, the barrage of horror mental health stories emerging at a time of enormous economic prosperity – it is all proof of what's become known as the Easterlin Paradox. Simply stated, the happiness-income paradox is this: life satisfaction does rise with average incomes *but* only up to a point. Beyond that, happiness does not trend upwards as income continues to grow, says economist Richard Easterlin, who became known as 'the father of happiness economics' after publishing his controversial 1974 paper *Does Economic Growth Improve the Human Lot? Some Empirical Evidence*. He concluded the paper by saying "Economic growth does not raise a society to some ultimate state of plenty. Rather, growth fuels ever-growing wants."

What the Easterlin Paradox gave birth to was an entirely new field of research. It asked economists, psychologists, anthropologists, sociologists and a whole lot of other people with long titles ending in 'ist' to consider the relationship between the economics, the policies, the social framework and the happiness of a country. For nearly half a century now, data pointing us toward a happier 'what next?' has largely been ignored in favour of sticking with what we know. The mantra 'growth is good' has become both a wish and a command.

The problem, as Easterlin's 2010 paper suggests, is that what we know is not working – not if happiness is the goal. "With incomes rising so rapidly in [certain] countries, it seems extraordinary that no surveys register the marked improvement in subjective well-being that mainstream economists and policy makers worldwide expect to find," says Easterlin, whose 2010 report analysed a sample of 37 countries, rich and poor, ex-communist and capitalist. For example, he says, in Chile,

China and South Korea, three countries in which per capita income has doubled in less than 20 years, life satisfaction has remained flat (or even slightly declined). "Where does this leave us? If economic growth is not the main route to greater happiness, what is?" Easterlin asks. "We may need to focus policy more directly on urgent personal concerns relating to things such as health and family life, rather than on the mere escalation of material goods."

Sitting in a cosy Melbourne cafe waiting for my favourite hot chocolate and falafel roll, as I tap at the keys of my insanely expensive MacBook Pro, I'm not for a minute intimating that governments (or individuals) need to altogether renounce money, GDP or materialism in order to discover our happiest state. No. What Easterlin, what I, and what a whole myriad of researchers are saying is simply this: **richest isn't always happiest.** There's more to it than that, much more, which is why this question of 'what next?' must begin with a thorough analysis of those societies that are getting it right – the happiest countries on earth. So who are they? (Take a look to the right.)

Let the search begin!

Curious to learn more about the politics, science, stories and the truth behind these rankings, I spent three months in early 2019 scooting, trekking, training, busing and biking through Europe, chatting to anyone and everyone I bumped into – including a Lord, a Prime Minister and a busker who blew my mind. Rather luckily, one of the first stops on my journey was the launch of the 2019 World Happiness Report (WHR) at Bocconi University in Milan, Italy. One of the guys I was particularly thrilled to meet was Professor Jeffrey Sachs, a man whose lofty titles refreshingly didn't seem to come with strings or a giant ego attached. From former-Harvard and now Columbia University Professor, to senior UN advisor and twice being named one of Time Magazine's 100 most influential world leaders, what struck me as Sachs' most impressive quality wasn't what he'd done, but why he'd done it.

"I grew up in a very socially aware family, my father was very much involved in civil rights movements, political rights. We lived in a culturally rich suburban community in Detroit. So, this was sort of the orientation to asking questions about *what makes for a good society?*. I remember asking

Ranking of Happiness 2016-2018

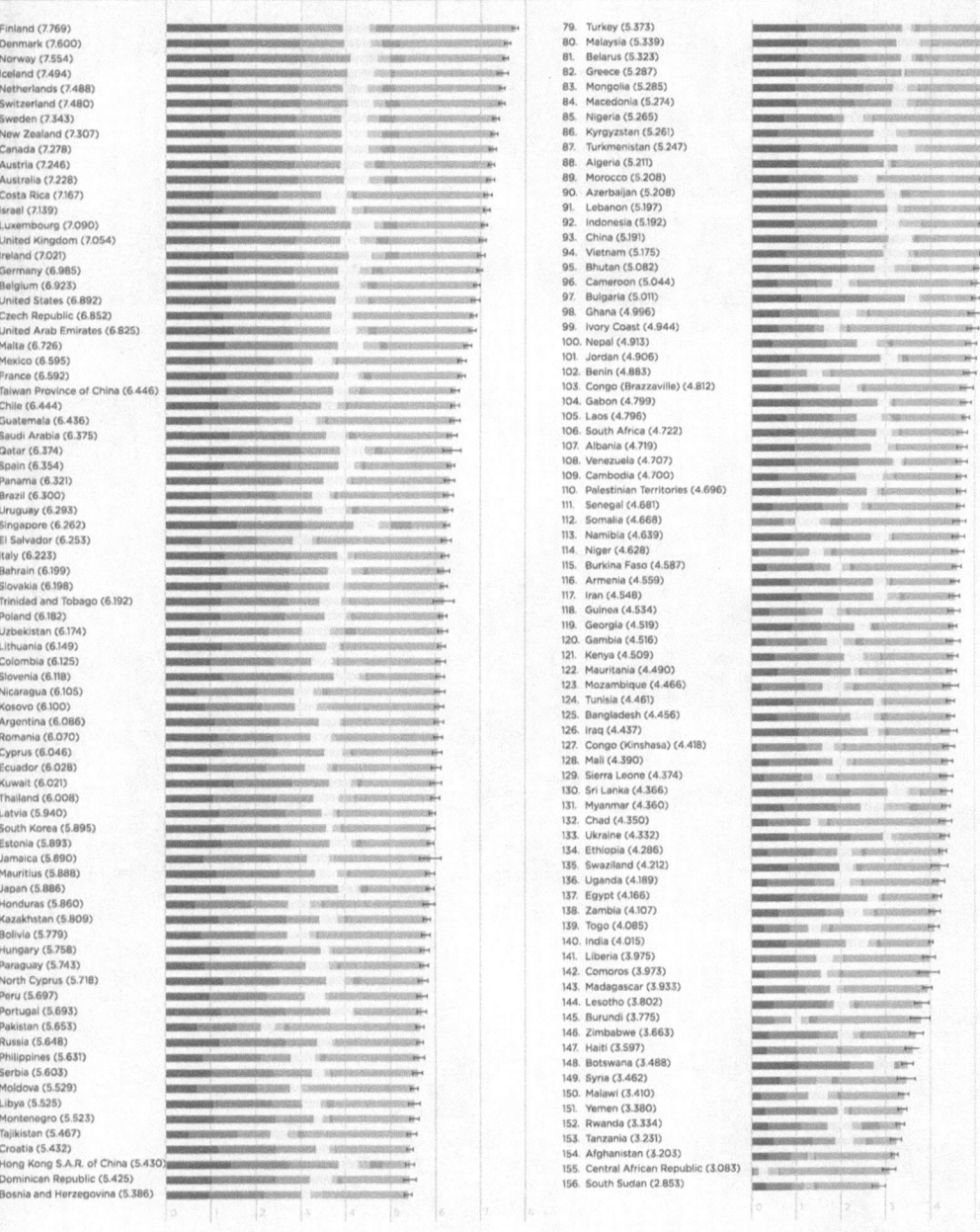

(Left to right) Gerry, our barmaid, their other fiend who left before the interview, and Ken at a bar called Lefty's in Windsor, Canada.

Oslo Town Hall, with statues of the workers that built it in front of it.

These buskers in Florence, Italy reminded me of what truly make a society richer.

Jeffrey Sachs speaking with Pope Francis at the convening of Finance Ministers worldwide to talk about Climate Change and New Evidence from Science, Engineering, and Policy. Photo by Gabriella Marino.

myself that question for the first time when I was 15, and I've never stopped asking that question," said Sachs. "I've been studying it since 1972. So that's 47 years of trying to answer that question." "And what have you discovered?" I asked. "My bottom line is very simple," he says. "I believe **the social-democratic ethos is the most successful model we know.** So, I think the Scandinavian countries are close, they're not perfect, but they're the closest on the planet to what we would actually regard as a basis for happiness, in that they combine prosperity, social cohesion, good work-life balance, and decency in relating to others and to the rest of the world."

> **What is social democracy?** A system of governance that balances inclusion and equality with capitalism and keeps capitalism in check through strict economic regulation while promoting income redistribution via a robust welfare state.

What baffles me, and what must frustrate the absolute hell out of a guy like Sachs, is that despite the irrefutable evidence that the social democratic system *does* create the conditions for happiness, countries such as my own (and we're not alone) seem to be veering further and further away from such a model in favour of this primitive 'everyone against everyone' approach. What, and most importantly who, is driving this? Well, what any good journalist knows to follow, is the money. Giant corporations want lax laws and governments that aren't going to stand in their way. The trouble with social democracies, as big business would see it, is they're defined by this pesky notion of 'governing for the common good', rather than individual gain. In Finland for instance, there are no private schools, no standardised tests and teachers are paid a very decent wage. It's little wonder their education system is considered the best in the world. In Iceland, 91.8% of employees belong to a labour union, the highest percentage in the world. As a result, Icelanders enjoy the most equal GDP per capita, as well as the most equal happiness ranking per capita. In Norway, new mothers and fathers can revel in a total of 49 weeks of fully-paid parental leave. They've also allocated 15 weeks of non-transferable leave for fathers, making it perhaps the most gender-equal system in the world. Oh, and this is all paid for by the government. If you think that's nifty, in Denmark, university isn't only free (as in no tuition fees, no loans, ever), but students not living with their parents are given $900USD a month (by the government) for up to six years, with no strings attached. Conservative politicians and economists might read all this and fret over delusions of 'unaffordability' or 'economic mismanagement', but the proof is in the pudding. Finland, Denmark, Norway and Iceland (all social democracies) are among the richest, the most stable and the most generous economies globally. They're also the four happiest countries on earth!

The only mistake politicians and governments across the world continue to make, is not copying these places. Though, in a way, that's our fault too. For 200,000 years we've been conditioned to look out for numero uno. Me, myself and I. Doing anything for anyone outside of our immediate blood line, or possibly our tribe (if they helped to guarantee our survival), was ludicrous. This 'me first' mentality has undoubtedly served a purpose. We are alive no less, but shedding that selfish cocoon we've been hiding in – and being willing to trust someone else and give over control of our health, security, education, transport and wellbeing to a government – that is the next step. I don't say this because I love governments or the bean counters, bureaucrats and policy makers that make them up. I say this because **in a true and proper functioning democracy, a government is answerable to the people** and is easily voted out if it's not. When it gets murky – and the reason the *2018 Economist Intelligence Unit's Democracy Index* says there's just 20 "full" democracies alive today – is because "transparency, accountability and corruption" continue to plague our "confidence in political parties." The report also suggests civil rights and free speech are slowly being eroded by numerous state and non-state entities, including the ever corrupting influence of the top 1%, who Sachs says are clearly answerable to nobody.

"We have an opioid addiction in the United States, which was incredibly caused by deliberate pharmaceutical industry behaviours, especially one company, Purdue Pharma, which paid doctors to addict patients all over the country," said Sachs, during his public address at Bocconi. "This is evidence that we're really not taking care of ourselves at all, as a society. Partly because the businesses are not self-regulating, to the contrary. And government is not at all regulating, to the extent that a company can create an epidemic before our eyes."

Purdue may have kicked open the door to a crisis officially estimated to have claimed 350,000 lives – roughly the same number of people to attend the past five Super Bowls – but the "national nightmare" as Trump put it, was effectively enabled by the medical industry, which is in control of America's healthcare system. "By 2012, doctors were writing 250 million opioid prescriptions a year, enough to supply every adult for a month – greatly widening the number of people exposed to the risk of addiction and leaving the country awash in surplus drugs to feed experimentation and the underground market," says Chris McGreal, author of *American Overdose, The Opioid Tragedy in Three Acts*. As daunting as this figure is, it paled into insignificance when in July 2019, a report detailing America's 'overdose epidemic' revealed the number of pills distributed in America in the six years from 2006 to 2012 was a mind-boggling 76 billion! "When a few doctors raised the alarm in the early 2000s, warning that opioids were more dangerous and less effective than the makers claimed – and particularly, that they did not work well as long-term treatment for chronic pain – the drug industry turned on the victims. It disparaged the addicted and the dead as 'abusers', even if they became hooked by following their prescriptions. The problem was the person not the pills, the drug makers claimed. It was pharma's equivalent of the NRA slogan 'Guns don't kill people, people kill people.'"

With federal regulators and corrupt politicians being lobbied (and openly bribed) to ignore the 'blizzard of prescriptions' to sell a drug described as 'heroin in a pill', the opioid epidemic, which continues to claim around 150 lives a day (in 2019), is just one example of why America is considered a "flawed democracy" by the Economist Intelligence Unit. Coming in at 25th place, below countries such as Costa Rica, Uruguay and Chile, it's fascinating that America still paints itself as the guiding light of democracy across the world, often waging wars to 'free' and 'liberate' countries, while their own civil liberties are eroded in the name of economic development.

"I think it's an interesting question for all of us in general," says Sachs. **"What's the point of getting so rich if you don't feel so good about it?** We have been in a strange experience now for 70 years actually, in the United States, which is that we've got richer, and richer, and richer, but we haven't been able to get that happiness scale to rise – and it's actually been on a decline."

Pointing to one or two things that have caused this paradox is difficult; that was, until I witnessed the solution for myself. Travelling to the five happiest countries on earth, what I noticed, which is also lacking in Australia, the UK and several other countries at present, is trust in government and our leaders. "That trust comes from faith in the system itself," says Andrè, an Oslo barman whose family has lived in the area since 600AD. "I think the government, the belief that we have almost always had in Norway, is in social democracy. Even if it's the 'right' who is in government, it's always the same basic value that governs us: equality." My first taste of just how deeply this was embedded in Norwegian society, was during my free walking tour of Oslo (the capital of Norway). As we approached the city hall, our guide pointed out six statues standing in front of the enormously imposing brick structure. "Can anyone guess who these statues depict?" she asked. "The founders of Oslo?" an older member of our group replied. "Viking warriors?" said an enthusiastic young boy. "Good guess," our guide responded. "But in particularly Norwegian style, the statues actually represent the six different types of workers it took to build the town hall. The architects and artists were clearly asked to portray the worth of having a noble working class laboring together for the good of society and the State." This simple gesture was to me enormously telling. Statues and landmarks will almost always tell you who is or was important or valued by a society. In Norway, even back in 1950 when the city hall was built, the tradespeople and the working class clearly mattered just as much as the politicians and conquerors who'd typically adorn such monuments.

"We are all equal in Norway, because we are. How could we not be? We all need one another to keep the society safe and running," says Andrè, who goes on to tell me about his mother. "She's been working her whole life by herself, for us, her four sons. She's gone without school. But again, she just worked hard, and because things are pretty fair here, she was able to become a manager and a hotel owner. Nobody's been holding her back. So, I think **we all have a chance in Norway, because we all have an equal standing and voice**." He wasn't wrong. In fact Norway ranks as the number one country on the Economist Intelligence Unit 2018 Democracy Index, with a score of 9.87 out of a possible 10. Unsurprisingly, all of Scandinavia's social democracies are amongst the top ten most democratic countries on earth, with Iceland in 2nd, Sweden 3rd, and Denmark and Finland coming in 5th and 8th respectively.

Asking Andrè what he would change about his government or country if he had the chance, he was the first person I've ever heard respond in this way: "If I could change anything [he pauses in thought], I don't think I would, because I think it's fine as it is," he says with a rare smile. "I've got nothing to worry about. If something doesn't work out, people will help me on my way back up. So, that's the safety net. You're safe if you fuck up once at the very least, or if you fall ill, so it's a good country to live in." Not only is healthcare in Norway free (other than a $246USD levy each year), but the country arguably has the most generous sick leave policy in the world. Employees receive 100 percent of their salary from day one for up to a year.

What's allowed Norway to become such a generous and enviable country to live in is a policy I can't believe more countries haven't followed. When Norway discovered large oil and gas reserves in its sector of the North Sea, the country decided that it would set up a sovereign wealth fund – a piggy bank for the people – to ensure current and future generations would reap the benefits of the unexpected bonanza. Britain, which also discovered oil in the North Sea around the same time, did not establish a future fund. The result is that Norway has amassed a $1,000,000,000,000USD (one trillion) wealth fund, which made the country $130 billion USD in 2017 alone, accounting for nearly one third of the country's GDP. That's a whole lot of money for doing nothing. If they'd invested their North Sea oil money in a similar way, Sukhdev Johal, Professor of Accounting at Queen Mary University of London, thinks the UK total might well have been in excess of $1 trillion USD (as of 2014). Australia too, made the same short-sighted non-socially democratic decision when consecutive prime ministers pissed away hundreds of billions of dollars we made digging up coal and iron ore. Rather than see these resources as something that should benefit all Aussies, or Brits, for the foreseeable future, our respective governments used the cash injection to provide tax cuts and incentives that would get them re-elected.

When I asked Andrè why he felt his country had made the decision they had, his response encapsulated why it is that any answer to the question of 'what next?' must include the words 'social democracy'. "Norway's more than a country. It sounds wrong, but it's our family. We're the same people. We are equal. We are a social democracy. That's why, when we found oil in Norway, we chose to put the profits in a fund to ensure this one-off find is shared among all of us forever. Because we believe our children and their children should also benefit from such a thing," he says.

Still, if you were to ask a Norwegian child or adult 'what next?' there may be some confusion, because, like the rest of us, Norway continues to wrestle with that age-old dilemma of finding the balance between GDP growth and sustainability. Like in March 2019, Norway became the first country on earth where electric vehicles (58.4 percent of sales) outsold petrol and diesel models. Yep, they're a definite leader in the adoption of zero emission vehicles, and all sides of Norway's government have agreed to the ambitious goal to stop selling new non-electric vehicles by 2025. Where the confusion comes in, is that at the very same time the country is reducing CO_2 emissions by going electric, Equinor energy, which is 67% owned by the Norwegian government, is hoping to drill a massive deep water oil well 370km off the coastline of the Great Australian Bight. Not only do such investments seem to undermine the will of the Norwegian people (and government), who say they want to see real action on climate change, but with the Bight boasting more marine diversity that the Great Barrier Reef – 85% of which can't be found anywhere else in the world – the prospect of a major leak or spill in this wild, stormy and remote stretch of water would be catastrophic. As it stands, the Bight attracts more than eight million visitors a year and plays host to a large local fishing industry, which all up contributes around $10 billion a year to the Australian economy, roughly twice as much as the Great Barrier Reef.

While a 2018 ACIL Allen report suggests drilling in the Bight could add $5.9 billion a year to Australia's GDP – if the region turns out to be a major oil field – the expected windfall wouldn't be realised until between 2040 and 2060, and would likely never reach the pockets of locals. Instead, Equinor (a company located 15,000km away) would pocket the majority of profits, but not before coughing up a hefty sum to the Australian government via the Petroleum Resource Rent Tax. What's concerning for locals, and the reason I think we continue to see growing distrust of governments globally, is that the needs of the people (especially those not from cities) are largely being ignored in favour of generating wealth for the few, including the State. In this case, 3900 fisherman and thousands more employed in tourism, bear all the risk if things go wrong, and yet, they will see none of the benefits. The money will not be reinvested locally and the 1361 jobs created in order to drill and maintain the 101 oil wells will be filled by highly skilled fly-in fly-out workers from Adelaide (the nearest capital city). While Equinor has engaged in a lengthy (and costly) two year process to get government and industry stakeholders on board, a 2019 study by The Australia Institute

(TAI) suggests that seven out of ten South Australian voters are still against drilling in the Bight.

"Equinor and the other oil giants looking to drill in the Great Australian Bight are attempting to do so in direct opposition to the wishes of the Australian people," says Noah Schultz-Byard from TAI. Even Norway's own MPs are beginning to question the project. In March 2019, MP Kristoffer Robin Haug asked the Norwegian Parliament to consider whether Norway would "become the enemy" if they proceeded. What's even more confusing in all this is that Norway's 1 trillion dollar investment fund – which owns $37 billion of shares in oil giants such as BP, Shell and Total – says it is also moving away from fossil fuels after a report by Norway's central bank in 2017 advised that dropping oil and gas investment would be a good economic move – as well as ease the pressure it was under to do so for environmental reasons.

If researchers are right and social and political trust is at the heart of what makes us our happiest, then decisions such as this – which go against the will of the people in favour of a small minority of voices with a vested interest – are like a social cancer. The disease begins to take effect the moment politicians and corporate lobbyists start talking in dualities: you're either a tree hugging environmentalist or you care about jobs and the economy – but you can't be both – or so they'd have us think. Most citizens sadly and unknowingly buy into this rhetoric, because as psychologists have shown, "enemies enhance the meaning of life." Research conducted by Mark Landau, Professor of Psychology at the University of Kansas, went so far as to suggest that **people literally create enemies in order to maintain a stable, coherent, clear view of the world.** There's good and evil, right!? Such a basic binary view helps us effortlessly navigate life without much complex thinking, and lets us freely attribute the negatives we encounter (which are inevitable) to our so called 'evil enemies'. Interestingly, in one study, people who had just been told to imagine a powerful enemy – Al-Qaeda – actually thought the world felt less dangerous and chaotic afterwards. "Having enemies even appears to make people feel, ironically, safer," writes psychologist Dr. Nathan Heflick in an article on Psychology Today.

Understanding our weaknesses as a society, those things that tear us apart – such as this primitive want or need for an enemy – is critical if we are to fight off this common social cancer, which writer and Atlantic Fellow Durkhanai Ayubi calls "othering." "The problem of othering is the problem of the 21st century. And the possible demise of the nation state and the planet as we know it," says Durkhanai, quoting Dr. John Powell from the University of California. "One facet of othering is about creating marginalised and dehumanised groups of people, so that a smaller 'we' continues to centralise wealth and power, but it is also about a disconnection from our own humanness and from the natural universe we are a part of – and the interaction of these three things," continues Durkhanai, during a speech at *newday*, a leadership forum I'm involved with.

This wedge being driven between us by the ruling class, who have long used our tribal instincts against us, has one clear motive – to distract and divide us – because if we're busy fighting each other, we're unlikely to rise up and fight or demand anything of them. While the modern ruler wears a suit, not a crown, and the level of sophistication behind their divisive manipulation has evolved with our knowledge of human psychology, the premise is much the same as it always has been. Those in power, or those seeking it, need not convince everyone that they're good or right, they need not even convince the majority, all they need to do (initially) is make it seem as though there are two sides, of which they are the more legitimate one. This is, of course, achieved surprisingly easily with enough money. First, you hire a team of marketing wizards to come up with a catchy messaging strategy: in essence, the unpleasant label you will give to your opponent, and the amazingly agreeable label you will give yourself. Next, you spend enough money to make sure your voice is as loud or louder than theirs. This generally, though not exclusively, involves acquiring media or advertising space, giving journalists a controversial scoop or sound bite, and buying up enough celebrity, scientific or political endorsements to make your argument sound 'legit'. To see just how effectively this works, we need look no further than the success of big tobacco, Brexit, Trump, Australia's 'stop the boats' policy and the illegal invasion of Iraq in 2003, which Bush somehow sold as being about (non-existent) weapons of mass destruction, not oil.

At the end of the day, while we continue to let crooked governments and greedy corporations convince us that they're not the enemy – and that someone else is – we'll continue to see this cancer grow. The poor will blame the rich, who'll blame the young, who'll blame the old, who'll blame the atheists, who'll blame the right, who'll blame the left, who'll blame the uneducated, who'll blame the migrants, who'll blame the newer migrants, and so on and so on until all trust has been eroded. Then, with everyone distracted, with our eyes firmly fixed on those we are told to fear – whether Muslim, Jew, Christian, Mexican, Syrian or Sudanese – those in power will be free to sell our rights, our resources and our future to the highest bidder. This is how the cancer grows. This is how inequality becomes the norm. This is how democracy crumbles.

What was abundantly clear in Norway and right across Scandinavia, was that people weren't caught in this cycle of fear, distrust and division – not in the same way the rest of the world is anyway. "We're not perfect, but we don't have to worry too much about what our government is doing behind our back," said Louie, a young disability support worker from the Philippines, who caught my attention because he and his client Kristoffer were laughing ecstatically outside the Oslo Opera House. "Norwegian society and how the politics works in my opinion is amazing. I trust them, yeah, I trust the system," said Louie, before Kristoffer chimed in. "If you come from a land with a corrupt system, it's much harder to depend on anyone I think. Because trust is fragile, you see. It is difficult to build, but easily broken," said Kristoffer, who was born with Cerebral Palsy, and has relied on government support his entire life. "Without a doubt we are better than most countries ... but we pay a lot in taxes too, so I think we expect more from our government." With an average personal income tax rate of 38%, Norway is one of the most heavily taxed nations on earth. They pay almost four times that of Hong Kong, and nearly twice the US rate. But maybe that's why things work. Maybe that's why people in Norway are happy. "What do you think?" I asked Louie and Kristoffer.

"Well, I am paid by the government to help other human beings," said Louie. "And Kristoffer receives the services he needs to get on with life thanks to the system here." "We have this kind of informal dictate here known as Jante Law," said Kristoffer. "It essentially says *'You're only as good as everyone else'*, and I think that is why we are happy here," continues Kristoffer, before Louie interrupts. "So that is why **the Norwegian tax system is based on the principle that everybody should pay tax according to their means and receive services according to their needs.**" If not for such a system, Kristoffer says, he'd either be dead, or dreadfully unhappy. "I think that's why I'm happier than most, because I am secure, regardless of my condition. I am better off than any of my relatives or Louie's relatives in the Philippines, or people in many other countries who cannot trust their leaders because they are not seen as equals by their government."

While capitalist Norwegian commentator Simon Black argues that "in keeping people at the same level, Norwegian society has lowered the bar for everyone," or that "there is limited economic freedom to achieve more," the truth is, Norway has tripled its number of millionaires in the past decade from 55,000 in 2007 to more than 169,000 in 2018. In 2017 alone, the number of millionaires in Norway grew by 13% from the previous year, while the European average was 7.7%. Black and others may want us to believe that "a system based on economic freedom" is better for our prosperity or happiness, but that's simply not what the data says. Norway's egalitarian ethos hasn't only made it one of the happiest countries on earth, but in 2018 it became the richest nation on earth per capita, with Norway's total wealth per capita being $1.67 million USD. What's particularly enviable, though Mr Black might not agree, is it's all been done while maintaining and even promoting a healthy work-life balance, something which three working women tell me is at the core of Norway's happiness.

"We have everything we want in our lives. We have free education, good jobs and a lot of time to have a good social life, a healthy love life, and just enjoy doing things that we want to do. Our passions. So our lives aren't just about work," said Hanne, a 30-something-year-old electrical engineer, who was sitting with two friends chatting about life, when I interrupted them. "We have these regulations in our work life regarding how much we must be paid and what hours we can work, to make sure we have a good work environment and we are protected," continues Hanne, before her friend Julie cuts in. **"We are given enough money, and enough time to spend that money,"** says Julie, whose job is to help others find a job. "Everyone is of equal worth here," said Margarete, a rehabilitation nurse, who was far and away the quietest of the three. "What laws or policies or government decisions have instilled this idea?" I ask. "I think that it's just in our entire community, we have these social ideals," says Hanne. "And this means that everyone is worth something, and we take care of everyone and so I don't, I can't say any specific laws or policies have led to this. We just have this kind of mentality ingrained in us that that's how we should live life."

In 2011, when Norway suffered a major terrorist attack at the hands of a crazed right-wing extremist who killed 77 people — eight in a bombing of the government's headquarters in Oslo and 69 young people who were gunned down while attending a Labour Party youth camp on Utøya Island – the harmony and solidarity underpinning the country's social democratic ethos was put to the test. Would this homegrown murderer with his anti-Islamic, anti-immigration agenda force Norway to change its colours? In the immediate aftermath it seemed likely. There were sudden and strong calls for Norway's police officers to be armed at all times, after a police officer stationed at the youth camp became one of the first people killed there; because, critics argued, he wasn't carrying a gun. This was standard procedure at the time. Norwegian police only carried firearms in response to specific situations – a move that engendered trust in the police force to resolve matters peacefully – evidenced in the fact that between 2001 and 2011 there were just two people killed by police. In Australia, where police routinely carry firearms, we had 43 fatal police shootings over the same period. Even when you take into account the difference in population, that's still six times more than Norway. Unsurprisingly, the media also played a major role in "unsettling Norway's tolerance," wrote Guardian journalist Richard Orange at the time. He said that unearthing every detail of the perpetrator's crimes, from his confidential psychiatric reports, to police interviews and the easy regime he faced in prison, was too much for some to bear. 'Where is the justice?', people began to query. "Why does he have to explain in the court what his ideology is? We don't care. We know it already," said Jarl Robert Christensen, who lost his 15-year-old daughter Birgitta on the island. "Why give him the satisfaction of letting him speak freely for almost a week?" he asked during an interview with Orange.

Just as New Zealand Prime Minister Jacinda Ardern turned the 2019 Christchurch terror attack into a unifying force, so too Norway's Prime Minister at the time, Jens Stoltenberg had a clear and unwavering commitment to do what was right. "We are still shocked by what has happened, but we will never give up our values," said Stoltenberg, in his address at the memorial service in Oslo cathedral two days after the tragedy. "Our response is more democracy, more openness, and more humanity." Norway, he suggested, would not seek vengeance as America and others had done after similar attacks. "We will answer hatred with love," he said.

After Stoltenberg's speech, Norway rallied around their prime minister. Even opposition politicians expressed support. "We all applaud the Prime Minister for the way he led the nation after this attack," said Morten Høglund, of the right-wing Progress Party. "It's important for many people not to let feelings of hatred take over, and not to expect that, since this is a very extraordinary crime, he should be handled in an extreme way," said 35-year-old Ali Esbati, who was a survivor of the Utøya Island massacre. "The idea of vengeance, that he should suffer very much, or that we need to be extremely harsh on him, is not very dominant in the Norwegian debate, and that's a strength of Norwegian society," Esbati told Orange.

"We cannot let the worst in our society dictate how we govern ourselves or what we believe in," said Julie, when I asked the three girls about their thoughts on Norway's response to the 2011 attack. "It's more difficult to do what we did if you're living in a country where you are more used to hate, and where there's been so much conflict and social inequality and everything. It's easier to hate when you feel as if life or your government or the system is against you. But here, where everyone is much more happy and where we trust each other, it is easier to forgive, or to move past our differences at least," says Hanne.

Searching for a balance, someone who might offer me an alternative view of Norway – something less positive, or something I hadn't heard – I approached a pretty serious looking businessman wearing an impressive navy blue suit. "I'm a fund manager," he said. 'Bingo!' I thought, before noticing that his particular brand of euro-English didn't sound all that Norwegian. Finding out that Pedro, 44, was Portuguese, but had lived in five countries and travelled to more than 60, including regularly throughout Europe for work, I felt he may actually be just what I was after: an unbiased insight into how Norway truly measured up. "So," I said, "what do you think of this place?" "Look around you," he said, "it is extremely developed, everything works, you can trust people. You could hypothetically come here, you could get a job, and you'd be able to raise your kids in a decent school. It may be expensive to do that, but the pay off is that things work, and that's really important, the system serves the people." "Do you think locals trust in government in these places, from what you hear in the business community? Is that the difference?" I ask. "That's a good point," Pedro says. "That's an indicator that, for me, is always very crucial. Perceived level of corruption in a given country. Even within Europe you get very different levels. Obviously,

Louie and Kristoffer.

Andrè the barman.

Manon with Josua and her daughter (Pg 342).

Lord Richard Layard (Pg 344).

Nehad and me (Pg 326).

Britt (left) and Aud.

Mikko with his wife and daughter in a forest nearby their house.

Pedro from Portugal.

(Left to right) Julie, Hanne and Margarete.

in the northern countries, things do work, the level of corruption is very low, and that, again, keeps a sense of confidence in the system, that you can trust your public services. That's an additional confidence for people, I would say. I would rank that as quite relevant. Because, like, if I compare it to Portugal, it feels peaceful. It feels as though people are working hard, they are going about their stuff, but still, it's peaceful, it's quiet, it's not noisy, whereas in London, you feel this kind of rush. The subway's crowded, the houses are falling apart. Here, you feel like you're in some future world."

The only thing that's strange about Scandinavian countries being labelled the happiest on earth, says Pedro, is that "they don't put themselves across as being that much happier than others." The thing is, locals agree. Asking dozens of people about this bizarre phenomenon, which was everywhere, most simply laughed and told me: "we are taught not to be show offs, not to gloat over our wealth or position, but to be content with our luck; we're also not very open people, we keep our distance, we respect personal space and we don't show our emotions much, not in public at least." The subdued, calm, quiet nature of Scandinavia was perplexing. It reminded me of a number of deeply Buddhist communities I'd visited, and yet, these Nordic countries enjoyed a material abundance that was usually accompanied by a busy, frenetic, anxious and discontent populace. So, what was different about this place? How had they struck this balance, this unique set of attributes that seemed to make them the happiest people on earth?

Two older women who cruised into an Indian restaurant where I was eating (on their motorised scooters) told me the size of Norway's safety net meant there was less to think about, which meant they could focus on icing the cake, not baking it from scratch. "It's very safe. I don't only mean from bombs and stuff, but we have good medical care, a calm environment, we're generally not fighting each other to get to the top, and that means you're free to enjoy the rest of the stuff, the beautiful landscapes we have, the fjords, even just coming here for our favourite Indian," said 75-year-old Aud. "We even got these things for free from the government," said Aud's friend Britt, pointing to their two mobility scooters. "All the people here even look younger and live longer, because we have good systems under us, doctors and everything, it's free."

It's strange, for all that I tried to find people who might speak ill of the government or the social democratic system in Norway – that's why

I targeted (as I always do) minorities, people with a disability, people in low paying jobs, homeless people, older people, wealthy business people, as well as of course the middle-class 9-5 type – I found nothing, one or two mumbles and grumbles, but nothing of substance, no one openly saying 'I'm unhappy and it's partly or completely due to the government or system.'

While a score of 7.537 out of 10 was enough to secure Norway top spot in the 2017 world happiness rankings, Finland, who scored 7.469 in 2017, has for the last two years outgrown and outranked their neighbour, taking out top spot in 2019 with a score of 7.769. The question I had was: what had Finland done in those years to see a 4% boost in their result? The first Finn I met, Nehad, who was a Syrian refugee working at the Helsinki airport as a chef, was in retrospect the perfect case in point.

If I were a refugee, I would...

One of the core topics that's been dividing and therefore eating away at people's happiness across the globe in recent years, is how to deal with the 68.5 million people worldwide who have been displaced from their homes. While most (40 million) remain in internal displacement camps, the remaining 28.5 million have become refugees and asylum seekers looking for a new place to live. The notion that humanity (particularly the privileged) should open their borders and accept and pay for these people to come and settle in their country is one of the most contentious talking points of our time. On the one hand, we have this innate empathy and desire to 'do unto others', while on the other hand we have our survivalist brain, which is terrified of the different skin colours and beliefs of these people, and tells us not to give money to anyone, let alone these strangers, who the media have condemned as 'our enemy'. It's not all the journalists' fault, of course. Those few refugees who perpetrate acts of terror or violence and those few more who refuse or find it difficult to integrate into their new-found land end up feeding the fear and scepticism, and smearing the image of all new migrants – even guys like Nehad, who turned out to be one of the happiest and most patriotic Finns I met.

"I think it [Finland] is the happiest country in the world, because the people here are very good. Very good. They help us too much. Too much. They are wonderful people!" exclaimed Nehad, as he graciously showed me how to get to the train station in Helsinki Airport. "We are from Syria. Me, my wife and two children. But we are Christians, so we were just a small minority. Life was not good for us. There was no help, because no one, not a lot, know there are Christians like us in Syria, being killed, being targeted," he said, in his own brand of broken English. "It was not so bad when the war starts in 2011. Not in our region. My two cafeteria businesses were doing good. Life was normal, until the war spread. And then it turned worse and worse and worse. One of my shops was bombed. And my city, Maharda – it is 22,000 Christians – was suddenly being hit by rockets everyday. Still, we have nowhere to go. We don't want to leave our home. But then, one incident changed this. My daughter saw her friend get hit in the head by a rocket at her school. Seeing her classmate dying, not knowing what to do, what had happened, it [Nehad pauses] ... she became a bit complicated [mentally]." His daughter Lisa was just six and a half at the time.

Making the decision to leave, to forfeit his two businesses and home (everything he'd worked for), was tough says Nehad. But it was just the beginning. The young family of four fled Maharda for Beirut, before flying to Moscow, where Nehad's friend said he may be able to help them seek asylum in Norway (where Nehad had a brother). Travelling to the tiny north-west border town of Murmansk in Russia, which borders Norway, the family were met by more bad news. The border was closed. "So the guy who was helping us said, 'what do you think about Finland?'" Nehad recalls. A couple of weeks later, with the backing of a sympathetic Russian judge who gave them a letter saying they could not return to Russia for five years, or Syria at all, Nehad and his family filed an application to live in Finland.

Despite being held in a camp and an old hotel for three months while their papers were verified, and despite being sent alone to find a home for himself and his family in Helsinki, before his wife and kids were free to join him, Nehad says he never felt worried, "because the government here, they care about you."

"It is not like my country," he says. "It is too safe, everything, any problems you have in your life, you can discuss these matters with some people who will listen to you, who will help you. My daughter especially is receiving psychological care. So they are giving us every chance of succeeding in this country, and of becoming a valuable part of Finnish society," said Nehad. "And isn't that the point?" an old Finnish gentleman who was walking his dog down by Helsinki Harbour commented. "We need these migrants as much as they need us. Without them, who will keep our ageing country viable? We need more people making money, paying taxes, else there goes my pension. We need entrepreneurs. People to come in and get things started, like the family who took over this old business [he points to a local grocery shop]. Regardless of our economic needs though, we should also help these people because we can, and because if we don't, if we leave them to be slaughtered at the hands of these mad men, like we did in World War II, then how far have we come?"

If we take the emotion out of it and look purely at the science and the sums of the refugee debate, what we see is decisively calming. Research not only suggests that helping others is 'the not-so-secret secret' to living a happier and healthier life, but financially, **"investing one euro in welcoming refugees can yield nearly two euros in economic benefits within five years"** according to a study led by economist Philippe Legrain.

"That is a key finding of this report – to our knowledge, the first comprehensive, international study of how refugees can contribute to advanced economies," writes Legrain. "The return on investing in refugees has been calculated using International Monetary Fund (IMF) estimates of the economic impact of asylum seekers and refugees on the European Union." So while the world may be facing the largest refugee crisis since the Second World War, Legrain says advanced economies should be seeing this as an economic and moral opportunity. "Welcoming refugees is not only a humanitarian and legal obligation; it is an investment that can yield significant economic dividends," he writes. Most refugees "fill gaps in the labour market" doing dirty, difficult jobs that locals despise. Others, says Legrain, "start new businesses that create wealth, employ locals, make the economy more dynamic and adaptable, and boost international trade and investment." Just look at Google co-founder Sergey Brin, who arrived in the US as a child refugee from the Soviet Union, or how about Asia's richest man Li Ka-Shing, who sought refuge in (then) British-run Hong Kong, after the Chinese Communist Revolution in 1949. "In Britain, migrants are nearly twice as likely as locals to start a business… And in Australia, refugees are the most entrepreneurial migrants," says Legrain.

So, why isn't this the story we hear when it comes to refugees and asylum seekers?

During my time in Europe I witnessed a number of newspaper headlines that read something like: 'Europe to spend more than €10 billion a year on unauthorised migrants'. Media organisations, who profit from propagating fear, clearly aren't interested in letting the truth (or their humanity) get in the way of a good story. Because 'Europe to make €10 billion from refugees over 5 years' or 'Europe spends €10 billion to help those legally fleeing war and persecution, knowing they will insert €20 billion into the economy within 5 years', just doesn't evoke the same selfish rage-filled response. Logic and decency don't sell newspapers.

> A small technicality I feel I need to clear up before we continue: the notion that it is unauthorized or illegal to seek asylum or refuge in another country is plain wrong. Just weeks before writing this chapter I visited Germany, a place where six million Jews, and countless other minorities were persecuted and slaughtered by the Nazis. To help prevent this sort of thing from happening again, or to at least stop minorities from becoming fish in a barrel – as the Jews were when many countries decided to deny them refuge – the 1948 Universal Declaration of Human Rights, the 1951 Refugee Convention and 1967 Protocol, were adopted by 148 countries. What these documents guarantee is: everyone has the right to seek and enjoy asylum from persecution in other countries. So just remember, anytime you hear the term 'illegal' in relation to refugees, it is propaganda and misinformation that has no legal grounding – it is also a hugely dangerous and divisive view to spread if our past is anything to go by.

Instead of buying into the fear and pandemonium of Europe's 'refugee crisis', which began in 2015, Finland's Prime Minister at the time, Juha Sipilä, decided to double the country's refugee intake to 30,000, and offer his spare house to host a refugee family. "We should all take a look in the mirror and ask how we can help," said Sipilä in a 2015 interview with national broadcaster YLE. Sipilä's comments were soon echoed by the head of the Finnish Lutheran Church, Archbishop Kari Mäkinen, who urged members to take in refugees. While 78% of Finns belong to the Lutheran Church and 21% voted for Sipilä, both were met with some outcry. Rather than kowtow to the populist far-right movement sweeping the globe by adopting a nastier approach to migrants (as most governments have), Sipilä backed the power of empathy and reason, two fundamentals of any social democracy. Such was his conviction, that when his coalition partners, The Finns Party, installed a hard-line anti-immigration spokesman as their leader, Sipilä threatened to break up the government, rather than work with them. After a brief stand-off, The Finns – the far-right party which was Finland's third-biggest political force – imploded and 20 of its more moderate MPs left to form the 'New Alternative' movement which continued to prop up Sipilä's government until the country's April 2019 elections. In a striking twist, Finland further bucked the populist far-right trend at their general election by voting in its first left-leaning government in 20 years, led by none other than The Social Democratic Party. The Finns (the only right leaning party in Finland) actually received 0.22% less of the vote than they did in 2015.

What all of this tells me, and what I could see and hear during conversations with so many Finns, was that their happiest state was not tied to wealth or abundance, but rather kindness and candor. "Finns," Nehad said, "enjoy the simple things."

The happiest country on earth

"Generally in Finland, man is evaluated based on his doing and his words, not based on what he owns," says Mikko, a Finnish man who hosted me during my stay in Sundsvall in northern Sweden. My favourite example of just how this uncommon phenomenon played out in reality was a story Mikko told me about a man he knew who was living in the countryside in Finland. "He was a wealthy entrepreneur and lived outside of a small town," recalled Mikko. "He owned two cars. One was this very old and simple thing he used to drive to the shops in that small town, but then the other vehicle was a luxury sports car that he'd only drive in other cities where people didn't know him, or if he had a business meeting in Helsinki or something. This wasn't to preserve his car, it was just because in Finnish culture it's not seen as good to show off your wealth like that."

While some may scoff and question why anyone should feel guilty for showing off the fruits of their hard work, the humble, modest character of most Finns is precisely what's let their country flourish. This is because when we're united – when we're not looking at our neighbour with envy or yelling at the rich or the unemployed for taking advantage of the system – that's when a society can come together and discuss what's best for everyone. "Social trust and good government isn't possible in a hyper-competitive environment," says Mikko. "And that's why our education system is so critical. This is where it starts. So we must strike a healthy balance of competition that doesn't exclude or unfairly advantage or disadvantage certain kids. That's why Finland, which has just one system of schooling [all publicly funded] from class one to nine, is superior to what they have here in Sweden, which is this kind of dual – public and private – system. The problem here, and we've seen this when trying to enrol my daughter, is that there are really good schools and there are quite bad schools, whereas in Finland, there are not these extremes." The other major advantage of having one publicly funded schooling system, is that each school is made up of a fair and representative cross section of students and teachers from the local area says Mikko. "There is no driving across town to attend the 'better' school or to get more pay."

Another thing that's often cited as a reason Finland's education system is considered the best in the world, is that the government invests heavily in ensuring its teachers are extremely well educated. All undergo a minimum of a five year master's degree (which is free, just as all higher education is in Finland), and all are provided with ongoing high-level teacher training, which allows young teachers to have a great deal of autonomy to choose what methods they use in the classroom. In contrast, Leena Krokfors, Professor of Teaching at Helsinki University, says teaching in a lot of countries falls "somewhere between administration and giving tests to students." The outcome of the Finnish system is that teaching is both a highly prized and deeply respected profession: two things that undoubtedly go hand in hand. But Finland didn't suddenly wake up and find itself on the top of the education pyramid. The decision to go 'all in' on a singular public education system in the 1970s was bold and included phasing out kansakoulu schools (which were public/mandatory) and oppikoulu schools (which were optional, competitive to attend, and the only path to university). The new system, which topped the world for academic results in 2000, 2003 and 2006, is unlike most. To start with, Finnish children don't enter a classroom until they are seven, because, put simply, playtime is more important for a child's development (and eventual academic outcomes) than formal classroom learning. Not only do countless anthropological, psychological, neuroscientific and educational studies clearly outline the benefits of this approach, but, as developmental psychologist and early childhood education specialist Professor David Whitebread from the University of Cambridge says, starting formal learning at age four or five can have negative consequences.

"Perhaps most worrying," says Whitebread, is that, "a number of studies have documented the loss of play opportunities for children over the second half of the 20th century, and demonstrated a clear link with increased indicators of stress and mental health problems." This is why Finnish educational expert Pasi Sahlberg says, "Kindergarten in Finland doesn't focus on preparing children for school academically ... Instead the main goal is to make sure the children are happy and responsible individuals." According to Whitebread, carefully organised play helps develop qualities such as attention span, perseverance, concentration and problem solving, which at the age of four are stronger predictors of academic success than the age at which a child learns to read. In fact, in New Zealand a number of studies have compared groups of children who started formal literacy lessons at ages 5 and 7. What the results show is that the early introduction of formal learning approaches to literacy does not improve a child's reading development, and may be damaging. By the age of 11 there was no difference in reading ability level between the two groups, but the children who started at five developed less positive attitudes to reading, and showed poorer text comprehension than those children who had started later.

What's even more telling from an equality and therefore happiness standpoint, is that there is evidence that high-quality, early years, play-based learning not only enriches educational development, but boosts attainment in children from disadvantaged backgrounds who do not possess the cultural capital enjoyed by their wealthier peers. "The better the quality of pre-school, the better the outcomes, both emotionally and socially and in terms of academic achievement," says Whitebread. Finland's early education system isn't only designed with equality and well-being in mind, but it's funded to ensure every child has a legal right to it. In all day-care centres, as in all their schools, there are children from a mix of backgrounds, because fees are subsidised by the state, and are capped at a maximum of €290 a month (or free for those on low incomes) for five-day, 40 hour a week care. What this means is that about 40% of 1 to 3-year-olds are in day-care, as are 75% of 3 to 5-year-olds. Optional pre-school at the age of six has a 98% up-take. Oh, and thanks to the very social democratic funding of pre-schools, the staff-to-child ratio is 1:4 for under-threes and 1:7 for older children. While it was initially envisaged in the '70s as a way of getting mothers back into the workplace, Finland's day-care system has today become a pivotal starting point from which "we should all progress together," says Gunilla Holm, Professor of Education at the University of Helsinki.

When kids do finally start school in Finland, they (and their parents) are not made to suffer the usual anxiety of applying to the best school and waiting nervously to see if they get in. No, in Finland, such is their commitment to equality (on both moral and economic grounds), that it outlaws school selection, formal examinations (until the age of 18) and streaming by ability. Competition, choice, privatisation and league tables do not exist. This may come as a shock to a lot of parents who've been convinced education is a competition, but the academic results and happiness spawned from this egalitarian system speak for themselves. Ninety-three percent of Finns graduate from high school, 17.5% higher than the United States, and 66% go on to higher education, the highest rate in the European Union. What's truly impressive is that they've done this while maintaining the wellbeing of young people and their families, by providing students with free school meals (imagine not having to pack lunch every day!), shorter school hours and light, if any, homework duties. Amazingly, it does all this while spending about 30% less per student than the US.

If we consider the alternative, somewhere like China, where parents start to drill their children from as young as two in a race for university places and jobs, what we see is disastrous. One, if not two, entire generations of people (or most of them at least) have grown up without properly forming or engaging the creative or social/emotional part of their brain. A rise in cram schools, enrichment programs, generally long school hours and even longer homework hours (two hours a night, compared with less than 30 minutes in Finland) have seen China soar into the top ten in the Program for International Student Assessment (PISA) rankings, but the path they've taken to get there has stifled the country's ability to be anything more than the factory of the world.

Desperately ambitious to lead and design the next wave of technological developments, rather than just build the stuff, the Chinese government is now working tirelessly with a number of international education specialists to redesign the country's uninspired schooling system. Beijing has even invited a bunch of early education start-ups, including Finland's Fun Academy, to open schools and kindergartens across the country.

"We are pooling our [Finland's] experience to develop the fun-learning environment, teaching tools and [game-based] learning tools for teachers and for kids. We have shorter school days and no homework but have a better result," said co-founder of Fun Academy, Peter Vesterbacka. "The very traditional education in China, I think, seems opposite to the nation's encouragement of establishing start-ups, which need creativity," continued Vesterbacka, in an interview at the Mars Summit technology conference. With between 40 to 60% of jobs expected to be taken by machines and automation in the next two to three decades, countries must prepare their workforces to be creative and innovative or risk being replaced, Vesterbacka concluded.

What China and others might take away from Finland's successes – socially, economically and in terms of happiness – is that it all started with a simple belief: **educating all youth equally well would be the best way to achieve economic success and societal wellbeing, because it could provide the small nation with the creativity, ingenuity and solidarity it needed to be able to compete on a global scale.** "The Finnish dream," says Pasi Sahlberg, a Finnish educationist at Harvard, was for all children, regardless of family background or personal conditions, to have a good school in their community – a focus that has remained unchanged for the past four decades.

While Finland no longer tops the PISA rankings – in 2015 it placed 5th, mostly behind cram and learn Asian nations – the gift that it continues to provide over others is what the system itself teaches, and what it embodies, which is equality over vanity, humility over arrogance. The success of Finland's education revolution isn't simply that it helped the small, relatively poor, agrarian nation develop economically, it's that it forged good human beings, who believe in the common good – the bedrock of a happy society. The reason equality or governing toward the common good is so important is because it builds 'social capital' – the extent to which we trust and feel connected to those around us, including government.

Free from the inequality that breeds division, Finland has prospered in every single way. According to a range of reports, Finland is said to be the safest, most peaceful and freest country on earth, with the least organised crime, the most independent judicial system, the soundest banks, the second most generous social welfare program and the best governance. Finland also offers the equal best (with Norway) maternity leave in the world – up to 161 weeks of leave at 25 percent of wages or the equivalent of 40 weeks at full salary. Unsurprisingly, Finns' trust in other people is the highest in Europe, while among EU citizens they enjoy the most human capital in the world. Finally, because I could go on all day (just check out stat.fi), Finland is the third most gender equal country in the world, has the second lowest inequality among children globally and also breathes in the cleanest air, thanks to having the most forests in Europe and the second best proportion of renewable to non-renewable energy in the EU.

Finland has even solved homelessness. How? By providing homes for people without them! Why? Because if we see a cancer and don't act – **if we ignore inequality – it festers and spreads and puts all that we hold dear at risk.** Peace, safety, freedom, trust, prosperity, happiness – these things all rely on equality, which cannot exist without unity – and if we are united (as the Finns are), then how long can we walk past homeless people and think 'it's their fault'? Because if we are truly united, if they are truly part of our society, then it doesn't matter if its drugs, mental health, job loss or family breakdown that brought them to that situation, it's up to all of us to fix it. Social harmony and happiness aren't the only upside to Finland's radical *Housing First* policy, it also makes economic sense says Juha Kaakinen, Chief Executive of the Y-Foundation, which provides 16,300 low cost flats to homeless people in Finland. "In a country like Finland or Australia, it's not a money issue," says Kaakinen in an interview with Australian journalist Cat McGauran. "Helping the homeless out of homelessness actually saves money – we have studies that show when one homeless person gets permanent housing, with support, it saves our society €15,000 per year." It is always more cost-effective to solve a problem rather than manage it, Kaakinen adds.

By providing homeless people with permanent housing on a normal lease, which includes paying rent (though they can apply for subsidies), governments can reduce the enormous costs associated with emergency medical care, shelters, social workers and the justice system, as well as give the recipient a fresh start. "People living in shelters and hostels are still homeless," says Kaakinen. "That's not a place where you can build your life and positive relations with other people. It's also very hard to get back to employment [when] living in temporary housing." A typical case in point is the story of Thomas Salmi.

Like a lot of homeless, Salmi had a rough start in life. As a child, he was forced to leave home to escape his father's uncontrolled aggression. Passed from home to home – nine in total – Salmi eventually slipped through the cracks in the system in his late teens. By 21 he was on the streets. "I lost the sense of a normal life. I became depressed, aggressive, angry and I abused alcohol a lot," said Salmi, in an interview with the Huffington Post. Drinking up to half a gallon of wine a day, Salmi regularly found himself getting into trouble with friends, strangers and the police. "I thought why would I care if I go to jail? [At least] then I don't have to be out there in snow and cold." When a social worker came across Salmi sleeping in Helsinki train station in 2015, he put him in touch with Helsinki Deaconess Institute (HDI), a Finnish non-profit that provides social services. A year later Salmi moved into Aurora-Tola, a 125-unit house run by HDI. Now 25 years old, he lives in his own studio apartment, works as a janitor and life is getting back on track, he says. "I know that if I am in my house nobody is coming to get me or telling me what to do," he said. "If I want to dance in my home, I can."

While many of those working in the homeless sector initially objected to the idea of giving their clients a home before sorting out any of their other problems, *Housing First* has effectively shown that it's much easier to solve those problems with a roof over their head. For this reason, Kaakinen says the focus of governments must be on affordable social housing. "You can see what happens when housing is the playground of finance and speculation, rather than seen as a social right, or basic social infrastructure that's needed to keep society functioning." In Australia for instance, roughly 0.5% of the population is homeless (116,000 people), while social housing makes up just 4% of total housing stock. Facing a similar rate of homelessness (0.4% or roughly 20,000 people) in the 1980s, Finland began investing in social housing. "To keep the society functioning, you have to keep everybody in," says Kaakinen. "It's a very strong cultural way of thinking in Finland … that you have to look after your fellow citizens." When signs emerged that chronic homelessness was once again rising in the mid 2000s, the conservative government decided to adopt *Housing First*. In the decade since 2008, Finland has spent €250million building roughly 3500 new homes (20% of all new development) and hiring 300 extra support workers. The result: Finland has seen a 35% decrease in homelessness at a time when every other European country has seen an explosion. In England, Germany, Belgium and Ireland, homeless numbers have more than doubled in recent years, while in Finland current figures stand at just 0.13% of the population – roughly 7000 people, of which 5000 are temporarily lodging with friends or family. "In Helsinki, for example, there were [in 2008] approximately 600 spots in temporary accommodation," says Kaakinen. "Now there's one service that has 52 beds, but that's really for emergencies. So it's been a major transformation of the system," he says. With a tangible example of how a coordinated, national strategy using *Housing First* and investment in social housing can end chronic homelessness and save governments money, it raises the question: why isn't this approach being adopted everywhere? "It is quite a mystery," concludes Kaakinen.

Finns aren't just designing the systems and programs to end unnecessary inequality and suffering, they're also showing us who should pay for it. Following a decade of austerity measures, Antti Rinne, Finland's latest Prime Minister and head of the Social Democratic Party, said his party's vision to increase pensions, healthcare and education funding, as well as become the first carbon neutral country (by 2035) would be paid for by closing extortionate tax loopholes, increasing taxes associated with fossil fuels, tobacco, alcohol and mining and a modest levy on capital gains accrued to foreign funds and tax-exempt entities. What it feels like Finland (and the EU) is finally doing is standing up to multi-billion dollar corporations who get away with paying $0.00 in taxes (in most countries). A question my editor asked me, which I then quizzed others on throughout my European adventure was, "if you could play god and introduce one law or policy to make the world a happier place what would it be?" My answer was a single global corporate tax rate (that's strictly enforced), because **if Apple, Amazon, Google, Facebook, Chevron, Microsoft, IBM, General Motors and the rest of the Fortune 500 were made to pay their fair share of taxes in each country they operate, then governments would have more money to look after the people, and less of the tax burden would fall onto the middle classes.**

I don't exactly blame big business for taking advantage of loopholes. In the highly competitive global market we've created you'd be silly not to seek out tax havens such as Ireland, which let Apple get away with paying just 0.005% in taxes on its $53.39 billion USD profit in 2015 (well below Ireland's corporate tax rate of 12.5%). Given Apple employs roughly 7000 people at its Irish headquarters, the company can naturally make certain demands of the government, which was actually found guilty of granting "illegal tax benefits to Apple," according to the European Commission, who consequently ordered Apple to pay €13 billion, plus interest, in unpaid Irish taxes from 2004 to 2014 (something Apple and the Irish government is still fighting in court, because neither want the tech giant to pay). This startling finding renewed calls for greater co-operation between governments, to tackle the challenge of tax avoidance.

"It is in Finland's interest that the EU makes a majority decision to combat harmful tax competition and aggressive tax planning. Otherwise, tax havens could torpedo reforms that benefit everyone," said Antton Rönnholm, the Party Secretary of the Social Democrats. Rönnholm emphasised that the middle class can no longer be expected to cover the cost of such practices, which are deteriorating the funding base needed to provide key services and promote well-being. "We need tougher measures to intervene in interest arrangements and country-specific public tax reporting. Finland alone cannot change the course, it needs partners in other EU countries," he said. With the world's super-rich currently hiding as much as $32 trillion USD in offshore tax havens and an estimated $500 billion in corporate tax being dodged each year globally, Rönnholm's words could not be more timely.

Finland's title of 'happiest country' doesn't solely come from its ability to lead the world in equitable taxation, education, housing and welfare policies, it's also got a lifestyle to die for. "Finland actually has the lowest GDP of the Nordic countries," says Mikko. "So, there must be something else, some other place we find happiness, and this is our summer cottages and our saunas. These things are not valued in our GDP of course, and this kind of lifestyle is not understood very much in financial calculations. But still, when I was a little boy, these were my happiest days. We'd get lost in forests, we'd go biking, camping, we'd find frogs, we'd go on all kinds of adventures," says Mikko, reflecting decades of research that tells us green spaces and nature makes us happier, and therefore must be a priority for all societies and governments seeking their happiest state. "As an adult, the cottage life has become even more important, because it's a way of balancing out life. Like, when I'm there, I'm sleeping better, connecting with nature, listening to the sounds of silence and just letting the outside world drift away." Of Finland's 507,000 summer cottages (one for every ten people), most are basic cabins with a median size of about 40 square metres or less. A lot of summer cottages don't have running water, electricity or indoor plumbing says Mikko, but all have a sauna.

"You asked why we're happy, why we're relaxed and calm, well…" Mikko smirks. "That's your answer. It's one of Finland's biggest secrets. We have three million saunas in Finland – that's a third of the world's saunas, or one for every 1.8 Finns. When I think about how much time we spend in saunas, either sort of meditating or meeting different people, then yeah, you can see this sauna culture is important. Public saunas next to lakes and seas are places where we can come together, there are wealthy, poor, academics, builders – and all get along. So, it's kind of a chance to discuss life and to relax with different kinds of people. You don't have to talk there, but a lot of people do, and that builds that community, which is dying off in other parts of our society due to things like technology. These public saunas also operate during winter, and winter-swimming in holes in the ice is an experience that unites people, gives health benefits and helps us forget about the stresses of work. That's one thing about our saunas, summer cottages and forests – which is where we spend a lot of our spare time – people don't have their mobile phones with them, so at least they can be stress free for one or two hours a day."

Interestingly, this topic of technology, and if or how governments should regulate or educate people about its potentially disastrous impacts, was actually why I travelled to northern Sweden to meet Mikko – one of the founders of a non-profit called Wireless Education. Graduating from a degree in IT and computer science and a master's in educational science, Mikko quickly landed a plush job with one of Finland's largest telco providers, before undertaking his PhD at Tampere University, where he looked at information systems, educational technology and bioelectromagnetics. "It was early 2000 when I realised something was wrong," he says. "I was working at a large telecommunications provider as a program manager in R&D [research and development], when I began looking at research databases that pointed to some fairly clear signs of health risk. When I was hired by the university to run pilots related to mobile learning, and then again when I was asked to work with the EU Information Society Technologies program on the world's largest mobile learning research project called MOBIlearn, I became more and more sceptical of what we were doing. As an academic, I told myself, 'this is not your area', so I left it alone. It wasn't until years later that I felt I was ready to oppose this development, while working in a bio-electromagnetics research group."

While I'd read about the detrimental mental health effects of technology for the past decade, Mikko (and hundreds of his research colleagues) offered a new and potentially even more catastrophic insight: Wi-Fi and mobile data (or more specifically the radiofrequency (RF) radiation, AKA microwave radiation, it exposes us to) could be making us sick, or even killing us.

Whenever a bunch of doctors or scientists tell us something may be harmful (such as tobacco, asbestos or burning fossil fuels), what we must ask ourselves is: one, is there a vested interest (who stands to gain or lose), and two, what do we risk if we don't listen? What will all this 3, 4 and 5G radiation do to us for instance? Nothing? Maybe. But personally, I wouldn't bet on it. Why? Because 300 scientists and another 1000 doctors from more than 75 countries have signed appeals warning governments of the dangers of RF radiation, and *particularly* 5G. The writing is on the wall. A range of independent studies have shown the effects of heavy and prolonged exposure to RF radiation (something most now endure) can include an increased risk of cancer, genetic damage, learning and memory deficits, and neurological disorders (among others). What's muddying these findings are hundreds of industry funded studies that have mostly found little or no cause for concern. This isn't exactly surprising given **the telecommunications, mobile technology and online shopping industry rake in more than $7.96 trillion USD a year (around 10 percent of global GDP).** To put that in perspective, that's roughly four times the revenue of the entire oil industry and 10 times what big tobacco earns annually. While I cannot tell you with 100% assurance that we're going to see some sort of 5G health-crisis (because there's not enough well funded, truly independent research into the long term effects), I would say we desperately need to stop rolling out the 5G network, which uses a far higher (more dangerous) frequency of RF radiation, until we are sure. Because if we're all sick, dead or dying no one is likely to be all that happy.

The problem we have, even in places like Finland says Mikko, is that what's in the best interests of the people, isn't necessarily in the best interests of governments or corporations. Nokia for instance, which is Finland's pride and joy, rallied 30% in 2018 off the news that they were going to be a key player in the global rollout of 5G equipment and software. That was particularly good news for the Finnish government, which bought a 3.3% stake in Nokia in 2018, at a cost of 844 million euros. "Why isn't anyone, including the Finnish government funding adequate research into the effects of 5G?" asks Mikko. "Because if the risks we've known about for years are verified officially, they stand to lose huge amounts of money, and thousands of jobs. They may even be held to account for what could be thousands of cancer cases and other health issues in the decades to come. So the government – carefully guided and manipulated by the telco lobbyists – buries its head in the sand, and tries to sweep our words under the rug. But the rug is getting very lumpy. The truth can only stay hidden so long," he says. "Because we're all part of this now, and there's no hiding what happens to eight billion people trapped by technology we never signed up to," says Mikko, reminding me of a profoundly farsighted line by the 13th century poet Rumi, who wrote: "Man worked things out and his devices trapped him, and what he took for life, would suck his blood."

"Even within the past five years," says Mikko, "to think that most people now have a smartphone, and these people are not aware that when they receive this smartphone there is Wi-Fi active, there is mobile data active, there is Bluetooth active – all of which transmit RF radiation continuously," he warns. "But we can switch these things off. So that's what I am focussed on now, is educating people about wireless technology, and particularly schools, because we know kids' brains are particularly susceptible to the radiation. That's why we see so many young people suffering sleep problems, hyperactivity, headaches and so on, because this radiation affects chemicals like melatonin, dopamine and serotonin, which are connected directly to depression, aggression and stress."

"But these effects are not just in kids, they're everywhere," he continues. "This is why we must also discuss more about happiness. Because now, what we hear from government and industry is so much about artificial intelligence, digitalisation and efficiency of systems, but to what end? Technology is not a solution in itself, it will not make us better or happier people, unless we make that the goal of it. Like, here in Sweden we are seeing children as young as one or two being given tablets in kindergarten centres, because the government made a law that educators have to use these technologies in the classroom. So, that is very unhealthy. It is not in line with best practice models for early childhood education, and research shows it is not adding to a child's happiness in the short or long term. It is just the dream of some technocrat."

"This is too early," says Swedish kindergarten teacher, Manon Li. "We need to teach kids many different things. Yes, computers are one of them, when they're old enough, but we must also show them how to play piano. How to run and play outside. How to be a good friend. Things we need to be a person, to be a human, because we are more than just a head. We people are more than just a brain. And I think in school, there's too little of this emphasis. Creativity and courage is not rewarded. The heart is ignored. **Beautiful things are being replaced by smart things**." The problem, Manon says, is that the human mind is not a computer. "We're overloading young heads. So they're not growing in a healthy way. Kids don't know how to listen anymore, they can't concentrate because they're spending so much time on machines that move so fast in order to entertain the mind, but they do not grow the mind. We need to slow down to do that. We need to write poetry, to draw, to invent, to build, to experiment."

"I feel like when I was a kid it was all about acting naturally," says Josua, Manon's 25-year-old son. "You were just yourself, and you spent time with your family or friends doing basic stuff. We had a simple farm life, my parents grew things, we didn't have tractors, so we used horses to plough the fields, and we'd spend a lot of time caring for the horses and other animals in between school and other things. But then when you grow up, and when you sort of enter into society, there's suddenly all these demands of you, from everywhere, including yourself. With so much stimulus, this intense oversaturation of people voicing their successes and thoughts on social media and just generally the 24/7 nature of most technology, it becomes hard to escape the whole 'I should become something, I want to have this, I need to do that', because now it's in front of us all the time. I think governments, and people in general, are too busy with this goal, with improving or striving to become better in the material sense, and so, they stop thinking about what it is to be human. It becomes a little bit like a big machine, like you need to just do your part to keep the cogs turning, the economy growing, and that's how you contribute to the society, that's how we become better, but that's kind of a myth. It's missing the point. Everyone knows this, but that is the problem. We don't get time to really look into ourselves, our existence and use our knowledge. Because everything's going too fast. We have no time to think about what's next."

The stress, anxiety and lack of 'me' or 'us' time that comes with being plugged into a digital world that never sleeps is clearly impacting human beings mentally, physically and societally. Being overly connected has been linked with psychological issues such as distraction, narcissism, expectation of instant gratification, low self-esteem, poor body image and even depression and suicide. Physically, technology can cause vision problems, hearing loss, neck strain, weight gain and most detrimentally, lack of sleep. Socially, the sheer time we're spending on our devices – which went from 3 hours a day in 2009 to an average of 5.9 hours in 2018 – means we literally have less time to engage and interact in the real world, face to face. What's particularly alarming about this is that now even when we do engage, research suggests we're doing it poorly – we're forgetting how to form deep and lasting bonds, due to the shallow nature of (most) online friendships.

A question of policy

One of the questions I was fascinated to ask both politicians and pundits across Europe was: if a government's primary role is to protect us – and if digital technology is causing us all this harm – if and how should we expect our leaders to intervene? "Wow, I've never really thought about that," was the most common response, before following it up with something like, "No," "You can't," or "Politicians would be too scared of the backlash of such an infringement." Generally, there wasn't all that much support for the idea of a policy that would limit use or require users to undergo a training course to understand how to safely and ethically use the internet. "Education is the key," most agreed, "which is why this must start in schools, or with parents." When I asked people if they felt teachers and parents were informed enough to do this, most looked at me blankly. "No," said all but two people I spoke to. And therein lies the problem. "How do we solve something most don't understand? Is this not the role of our government or leaders?" I asked. "Well..."

"Mmmm, I guess it should be," most said, with a certain degree of hesitation, fearing such a law may encroach upon their freedom. One of the few people to add a fresh and insightful voice to this debate was 85-year-old Lord Richard Layard, an active member of the House of Lords and distinguished Professor at the London School of Economics (LSE). "I've just been writing this book which discusses the immense damage being caused by social media," says Layard, another co-editor of the World Happiness Report. "When enough people come to see the damage, I know we'll get around to regulating it, because that's what human beings do. I was just researching how many people were killed in car accidents in 1930 for example, because it was a huge public health problem, like technology is today. You'd never believe what the numbers were. If I were to tell you we had roughly 1800 fatalities last year in Britain, what would your guess for 1930 be – given of course there were far fewer cars?" "In 1930?" I pondered aloud. "Seven thousand three hundred," Layard interrupted. "So we've cut that by three quarters, despite there being millions more cars driving millions more miles every day. But this is what regulation does. It likely wouldn't have occurred to people that you could regulate a car [because like technology they were so popular, so necessary and so good – when used well], but when something is harming us, even killing us, that's what we must do. We regulated the inside of the car, the roads, even how you get your license, everything."

While Apple CEO Tim Cook admits regulations around the use of personal data are "inevitable" and governments are starting to introduce laws that require online platforms to do a better job of self-regulating inappropriate content (such as the New Zealand massacre, which was live-streamed on Facebook), the concept that most fascinates me (maybe because I thought it up) is the idea of an 'internet license', similar to a car license. Like, if people had to attend training sessions on how to use the internet safely (how to avoid addiction, social media envy, security issues and so on) and responsibly (how to interact ethically and within the law) in order to get their license; and then, if that license could be revoked when users broke certain rules, like bullying, propagating hate speech, addictive/excessive use or setting up fake/anonymous accounts, maybe we'd start to stem the number of cases of anxiety, depression and suicide being linked with its prolific and unsafe use.

"Where is the line on this? How much of an active role should governments play in teaching people how to live their happiest life?" I ask Layard, who played a pivotal role in convincing former PM David Cameron to start measuring general well-being (GWB) alongside GDP. "Obviously, governments must have values and objectives, but you've got to be slightly careful of the 'Big Brother' thing. I think we need governments to fund people who are doing the right kinds of work. Experts like clinical psychologist David Clark, who is behind the Improving Access to Psychological Therapy (IAPT) program, which started 10 years ago and is now treating more than 600,000 people a year using evidenced-based cognitive behavioural therapy. So it's not about government lecturing us, it's about government offering us and our children services that will enable us to become happier people. I've been very keen, for example, on parenting being taught in schools. And we saw that get started under the very hard-nosed government of Theresa May, which moved to make 'life skills' compulsory in schools, as well as openly prioritising mental health. So it's promising, and we're seeing both sides of government – in a lot of cases – coming to understand the economic and moral sense in prioritising something other than GDP."

What was apparent in Scandinavian countries, and what Layard hopes his own government can realise, is that policies that prioritise wellbeing aren't only better for society, they're often better for the bottom line too. Take for instance the IAPT program, he says. "What is the greatest source of misery in our society?" he asks. "Poverty, unemployment or mental illness? Surveys tell us the answer is mental illness. Did you know nearly 40% of all illness in this country is mental illness, yet under a third of people with these problems are in treatment. If you break a bone, you receive care automatically, but if your spirit is broken, you don't. Even if we forget our core responsibility [as government], which is to look after citizens, and even if we focus on the economics, we can see that inaction is costing us a fortune." A 2018 OECD report put the cost of this epidemic, which affects one in four people across the UK annually, at 94 billion pounds ($119 billion USD) a year, nearly half of which is indirect costs related to lower employment and productivity. With the gross cost of cognitive behavioural therapy (which cures one in two and substantially helps others) being a meager 650 pounds ($829USD)

THE HAPPIEST

per person on average, Layard says there are huge savings to be made. "Instead of asking: 'can we afford to?', the question should be: 'can we afford not to?'" **Can we afford not to help the 800 thousand people committing suicide every year, or the 300 million suffering depression, or 260 million living with anxiety at any one time?** Can we afford not to do anything about a recent UNICEF study that found only 43% of British kids answered "yes" to the question: 'are most of your classmates kind and helpful?' Can we afford not to learn from the Scandinavian countries where more than 70% kids answered "yes" to the same question?

"That's just it," says Layard. "We have 30 years of research now, to guide us in the matter of 'what next?'. In Scandinavia, for example, young people grow up looking for the things they have in common with other people. Whereas in the rest of the Anglo Saxon world, certainly Britain and America, you're really encouraged to think of how you can make yourself different from everyone else. And preferably, superior. And that's not a very good way to produce a happy society. So then the question becomes, how do governments unravel this. Wind back the self-interest that's tearing us apart [he pauses]." "And?" I interrupt eagerly. "Well I think governments play an enormous role because they can set the tone of a society. I mean, surely America and to some degree the UK is going to suffer for some years over the way the tone is being set at the moment? All this blaming and name calling just legitimises all the worst aspects of our human nature, which should never be legitimised. So, I think there's a tone setting. But there's also, of course, the policy, where they spend our money. Do they spend it on something material which we can see – like costly high speed rail which will save us a few minutes – or do they spend it on something we'll feel for generations, like maintaining a decent system of social care, mental health interventions and getting some equality back into our schooling system? Now, I've probably spent more time on this than anything else – on working out how a government would organise itself and prioritise policies if it's aim was wellbeing." "And?" I push.

"Well, there are hundreds of dominoes that need to fall in line in order to reach the likes of Finland, but here are five actions most countries could take immediately to boost their happiness. On the **education** front, we must aim explicitly at developing young people who are emotionally resilient and eager to contribute to the social good. We need to deliver policy that guarantees more **equal income**, because extra money improves wellbeing more for the poor than the rich. Moreover, engendering a greater spirit of equality increases mutual respect and trust, which are crucial for happiness. All measures to promote economic growth should be accompanied by explicit policies to **build and sustain community**, social cohesion, stable family life, and personal security. If or when these above measures fail, societies must have **evidence-based treatment** available for mental illness, as well as a **system for supporting couples or families** in conflict, because healthy, stable people and households are at the heart of every happy society."

While governing towards something other than GDP, such as happiness, might sound like a luxury – something the wealthy can spend their time contemplating (because their survival is all but guaranteed) – the truth is, it's arguably just as (if not more) important in developing nations, where gross inequality breeds distrust, death and dictators (who threaten global cohesion and happiness). "If you consider somewhere like Bhutan, which sort of founded the whole Gross National Happiness (GNH) idea, they just seem much happier than comparable countries, because they have this moral rather than materialist ethos," said Layard. "Relationships are rather equal, and there's very little status anxiety. I think that comes back to the four pillars of Bhutan's GNH: the promotion of equitable and sustainable socio-economic development; preservation and promotion of cultural values; conservation of the natural environment; and establishment of good governance. What really struck me, in terms of policy, is that there is very little extreme poverty (just 1.6% as of 2017), because Bhutan realises that a redistribution of wealth that favours the poor is better for producing happiness."

Does Gross National Happiness Work?

Travelling to Bhutan in May 2017, what I immediately detected frightened me a little. Before even setting foot in the country, the tight (almost authoritarian) grasp of government was everywhere. The first indication was the near impossibility of travelling independently within the country – without a paid tour guide. The next was the Visa process – a government registered tour operator was the only way you could get one – you could not apply via the Bhutanese embassy directly. Then there was the price: all foreign tourists (except Indians) had to pre-book a trip that costs a minimum of $250USD per day. As an individual traveller (that didn't want to join a group), I had to pay a further levy of $40USD a day.

Setting off from Kathmandu in Nepal (where I'd been filming with the Fred Hollows Foundation), the first hint I got that Bhutan was going to be worth the money and effort came when I looked out the left hand side of the plane and saw Mount Everest. Wow! It was chilling. After a series of death-defying turns that took us over and through the peaks and valleys of the mighty Himalayas, I landed in Bhutan with a sense of reverence. Greeted by my guide Tshewang, a 43-year-old man who was born in a rural village in east Bhutan before studying in Australia and spending time in the US – his opening insight told me I'd made the right choice.

"It was a cultural shock at first," Tshewang says, as we pass by a number of ancient monasteries, fluttering prayer flags and staggering mountain passes on the way to Thimphu, Bhutan's capital. "Seeing the hectic lifestyle of Australia and America, and the rush to acquire and achieve so much in life, whether we need to or not – everything seemed so busy and unsettled. Things were so abundant and easy to get and consume, as long as I had the money. You also learn to be emotionally detached from what you do. It was so different from my village, where you could get something even if you didn't have money, 'cause what you got was from the very little all of us had, and so it meant a lot to both the provider and the recipient, materially and emotionally. The abundance and frantic life abroad did not have that connection and feel for me and I began to appreciate the pace of my life and value in Bhutan. This doesn't mean I hated the lifestyle abroad. I just thought that doing so much abroad will mean very little to others, and my efforts would be lost within the massive stream of things. So I came back to Bhutan, because what little I can do here will mean much more to my country, my family and my existence."

Journal entry 12.5.17: So many interesting observations!!! Their expressway had speed bumps, because Tshewang says time isn't as important as ensuring everyone gets there safely. Thimphu had a free outdoor gym, zebra crossings for pedestrians that were manned by police, and yet, the banks had no barriers and no security – you could literally walk behind the counter if you wanted. Crazy

Three women doing lap after lap of a temple in Bhutan, meditating on peace and happiness.

Tshewang and me in front of Tiger's Nest.

Thinley Yan Gzon, one of my hosts.

Buddhist prayer flags added a burst of colour to Bhutan's landscapes.

An old Bhutanese man doing a walking meditation.

A mother and daughter outside a temple in Bhutan.

At a market in Bhutan I came across one of the biggest smiles I've seen anywhere.

A woman sips on a cup of butter milk at a market in Bhutan.

The man who invites me to take his photo after saying, "We are given what we need to be happy here."

Ara, the lady that feeds us rice wine and tea.

Ara's daughter picking beans.

Ara's daughter and her mischievous granddaughter.

trust! Sitting, eating lunch at a well fitted out, modern restaurant in Thimphu, a bunch of half-naked boys ran past the window. One even stopped to take a poo (not once but twice) on the front lawn of the adjacent property. Just above him was a fancy sign advertising Zumba. I'm not sure if this place is poor, rich, free or regulated – or maybe it's the perfect balance of each?

Bhutan (as you might have guessed) instantly mesmerised me. Geographically, the tiny mountainous nation of little more than 700,000 people is wedged between two enormous and hugely overpopulated super powers, India and China. Seemingly, the country has sided with its southern neighbour India, who make up 81% of its exports – up to 80% of which is hydro-electric power. Bhutan itself uses just 6.5% of the 24,000 megawatts it generates – not surprising given 80% of its population are subsistence farmers. Bhutan isn't only the sole carbon negative country on the planet (offsetting 17 million tonnes of CO_2 annually – enough to power 2.9 million homes for a year), it's also batting well above average across a number of other areas. GDP per capita, for instance, is $3110USD in Bhutan, while in India it's $1939, Bangladesh it's $1888, Myanmar it's $1490 and Nepal it's $918. Bhutan's GDP actually grew by an average of 7.13% between 2015 and 2017, well above the global average of 2.8%. As Layard eluded, poverty rates are also well below the average of the region, with just 1.5% of Bhutanese living in 'extreme poverty' – which is classified as less than $1.90USD a day. Comparatively, India has 21.2% living in extreme poverty, while Nepal has 15%, Bangladesh 14.8% and Myanmar 6.2%. Again, Bhutan's not perfect – as I suspected, it comes in at 94 on the *Democracy Index*, below India (41) and Bangladesh (88), and just marginally above Nepal (97).

What was interesting, I found, was that the problems facing Bhutan, according to one local journalist named Rabi, were much the same as those facing the rest of the world. "If you go to the clubs you'll see a lot of drug use, in the streets we're seeing technology addiction, in the villages we see climate change, and then in our government we see corruption and abuse of civil rights," said Rabi. "But the big one, and what this all goes back to, is consumerism, or materialism. Some people are wanting more, or something else than what we've had for hundreds of years. Bhutanese people have long felt a connection to the environment, because most are farmers, and we have long held strong social connections, because, as an example, today we [a group of neighbours] will plant my paddy field, and then tomorrow, we will do it for my neighbour. But these things are degrading slowly. Kids are wanting white collar jobs. They're leaving the farm behind. Some are even going to the Middle East for money. They're working in massage businesses, but then they are being sexually assaulted."

What was different about my conversation with Rabi, compared to most discussions I've had with people in poor and disadvantaged nations, were these seven words: "we are trying, the government is trying," he says. "The new king is working on bringing peace in the south, and I think largely, you asked are we happy, yes we are. Because even when we go overseas, as my wife and I did to England, we and a lot of friends have returned, because working all day and night just to survive, and not being able to take time off when your family or community needs you, that is no way to live. And really, governments should stop announcing this as the way forward, because like we've found here, and why we started this GNH thing here in Bhutan, is because studies have told us that being rich doesn't make us happy, but being content and connected does."

Journal entry 14.5.17: As we trekked through abandoned paddy fields, up cow trodden paths, we saw a mother watering her veggie patch, while her daughter climbed a small rickety wooden ladder to pick beans from lush green vines. I'd begged Tshewang to take me to a tiny village that stood above our remote mountainous accommodation. Having never been there, he was nervous, but it didn't last. The old lady watering her plants invited us in immediately. Ascending a ramp, then a few steps up to a kind of large attic living space, a baby squealed with glee. The little 18 month old was smothered in white cream. She'd obviously got into mum's make up or cooking. Unperturbed by her granddaughters mischief, Ara (the old lady) fetched what appeared to be a bottle of water in an old rum jar. The cloudy quality of the liquid made me nervous – am I going to be asked to drink this? I wondered. Grabbing a coffee cup and filling it to the brim with the murky water – floaty bits and all – Ara gestured for me to do exactly that. I looked to Tshewang who said, "cheers!" I quickly shut my eyes and drank. "Holy shit!" I coughed and sputtered. "This is the local welcome drink," said Tshewang. "Home brewed rice wine."

Slowly making my way through the grassy-tasting throat-burning fluid, I asked Ara, "Are you happy?" Through Tshewang, who translated, she said, "Yes. I have all I want. I am loved by my community. That is why the village is the happiest place. We don't need things, only people." More than the wisdom of the

GROSS NATIONAL HAPPINESS AND THE RICE WINE HANGOVER

> *words being passed back and forth, what I was taken aback by was Tshewang's response. "I have never done this sort of thing," he told me with child-like enthusiasm. "You can forget what's important sometimes about a country," he said, referring to the usual path he takes tourists on, from landmark to landmark.*
>
> *As we continued to explore the village, and were invited in for more rice wine and what they call milk butter tea — which tastes as it sounds — I found out that every house in Bhutan that wasn't connected to mains electricity was given free solar from the government. Little satellite dishes also littered the rooftops — something locals tell me is good, "because it keeps us connected to what is going on, and entertains us at night." "We are given what we need to be happy here," said a middle-aged man who invited me to take a photo (top left).*

While I probably didn't need, nor want, any more rice wine or alcohol of any sort, Tshewang had called our accommodation as we walked back down the mountain, and that was exactly what confronted us on our return. And I'm glad it did. Because (in retrospect) it allowed Tshewang to let down his walls, and to trust me with his thoughts on Bhutan's leadership. "We all want to be happy no matter where in the world we are," he tells me. "And that was the basic truth that our Fourth King envisioned and propounded as what we should strive for rather than all out economic prosperity. It is our core philosophy, and it has helped Bhutan in developing policies and plans that are people friendly rather than just economic boosters." Under this guise, Tshewang somehow even managed to convince me that all the money and control I'd loathed as a tourist was justified. "When you consider the alternative, which is to open our country (for profit's sake) to any and all foreigners — like Thailand, Bali or Nepal — all of which now have chronic drug and prostitution problems as a result, then yeah, you can see the power of our GNH Commission, which makes sure all developmental plans are scrutinised and fulfil the GNH parameters. It's not perfect, but most people are fairly happy, because we are looked after well by fairly good leaders who are led by these core philosophies and values."

Having spent a lot of time in India, my final host, a 32-year-old farmer by the name of Thinley Yan Gzon provided a glaring insight. "Here we have free healthcare, free education, you don't need to worry. You can spend all your money if you need to buy something for the farm," said Gzon. "In India, no one cares for you or will stop for you if you need help. You'll never starve or be left for dead here, whereas in India a lack of money can kill you. When we lived in India, where my son was born, we had to spend $1000 on his medical costs, like vaccines and things, which was a lot. I think why we see this kindness [the way] we do in Bhutan is because Buddhist values are ingrained in you as a child, and then Gross National Happiness means you don't forget this as an adult. We are not led by greed. We have not gone the same way as others, and sold off all our resources. **We may develop slower, but it is sustainable and led by social values, which means we're happier, because one is not benefitting more than another, one is not profiting off another.** Doing more for others – not yourself – is what makes us happy, so our government must reflect this, and mostly they do. As a farmer, if we don't have money for a plough, the government will send one we can borrow. Privately we might spend $100 per day if we needed this machine, but government equipment is $25 a day. Even if I want to set up a business like we have with our farm-stay, if I needed some money, the government will give us a low interest loan. So we are supported, and we are all working together," concludes Gzon.

The following day, as I laid eyes on Tiger's Nest – a dazzling monastery clinging to a rocky cliff face way up in the mountains – I felt a clatter of goosebumps creep across my body. "Isn't it amazing what we can do when we work together towards a common goal," I said aloud to Tshewang, who must have seen the mystical Buddhist temple hundreds of times. "That's the one thing I can't get past each time I visit," he says, "the hope and wonder co-operation spawns." Not just when we build beautiful things, but when we defeat dictators, donate organs, free people from poverty or discover new galaxies. What's defined human evolution, interestingly, isn't our ability to work together – we know chimpanzees do this – but according to evolutionary anthropologist Michael Tomasello, primates will only co-operate if there's something in it for them. "Humans do that too," said Tomasello, in an interview with the BBC. "But in addition, they care about what their partner gets. In some experiments we have children as young as 14-18 months who seem to expect their partner to collaborate in certain ways, and who share in ways chimps don't." Humans are also far less selective about who they share with, says Tomasello. What gave birth to this behaviour, and what's allowed us to grow from small hunter-gatherer tribes to larger groups of 50-150 (the limit of the number of people we can form deep connections with), are the stories our ancestors told. "The real difference between us and chimpanzees is the mysterious glue that enables millions of humans to co-operate effectively," says Oxford History Professor, Yuval Noah Harari. "This mysterious glue is made of stories, not genes," and it was through these stories that our early ancestors figured out who they could trust and which friendships/relationships to build, which in turn facilitated our ability to come together and survive more efficiently. In order to more happily advance our 'human journey', we must see through the imaginary boundaries drawn by those who benefit from 'othering'. We must remember how far we have come.

Our new story must include the fact that every second, humanity donates more than $52,000USD to charity, and roughly 78 billion hours are volunteered each year worldwide.

"In general, most people are intrinsically good anywhere," said Tshewang, as we traversed back down the mountain path. "There are a lot of good people in the West, I've seen it, but I think it's the cut-throat race that makes people blind and act bad. That's why you need to find leaders who are brave enough to say 'no, this is not working, we need another way or another goal'. Leaders who can see and then convince others that what's easy may not be what's best." It's a tough call to make, to deny people the obvious path in favour of a lesser known avenue – but that's what we're in desperate need of. Leaders who can see that **cutting, burning and rebuilding the face of this planet out of concrete and steel – as we have done for the past 200 years – is no longer progress.** Because even if we eradicate poverty, cure cancer and give everyone their dream house and job – if the cost is our common home here on earth – we'll still go down as the smartest, wealthiest and most stupid species to have ever ruled this place.

The smallest biggest leader I've ever met

Searching for a leader who might offer some answers or inspiration in terms of 'what next?' and how we solve some of the shit we're facing, I headed to Iceland (toward the end of my Nordic jaunt), to meet one of Europe's youngest female leaders, Prime Minister Katrín Jakobsdóttir. What struck me the moment I entered the 42-year-old's office building was the distinct lack of metal detectors or security guards. There was nothing. The door was literally open. So I walked in and sat down. A short time later, I was met by a petite, spirited woman wearing a curious smile. "Hello, I'm Katrín," she said graciously. "Please come through." If I hadn't known what she looked like, I would have never assumed the women who greeted me was a prime minister – she seemed far too warm, humble and human to hold such an office. So what made Katrín (as she asked me to call her) different? Was it her age? Gender? The choice to do her master's thesis on Icelandic crime fiction? What about her background made her such an ideal leader?

For starters, she tells me she "never intended to go into politics." Pretty self-evident if you consider her course of study. But why is this important? It's not just that the path to power corrupts – because every campaign needs a sponsor and none come without strings – it's also that "power attracts the corruptible [because] the sane are usually attracted by things other than power," says scientist and author David Brin. To attract more everyday folks to run for office (rather than marauding career politicians), and to effectively restore democracy – a government of, by and for the people – **we plainly and simply need to demand a system that bans political parties from taking private funding, period.** If we want governments and leaders that serve us – the people – then we must take industry and corporate funds out of the equation. Election campaigns *must* be publicly funded. A simple model that could work would be to allocate a kitty of $100 million of public money (or whatever makes it economically viable in each country). Registered parties would then be allocated a share of the kitty based on how many supporters sign a petition registering their intention to vote for them (each signature would of course be verified securely). To stop any Tom, Dick or Harry with a few dozen mates being able to register and receive public money, there would of course be a minimum number of signatures needed (let's say 20,000) before you could be classified as a contender and are able to collect funds.

What shouldn't be forgotten is that most developed countries already do this in some form or another. For example, in Australia after the 2013 election, political parties and candidates received $58.1 million in election funding (roughly $3 per voter) from public coffers. The undeniable flaw of this system, or any system that awards public money post-election, is that by this time, politicians are already selling off our democracy as they work out how to repay campaign-donors with lucrative government contracts or changes to legislation – none of which serves the general public, despite us involuntarily forking out millions to prop up our political parties.

Iceland, which is the second most democratic nation on Earth, has unsurprisingly adopted a model that's better than most. Under their current system, the maximum donation that can be made by a business or individual is $4000USD per year – an amount unlikely to buy much political influence. By contrast, the top campaign contributor in the 2018 US mid-term elections donated $123 million USD to the Republican Party. Iceland doesn't only cap donations, it also provides a pool of $5.9 million USD in public funds that is divided among political parties based on how well they do in independent pre-election polls. Iceland strictly forbids donations from state, foreign and anonymous sources, as well as enforcing a spending limit for candidates of $8000USD plus $1.30 for each voter in their electorate (electorates vary from 21,000 voters to 58,000). However you look at it, there's little reason for Icelandic politicians to get in bed with big business. There's also less opportunity for any one party to gain a significant advantage based on how much money they pull in, because there are caps and restrictions in place to limit campaign spending in general. The only thing missing in Iceland (and 173 other countries) is mandatory voting – because how can you have a government of, by and for the people if 44% of eligible voters don't cast a ballot – as was the case in the 2016 US election (where Trump was elected). What's critical about voter turnout – which was 81.2% in Iceland in 2017, despite it being voluntary – is that it gives our elected officials a mandate to feel as though they're speaking on behalf of the electorate or nation, not just those who were lucky (or smart) enough to find the time to vote.

The notion of having to vote or of giving some or any of your hard earned tax dollars to a party you disagree with may be frustrating for some, but the upside of a system that is publicly funded and voted on by all is that when you hear a leader or MP speak, you know their words are not being manipulated by some self-serving puppet master. I think that's why I found Katrín's approach to my questioning to be so genuine and refreshing – she was truly free. Free to tell me that welfare states are happier. Free to agree with the idea of governing toward something other than GDP. Free to proclaim her country would be carbon neutral by 2040. Free to speak openly about her own technology addiction and the role governments must play in ending this epidemic. She was even willing to say an equal representation of women in politics is essential if we ever hope to see a more peaceful global society.

"I think that's a very good thing for all decisions," says Katrín. "Having the number of men and women as equal as possible is good for decision-making, because we are different. We talk different and use different methods. And I think when we look at peace you can definitely see, you know, research shows that having more women at the table increases peace and makes societies more peaceful, because they are the ones responsible for the consequences of war. They're the ones left to defend their home or fend for their children and family." While global media outlets described Katrín as a feminist, environmentalist and anti-war activist when she was elected, the truth is, she's an equalitist. "If I had the power to introduce one law or policy globally, and the goal was happiness [she pauses], it's equality, and it's not just gender equality, it's equality in general. **Inequality is a reason for so many bad feelings because as a society you're losing so much from people who don't get the opportunity to use their talent for the greater good and for their own good.** So I think what we have learned here in the Nordic countries is that equality is really the key to creating better economies, but also better societies."

Iceland wasn't only the first place to democratically elect a female president, a lesbian prime minister, or to ban strip clubs for social rather than religious reasons (in 2010), but the former mayor of Reykjavik was a punk rock taxi-driving comedian whose famous pro-gay tweet read: "Homophobia is not a phobia. They are not scared. They are just a bunch of assholes." The country also leads the world in a range of other social measures. They publish and buy more books per head than any other country, their police have no need to carry guns, they're the most web savvy country on earth (with 97% of the population connected to high speed broadband) and they plant the most trees per capita of any nation. The government even encourages people to paint their houses in bright colours to give the streets a happier feeling (an important measure for those dark winter months). Last but certainly not least, they have one of the coolest high school graduation rituals in the world: *dimission* (as they call it) involves everyone dressing up in Elmo suits (or whatever costume the class picks) and then racing around the city in groups completing tasks, such as sniffing or even kissing a stranger. How do I know this?

Because both of these things were done to me. In return for my co-operation though, I of course demanded some of them tell me more about their country.

"What makes Iceland such a happy and good society?" I asked two separate groups of Elmos. "What I think keeps Iceland happy is that we have a very distinct culture and language that we relate to, and we have importantly held on to those traditions and our holidays and all that," said a young man named Karl. "We are even keeping just the traditional names, you cannot name your child after a fruit or spice or inanimate object here. There is a register of Icelandic names, which you have to choose from. It might sound strange, but it helps us maintain our identity which makes us unique, and so that makes us happy and proud to be Icelandic," said Eiríkur. "What makes Iceland a very happy country is probably because it's very peaceful, and the people are very nice as well. The education level is also pretty good, so you get a lot of opportunity. You can really do whatever you want to or be whatever you want to become. It's all possible because the teachers and people here are willing to help you to make it through," said Kristófer (the boy who kissed me). "That's because we have this thinking that when we are all able to grow into who we are, then our society will be healthy," said Kári. "We don't have private schools, and we don't have too much rich or poor, so we feel we are equal together," Kári continued, before a girl with a long name beginning in V interrupted. "We can trust each other, because we are the same," she said. "Yeah, the government will support you here, all of us, to be good and safe," concludes Kristófer.

The importance of this communal bond and trust that Icelanders share was particularly evident whenever these conversations inevitably turned to the one thing Icelanders could not avoid, nor control – the weather – or more specifically, the 'dark days'. Those chilly winter months where the country receives as little as three hours of sunlight a day. "Depression is common-place during this time for a lot of people, at least at some point in their life," said Aron, a local fireman I met working in a remote, abandoned cave-home turned cafe/historical site. "But we have a mind-set too, from this life," he says. "I mean, people used to live in this place [he points to the cave behind him]. All this isolation, deprivation … living on an island of volcanoes and ice, where the sun barely rises in winter and barely sets in summer – it is what makes us happy – because it teaches us to see the positive things in life, to not focus on the problems, but to see them as a chance to become more." This culture of embracing its challenges as an opportunity to unite or grow as individuals, or as a society, was perhaps most evident in Iceland's response to the 2008 global financial crisis (GFC).

Even if we forget the $22 trillion USD and millions of jobs the GFC wiped from global markets, it's worth remembering that **10,000 people killed themselves in the US, Europe and Canada as a direct result of the economic crisis.** In my opinion at least (given that's three times more people than were killed on 9/11), this should have been enough to land thousands of dodgy bankers and investors in jail. Instead, all we saw were a few choice words and the odd tokenistic fine being handed out – often to the very same banks that were receiving billions of dollars in government bailouts (our tax dollars), even after fleecing people out of their invested money. One of the only countries to stand up and say 'enough is enough', was Iceland. Of the 47 people who were jailed as a consequence of the GFC, 25 were in Iceland. Their combined sentences were 74 years.

"In terms of happiness," says Katrín, "what we saw after the crisis – which came as such a shock to us because we were in an economic boom – was just this wave of people making Icelandic sweaters and old Icelandic foods from the insides of the sheep – blood sausage and liver sausage. So everybody was just doing that, going back to what we knew – stockpiling – because we were in a crisis. I think that period shows a little bit about the Icelandic mentality. That we were like OK, we are in a crisis, so let's do this right, do this as a group – because we're a small society. So we even saw that more people went to the theatre and to concerts because people had this need to go out and meet other people. I was the minister of culture at the time and we were like, 'what's happening?'"

"And…?" I asked, "do you think the crisis reminded people of what's important?" "I think it did in a way. A lot of people said 'well, this didn't fall apart – our society is still here – we're together, at the theatre or eating a meal, so maybe we'll be OK.'" What's fascinating is that studies actually confirmed that Iceland's overall happiness dipped only slightly during the crisis, while 25% of the population actually reported an increase in happiness.

If we take a brief look at human history, this Icelandic phenomenon seems less peculiar, for we are without doubt a species that thrives under pressure. What this made me curious to imagine is: **if the battle to**

The Prime Minister of Iceland Katrín Jakobsdóttir.

Some of the Elmos I interviewed in Iceland.

The Prime Minister's Office in Iceland.

The Chinese Embassy in Iceland.

Aron, in front of the cave-home cafe he runs.

Sigurdur Gretar explaining that the Sólheimajökull Glacier we were standing on used to extend to the ridge next to his shoulder 20 years ago.

Michael Birkjær.

Durkhanai Ayubi speaking at *newday* about the earthrise image to the right.

Carl.

survive as individuals, tribes and nations led us to create language, medicines and unbelievable technologies, then what might we discover if all of us were to unite? Cheap forms of perpetual energy? The end of all known diseases? The end of war? The end of inequality? The beginning of an unprecedented era of peace and acceptance driven by leaders (and supported by the population) who are wise enough and brave enough to put their egos and agendas aside in order to let us all see just how similar we are? Resisting our selfish survivalist-based urges isn't just imperative if we're to save our planet, it's imperative in order to save ourselves – because without solidarity and connection, we will either kill ourselves, or one another, long before we work out how to inhabit another planet.

"People often say we need to save the planet," said Sigurdur Gretar, a local adventurer and tour guide who grew up at the base of the Sólheimajökull glacier in Iceland. "But the truth is, we need to save ourselves – the planet will be just fine without us. The universe will go on." Standing atop Sólheimajökull, listening to Gretar tell me and my tour group about the glaciers' rapid retreat, it was hard not to feel a little terrified. "When I was 12 this place was my playground," said the now 40-year-old. "Back then, it was this huge white chunk of ice that stretched up above those peaks, and way out past the pools of water near the car park. Now, as a guide, I come here nearly everyday, and I see daily changes to the glacier – paths being washed away, new holes or ravines opening up, even this black ash from the eruption of Eyjafjallajökull volcano in 2010 is causing the ice to melt faster – so yeah, it's changing quickly," concluded Gretar.

"This is the challenge of our time," said Katrín. "Ten years ago, when I was studying and presenting arguments on climate change, people in parliament were like 'Oh my god. This crazy person here'. But now, everybody is feeling it and we're seeing it in the dramatic changes in weather here and in Europe. So it's kind of unmistakable – it's happening. Now we need to decide how we respond to it, not just as a country, but as humanity." Because we will not solve this or any of the world's current list of problems alone, she says.

The climate crisis, drug crisis, inequality crisis, refugee crisis, corporate taxation crisis, mental health crisis, technology taking our jobs crisis, technology killing us crisis – these things all require a coordinated global approach. They require tenacious and innovative leadership that shifts the status quo, says Katrín. "With regards to technology for instance, we have clear opportunities, but I think the challenge for politicians is trying to ensure that technological changes are going to ensure more equality and not less. The danger is that we will have more wealth and more power in fewer hands ... the people who own the technology. I think that's the heavy battle ahead, to maintain this line of questioning – of 'who does this or that benefit?'... And 'does it make us happier?', as you say." The frank and honest conversation I enjoyed with Katrín was a stark reminder to me of what is so often missing from the social and political landscape today – which is open, heart-felt dialogue, that's not censored by panic over political correctness.

"We used to be free to just say what was on our mind," said Carl, a super-talented young busker I met in Copenhagen, Denmark. "But now we are so worried about our words offending someone or being yelled at online, and so we've stopped having these important conversations, you know. The stuff that's not easy to talk about, like refugees or technology dependence or drugs and mental illness – everything we've just been talking about. We're told this stuff is too sensitive. 'You can't say that,' people say. But addressing these taboo topics is what's made Denmark a strong and happy country. We've confronted our troubles, our differences, and it's made us more connected, more equal, because **when we're silent nothing happens.** People or issues are ignored, and then some communities branch off and things get worse."

The 20-year-old singer-songwriter wasn't only one of the most fabulous buskers I've seen, he also raised a point that I've long considered to be one of humanity's fastest growing obstacles when it comes to establishing trust, cohesion and therefore our happiest state – political correctness. If we let political correctness rule us – like if I'm berated as a 'fat shamer' for suggesting obesity is an issue, or if I'm accused and even blocked (as I have been) from presenting the terrible truth of what I've filmed in places of abject poverty, because it makes people look 'too poor and desperate' – then how can we ever hope to address all the elephants in the room that are currently running amok. 'Wishing' people to be thinner or richer or less desperate looking won't solve anything. Only the truth will set us free. Which means speaking openly, honestly and responsibly. Political correctness undoubtedly started off as a means of doing this. Of recognising the derogatory nature of the N-word or the difference between 'disabled person' and 'person with a disability'. What's cause for concern though, is that it seems to have been weaponised by limited minds and angry online trolls in order to stir up hate and division, or to make or avoid arguments against which they have no other defense. 'You can't say that!' or 'You're just a racist/sexist/bigot!!!' isn't going to lead to anything good. It's just another form of *othering*. Another hateful narrative we don't need.

"If our leaders, or we, hadn't talked about homosexuality, because we were scared of offending them, we wouldn't have become the first country in the world to legalise gay marriage," said Carl. "We also have a minimum wage that is good, and we have this thing we call *janteloven*, which means we are all equal, but this does not happen if you ignore the hard conversation about privilege, poverty and responsibility. So there is mutual benefit in talking about this stuff truthfully, because it leads to solutions and common ground ... Now look at us." "Don't worry, I have been," I laughed. "You're the best looking country on Earth. Because you're all so fit and healthy from cycling all the time." This wasn't just some brash observation I'd made – it was fact – despite there being roughly 170 days of rain a year in Denmark, the country has more than twice as many bicycles (4.2 million) as cars (1.8 million), with the average Dane covering 1.6km per day by bike. It's no wonder Danes enjoy the lowest childhood obesity in Europe and the OECD (of 10%) and one of the lowest adult obesity rates in the world (with 14.9%). An unrelated but equally telling figure that sheds further light on why Danes are so happy, is that the average salary of CEOs in Denmark is just 48 times higher than those of the company's workers, where as in the USA, it is 354 times higher. While these statistics paint a broad black and white image of the society, Carl's smile as he told me his story – of having sufficient faith in the system to quit his job at a coffee shop to pursue his love of music full-time – was like a vivid splash of colour that highlighted to me just how special this place was.

"Taking the leap," said Carl. "When I look at what it has shown me – well for one it has enhanced my belief in the goodness of people, because it's only due to them stopping by and donating that I can survive. And then to be able to go back to university and study English – to help my music career – without the worry of the economic side of it, without going into debt, or without having to work several jobs as some people in other countries do, that's a sign that our system is well built. Because every Dane can easily go through school and university and make a nice living, but then even for someone like me, who is kind of going a different route, I am still given the opportunity to do that, and that's kind of the happiest situation: for everyone to be able to go with the flow of who they are. That's freedom, and that's what we're about."

According to Michael Birkjær, a senior analyst at the Happiness Research Institute in Copenhagen, it is this Danish appetite for freedom that is at the heart of it's robust welfare state. "We have access to the basic needs, which means we don't have a lot of people suffering," says Birkjær. "This builds trust, because it eliminates the need to fight among ourselves over who should be able to access simple human rights such as healthcare, housing, food or education. The system guarantees just about everyone gets this stuff, which is why there's a lot of trust between people, which is often quite visible. You'll see, for instance, some people don't lock up their bikes, and actually if the weather was a little warmer and you went to a café like this one, it wouldn't be uncommon to see baby carriages [prams] standing outside the café with children inside of them while their parents drink coffee inside. **So when people ask 'what do our higher taxes pay for?' it is that – a safety net that builds trust by collectively looking after one another.** And we know more equal, more trusting societies are happier societies. And when you have happier citizens, you also notice this cycle start to build, because research tells us happy people are kinder, more productive, have better relationships and are healthier, which is better for a society, and leads to more happy people within that society, which continues to feed this cycle."

Denmark's ability to turn their collective wealth into a cycle of well-being wasn't the only reason I found it to be the happiest country in my European travels. Finland, Norway and Iceland had arguably done that too. No, what made Denmark a happier place to me – and this is based on my preference and personality – is that there was a bit more life on the streets and in the people. Don't get me wrong, the Danes were still calm, measured and enjoyed their personal space, as all Scandinavians seemed to, but they did feel a degree or two warmer in their interaction, as well as being a bit feistier and more willing to express their emotions too.

A young woman who more than fitted this bill was 26-year-old local Ida, who shared a particularly telling tale of how the collective desire for good can overcome evil. "There's this Danish guy who's a convicted racist and attention whore, who's been making these really aggressive anti-Muslim, anti-refugee demonstrations where he's been marching into certain neighbourhoods and burning the Quran," said Ida. "When Danes saw this, they became frustrated and began protesting at his rallies. But all this did was make them bigger, more violent and destructive spectacles, which attracted the media, who up until that point had largely ignored his events. Seeing the flaw in their plan, protestors decided to follow the advice of politicians who called for people to ignore Paludan [the racist] and instead donate to local refugee organisations each time they saw his hate speech being televised. And so that's what we did. We used his evil to raise money for good." "What's ironic," she continued "is he goes around calling Muslims thieves and violent extremists, while he and his supporters pick fights and set fire to things. It's funny you know, these refugees are more Danish than him. They're more kind, more accepting, they contribute more to the common good. There was actually this story that emerged where Paludan had dropped his Mastercard during one of his rallies, and a Muslim boy who was walking with his father picked it up and handed it back to him, saying, 'Oh, you dropped this.'"

What Ida's words made me wonder, and a question that's enthralled me for years, is: how do we shape or change things – namely the future? How do we make the happiest society possible? Do we wait for governments to act or do we take it upon ourselves? In the US for instance, I've long imagined what might be possible if all the super-wealthy supporters of a 'more equal' America – like Oprah, Ellen, Beyonce, Lebron and so on – pooled their available money into a trust account (similar to Norway's wealth fund) in order to provide the free healthcare, education and more generous social welfare policies they desire. The economic impact of such a scheme may not change things overnight, but the notion of banding together to do what we can for our neighbours is arguably more telling for a country's happiness than the mere accumulation of wealth, says Birkjær.

"I think what we need to do, and what we're missing in Denmark and most Nordic countries, is to create more collectivist communities," says Birkjær. "So in fact, and this is one of the most interesting, striking things for me personally from all the data out there, is that you have so many countries that are doing extremely well – in terms of happiness – compared to how rich they are. So like Mexico is just as happy as America and Costa Rica is almost in the top ten. So we say that the Latin American countries are definitely the best countries at converting wealth into wellbeing. They're doing it much better than even the Nordic countries. When we look at why, the research conducted all points toward their collectivistic culture, which we don't have a lot of in the West. And so I think there's a lot to learn from that, from the family ties and the way they work together in their neighbourhoods, to the way they develop communities where everybody has a purpose and everybody feels a sort of social connection because their problems are seen as shared."

"In contrast, the Nordic countries and much of the developed world is experiencing a sharp rise loneliness and mental health problems, which are the most potent sources of misery," says Birkjær. What this tells us is that **the wealthy welfare-state alone is not enough.** "It's a myth that people in Denmark are just bursting out laughing all the time, or are extremely happy. This is not the case. The cantril ladder asks us to evaluate our life on a scale of 0-10, and Denmark is a top performer on that. But the World Happiness Report also looks at the number of positive and negative daily emotions one feels, and on this scale, Latin American countries are the top performing, because of their social bonds and collectivist culture."

While you can't force people to interact, Birkjær says civil servants, business and policy makers can work to develop and design cities, workplaces and communities in a way that promotes human connection. "We need to make spaces and experiences where we're kind of nudged together," he believes. "It should be very practical and intentional. You know, one very concrete thing that inspired me a lot was a project in America that I visited a couple of years ago called the Bridge Meadows Project. It's actually an inter-generational living community for foster children, adoptive parents and elders. So they argue that there's a problem with mental health for children in foster care – but arguably also children and young people in general. There's a problem with parents who just don't have enough time to be parents and work at the same time, and there's a problem with elders who are isolated and don't feel they have a purpose in society anymore. How can we solve these three things at once? Well, they're building these communities where the elders dedicate themselves to be additional grandparents, providing several hours a week of care or babysitting for all these young people who are living there with their [adoptive] parents. The parents then have less parental burden you could say. So they are free to pursue further education or to work, because there's somebody to take care of the kids, who just length in the following chapter). The social democratic ethos engenders kindness, responsibility, contentment and a belief in something greater than ourselves. The motive for this larger societal vision is not fear of punishment, but rather the belief in doing the right thing. Social democracy is the secular faith we can use, not just to govern us, but to help inspire and unveil a new narrative. Because, as Yuval Noah Harari points out, "We are still in the nihilist moment of disillusionment and anger, after people have lost faith in the old stories, but before they have embraced a new one."

"I believe the call of our time is to find narratives that fit," says Durkhanai during her *newday* address. "The question is, can we morph into a narrative that reflects our potential for boundless horizons? Without an overarching narrative that can do so, then anything we come up with, 'our solutions', mean little – they are tainted, ineffective and out of step with what is required of us at this moment in the field of time." To solve our most complex and difficult problems – of *unsustainability* and *othering* – we must consider the NASA image of an earthrise from the moon, says Durkhanai, because there are no boundaries on our planet from there. "We are bound by this common fate," she continues. "All dividing horizons on this planet have been shattered. We can no longer hold our loves at home and project our aggressions elsewhere, for on this Earth flying through space, there is no 'elsewhere' anymore. And narratives that continue to speak or to teach of 'elsewhere' and 'outsiders' do not meet the requirement of this hour," says Durkhanai, paraphrasing writer Joseph Campbell.

It might seem an odd way to end a chapter about policy and governance, but when I heard Durkhanai speak (just as I was searching for a way to tie these giant and often intangible ideas together), her words let me see the link. "I want people to know that our history is shared. It is misguided to believe in this present fiction of a deep and ever-present schism between East/West, Islam/Christianity, women/men, black/white – we are bigger, more intuitive, more interesting and more complex than this fiction," says Durkhanai. "I do not believe we need to be overwhelmed. **Our mind is sufficiently capable of taking us anywhere, it is only a matter of re-awakening the primal language of our soul, which knows we are all part of the same patchwork."**

"The water in your body once flowed down the Nile, fell as monsoon rain onto India, and swirled around the Pacific. The carbon in the organic molecules of your cells was mined from the atmosphere by the plants that we eat. The salt in your sweat and tears, the calcium of your bones, and the iron in your blood all eroded out of the rocks of the Earth's crust; and the sulphur of the protein molecules in your hair and muscles was spewed out by volcanoes," says Durkhanai, quoting Lewis Dartnell's book *Origins*.

We must know that there is no utopian past. Retreat or regression is not an option. Things were not better before globalisation or technology, or cities or governments. They are not the problem. And they are not the solution. We are! We are the ones who must demand or become that 'better leader'. We are the ones who must deny our ego in favour of the common good. We are the ones who must stop buying into all this othering. Because I assure you, when we do, when we speak with one voice – a common narrative – that's when we'll see business and government embedding equality into education, ethics into algorithms and happiness into every single policy they write.

"Being a leader today is not about assuming you have the answers," says Durkhanai. "It's about following and learning and observing, and then returning to share the boons of your experience with all as a weaver – knowing we can all contribute, strand by strand, in shifting our narratives, through shifting our definition of ourselves. In this way, true leadership is merely a symptom of an affair of the heart, which is something we're all capable of – and in fact, I think our deepest nature requires it."

"Finally," Durkhanai concludes...

"We stand at the cusp of a precipice,
with the long chain of the human story behind us, watching;
beckoning us to bound forth
in answer to the call of our time –
to transfigure;
knowing that we are each notes
in a grand and primal symphony,
and that we must find a way to harmonise."

Because isn't that the most logical path to our happiest state: to find and learn and get there together?

Beyond country and self, lies our spirit and faith,

each begging us to love and connect.

9

A MAN UP A MOUNTAIN AND THE IDEA THAT PUT HIM THERE

Religion. I was warned not to write about it. "It's too dangerous," I was told. "Don't place that bomb in the middle of your book." Why? I debated for months. Isn't religion a tool to teach us how to love, live and discover who we are? Doesn't it bring together the happiest ideas humanity knows? So why should I fear it? Don't most sects teach non-judgement and forgiveness anyhow, if I should 'say the wrong thing'? My own faith tells me that if god didn't want me to write this, it wouldn't exist. You wouldn't be reading it. But here we are.

So why did 'the world' or 'god' – two terms that to me mean 'the energy of all things, not 'a man in the sky pulling strings' – drag me to the far corners of the globe to meet all these fascinating human beings with such diverse, yet similar beliefs? What was I meant to see? Learn? What am I meant to tell you? As I have done throughout the process of writing this book, I shut my eyes and meditated, prayed, connected with god, whatever you want to call it… no answers yet. So I continue.

'Start at the beginning,' my heart, or god, tells me after some minutes of looking like a weirdo shutting my eyes in a crowded cafe. I suppose my journey to 'find god' began at the age of 12 or 13. I was decidedly unhappy with everyone and everything. How could this 'loving god' Christians talk about let me suffer like this? What sick sense of humour did he (this is not to be sexist, I'll explain later why I use the male pronoun) have that he'd let suicide, poverty and war reign over humanity? And why was it that the worst people so often seemed to be given the most? What a prick this god was!

As a pissed-off youth searching for truth, these questions didn't let up, and my feelings became more and more spiteful as life and my knowledge of the world drew me to darker and darker realities. My first brush with faith was actually the result of that failed suicide attempt, where, with a knife to my wrist, something drew me to that photo of my sister, which eventually made me stop.

I'd long felt I was on Earth to 'do something important'. Even as a 10 or 11 year old I'd say this to my mum. But until this brush with death, there'd always been a certain degree of doubt as to who or what was putting this thought in my head. Was it society? My teachers? Or that awful god I'd come to loathe? My eyes water as I write this, but letting me live, that voice that told me to stop which I heard through my sister, was the first time I felt god's love. This didn't mean life was suddenly better, or those scars within me had been healed. It merely sparked a new thought: perhaps god was both light and dark, because he was reflecting us.

> At the age of 16, I wrote a passage in my journal that read: *God is real, he is the sum of us all. The good, the bad, the ugly and all shades in between. God would not exist without us, because he is us. We are all each a part of the whole, which means we are creators ourselves, tiny gods that need to understand our responsibility as part of this entity. God is the energy of everything, all souls, animals, every living cell and atom in the universe.*

Ever since this revelation, learning about religion has become a kind of drug for me. A way of expanding my mind, growing my heart and uncovering the secrets of the universe. While I don't belong to any specific religion or church, without this spiritual path and the belief it's developed in me, I never would have found my happiest state. **At its core, I think this is what the journey toward faith, god, philosophy or connection to something beyond one's own self can do – make us happier and more complete beings.**

Heaven is a place on earth

What better place to start this story of miracles, morals, death, demons, rituals, rebirth, sacrifice and sacred texts than one of the oldest cities in the world, Varanasi in India. Inhabited continuously for more than 5000 years, this holy city located on the banks of the River Ganges in north-east-India, is important to Hindus, Jains and Buddhists. It's also one of the craziest places I've ever been – the India of my imagination – where magic and intrigue is met by the rawness of lepers, beggars, half-naked gurus, conmen (they were clothed) and queues of dead bodies hoping to escape the endless cycle of rebirth. Ironically, my Varanasi epiphany was forged when all these things met.

Walking through a swarm of coloured robes, men chanting and young boys frolicking in the holy waters of 'the Ganga', the jarring odour of an unfamiliar smokey smell told my travel companion and I we were nearing our destination. While Varanasi has 85 enormous ghats – sets of steps leading down to the river – travellers to the city are most often interested in just two, which are reserved for the burning of bodies.

Death, and what happens after this life, is of course a contentious selling point for most religions. Who wouldn't want to go to heaven or paradise? And what better way to recruit non-believers, or control the dissident masses, than to promise them an eternity with their loved ones or the chance of being reborn into a better life, if they behave themselves in this one. To me at least, it is an area riddled with doubt. More questions than answers. Because how can we know? There is no consistency among the stories of those who have technically died and come back to life.

Interestingly, for these bodies being burned right in front of me, the purpose was not a happier re-incarnation. Rather, the Hindus believe that if a deceased's ashes are laid in the Ganges at Varanasi, their soul will be transported to moksha (the divine) and will be liberated from the cycle of rebirth. Operating 24/7, burning hundreds of bodies a day in plain sight, what dawned on me as I uncomfortably documented the last private moments a family had with their loved one, was there were no women anywhere. Taking my phone out to google the answer, a man rushed to warn my companion and me not to take photos. "Last week a German man was deported for photographing the dead, because this interrupts the soul's journey to Nirvana," he warned us, before blabbering on endlessly about this poor German guy's fate. "Anyhow, we [his friend had joined him by this stage] are two of the government officials here to let you know about this site, so if you want we can tell you more?" I was still so transfixed on the ritual of it all I barely heard him. "No, not yet," replied my companion. There was something so wrong about what we were doing – it was like catching your neighbours having sex – you know you shouldn't look, but something draws you in. Perhaps it was the simple commonality of it? Because no matter what we do or don't believe, none of us can escape death.

Having just attended my grandfather's funeral, another thing I noticed was the close physically-involved nature of the Hindu ceremony. There was no hiding death in this place. It was literally in your face. Male mourners shuffle past locals, tourists and other pallbearers as they carry the remains through the tiny alleyways of the old city on a bamboo stretcher swathed in colourful cloth, down to the Ganges. Wrapped in white cloth and covered in flowers, herbs and oils, plus a mouth full of rice (nourishment for the journey), the body is then transferred from the stretcher into the water, where it is purified, before being laid out to dry for two hours on the steps. Once it has dried, the body (still wrapped in cloth) is placed on the pyres (piles of wood), which have been carefully selected and weighed depending on the amount of money the family can afford to spend on the ceremony. The entire time family members recite prayers, hymns and chants asking Brahma (the Hindu god) to accept the deceased on his or her journey to Nirvana. The atmosphere at the giant funeral site is surprisingly not one of sorrow, as mourners instead laugh, chat and play cards as the rituals are carried out. A positive and happy environment is thought to provide good karma for the deceased's spiritual migration.

"Are you coming now?" says a distant voice. "Hello sir, please come," says the government official from earlier, as my friend and I finally stop staring for long enough to take a few steps forward. "You can come closer, please, don't be shy, we will not bite and we do not charge you," says the pushier of the two men, gesturing for us to enter the inner sanctum of Manikarnika, the biggest burning ghat in Varanasi. "So what do you want to know?" he asks. "We're OK, we're happy just observing," my friend replied. "Do you know why some of the bodies are wrapped in different colours?" Damn he's got me, I thought, I do want to know that. "Why?" I asked. "If the deceased is a married woman whose husband is still alive, or an unmarried younger female, the clothing will be either a red or yellow dress. You will also not see holy men and children who die before reaching two years old here, as it is believed that their spirits are pure and don't need to be cleansed by the fire. Criminals and people who have committed suicide are also buried, as their sins are too great to be cleansed."

Thirty or so minutes later, having heard the entire spiel, I felt like a guru of Hindu funerals. I wonder what they'd say if I went down to help the Doms, the only sub-caste of Untouchables who are allowed to come into contact with dead bodies. "If you want to see more, we can take you up there, to the flame that has been burning for 3000 years. There is a hospice for the poor too, because not everyone can afford the wood for a pyre, so they can never reach Nirvana." Squirming at the injustices of poverty and the caste system (which the government will tell you doesn't exist anymore), I felt the need to do what little I could to give one or two of these economic outcasts (I wasn't sure what I could afford) a shot at Nirvana, so we followed the men.

Passing hundreds of mourners, bodies and nearly dead patients of the hospice, my heart writhed in pain. "Here you must give some money to this woman," one of the government officials suddenly said. "Why?" I asked, feeling a bit uncomfortable. "She is a nurse for the hospice, you can trust her." I hadn't yet shared my intentions to give with 'the officials' – I wanted to do it in private – and something was off about this shabbily dressed nurse who looked like a beggar. "What's going on?" I asked my friend, who'd been accosted by the more quiet of the two men, while the louder suggested I "must" turn over my money to this strange woman. "It is very good karma sir," he said, before his tone all of a sudden changed. "We give you good karma," he yelled. "We don't take you to the police about your photography, like the German man, now you do some good karma for the poor elderly people here to say thanks." Wait a minute I thought, why is he bringing up the German guy? "I am happy to give, but I do not feel comfortable that this woman is a nurse for the hospice. Why is she sitting outside in a different uniform to those nurses up there?" I asked. "That's it, we are going to have to take you both to the police station where you will be fined and deported, all because you are too greedy. 'Greedy foreigners get bad karma,'" he repeated numerous times. "Greedy foreigners, get bad karma." To be honest, my scam-dar had been curious about these men right from the start, because in my experience, India never provided government officials to guide tourists anywhere. Grabbing my friend and walking away as the men abused us, saying "karma will get you, karma will get you," I couldn't help but turn around and ask them: "do you think it is good karma, to use a sacred funeral site in the most holy place in India to run a scam? Do you think this is the sort of karma that lets you attain Nirvana?"

This highly sophisticated and successful long-running scam (which is almost never spotted according to travel forums) let me see an often hidden truth. **Heaven/Nirvana and hell/Naraka are not places we go when we die, but are states of being we can achieve right here on Earth, depending on our choices.** The anger, shame, fear, lies and disconnect that tortured these con-men everyday, is the bottomless pit of darkness we often refer to as hell. For much of my life I've actually held similar views to most major religions, which see this life as a kind of suffering or test. The downside to my beliefs however, are that I never bought into this notion of an afterlife spent in a garden, cloud or fiery pit, so there was no escaping the challenges I faced. What this taught me, and it didn't happen very quickly, was that I needed to find absolute peace and happiness in the here and now, because there might not be anything else. Seeking to drag the beauty of heaven down here to the living realm was actually a big part of what moved me to change course as a 23-year-old, and to start capturing and sharing the most inspiring stories the world has to offer. Because the news will always show us the horrors of hell, but it's the news of those angels, saints and prophets that can bring heaven closer to us all.

"We can all be holy when there's no inequality," my editor tells me, during our first discussion about this chapter. And I agree. It is my privilege, faith and luck that allows me to pursue a more heavenly state of being. That's why I do not judge or blame the actions of these con-men or anyone for their devilish deeds, for we are all a product of our upbringing and environment. India's injustice and inequality for instance, fuelled by the competition of capitalism and distrust of government, lead many to seek their own ends; lying, cheating and stealing in order to survive. Most people might think they'd behave differently, I certainly hope I would, but until we're faced with the prospect of losing a family member to starvation or a lack of medicine, we'll simply never know.

With all the time in the world to think about their predicament – the luxury of my conscious/opportunity-based existence – I was sure these men could use their flawless English skills and sparkling personalities to become actual tour guides, likely making them far more money than running this scam. Two days later I had a local guru pass a letter to them, which outlined my thoughts. I don't know if they ever read it, but I do know that this same hellish suffering they endured was commonplace in the West. For it was a hell of their own making.

A hell born from what I've coined as 'meego', the point at which one's ego fails to let them see past 'me me me'. Such a state is the most destructive force on the planet. Meego has splintered religions, laid waste to entire civilisations and spilled the blood of millions. But for what? How could hurting god's creatures ever be considered god's work? Surely if god wanted us to piss and fight like rabid dogs over territory, he wouldn't have given us a mind that's made happier when we act with compassion? Isn't that why faiths teach us to be kind? To do good? Because it's good for us? Because it's good for everyone? Still, despite all this, religious wars rage and hate swells, to the detriment of all **religions, who (at times) seem to have forgotten the love, actions and words that made their founders such popular and prophetic beings.**

Take Prophet Muhammad (Peace Be Upon Him), who said, "You do not do evil to those who do evil to you, but you deal with them with forgiveness and kindness." Or ancient Rabis who stated, "In God's eyes the man stands high who makes peace between men. But he stands highest who establishes peace among the nations." Jesus too seems in sync, "But I say to you, Love your enemies and pray for those who persecute you, so that you may be sons of your Father who is in heaven; for he makes his sun rise on the evil and on the good, and sends rain on the just and on the unjust." While Buddha warns us that, "The method of trying to conquer hatred through hatred never succeeds in overcoming hatred. But, the method of overcoming hatred through non-hatred is eternally effective. That is why that method is described as eternal wisdom." And what about Hindu scriptures, which tell us to "Do everything you have to do, but not with greed, not with ego, not with lust, not with envy, but with love, compassion, humility, and devotion."

Climbing aboard a small wooden boat in Varanasi to watch the nightly Ganga Aarti ceremony – a devotional ritual and prayer to the Ganges that uses fire as an offering – I was shocked to see there were two shows going on simultaneously. "Why are there two stages?" I asked our guide. "Mmmmm, we have two warring brothers in this city. Both believe they have the right and were called by God to host the Aarti. A lot of money and power comes from being in charge of this, so neither will give it up. Locals must now choose who to support, and the city is divided. Nobody can even hear what the priests are saying, because the ceremonies are side by side, so it is a noisy mess."

Extorting money and power in the name of prophets and gods is nothing new. From ancient Egypt, The Crusades, The Inquisition, the

Vikings, the Middle East, the Buddhist uprising (in Vietnam), Pakistan's split from India, Northern Ireland, Nigeria, Sudan, Somalia, Yugoslavia and ISIS, to Israel's annihilation of Palestine, the slaughter of Myanmar's Rohingya Muslims at the hands of Buddhist leaders, Hindu extremists attacking Christians in India and of course, the institutional rape and abuse of children at the hands of numerous churches and faiths. Keeping in mind that all it takes for evil to prevail is for good people to do nothing, there are few hands (whether through complicity or direct action) that have not been muddied by the ego maniacs – the unholy clerics and gurus – who use false claims and misguided scriptures to push their followers to do unthinkable things. I don't say this to be mean. I'm not going to sit here and suggest religion is the cause of all or even most wars and suffering, it is not, but to be responsible for any wars, any suffering, is enough to turn many would-be followers away. And to me that is a problem. For at its pure unfiltered centre, religion/belief/faith is perhaps the happiest idea on Earth. It is also one of the few forces that might stand in the way of materialism, individualism and capitalism-without-conscience – all of which, when left unchecked without a counter-weight, lead to our unhappiest state.

Just as cultural, political and governmental systems are made or broken by the people who make them up, so too the flaws apparent in religion are not the fault of sacred texts, rituals, the church or the emotions faith evokes. The flaws are human. All of them. But so too are the strength and joy religion brings. And that's what I've travelled the world to find: the happiest believers and non-believers.

The jackaroo who fell in love

Journeying through the mountains outside Yogyakarta in late 2013, rice paddy soon turned to jungle, which turned to thicker and darker jungle, before suddenly we (Sash and I) came across the man we'd come to meet.

"As-Salaam-Alaikum (peace be unto you) and welcome to Bumi Lingit," said Iskandar Waworuntu, a tall lanky figure who resembled Gandalf from Lord of the Rings, only in Muslim attire. He'd barely opened his mouth, but already Iskandar had told me everything there was to know about him – he was one with all things, including god. How

People congregate around Manikarnika Ghat, where smoke rises from bodies being cremated. We stood watching half way between the bright blue structure to the left of the image and the ghat. Image by Sondipon.

Two bodies wrapped in cloth await their journey to moksha. Image by Salvacampillo.

A religious man I met in Varanasi.

A view of the duel Ganga Aarti ceremonies from my boat on the river.

Iskandar (in white) with his wife and kids.

Iskandar and his wife sorting and chopping the veggies they just picked.

Angela and Zia (Pg 380).

Teachers visit a Buddhist temple to learn about the religion's history in Indonesia. This was a common and inspiring sight.

had he come to such an understanding though? Was it Islam? His wife? Who or what had instilled the peace and love that radiated so effortlessly from him?

"You know I was a jackaroo (sheep/cattle station worker) in Australia for about three months in 1968," he tells me, immediately peaking my interest and drawing me closer to him by finding our common ground, as all good leaders do. "I'd never ridden a horse in my life. But there, I have to be on the top of a horse maybe 8 to 10 hours a day," he said in his own brand of slightly broken English. "It didn't last very long, but that was the beginning. I joined the problem generation at the time. This is in '69, the peak of the hippie era, and I was part of that. I stayed in backpackers. I hitchhiked to Byron Bay or to Queensland just to look for magic mushroom and things like that. That's very much my young days. Right from when I was 14, I took off from mainstream culture, and I think that's basically the right age when everybody should go off in search," he tells me during a videoed interview (part of which you can view on thehappiest.com).

"The older I got, the more I got captured into the serious element of life. I wanted to find out more of the meaning of life. Hinduism, Taoism, and Buddhism was of most interest to people in those days. I touched a little bit on those religions through friends, through reading, and things like that, but never really took it too seriously. Then in '82 I decided to move from Yogyakarta to Sumatra (Indonesia) with a friend from the revolutionary theatre group I was a part of called 'Bengkel Teater Rendra'. We opened *The Clearer Jungle*, a kind of place where we tried to be self-sufficient. It lasted for about five or six years, but the experiment never really went very well because we were so naïve. We didn't know anything about agriculture or local customs. The only success was that I found my wife there."

Loved up and not ready to let go of this dream of self-sufficiency, Iskandar moved to Bali and became an organic farmer. "That's when I learned about permaculture," he said. "I also came to know Islam is the answer I was looking for, for a long time. I was almost 50 years old by this time (2001), but we cannot rush to find truth, it will find us when we are ready."

Reading some Islamic literature that related to Ihsan (one of the three dimensions of the Islamic religion), which means 'to do beautiful things', Iskandar said he started to fall in love. "Islam has become my love affair. And **when you fall in love, you're ready to sacrifice your own existence for something greater in life, which is love**. Because that is what Islam tells us. To be Muslim is to live with love, because that is how you 'do beautiful things.'"

Iskandar, now a renowned figure of his faith, says the continued manipulation of followers who are taught to focus on the other two dimensions of Islamic belief – Islam and Iman – is draining the heart out of the religion. 'Islam' encompasses the rules, such as praying 5 times a day, Zakat (giving a portion of your wealth to charity), fasting in Ramadan, visiting Mecca and declaring there is no God but Allah and Muhammad (PBUH) is the messenger of Allah. 'Iman' means faith, and according to the Prophet, Iman is, "To believe in Allah, His Angels, His Books, to believe in meeting Him, to believe in His Messengers, the Resurrection and the predestination." Ihsan, sometimes (but not often enough) referred to as the 'highest status' of the Islamic religion, is discussed in the Quran by Allah, who says: "Indeed, Allah commands justice, good conduct (Ihsan), and giving to relatives (and He) forbids immorality, bad conduct, and oppression. He admonishes you that perhaps you will be reminded," (Quran, 16: 90).

"Ihsan is the path of the heart, the path of love," says Iskandar. "It's a very important aspect of Islam, because only then I think you will touch on happiness. See Ihsan, it is what you practice, not because you're afraid of being punished for not doing it, but just because love is so beautiful and happiness is part of you, so you want to give it to others."

While Ihsan was what drew him to Islam, and remains his focus, Iskandar says the structure, symbolism and rules of the religion have helped him to express his love of God with an added intensity. "For somebody to be obliged to pray five times a day is a big commitment. It feels like the opposite of freedom. I know I felt like this before I became Muslim," he says, before opening a window and inviting me to look outside. "Now, if you put some imagination into it... because Muslims pray with the position of the sun – at dawn, midday, afternoon, sunset and night – you can picture from space there are these consecutive waves of prayer circling the planet, like in a stadium as people raise their hands and stand up and then sit one after another [a Mexican wave]. Spending some time in the theatre world, I think this performance by God, where he has us giving the selfless good of prayer together, non-stop, around the world... to be part of that is my happiness."

Witnessing Iskandar, his family and members of the Bumi Lingit community pray together, as one, was beautiful. I think the commitment too, to think of others and to disconnect from our busy, noisy, often self-indulgent lives five times a day is something that would make us all happier. My only thought was, why were the women segregated at the back? The answer I've heard every time I've questioned this phenomenon, which is a lot, is essentially: to stop the mischievous eyes of men from becoming distracted during this holy act by the bowing, bending and prostrating women. It seems even Muhammad (PBUH) knew of the weakness of men, when he said, "Do not prevent your womenfolk from going to the mosques, although their houses are better for them." Iskandar's response was slightly different, "if it is not a sign of disrespect, but the opposite, part of the protection to women due to male weakness, where is the debate?" "The debate," I said "is in how Islam, at large – not so much in Indonesia – treats women." "Yes, well, I admit, you can't find a more dominant and negative male culture than the Arabs," he says, echoing my own observations of the arrogant, sexist, material-loving nature of (most) men in the Middle-East, who use and abuse their women nearly as much as they do their religion.

"You know, woman there are so badly treated, despite the prophet actually giving such incredible rights to woman. **In Islam, for instance, nobody realises that the obligation of cooking, cleaning, all the household things, it's not the obligation of women. It's the obligation of men.** Women can even refuse to nurse their baby if they want to, and the husband would have to find a wet nurse. Another example is, before a wedding, the woman can ask for whatever she wants from her husband, like what you call a prenuptial agreement. This is all part of the tradition of Islam. But nobody really talks about this, because it is a male dominated world, particularly in the Arab countries where Islamic culture is propogated." Not only did Iskandar shed a light on the rights of women in Islam, he also raised an idea my wife and I have long since discussed with vigor. "In the Western world, the meaning of happiness and freedom has become distorted. Now, opening up your body has become an expression of both of these things, especially for women. But is it a true happiness?" he asks. "I think it's more a form of exploitation by the cosmetics, the fashion industry, to shape women to buy more things. It's just a pity that human beings seek to find happiness through such vulgar, indecent ways. Surely there must be better means to express beauty?"

When I asked him about the views of Islamic theologians in Saudi Arabia, who have issued death warrants in the form of fatwas against those who allow the mixing of the sexes, his thinking and words were both novel and telling.

"This is why they sent our prophet in that culture, I think, because of that aspect. Because of how corrupt that place was at the time of the prophet Muhammad (PBUH). So they needed his guidance. His example on how to treat people, women particularly. But Islam failed to help them. And now, history shows us that politics distorts Islam and puts us in conflict, because the Saudi's new version of Islam is very, very corrupt and self-serving."

Worried about the mass of Saudi money and mosques pouring into Indonesia and the influence that buys, particularly among the poor and uneducated, Iskandar says nothing good can come of Arab wealth, because of its impure origins.

"One teaching in Islam that I take very seriously, that can make people happy or miserable, is 'halal'. Halal is a word that people in the West have heard, but nobody really knows that halal actually doesn't stand alone, it's always attached to 'toyib', which means goodness or wholesome. This encompasses the background on how something manifests in this life. The intention anything begins with. The problem is, industry has the wrong intention, because the intention is just to make money, to double the profit. So the phone, the food, even the home, if it is manifest through exploitation, it is not toyib. It has no goodness. That is why you can't hope anything good will come out of the [Saudi] money that came from petroleum. It's a dark money, it's an evil money. It is without toyib." It's little wonder oil money is so often linked to radicalisation says Iskandar, which leads only to the death and suffering of Muslims and non-Muslims alike.

What many Islamic scholars and ordinary people fail or refuse to see is that "our happiness and our religion is being destroyed from within, from our lifestyle," says Iskandar. "Take the environment, I have always had a special relationship with nature. Its destruction hurts me. But Islam gives us a timeless guidance on this. It tells us there are basically two types of environment. One is the internal environment, which is our internal system within our body, our blood, digestion, respiratory, emotional, spiritual, all the internal element of our life. Then we have the external environment, which is the whole creation of the universe. What's misunderstood is that these two are very much linked. Basically the external and the internal is a reflection of each other. If you can deal with your internal environment in a good way, that means you're dealing with your external environment also, and vice versa."

Our current *newer, bigger, faster, cheaper* consumer-driven lifestyles seldom gives us time to think about the forests we're laying waste to or the modern-day slaves who make our clothing or technology. And it certainly doesn't give us a chance to contemplate the inequality our greed makes us complicit in perpetuating. The problem is, Iskandar says, "happiness exists in the balance of life," and right now, we all want more scoops of ice cream than the cone can hold.

Unlike many of us (me included) who might think we're living in balance because we compost, ride a bike, recycle, eat vegetarian or drive a hybrid, Iskandar and every single thing he owned (bar his watch and T-shirt) was part of a cyclical structure of birth, death and rebirth. Bumi Lingit – Iskandar's communal property, where people can witness and learn about the importance of mutual living between man and nature – was and still is the most sustainable house I have seen. Given how many eco-villages and projects I've visited, that says a lot.

"Most creatures will live and die in their usefulness, without waste," continues Iskandar, as he points out his flourishing fish farm, poultry hatcheries and veggie patch. "But for humans, the whole characteristic of the modern time now is basically being excessive. Due to this we cannot be happy. Imbalance brings fear, like burning too much fossil fuel, because it is now killing us. So who can be happy in the future? Nobody, maybe. Unless we say 'no' or 'enough.'"

"Because when you talk about happiness, it has to be unconditional. If you are happy but it's a conditional happiness, there's something wrong, something lacking. God does not disappear, He is in nature, in the miracle of the sun's light, the moon's tides, the forest, our food, the spontaneous activity and togetherness we receive when we return to our village roots." As Prophet Muhammad (PBUH) said, **"Riches are not from an abundance of worldly goods but from a contented mind."** That's why "The greatest jihad [struggle/striving] is to battle your own soul, to fight the evil within yourself," concluded Muhammad (PBUH).

How similar this sounded to Buddha, I thought, who said, "to conquer oneself is a greater task than conquering others [for] to bring true happiness to one's family, to bring peace to all, one must first discipline and control one's own mind." If these two great leaders were basically saying the same thing, then why is it that Buddhists in Myanmar are killing Muslims? And how is it that crazed monk Ashin Wirathu was allowed to fan the flames of hatred, calling Rohingya Muslims "rats" and "vermin" (the same language used by Nazis in reference to Jews). Keen to discover how Buddha's words had manifest, for good and for bad, I headed to Myanmar (and eight other majority-Buddhist countries) in late-2012, and again in early-2015, to see for myself.

Buddha's legacy, 2419 years later

Before I'd even laid eyes on a monk, Zia and Angela, the father and daughter I sat next to on my flight to Kuala Lumpur, had introduced me to their own religion, called the Baha'i Faith. Heading to Israel to volunteer at the Baha'i World Centre, the two gave me a stirring glimpse of their god. "We see God as a prism where one religion sees one side of the divine light, while another sees the other and so on. But all see the same light, just less of it, because to be close to the light is to be close to all beings and at peace with all sides of the prism," says Zia. "So what is happiness then, for a Baha'i?" I ask him. "When the inner being reflects The Light, when you see with your inner eyes, hear with inner ears, when the motive is pure, when the conduct is seemly, when the action is praiseworthy and when you rise above human limitations and enter the plane of sacrifice, preferring your sisters and brothers and placing their needs above yours. Then you are happy." "And you?" I look to Angela. "Happiness is rejecting racism and nationalism because that is how we draw closer to the divine in all, is through removing our human flaws and being one with love, which is the glue that binds us, that is The Light."

Handing me a small book called *The Hidden Words and Selected Holy Writings* (a pocket bible for Baha'i), I found the words profound. This favourite passage says it all: "Be generous in prosperity, and thankful in adversity ... Be as a lamp unto them that walk in darkness, a joy to the sorrowful, a sea for the thirsty, a haven for the distressed, an upholder and defender of the victim of oppression."

A MAN UP A MOUNTAIN AND THE IDEA THAT PUT HIM THERE

Incredible words, but still just words. Without tearing them off the page and stitching them into your hands, your heart, your every vein and action, they are worthless. I suppose that's why I've always trusted my eyes more than my ears when it comes to religion, because seeing is believing.

Witnessing the sunrise over 2230 mist-shrouded stupas on the ancient temple plain of Bagan, Myanmar, gave me a chill I'll never forget. Fervent believers in Theravada Buddhism, the Bagan kings and their subjects built more than 10,000 stupas throughout their metropolis between the 9th and 13th centuries. With each considered an act of merit, the middle and upper classes, including royalty, spared no expense erecting these symbols of faith. Standing atop one of the larger temples filming the stunning sunrise, a father and his two sons (who were monks) crouched awkwardly trying to take a selfie. Seeing their trouble, I offered a hand. Unable to communicate in words, we spent some minutes laughing together as we mimed a few thoughts, before trying to find someone with a pen, as one monk in particular was curious to discuss more than mime would allow. Scribbling several lines in my journal, which I later had translated, I discovered Moe Myint Thu (the monk) had written, "The purpose of our lives is to be happy. The monastery teaches us the path is in detachment from self, from want, desire. The path is kindness, because peace of mind comes from good energy, good karma, and this comes from compassion and kindness." Despite our severe language barrier, the ease, the love and the innocence of these men was warming, and is telling of most devout Buddhists I've met.

A small but memorable aside: when I returned the pen to the Swiss couple who'd lent it to us, Flaviu and Ruth told me they had been on honeymoon for 15 years. Touched by what they saw in India, Nepal and Tibet in 1997, the pair began volunteering in local communities and have done so ever since. I didn't ask their religion, I only know they felt godly, because they oozed love.

Naked, vulnerable and open to both the good and the bad intentions of man, I think the best way to test the moral fibre and happiness instilled by a religion, is to simply walk the streets of its followers, and see what happens. Barely a minute in, a rowdy group of young men whistled at me, clapping their hands and gesturing for me to come closer. "Come, you want to play?" asked one of the boys. The reason for all the commotion became clear when I poked my head behind a couple of thick bushes and saw a table tennis table. "OK, I'm in," I said, secretly buzzing with anticipation, as I love table tennis. Forty five minutes later, after finally adjusting to the wind, the weathered table and the roaring crowd, one of the guys pulled me aside. "Wow, we don't know you can play so well," he said. "We just like to invite foreigner to play with us, but most, they cannot hit the ball too much." "Why do you invite tourists to play?" I asked the boy, who said he studied English at university. "We all go to monastery in this country when we are small, maybe 7 or 10 years old, so we learn the ways of Buddha," says the 20-year-old. "Buddha tells us 'generosity brings happiness at every stage of its expression'. So this is why we must include the foreigner in our game. Because 'to live a pure unselfish life, one must count nothing as one's own in the midst of abundance'. He says this too, Buddha does."

Following the banks of the Ayeyarwaddy River, which snaked and curved through the ethereal plain of temples, Buddha's words were everywhere. His teachings on appreciation and contentment filled the hearts of local women as they washed clothes and bathed their mischievous children in the river. His philosophies around being present and living without fear shone as children crawled, climbed and clung onto my every limb as parents sat back and laughed as this strange foreigner – me – raced, wrestled and threw their kids through the air. Buddha's guidance on generosity, kindness and service to others was also self-evident as numerous monasteries opened their doors and without a second thought gave me their time, even offering me food and drink. U Dharmma Piya, a 36-year-old who ran Lawkananda Monastery, which was home to 12 monks, 80 novices and a family of dogs, told me he sees "many tourists worrying over everything, but what problem did worry ever solve?" He laughs. Drawn to explore the unexplored, I think Mauk Gutala, a 50-year-old monk who was living in a little-known run-down monastery called Nayubaka, was surprised to see me and my bloodied feet (thanks to the thorns and thick bush) as I stumbled upon his dilapidated stupa. "My brother and I take the ruins of this temple and make it OK to use again," he tells me. "That is our home," he points to a rustic shed that's around 12 square metres. "This is where I come to meditate," he says, taking me to stand atop the ancient structure, which had succumbed to both war and Mother Nature. "For me, I like this place, because it tells me nothing is forever. In Buddhism, we call it impermanence. You can find peace in this. Because then you do not attach to things in a bad way,

Flaviu and Ruth.

Moe Myint Thu with his father and brother.

Some kids I met at a temple on the banks of the Ayeyarwaddy River.

Their favourite game was being thrown up and down and spun around.

My table tennis friends from Bagan.

1, 2, 3... Run!!!

Mauk Gutala standing atop the ruins of Nayubaka monastery. Bagan's temple plain in the background.

Mauk Gutala.

Papak Hing.

Hinn Oo Shwe Yie.

U Dharmma Piya meditating under a tree.

The monks I met on the bus in front of Kyaiktiyo Pagoda, AKA Golden Rock.

A stunning bamboo forest I came across in the mountains of Myanmar.

Kyaiktiyo Pagoda, AKA Golden Rock.

then even death is OK, 'cause no one is permanent. Nothing. Not brick and cement even you see," he crumbles some old mortar in his hand. Papak Hing was my final teacher in Bagan. The cheeky 10-year-old, who had to work to be able to afford school, had tried to sell me a postcard, before ducking and diving in her bright pink dress to avoid me getting a photo. An hour or so later, after I'd finished speaking to everyone else in the area, she resurfaced, jumping out in front of my camera with a giant grin, before saying the one thing she knew might be relevant, having eavesdropped on my prior conversations. "We must do loving thing, good thing," she says, having clearly learned a little English at school.

Trying to hop a bus to Mount Kyaiktiyo and the precarious overhanging Golden Rock that is said to be balancing on one of Buddha's hairs, I was met by men who revealed, rather sadly, that Buddhists too have flaws. Sent on the wrong bus not once but twice, because it would make the operators an extra buck or two, these vultures were the first decidedly unhappy and decidedly non-Buddhist Buddhists I'd encountered. Don't get me wrong, these tour operators worshipped the monks who got on my bus, offering them additional favours, food, even money, in exchange for prayers or holy words. The problem was, by cheating me and likely other tourists in the name of the almighty dollar, they took such words and made them empty. Because it's like Buddha said, **"However many holy words you read, however many you speak, what good will they do you if you do not act upon them?"**

Not only was I determined not to let this get me down, but it seemed like I had the support of all of Myanmar, who upon noticing I was the only foreigner on the bus, seemed to sort of gravitate their kindness towards me. Peeking through the gap in the chair, Hinn Oo Shwe Yie, an 8-year-old girl, started to laugh as I smiled and then poked my tongue out at her. Within minutes we were having an all out face-pulling competition. Every silly move I made she mimicked. Back and forth we went, getting more and more ridiculous until the entire bus were in stitches. Even the five young monks who were on the back seat had become curious, gesturing for me to come and sit with them when I was done. "Would you like food?" asked 21-year-old Zuly Phyoe, who opened his alms bowl. Before getting a chance to say no, he'd placed a small portion of rice and a local fruit in my hand. "Thank you," I said, before asking them about the newspaper they were reading. "We just look at football," says Tin Tun Win, the oldest of the monks at 44.

"Some say not to indulge in this thing [soccer], but it is a unifier of all people, universal religion is the ball [he laughs]. **We need this. To come together, beyond religion**," he continues in broken English, with the help of his friend who translates. "Like you are doing playing with the little girl. You are a stranger, she is a stranger, but you smile and laugh in same language. Buddha talk like this, universal truths. We are same," says Ueindar Sar Da, who was 25 and had one of the biggest smiles I've ever seen.

The following day as I made the pilgrimage to see the Golden Rock, this line *we are same* seemed poignant. I didn't notice it to begin with, but as I went to place a piece of golden leaf on the giant glistening boulder, something was off. Standing back and observing others perform this most sacred ritual, what I noticed was there were no women. Bumping into the group of monks from the bus, who'd been joined by some additional friends, I asked them why. "That is the rule, women can only go to that area to pray, [they] cannot touch the rock," Zou Win Nang tells me, before I push them for a reason. "It is since ancient time, and in that time men are regarded as more noble than women, this is also why women cannot be in the room with the images of Buddha," says 30-year-old monk Ashin Pa Di Ta. Searching out the origins of such misogyny, it is impossible to determine with certainty whether it was Buddha who held this bias against women, or whether it was simply the chauvinistic society of the day. Certainly, if he were alive today, I would ask Buddha why he only ordained women as nuns five years after first ordaining men into the sangha (Buddhist church) as monks. I'd also love to know how he felt about those who poisoned his wisdom by adding their own self-serving rhetoric, which says it is impossible for women to be 'the perfectly rightfully Enlightened One', 'the Universal Monarch' or 'Brahma'. Furthermore, as author Diana Paul points out in her book *Women in Buddhism,* the religion inherited (and in my experience maintains) a view of women whereby if they are not represented as mothers, then they are portrayed as either lustful temptresses or as evil incarnate. Knowing perhaps that his words would be muddied by weaker men, Buddha (unlike other prophets) invited us to question everything. "Do not believe in anything simply because you have heard it ... because it is written in your religious books. Do not believe in anything merely on the authority of your teachers and elders. Do not believe in traditions because they have been handed down for many generations. But after observation and analysis, when you find that anything agrees with reason and is conducive to the good and benefit of one and all, then accept it and live up to it."

Those who abide by this quote will find the religion or belief that brings about their happiest state. For in faith, as in life, we must seek out *our* path, not somebody else's, which means we need to question if something is right for *us*, not some version of ourselves that we think we're meant to be. And certainly not to please those in authority. For when we give up our right to observation and analysis, to question what is conducive to the good and benefit of one and all, then things get ugly, fast. Three years later, when I returned to Myanmar, that's unfortunately, exactly what I found. Though, there was some other pretty awesome stuff too.

On 4 January 2015 I arrived in Myeik, a small city located on the remote Tanintharyi coast of Southern Myanmar. I'd travelled there hoping to learn more about the indigenous Moken people, who were nomadic sea gypsies that roamed the Mergui Archipelago in fragile canoes searching the sea bed for their livelihood. As it turns out, the gruelling 46 hour bus trip aboard the 'Express Air Con' from Yangon (which didn't have air con and was decidedly slow) was a giant waste of time, with the local authorities in Myeik telling me I needed a permit to visit the Moken people. With a 14 day turn around on the necessary paperwork, unless I was willing to bribe them (something I try to avoid), I decided to change tack. Roughly 110 hours by bus from where the Rohingya Muslims lived, I figured this might be a good place to get an unbiased view of the conflict (whereby Buddhists and Muslims are warring over land/power in the countries north west), as well as dive a little deeper down the rabbit hole of Buddhism.

Walking along the coastline in Myeik, men cackled raucously as they enjoyed a local game that involved throwing tiny shells into squares etched onto the pavement. Passing by the one shopping mall and through an empty field that was destined to have a new housing development lopped onto it, I found a young boy whistling. Quietly observing his sheepish smile as he hauled a large garbage bag along the dusty dirt road, I knew I needed to speak to him. Thankfully, he stopped to talk to a group of kids and parents who seemed intent on working out what I was doing there. Dragging a neighbour out of his house to translate, I quickly wanted to ask the boy what he was doing. His reply was ever honest, "Carrying garbage," he said. "But why are you smiling?" I asked. "Because I'm happy," he concluded.

Playing with a few rocks and an empty plastic cup, I queried a congregation of younger children about their activities. "This is what we use for our game," said a squeaky, shy voice. "We don't need any more things in the village," interrupted one of the men who'd been listening in. "In Buddhism, happiness comes from within, so you will see our village is poor, but we too have riches in here," he says, holding his hand to his chest. Continuing to walk the dusty streets of this shanty town, which is littered with men doing odd jobs, women preparing and selling food by the roadside, and kids hunting for that perfect cardboard box to play with, I'm invited into what appears to be a house that sells ice cream. Hurrying to brush her daughter's hair so I can take a photo, the mother pulls up a chair and gestures for me to sit. "Wait," she says in a distorted form of English. "Here, you eat." She passes me a pink ice cream in a cone. "Best in Myeik," she laughs. Not interested in my money, just in my happiness, the woman looks intently at my face as I taste her local delicacy. "Yummy!" I scream, and I wasn't lying. "Good, you happy, then me happy," she smiles. "You want to take photo of children, you can, they like, all kid in village like. We don't see foreigner here, so we like you to visit, we show you our home." Welcomed at every turn, and offered accommodation, food, tea and even marriage throughout the three days I ended up spending in this impoverished village on the outskirts of Myeik, there was a relishing of the small things, a belief in *enough*, that made this place feel truly like a Buddhist sanctuary. One of my favourite interactions, which sums up the ethos of these people, came when I approached a young, shabbily dressed couple who sat on their porch sharing a smoke. "We don't have much," they told me. "What else would you like?" I asked. "Nothing. We don't need much to be happy, just life, love and enough time to enjoy both." Even a 38-year-old single woman (a rare thing in such a place), had a particularly Buddhist way of rebutting her friends, who teased her. "They are worried I am still single," she tells me, gazing at her friends. "Are you?" I asked. "No, because I am happy in myself and if I am patient good things will come to me."

Just when I thought this community had given me everything, a number of the women insisted I join them at a Buddhist ceremony where they would offer rice and other foods and resources to the local monasteries. Not quite understanding just how big a deal this was, when

The boy carrying garbage.

The group of kids who were playing with rocks and a plastic cup.

The lady who gave me ice cream brushing her daughter's hair.

The 38-year-old single lady.

The young 'shabbily' dressed couple.

Ko Than Zaw Min.

Ashin Nasada. Ko Than's guru.

Ravinatha Gurukkal, the Chief High Priest of Batu Caves Murugan Temple (Pg 398).

A young girl caring for her sibling in the Myeik village I visited.

Villagers line the streets to offer rice and other goods to local monks and nuns.

The 83yo leader of Kiladayama Monastery (left) with her 77yo counterpart (right).

Deau Punnawati (top) and nuns from Shaw Kyin Monastery.

Gowe Nawe, leader of Para Nu Su Monastery.

Novices at Para Nu Su Monastery.

My 35-year-old guide/translator.

Tongwe, the monk I met on the bus in Thailand.

My guide helping me to interview the three leaders from Kiladayama Monastery.

A MAN UP A MOUNTAIN AND THE IDEA THAT PUT HIM THERE

I arrived, I was ushered into the 'holy (tent) sangha', where a number of older monks said a prayer with me, before blessing me to take photos. Something about going that extra step to connect, to hold my hands and offer me welcome, rather than just say 'yeah mate you can take photos', really made me feel as one, at peace. With thousands of locals lining the streets, an impeccable, well ordered line of maroon-clad monks and pink-robed nuns started their colourful procession through the village. Each layperson saw their sacrificial offering (especially given many could barely afford enough food for themselves) as a reminder not to be greedy or selfish, which draws them closer to Buddha.

Keen to show me more, a former monk and now school teacher Ko Than Zaw Min told me to jump on the back of his motorbike. Such was the selfless and kind intentions of 99.9% of Buddhists, that I was happy to be whisked away by this complete stranger. And I'm glad I was. Ko Than took me to visit his former Preceptor (guru) Ashin Nasada, the Abbot (head) of Maw Taung Monastery in Myeik. Draped in orange robes and sporting the customary shaved head, Nasada spoke of the tolerance we can find in "denying ignorance" through practicing love and kindness "because it reduces the gaps between us." Once mastered, he says, "you must then help others to practice love and kindness," which he exclaims is the primary purpose of a monk, "for it is the path to enlightenment." Spending some time discussing the idea of 'the right view' – how we can grow and maintain a positive and generous perspective – I felt it was the right time to broach a touchier topic. "Do you think Buddhists in this country have the right view when it comes to the Rohingya Muslims?" I asked calmly, not wanting to cause insult. "With regards to right view of Muslim [he pauses], we feel we must protect ourselves in this case, because it is something [he pauses again], it is something we cannot avoid, even if we run, because they will spread too, so the problem will chase us," he said, with a great deal of reflection and angst. "Will love and kindness not work?" I ask nervously. I'm not sure if it was a sigh or a sad spurt of 'if only' laughter, but his response was not a happy one. "It is hard because you cannot stop a boulder with love, and Islam is like a boulder – very hard, that black, this white – and so it squashes other things when it rolls." Engaging in conversations with more than 30 monks from 9 monasteries over the following 48 hours (thanks to another monk I befriended who offered to take me around and act as my translator), I can tell you that all spoke of "kindness, oneness and helping others" as being central to our happiest existence, and yet, only a handful expressed solidarity or compassion for the Rohingya Muslims. And only one called on the sanga (Buddhist church) to be more vocal in demanding a peaceful resolution.

"We must learn to love more," said Gowe Nawe, the leader of Para Nu Su Monastery. "That is Buddha's message for all, compassion is solution to everything. Because more hate just make more hate, this is what military and government do. So we as Buddhist, we know, so we must show that only compassion and acceptance can cure hate. This is eternal wisdom of Buddha."

It's interesting, because the two Female Nunneries I visited, Shaw Kyin and Kiladayama Monastery, were utterly perplexed by the notion that a country of Buddhists could inflict harm on anyone or anything. "We have clear guidance," says the 83-year-old head of Kiladayama Monastery. "Buddha tells us we must respect each other and refrain from disputes; he says 'you should not, like water and oil, repel each other, but should, like milk and water, mingle together.'" Her 77-year-old counterpart agreed, **"Treat others with respect, this is what Buddha said, because how you treat others will be how they treat you."** These words might sound familiar or cliche, but it was the hearts from which they danced into the world that was different in this instance. These women were beyond this worldly plain. If they hadn't attained enlightenment, I don't know who could or had. In my journal at the time I scribbled: *"in awe of the peace and kindness of their auras, they need not even speak and I am being loved."* I wonder whether this goes back to Iskandar's point, whereby all love is only equal to the sacrifice we are willing to make for it, because as 75-year-old Deau Punnawati said, nuns faced a number of extrinsic pressures monks did not. "Many girls in this culture, they are told 'you must be a mum', but as nuns, we cannot be. We must also shave our head and for most young girls this is not seen as beautiful, so there are less girls educated in the Dharma, because it is still not seen as 'right path' or as dignified for a girl to be a nun, like it is for boy to be a monk," says the head of Shaw Kyin Monastery. "This is sad, because our happiest way is the way of the Buddha, which is to do away with worldly desires, to make extinct the flames of passion, aversion and ignorance."

To best understand my feelings towards Buddhism, and the role it has played in my own path to happiness, I dug up this journal entry I wrote after finally digesting the many interviews, observations and

Buddhist books I was given by several abbots in Myanmar, Thailand, Cambodia and Sri Lanka.

> *I see and feel impermanence everywhere. This Buddhist belief that all things, including 'the self' are transient, inconstant and ever changing, is freeing. Perhaps it helps with Buddha's notion that we must free ourselves from attachment to reach our happiest state – Enlightenment. What impermanence tells me is that no matter how much shit you're dealing with, it won't last forever. The flipside is, the happiest most awesome times won't roll on forever either. So we should embrace and find what good we can in each moment, for either way it won't last. Does this mean nothing matters? Or does it mean everything matters? I mean if we are, if everything is impermanent and doomed to change for better or worse, does our own purpose or existence matter? This is where this Buddhist idea of finding peace and Enlightenment by sitting on a mountain or in a cave somewhere doesn't seem like the happiest path to me. Sure, you might detach yourself from worldly possessions and suffering, but is the absence of suffering happiness? If I liberate myself, who or what am I serving? I get that I may not harm anyone, but do I help anyone? The greater path, as Buddhism further suggests (the notion of the Bodhisattva), is to purify one's thoughts, to serve with compassion your fellow man, and to love friends and family with all your heart, while remaining unattached and at peace with the impermanence we all face. It may be much harder of course. But that is the reality I face. That is my truth. Is it the ultimate truth? I wouldn't 'know' and I don't think Buddha would profess to either (that's why he tells us to question everything and to seek our own answers). His followers of course, might argue that he 'knew' what the universe holds, or where we are destined to go when we die. Buddha, thankfully, only tells me through his words and life that we can and must prepare ourselves for all ideas of life after death by living and finding constant peace in our present and impermanent being.*

As if wanting to put my impermanence and faith in Buddhism to the test, on 23 January 2015, having just crossed the border from Myanmar into Thailand (where a monk saved me from a violent, alcoholic, mentally-deranged con man trying to steal my money and passport), I got a phone call from my now wife. "Mama is really bad Mike," said Sash through unrelenting tears. "I'm scared, she's got some new thing, not the cancer, it's some spinal, brain infection caused by the chemotherapy. It's bad Mike, the doctor's are worried, you should see how many nurses were around her. They've taken her to the ICU. I'm so scared. Mama thrive you know, because they have a lot of focus on them and they have older role models and other kids to play with. So everybody living in the community has an interconnected role in making the society work. So that's a very concrete and practical way of thinking about how we can design cities or communities to fit the needs of the 21st century." "Is it essentially about re-inventing the village for the modern age?" I asked. "Yeah, basically, right. I think we have to be quite creative and open-minded on these fronts, because that's how we create solutions that can deal with several problems at once," concludes Birkjær.

The notion of killing two or three or even ten birds with one stone is not only the key to sustaining life, it's also the key to achieving a life worth sustaining. Our problem, or a fairly big part of it at least, is that for centuries we – and particularly businesses and governments – have quashed one problem, only for it to create another (often bigger) problem somewhere else. In Australia, for instance, we introduced a number of animals to make money or curb agricultural problems, only to have those same species turn around and decimate our environment, industry and cost taxpayers billions. Similarly, in the US (and they're not alone), oil and gas companies continue to rake in $100 billion plus in profit every year – which is great for those sharing in the spoils – but I wonder how Americans in 2090 will feel when the effects of climate change are expected to cost the country $500 billion annually. The biggest, most awkward and most immediate problem we face is that we've worked out how to live for twice as long, without working out how to live twice as sustainably – in fact, we've done quite the opposite. What I think is pretty obvious, and what we seriously need to ask ourselves, is: what is progress? What are we aiming for? And why?

If the answer is a system that perpetuates gross and ever increasing inequality, then the path of pure capitalism, with a fully deregulated market, and individual freedom at all costs, is the model we should follow. If you're more interested in establishing a society and world that gives us all a chance of achieving our happiest state, then we must vote for governments willing to learn from and adopt the fundamental ingredients we see working in Scandinavia, Bhutan and Latin America. **Social democracy (with a healthy side of collectivism) must be our goal.** Not just because it's the happiest system we know, but because it may also go some way to addressing another massive problem, which is the growing void left by the death of religion (something discussed at can't speak." Sash was actually meant to be with me on this trip (which was meant to be a three month jaunt through Myanmar, Cambodia and India), but when her mum was diagnosed with breast cancer a month before we were set to go, she decided to stay in Australia to support her through the chemo and radiotherapy. Standing at a bus stop in far-north Thailand when I got that call from Sash, a monk, perhaps sensing my distress (or seeing the *What is Buddhism* book in my hand), offered to sit with me on the bus we were both about to board. Dressed in an orange robe, orange beanie and carrying a yellow rucksack, Tongwe was terribly curious to observe and question my every move and word (particularly those I was reading). As it happened, he got plenty of time to do this, when our bus unexpectedly stopped working in the middle of a mountain pass. With nothing to do but read and think, and think and read, I encountered a chapter I felt may be of some use given my mother-in-law's situation. It essentially said that with enough practice in meditation, those who have it, can choose to pass on their good karma. It was the first I'd heard of this, so I asked the monk his thoughts on it. Through a few broken words of English and a bit of help from a local who could translate, he said, "yes you must meditate much, that is how you send your energy to another." With my own beliefs telling me energy can't just disappear, the thought I meditated on for three hours while our bus was broken down was this: *take all I've done, the good karma, the love within me and pass it to Twinkle (my mother-in-law), and let me absorb her pain, no matter what it means for me. If I should suffer, die, then let that be, but let me give her all the goodness in me and let me take all that is needed for her to live.* Concentrating and focussing on the transition of energy between us, I rarely opened my eyes for several hours. When I did, the monk gestured for me to keep going. He knew what was at stake, I'd shown him a photo of Twinkle and Sash. "More," he'd say. "More." So I did. I blocked everything out and just repeated those thoughts.

"We must go," said Tongwe, tapping me on the shoulder to wake me from my meditation. "Another bus," he said. Hopping on a new bus, that was set to get us to our destination at 11pm, instead of 3pm, I was a little worried, as I hadn't yet booked accommodation. Sharing my concern with Tongwe, I wasn't sure he'd understood me, saying instead something about firemen and drawing a picture of a tent in my book. Finally arriving in Nan, a town in north-east Thailand, it turns out my new friend had done more than just understand me, he'd arranged for his English speaking cousin (who was a fireman) to meet us and help me find somewhere to stay. Offering for me to sleep in a tent at the fire station, I originally said yes, before reconsidering, as I felt I really needed a good night's rest. I didn't want to tell him, but I was exhausted from the meditation. Dropping me at a cheap motel, where Tongwe and his cousin ensured I paid local rates and was treated like royalty (or a monk in this case), I was out like a log by midnight.

Waking to raging stomach cramps, I didn't even make it to the toilet before vomiting. Sitting on the toilet, spewing that day's lunch out my arse and mouth uncontrollably, I remember being glad for the hand basin next to the loo, because it meant I could do both at once without having to stick my head in the stinking bowl of filth. Win! What the hell had made me sick though? I'd eaten nothing unusual or unsafe. I'm vegetarian, so it wasn't spoiled meat off the street, and the rice at lunch had been cooked fresh (I think). Four or five more trips to the toilet and these thoughts had left my head. All thoughts had left my head. It was only about survival. With a chronic fever forcing water from my body, I knew I needed to stay hydrated, but nothing would stay down. Not 5mls, not 50mls, which unfortunately meant the anti-diarrhoea and nausea tablets I had didn't have time to take effect. My head soon began to float, and I was forced to crawl around the room as I feared passing out and cracking my head. It's probably lucky I did drag myself across the floor, because there were three occasions where everything went blank. Coming to, all alone in a room in a village somewhere was confusing. My mind wasn't operating properly. I was scared – which is unusual.

Transfixed by the pain, I remember smiling. "I asked for it," I thought, "the pain and the suffering." Then, I passed out again. The troubling thing was, each time I blacked out, I wasn't sure I'd wake up. This didn't stress me out all that much, I was more at peace than ever with the idea of death thanks to Buddhism, but I knew my wife might not be, so I bunkered down and decided to sit under a cold tap hoping to lower my body temperature and stop myself from passing out. Going half an hour without excreting bodily fluids, I decided to try and head to bed. Some hours later I woke up to a knock on my door. It was the motel manager checking what I wanted for breakfast. Slowly walking to the door, I remember his face as I opened it, "Sir, you are not looking well, what is wrong?" Explaining what had happened the man assembled a group of people to attend to my needs. A can of coke, a few biscuits, some medication and a loaf of bread later and I was out of the woods. Not wanting to alarm my wife, I didn't tell her what had happened, but I was glad to hear that her mum had survived a terrible scare that night.

Several months later, having recovered from her chemo, radiotherapy and what doctors found was meningitis (the thing that nearly killed her), I was curious to learn more about that specific night. "I thought I was gone, honestly, it was the worst time in all of it," said Twinkle. Not wanting to sound cuckoo, or as if I'd had anything to do with her recovery, I told Twinkle my own story of that night. Three years later (at the same time I'm writing this chapter), as my mother-in-law (a devout Christian) recounted this tale to her Buddhist friend Sanduni, she sounded unsurprised by what had happened. "Yes that is possible, we believe karma can be used in that way," said Sanduni.

On the surface, such an idea may sound fantastical, but there is some science to it, and that's why it sits comfortably within my beliefs around god, which again, to me is: the energy of all things. Physicists tell us that there is nothing in the universe that is not some form of energy. When we cook food, use Wi-Fi or listen to music we can see that energy may be transferred both through direct contact and invisibly. If we can send huge amounts of data and information via an invisible network of radio waves (Wi-Fi), why is it not conceivable that we may be able to transmit our thoughts (a form of energy) through the invisible network of energy that surrounds us?

Call me nuts, maybe I am, but Dr. Masaru Emoto has shown that human thoughts and speech can change the molecular makeup of water. His research has even illustrated how polluted and toxic water, when exposed to prayer and positive intention, can be altered and restored to the beautifully formed geometric crystals found in clean, healthy water. In fact, when Reverend Kato Hoki, chief priest of Jyuhouin Temple in Japan, offered an hour-long prayer over the Fujiwara Dam, he did just that: he purified the water. There may never be concrete proof of whether or not my thoughts and meditation had impacted Twinkle's health, but I guess that's why faith is part of every religion.

Faith, the mother of religion

Like it or not, believe it or not, I think we've barely scraped the surface when it comes to what the 100 billion neurons in our brain and 40 thousand neurons in our heart can do. A telling sign of this is the very fact that scientists didn't even know we had neurons in our heart until the 1990s. Something I think religions do, at their best (and this is something I've noticed about the happiest people of all faiths), is that they search the heart, not just the mind, for truth. Because that's what origin stories and the mythology surrounding religion forces us to ask: what does your heart tell you? Was Jesus born to a virgin mother? Will I receive 72 virgins in paradise? How much milk do I need to offer Murugan before he grants me a wish? What happens if I reach Nirvana? While most choose to see or seek absolute resolutions to such matters, I think the happiest followers let the unseen charm of faith and the unknown open their heart and mind, allowing them to examine and feel more of the world. What this reveals, or it has to me at least, is that there are no absolutes. No guarantees. We can't *know* god's plans. What he has seen. Jesus may have been born to a virgin mother, I might get 72 virgins, Murugan could grant my wish and Nirvana may be a place of perfect peace and happiness.

What I'd ask is: does it matter if all or none of these things are true if your heart tells you they are?

If it makes you happier, if it builds love and togetherness... Believe, believe, believe. But, and here's the part that stands in the way of humanity achieving its happiest state: if your beliefs harm others, ask yourself, 'would god want me damaging one of his creations?' Would he? Would Muhammad (PBUH), Buddha, Kamadeva, Jesus? Would anyone look upon that favourably? The solution to this absolutist, fundamentalist attitude, which spits in the face of the diversity god designed us with, is just to **leave a tiny space in your head with a '?', because there are infinite questions we don't and may never have answers to.** If we can admit this, if we can rid ourselves of the arrogance and ego of thinking we know everything, then we give ourselves a chance to learn and grow, which brings us closer to god. For god is truth.

On a flight from Salt Lake City to Kansas City in the US, that little '?' in the heads of a young couple sitting next to me was obviously burning hot. I'd been editing a video about the largest refugee camp on Earth – Bidi Bidi, in northern Uganda (which I'd recently visited) – when the woman next to me, Allison (who'd been staring at my computer screen), asked me what I was doing. As I looked across at Allison and her husband

A MAN UP A MOUNTAIN AND THE IDEA THAT PUT HIM THERE

Mark, I probably should have warned them of what I was about to say. But, then again, the truth should need no introduction.

"This girl Nisa who was 16-years-old was fleeing South Sudan with her mother, older brother and younger sister Nimala who was 8-years old," I said. "In their first week trekking through the bush to the Ugandan border their mother was raped, abducted and hasn't been seen since. In week two, the older brother was shot dead by South Sudanese militia right in front of the two sisters, who quickly fled. Lost, and without anyone to protect them, they hid under a tree for two days until they heard someone speaking their tribal dialect walking close by. These people were also fleeing as refugees – as were more than 3.5 million South Sudanese who have fled to neighboring countries since civil war broke out in December 2013. That night, four of the men who had offered to help the sisters ended up taking Nimala, tying her up and telling her to be quiet. They then gang raped Nisa. The men abandoned the girls in the early hours of the morning, leaving them in the middle of nowhere, with no one. Trapped, terrified, broken and confused, the pair hid in dense bush. Unable to mourn her pain, for risk of further upsetting her younger sister (who was still visibly shaken from the experience even when I met her four months later), Nisa took on the role of mother and carer, and eventually found some women who were headed to Uganda, as they'd originally set out to do." The look on Allison and Mark's face at this point was probably similar to your own – a mix of horror and disbelief. This was not an easy story to hear when Nisa sat in front of me sharing it, and it should absolutely eat away at our humanity. But it was about to get even worse.

"When I met Nisa, she told me they were walking for 28 days before they reached the refugee processing centre in Uganda," I continued telling Allison and Mark. "For the first time since they left their home, Nisa said she felt safe. But that didn't last long. When she was examined by doctors as part of her processing Nisa was told she was pregnant. 'But I did not want to have that child,' she told me. Unfortunately though, she was given the news that it was too late to have an abortion. 'I just wanted to go to school'. 'I am Christian, so I know it is wrong to kill my unborn baby, but I just want to be a child and to get a good education so I can help my country,' she said. 'That is why those men did this to me, because they do not have the knowledge, the spirit of how to do good by others, because they are not educated,' said Nisa. 'That is why I forgive them,' she told me. Nisa's wisdom and intelligence was beyond words. **She'd already forgiven the men who kidnapped her mother, killed her brother and raped her, not because she had to, but because somehow she knew that hating them would not help her or her country to heal.** It would not bring her happiness to see them suffer," I told the spellbound couple. "While I was meant to be there as a filmmaker, something inside me wouldn't let me just be OK with what she'd told me, so after our interview, I asked her if or how I could help her and her sister."

In tears by this point, Allison and Mark prompted me to continue, "So…?" they asked. "The math's didn't add up to me, if she'd been on the road for just 28 days, then why had local doctors told her it was too late to abort? Was it the strict religious beliefs in the area? Was it a case of 'too hard'? I knew in Australia it was safe and legal to have an abortion up to three and a half months into a pregnancy. Something felt off. But I was leaving Bidi Bidi the following day, so I quickly wrote and stashed a note and some cash in a jumper for Nisa, because she'd also said she was freezing cold at night, so leaving what warm clothing I had was the least I could do. I also gave Nimala my travel pillow, which was the first time I saw her traumatized face smile. The note I'd left told Nisa to buy a phone with the money I'd given her, so I could keep in touch.

To be honest, I assumed I'd never hear from her again. But low and behold, I was sitting in Dubai Airport when my phone rang. Nisa had proven yet again just how smart and resourceful she was.

That day I emailed Nisa's story to Marie Stopes International – a charity that provides family planning, contraception and safe abortion services in 37 countries around the world – including in far northern Uganda, nearby Bidi Bidi. I knew they'd give Nisa the frank assessment she needed, so I gave them her number and asked them to call Nisa to book an appointment. When the people from Marie Stopes got back to me they said they'd tried to contact Nisa, but her phone number was not connecting. I tried to call Nisa myself and there was nothing. Shit, I thought. Some days later she messaged me from a new number and said she'd got a new SIM card. Long story short, by the time she got in to see the women at Marie Stopes it was indeed too late to abort. If however, she had not changed her phone number and had been able to see them ten days earlier when they called her, she could have ended her pregnancy." "Oh wow!" said Allison. "How sad. We are actually

Mormons so we would normally look at this as going against our beliefs, but I guess Nisa's story shows that nothing is absolutely right or wrong."

For most Christians (and I've met a lot), abortion is a major point of contention that is most often answered like this: "well we are told we cannot kill, which means abortion is wrong, so my hands are tied." Forgetting (it seems) that their first two commandments were to "love the Lord thy God with all thy heart, might, mind, and strength" and "to love thy neighbour as thyself," I couldn't help but feel perplexed – what love did this show toward "thy neighbor" who felt they needed to have an abortion? What love did it show for Nisa who could have quite easily died in childbirth? And what love or faith did it show in god, whose clearly given us this ability to stop a child being born, because who knows, maybe Nisa's inability to raise him right might have made him the next dictator of South Sudan? Plus, with 7000 newborns dying each day, mostly from preventable causes, it's clear god (or we) aren't that worried about saving defenseless babies.

"What's horribly ironic," I continued telling the Mormon couple, "is that conservative Christians who typically vote to the conservative right actually kill millions of people when they elect guys like Trump." The couple looked perplexed. "When I was in Bidi Bidi and other refugee camps, the greatest fear among charities working there was that the US and other countries would follow the nationalist rhetoric at the time and would withdraw aid funding for the region, which many have since done. When you talk about policies or decisions that kill innocent babies (and adults), the choice to vote for a party who might outlaw abortion, rather than a party who supports those in most need in the world, is guaranteed to leave you with far more blood on your hands – if it is *all* lives you're concerned about, not just white ones."

"Wow. I'm speechless. I've never heard someone talk like this before," said Allison. "I didn't know, didn't ever think like that. I suppose there is some uncertainty, some grey in everything. I mean I couldn't say 'no that's wrong' to someone like that girl."

If there were one thing I could gift everyone, it would be that: the ability to **see every decision, belief and action as neither 100% right or 100% wrong.**

What humanity's dangerous cocktail of ego and religion is teaching, is unfortunately the opposite. There is no room for the '?' box in the minds of many followers, because they want to believe *their* god, *their* beliefs or *their* story of creation is right; as if that somehow validates their position with god, or assures them the splendours of heaven, nirvana or paradise.

Something that can draw us closer to god is sacrifice. All prophets and gurus have known it. That's why we see fasting, philanthropy, pilgrimage, prayer, patience, humility, chastity and silence as necessary and endemic aspects of faith. Conditioning our mind to see the wisdom and spirit that lies beyond what's easy and pleasurable is essential if we're to reach our happiest state. Abstaining from alcohol, sweets, food and money at various times each year; sharing what little wealth I have with others I meet in my travels; and forcing myself to endure 30-45 minutes of grueling exercise a day – during which time I pray and connect with god; are three key elements that bring me closer to god.

On the slopes of Batu Caves in Malaysia, I witnessed a million Hindus partake in one of the largest sacrificial rituals in the world – Thaipusam – which sees pilgrims walk barefoot for several kilometres before climbing 272 stairs to the temple of Lord Murugan, located in the middle of the ancient cave.

"Murugan, the god of courage, wealth and wisdom, defeated great demons using a spear named Vel, thus saving humanity," says Ravinatha Gurukkal, the Chief High Priest of Batu Caves Murugan Temple. "Hindu devotees pray to Murugan throughout the year, asking for help in various aspects of their lives, and vow to fulfil a pilgrimage during Thaipusam, if their wishes are granted. The pilgrims carry offerings that vary from bowls of milk to elaborate contraptions that can weigh up to 80kg known as 'Kavadi'. They often perform acts of self-sacrifice, piercing their skin with silver skewers that symbolise the Vel, or with hooks from which they hang fruits or bowls of milk. The ritual is intended to defeat the pilgrim's inner demons and gain the god's blessings."

Inviting me into the inner sanctum of the temple for our interview (which you can view on thehappiest.com) and taking me through the ritual of Thaipusam from start to end, what stood out from all the pomp and ceremony were Gurukkal's words, and his loving, peaceful, happy demeanor. This isn't to say the smoke being waved and water and milk being poured over various Hindu gods wasn't interesting, it was. And the level of sacrifice was next level. Most men and women had shaved orange scalps. One man wore wooden shoes with nails inserted in the soles as a self-penitence. Some bloke even pulled a wooden shrine attached with hooks to his back. I guess the white and red pottu/bindi on my forehead and the few prayers I offered over a candle was tame by comparison, but again, as Gurukkal tells me "there are many ways to free ourselves of 'aham' or ego as you say in English."

Said to predate the existence of water, dust and the first forms of life, Hinduism is often referred to as 'the eternal law', as it has no beginning and no end. While Western academics often label Hinduism as a complex fusion of ideas, difficult to call a religion, Gurukkal suggests that while it is open, embracing of other religions and deeply rooted in science, there is no religion with more clarity or direction on how to live a happy and peaceful existence.

"To treat one another with brotherly and sisterly love, is what Hinduism teaches us all to do," he says. "This means we must respect other religions. Even if you were to pass a mosque, pay your respects as it's a sacred ground to Muslims. Believe in the powers of other religions, even if it's not your own." Such an embracing vision meant that during Thaipusam, Batu Caves was littered with Muslims, Christians, Buddhists and Nones (non-affiliated believers, like me) all there to pay their respects to their Hindu friends or Lord Murugan himself. Maybe I could be Hindu, I thought. But how, with such a smorgasbord of bright and colourful deities, did their Chief High Priest see god?

"God is invisible, he has no form," Gurukkal tells me, despite being surrounded by bright-green walls covered with images of various gods. "All the gods that we worship today in Hinduism were all given their forms by mankind. All the gods have one thing in common and that is energy. Energy is god," he says, wobbling his head enthusiastically – I was probably doing the same. "Why we have all these forms to represent god is so that we're able to focus our energy with a visual. Because with the aid of a visual, we're able to better control our heart and mind," he continues. No doubt this is why so many use crosses, prayer beads and Buddha statues to centre their thoughts onto god. "If we're seeking our happiest state, what should we be praying about when we do connect with god?" I asked Gurukkal.

"Human beings need peace," he says. "But these days we're all too busy running after material possessions and money to find it. The issue is, once you earn your first million, you will want to earn your second, then third, and so on. So this out-of-control thirst for more and more is destroying the peace that appreciating god's gifts can bring. To find satisfaction and peace in life, we must understand that every action, whether good or bad, begins with a thought. Therefore we must pray and focus on being grateful for what we have. Only then will we find happiness within our mind and our life," he concludes.

If Gurukkal had remained the only Hindu I interviewed and this Malaysian Thaipusam the only festival I attended, who knows, maybe I'd have become Hindu. But when I travelled to India a few years later, as you've already read, things changed. The Hindu caste system, was evil incarnate. Dividing Hindus into Brahmins (priests, scholars and teachers), Kshatriyas (rulers, warriors and administrators), Vaishyas (agriculturalists and merchants), Shudras (laborers and service providers) and Dalits or Untouchables (who were considered the lowest form of life), this scheme stood in absolute opposition to the harmony and oneness Gurukkal preached. The Indian government may claim the caste system is a thing of the past, and perhaps in some places it is, but in the India I saw, the sickening lack of compassion and generosity between rich and poor told me it was very much alive and well.

While one wealthy businessman in Delhi told me "the groups originated from Brahma, the Hindu God of creation," it sounded more like a brilliant marketing ploy to keep the lower castes subdued and in-line. The ingenious system did this by telling the Untouchables, Shudras and Vaishyas that if they behaved honourably and well in this life, then they would come back as Kshatriyas or Brahmins in their next incarnation. The result of such divisive labels (as films like Divergent have shown) is an ungodly level of suffering, the likes of which overshadowed even the frightful inequality that characterised much of east-Africa and Asia. The blatant sexism, homophobia and lack of morals I observed within several communities also told me that Gurukkal's words and his peaceful happy aura were not shared by those Hindus who called the shots in India. People such as Baba Ramdev, a prominent guru with close ties to Prime Minister Narendra Modi, who, in 2015, told the press "homosexuality is not natural." That's not to say that Hinduism condones discrimination, but that same-sex relations go against the Vedas of Hindu scripture, he added. Ramdev's assertion however, is, contradicted by ancient temple carvings that openly show homosexuality, or a passage in the Vedas which says "Vikruti Evam Prakriti," which roughly translates to "What seems unnatural, is natural."

This perpetual quarrel over who is and who isn't equal in god's eyes is as damaging as it is cruel. I mean, **how would you feel, if who you were or how you were born was deemed wrong – not by god, but by self-serving human beings, who feel they have the right to discriminate and oppress on god's behalf?** While most want to justify or excuse such behaviour – claiming it's cultural or political conservatism, not religious – the argument could not be clearer. If you're opposed to homosexuals living their lives openly, then you're in the same camp as the Nazi's who felt Jews were ungodly, Joseph Kony who felt justified abducting and enslaving an army of 60,000 child soldiers because it was 'God's will', or the millions of men throughout history who have used religion to objectify and oppress women. Condemning anyone for matters over which they have no control – race, sex, skin colour or sexual orientation – is at best bullying and at worst, persecution that leads to suicide, depression and war.

One conversation that probably sums up hundreds of others I've had on the topic of LGBTQIA+ rights, was with Laura and Aaron Evans (the semi-progressive Mormons from chapter 7). It started in typical fashion: justify and or distance yourself from the discrimination. "In the doctrinal sense, as LDS (Latter Day Saints), no, they [same-sex couples] can't marry, but as a person I would still be kind, I would not treat them badly or like them less. Our son actually has a close friend who's gay and he's very supportive of him and we are as well," says Laura. "I actually grew up in a time when a lot of Mormons believed it was a choice, like this was not an innate quality in someone, it was just a sinful thing they were choosing to do, and so I think there's been a transition now where more and more LDS are realising, 'maybe I was wrong. Maybe this isn't a choice, maybe this really is who they are'. What's tricky is the LDS church teaches it's still wrong regardless of whether you choose to be that way or not, so not that the person's a bad person, but they just need to choose not to act on it. I think regardless of whether they do or not, the ideal is that they would be treated equal to anyone." But, but, but … **surely if someone is equal then they should have equal opportunities, equal rights, otherwise they are not equal!** No matter how kind or good your intentions are.

"Do you believe that Jesus would have shunned these people as most Christian groups have?" I asked. "Jesus taught that we should love everyone, that we should treat them with love and compassion," says Aaron. "I don't think there's an exception to that." "Doesn't that conflict with the church's belief though?" I butted in. "The decision [around LGBTQIA+ rights], or my faith, resides in a living being which is Jesus Christ, that ultimately he is the judge, he is ... and he's a perfect judge," continues Aaron. "Why are there so many things in the world, right? So many injustices," he asks rhetorically. "There's no consistent experience for us all. Her [Laura's] brother passed away at 17. I've met others who've experienced World War II and lived in Germany and the injustices of that time ... One thing that's common is everyone is going to experience adversity. I do, you do, everyone does." "Yes, but if you're part of a belief system that's causing that adversity, how does that make you feel? Happier?" I questioned. Aaron looks to Laura. Both are visibly uncomfortable. "I know I'm a pain in the arse," I say to ease the tension. "No, no, no, don't worry," they respond in sync. "I don't like anyone to feel like they're less or like they aren't being treated equally," says Laura, before Aaron interrupts. "Ultimately, in answer to your question, God is at the head and as..." "So why did he create gay people then?" I pushed. "Well, that's a good question," says Aaron. "That's a very good question," adds Laura. "These are all fair questions, they are."

"Does it make your marriage feel more special or sacred that they can't get married?" I asked. "Honestly, no," says Laura. "I mean, I can honestly tell you there's a lot of Mormons who disagree with that teaching [against marriage equality]." "If you were a leader of the LDS church, would you allow gay marriage?" I continued probing, searching for *their* thoughts – not that of the church. "I don't have the answer," says Laura. "If you shut your eyes and try and feel what God would tell you, what comes to you?" I asked, shutting my eyes. "Well, I guess..." Aaron pauses. "I'm not trying to get you in trouble," I said. "No it's fine," says Laura. "Me personally, I agree with you ... If I just took God totally out of the equation, that makes total sense. Why does it matter? Let whoever get married to whomever, it doesn't matter, we just want everyone to be happy and I'm totally with that, but I have to go back to my beliefs and say, 'OK, I believe in God, I believe we have a living prophet, and this is how they've interpreted the scriptures'. I don't think it was ever intended to hurt, I would say 50 years ago, they really felt like it [being LGBTQIA+] was a choice, and so I think I don't know where this is all going, but ... there's a lot of things in our church history that I don't agree with. But I don't need to have every piece fit to stay with it. I challenge you to find a church that has everything that fits perfect. I don't think there is one," concedes Laura.

"It's not my decision," says Aaron, in reference to what he'd do as LDS leader. "That's all I can say. In terms of the church, what you're asking is very core, because that's how we, as Mormons, are different." "It actually goes back to your very first question," says Laura. "You asked about the most important thing for our happiness and we spoke about families and the family proclamation, and I think that's part of it. The [LGBTQIA+] lifestyle doesn't quite work with that ... And yet, there's arguments of, 'Well, what about someone who can't have children? Do they automatically get excluded from that?'"

"I guess that's the question," I said. "Would god want us to exclude anyone?"

F*ck the asterisk *u

When I was thinking about how to write this chapter, what message I most wanted to convey, I kept coming back to this assumption most make of me that I am religious. When asked why I am not, I come back to one idea: **love can have no *asterisk. No terms and conditions.** For if we are to be one with god, then we must love all of him. Accept all of him. I think this is why Jesus, Muhammad (PBUH) and Buddha were prophets and leaders worth following – they called us to love unconditionally. That doesn't mean we have to love the *actions* of rapists, murderers or thieves, but we must love *them*, because they are as much a part of god as I am, which means they are as much a part of me as I am of them. That is what it means to be one with god. You surrender to his suffering, just as you surrender to his love.

But what if we could undo the suffering part? What if Buddhism, Hinduism, Islam, Christianity and all faiths got rid of their asterisks? What if these institutions got rid of their engendered oppression?

The sexism that means a woman can't be Pope, or that the first female rabbi was ordained only 3500 years after Judaism began. And what about Abdel-Qader Ali, who stomped on, suffocated and stabbed to death his 17-year-old daughter for becoming infatuated with a British soldier. "Death was the least she deserved. I don't regret it. I had the support of all my friends who are fathers, like me, and know what she did was unacceptable to any Muslim that honours his religion," the Iraqi father told reporters. Even in America, the Southern Baptist Convention declares in its faith and mission statement: "A wife is to submit herself graciously to the servant leadership of her husband." If this is what god has told his messengers, then (as I said earlier) god, must be made of the same horrible misogynist 'He' energy we've seen dominate human history. That, or the weakness of man has distorted god's intentions?

For much the same reason, **classism** continues to plague many religions, but most notably Hinduism. Though it would be remiss of me not to mention the many impoverished and often homeless Christians, Buddhists and Muslims I've met who have told me they feel too ashamed to go to their church, mosque or temple, because people look at them unfavourably, as if they're impure or not worthy of being in 'god's house'. I often wonder, if churches, temples and mosques stopped spending billions on illustrious buildings and decor in order to 'one up' their competitors (in the name of ego), and invested that money in helping the poor and disenfranchised, would we see more people believing in and worshipping god?

The LGBTQIA+ community has also been an ongoing target of religious hatred. Described as "a cancer on society" by one Muslim I interviewed, or "just wrong" by many Hindus, Buddhists, Christians and Jews I met. Lesbian, gay, bisexual, transgender, queer or questioning, and intersex people are outright denied their happiest state by these establishments, which instead of being beacons of tolerance, love and acceptance, perpetuate the awful persecution their founders suffered: including the Jews/Romans who killed Jesus, Pharaoh/Egypt who sought to slay Moses, and Meccans who forced Muhammad (PBUH) to flee. There's also the great anti-Buddhist persecution initiated by Tang Emperor Wuzong of China, which arguably continues today in places like Tibet.

If this hypocrisy and distortion of god's intentions frustrates me, and I don't belong to any specific faith (I don't have skin in the game), I wondered just how much it must upset those believers who don't wish to put an *asterisk at the end of every conversation about love or equality that reads *except for these people. And yes, * usually means *LGBTQIA+, *women, *the poor, *other religions or *non believers.

"Religion is something I don't enjoy," says Pastor Brad Chilcott, a man I've long revered for his work with refugees, through his organisation Welcoming Australia. "Religion is a series of institutions, or rituals, or intellectual truths that help you make sense of the world, and give you a sense of identity and your place in the world. But for me, I want something more than that. I believe that I have a relationship with a living God, and I believe that's interactive and experiential, and is something beyond just academics."

"The story of Jesus coming as a baby, born to a working-class family, working a trade and then spending three years as a teacher who touched the socially untouchable, welcomed the outcast and included those the leaders of his religion rejected is, as Christians often say, the story of 'God moving in to the neighbourhood'. His death as a criminal, according to Christian theology, paved the way for all people to be welcomed unconditionally into the life and love of God, removing the barriers between humanity and deity imposed by religious dogma."

But the church established in the name of Jesus has struggled to fulfil the promise of the new way of life that his example represented, says Brad (during an interview you can watch on thehappiet.com). "Despite his request that his followers 'love others the way I have loved you', and the Apostle Paul's assertion that there is 'no longer male nor female, slave nor free person, for all are one in Christ Jesus', the church has a long history of finding ways to exclude women, divorcees, people of colour and those deemed 'sinful' from full inclusion in the life and leadership of Christian community and institutions," he continues. "Apartheid, anti-semitism, slavery, the massacre of people of Muslim faith, banning interracial marriage, domestic violence and the subjugation of women, child abuse and the destruction of Indigenous cultures have all found theological justification in various incarnations of the church throughout Christian history across the world."

Too liberal for the hard-line Christians, and too Christian for many hard-line liberals, Brad faces a similar dilemma to Jesus, who was trapped somewhere between the Synagogue and the prostitutes. Just as Jesus did two millennia ago, Brad has sided with the ill, the lost, the forgotten in society – those whom his abundant love could serve. "People tend to want to use religion to define who's in and who's out. It helps them make sense of the world. But Jesus' style was not like that at all. **Jesus' style was that he turned the outsiders into insiders, and he taught all of us to do the same.** He intentionally aligned himself with the people that society pushed to the outer. So when we interpret our Christian faith in any way other than that, we're not following in the footsteps of Jesus."

Embracing refugees, the destitute and non-believers is one thing, but when Brad's Adelaide-based church *Activate*, decided to allow LGBTQIA+ people into their community and leadership, it was forced to split from the Australian Christian Churches (ACC) denomination, which has more than 1000 churches nationwide.

"The next frontier in the battle for full inclusion is being waged by the LGBTQIA+ community and their allies and is seen by many Christian leaders as an existential threat to orthodox Christianity and the church. We've had members of the LGBTQIA+ community as part of our church for quite a long time, including in leadership positions. We knew from the outset that this was outside the rules and the position on human sexuality the ACC has," explains Brad. "Initially we hoped we may find common ground, but when the ACC joined the Marriage Alliance, an anti-marriage equality group, that was a big red flag for us. It went against our understanding of Christianity, so we parted ways."

Church leaders may have the 'best of intentions' when it comes to trying to help LGBTQIA+ people says Brad, but they often fail to sufficiently reflect on how the things they say might hurt. "They say 'We are welcoming, we want people to come and feel at home and feel loved', but there is a limitation or terms to their involvement. That might sound conceptually nice to the straight, married pastor... but if you're the person on the end of that message, it can sound like 'You're half welcome here. You're a bit welcome here,'" says Brad, who stresses Activate's support of LGBTQIA+ people is not "despite our faith, but because of it." "If standing in solidarity with the excluded in society was good enough for Jesus, it's good enough for us," he says. "It is time for the church to extend the gift of love to LGBTQIA+ people, as much as it has to women and people of colour – albeit often with great reluctance – so that they too may experience the 'thrill of hope as a weary world rejoices'. A world that is weary of division, of hatred, of inequality and exclusion. A world that is weary of a church that looks to the self-sacrificial love of Jesus for guidance and then fights to maintain its cultural privilege and legal right to discriminate against those it is uncomfortable with."

One of the more common beliefs Brad says he hears to justify the hatred peddled at LGBTQIA+ people, and I've heard it more times than

I can recall, is that being gay is a choice that is unnatural and therefore ungodly and immoral. What more than a century of scientific research into sexual orientation has shown is that being Lesbian, Gay, Bisexual, Transgender, Queer, Intersex or Asexual (LGBTQIA+) is part of the normal biological range of human sexuality. Just as there are genetic regions that determine hair colour, height or the size of your lips, research conducted by the NorthShore Research Institute in the US found clear links between sexual orientation and two specific regions of the human genome, causing lead scientist Alan Sanders to declare that these findings "erode the notion that sexual orientation is a choice." The study, which analysed the genetic code of 409 pairs of gay brothers for common markers found that Xq28 and 8q12 were the two regions that were most frequently identified among the 818 gay men. Seventy-six-year-old neuroscientist Simon LeVay said, "This study knocks another nail into the coffin of the 'chosen lifestyle' theory of homosexuality."

Reviewing more than 500 studies and papers in human sexuality, the Academy of Science of South Africa (ASSAf) says it is clear that the so-called 'gay gene' is completely natural, and this is why **the percentage of homosexual people remains consistent across all societies, at 5-8%**. That's because biological gender is set in the first trimester of pregnancy, and psychological gender is set in the second, when the child in the womb is exposed to varying levels of testosterone. I suppose that's why same-sex tendencies have been observed amongst 1500 animal species, including lions, dolphins, deer, crabs, worms, giraffes, penguins and one of humanity's closest relatives, the dwarf chimpanzee, which is entirely bisexual. To those who feel there has been a 'sudden' or 'unnatural' spike in LGBTQIA+ people (as many religious figures told me), that is simply an illusion, born of two factors: more media coverage on gay rights, and the 5-8% of LGBTQIA+ people actually feeling safe enough to come out publicly.

While many societies still discriminate legally or socially, change in public opinion across the world has in fact come remarkably swiftly: 15 years ago, no countries allowed gay marriage, now 19 do (the nineteenth being Catholic Ireland, which racked up a vote of 62% in favour recently). What this points to is not only the rise of pro-equality millennials who are blind to differences, but it also tells me change in the church is inevitable. For if faith groups don't adopt the selfless, generous, boundless loving spirit of Jesus, Buddha, Muhammad (PBUH) and other prophets, they'll simply die out. How do I know this? Because I know I am not alone in my thoughts.

The religiously unaffiliated, called 'Nones' (like me), are now the second largest religious group in North America and most of Europe. France, the Netherlands and New Zealand will also have a majority secular population soon, and the United Kingdom and Australia will shortly lose Christian majorities. Religion is rapidly becoming less important than it's ever been, even to people who live in countries where faith has affected everything from rulers and borders, to architecture and music. There have long been predictions that religion would fade from relevancy as the world modernizes. What is surprising is that recent surveys are finding it's happening startlingly fast (particularly in the West). As a 'None', you may assume I support this, but the truth is, I don't.

I feel sick to the core that greedy evil men have bent and perverted the words and actions of prophets. It upsets me that **religions have failed to adapt and evolve as humanity has propelled itself ever forward, opening its heart and mind to ideas of equality, justice, science and acceptance for all**. I'm particularly angered because the hypocrisy and *asterisks associated with religion are turning people away from the love, generosity and community that faith and a relationship with god can bring. What this is giving rise to is a callous self-reinforcing system called materialism. That emptiness within us, that religion told us could be filled through selfless service and belief in something bigger than our own ego, is now being replaced by sophisticated marketing campaigns that tell us wholeness can be found in a new TV, Jeep or diamond ring. 'If only I had *that thing* I'd be more complete', we foolishly think, as false-prophets profit from our spiritual desolation.

Asking Brad how and where religion went so wrong, and what the solution is, he told me it was not the words or life of Jesus or other religious figures that was the problem. "It's people taking their own value system, their own self interest, their own sense of insecurity and fear, and imposing that on a religious framework and then using that as an excuse to be horrible to one another. That's what is causing the problems in the world today. People – not prophets," says Brad.

Over the years, Brad says Jesus' radical idea of a love without limits, acceptance without question and a world without suffering, has been overcome by claims to ultimate truth, and a want to go to heaven.

"We have turned Christianity into something that is more about a disembodied afterlife than about the here and now, something that makes the world better today. That is, I think, a misunderstanding that Christians have had, but it's also influenced the way people see Christians, as a faith who are not invested in making their community better or happier, but instead are more interested in getting people to sign up to their religion, to sit in a seat every Sunday and make sure their soul goes to heaven when they die." As Brad and other religious figures have often confessed, the problem with promising people their reward in heaven is they're liable to sit on their asses here on Earth, doing stuff all, hoping they'll somehow grow wings.

With a huge number of friends from a range of faiths or no faith at all, Brad says any who journey towards reflecting the character of god, "acting in a way that shows compassion, togetherness, a love for the natural diversity He has given us, I think it will lead to happiness, otherwise I wouldn't be a part of all this. There are enough challenges in being a religious leader, a charity worker, or an activist, that if it wasn't a source of inner peace and happiness then you wouldn't do it. To me, hope is the great provider of smiles, or the great provider of happiness. It means that when something is challenging that you can get up the next day and think, 'Today is a new day, tomorrow is a new tomorrow and I can go into this day knowing that good things are ahead,'" concludes Brad.

Actively living out his unadulterated faith beliefs every minute of every day as a husband, father, Pastor and political figure, Brad is a timely reminder of the clarity and happiness that can be found in following the timeless actions of prophets, rather than the impure, often dated words followers have handed down. When we look at the life of Jesus and Muhammad (PBUH) for instance, we see clearly that they were revolutionary leaders of their time, driven by truth, love and kindness. Jesus himself flat out rejected the status quo and challenged the authority of religious leaders and politicians, and urged his followers to do the same: to ask questions, to demand justice, and to stress their desire for equality and freedom. He did this by railing against the synagogue, which had in his mind become more focused on rules and regulations than people or love – the religious leaders who preceded him had turned 10 commandments into 600 laws. It's for this reason, I think, that Jesus seemed to find such comfort in disobeying social norms: in touching lepers, letting prostitutes wash his feet or intentionally healing people on the Sabbath, because he knew it would violate Jewish law. Jesus even allowed women to follow him – a complete 'no-no' at the time – as it was commonly believed that girls could not learn and that you were only born female because you did not mature completely in the womb.

Following suit, in his final sermon in 632 AD, Prophet Muhammad (PBUH) stood firmly against the established power structures of the day as he declared complete equality amongst all humanity: "O people. Your Lord is one and your father [Adam] is one. An Arab has no superiority over non-Arab, nor a non-Arab has any superiority over Arab, also white has no superiority over black nor does black have any superiority over white, except by piety and righteousness. All humans are from Adam and Adam is from dust."

Not only did Muhammad (PBUH) literally fight against the tyrannical rule of kings, queens and emperors in battle, but upon defeating them, he lifted slaves from the gutter and welcomed outcasts into the community – tearing down the divisive cultural and political structures that were often required to rule.

Looking extensively at the lives of both Jesus and Muhammad (PBUH), I find it hard, near impossible, to imagine either of them not joining Brad and others in welcoming gay and lesbian people into their congregations. Some may disagree of course (and you're welcome to) because yes, the Bible and Quran do say 'man and woman' when referring to marriage, but remember, Jesus and Muhammad (PBUH) didn't write these books, men did. They also changed them repeatedly – and we all know how Chinese whispers ends.

What I feel such texts, written a couple of thousand years ago, don't take into consideration is what Jesus or Muhammad (PBUH) would have felt or said if they were alive today. If they had the knowledge we do – that around 5-8% of people are born LGBTQIA+ – what would they think? Would they be on the front lines of pro-equality marches, as they were in their own time? Or would they persecute LGBTQIA+ people for being made 'wrong' by god, who by the way 'made us in his image' according to Christianity, Judaism, Islam and a host of other faiths. So does that mean god was or is a little bit gay? Or are we to believe that LGBTQIA+ people are somehow the devil's doing? That all the lifesaving doctors, volunteers, researchers, writers, artists, teachers and TV personalities who belong to this community are in fact evil? Simply

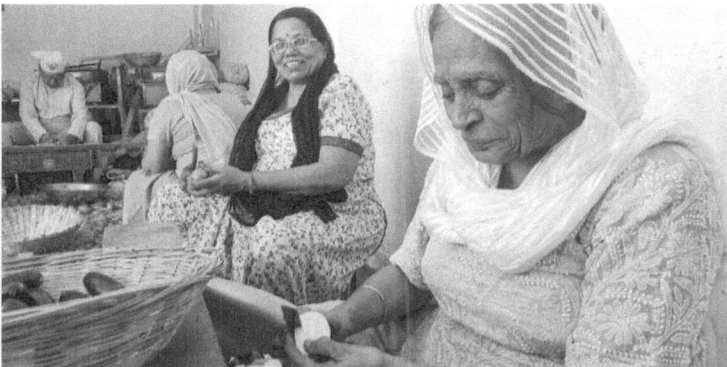

Ranvir (Pg 420). Amita (right) and Rajathi cutting vegetables at Gurudwara Bangla Sahib (Pg 420).

Brad (second from left at the front) attending the Adelaide launch of Australian Christians for Marriage Equality. Brad at Multicultural Australia's Luminous Lantern Parade event.

People waiting to be fed at Gurudwara Bangla Sahib in Delhi, India.

because they don't fit into the archaic definition of 'man', 'women' or 'marriage' perpetuated by religion.

The missing piece

"There was a woman at the time of the prophet, peace be upon him (PBUH), who cleaned the mosque," says Islamic faith leader, Saara Sabbagh. "Now nobody knew her name, and one day she passed away, and the prophet asked 'What happened to the lady?' And they said to him, 'She passed away'. 'So why didn't you tell me she passed away, I would have led her funeral', said the prophet, to which his companion replied, 'We didn't think you would care as nobody knew her'. And he turned around and said, 'Do you know who she was in the eyes of God?'"

What I think this story asks us to consider, and what I'm questioning too, is **who are we to judge another on god's behalf?** And how dare any of us deny the right for any one of god's creatures to live their happiest life?

"At the end of the day, there are so many paths to the creator. It's up to each of us to find our journey. We [religious people] can't claim to own the way, we must let people discover their own," says Saara, who was born and raised in Beirut, before fleeing to Australia due to the Lebanese Civil War. "Acceptance of other religions, and non-believers, is central to Islam. At the time of the prophet we saw him actually living with the Christians and the Jews. The Christians came and worshipped in the mosque. His people went and sought refuge in a church ... Because the search for happiness or contentedness or a more purposeful way of living is the quest of every human being. Muslim or non-Muslim. We're just using our toolbox, while a Buddhist uses theirs, Christians theirs, atheists theirs, agnostics theirs. Why is it today that we see the 'other' so differently? Why is it that we suddenly can't live together? That we can't accept that there are multiple paths to the divine? Is it the religion that's at fault, or is it something within us that has changed? I would argue it's something within us," says Saara. "And that's based in ego."

In Islamic tradition, there is nothing standing between you and the divine, except your ego, says Saara. "So your ego is your false sense of I, which the consumer world has now manifested globally. To eliminate the 'I' is the journey of a Muslim," she says. The tool Islam tells us we must use to do this is jihad. "Jihad is a very powerful and meaningful word because it means to struggle with your internal self, with your ego. The word jihad means to battle, to struggle, both with the internal and external. External jihad is when you protect your family or yourself from physical harm. That's the easy one, because it's clear cut. The internal jihad is the higher jihad, and it's more complicated, it's more nuanced. Because it's battling your ego. It's deciphering whether you have arrogance and how to overcome your arrogance. Whether you have traits of selfishness and how to overcome those traits. That is why we fast and refrain from speaking – to tame the ego."

Why is it most will have never heard of the term internal jihad? Why does our mind think 'terrorist' when we hear 'jihad'? Saara says the answer is the same reason the Islamic tradition has been going through its "dark ages."

"Our scholars have been saying that for the past hundred years or so, that we've lost the strength of our spiritual tradition. Today there's just this exoteric manifestation of faith. So within Islam, for the past century, all we've been concentrating on is the outer form: headdress, our prayer, dress code, a man's beard, and so on. The other reason our scholars say **Islam is in the state it's in today is because we've taken women out of the equation.** I'm not saying that because I am a woman, male scholars have said the place of women as scholars and leaders must be restored, because we have lost female input into this discourse, and women innately carry mercy. The word for womb in Arabic even means mercy, which is the name of God. God's name is the Most Merciful. But now we are seeing people leave the faith because there's no gentleness, no mercy in the religion, because of this emphasis on the external rigid form, which is devoid of the feminine energy of compassion."

Ostracised by her faith, oppressed by her community and targeted by Islamophobic abusers, the chances of a Muslim woman finding her happiest state seems slim in the modern context. Adversity though, if we let it, does have a strange way of drawing us closer to god, says Saara.

"The first time I experienced happiness was after the loss of my mother," she says. "I was 14, and it was through that pain, that tragedy, and the darkness that I was able to emerge with a feeling of immense peace and contentment. I was able to put life in perspective and I realised it wasn't my external circumstances that defined my internal state. So at 14, I was able to see that if I found inner peace, whatever happens on the outside, my internal state was unshakeable and, from that moment on, I realised happiness or contentment was not about the external factors of life."

Fasting from consumerism for a year in 2015 and heading to Syria to study the spiritual side of Islam alongside Dr. Rufaida Habash in 2001 (and several times since), Saara says it is when we strip back our wants and needs that we reveal our happiest state. "Why do people with less, give more? Why is it that those who were struggling to make ends meet were the ones who would open up their homes offering all they had and not worrying about the next day? It's because they put their trust in something beyond themselves. They knew they were not the ones providing their food for the next day, so they had this immense trust that 'God will provide for me, and God will provide for the others'. I found that people who had this deep sense of faith, also felt a deep sense of community, that there's no such thing as 'what is mine'. It's ours. Everything is 'ours'. **Trusting in a higher power I think lets us see that we are a 'we' and not an 'I.'"**

Without this connected 'we' culture, Saara says humanity will continue to priorities the external (things or how we look) over the internal (love, generosity, forgiveness), leaving us with a gaping hole we just cant seem to mend. "We try to fill it with consumerism, but still the hole is there." And according to Islam, the hole will remain unless we find what we are doing here, where we came from and why we exist. "I understand that God may not fill that hole for everyone," says Saara. "But we've gone in the other direction and taken God out of the equation entirely."

Believing in a god full of goodness and love might not be everyone's cup of tea, but for many like Saara, the unconditional nature of this relationship acts like a security blanket. And if you've ever observed a child cuddled in their mother's arms, you'll notice they're never afraid to be their crazy, loud, outspoken self. "Knowing I won't be rejected by God allows me to be courageous, because people who are beloved by God are in a state of bliss, and are fearless," says Saara, who boldly seeks and speaks truth – god's words.

"I completely reject the imposition of a dress code as a woman. Because people have said in the past and it's usually interpreted by men that a woman's dress code is about protecting her from abuse and sexual assault and rape. I reject that completely. Rape and sexual abuse are acts of violence and have nothing to do with a woman's dress code," says

Saara, who is wearing a cream hijab and full length black dress. "Babies are raped. Eighty-year-old women sitting at home are raped. It has nothing to do with what they wear. I feel very passionately about this, and it's a complete misuse of the purpose of our dress code. Complete! And it's seen from a patriarchal lens. So I reject that completely. It's demeaning and it's putting the onus on the woman yet again."

How can women feel safe, let alone happy, when sexual misdeeds are justified, she says. "There's also a lot of misplaced emphasis in Muslim communities about entering paradise. There's a great Sufi master by the name of Rabi'ah al-Adawiyah, who I love dearly. She was a poet and a spiritual master. She said, 'Oh God, if I worship You for fear of hell, then burn me in it. And if I worship You in hope of paradise, then exclude me from it. But I worship You for your own sake, therefore grudge me not your everlasting Beauty'. This is the higher realm of conversation, which unfortunately the Muslim world has moved away from. Because to me, aiming for paradise and keeping away from hell fire, is not seeing The One behind them both," says Saara, echoing Brad's sentiments.

Speaking to Saara just a week after Australia voted on marriage equality, which eventually passed 62% yes to 38% no, I was curious to hear her thoughts on the topic, particularly given so many Muslims in Western Sydney voted no despite their god being the 'Most Merciful', and despite this population knowing exactly how it feels to be unjustly persecuted. "We live in a secular democratic society, and therefore, of course, people have the right to live according to their own set of values, so there isn't an issue there. But then you put a faith hat on, and it can be tricky, because from a faith perspective, we believe that God created man and woman to be together ... so people who voted 'no' possibly felt like they were being asked from a faith perspective. Those who voted 'yes' maybe felt more like they were being asked as a citizen of a secular democracy. It depends how the question was received," says Saara, who seemed uncomfortably reluctant to ostracise the Islamic or Australian community with any sort of definitive answer. "Should it matter how they interpreted the question? What are your thoughts, personally?" I probed. "For me, you need to go back to the premise that God is all-loving, all-compassionate, all-wise, all-knowing, right? That **I do not know what God knows**, and I trust what God has revealed, and so, with that premise, you have to come from a place of non-judgement and compassion, and see where the law fits into that. It's not black and white. And that's why Muslims have mixed opinions about it." "Yes, but what are your thoughts? Do you agree with same-sex marriage?" I pushed. "If I'm being asked as a Muslim, then I go back to my value system, and I don't. It [same-sex marriage] doesn't exist [in Islam]. But if I am being asked as an Australian, then of course I believe they should marry. Do you see what I'm saying? There's a difference. But I feel I can comfortably hold both views simultaneously, without contradiction," she says, before adding a kind of *asterisk on her own thoughts. "But the Muslim community's very much behind the eight-ball when it comes to these conversations. Very much behind the eight-ball. The wider community is having conversations around gender as being non-binary and yet the Muslim community is struggling to discuss the complexities that come with an open secular society."

Saara's reluctance to publicly support same-sex marriage (as Brad had), was, in my opinion, less about her holding an *asterisk that read *LGBTQIA+ people, and more about her much longer, more calculated, deeper path to affect change. As a well-known figure in the Islamic community, Saara is able to influence hundreds, if not thousands of hearts and minds. To risk losing that, by speaking out on such a divisive topic, would destroy her chances of slowly but surely moving her religion toward a more loving, peaceful centre that will let all people enjoy a happier state.

"What would Muhammad (PBUH) think of all this? If he was alive today, what would he write if he had just one tweet?" I asked Saara. "Oh. I don't know. That's an interesting question," says Saara. "Something to do with love. Actually, no. You know what? He'd be a social justice advocate. Actually, he'd be in the forefront of reform and justice, and if he was in Australia right now, he'd be standing alongside Indigenous leaders in their struggle. He wasn't all about just peace and love, he was about reform and change." When I asked why the Islamic community wasn't doing this, why they were silent on women's rights, LGBTQIA+ rights, indigenous rights and other social justice areas, she said it was because people had forgotten who Muhammad (PBUH) was.

"We mustn't forget how he was as a person, as a husband, as a father, as a leader, as an activist, as a prophet … he was revolutionary. He was revolutionary with compassion and mercy. He wasn't a revolutionary because he went to war or took over countries as has been said. He won hearts because of his heart. People embrace Islam because of his condition, not because of his power or wealth. He was a simple man who slept on the floor, who ate barley, a simple man who practised what he preached. He had the choice of being a king on a throne, but he chose to be a simple man because he wanted to feel for the people." Because he knew love was what bound us to God, says Saara.

"Love cannot be faked. It is the greatest power. Rumi says, 'My religion is love'. He also says that God has been in love with love since the beginning of time and only love will suffice him. I believe beyond religion and beyond culture and beyond countries and beyond even ancient wisdom, beyond everything, there is a place that we can come to that doesn't require anything else but to become vulnerable and to connect and to express love, and it takes a lot of energy and openess to do that. But I think when we get there, that's what's going to change us – love – because if we really love one another, we wouldn't hurt one another," Saara concludes.

What if god was one of us?

What seems easier? What I love about being a 'None' is I'm not beholden to words or actions I don't agree with. If I don't want to hurt someone, I can simply choose not to. I'm not part of a team. I don't need to toe the line. I am not complicit in causing unnecessary oppression and suffering. I can think for myself and love without *asterisks – as I believe god intended us to. Another person who shares a similar view, despite us arguing quite a bit about god, religion and the origins of man, is my editor, Andrew. "The absence of organised religion in my life puts me in control," the 70-year-old staunch atheist tells me. "I am responsible, or, at the very least, complicit in world events from environmental destruction to the waging of wars. I can be persuaded by good argument to change my ways because my worldviews are not carved in stone but rather written in wet sand. **My commitment is to what's right and what's right changes with time.** I do not have all the answers, and because I know that, I am always willing to listen, to be persuaded and to change, which would be less likely were I chained to a set of rigid, imposed beliefs."

The pool of atheists I could have chosen to write about is endless, I've met and interviewed hundreds, but to this day Andrew remains the happiest – and that's what I was seeking. So, what role had religion, or the lack thereof, played in shaping his unnaturally optimistic disposition? How did he forgive his business partner who stole millions from him? Why does he do good if there's no threat of heaven or hell? How did he feel about gays, women, and other dejected creatures of god?

Born in Pune, India in 1948, Andrew soon moved to Kolkata where he lived until he was sent to boarding school in Darjeeling at the age of nine. The great 'religious' influence in his life, Andrew says, was his father, a devoutly religious man who prayed on his knees, read from his well-worn Bible every morning and evening and went to church every Sunday and every holy day. "He was Irish Catholic," says Andrew. "So when he fell for a Catholic convent girl they quite naturally went to the Catholic bishop of Bangalore (where they lived) and announced their intention to get married. The bishop pushed a contract towards them and my dad asked what it was. It was, said the bishop, an agreement to bring up any children of the union as Catholic. 'I can't sign that', said my dad, 'I don't know what my children will want to be'. 'If you don't sign it', said the bishop, 'then you can't get married in our church'. My mum and dad walked out of the Catholic church and into the welcoming arms of the Anglicans who made no such demands."

When his dad died, Andrew's death notice in the paper read: 'To my dad, who showed me the paths to heaven and to hell and loved me even though I forged my own'. "You see, despite his extreme religiosity, my dad never attempted to implant his religious views on anyone. On Sundays and other holy days he would rise early and get himself off to church. If we wanted to go we needed to get ourselves up and ready to go and the consequences of any reluctance on our part were absolutely zero. All my father showered me with was unconditional love and total acceptance."

At 13, Andrew decided he was an atheist, and in the almost 60 years since, he's never wavered from that conviction. "An atheist is merely a person who has seen no evidence of a creative god. To me, god and the devil are concepts. Both live within me. Everything good I attribute to the god within and everything bad to the devil. They are the different moods of the same person, but because of my ridiculously optimistic disposition I have spent more time praising god than cursing the devil."

While he didn't inherit his father's beliefs, Andrew says he did absorb his fantastically strong moral compass – a very necessary tool to reach our happiest state. "The mere thought of doing wrong to anyone is an anathema to me. **I constantly seek to do good not because of any fear of a vengeful god but because doing good makes me feel good.** I'm selfish that way!" he laughs. "You know how the only people who can quit a bad habit are those who decide for themselves that they want to quit, and without that conviction quitting is almost impossible? Well, happiness is achieved with a similar bargain. Only when you are living life on your terms and not by rules dictated to you, can you be at peace with your choices. And peace is the great precursor to happiness."

Religion is merely a way of life, a set of guidelines to live by, says Andrew, who believes problems arise when absolutes are included in the directions. "Every person has a religion, it's just that some people pick up a rule book written by someone else, and others write their own," he says. "The problem with picking up someone else's rule book is that you're denied the opportunity to alter the rules as you journey through life, while if you're the author of your own rules, then you're free to rewrite them as often as you like."

Interestingly, I think it's actually people not wanting to go to the effort or not knowing how to write their own rules or find their own hope (in humanity or the world) that seems to be drawing some people back to religion in recent times. "They see or hear hope or this sense of moral superiority in followers and naturally they want that too, so they say 'ok, I'll try that, I'll believe that,'" says Andrew, echoing my thoughts. The church also seems to have become one of the few remaining places where the everyday person can feel valued. The problem is, modern society (led by big business, which puts profit before people) has continued to tell more and more people that their job and who they are as a salesman, butcher, builder, hairdresser and so on is unimportant. It's not valuable. They are simply a replaceable cog in the giant capitalist machine we've come to call society. "We're seeing this new brand of believer, who seems to be looking at the church as a way out. A way to feel valued or superior or hopeful, and that's sad I think, that people blindly adopt someone else's beliefs rather than forge a life that lets them find or feel this stuff organically."

"Does religion promote happiness?" Andrew asks rhetorically, before answering his own question. "Only in the way that drugs do, by providing an escape from reality. Would I ban religion if I could? Of course not, but I would forbid it being imposed on children and allow people to decide for themselves, without coercion, what they want to believe. Would I ban drugs if I could? Of course not, because, like religion, many people need them to make sense of their lives."

While our happiest state might be one where people are simply left to believe what their life experiences revealed to them, I do see religion as a beautiful way to ensure we meet morality and goodness along the way. Arguing with Andrew that religion gave the world morals and hope and charity, what he tells me is: we are savages no more, we've evolved a higher mind, and can learn to be kind, without the threat of god to punish us.

"When we see that there are something like 7.5 billion parts to god – each of us – and we have the power to punish ourselves, or others, or this planet, then it becomes obvious that what you 'believe' doesn't matter a hoot, it's what you *do* that dictates your reality," says Andrew. "My father had a complex set of beliefs, but what he did – love unconditionally and be totally non-judgemental – is what truly defined him. It didn't matter *why* he did what he did, because only what he *did* mattered. There were many instances when I could have been estranged from a devout parent. The first was when I became an atheist, but he met my difference with total acceptance. Then, when my parents thought I might be gay, he said to my mother (she told me years later), 'If he's homosexual so what? He's still our son'. Finally, when I made my first wife pregnant before marriage at a time when pre-marriage pregnancies were generally frowned upon, my father said, 'well at least we know he's not gay and now we've got a grandchild to look forward to!'"

What organised religion does, says Andrew, is it stops us from learning, keeps us ignorant of developments and, ultimately, it is ignorance and the failure to adapt that will result in the end of humanity. "The idea of a creative god is a beautiful idea to cling to, and so is the idea of there being a tangible Father Christmas or Tooth Fairy, but when the alleged mandates of this imaginary being are used to oppress people, the source of these 'rules' must be questioned, and the divinity of their power rejected," he says. "Anything or anyone claiming a higher/superior path is dangerous. Personally, I have always seen myself as one with beggars and kings. I learned at school that **'It is the last and final test of a gentleman to be of service to those who can be of no possible use to him.'"**

To Sikh more

One of few places I have found such gentlemen (and women) working for those who can be of no benefit for them, is Gurudwara Bangla Sahib, a prominent Sikh house of worship in Delhi, India. There, the moment I set foot in the door, I felt the presence of god. He was living in the wrinkly weathered hands of 87-year-old Amita and 64-year-old Rajathi, who were two of the volunteers preparing food for the 15,000 hungry mouths that the temple fed for free every single day! You could literally see and smell god in each life-giving bite the thin, brittle souls consumed. But that's not entirely surprising. In 1664, the eighth of ten Sikh gurus, 8-year-old Guru Har Krishans gave aid and fresh water to victims of a smallpox epidemic that was raging in Delhi at the time. The young Guru, who used water from the well of a wealthy ruler's property (which was transformed into Gurudwara Bangla Sahib in 1783), is said to have healed thousands before ultimately succumbing to the disease himself. Today, a large pool that sits at the centre of the temple is said to contain the same healing water Guru Krishan used.

After dipping my feet in the holy pond and spending some time making naan bread for the needy, I asked our volunteer guide, Ranvir Sharma, what Sikhism could teach us about finding our happiest state. Speaking at 300 plus words a minute and barely pausing to breathe, Ranvir's big bushy eyebrows and black turban bobbled back and forth frantically, almost hypnotically, as he told me that it is what we do that counts. "We must act," he says rapidly. "Because **an idea is neither negative nor positive. It's how you apply it**. Look at this [he shows me the packed dining room], if the Guru had this idea to feed people and he does so for positive purpose of serving the under-nourished and oppressed, then we see happiness. If the Guru thinks he will do it to make money, or to influence these people to be Sikh, then it is negative and you will not see happiness. When you understand that point, from every aspect, you don't rush off to here and there. That's what makes your happiness stable. Not running after glitter."

I didn't ask Ranvir about homosexuality or misogyny specifically – but I did need answers on such things – so I decided to speak to a series of Sikh Uber drivers in Australia, who all told me the same thing. "Our Gurus, they did not see human in male or female, or by sexuality. They say 'God is without form or gender, and everyone has direct access to

God, and everyone is equal before God'. This is why for Sikhs, a good life is lived as part of a community, where all help all, Sikh or non-Sikh. Regardless of gender, class, deformity or sexuality." Free from empty religious rituals and superstitions, Sikhs are some of the most active and practical believers I've met. "We are close to God when we do good deeds, as well as when we meditate on God and goodness for others," a 27-year-old Sikh tells me on the way back from Melbourne Airport in January 2018. "This is the only way to escape bad Karma and rebirth and find mukti (liberation), we switch the focus of attention from ourselves to our neighbours."

Unlike many faiths, Sikhs don't think it pleases god if people pay no attention to others and simply devote themselves slavishly to religion. For this reason, Sikhism doesn't ask people to turn away from ordinary life to get closer to god. In fact, it demands that they use ordinary life as a way to get closer to god. A Sikh serves god by serving (seva) other people every day. By devoting their lives to service, they get rid of their own ego and pride. "So why do Sikh gurdwaras (churches) not permit same-sex weddings?" I asked several Aussie Sikhs. "I don't know," was the most common response. "It is the culture in India, not the religion." Perhaps this is why in 2016 – during a spate of violence against homosexuals in India – the openly gay Premier of Ontario, Canada, Kathleen Wynne, was still honoured and was photographed receiving the 'siropa' – a garb given as a form of respect – during her trip to the Golden Temple in Punjab (the most holy Sikh house). Officially, Sikhism has no teachings about sexuality, and the religion's holy book – the Guru Granth Sahib – does not mention homosexuality. You might think this gives the religion clarity, but it's quite the opposite. There is not one consistent teaching on LGBTQIA+ people in modern Sikhism, with some Sikh groups preaching acceptance of everyone, while some others take a more conservative stance.

The notion that any one religious path is more equipped to teach us why we're here, or how we might do our best, is absurd – and comes from the very egotistical, selfish nature that faith promises to free us from. Fortunately, what witnessing the happiest believers and non-believers has taught me is that **we're all destined to follow a different religious or spiritual path whether we like it or not**. Because even if I call myself a 'None' or a Muslim, Hindu, Buddhist, Atheist or Christian, and even if I read the same prophetic words other followers have, I will never be the same as them, because as author Edmund Wilson said, "no two people have ever read the same book." Our happiest state therefore, must come from seeing the beauty in god's diversity. To think or behave in any other way — such as discriminating against women, gays or the poor — is to reject god or suggest he or she got it wrong — which again, if you believe in a creative god, is absurd.

The truth, as all of the figures in this chapter have alluded to, is that god is not mean, *we* are mean, and god does not discriminate, *we* discriminate. When *we* awaken to this, then *we* will see that 'god is good' is an aspirational chant, not a foregone conclusion. There can be no ultimate claim — because we don't know. We never will. No one can tell us they have been to heaven, hell or nirvana. No one knows if Jesus was born to a virgin mother or if Muhammad (PBUH) was the last prophet. These things are neither true, nor untrue. They are simply part of the human story, which is the mysterious glue that has let us become the only creature on this planet that can co-operate in large numbers. "Societies are constellations of prayer," says author Wayne Cristaudo. We co-operate effectively with strangers (for the most part) because we believe in things like gods, nations, money and human rights. Yet none of these things exist outside the stories that people invent and tell one another. There are no gods in the universe, no nations, no money and no human rights — except in the common imagination of human beings. "You can never convince a chimpanzee to give you a banana by promising him that after he dies, he will get limitless bananas in chimpanzee heaven," says best-selling author Yuval Noah Harari. Only human beings believe such stories, he says. This is why we rule the world, and why we must continue to believe in those stories that can deliver us from our evil, selfish nature to a state of generosity and service to a greater good. For it is there that we will find our happiest self and create our happiest society.

*Deliverance from evil
begins with letting go of it.*

Me holding a crab during our trip around Australia.

10

MY BROTHER AND THE TALIBAN

Can you be a good person if you've done bad things? What about *really* bad things? The sort of things that shatter and tear at even the most resolute fibers of our being.

What if it was you? What if by some chance encounter or mistake you found yourself at the centre of an awful act? Is it solely you we should blame? Were you influenced by others? Your upbringing? Maybe it was just a mistake? Does any of this even matter?

If someone killed your father, could you forgive them? What if they beat your mother or shot your sibling dead? If your brother raped you, could you ever look at him, let alone love him the same again? What is lost when we hold onto that pain, that anger, that fear?

And most importantly, how do we get rid of that incessant burrowing worm of hatred and revenge – the one that feasts on our ever-decomposing happiness, eating us from the inside out?

The solution is simple. We kill it with light. With love. With honesty.

Of course, the application of such a simple solution is not always so simple.

In the backseat of a car on my way to a tiny village in rural India, in May 2017, I told a stranger the following story. Two days later I knew I needed to share these words with the world, so here goes:

When I was 12 years old – during that six month trip around Australia – the first few weeks were full of fond memories. From walks, waterfalls and endless putt-putt courses, to a huge dry-toboggan ride in the blue mountains, and using an old car-tyre tube to go rafting on the mighty Snowy River. This was the sort of adventure I constantly longed for as a kid. Every day was different, it was fresh, with challenges, lessons and opportunities to refine my new-found understanding and sense of self.

Nights were spent around the scrabble table with mum, Kane and I fiercely battling for supremacy. Dad often spent this time buried in books, investigating and conceptualising the utopia my parents hoped to create.

But then, something happened. Something that would change our family forever, though most wouldn't find out about it for 18 long years.

Staying at a fairly modern campground on the outskirts of Canberra (our nation's capital), I went to take a shower and my brother followed. The exact details escape me, perhaps I've blocked them out, but the next thing I knew he'd jumped over the wall of my cubicle and began approaching me in a strange way. He mostly laughed and made it seem like what he was doing was an everyday, normal occurrence. But I knew it was wrong. Even as a 12-year-old, you know that's not right. When I refused to touch him or let him touch me, he got angry. He'd always had a horrible temper and I often wore bruises as a result, but this was different and he knew it. On this occasion I called him out: "What are you doing?" I cried, as I said "no" repeatedly. I played on his fear of being caught and said I'd scream and get us both in trouble if he came any closer. He tried to negotiate, as if he thought he might convince me it was OK for brothers to touch one another in the way he obviously wanted to. In the confusion of my negotiating tactics, he'd moved away from the door of my cubicle, and I managed to escape before anything could develop further.

Over the following months I wasn't always so lucky. There were times I couldn't escape. There were times I couldn't persuade him to stop. There were times he was too violent to fight off, and there were times I felt too alone and helpless to do anything. When I threatened to tell mum and dad, he said he'd kill me, and if you knew him in his fits of rage, you'd believe him, as I did. Even if I did tell my parents, he'd convinced me they wouldn't believe me, and he was probably right. After all, he was a great liar. There was also the shame factor. How do you tell people such a thing? What would my parents feel? Would they still love me? Rational thought and reason were not my companions at 12.

The next few months were a blur of me trying to avoid being left alone with him. I'd become wrapped up in a set of circumstances hard to explain to those who have not experienced it themselves. I knew I needed to find a way out. I knew rape and sexual abuse were not OK. But as a 12-year-old with nowhere to run – we were literally living in a car and campervan together all day, every day – and no one I could talk to, my options seemed limited. In the end, I was raped and sexually abused more than a dozen times before I broke. Before, death seemed a better alternative than the life I was enduring. "I don't care if you kill me, I'm going to tell mum and dad if you don't stop," I told him, the night he finally stopped.

When I think about how I survived that period, I guess I simply ignored what was happening to me and continued to find and focus on the good in life. The beautiful beaches, rustic Outback landscapes and wholly enthralling experience of learning about one of the oldest living cultures on Earth – Australia's Aboriginal people.

I don't recall my precise train of thought during this time, but as a fairly complex thinker, even as a 12-year-old, I remember one idea that repeats in my mind still today: If something is beyond our control and we do not have the ability to change it – such as my brother's horrendous actions – then we must let those things be, and remain focused on taking what positive lessons we can from them.

A lot of people, like the lady in the car in India, have asked me: "how can you just forget about it?" But this idea doesn't quite mean doing that. Rather, **it is about accepting those parts of your reality you cannot change, and trying to find some good, before removing them from your mind's field of vision**. Because the danger with allowing these things to simply float around in our head, forever unanswered and unchanged – which is the nature of them being outside of your control – is that they begin to cloud everything. Life and everyone in it quickly becomes dull, broken and blurry if you can't see past the scratches that pain has inflicted upon your eyes.

Of course, there is an extension of this idea. One that provides a much more long term solution. One that mends and wipes clean the scratches that cloud our ability to live, to love and to find peace. That idea is *forgiveness*.

As I sat in the backseat of that car and divulged this shocking tale to the relative stranger sitting next to me, I could sense her growing discomfort with what I was saying.

"How could you possibly forgive him?" she asked, almost indignantly.

"If I don't forgive him, who am I hurting? To do something like that – to rape and abuse me – said to me that he clearly hates himself already. After all, good, kind and happy people don't harm others. The vast majority of people who cause pain no doubt feel it tenfold themselves. So ultimately, the only person I would have been hurting by not forgiving him, was me. But why should I suffer for his wrong doing, it doesn't make sense? So even if you want to look at it selfishly, forgive them because you don't deserve to live in a misery caused by their mistakes," I said.

"But what was the process, how did you come to that decision to forgive him?" she asked. I could see by this stage that she held a great deal of pain inside her, so I continued.

"We are all a product of our upbringing, and we are all prone to mistakes. While we enjoyed a similar childhood, he'd always struggled with self-esteem and fear of failure. He'd lie about anything and everything. Despite being a straight-A student who excelled at sport, Kane always felt inadequate. There was always a need to bend the truth in order to fill that hole in his soul, but it never quite worked. In his early teenage years, he began making bad choice after bad choice, and this was just another one of them. His need to commit these heinous acts was not my fault. It had very little to do with me at all. Rather, I'd say it was another attempt in some strange way to feel in control or to have power over someone, which perhaps was a band-aid fix for his self-esteem problems?" I questioned.

"So often I think people inflict pain on others, not because they want to hurt that person, but because something is hurting inside of them, and that's how it manifests," I continued. "I think the more I have travelled and seen war zones, and humanity at its very worst, this is a common thread. **People only know what they know, and if that is pain and suffering, then how can they create love and kindness?** I don't know why my brother felt such pain, to be honest. It seemed to me he had everything, all the love and talent in the world, but still something caused him to make the decision he did."

"I think forgiveness was pretty simple once I wrapped my head around this train of thought. What was a hell of a challenge was when one night, a few years after our trip around Australia, he returned home drunk from a party and tried to repeat the behaviour. He even recalled to me that he'd done it before. Being much older (15), I was sitting at the computer and grabbed the keyboard and told him I'd kill him if he came near me. 'Go to bed you sad piece of shit,' I hissed, with all the menace I could muster. This was far more difficult to forgive, because he acknowledged what he'd done and tried to do it again. Was he so innocent I wondered? But, I guess, once more understanding that it wasn't about me, but rather about a deep emptiness inside him, allowed me to forgive him."

"I don't understand how you can forgive that though, how you can think what he did was OK?" asked my travel companion.

"Let's be clear, forgiveness is not about saying what he did was OK. Far from it. Forgiveness is about truly understanding and accepting the decisions and actions that someone else has perpetrated upon you. It is about ridding yourself of hate and anger towards that person and the world for what was done to you. You don't have to be happy about anything that happened, you just need to find peace with it."

"I guess knowing who my brother was then, and seeing who he is today, under all that pain and suffering he has caused himself, I can feel empathy for him. He still has good in him, he always has, he just needs to realise it – we all do. I think maybe if I felt he could have done this to anyone else, forgiveness might have been more challenging – and I would have gone to the police by now – but I've never really felt he was capable of that. Or at least I dearly hope that's the case."

To give you all a bit of background as I did my friend in the car that day, here's a snapshot of my brother's life to date.

Making a monster

For the most part, Kane and I enjoyed pretty uneventful childhoods. We'd go to school, come home and fight for supremacy on the trampoline, skating-rink or backyard cricket pitch, and then play endless sports on weekends. Literally as much as we could pack in. Mum even held coaching roles in our T-ball, baseball and cricket teams. Needless to say, both mum and dad were keen sportspeople in their day and provided us with every advantage we could dream of, both genetically and in terms of support.

Kane was gifted across a variety of fields, from mathematics and language in the classroom, to cricket, baseball and Australian Rules Football. He could do it all, and I idolised him for it. I was three-and-a-bit years younger than he was, so I could never quite run as fast, throw as hard or kick as far, but that didn't stop us spending nearly every day in a park or backyard with a ball or bat of some shape and size in hand.

The first whiff I got that something wasn't right with Kane was high school. He had a few really good friends who we all knew well, then one day a new acquaintance showed up on our doorstep – Jeremy. As the youngest, I'd often spy on my brother and sister when their friends were over to see what 'cool' things older kids did. On this occasion however, all I remember was the smell of smoke. Jeremy had convinced my brother it would be a good idea to drop a lit match in the charity clothing bin next to our house, because as he explained "it wouldn't actually set on fire because there was no oxygen in there." The fire that erupted was so hot it nearly melted the metal bin to the ground. This was the first time I'd seen my brother do something terribly destructive, for no reason other than because someone he thought was 'cool' told him to.

My brother's lack of self-esteem saw his behaviours go from bad to worse in the years that followed. They manifested as a sort of social weakness that made him susceptible to anything that would give him a thrill and sense of fitting in. As a teenager this means being cool, which is all about sex, drugs and rock'n'roll. Unfortunately, it was the middle of these three things that caused the biggest problem – marijuana was his substance of choice. Like most addicts, he'd do anything to get it. I'd often catch him stealing from my parents, or selling or trading things he'd been given as birthday or Christmas gifts.

By the middle of year 10, his grades had slipped and he was furious. His academic position was the one thing he always seemed in control of, but some of his extracurricular habits had obviously started taking their toll on his ability to study or think critically. Unable to cope with the thought of failing, he quit school, and for the next six months worked full-time at Hungry Jacks (AKA Burger King).

By the time we were headed off on our trip around Australia, Kane had established a steady stream of lies to cover his various evils. However, anyone could see that underlying this 'naughty little boy' image he'd created for himself, was still a good heart that just wanted to be loved. That just wanted to be accepted. That desperately needed to fit it.

While I've never fully understood what happened next – this book forced a conversation I'd long wanted to have.

"Why do you think it happened? Was it, as mum suggested, that you were sexually abused?" I asked my brother on 16 August 2017.

"No, I was never abused," he said. "I've thought about this a few times in my life, and to be honest I don't know why. There is no reason, no excuse. I think I have made some strange sense of it recently, since learning more about the nature of alcoholics at AA. There's a thing in the alcoholic psyche where we feel like there's something fundamentally wrong with us, and so we'll do anything to fit in, to be liked, to feel normal."

"So much was out of control in my life back then – with dropping out of school, smoking pot and being forced to go on that trip – that I probably just wanted to control something, as sick as that sounds. It was probably my way of feeling liked, even though obviously looking back it would have had the opposite effect. There's nothing that excuses my behavior, you know how sorry I am, but I can't change what happened. I was a teenage kid going through puberty with a fucked up head that made a shit choice and I've hated myself ever since for doing what I did," he said, in a surprisingly calm manner, given his typically harsh, hate-filled tone he uses when discussing the many wrongs he's committed.

When we returned from our Australia-wide search for utopia, mum decided she and dad needed another look at a small 'sustainable eco-village' we'd visited in Gin Gin, Queensland. When they got back and told us we were moving there in a few weeks, all hell broke loose.

This was the place Kane and I had hated the most out of anywhere we visited in Australia. It was a rural, racist, shit-hole. The idea of leaving everything I knew and everyone I loved for *that* was nearly unbearable for me. Then there was my brother, who was in a highly turbulent period of his life, and arguably craved stability. While the decision was never about pleasing us kids, the damage it did, in my opinion, was unfathomable, and it continues to wreak havoc on our family two decades on.

To begin with, Kane remained in Adelaide, living with Bek and Cin, while he attended a training college (TAFE) to study carpentry and joinery. But it wasn't long before trouble found him – if it ever left him. There were two boys in his class who'd befriended him. I'm not exactly sure how or why, but like almost every friendship he's ever had, these guys turned on him. Whether it was his poor self-esteem which often comes across as weakness, or his incessant need to fit in, which can make him seem desperate, like a bit of a loser – no one deserves what happened next. Over the course of about a month, these psychopaths tortured Kane, both mentally and physically. They mugged him, stole money, bashed him, left him for dead and even set him on fire. But somehow, as he has done time and again, he survived.

My eldest sister struggled to cope with the growing list of problems surrounding my brother, leading him to seek refuge with our grandparents (on my dad's side). Despite their absolute and unconditional love for him, my grandma and grandad couldn't handle Kane's behaviors either, especially his constant lying. I remember the straw that broke the camel's back was when grandma discovered that he'd taken one of grandad's beers. It wasn't necessarily what he'd done that upset her, but rather his inability to own up to it. Within a few weeks he'd exhausted his lifelines in Adelaide and was forced to move to Queensland, where mum and dad had just finished building their 'dream home'.

In the three years my brother lived with us in Queensland, he was like poison to everyone, including me. He was expelled from school for (consensually) fingering a girl in my year level with whom I was friends – this was hugely embarrassing. He didn't turn up for work experience with a local carpenter, who just happened to be the father of my first love. Unfortunately, this guy assumed I was a useless druggie like my brother, so he didn't let me see his daughter. Then there was the usual tendency of getting involved with the wrong people, which ended up with Kane being tied up and bashed by a local drug dealer, who thought he was some tough guy boxer, but mostly resembled a low-life scumbag.

"I honestly don't know how I survived that period of my life. That guy, Chris (the drug dealer), just had it in for me and nearly killed me a few times," said Kane. "He literally tortured me, but still I wanted to fit in, so I kept going back to him, because that's how an alcoholic or addicted brain works."

During this time, I was also grabbed on the street and slammed against a local shop front by the same guy, who threatened to kill me, simply for being my brother's brother. Explaining rather frantically that I was nothing like Kane, and was ashamed to be related to him, the hand around my neck slowly loosened. While in some ways what I said was true, I was ashamed of who he was on the surface – a dickhead druggie – underneath I knew he was still just a kid that wanted to fit in.

Just as we were finally preparing to leave Queensland (utopia having failed to eventuate), my brother's need to feel connected saw him make yet another ill-fated decision. He invited a girl he'd just met and started living with – Jessica – back to Adelaide to live with us. The problem was, her best, was like his worst. But I think that's what attracted him to her. She was less capable and less wholesome than he was, and it made him feel good, or at least marginally better, about himself. Jessica also gave him that sense of fitting in or being loved he so badly craved. Their relationship, unfortunately, was nothing but a co-dependent disaster.

The domestic violence and emotional abuse went both ways, as they slowly tore each other apart. Limb from limb, brain cell from brain cell. Jessica's dreams of becoming a nurse crashed and burned as the turmoil of their relationship grew. While for Kane, being told he was a "piece of shit" often enough destroyed any sense of self he had left. Substance abuse became his (and their) only way to cope.

My brother's addiction quickly progressed from marijuana with a sprinkling of alcohol, to alcohol with a heck of a lot more alcohol and a sprinkling of cigarettes. At the time, he was actually proud to have quit marijuana, not realising immediately what he'd begun to replace it with. Before long he was entirely useless, on a whole new level. Unreliable, unable to hold down a job and readily dispensing his pain onto anyone who tried to help him, I wondered if he'd passed the point of no return?

Did those brash moments in which he'd lost all semblance of a moral compass mean he was and would forever be bad? Again, I think this is a case-by-case thing, but at that time my heart still said 'no'. He had made errors of judgment. Severe errors. He had lost control of his mind. He had committed several crimes. But in his heart, beneath the alcohol and THC (the active drug in cannabis), he was still not a person who wanted to harm others. He was a piece of shit at times, and worse when he was drinking or smoking, but his centre point, where he returned to when he was sober, was a kind but lost and broken soul, caught in a cycle of endless suffering worse than death.

This cycle, which has been on repeat for more than two decades now, goes like this: feel lost and depressed > turn to alcohol and drugs > do bad things while under the influence > feel more depressed > slowly become increasingly addicted to alcohol, which causes you to make more and more poor choices > and so the hole gets deeper and bigger, until no light gets in at all and you forget you're even digging. The darkness totalises as reality.

As I finished explaining this shocking tale to my travel companion in India, she had one last question: "Do you love him?"

"Yes," I replied candidly. "How!?" she said. "Because that's what he needs. It's all anyone needs. And he needs it so, so badly. So showing him anything but absolute and unconditional love would serve nothing and no one, not even myself. Revenge or hate is only ever self-serving, and as such, no happiness can come from it. It's like Martin Luther King Jr's wife said: 'Hate is too great a burden to bear. It injures the hater more than it injures the hated.'"

"That's why, when Kane and my parents experienced a big falling out and he was left homeless – after failing to finish one of many stints in rehab – I thought I'd see if I could be the spark that ignited a new fire in him. A different perspective. At the time (2011) I was in the midst of running Our World Today, so while I didn't have a lot of time, I did have a spare room and wondered whether him being around someone who was pursuing their passion for justice and happiness could rub off on him. I was also listed as his primary contact when he was homeless, which meant the police, ambulance and hospital would regularly call me at all hours of the night to request I come and pick him up or 'deal with him', or he'd go to jail. So maybe there was some self-preservation in there too – I knew, or hoped, there'd be less late night emergencies – or at least that was the plan."

"But sadly, nothing changed. He actually got worse. He was more suicidal and violent than ever. He smashed holes in the walls of my rental home, which I had to pay to fix. When police dropped him home because he was passed out in a gutter, I ended up having to wrestle him inside to stop him abusing and chasing after the cops. I'd also regularly come home from work to find him passed out in the yard, and I'd have to bend down to check his pulse. Don't get me wrong, he was fucking poison, but still I loved him. Enough to use our past as a bargaining chip, as I pleaded with him to go back to rehab, because that was his only hope of redemption. 'The only way you can make things right between us,' I told him, 'was to start doing good, to live up to the potential you have, because those who have suffered are those who can end suffering, just look at Gandhi, Mandela or Martin Luther King' I'd say. 'What if you could be the equivalent for those with addiction?'"

"Oh how I wished he could see what I could see," I said to my friend, just as our car pulled up at the village we'd come to visit. "Shit, I couldn't do it," she said, through painful sighs. "Don't worry, you're not alone," I concluded.

Love is rarely unconditional. Typically, and understandably, there's only so much people can put up with before the heart wanes. In the twelve months I acted as the primary carer for my brother, I came to see and feel the challenges my parents had faced for more than a decade as my brother's frightening violence and utter disdain for life, wreaked havoc. He was, as my parents said, "too hard to deal with." A cancer on our family and society. Part of me wished he'd follow through with his suicide threats. The other 99% of me prayed he would find something to love about himself.

Oh how I wished he would change.

But my unconditional love was not enough, nor was my parents'. Nothing was.

Five or six suicide attempts and a few arrests later, I told my brother he could either choose jail, rehab or homelessness – because insanity is trying the same thing over and over and expecting a different result. I'd done my time, I thought, I'd tried something new – him living with me – and now I'm out. Not because I didn't love him, but because **this is what love looks like sometimes – doing what's good for someone even when they won't do it for themselves – even when it brings them discomfort.**

"That's the longest I've gone without grog," my brother tells me, referring to his stint in rehab after I kicked him out. "It was 11 months." Sadly, the rehab program was twelve, though he didn't tell us at the time of course. Rather, he said he was leaving early because he felt ready (fear of failure still haunted him). Some weeks later, he publicly jumped off the wagon during our family Christmas party, though we all knew he'd long veered from the straight and narrow. "What do you want me to say, I'm a fuckhead, I've destroyed this family, I'm worthless, I just want to die, honestly, you'd all be better off," he lamented.

"That may be true," I told him, "but I wouldn't be me without you. And who knows, maybe the pain you inflicted on me, and the lessons it has taught me, can help others." It's not an easy thing to tell the person who raped you – your brother no less – that you are going to tell the world about it, but when I sat down at TGI Fridays in Kolkata, and that woman I'd met in the taxi in India opened up to me about her mother, who had molested her, I suddenly realised that by exposing my wound

I could help others heal theirs. "I've told nearly no one about this until you," she said. "Because I suppose we think we're alone. No one could fathom that this happens."

In reality, roughly 20% of girls (1 in 5) and 8% of boys (1 in 12.5) are sexually abused before their 18th birthday, with 95% of victims knowing their abusers. Of those molesting a child under the age of six, 50% were family members, while for children 12 to 17 (like me), 23% of perpetrators were related. Shockingly, the most vulnerable age for children to be exposed to sexual assault is between 3 and 8 years old, and as many as 40% of children who are sexually abused are abused by older, or more powerful children. With the rise of pornography, there's actually been more and more cases of child on child sexual abuse, and older children or siblings sexually abusing younger children. What stood out to me, as an Australian, was that we (an educated, developed, supposedly decent country), have the highest prevalence of female child sexual abuse, with 37.8% of girls reporting some form of abuse by the age of 18. This was followed by Costa Rica (32.2%), Tanzania (31%), Israel (30.7%), Sweden (28.1%), the US (25.3%) and Switzerland (24.2%).

If you're disturbed, even angry, reading this research (I know I was), congratulations, you're human. So why aren't we humans talking about this? Why aren't we doing something to stop it? Is it too disgusting? Too taboo? Too overwhelming?

Thinking about your kids raping one another, or being abused by strangers, teachers, priests, friends or family is a thing of nightmares, but I can tell you this nightmare is real. In fact, 98% of child abuse cases reported to officials are found to be true. Problem is, just two thirds of adults said they would believe a child if they disclosed sexual abuse, according to an Australian study. I suppose this is why 73% of child victims don't tell anyone about their abuse for at least a year, while 45% don't tell anyone for five years, and many of course never disclose their torture.

My teenage girlfriend of five years, Megan, was the first person I told. I was 19. As a stoic, macho Aussie bloke, this was tough. Seven years seems a long time, and I think I'd mostly dealt with it, but to reveal such a thing is forever terrifying. It's like admitting you're an alien. You want to seem as normal and peaceful as you can, but underneath I shook, petrified she'd see me as different, a freak. Then the tears came, and I knew I'd lost. 'Weirdo!' I imagined her saying. 'Filthy creep, I'm never having sex with you again'. Thankfully, these words never came. Instead she just held me and we cried.

The next to find out was Sash, who was furious. Laying on my chest on her bed as I calmly recounted my story (I was much more well thought out and at peace by this point – aged 26), Sash immediately dove off me and began screaming into her pillow. "Ahhhhhhhh! No, no, no. Why? How could he. No, no, no, you poor thing. Mike, why would he?" she yelled, as I consoled her. "I'm OK. Look at me, I'm not even crying. I forgive and love him, as I hope those I have hurt forgive and love me. I am happy Sash, it is of no consequence to me, I mostly love who I am and would not be this way if not for the darkness. Don't worry, he is the one who suffers, not me." "Well he should!" snarled Sash, who readily absorbs the agony of others – a beautiful but painful trait. "How..." she muttered, ten or so minutes later, "how can you look at him, how can you treat him the way you do? Where the shit (she never says fuck) were your parents?"

Sash's anger towards my brother, and parents, is probably telling of how I think most might react to such a sickening story. Justice is, after all, a human instinct (one of the most important). The problem is, if pain must have pain, if victims see the suffering they might want to inflict on their perpetrator as 'getting even', then the cycle continues, and we become no better than them, or anyone else who might knowingly (or unknowingly) inflict misery on another. I get it, there is a difference. And just to be clear, a sense of justice (in all areas of life) is central to a human being reaching their happiest state – because it brings peace of mind. All I'm saying is: sometimes the only truly 'just' solution is fixing the root cause of the pain or crime, so it doesn't happen again, so others don't get caught, as I did, in the whirlwind of a broken soul.

My sister Bek was the next to find out. She seemed distinctly unsurprised. "Well Kane hating himself definitely makes more sense now," she said in a roundabout way. "Do mum and dad know?" Bek asked. "No, not yet," I replied, "but I'll have to tell them soon, before writing the book, as I want to know their thoughts."

A little over a year later, sitting in the courtyard of my parent's home sipping a cup of tea with my mum (dad wasn't around), I spurted out those gutting words: "There's no easy way to say this, but I think you know there's been something I've wanted to tell you about Kane for a while (I'd often gone to tell mum but chickened out), so... When we were travelling around Australia, Kane raped and sexually abused me, many times, on and off, depending on whether I could fight him off or avoid him. You know how crazy and aggressive he was." Without a trickle of a tear or hesitation in her breath, mum replied, "Well I guess it must have happened to him." She didn't come to console me, give me a hug, nothing. There was no 'sorry' no sign of remorse. Was it me? Was it her? Did I fail to see something? Say something? What had my words triggered? Where had this foul truth taken her? Where was my mum?

Mum and I had long shared a tender, close bond. I was unashamedly a muma's boy. We'd share cuddles, massages, chats about girls, friends, teachers, all of life's intimate details. Never had she been so cold.

Weeks later, when I told mum that Kane hadn't been abused – that she was wrong – he had simply chosen to sexually abuse, in the worst possible way, his baby brother... nothing. There was still no apology. Not even when I detailed the role their self-absorbed neglect played in making me feel even more alone and unable to reveal what was happening to me during that trip. All I got out of dad was, "you can't write about this, some things are meant to remain private." You could see his anguish as he argued his position, devoid of any conviction. The shame of others finding out seemed to be the only thing that got any rise out of my dad. Again, there was no apology or compassion forthcoming.

My parent's reaction hurt me... a lot. But to me, mum and dad had always been perfectly-flawed. They'd taught me so much of what I wanted to become, and inevitably, a bit of what I didn't. That's why I am the happy person I am, I think. Because I've long learned from other's triumphs and mistakes.

On 21 January 2019 (as I was writing this chapter), my dad called me to tell me Kane was in the Intensive Care Unit (ICU) at Flinders Medical Centre in Adelaide. "We don't quite know what happened," said dad. "Kane's been pretty bad lately, his repeated calls to LifeLine threatening suicide mean he's ended up in hospital where something's gone wrong. We don't know much, just that he was unconscious and wasn't breathing for some time." Not breathing, I thought. Could he be brain dead? What could that mean for mum and dad? The family? Is he destined to die as a shadow of the young boy I once idolised? Or, could this be the wake-up call that breaks his addiction? Will he wake up a new man? Will the fear of death finally get to him?

Unfortunately, the answer was no, no and no. A week after he left hospital, he was back to business as usual, maybe worse… (mum sent me a photo of his wardrobe, which was stacked full of 4 litre goon (cheap wine) casks). The only good thing I'd say about him being in a prolonged bad streak whilst I wrote this chapter, is that the decision to reveal his horrendous truth feels easier. Because nothing is being lost on his end – he has no job, self-respect or decency as it stands. Two and a half years ago, when he was trying really hard to get better, I considered scrapping this story from the book entirely, because it didn't feel right, just as his head was nearing the surface, to push him back down again. It was actually during this period of sobriety that I met the woman in India, and saw, through telling her and others, the power of this truth I'd long held onto – and its ability to set others free. **I also hoped it might ignite the long-overdue discussion necessary to begin addressing such heinous behaviour.** Calling my brother to relay my decision (to publish this story), I told him two things: one, our happiest state exists only within our truth. And two, what if this is the only good thing you do? What if this was god's strange plan for you? What if all our shared pain can free others from suffering? Is that not worth the bad looks or stigma we'll both confront? And really, who knows, maybe it will set you free, from that one lie at least.

On 9 February 2019 (a year or so after I told him I would publish this story) Kane called, and unusually I picked up. He talked about getting free of mum and dad by going into rehab and then supported accommodation in the city. For years he'd been living in my parent's investment property (barely paying rent) as they kept his head just above water (paying his bills, buying him food or furniture when he couldn't afford to, even an electric bike). When Kane told me he needed to take charge of his life if he was to ever get better, I agreed and told him to go for it. "It'll be good for you, and mum and dad," I said, before adding my usual spiel about filling his life with good, and using his story to help others. Then, given his growth-seeking mood, I sent him an early draft of this chapter.

The following day Kane called me, having said he'd read his part of the chapter. His immediate feedback was surprising. "It's a hard thing to say, but I can see that this story can do a lot of good for a lot of people," he said. "I'm not stupid, reading through it twice now, I can tell you it is a story that has to be told. Whether I'm better or not. And no matter the damage it might do me or our family." Insisting he read the entire chapter, to put his own crimes into perspective, he called me back some hours later with a stirring sense of hope in his voice. "Mike, I can see it now, the greatest gift I could give myself, would be to forgive Jessica. I'd never thought of it before, but that's what I took from your writing." He then went on to tell me he wanted to be the one to disclose his crimes to my sister Cin, who didn't know, as well as our grandma. "Because I need to own up to this," he said.

The decision to 'out him' to the world seemed strangely as if it might provide just the push he needed to confront and overcome his demons. When he bravely decided to tell his AA sponsor and our family doctor about the rape (in the hope of getting professional help), we all felt the gears of his suffering shift. His stagnant self-loathed soul seemed to be unhinging itself from the lies that had long fed and protected it.

In early August 2019, with the book inching ever closer to completion, Sash asked me a couple of questions about what Kane had done to me. Shocked to hear just how bad things got (because I guess I was often quite calm, emotionless and sanitized things when speaking to people) Sash insisted I needed to tell my parents the extent of his evils.

Days later when I revealed all the sickening details about what Kane had done to me to mum, dad and Bek the absolute devastation and disgust was written all over their faces – the pain almost physically oozing out of them. My dad's reaction was instant empathy born of a rage at his inability to go back and change what he wished he could. "Maybe it's lucky you didn't tell me at the time [dad pauses], or I might have killed him," he said. Dad's words – finally – told me I was loved. His hug – finally – told me I was safe. Mum's tearful warm embrace and her acknowledgement of her (and dad's) poor reaction to hearing the story for the first time, was soothing. This was the mum I knew. The mum that had been there for me during some of my toughest days. Two days later mum wrote me a letter:

> **My response** – you can say you don't like it, you can say why, bringing in your past experiences of me and my emotions. You've demonised it, made it seem as if I love you less, but I don't. I'm at the bottom of a hole that's dug in our garden of life. It's a hole I climb up out of and I live in the garden some days. But sometimes I'm so close to the edge I fall in and can't see light. That's where I went after reading Kane's chapter, where I've been while laying in bed late at night, where I was

when you first told me. Revisited – I would hold your hands in mine, look you in the eyes and cry. Cry for the pain and hurt that you've endured, that we are all currently enduring.

The openness with which my family began to embrace this heinous act soon led someone to come forward and tell me that Kane had tried to abuse someone else (when he was 18), but that this person had escaped without harm. The moment I heard this I told my parents and sister we needed to confront Kane and tell him he either needed to commit himself to a secure facility away from society where he could get help, or I'd pursue the case through the legal system (which would likely see him go to jail or at the very least a similar secure facility). Sitting there in front of mum, dad, Bek and me, Kane calmly and firmly told us he'd never hurt anyone else, despite us knowing otherwise.

"We know you tried to abuse someone else Kane," I said abruptly. "So STOP lying!" "OK," he conceded. "But nothing happened," he insisted, as if that somehow excused his criminal behaviour. "Who else have you abused Kane?" I asked, as I listed off potential suspects. "I swear on my life, there's no one else," he said. "But you just lied to our face about the person you tried to molest. So how can we trust you? [I paused] We can't, you need help, and you need to be locked up somewhere until we can be sure you're better. If not, I'll make sure you go to jail."

The next day, in a psychotic drunken state, Kane turned himself into police and confessed to raping me when we were younger, as if somehow it might make things right (or maybe he just wanted attention or control), despite me pleading with him not to put us all through a drawn out court case, because it would only inflict more pain on the family.

With the police failing to apprehend him (saying there was nothing they could do until the courts ordered it), Kane returned to his same-old same-old, before finally getting himself admitted to the one rehab facility he hadn't yet tried in the state.

Then, on 28 December 2019, sitting in a hotel room in Hoi An in Vietnam, I received a text message from my mum that I'll never forget. It was a photo of a letter that my brother had left at my parents house which read: *I touched _____ in a sexually inappropriate way on four occasions. I disclosed this to a staff member. Possibly contact police or whatever you deem appropriate. I hate myself for what I have done. But I was in a program of complete honesty and the guilt was eating me alive. Sorry doesn't cut it and I realise this. Probably notify police is the only appropriate course of action. I would at least rather you hear it from me than elsewhere.*

Fuck, just fuck. The only way to conceive how I felt upon reading this is to stop reading and just be silent for a moment. The initial anger was the result of him somehow (as he's always done) trying to make himself sound like he's doing the right thing or that we should feel sorry for him. The overwhelming rage that made me want to drive a fucking knife through his face was that this person was one of the most beautiful and innocent beings I'd met and was someone we'd directly asked him about just months earlier during our 'family interrogation'. The pain too, in knowing that I could have prevented this if only I'd spoken out about this earlier is tough to live with (don't worry I know it's not my fault, but it is the truth).

Learning over the coming weeks (as police became involved) that my brother was in fact a serial sexual predator who'd abused a young child from the time they were six or seven for many years (NOT the four times he confessed to – yes, even in admitting the truth he lied) was gutting. I felt physically ill for days. Nearly two months later as I write this, the idea of forgiveness is a struggle. How can I forgive him on behalf of another? The simple answer is, I can't. I think too, this experience has shown me that forgiveness is a fluid thing. Right now, I feel some peace and forgiveness because the person he molested is getting on with their life, largely free of his darkness. If and when the agony of his actions take hold of this person's life – when his actions and the impact of those actions move from their subconscious mind into their conscious mind – then I will need to re-evaluate whatever level of forgiveness I may feel for him at that time.

While my family may never fully recover from the inconceivable horrors that the process of writing this book has uncovered, there are three things I think we're all glad of: one, with two pending court cases against him (mine and the other person's), my brother will go to jail for a long time (hopefully forever, if he can't overcome his sickness), which means he won't hurt anyone else; two, my family (including my parents) have finally disowned Kane, and can be free of his mental and emotional torture; and three, **we desperately hope other people and families can learn from these tremendously-difficult-to-share words**.

Words I know I will need to seek forgiveness for making public, because some people in my family still don't agree with me sharing them. Then there's the friends, colleagues and Sash's family, most of whom don't know about this (and probably don't want to). But, in a way, that's the problem – the silence. Rape, abuse and domestic violence, and the ensuing mental health issues these things cause, are quietly paralysing millions of lives – and not just victims. Left untreated, without forgiveness, anger born of injustice all too often festers into a kind of lonely all-consuming rage, that's defined by the narcissistic assumption that no one else is, or has ever been, through this.

When all seems lost

Take Aly, the guy you met in Chapter 7 from Chicago (from page 284), with the Muslim father from Senegal who died when he was young, and the Catholic mother from Mali, who went on to work for the UN in New York. Well, through her role at the United Nations, Aly's mum Claudette eventually met her second husband John. "He was a very impressive man on paper," says Aly. "Very high achieving, extremely smart, extremely charming. He was actually the head of the entire African continent for the United Nations Development Program (UNDP), so he was a big deal. But that was his problem, too. He had to be 'the man', to keep his ego fed. This made him terribly unbalanced. Like, for instance, he would use religion as a way to kind of cut himself off from the deeper parts of himself, and especially the darker or more fragile parts – because that's where we see weakness. For example, when they [John and Aly's mum] would start getting into a fight he'd just be like, 'well, I'm just going to go pray'. He couldn't go there, couldn't talk it out, or look inside. Emotions were kind of out of bounds."

Some years into their relationship, Aly says things turned south. Leaving his role at the UN to run for president in his home country, Burkina Faso, John convinced Claudette to put everything she had into his campaign, including money from the education fund she'd established for Aly and his sister, both of whom remained in the US. When his campaign failed, the couple moved to Zimbabwe, where John used his vast connections to land a plush job with a big bank.

"I hadn't seen mum for nearly four years by this time, but I had questions about my childhood, and hers, so I'd been trying to get in touch, so I could go see her," said Aly. A few weeks later he received a phone call telling him his mother was dead. "What happened to mum is what happens to a lot of women in these domestic violence situations, which is that she loved him, so she tried to make it work. She tried to change him, but ultimately she got to that place where she realised, 'I can't change this guy and I need to leave'. When she finally confronted him and said that she was going to go, he stabbed her to death." Just two days later – the time it took him to pull the necessary strings – John walked out of jail a free man, exonerated of Claudette's murder. Officially, Aly was told his mother died of 'natural causes'.

"I was in this place of sort of double darkness. The person who raised me as a single parent was gone. On top of that, my sister and I lost our legal right to be in the US. Suddenly we were undocumented migrants without any avenues to become legal, because mum had all our papers. Then, because mum gave John all our education money, we had to drop out of school. In a matter of weeks, we plummeted right to the bottom of the pile. The middle-class existence we'd known was gone," said Aly. "I went through two years – I call them my underwater years – because I suffered a major depressive episode that made me feel like I was drowning. It was the type of depression that you get up in the morning and your to-do list is – take a shower, take a walk, go to bed – and half the time you can't even do that. Those years felt like a trial of the soul, and I was losing. I could feel myself giving up on life, and you add to that the fact that being undocumented meant I would go to job interview after job interview and I would always get the same result: 'You're very well qualified, and we like you, if you were a US citizen we'd hire you, no problem. But, well, sorry'. I felt very trapped, and this is maybe the lesson I keep learning over and over again – the thing that started to dig me out of the hole was the thought that, 'I need to do something.'"

Within days of starting a number of volunteer positions, including one at an AIDS clinic called *Better Existence with HIV*, Aly says he began to notice a change. "All of those questions that I was asking about life, like, 'Why did this happen to me? Why is life so unfair. Why should I suffer?', suddenly took on new meaning. Like here I was dealing with all of these young people who were diagnosed with this terrifying disease, and was it anymore fair that they were going through that? It strangely sort of reconnected me to life, it was like **there was nothing unique**

about my suffering and it was connected to the suffering of others. That's when those other questions came up, which were like, 'Why the fuck not me? Why not? Why would it happen to these people? I care about these people, it's not fair that they're dealing with this, they're good too.'"

"I guess I just sort of looked around and was like, 'Oh yeah, obvious lesson, terrible things happen to good people all the time', but if you can connect with others and particularly when you can relate with their suffering, you can stop yourself from drowning. That's been my ethos my entire life: yeah, sometimes life sucks and it's painful and it's terrible, but we're here for each other to weather through it, because we're not meant to be these individuals trapped all alone with our pain."

Seeking to free himself from the anger and rage that had seen him consumed by thoughts of murderous revenge, Aly made the brave decision to pursue professional help. "I wouldn't say I feel at peace with how it [the trauma surrounding my mother] turned out, but I don't feel any tension around it anymore, because I've done enough counselling around it," he said. "How did you let go?" I asked, "and how did you find any semblance of happiness after that?" "There are several layers to that, but ultimately just two paths," Aly said. "I could either measure my life by how much retribution I could find in taking this guy out, or I could measure my life in terms of what I can achieve if I let go of the pain and pursue the path my mother, and I, had always wanted."

"I actually remember I wrote him a letter of forgiveness. Boy, I hadn't thought about that in a long time [he chuckles, then sighs], but I did write him a letter once and I... I don't know if he 'deserved forgiveness', but for me it felt like I needed to let go of this energy of hatred towards him, so that's what I did, and it freed me. The weight – all that water trapping me – was lifted." This reflex we have to curl up when hurt – to ignore our neighbours, our friends and our morality – is the very thing that makes it feel as if the world is collapsing. Because when you look, think and obsess over you – your pain, your outrage, your loss – everything and everyone naturally feels as though it is against you. "When mum died, and especially in the way that she died, it felt like god giving me the finger," said Aly, "like he was saying, 'here are your prayers, here is your love, I'm going to throw them in the trash now and I'm going to kick that trash down through the canyon.'"

Such events often lay waste to one's faith, because all meaning and reason seems lost. We also tend to be drawn closer to the evil abyss, because we confuse 'justice', 'revenge' and 'doing what's right'.

Justice is a concept of ethics and law whereby people behave and are treated in a way that is fair, equal and balanced for everyone. The problem is, when an act of rape, abuse, domestic violence or murder is committed, justice for the victim(s) is forever lost. I mean, even if you pursue the matter and win your day in court, what you get back will never be fair or equal to what you gave up. Aly will never get his mum back. I will live forever knowing my brother raped me. The highest form of justice we can and should hope for, therefore, is that another person doesn't have to suffer that pain – which is why dobbing-in would-be serial criminals is so critical to establishing a happier society. Because perpetrators of serious crimes need psychological help, and should not be free to live amongst society until they get it – if ever. That is the only justice. The only way to stop the cycle of suffering – whereby sufferers (often unknowingly) pass their suffering onto others, who then do the same. The issue is, jails aren't designed to rehabilitate – they're designed to punish – which simply further damages the already damaged. That's why most felons cycle in and out of jail like the wind. It's also why I see our current criminal justice system as a front for getting revenge, not justice. Perhaps if we had secure rehabilitation centres that specialised in curing rapists, domestic violence abusers and other criminals, we'd see true justice – and an end to the cycle of suffering – because fair, equal and balanced for 'everyone' must surely include those poor broken souls who become criminals.

Revenge is defined as: the action of hurting or harming someone in return for an injury or wrong suffered at their hands. Just as the Bible instructs us to take "life for life, eye for eye, tooth for tooth, hand for hand" to punish an offender, evolutionary psychologists tell us the instinctive urge to seek vengeance is hard-wired, and comes from our earliest ancestors who relied on the fear of retaliation to help keep the peace and correct injustices. "Acts of revenge not only sought to deter a second harmful act by a wrongdoer, but also acted as an insurance policy against future harm by others, a warning signal that you're someone who will not tolerate mistreatment," says Michael McCullough, a Professor of Psychology at the University of Miami, in a Washington Post interview. This makes sense right!? Someone hurts you, you hurt them back. A colleague steals your idea and undermines you in front of the boss –

you post compromising pictures of them around the office. An eye for an eye seems fair, doesn't it? Well, maybe, but psychologically, there is no such thing as 'getting even', and passing on the baton of pain will not bring you closure. Even that buzz you think you might get when you lay some crazy revenge-smackdown won't last. "Revenge can feel really good in the moment," explains David Chester, who studies the psychological and biological processes involved in human aggression. "But when we follow up with people five minutes, 10 minutes and 45 minutes later, they actually report feeling worse than they did before they sought revenge."

In a 2008 study looking at whether revenge makes us happier, University of Virginia Psychology Professor Timothy Wilson and his colleagues set up a group investment game with college students where if everyone co-operated, everyone would benefit equally. However, if someone refused to invest his or her money, that person would benefit at the group's expense. A secret experimenter within each group (called a free rider) convinced the group members to invest equally. But when it came time to putting up the money, the free riders didn't go along with the agreed-upon plan. As a result, the free riders earned an average of $5.59, while the other players earned around $2.51. 'That's not fair,' participants must've yelled, and they were right. So researchers gave a select number of groups (not all) the chance to retaliate. These groups could choose to spend some of their own earnings to financially punish the free rider. Everyone who was given the chance for revenge took it, predicting that they would feel much better after they got even.

When surveyed afterward, those who had chosen revenge reported feeling worse than players who didn't get the opportunity to punish and so had 'moved on'. Wilson theorises that seeking revenge may remind us of the pain we experienced when we were wronged, and can make an event appear even larger in our minds. "By not retaliating, we're able to find other ways of coping, like telling ourselves that it wasn't such a big deal," he says. What's more, ruminating about getting even – stewing over what the person did to you and what you would like to do in return – delays the process of letting go and takes up important cognitive resources, depleting you of time and energy that could be better spent on healthier, more constructive ways of dealing with the anger, such as learning to accept the injustice, putting yourself in the other person's shoes or acknowledging that you too may have hurt someone in similar ways.

Doing what's right is about finding a way for all parties to heal, because without a relentless focus on mending the broken parts of ourselves and others, we will all continue to suffer. To stop this heinous cycle of victims becoming perpetrators and perpetrators becoming serial perpetrators, we must approach all suffering from a place of empathy. Because other than psychopaths, sociopaths and the mentally deranged, the pain most incidents incite is split relatively evenly between perpetrator and victim. "To hurt others is not without a cost," writes Danish Psychologist Simon Moesgaard. "We are social animals, so hurting others hurts us too." When we come to see this, we can let go of this need for revenge, for within our human mind – which is innately empathetic – justice is served upon any wrongdoer the moment they harm someone. "Punishing the other person is self-punishment. That is true in every circumstance," says Buddhist monk Thich Nhat Hahn. And Roman emperor Marcus Aurelius agreed. "What injures the hive, injures the bee," he said, believing we were part of an inter-connected organism. "The best revenge, therefore, is not to be like that," said Aurelius. Because when you hurt others, you hurt the group and you hurt yourself. Doing what's right, therefore, is about ending this cycle.

"The only way out of this morass is to stop viewing emotional pain as a punishment inflicted by someone else and learn to act on it as an internal motivation to heal, correct, and improve," says Dr. Steven Stosny, who has treated more than 6000 clients with various forms of anger, abuse and violence. "This will lead to a deeper self-compassion and put us more in touch with our deepest values, which will, in turn, inspire more compassion for one another." It was precisely this ability to turn pain into something positive and meaningful that gave Aly the final pieces of his life back. "When I connected with people from *Murder Victims' Families for Reconciliation* – which was a group of people who had lost family members to violence, but who were advocating against the death penalty – I saw that there was another way. I haven't thought about it in a while, but that community of mourners who were all grieving deeply, were so clear about saying, 'no, we still have this ethos of life, we're not interested in inflicting this kind of suffering and pain on any other family, even the families of the people who maybe took loved ones away from us.'" That really helped to reorient me and also just made me feel sane and safe again. Like I didn't have to want someone to die, just because my mum was murdered. And actually I shouldn't want him to."

With the largest ever study into the genetic basis of empathy suggesting that just 10% of the variation between people's compassion and understanding comes down to genes, forgiveness of and empathy for criminals seems to make even more sense – if the goal is healing. This research tells us that 90% of a person's empathy is learned – it is shaped by our upbringing and environment – which means it can also be altered by these things. For example, in Afghanistan I met a young woman whose father was killed by the Taliban. Upon hearing about this, her uncle sought revenge, in her name. "No, no," she said. "If we attack them, then no one will win. The hurt goes on. But if we can forgive him, and tell him of our forgiveness, perhaps we can change his heart. And that is how we will win this war," said the 19-year-old. She might not have known the science behind it, but what this young woman was proof of, was the cure – empathy is the solution to suffering. "If we can teach those who lack empathy, however hard it may be, what it looks and feels like to show and live with empathy, perhaps the next time they are told to raid a village, they will object," concluded the young Afghani, who said the only happiness she salvaged from her horror came from "doing what's right" (she was actually my inspiration for using this term).

What's often misconstrued about forgiveness (a major part of doing what's right), is that it doesn't mean forgetting or minimising the pain we feel, and it is absolutely not about excusing others. Forgiveness means making a conscious and deliberate decision to let go of any feelings of resentment or revenge, regardless of whether the person who has harmed you deserves it. "Forgiveness is, in the first place, not about others," write psychologists Alfred and Maria Allan, of Edith Cowan University. "It is about stopping us from allowing resentment towards others to make life miserable for us." That's how we return to the way we felt before the offending incident occurred, they write. "We must start by forgiving ourselves for any contribution we think we might have made to the incident. People often blame themselves partly for what may have happened. Survivors of sexual abuse or harassment say the most difficult part of the forgiveness process is accepting they were not to blame and to stop being angry with themselves. After forgiving yourself, it's easier to then privately forgive other people involved."

But what if the person you're forgiving can't see or won't admit to what they have done? Research suggests that "what the angry mind ultimately wants is a change of heart from the transgressor," McCullough says, pointing to studies showing that when a victim receives an explanation and an apology, the desire for revenge weakens. So what if an apology never comes? If there is no explanation given? What if, like disgraced film producer Harvey Weinstein, the perpetrator of your pain denies or cannot see their wrongdoing? This is exactly what happened to Evelyn, a homeless woman I met and took to lunch in Salt Lake City, Utah.

Under the surface

Smelling less than pleasant, and with scars etched deep into her face, I could see and smell her pain, but as she spoke I couldn't hear it.

"I was born in Arizona to a mother and father who were not the best of parents. My mother would beat me severely with anything she could find. My father, if you could call him that, molested me from as early as I can remember, age five, until I was placed in a foster home," said Evelyn. "In foster care, nothing much changed. I was raped on several different occasions. When I finally ran away, when I got out of all that and married my first husband, that's when things got even worse. Trying to reconcile with my mum, and forgive her for what she had done – I found out she was also abused by my father. I let her move in with me and my ex-husband. Bad idea, bad idea. All he wanted to do was have a threesome with me and my mother. 'You know, you can have her. See you later', I said. Then I went to Iowa for a few months, before coming here to Salt Lake. And that's when I met the monster himself."

Like most ghoulish and evil men, Evelyn's second husband (of 13 years) didn't present as a bad man with ill intent. "At first he was charming," she recalled. "But I guess I should've paid attention to the details... 'Cause he asked me to marry him pretty quick and I was like, 'You know, I just got out of a relationship not too long ago. Not yet'. And he said, 'Oh, well ...', you know, kind of like giving me a guilt trip. So idiotic me, I agreed to marry him. We went from being in a homeless shelter for two years to staying in a motel at first. And that's when it started, the hitting, the constantly accusing me of cheating, not doing what I was supposed to be doing, not checking in at certain times when I was supposed to check in. I should've paid attention to all these

Evelyn.

things, but I didn't. I shrugged it off. I thought, 'Oh, it's alright. He's just possessive. He can change, he can be a better man. I know he can.'"

Unfortunately, that wasn't the case. Throughout the course of their relationship, Evelyn suffered three broken noses, a shattered jaw, deep facial scarring and a massive seizure when her husband stomped on her head with steel-toed boots. The worst part of it was, he never let her go to the hospital and get anything fixed, which means she's been left disfigured. "He even tried to bite my nose off when I went to the domestic violence women's shelter. I was there two weeks and they want you to become self-reliant, which I think is wonderful. But as I was leaving one day he was waiting about two blocks away and grabbed hold of me, and tried to bite my face. I've put him in jail three or four different times, but it didn't seem to do no good. It made him more violent. One time when he got out, he stabbed me with a steak knife in my hand and in my leg [she shows me the scars]. The things he did were monstrous, and that's the best way I can describe him, is a monster. [She pauses] But..."

"How do you recover from that and find some sort of semblance of happiness in your life? And what was that 'but' about to be?" I asked.

"The 'but' was.... but I have come to forgive him, all of them. My first husband, who was just an abusive horn dog. My second husband – for a while I struggled to forgive him – but now, it's like for both of them, they knew not what they were doing – their own suffering didn't let them see the pain they inflicted on others. And anyhow, I can't seek out vengeance on anybody 'cause it's not my place. I'm not your judge, I'm not your jury. I'm just somebody here, for you to be tested upon, but I'm not the one that's gonna grade the paper," she says. "It's not to say it was right, what they did, but God created them, and me, and for some reason I was made to endure that. But I'm still here, so I guess he's still got a purpose for me. He's still got a reason for me to be here or a lesson I've gotta teach to somebody, or something."

"In terms of my parents, I said the same thing to both of them, you know, and asked God to forgive them, because again, they knew not what they did. They did not understand how to love, because they were not loved. They only knew what they had seen or been taught themselves. And so, luckily I broke that pattern, so the cycle of abuse could stop with me. It helped me to see that. To see that **we are all victims of** circumstance, just some have the wisdom or will to overcome it. And they, or we, are the lucky ones."

It might seem an odd thing, to hear a rape, abuse and domestic violence victim describe themself as 'lucky', particularly given Evelyn remains homeless as a result of all this, but there is something strangely beautiful about those who manage to emerge from the darkest holes. "I've always been an optimist. No matter what the situation is, what's going on, I've always been a glass is half full person," she continued. "Knowing all of the darkness and bad that's happened in my life... You know what? It's OK. I'm still here. I'm still as nice and caring as I was before. Maybe more. Because I see the suffering of others. So it hasn't altered, it hasn't changed me. So why condemn somebody for what they did, especially like I said, if they don't know any better?"

"What's your dream?" I asked. "For me, I just want to see everybody in this world be able to look at one another, and not have prejudice in them, not have hate, not have sorrow, not have any pain, but just be able to have love and compassion and an understanding for each other. You know, out of all the species on this planet, we are the only ones that kill for the joy of it, or because we want to. All the other species in this world kill for protection or food. That's it. And that's sad." "So how do we fix this, how do we be our happiest selves?" I asked. "By not holding grudges, letting things go, not letting them burrow into your soul so hard and so deep that you can't climb out of the hole that you created. Learn to just say, 'It's all right. Tomorrow's coming. We can try again.'"

By this time, I knew I wanted to do something to help Evelyn get through the next few days, as she said she would be fine (off the streets) once she started her new job on Monday. It was Friday when I met her. "What would be your instant wish, right now?" I said, fishing for answers on how I could help her. "To be honest with you, just that people will stop and say 'hi', like you did, just because. Without wanting something in return," she said. "Because connection is everything, you know, you see that when you're homeless, because out of 100 people, 99 will ignore you, but the one that acknowledges you, or asks you if you're ok, they are the cement that mends society, that moves us towards that happiest place you were talking about."

I could see by now that Evelyn didn't have a selfish bone in her body, she literally didn't know how to ask for something for herself. Maybe that's why she'd stayed with such horrible men for so long, I thought, before asking her how she felt about the grave disfigurement and scars she'd been left with.

"Well, at first it made me really embarrassed and really ashamed, like it was my fault, because I stayed with him for so long and allowed him to continue to do it. But now, I look at it like this... my scars are a blessing, for they will deter people from looking at me like, 'Oh, I can use her like a piece of meat'. More likely they'll say 'Ew,' you know, 'She's got some issues there, so let's stay away from her'. That's why I'm happy now, because I know that if I meet somebody, they will need to see past all that, and know me for who I really am on the inside, and that all the disfigurements don't matter. I'm actually [she pauses], that job I'm starting on Monday is doing waitressing, so I'm a little nervous about my scars. But that's gonna be a good test for me on my self-image."

Telling me scars are like dirt that will be washed away with all our sins when we die, Evelyn began to tear up. "What's wrong?" I asked. "The saddest thing I'll tell you is all the judgement, because it lets us hate and think we're somehow different, but no one is outside this human existence. We're all walking the same road, you're just over there, and I'm over here. But what's happening to the homeless, is people think they're not part of it. Somehow their suffering is less legitimate, or is a choice, as if drugs or being beat up, or not having a job is the life anyone would pick, given the chance. No one wants this life. But like the Jews under Hitler, the poor class are becoming demonised, so that certain groups, like our president (Trump) can exterminate us without a peep. To go back to that one wish, I'd say this: to stop putting price tags on things, to end the blame game and forgive whatever is causing that gap between you and another person, any person, family, friend or stranger."

Telling me with enormous pride about her 22-year-old daughter and 19-year-old son, who are both in college, it made me wonder, "what or who do you want to be?" "I want to be hope for those who are facing, or have faced, what I have. To be able to take anybody who has had any of those issues, and be able to, while it's still fresh and it's just starting, to be able to have them come to me and say, 'OK. What do I do?' And help them to get out of it before it gets worse. To help them to change it before it causes a mental or a physical breakdown, or even the emotional and the spiritual breakdown. To be able to prevent the things that I have gone through as far as repressing all my emotions and not letting anything out. Because it's only more recently, thanks to this very sweet psychology guy who's helping me, that I'm learning to love myself, which I didn't do before. To be able to be that for someone else would just be my happiest day." "Thank you so much for being who you are," I said, before promising to tell others about her gorgeous soul, in the hope that it might land her in a position where she can help others. (In that vein, if you're in or around Salt Lake City and want to meet or recruit Evelyn, please do, and say hi to her from me while you're there.)

With a plethora of movements such as #MeToo, #HeForShe and #BlackLivesMatter shining a tiny light on the enormous suffering so many people face on a daily basis, it can be overwhelming to know where to start. How do we forgive? Let go? How do we find peace? How do we heal ourselves? How do we heal others? How do we start doing what's right?

Before we can even start down that road, we need to take a step back and let go of the shame, guilt and blame associated with our dark nature. As renowned psychoanalyst Carl Jung said, **"wholeness for humans depends on the ability to own their own shadow."** Because it is only when the individual strives to 'know thyself' fully that we can begin to unwrap the psychological reasons for why we humans have not been ideally behaved. From there, and only from there, we can begin the process of healing, of becoming 'whole'. I think this is why knowledge, specifically self-knowledge, is what the human race has been tirelessly working towards since the dawn of consciousness some two hundred thousand years ago.

If we can grasp and accept that uncomfortable side of ourselves, and others, and realise no one is free of it – the darkness that inflicts suffering – the process of forgiveness and doing what's right becomes easier. Namely because the choices you make become rounded, thought-out and steeped in a calming truth. Suddenly, it seems effortless to say 'no' to your ego, which you notice is the culprit blindly seeking revenge on your behalf, not realising it is only adding to the cycle of suffering by doing so. With your ego in check, it also becomes easier to say 'yes' to seeking help – it could be a friend, a professional, a stranger – whatever or whoever lets you spew out all that hatred, go for it. Pain needs to come out before you can make peace with it. Next, and most critically, you will see (just as Aly, Evelyn and I did through opening up to others) that all suffering is connected, like a flu of the soul that's transmitted from one damaged being to the next, until it meets someone who holds the vaccine to defeat it — empathy. The reason empathy is such a telling cure for suffering is because someone with enough of it will never hurt another. Conversely, what lets a damaged soul pass on its pain is a lack of empathy, which is typically born of a loveless, disconnected upbringing or experience. That's why the choice to let go, forgive and, if you can, love the perpetrator of your pain, is so transforming, because that's what they've lacked throughout their life. That's what let them hurt you.

The thing is, even if you can't get to that point, the choice to pursue peace, and to not pass that pain forward, is world changing. It is the cure for war, rape, division, abuse, murder — all suffering. Because forgiving your friend for those hurtful words is just as critical to your and our happiest state, as making peace with the person who caused you to write #MeToo.

We must let go of hurt,

before we can grab a hold of love.

11

MR SMITH AND THE GIRL WITH THE BIG BUM

Love and relationships haven't been my strong suit. I've hurt a lot of people. Unintentionally. Though I doubt that fact helped them much. The problem... well, there are several. One, victims of abuse can often come to feel they're deserving of their abuse – as if there is something inherently wrong with them, rather than the abuser. The twisted logic damages the soul by inscribing onto the subconscious-mind the notion that somehow the abused (me) is unworthy of love and goodness. This, coupled with that old foe, testosterone, and my parents – who, at times, neglected us and didn't exactly know how to give us the love we needed during our teenage years – saw me bescame a person who craved connection, despite being a ticking time bomb terrified of commitment.

The question I'm curious to explore and ask myself – as painful and troublesome as it may be – is how am I now married? And what is it that's given me such a deep and abounding love for – and such happy and healthy relationships with – my parents, my family, my friends, my wife and the 8 billion strangers I consider companions?

Rewinding a little... my earliest memories of love were joyful – long cuddles with mum; sport and heaps of laughs with dad – but as I transitioned from child to adolescent, the expression of that love became more practical and less emotionally connected. It's as if they slowly turned into the stoic providers their parents had been for them. I think my grandparent's generation was probably more interested in securing 'a better life for their children', rather than smothering them with kisses, cuddles and 'love yous'. They were survivors of the Second World War after all, which meant they were highly practical people who knew what it was to go without, so being providers of *stuff* probably felt more important than being providers of *love*. "It was all about survival," mum tells me. Fascinatingly, what happened next was what I refer to as 'the flip'. As the disconnection with my parents manifested more and more (during my teenage years), my grandparents became what my parents could no longer be – providers of love.

"We weren't prepared when we had you kids," confesses mum. "We could easily love you as children, but I'd never had the example of what it meant to meet the emotional and intellectual needs of a teenager. Your dad might have known better, but he had to work long hours to provide for us. And I think overall there just wasn't the psychological knowledge available that we have today."

Despite the many advantages my parents had over their predecessors – in that they were richer, smarter and more exposed to the ideas of free love and expression that defined the hippie counter-culture movements of the 1960s and '70s – they weren't able to give us what they had never been given themselves, which was genuine, unabated, fully-expressed love. What's telling is that while we didn't get it, they were able to share this sort of love between themselves, which goes to show that change is possible, if we're exposed to the right stimulus.

"We famously had Princess Margaret wanting to marry a divorced man, which wreaked havoc for the Queen [of England], who had to deny her sister the right to wed the man she loved, due to her position as Head of the Church, which forbade re-marriage after divorce. What this sparked was a massive debate that began to see a snowballing shift in the moral narrative," says mum, who could have quite easily followed her parents' unhappy example of how to do love. "Suddenly, the way an entire generation viewed the importance of love in relationships and marriage changed. So we lived through the emergence of this radical notion of free love, which was that people should be able to marry or get divorced as their heart desired. What this meant for people like your dad and I was that we held each other to a much higher standard of love than what my mother endured, and this was a transformative thing. Because when you love someone deeply enough, you're willing to accept them, flaws and all, so it led to more fulfilling relationships and more open dialogue between couples, which had never been a very common thing."

Having stood the test of time – 40 years – one of the most priceless gifts my parents bestowed on me was an example of what it takes to stick together. "You definitely have to love profoundly," said mum, when I asked her what their secret was. "And you need to be able to be yourself, which means accepting the other person. This is the glue. But it is also where sacrifice comes in, because there will inevitably be things you wish the other person would do or wouldn't do. The hard part is taking your wants and ego out of it. **A relationship isn't about one person, it's about the meeting of two souls.** Who ever goes in and thinks this will be great when I get in and change the other person is kidding themselves." "Your mum's never been able to change my brilliant sense of humour," laughs dad, who was listening in the background. "What about when things get difficult?" I ask. "When you get to that point, and that happened to us when we were looking after Dylan (their first foster child) ... he became impossible for me to manage or be around, because he had this disdain for women, due to his mother's abuse and neglect, which landed him in our care. As you know, dad didn't want to budge, he had formed this bond with Dylan, so that was hard. What I asked myself was, 'why would I start again when I have put so much in?' So I hung in there, we both did."

Two and a half years after taking Dylan on, his unyielding anger and violent tendencies toward my mum, coupled with the fact that he was getting to an age and a size where he could overpower her, meant he was eventually taken away from my parents, and placed back in the system. The decision nearly killed my dad. Here was this innocent child who had helplessly developed a condition called *reactive attachment disorder*, which essentially comes about when a baby is not loved and held and therefore does not bond or attach to another human being within their first 1000 days of life. What my dad managed to do to some extent – by listening to and following hundreds of expert psychologists in the field – was become the first person Dylan had ever loved or attached to. "What's missing in a kid like Dylan," says dad, "is an understanding of our world. The human world. They haven't been able to develop emotions as we have. They exist in this parallel place, by themselves, because due to the neglect, they've created their own meanings behind certain feelings and emotions. That's why they say they're dissociative. Because my role with Dylan for instance, and the way you help these kids, is just by bringing them into an understanding of me, my being, who I am, how I behave, and then gradually that lets them see how human beings behave. The more time they can spend living and feeling and relating in *this* world, rather than their parallel world, the more chance they have of feeling or living a life that's somewhat 'normal.'"

Witnessing the 'reactive' part of Dylan's condition – manifesting as uncontrolled outbursts of sheer animal-like rage, usually as a result of feeling threatened – what becomes obvious is that our ability to relate and feel love – as babies, kids and adults – is what makes us distinctly human. Left to our own devices, to raise ourselves, we become more animal than human. In fact, a defining feature of reactive attachment disorder kids is that their amygdala – the part of the brain responsible for our fight or flight instinct – becomes more dominant, because that's what has kept them alive as a baby: the ability to avoid danger, and to seek out food scraps (often even dog food) on the floor.

What's troubling isn't just that this sort of thing is becoming more common due to a rise in drug addicted parents, but milder forms of what psychologists' call 'benign neglect' is also becoming more frequent as a result of parents constantly fiddling with their mobile phones and iPads in front of their children. "Family over-use of technology is not only gravely affecting early attachment formation, but it's also having a negative impact on child psychological and behavioral health," says biologist and pediatric occupational therapist, Cris Rowan. "Learning to read people's faces and expressions and body language is absolutely essential in order to develop empathy," adds Sue Palmer, author of the book *Toxic Childhood*. But kids are simply not getting enough time or opportunity to experience this, she says.

Parents aren't the only ones to blame of course, tech designers and video game makers have constructed this stuff to addict us. "What's the difference between half a line of cocaine and an hour playing a video game?" asks the author of *Digital Cocaine*, Brad Huddleston, "nothing, as far as your brain is concerned." Having demonstrated this with neurological scans, the World Health organisation (WHO) recently added online and offline 'gaming disorder' to the group 'disorders due to substance use or addictive behaviours', within the International Classification of Diseases. "After consulting with experts across the world, and reviewing evidence in an exhaustive manner, we decided that this condition should be added," says Shekhar Saxena, director of the WHO's department of mental health and substance abuse. "We are not saying that all gaming is pathological," she continues, but with 2.5 billion people – one-in-three worldwide – playing some form of screen game,

Some of the happiest relationships I've come across.

"What makes you happy?" I asked. "Love. All 72 years of it!" replied the Cambodian couple.

This was the first time these three friends in Timor Leste had ever seen a photo of themselves.

"How could anyone think our love any different from any other?"

A family sitting and chatting in Indonesia.

Three novice monks in Myanmar.

It's not the toy, it's who you play with.

That random friend you meet on a bus in Fiji.

Two friends bump into one another in the street in Mozambique.

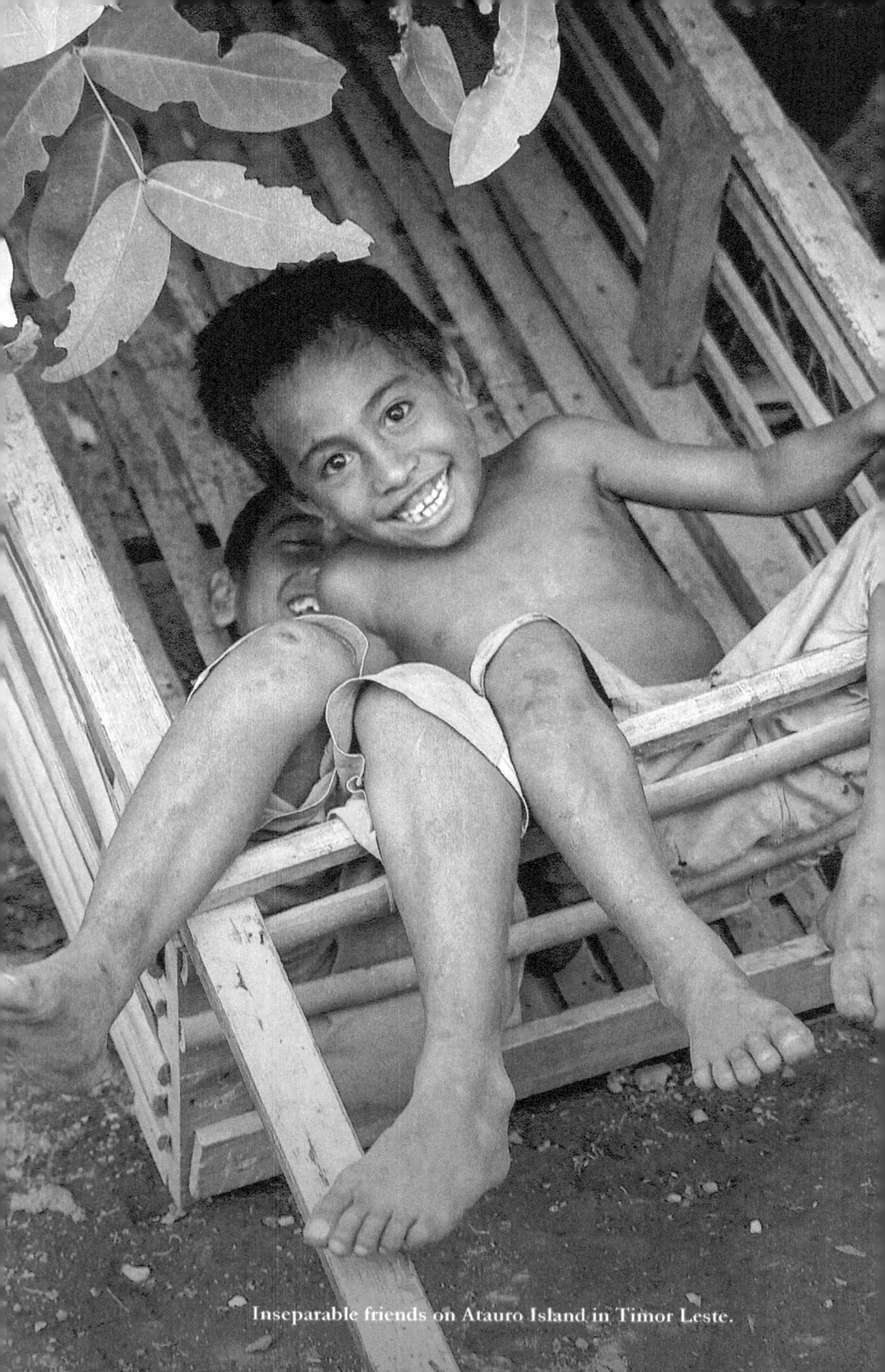
Inseparable friends on Atauro Island in Timor Leste.

especially on cell phones, this is now something that is clearly getting in the way of building healthy and happy relationships (or people), because as we all know, love and friendships both require time to flourish.

The problem is, that by the time they turn seven, most children born today will have spent the equivalent of an entire year of their lives watching some form of small screen (this doesn't include TV). "It's just a mild form of what we could see in Dylan," my dad says. "Which is that kids – and adults – are forming these parallel realities and we're spending huge amounts of time in them, which is causing two issues – one: kids aren't learning to relate to their parents or other kids and visa versa, and two: there's this mild ADHD evolving in children – and all of us – where we're not entertainable in a normal way anymore. Kids are used to this sensory overload, which means they're struggling with self-regulation and attention skills necessary for learning at school, and this is causing significant behaviour management problems for teachers in the classroom. Like any drug or addiction, screens have caused us to stop prioritising what we know is right, which is family, education, our health, our passions, even each other. All for that rush of endorphins that comes with 'likes' and killing baddies."

"The catch," says Rowan, "is that technology is killing what we love the most… connection with other human beings." Spending time with people we like, love, even those we clash with – it's all good! In fact, Harvard's longest study into adult life – which began in 1938 – found one overwhelming takeaway: **"Happiness is love. Full stop,"** said George Vaillant, the Harvard psychiatrist who directed the study from 1972 to 2004. The only other requisite for happiness "is finding a way of coping with life that does not push love away," Vaillant told *The Huffington Post* in 2013. Four years later, the now current director of the nearly-80-year-long study, psychiatrist Robert Waldinger, told The Harvard Gazette that, "the surprising finding is that our relationships and how happy we are in our relationships has a powerful influence on our health." Waldinger said that "taking care of your body is important, but tending to your relationships is a form of self-care too. That, I think, is the revelation." Lack of social connection isn't only being labelled "a greater overall health risk" than smoking, but a more recent review of 148 studies concluded that on average, having stronger social ties increased likelihood of an individual's overall survival by as much as 50%.

"Human beings are an ultra-social species – and our nervous systems expect to have others around us," says Emiliana Simon-Thomas PhD, Science Director of the Greater Good Science Center at The University of California, Berkeley, in an interview with NBC. In short, what biology, neuroscience and psychology tell us is that our bodies and our brains actually tend to work better when we're around others. Though the benefits don't stop there. A 2008 study, aptly titled *Social Support and the Perception of Geographical Slant*, found that **individuals actually perceived a hill to be steeper if they were standing at the bottom alone compared to standing at the bottom with a friend**. "Just having another person there and present, who you trust and feel safe around makes the world look like a less challenging place," says Simon-Thomas. Studies not only reveal that lonelier people have higher levels of the stress hormone cortisol (which is bad for lots of stuff), they also tell us that the simple act of holding someone else's hand reduces that cortisol and lessens an individual's emotional response in the brain to a perceived threat. And yes, the effect was even greater if the person's hand you were holding was a spouse. No wonder people keep applying for *The Bachelor!*

The thing about love and connection that I love most, is that like germs it's contagious – because it breeds happiness and kindness, both of which are known to spread up to three degrees from the host. One now-famous experiment that illustrates this, began when Jonathan Stark made his Starbucks card information public and encouraged others to use it or "pay it forward" as they saw fit. Between 14 July and 13 August 2011, more than 500 strangers contributed a total of $8,700 to the card, while there were 900 people who made withdrawals. "I would have thought the ratio would be more like 10 to 1 [drinkers to donors] ... So it's been extremely uplifting," said Stark during an interview with *good.is* at the time. The only anomaly, he said, was what happened when people were too generous. "Every time the balance gets really high, it brings out the worst in people: Someone goes down to Starbucks and makes a huge purchase," Stark told the LA Times on 8 August 2011. "But as long as the balance stays low, say $20 to $30, it seems like it manages itself. I haven't put any money on it in a while. All the money going through the card right now is the kindness of strangers." Lamentably, 30 days of human kindness and goodness came to a grinding halt when Starbucks shut down the social experiment over concerns about "fraud" and because it "violated Starbuck's terms of use." Yep, corporations suck, and don't understand love or relationships. But hey, they weren't the only ones. Stark's tremendous notoriety also attracted a number of haters who wanted to suggest that his feel-good social media experiment was actually a stealth campaign for the coffee giant or some effort by Stark to boost his credentials as an app developer.

What might sound obvious is that whether we like it or not, we're bound to encounter strangers, co-workers, friends of friends or relatives we just cannot stand to be around. Or maybe they can't stand us. The challenge, says Simon-Thomas, is to see this confrontation as an opportunity to expand our perspective. "These 'being driven crazy' moments are truly well thought of as opportunities for growth and transformation, which can ultimately be a more poignant source of sustained happiness," she explains. That's because having a diverse variety of emotional experiences – including feeling sad, angry, anxious, or irritated – expands our capacity to feel good too, says Simon-Thomas. Being grateful for your relationships (including those that challenge you) will tend to make you more resilient and more well-liked she adds. "Make a point of noticing who around you is contributing to the goodness in your life and actually express it by saying 'thank you,'" concludes Simon-Thomas, who studies the biology of our emotions and thinking.

If I think back to my own journey, finding light in the scars being etched onto my heart by others has been critical to my survival, and transformation. One of the more difficult nights I've faced followed news that the girl who'd relieved me of my virginity was pregnant. When the girl, Emma, and her friend Kathleen, called and then messaged me on MSN to tell me, adding that she would definitely have the baby (at age 14), I immediately thought, 'how do I escape?' Do I run? (I was due to move back to Adelaide from Queensland within weeks anyway – that's actually why we'd rushed into sex, because we were in love and I was leaving). Or do I do what I'd been threatening to do for years – kill myself? I was trapped somewhere between who I wanted to be (a decent human being and father) and who I needed to be to survive (which was a student back in Adelaide). Having sat there for ten or so hours, with a bottle of cheap bourbon in one hand and a knife in the other, Emma and Kathleen sent me a message I'll never forget: 'we were joking Mike!' Enter a loud breath and a lot of tears. What I learned from this harrowing experience wasn't not to trust people – I've never grasped that idea – no, all I can remember thinking was 'god, how lucky!' There must be some poor, stupid 15-year-old somewhere waking up to the message 'I'm pregnant', but it wasn't me. I guess I'd also proven I could survive the darkness that comes with confronting our greatest fear, which in my case was feeling trapped.

From facing the horrors of being a 15-year-old dad, to the ongoing burden of being my brother's brother or the child of parents lost in their own world – none of these things actually felt as scary as confronting my own declining popularity, which was the result of not wanting to take drugs with my mates (how uncool was I? Right!?). What this period of my life in Queensland taught me about myself and my place in the world was that I was not invincible and could not control the thoughts or actions of others, all I could do was be me. These words might sound wise or easy to say now, but back then it felt as if the reality I knew was crumbling. For as long as I could recall, life, and my position in it, had been easy – I was smart, good at sports, popular with mates and girls and was basically untouchable, because I'd always been the leader of the 'cool kids'. No one had ever questioned my infatuation with art, drama or poetry (a strange thing for a jock). What would I do if people noticed and poked at my insecurities? Would I change who I was? Would I sit there and sob? Would I find new friends? All I wanted was to be loved, as we all do, though it should be said that my background and home life probably meant I lusted after it more than most.

Packing up and leaving everyone I knew and loved and connected with for the second time in four years (because we were heading back to Adelaide), what I came to learn from this shitty experience – in retrospect – was that **I needed to find love in the only person who wouldn't leave me – me.** At the age of 15 you don't exactly think in these words – I'd basically been forced to learn this or collapse in a heap – but it didn't make the lesson any less valuable. "You have to learn to love yourself before you can love someone else. Because it's only when we love ourselves that we feel worthy of someone else's love," says Alyssa Sheinmel in her book *Faceless*. The ability to (mostly) love myself – because it will always be a work in progress – didn't only let me enter into two soul-enriching long-term relationships (of 5.5 years and 1.5 years respectively), but my inner dialogue and trust in who I was also ended these relationships. It might sound peculiar (even a lie), but the same day I broke up with Megan and Alex, I could have quite easily married them (and likely gone on to live quite happily). Telling them this didn't help, of course. All it did was prolong the breakup sex, because other than that little voice inside of me screaming 'you've gotta do this!', I didn't have any justification for leaving. I literally loved them till the day we broke up (and beyond), and they knew it. It's what made me such a prick. Because 'it's not you, it's me' is a bullshit pill to swallow, and yet, in this case at least, it was the truth.

Jumping from heart to heart (and bed to bed), my singledom saw me leave a line of scars a mile long. What I came to realise, however, was that these wounds weren't only left on those I was with, they were being imprinted on my heart too. **It's not a nice thought – to think that we hurt people – and yet it is a reality of life. We will all do it.** Filming the Dalai Lama in the lead-up launching Our World Today, one of the ideas he discussed hit me hard – like a well overdue punch in the face. "To be happy with yourself, you cannot do that thing in private that you would not do in public. If you cannot tell your mother about your conduct, then how will you tell yourself? How will you live with your truth?" he said, or thereabouts. At the time I heard this, I was a single footballer with lots of beer buddies who I desperately wanted to impress and fit in with. Yes, I knew myself, and loved myself, but maybe too much or in the wrong way. My ego and sense of entitlement – that my feelings mattered more than others – was not something I was proud of. My mum would not enjoy hearing me talk about using girls to satisfy my desires or need to seek control/power through sex (a symptom – I think – of my brother's abuse).

For the next four years (not that I ever did it as much as most of my mates), I banned myself from watching porn (something I'd never do in public), and vowed to try and foster better, more loving thoughts and relationships (which my mum would be proud of). There were slip ups (lots in fact), but I do feel that what happened next was god's way of telling me I needed to keep trying.

She was a skater girl

In October 2011, I saw a Facebook post from a girl we'd written a story about for Our World Today (OWT). She was seeking donations for a raffle to support a climate change event she was organising. Keen to help this girl out – because there was something about her that went way beyond her simple beauty – I told her I'd contribute a couple of paintings I'd done. Rocking up in a singlet and tiny footy shorts covered in paint – because we were painting the OWT office – the girl was less than impressed. Not because my face and shabby clothes were covered in paint, but because I hadn't correctly filled out the form about what I was donating. "You need to do this," she said abruptly. "Sorry," I replied, as I scampered to rectify things. A week later, I was storming out the OWT office – angry as hell that no volunteers had rocked up that day – when I saw this same tiny brown girl (with a teeny waist and big bum) wearing a flowery summer dress skateboarding awkwardly towards me while trying to carry a large painting. "Sash," I said, as my frown turned around, "what are you doing? Let me help you." It might not have been enough to undo her first impression of me as an annoying slob who can't fill out a simple form, but I was smitten. Who was this girl? How had she turned my whole mood around in an instant?

Hoping to find out, I began chatting to her online about her work with the Australian Youth Climate Coalition and a trip she had planned to attend the UN climate talks in Durban, South Africa. I was asking in my journalistic capacity, of course… Anyway, on the 2nd of November 2011, this crazy young girl (who was six years my junior) came walking up the stairs of a chocolate shop we'd organised to meet at with a deep gash under her lip. "What have you done?" I said. "I was skateboarding down through the university and there was this wall," she said in her bubbly speedy little voice. "So why didn't you stop?" I asked. "Mmmm good point. I'm not very good at stopping. I am good at going though," she laughed, as I stared at the blood under her bottom lip. "Well it's a good look," I laughed – nervously testing her sense of humour. "I know right!" she giggled loudly. As it turns out, Sash didn't know she was on a date. Her friend Rachel had told her, "I think it is", but Sash's innocent view of people and the world didn't let her think in this way. "I thought you just wanted to catch up for chocolate, and who would say no to chocolate?" she asked me, when I interviewed her for this book.

Our first more formal date – dinner at Mr Z's restaurant, the place next to the OWT office – was a bizarre thing. Mr Z had crayons on each table so people could draw on the paper table cover. Bravery or stupidity and a complete lack of thought soon saw me drawing Sash, who wore a bright red dress and giant smile that filled the room. I'd always been an open book who (generally) expressed his emotions freely, but this was something else. Sash just knew me. She was the beauty I sought. She embodied the innocence of an infant and wisdom of a mystic elder. She was love itself. Pure and sublime.

Sash's nearly month long trip to South Africa clarified – in both of us – that we were onto something good. Despite us going on only two dates before she left, and regardless of the fact we hadn't put a label on us, I found myself doing something odd. I said no to a perfectly good-looking girl who was fiercely trying to sleep with me. That's right, mum, I didn't even kiss her. And boy was I glad. Liaising back and forth via a long email chain that included 107 correspondence about life, love and a few stories she felt I should cover on the conference, one thing was obvious – I was in love (and yes, the internet did help us stay connected, because that's what it can do, when used thoughtfully).

When Sash returned to Australia, I took her on a romantic picnic to my favourite park in the Adelaide Hills. Less than three years later, I had blindfolded Sash in a car outside the same park, telling her I had a belated birthday present to give her. The blindfold, I said, was because I was going to hide her gift and give her a map to find it (something I'd done before). In reality, I had placed a tiny box with a ring in it, inside a much larger box that I then sat on the end of a jetty that jutted out over the picturesque lake in the park. Taking forever to set up some cameras (because I'd loaned my usual filming equipment to someone and hadn't been able to get it back), I eventually ran back to the car where Sash was eagerly waiting. Walking to the exact spot we'd had that picnic years earlier, I was about to say, 'OK... take it off', when the unthinkable happened. A gust of wind had blown the giant, mostly empty box off the jetty into the water. "Oh shit shit shit," I said, as I ran toward the lake undressing myself. All the commotion was too much for Sash, who promptly ripped off her blindfold and started laughing. "You'll laugh even more when you know what it is," I said, as we ran around the side of the lake closest to where the box had been carried. "Why will I laugh more?" she said. "Is it scuba gear?" Haha if only, I thought, as I handed her my clothes and begrudgingly trudged through the mud filled lake holding a long stick to pry the box out from the reeds it had embedded in. Just as I neared the box (maybe 5 metres away) it began to sink. Oh no, I thought, knowing the tiny ring box could easily slip through the gaps left by my shabby wrapping effort. The worst thing was that this wasn't even a ring I could replace – it was my gran's engagement ring – which was a massively important thing to me. "Got it!" I said, as I rattled the big empty box to see if there was still something inside. With duck poo and mud up to my waist, I placed the box on the side of the lake and burst out with laughter. "Fuck me," I said. "This may just be the funniest thing, assuming the gift is still usable." "What is it, what is it, what is it?" she screamed excitedly.

Placing the box on the end of the jetty again (don't worry the water had made it heavy enough not to be blown off once more), I re-blindfolded Sash and ran down to my laptop which was hiding behind a tree. You've got to be kidding me, I thought, as I went to play our favourite song, *You've got the love* by Florence and the Machine, only to have it not work. We must have listened to this track a hundred or more times on my laptop, but lo and behold it just wouldn't play. "Grrrrrrrr," I roared, and I played another song we loved, *Let her go* by Passenger. "OK," I said to Sash who was seated on a bench blindfolded. "Take it off." Meandering down toward the lake curiously wondering why there was music on, I said "you'll never believe how funny this will seem in ten minutes time."

Just to set the scene, all the commotion I'd caused had drawn a small crowd of people who'd been walking in the park, so there were eight to ten people standing wondering what on earth was going on. This was a surprisingly common thing for us, as we had a tendency to fail comically in a lot of our more bold and public romantic gestures. Sash had actually once told me – again, while blindfolded – to "walk forward that way when the alarm on your phone goes off," only she'd forgotten I couldn't see the direction she was pointing (which wasn't straight ahead as I'd thought). Having used the five or so minutes I was blindfolded to set up a surprise picnic in a secret garden at an old winery, Sash naturally waited for me to arrive. Two hours later, after walking "forward" through the woods and being chased by dogs, I finally found my way back to where I started. Sash, not surprisingly, was sitting on the front lawn of a random house across the road from where we parked, bawling her eyes out as the owners of the property comforted her.

Back to the jetty. Even as she opened the giant box, which she thought was empty until she spotted the much smaller package inside, Sash had no clue what was happening. She was well aware of my fear of commitment after all. "Wow! That's a nice ring," she said. "Thanky...."

she began to say as I got down on one knee and said, "I think I'm meant to do this, right? So," I paused "will you mar..." before I'd even finished she yelled "yes!!!" for all to hear. "Let me ask you properly at least," I laughed, as she began to wail with tears. "You know how I adore you, and to this day I see all the beauty in this world embodied in you. Will you marry me my love?" I said. I don't know how to spell the sound she made, but it was something like "yyyaaaeeeeeiiiiiiiiiiiiiyyyyeeeeeeee!!!!!!!!!"

Not to burst your bubble or anything – we were (and are) ridiculously happy, a real-life fairy-tale – but we've had our fair share of troubles too. From the inevitable struggle of binding two souls together (one housing significant damage), to balancing the demands of work, life and love – what I've come to see as the quintessential ingredient of a good relationship is the ability to turn those shared challenges into growth. The alternative is to let that stray word, frustration or dishonesty ignite a fierce cycle of suffering, whereby one side punishes the other – and back and forth it goes – until nothing of value is left.

Thirteen months into our relationship when Sash and I had our first argument, I went into a dangerous spiral of self-sabotage. Drinking. Distancing myself. Thinking about my next shag. I exhibited all the trappings of a man terrified of rejection, but equally terrified of commitment.

In the past, ending relationships had mostly been a swift, emotionless affair – I'd never needed to drink or distance myself – I simply disconnected or disappeared as soon as I sensed trouble or got a whiff of obligation or constraint. This subconscious defence mechanism was both a symptom of my being human, and a sign of my damage. **Being hurt by those closest to me had made me terrified of emotional exposure – of wanting or needing anyone more than I felt they wanted or needed me.** I suppose that's why I tended to seek out and maintain control within relationships (often through huge romantic gestures that ensured my partner loved me unwaveringly), because then I could decide when and where we grew, and when and where we departed. To this day, I've actually only had one girl break up with me. The other several-dozen times were on me.

What's important to remember is that none of these thoughts were front-of-mind during my teens and early twenties. I was young and ignorant, and I loved hard (most of the time). I was a typical old-school romantic: for Sash's 19th birthday my mates gave me shit, because I got her 19 gifts – and hid them in our favourite botanical gardens – to make up for the 18 birthdays I'd missed. The problem – as I've come to see it – was never my inability to love others, it was my inability to feel as though I deserved their love in return.

I don't quite know how to explain it, but when you've been raped or abused *you* (subconsciously) feel as though there's something wrong with *you*. As if somehow *you* deserved it. What this led to in me was the most awful feeling of unworthiness. Particularly in love. Because there was something in me that I was ashamed of, that I hated. No one could love that part of me, I thought. The dire result of this was that whenever I sensed someone pulling away from me or loving me less – normally after an argument – that feeling of unworthiness bubbled to the surface, bringing with it the most crippling pain. 'There is something wrong with *you*,' my mind would tell me, in a snarling cruel tone that reminded me of Scar from the Lion King. 'You can't be loved,' it would repeat. And eventually, I'd run. Time and again, I'd run, pre-empting the torture of rejection – of someone telling me I was unworthy – which threatened to rip open that old, festering wound.

What was different with Sash, was Sash. She was and remains the embodiment of love… and acceptance. And I desperately wanted to be with her. That's why, nearly a month after our argument, just as I was about to break up with her, my heart screamed 'stop!'. At the time, I couldn't fathom why that little voice inside me was compelling me to own up to my past and present transgressions, rather than just run away from them. Just to set the scene: I'd lied directly to Sash's face about my drinking and why I was distancing myself, and had never been brave enough to disclose the darkness of my childhood to her. 'Why would my heart want me to go through the agony of revealing my flaws and sins to this creature of light who I loved?' I thought. 'No. You vowed to protect her beauty and innocence, and this would crush it. You can't do it,' my logical mind argued. But my soul dragged me in another direction.

Before I knew it, I was laying there on Sash's bed retching up my wrongdoings and my heinous past, while simultaneously seeking forgiveness and affirmation that I wasn't too far gone. All Sash did was weep, for me, and us, as she squeezed me increasingly tighter to her chest. When she finally released me, it was as if she'd exorcised my pain and scars, and left me with her light and love. **Just as suffering was a cyclical phenomenon, so too, it seemed, was love.** Sash, who was

Our wedding day.

On our four month honeymoon through East Africa with one tiny backpack each.

The first photo we ever took together.

Couples that protest together, stay together.

Being our childish selves with some kids in a slum in Sri Lanka.

Mike and Tanya.

born of love, and who had bathed in it her entire life – thanks mostly to her parents – had given me a glimpse inside the most powerful and transformative force on earth. And it was glorious.

Her love gave me a reason to overcome my terrible fear of commitment, because suddenly I wanted something more than I wanted to be free. Her forgiveness too, told me she accepted (with a heavy heart) the darkness within me, because she knew it was part of what made me who I was. This wasn't, and hasn't been easy. Sash didn't need to take on my shit. She had a joyous, innocent, purposeful, love-filled life. I too was comfortable with my impassioned, free, expressive and slightly less wholesome existence. What both of us decided, however, as all couples (and friendships) must if they're to survive, is that we were better together. **Our differences were just as necessary and just as complementary as our similarities,** and therefore we would need to be willing to make the sacrifices necessary in order to let one another flourish in who we were as individuals, as well as who we were collectively.

Finding the right balance, or the line in the sand, when it comes to when, where and what we should be willing to sacrifice – and what we should not – is an evolving challenge. If Sash demanded that I sacrifice my freedom – by saying you can't travel alone, you need a more reliable 9-5 job or you can't spend thousands of dollars on hiring an editor for your book – we would have never survived. Similarly, if I didn't give up my manic need to work 16 hours a day (on my numerous ventures), and if I continued with the weekend binge drinking and debauchery I'd grown accustomed to, then we would not be together today. While much of this went unspoken, there are some conversations we can't and mustn't avoid, because when one side is made to bend to the other's will – to sacrifice too much – it never ends well. Children for instance, or more specifically if/when we'd have them, is something Sash and I have regularly discussed since being together. Because if we'd committed or fallen madly in love and then one side wanted one thing and the other wanted another, one of us would have wound up dreadfully unhappy. The same goes for other insanely complex things such as marriage expectations, when and where you hope to buy a house, what lifestyle you want to live, who will stay at home if/when you have kids, and even how each of you hope to raise those children. Knowing that our happiest state is achieved when our expectations are met by our reality, we should try to discuss all these big decisions as openly and as early as possible in a relationship, to avoid getting to that situation where one side is forced to sacrifice their happiness – their expectations – for the other.

A man who taught and challenged me on a hell of a lot of things I thought I knew about love and sacrifice was Mike Smith. Three years before I met him, the 48-year-old experienced the worst day of his life.

An indomitable force of nature

"My wife was having some chronic coughing problems, and over the space of about five months it just couldn't be resolved, so she went in for day surgery," said Mike. "It was fairly minor, routine stuff, so I dropped her off, and was told I'd get a phone call later in the day to pick her up. When my phone rang, it was her surgeon. He said 'something had happened' [Mike begins to tear up], and it was immediately apparent that things had gone horribly, horribly wrong. Over the course of the next two weeks we found out that Tanya had suffered an anaphylactic reaction to the anaesthetic, which led her to start thrashing around as doctors desperately rushed to intubate and sedate her in the critical care unit. Unfortunately, what we know now is that during this period she'd formed a blood clot, and in the process of thrashing about she threw part of that clot into her lungs, while another part travelled through her heart and ended up in her brain stem. The rare form of stroke [she suffered] left Tanya with a condition called 'locked-in syndrome', which pretty much means that she can feel her body, and she can hear and see, but she can't move anything, anything at all, except for her eyes and she can only move them up and down. Up for 'yes', and down for 'no'. So we can communicate, in a fashion. But she can't open her mouth, she can't eat. She can breathe by herself. So yeah, it has all taken a lot of getting used to."

Of all the confronting things I've filmed or been a part of – from refugee camps and rape to cancer hospitals and homelessness – Mike and Tanya's story remains one of the absolute saddest. And yet, I'd be lying if I didn't tell you it has inspired me to be a better husband and human being. Mike himself will never admit to it, but he is a hero. He didn't want to be, of course, but faced with this impossible situation and pain, he did what few might – he pushed and endured and sacrificed for the one he loved. Don't get me wrong, I'd like to think I'd do the same, anyone would, but met by the reality of never hearing your partner's voice, never feeling their touch, never doing the things you both love the most – ever again – who really knows?

"Tanya and I used to be extremely active. We lived in Colorado, next to the Rocky Mountains in the United States, so snowboarding, snow shoeing, camping in the snow – our idea of a great weekend was in an expedition tent in the middle of the wilderness, in the snow, rugged up together in a sleeping bag, and we were happy [he pauses, fighting off tears] with basically only what we could carry on our backs. And that was a realisation for us very early in our relationship. It didn't matter what happened – whether we lost our jobs, our home – so long as we could be together. And that was the worst thing about this entire journey, not being together."

Spending 54 days in a critical care unit, nine months in a stroke ward and another year and a bit in a care facility run by SACARE (the organisation I was filming for), Mike and Tanya were finally reunited – back sleeping under the same roof – on the 5th December 2016. "I'd been pulling out a camping mat and staying the night when I could, but there was nowhere we could find that offered spouses the opportunity to live in care 24/7 with their partner. I was distraught, constantly. But then, we found someone who would [he breaks down, letting out the pain of being apart for those two years], and that was SACARE. I'll never forget the day the owner, Andrew Marshall, pulled out a blueprint of a new house they were building and said 'what do you need?' It was just before Tanya got out of the hospital, and I was tired, a basket-case, but just the kindness and love they offered in that moment was life changing. Because it meant we could be together again!"

Living in a 24/7 care facility alongside his wife who was trapped in a silent motionless bubble may sound like one of those unfair sacrifices, but again, it's about finding *your* balance, which means knowing *your* self. "We moved back to Australia [from the US] in mid-2002. We knew Tanya could get a job in Sydney, but I didn't manage to find anything there. I was offered a contract in Canberra (300km away), so I was travelling there during the week and that was horrific. So after a few months, I gave up my contract and we both moved back to Adelaide, which was home for me. We lived with my parents for a short period while searching for work, and at one stage we got down to $80 in the bank and we had this moment as a couple where it didn't matter. We both went on to get well paid jobs and then the global financial crisis happened and we thought we might lose our jobs, so we thought, how are we going to get through this, and we pooled our money and bought a rural block of land for $15,000, knowing we could always pitch a tent and live there. Again now, it's a shitty situation, but **being together is what's important**. Because we might be completely different people than what we were before, but we're still fundamentally the same couple, and that's thanks to SACARE letting us live together [he pauses, as tears fall], and so because of that we feel fortunate. We consider ourselves quite fortunate, yeah."

I'd never heard the phrase before, nor since, but something I scribbled in my notepad during my interview with Mike was: *sacrifice is gratitude in action*. One specific visualisation solidified this for me. If Mike wanted to have a conversation with Tanya, or if he wanted to understand the terror she felt living with her condition (something he described a lot), he would have to spend hundreds of hours spelling out each letter of the alphabet until her eyes looked up to say 'yes that one'. So the easiest word would have been something like 'dad', which would have involved Mike saying: a-b-c-d [then she'd look up], a [then she'd look up], a-b-c-d [then she'd look up]. You could imagine the patience and sacrifice necessary for them both to have a decent conversation, let alone carry on a loving relationship. Still, their gratitude for one another, for life, and to be able to communicate at all, meant they were both willing to give or do whatever was needed to make it all work.

"What wouldn't you do for true love?" Mike asked me some months later when we caught up for a bite to eat. "Nothing," I promptly replied. "Exactly!" he said. "Because you never know how long that love is going to last or if you'll ever find it again." Asking Mike about how he'd coped with everything, he openly admitted to "barely scraping through." What kept him going, he said, wasn't just his undying love, but the knowledge that Tanya had it so much worse. She was literally a brain – a fiercely intelligent one at that – trapped in a piece of immovable flesh; and she knew it (can you possibly imagine the feeling!?). While Mike had been told recovery was an impossibility, he wanted to be sure they were doing all they could to make sure their life was as meaningful and happy as it could be. Just prior to that first interview I conducted, he'd actually gone back to part time hours at work, so he could investigate new technologies and supports that might enable them to better communicate and manage Tanya's condition. "She's only 46," he said, "so we've got to plan for the future." Shockingly, just eight months after I met Mike and Tanya – on 6 February 2018 – Tanya passed away peacefully with Mike at her side. As a testament to everything they were together, Mike and Tanya enjoyed one last voyage to their favourite camping spot on the Chicago Lakes, where he scattered her ashes. This woman, who Mike described as "an indomitable force of nature to all who knew her," was gone. Their 19 years of love felt way too short.

The reason I cried so much when I heard this wasn't because she was young. It wasn't even because it was tragically unexpected. It was because Mike had let me in. He'd been vulnerable. He'd let me feel what he felt. And it drew me closer to the both of them. I genuinely felt love for Mike and Tanya – and pretty soon I wasn't alone. Within months of its release, the highly emotional interview and story we'd filmed had been viewed by millions of people across the globe (see the video via thehappiest.com). While Mike's will to bare his soul took vulnerability, his decision to double-down on his love and commitment for Tanya – in spite of the uncertainty, risk and emotional exposure he faced – was one of the most courageous things I've seen a human do. "To give someone your heart and say, 'I know this could hurt so bad, but I'm willing to do it' ... that's courage," says renowned author and researcher Brené Brown. "But there is an increasing number of people in the world today who are not willing to take that risk. They'd rather never know love than to know hurt or grief, and that is a huge price to pay." It's not only causing billions of little barriers to form between us – because we're terrified to let people see inside – but by numbing ourselves to painful emotions, we're also numbing ourselves to positive emotions, and that's paralysing our humanness.

Naked, for all the world to see

"We're wired for love and we're hard-wired for belonging. It's in our DNA," Brown explains. "From the research, we know that the opposite of belonging, is fitting in. Fitting in is assessing and acclimating. Belonging is belonging to yourself first. Speaking your truth, telling your story, and never betraying yourself for other people. **True belonging doesn't require you to change who you are. It requires you to be who you are, and that's vulnerable.**" What's often misunderstood, says

Brown, is that vulnerability is not weakness, it is our greatest measure of courage, because it's about showing up even when you can't control the outcome – even if there's a good chance you will fail – because that's life. "There are no guarantees," says Brown; and Mike is the perfect example. The prize for his courage and vulnerability was terribly short-lived, and yet the gift he will forever be able to hold onto is the knowledge that he entered the arena and fought for Tanya in spite of the fear and the odds.

"If you're brave with your life, if you choose to live in the arena, you're going to get your ass kicked. You're going to fall, you're going to fail, you're going to know heartbreak," says Brown in her Netflix special *The Call to Courage*. "These are the words I say before my feet hit the floor every day, 'Today, I'll choose courage over comfort. I can't make commitments for tomorrow, but today, I'm gonna choose to be brave.'" The alternative, she says, is that we get to the end of our lives and wonder – 'what if I had shown up?'. "A lot of cheap seats in the arena are filled with people who never venture onto the floor. They just hurl mean-spirited criticisms and put-downs from a safe distance," writes Brown in her book *Rising Strong*. "The problem is, when we stop caring what people think and stop feeling hurt by cruelty, we lose our ability to connect. But when we're defined by what people think, we lose the courage to be vulnerable. Therefore, we need to be selective about the feedback we let into our lives." Because as Tay Tay says, "haters gonna hate," and that can suck.

When I was crowdfunding to raise money and awareness for this book (and a large photographic exhibition), a distant friend of a friend actually took it upon himself to publicly post a terribly false, misleading and hurtful message on my personal Facebook page. "I am sorry to say Mike, but I hope you do not achieve your Kickstarter goal. That way people will not be conned into supporting your travel and lifestyle … If anyone wants to donate to an organisation that will actually make a difference, here is a list of Australian accredited non-government organisations … Also if anyone wants a book of smiling faces, here is one that was published in 2012 – unfortunately this book did not rid the world of poverty and suicide," said the guy, who works as a migration, globalisation and climate change lecturer and researcher. 'No, I won't let this affect me,' I thought. 'He's just ignorant and unaware, so I'll listen to him and then slowly piece together the puzzle for him on how my book and my work can help to end suicide, poverty and war (as well as climate change, problems associated with globalisation and fear of migration – his passions)'. Some hours later, I'd gotten nowhere, there was no 'sorry' forthcoming. He didn't even seem to care that I'd donated hundreds of thousands of dollars of my own money to fund my life's passion to inspire a more peaceful and happy world. It honestly makes me uneasy re-reading his comments, because there's a venom in them that's simply designed to cut me down. What ever happened to: if you don't have anything nice to say, don't say anything at all? Maybe I just needed to channel Brené Brown, who said, "if you're not in the arena getting your ass kicked, I'm not interested in your feedback."

What this incident told me, and what I've increasingly come to realise, is that I'm not immune to the fear, the shame or the criticism that's an inevitable part of life. While self-doubt has rarely stopped me from taking chances or putting myself out there, what's become clearer of late is that the veneer of confidence and the conviction of purpose I exude, and feel inside, is not impervious to the pain of judgement. If anything, caring so much about the work I do, coupled with those subconscious feelings of shame and being unworthy, has left me more terrified of rejection than ever. The inverse of this (and how this fear manifests in reality) is again this need for love and acceptance – someone to tell me 'you're good, you're enough, I'm here for you'. Embarrassing as all of this is to admit, it's not nearly as torturous or regretful as the subliminal reactions this damage has unleashed.

When I started writing this chapter, I chose to disclose a bunch of my most hideous and most recent shortcomings to Sash, because I knew it was time to stop running from my story. The most difficult transgression to own up to (because I'm someone who prides himself on learning from his mistakes), was that I'd done my usual bullshit of drinking, female-attention-seeking and distancing myself, because I wrongly blamed Sash for the feelings of rejection and not-being-enough that consumed me during our 2019 trip to Europe (the result of being denied lots of interviews and feeling alone during my period of solo travel). Letting Sash hold all the cards to my heart did make me vulnerable to being hurt by her, but in truth, my enemy was not the woman who loved and adored me, it was me. My shame. My pain. My past. The problem is, **it's so much easier to cause pain than feel pain**, and that's what I'd done for far too long. I'd let my pain haunt our relationship, and that was not OK, nor sustainable.

"I can't keep doing this," said Sash, "if I love myself, which I do, then I need to stop you from hurting me. I need you to change, or I need to leave. I'm not going to be one of those women who stays around putting up with being hurt." When I terrifyingly let Sash read this chapter, and when I asked her how or why she had kept loving me, her answer spoke of love's true nature – as the roller-coaster ride of your life:

"Well, I guess loving you has made my life spectacular. Choosing to keep loving you hasn't been easy. It's been so scary because it could hurt so, so bad. But not loving you would mean life would go back to being good. Only, I don't want to settle for good, especially now that I know what spectacular is like... I've also seen it as an opportunity to be better myself. To not worry about what others think, but to only think about how this impacts you and I. **I will never go to my grave regretting that I loved you too much.** But I would regret not fighting for our love. I also think you deserve that love. That you want to open yourself to the love I can give you and you can give me. If you didn't truly want that, I don't think I'd chose to keep loving you. Plus, you've made me better too."

In order to figure out how I could stop hurting us, and how I could stop betraying the 99% of me that is good and so full of love, I recently found myself doing something I never thought I would – I went to see a psychologist. It felt odd, and massively confronting, walking into his office – because I am a highly resilient and genuinely happy guy – but I knew I needed to air my shortcomings, and work through that 1% of my story that was plaguing me. "You either walk inside your story and own it or you stand outside your story and hustle for your worthiness," says Brown, who goes on to describe shame as: the intensely painful feeling or experience of believing we are flawed and therefore unworthy of acceptance and belonging. "Shame hates it when we reach out and tell our story," Brown continues. "It hates having words wrapped around it – it can't survive being shared. Shame loves secrecy. When we bury our story, the shame metastasises." In my case, this psychological-cancer had spread from me, to us (my marriage). The only cure for such shame, says Brown, is to find someone who loves you enough to let you bare your soul, darkness and all (so thank you Sash!).

"Through my research, I found that vulnerability is the glue that holds relationships together. It's the magic sauce," says Brown. "If we have one or two people in our lives who can sit with us and hold space for our shame stories, and love us for our strengths and struggles, we are incredibly lucky. If we have a friend, or a small group of friends, or family who embraces our imperfections, vulnerabilities, and power, and fills us with a sense of belonging, we are incredibly lucky." And yet, the fact that Sash loved me didn't rescue me from the more onerous task of loving myself (or more specifically, that final 1%).

Taking a step back and to the (out)side

The need to love our friends, our family and ourselves seems clear enough, but what about our need to love and relate to nature, strangers and all living things?

"We are hurting ourselves by not prioritising our deep human connection to the natural world," writes Florence Williams, author of *The Nature Fix: Why Nature Makes Us Happier, Healthier and More Creative*. "We've lost sight of how natural spaces – even citified versions of them – can help us feel psychologically restored (even after just 15 minutes)." More than 100 studies tell us that being in nature – or even watching it in videos – benefits our brains, bodies, feelings, thought processes and social interactions. "Humans have long intuited that being in nature is good for the mind and body. From indigenous adolescents completing rites of passage in the wild to modern East Asian cultures taking 'forest baths', many have looked to nature as a place for healing and personal growth," write psychologists Kristophe Green and Dacher Keltner in *Yes Magazine*. "Nature often induces awe, wonder, and reverence, all emotions known to have a variety of benefits, promoting everything from well-being and altruism to humility and health. Regrettably, however, people seem to be spending less time outdoors and less time immersed in nature than before. It is also clear that, in the past 30 years, people's levels of stress and sense of 'busyness' have risen dramatically. These converging forces have led environmental writer Richard Louv to coin the term 'nature deficit disorder' – a form of suffering that comes from a sense of disconnection from nature and its powers."

Recent studies led by Gregory Bratman out of Stanford University not only concluded that a 90-minute walk is a valid way to protect against depression, but a second study illustrated that being in a park (but not on a city street) reduced blood flow to the subgenual prefrontal cortex, a part of the brain associated with negative thought patterns. Adding to this are the results of the UK's first month-long nature challenge, which took place in 2015 and involved people 'doing something wild' every day for 30 consecutive days. Director of the study and Head of Psychology at the University of Derby, Dr. Miles Richardson said the number of people reporting their health as "excellent" increased by 30%, while rates of happiness, vitality, meaningfulness and mindfulness also improved. "These correlations are of a similar magnitude to those found between wellbeing and other variables, such as marriage and education, whose relationships with wellbeing are well established," says Richardson in an interview with *BBC World*. "It's time to realise that **nature is more than just a material resource, it's also a pathway to human health and happiness**," Green and Keltner conclude.

While many of my happiest memories as a child revolve around trees, sand, snow, dirt, lakes, fish, frogs and stars (and they still do), the incredible satisfaction and abiding joy I've felt as an adult comes largely from one central belief – we are all one and the same. If we are all connected, as intuition and research tells me we are, then denying any being love, means denying yourself that same love. To put it simply (well sort of), if we're all human then there is no distance between us except that which our love, or lack of love creates. When I tried explaining this concept to Sash… well, here's a story I wrote a while back about how it went.

> Four years ago I got in trouble for saying "I love you" to my fiance Sash. The problem (I must disclose) wasn't those three words, but the next hundred or so. "I love you," I said. "Just as I love all human beings. From members of ISIS to my worst enemy, I feel a deep, profound and unconditional love for all people and things, because true love must be boundless, unperturbed by our flailing emotions." The palpable anger on Sash's face forced me to speed through the insanely complex belief I was trying to flesh out.
>
> "What we share is a remarkably rare bond. A crazy connection and relationship that takes us to places unknown. This is the epitome of our existence – what we have – it goes beyond that which we can explain with mere words. Beyond love. It's as if we've given birth to an entirely new entity that didn't and wouldn't exist without our relationship – like there is

me, you and 'we' – and this third thing is magic. It's another creature of sorts. And that's what is so special about what we refer to as 'love between two people' or that special kind of love, bond, connection or relationship that we have," I said.

By this stage Sash looked as if she might throw her engagement ring right back in my face. "How do you think this makes me feel?" she asked me. "I don't know," I replied. "You know how I feel about you. All of this is just words. Ideas. It's semantics. I guess I just see love as a more universal bond between all beings, whereas what we have is specific, special to us, a unique relationship that probably can't and won't ever be described adequately." "It's lucky I know you love me and that you're not saying 'I love you' to everyone you meet," she interrupted with a stern face. "Like you told me a while ago, you said there was a language that had 12 different words for the various kinds of love. What was it? Maybe you need to learn to speak that language!?" concluded Sash. And she was probably right.

English really doesn't have the right words to paint the picture I was (and am) attempting to depict. Perhaps I should have learnt Tamil, the language Sash was referring to, which actually has more than 50 words for love. In Tamil, there is actually a specific word for that 'all-encompassing love in the deepest sense,' which is anbu. There are also several words to describe the love Sash and I share: from imil (loving bond, attachment, dear-bond, also means fullness of love), to aṇi (sweet, closeness type of love), aḻi (melt in love), āṇam (affection, feeling soul-embracing love), iṇpam (love in happiness or fulfilling relation), uḻuval (love soaked in deep feelings) and vēḷ (love, endearing love, friendship) just to name a few.

While my wife probably remains a little confused by my ongoing definition of love, I suppose in a way that's my point – human relationships are indescribable – other than to say they are highly complicated and absolutely essential to achieving our happiest state. Whether it's your child, partner, sibling, parent, friend, teacher, colleague, stranger or life-saving doctor – feeling connected to or loved by someone is the prize in this game of life.

It might sound odd or a bit idealistic to say 'we should all love one another unconditionally, even our enemies', but the truth is, this is the means and the path to our happiest state. What is often misunderstood about this notion of unconditional love, says writer Denise Hill, is that it does not mean neglecting yourself or becoming a deaf, dumb, blind and abused doormat. "Unconditional love is a gruesome, painful and sacrificial way to care for another human being. It isn't butterfly kisses, a steamy night of passion or the joy a son brings to his mother's heart. It is so much deeper than that. It is endless. It is profound. It's powerful," she writes in an article on *Life Hack*. "Loving someone unconditionally means loving the very essence of the individual. Just as they are. Despite what they do or fail to do, with no expectation of anything in return – including love."

Interestingly, in 2009 scientists studying the relationship between brain activity and unconditional love found that caring for someone without needing to receive any kind of reward involves a complex interplay between seven separate areas of the brain. Given just three of these areas showed up in similar scans that measured romantic or sexual love, researchers concluded that unconditional love should be seen as an entirely separate emotion.

'Aha,' I thought. For years I'd wondered just how I could, on the one hand, effortlessly love all human beings unconditionally, while on the other, struggle to maintain a single intimate relationship. But it kind of makes sense now – they're not linked. In fact, if I were to hazard a guess, I would say that the very same damage and imperfection that makes me naturally empathetic – a prerequisite of unconditional love – is the same thing that's shaken my marriage. Similarly, unconditional love doesn't necessarily require me to receive or accept too much love in return, which is often a discomfort or point of tension in relationships, when you feel unworthy. It may well be my darker side that drew me into this unique form of love, but as the lead researcher Professor Mario Beauregard suggests, there is immense lightness and good that can come from it.

"Unconditional love, extended to others without exception, is considered to be one of the highest expressions of spirituality. However, nothing has been known regarding its neural underpinnings until now," said Professor Beauregard of Montreal University's centre for research into neurophysiology and cognition, in an interview with *The Times*.

What Beauregard's findings showed specifically is that some of the areas activated when experiencing unconditional love were also involved in releasing dopamine – a chemical inherently associated with profound pleasure, and even feelings of reward and euphoria. "The rewarding nature of unconditional love facilitates the creation of strong emotional links. Such robust bonds may critically contribute to the survival of the human species," Beauregard wrote in his research. Arguably, this discovery flies directly in the face of evolutionary theory, which says we should only feel the above-mentioned emotions for people who pass our genes to future generations, such as partners and children. In reality, what we're seeing is a surge in unconditional love being experienced between people with whom there is no blood connection, such as carers and clients, mentors and mentees, benefactors and beneficiaries, blood/organ donors and those still alive because of them, even foster families and the children they take in.

Looking at my own life, and when, why and how unconditional love has shaped my happiness, I'm immediately taken back to the arms and the oversized boobs of my eldest sister Cindy, who would smother me with both whenever I needed a cuddle. My grandma too, was forever willing to blow up her food processor making me and my friend, Sam, milkshakes, while my grandad would happily stand there for hours on end bowling, hitting or catching a ball with me. My parents, and particularly my mum (because dad was often at work), would do all the same stuff – we were showered with love and joy as kids – but as we got older and they started chasing their own dreams (such as moving to Gin Gin) they invariably made it feel as if supporting us was a chore. They were doing it because they *had to*, not because they *wanted to*. In that sense I guess their love felt quite hard and practical, rather than soft and gushing as it was with my sister and grandparents. What these kinds of recollections taught me in my late teens and early twenties, was that unconditional love wasn't enough – it needed a condition – not on the person being loved, but on the person doing the loving; and that condition is that the love is genuine and fully expressed. **"It's not enough to tell someone you love them, you need to show them, make them feel it in their stomach,"** says Sash.

She wasn't the first to show me this, but Sash is the best example I know (or have seen) at conveying her love for others. She simply won't take no for an answer – if she loves you, you're going to know about it, and it's going to be loud, colourful and a bit wacky. While this boisterous sort of love isn't in my repertoire (other than when I'm playing with kids), one of the colossal lessons and behaviours Sash has imparted on me is how to be more vulnerable in showing my love.

"I was showered with affection, my parents literally drenched me in their love, and it filled every part of me. From my cheeks, which my dad would pinch and kiss and rub and hold, to my arms which to this day crave my mum's belly to hold – no, there was no questioning their love for me – not even when they refused to buy me what I wanted," said Sash. "Being an only child, people often thought 'oh, she must be spoilt', but that wasn't true, not for me. Well, I hope not [she laughs]. We lived comfortably, and my dad said the hardest thing was saying no to me, but he did, because he loved me. For example, he knew if I ate McDonalds every day or every week I might not appreciate it, or I might become unhealthy or entitled, so we got it once a month. When we did get it though, he would make a big song and dance and get me all excited about it, and that was typical of my childhood, I was spoilt with the thing that mattered most, which was love."

"Being loved so much, meant I wanted to be worth loving – because I loved being loved – which inspired me to work to be my best. What this did in turn, was let me truly believe I am worthy of love," said Sash, when I asked her how she thinks love works.

"I remember a conversation I had with my mum once. She said, as she and my dad had so many times, 'I love you no matter what'. Trying to be a smarty pants I said 'well, what if I kill someone!?' And mama said 'well, I'd be very disappointed and sad, but I'll still love you'... I guess I want people to feel that same love. Because I was not perfect. But I was loved regardless. And maybe that's what made me a decent human being. So, that's the love I want to show others – that no matter your flaws, you deserve love – and that love might actually consume any flaws. You know, it's like darkness. If your in a pitch black room, you can't see anything in front of you. But even the tiniest crack in the door, or hole in the curtain will let light in. No matter how small the crack or hole, the room will never be pitch black again and suddenly you can see – even if just a little. Love is like that. Even the tiniest bit of love is the light we need in our darkest days."

Sash with her mum during cancer treatment.

Sash sharing her love and joy with a stranger in Uganda.

Sash's dad holding her as a baby.

Sash with her mum, grandma and great grandma.

Sash's dad walking her down the isle at our wedding.

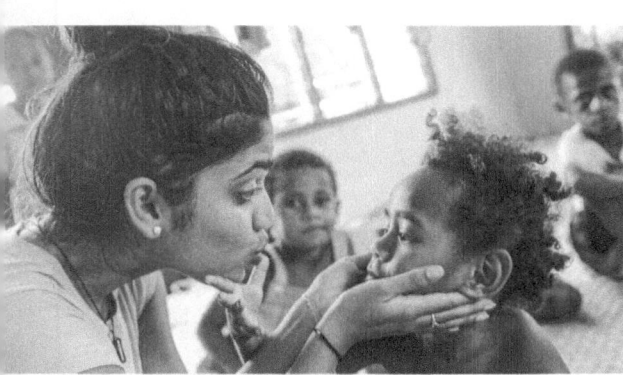
Sash cheering up a young girl called Evy in Yako Village, Fiji.

Sash playing soccer with a boy called Senura in Sri Lanka.

(Left to right) Sujith, Senura, Tharangani and Sasinda.

The price of love

Someone who demonstrated Sash's words in every way, everyday, was 29-year-old Tharangani Priyanka Perera. When I met her, Tharangani was living on the streets of Colombo, Sri Lanka with her husband Sujith JL (37) and their two children, Sasinda (5) and Senura (3). Every night the family would sleep outside a shut tailor's shop at the end of Sash's grandfather's street (where I was staying). Speaking to Tharangani (as much as we could, given the language barrier) and interacting with her kids on my way to and from getting lunch and dinner on a number of occasions, it wasn't long before I started buying a little extra of whatever I was having, and dropping it to them on my way home. Then, as part of our 'Selfless Santa' adventure, we bought the family a plastic picnic blanket (to stop them from laying directly on the ground), some pillows (as they had none) and some toys for the kids. We also invested in buying them one nice new set of clothes each, for two reasons: one, to appear presentable in job interviews (something they said would be useful), and two, because they felt too embarrassed (or judged) to attend church in their tattered outfits. Still, even without our help or 'things', Tharangani said they'd always found plenty of reasons to smile.

"Even though we don't have much, we like to live smiling," she says, showing off her giant, surprisingly white teeth during an interview we conducted for an A Million Smiles video called *The Happy Mum* (see thehappiest.com to watch it). "We always like to stay happy," Tharangani continued. "There's no point dwelling on our past problems, because our family life will get affected, and our children's minds also get affected, so **it's better to live within our means and be happy with our children**."

The 'past problems' Tharangani eludes to, began roughly 15 years prior to our meeting, when she decided to 'disobey' her family's wishes by marrying for love, and by choosing to wed a man who was seen as 'much lower' on the social pecking order. Rejected outright by her wealthy family, Tharangani (14) and Sujith (22) were left to fend for themselves. With Sujith unable (or unwilling) to find work – he didn't seem to want to do much other than sit around, gamble and drink when we met him – Tharangani took on the role of 'breadwinner', and then, three years later, of 'mother'.

Despite giving birth to four children in nine years, Tharangani has remained the sole earner for the family – selling food on the roadside

– while desperately trying to pursue other opportunities (without much luck). With their financial hardship forcing their two eldest – who were 12 and 8 (as of early 2013) – to be taken in by a monastery several hours away, it was hard not to be critical of Tharangani's husband, or her choice to blindly remain with him. The predicament led to an interesting discussion between Sash and I, as we debated the merits of 'arranged' or 'semi-arranged' marriages versus 'letting kids do their own thing'. Personally, I don't agree with wholly-arranged marriages, whereby the children have no say, and are often promised from a young age, without any consideration of who they might become and whether that will suit their future partner. I'm also dead against the dowry system – a common reason for arranged marriage – as it plainly and simply turns love into a financial transaction. So far as semi-arranged marriages go – whereby parents help to introduce or find a possible match for their kids – I can see some merit. Because without some distant, seeing eye, love can be blind, as Tharangani was proof. Regardless, and in spite of our and her parent's judgement, Tharangani was at peace with her choices.

"There are people who live for the happiness of their parents, and I know I could have taken up that situation. My mother said that if I left my children and my husband they would accept me back home," she recalls. "That might have made my parents happy, but not my children, and certainly I could not have found happiness in that."

Shockingly, this isn't the only incidence where Tharangani has been asked to choose between love and money: "When I was about to have my youngest son, a Maldivian couple came and offered to help me when they saw that I was pregnant. They offered to buy me a house, and give me money, if I would let them take my baby and go abroad." But the unborn Senura was not for sale, she asserts, before promptly adding, **"Love has no price."**

Despite the absence of her eldest children bringing her to tears, and in spite of the couple's nightly ritual of burying what few valuables they have in the sand to avoid robbery, Tharangani was happier and had her head screwed on tighter than most.

"My husband and my children are more important to me than money," she reiterates. "Happiness comes from your heart, from our experiences, and from our children. So, I am living as best as I can with my children."

This most unlikely of role models – a homeless mother of four

– to me typified just how simple life and happiness can be. **"Love is everything,"** she said, echoing a truth it's taken Harvard researchers 80 years to figure out, "and so we must make time and space for it, regardless of the challenges we face."

Being able to combat the daily adversity of feeling 'lesser', or as if they'd be dealt a bad hand, Tharangani said it was all about being grateful for what they *did* have. "There are many people without limbs and who can't even walk, and some are sad because they can't see the world [the blind]. I feel that God has given my family, a life without disabilities, and for that I tell my children 'we must be happy,'" she said, as she began to smile. "Because when we are happy, and when we smile, our pains disappear."

Tharangani's ability to let go of the torment of her parent's abandonment, had actually freed her heart to try and revive the relationship she'd once shared with her mother. "Because my father has already passed away and now my mother can't do things anymore, I would like to be there for her, but they don't like me," she admits with difficulty. "Still, I will try to show her my love, because I know she needs it. We all need it…"

The love evolution, or should it be revolution…

Having seen and felt what simple, fully-expressed, unconditional love can do for a person, my focus for some years now has been to share this gift with others; none more so than my family. In fact, right now as I write this I am sitting on the back porch of my parents' house, because I am baby-sitting the four foster children they look after for two and a half weeks. Roughly four months ago, during an interview with my mum for this book, she told me her and dad were not OK because it was "too hard to make plans, so there's nothing to look forward to," said mum.

I was genuinely worried that this would kill them if they didn't do something to diffuse the stress. "Tell me how I can help," I said. "I can drop everything almost anytime, so just pick a date and a location and give yourselves a break and something to look forward to. Please, it hurts me to hear you like this, I love you guys, and you need to be happy to be able to do what you need to for those kids, so if you don't want to do it for yourselves, do it for them," I pleaded.

It might sound an odd thing to say, but it was the truth. Plus, I felt mum and dad housed some of that same shame and guilt I did – again surrounding my brother, and as a result of their own childhoods – which made the thought of doing anything for themselves difficult, because they felt unworthy of love – as if somehow, they deserved to suffer. Knowing exactly how they felt, but also the precise solution to that pain – the love and sacrifice Sash had shown me – I was determined to pay it forward. Not just because mum and dad were good people, but because they deserve to feel that way too. Happily, I can report that right this minute, my parents are in Kochi, India, reinforcing their 40+ year bond and letting the stress drip out of them with every sweat inducing curry they consume.

I may not be able to delete my past or erase the suffering I've caused myself, Sash or other victims of my damage, but I can endeavour to heal myself and become a better and more loving person. Someone who doesn't just diffuse cycles of suffering (with forgiveness), but who ignites cycles of love (as Sash has in me).

At the end of the day, **I am the common denominator in every relationship I will ever have. So, if I fix myself, I fix them all.** Mending ourselves or becoming more whole isn't about blocking out our agony, fear or imperfection, it's about seeing our pain and our vulnerability as the culture from which we grow. As poet Kahlil Gibran said, "Out of suffering have emerged the strongest souls; the most massive characters are seared with scars." Just look at Elton John, Beethoven or Mother Teresa, all "made gold out of shit" says Vaillant, the former Harvard psychiatrist. This doesn't mean we should intentionally seek out or cause pain, only that we should see it for what it is – a teacher. If we can do this, and if we can accept that no one is perfect, and that misery and ecstasy are two sides of the same coin, then perhaps we can reduce the space between us – the shame, guilt and hate, which plagues our ability to connect more closely and more deeply with friends, family and all beings. In the words of Brené Brown, it all begins with entering the arena: being willing to say 'I love you', not knowing if they'll say it back, or being open to disclosing your imperfections to a friend even if it's scary as hell. Ultimately, there is no progress without discomfort. No love without pain. It may be easier to fear the world than trust it, but what basis for life and growth is that?

Without love, we'd be just another carnal, savage, self-obsessive creature consumed by our ego's need to pass on our DNA. Without relationships, we'd never have left the cave, and would likely be extinct. Our ability to relate, love, organise and connect is what's allowed us to become successful hunter-gatherers, farmers, builders, inventors and now this complex global network of cultures, races and economies bound together by common stories, systems and desires. A common love. Because that need we all feel to belong, to be held, to sit in nature – it isn't a mystery or an illusion, it is the quintessential ingredient to our happiest life. "The conclusion of the study, not in a medical but in a psychological sense, is that connection is the whole shooting match," says Vaillant, referencing the 80+ year Harvard study.

Here are 9 things you can do to have better and more loving relationships:

1. Forgive.

2. Empathise.

3. Learn to love yourself.

4. Be vulnerable. Practice open and honest communication.

5. Realise love isn't one-size-fits-all – what might be love for one person could be harmful to another.

6. Accept yourself and others 'as is'.

7. Love is a choice. Ask yourself in each situation, what is the most loving response?

8. Suffering is such an important part of life. Embrace it, and help others to do the same.

9. Make love unconditional. Perform daily acts of service.

What is love, what is anything,

without a mind that can see it?

A roughly seven-year-old girl from Cambodia, just to put things in perspective.

12

THE PRIME MINISTER AND THE SEX SLAVE

You can't imagine what I'm about to tell you. No one could. I certainly couldn't – not until I heard it for myself. Pai Somang's story is... well... it sits so far outside the realms of vulgarity we are used to that my editor tells me I need to include this: **WARNING! Do not read the indented section below if you're at all susceptible to tales of childhood torture, utter betrayal and violent rape.** This is not a run of the mill trigger warning, this is intended to alert you to some seriously disturbing and distressing stuff.

Knowing even just a bit about Pai's tale before I met her, I had wondered how I'd ask her what I needed to? Showing me to her room where we were to conduct our interview, I stopped nervously outside the door, recognising that this must be a sacred space for her. She laughed at my awkward pause and gestured for me to come in. Then, via a weary translator, the normally bubbly Pai relayed her horror.

> "When I was seven, my mother unknowingly sold me to a brothel," says Pai. When she attempted to deny her first customer by telling one of the brothel gangsters 'no', Pai says her captors set about breaking her. What began with drinking that customer's urine soon escalated, as the owner ordered her to be tied up and whipped until she bled. Still saying 'no', she was soaked in a barrel of stinking sewage water, before being thrown on the ground and stung by scorpions and poisonous ants. Pai was then taken to another room and electrocuted. Faint and suffering unthinkably, the seven-year-old finally submitted, as she uttered the word 'yes'.

THE HAPPIEST

As the Asian pedophile hoping to rape the young virgin walked towards her, she again refused, crying and screaming to be let go. Infuriated by her actions, brothel thugs jammed a handful of hot ground chillies in her vagina, before taking a scolding metal stake and shoving it inside the tiny seven-year-old. Shortly after, she was tied to a bed and raped.

Unthinkably, this would not be the only time a man would pay hundreds of dollars to be her 'first', as the brothel owner – a woman – twice stitched her vagina closed (with no anaesthetic) so she could be resold as a virgin. This excruciatingly painful practice is common in Asian brothels, with girls screaming in pain as their stitches rip, tricking clients into paying a higher price.

Pai, who was in high demand due to her young age, was soon forced to "serve 20 to 25 clients a day," a figure she said her tiny body simply could not handle. "At that time, I could not afford it as I was so young, I was only 7 years old, I wasn't able to serve that many customers, so they tortured me by hitting me, electrocuting, and giving me no food or water," she said. "When I could not serve their clients, as many as they wanted, then the brothel owner would ask all of her gangsters to rape me, to teach me a lesson."

At this point in the interview I broke. "Why? What sense does it make for her to get her goons to rape you? Why inflict more pain on your broken body? How could a human do this?" I cried. Seeing my rage, Pai lent over and placed a gentle, consoling hand on my shoulder. "How could anyone watch on as a seven year old was made to go through this? Who's doing this? And where the fuck are the authorities?" I mumbled through my tears.

Twenty-one-year-old Pai Somang (whose name I have changed for security reasons) was one of several former sex slaves I met during my inaugural trip to document the happiest people, places and ideas on Earth. The reason I chose Phnom Penh, Cambodia as my first stop, and sex trafficking (and abject poverty) as my first topic, was to test a theory I'd long held, which was this: perspective, or the lens through which we choose to see and frame our world, is invariably more important to our happiness than the world we actually experience.

Take Pai's life. Through 96 of 100 lenses there is only misery. For her, and for me.

When we look at the statistics for instance, we see that more than 40 million people are now victims of forced prostitution, labour and slavery across the world. That's more than three times the figure transported during the entire trans-Atlantic slave trade (which lasted for 400 years). In fact, as we speak, there are roughly 10 times as many girls being trafficked into brothels as African slaves were transported to the New World in the peak years of the slave trade.

Seeing too, just how insidious a part poverty and the resulting lack of education played in human trafficking was troubling. It's why Pai's mother — following the death of her father, who was the breadwinner — decided to sell Pai to a stranger who promised she would become a housekeeper in the city. Sadly, for ignorant starving families, daughters are a resource to be used in any way possible, in the battle to survive.

I could continue to list out another 94 miserable truths I witnessed during my time with Pai and others who'd escaped this insidious trade — and don't get me wrong, all are necessary, valid and have played a part in shaping my perspective — but **where we must learn to focus our attention is on the specks of happiness we can sift out of the rubble**. Because that's what the happiest minds do so effortlessly: they let the shit we can't or won't change pass through their mental sieve, without getting rid of the stirring questions or lessons that may drive us to think or act in a way that leads us (and others) to a happier reality.

For example, listening to Pai share the details of her tragic childhood, I knew there was nothing I could do to undo it, and yet, the puddle of tears in my hands told me I needed to do something. My heart, soul or conscience (wherever that inner dialogue comes from) wouldn't let me rest until I had. Initially, with steam still pouring from my ears, I got back to my hostel room and checked my bank balance to see how many police or rogue gunmen I could rent, to help me raid some of these brothels. With a $25K pay-out from my former employer just landing in my account, I figured we might be able to rescue a couple of hundred girls. But what if just one girl dies in my reckless attempt? I thought. Or, what if I die? What if I'm jailed? What if I don't save anyone? Where do I look for armed men? How should I approach the police? Half of them are on the payroll of the brothels. What if I choose the wrong one? Will the girls be hurt? What the fuck am I thinking? I can't become a killer.

That's not helping anyone. Fuck, fuck, fuck. Why do I have to have a conscience? People without morals so effortlessly tear this world apart – why does doing what's right have to be so hard?

By 1:00am, the anger-fuelled adrenaline rushing round my head had died down just a tad, and I began to concoct a plan that I thought could truly work. I was going to launch an organisation that would get volunteer photographers from Australia and other developed countries to travel to Cambodia (and other sex trafficking hot spots,) and photograph the men using the brothels. Their images would be placed on a website and shared via social media. We'd then invite people to name and shame the sick individuals who fund this horrific trade, which is worth $32 billion globally. With one estimate suggesting 25% of foreign visitors to Cambodia are sex tourists, I felt this 'public shaming' approach could both scare off and potentially catch offenders. If people knew they were risking their photo being seen by their friends, family or boss, who would be part of this filth?

That night I tossed and turned furiously, as I contemplated whether I was willing to give up my life as a writer and filmmaker who could expose innumerous inequalities, in order to focus on this singular injustice. Hearing and trusting that little voice inside me as it said 'you need to stay the path you're on', I decided to email my plan to the anti-trafficking NGO that had hosted me, in the hope they might consider it as a means to alleviate the demand for girls in the first place.

Walking a well known strip for prostitutes and brothels the night after my interview with Pai, the sea of pimps, barely dressed girls and men on the prowl for a cheap root floored me. Literally. The anger was paralysing. Sitting there on a filthy street corner in Phnom Penh, an older lady holding the hand of a prepubescent girl she was selling, approached me. Her eyes (the girl's) glanced my way. I could barely breathe. Do I kill the old bitch and snatch the girl? What if I offered her $10K for the girl's freedom? Was this perpetuating the underlying problem though – that girls were an object to be traded – or was it saving a young woman from a world of suffering?

Out of nowhere, one of those specks of happiness I'd held onto floated into my view. It was Pai's response to the question: how do you feel towards the owner of the brothel you were tortured in? "My anger wants her to be tortured like she did violently to me," Pai began. "But dharma [a Buddhist word meaning 'the truth about the way things are, and always will be'], says that because she has no education, she never understands about law or what is right and she is poor so she needs money," says Pai. "So, I forgive her as she did it blindly [she pauses]. It doesn't mean I omit my pains, I can never forget about it, but **if we let hate consume us, we become useless to others**, so we must try to return to having love inside us, so we can help other survivors smile too. That is my mission now, to give others their life back, as mine was to me." This remarkable lens through which Pai had chosen to see her world not only gave her purpose and peace, but profound happiness too. It was also one of two things that stopped me from belting that old lady and making off with the girl.

The other reactive-anger-restraint was something one of Pai's colleagues, Mey, had told me: "No one chooses this, but some know nothing else, so we must be careful when rescuing the girls, so we don't scare them into thinking they have done something wrong, because that is when they return to the streets. That is why we set them up with another source of income, because poverty and a lack of knowledge in how to make a business is normally what forces them to become trapped in this life." That's why going around grabbing girls out of brothels doesn't work, she says, "that's why organisations like ours exist." "Because keeping these girls out is about giving them a family they can rely on [she looks at her colleagues] and another means to survive. That's why we're happy here, because we have both." Remembering these words and the selfless, hopeful, happy lens from which they were born, slowly let me reclaim my calm.

Sitting down at a local restaurant for dinner, searching my mind for any other signs or specks of happiness this experience might gift me, a grave disgust grew inside me as a waiter brought me the bottle of beer I'd ordered. Clearly, and quite suddenly, my relative comfort in life had left me feeling utterly uncomfortable. Who the hell am I to sit here sipping on a beer, while millions of girls are forced to lay there as their bodies are defiled by empty, pitiful, weak men? I knew if a girl like Pai had the money I did, she'd be "helping other survivors", because that's how every single girl I spoke to answered the question, "what makes you happy today?" If helping other survivors had let these girls restore some semblance of happiness in their lives, maybe it would do the same for me? Maybe if I took the superhero cape off and focussed on doing what

I could for them – Pai and her colleagues – not my own sense of self, then I'd see the world the way they did.

That night I plainly and simply gave what I could to the organisation that Pai worked for. The result? It was one of the happiest things I've ever done.

You may think I was acting solely out of guilt, but that's not entirely true. What happens when we see or experience new things – particularly things this shocking – is that we change our perception, which gives birth to a new reality. New rules. New behaviours. New attitudes. A new lens. Because when the dust stirred up by significant life events eventually settles, that's when the specks of happiness emerge.

Like when I found out it costs around $3000 to rescue, rehabilitate and keep a girl out of sex trafficking, all of a sudden money took on a new value – I began to measure the worth of something by, 'how many girls I could save for that amount? Or, how many of that thing would let me free a sex slave?' I didn't do this forever, it would drive you nuts, but for a short time it did let me see the price of my own selfish spending habits, namely blindly pissing away money on booze (which did no good for anyone). Now, don't stress, I didn't give up alcohol, and I'm not suggesting you do either. Rather, it's about being open to the continuous changes life demands of us in order to strike an ongoing balance between your soul and the perspective with which you see the world. Without that bargain – which saw me limit my drinking to no more than a handful of beers a week – you'll never arrive at your happiest state. Because the little angel and devil inside you will forever be screaming at one another.

One of the more sizable specks of happiness that Pai and other victims left me with was a deep sense of gratitude and appreciation – even when I considered my gravest injustice. Because, yes, I had been raped and abused, but the torture, the solitude and the life that led to their abuse was not comparable to my own. I never lived in poverty. I was not sold off by my mum. I was never electrocuted. I was never stung by scorpions. I was not 7 years old. It might sound a little obvious or even distasteful, but *not* being a sex slave, was (and is) a huge reason to be happy. When you consider that right now, the UN estimates there are 4.8 million girls trapped in situations like Pai's, all of your problems will seem smaller. And that's the true beauty of growing our perspective – it enlarges our sphere of relativity. Because for those who have never met a former sex slave or witnessed abject poverty – missing your train or being served overdone poached eggs might seem like a big deal.

The thing is, sometimes even if we do technically 'know' there are others doing it tougher than us – because we've seen a documentary, World Vision ad or travelled to a poorer country – it doesn't necessarily mean that those thoughts automatically come to our salvation in the midst of a stressful or unhappy situation. That's because we don't always absorb or adopt those things we see and experience into our perspective. Changing our lens or thinking relies on a proactive attitude – and most often we can't be bothered updating the software in our head to reflect the new program we've just been a part of. It's too hard to keep Pai's story at the front of our mind – and I agree – but rather than let the entire thing slip into the partition in our mind labelled 'too hard', we should consider what elements of that experience can help us become more whole or more happy, and which bits are worth sieving out? Because I guarantee you, **the darkest, shittiest experiences we go through are where we will find the biggest nuggets of happiness**. It's just about giving yourself the time to think, and being open enough to be broken, bent and remoulded by the situations we go through – because *our happiest state is fluid*. Maintaining it therefore requires a certain degree of psychological gymnastics. Our brains need to be flexible. They must be able to change and expand and reprioritise our ever growing playlist of knowledge – which is our perspective.

What happens if we don't, is that we become restless and unfulfilled. It's like watching someone painfully tying their shoelaces the wrong way, only that person is you. Your heart or mind or soul (wherever our perspective lives) knows there is a better way – not to tie your shoelaces, but to live your life – only for some reason you're not doing it. That's what causes that inner angst. Because when we deny the messenger of our perspective – that inner voice – as it screams 'this job isn't right for you anymore' or 'you know money won't make you happy', we risk facing a messy argument, as our ego (which is fearful of change and just wants us to survive) tries to prevent our heart from showing us how beautiful the world could look through our newfound lens.

Addicted to the pursuit of new knowledge, I know just how hard this process can be. Our ego is a beast, after all. It's not its fault, it grew up in different, much darker times, when new was always scary. Like when 'that's a new tribe' meant 'we need to prepare for attack', or 'that's a new idea' meant 'you're a threat and must be killed'. What our ego has failed to do is to let go of those urges – the ones that tell us to stay put, nest and dread what's different. This might have helped us survive the past 200,000 years, but in order to continue thriving as human beings (or maybe even just to survive, if I put my pessimistic hat on), we must see and accept what our ego finds uncomfortable, which is that **we are more than singular physical entities with nothing better to do than pass on our DNA**. What lets me say this with such conviction, is my perspective, which has been informed by two decades of searching for answers to the question: why do we exist… and how could we do so more happily?

What a dump!

Bouncing up and down in the back of a pink tuk tuk as Bob (my driver) navigated us down a dodgy dirt road in the outskirts of Phnom Penh, my ego wondered if I was safe. 'Aaaaaah, where are we going!?' it yelled. 'Calm your horses,' replied my heart. 'Shut up you old toss,' added my soul, as both longed for what I might find. I'd shown Bob a photo of people living on a garbage dump, and he'd said "OK." As we jolted over a rush of potholes and neared the end of the road, he stopped. "OK, you can walk now," he said. "I stay here." My ego churned uncomfortably. "Over there you will find these people, living on the trash," he said. Cautiously approaching a small lane way that was meant to lead me to the rubbish tip, the smell became intense. I must be close, I thought. Then, two girls popped out from behind a cement wall that lined one side of the laneway I was about to enter. With a giant grin smeared across my face, as well as a few childish tongue-poking-outs and hand waving gestures, the kids came closer. Why didn't their egos tell them to run? Did they not see me as new and scary? Had they been raised in a different way? What way was that?

Words will never do justice to what happened next, as two kids became three, then five, then twenty five, and the unabated laughter of humans connecting echoed through the neighbourhood. "Hello mister, where are you from?" asked a loud and cheeky girl wearing a bright orange top, with her best friend under her arm. "Australia," I replied. "You know kangaroos," I said, jumping around mimicking the bouncy

The younger children who ran through the trash to say hi.

Two kids sit in the cement laneway that borders the old dump. Behind them is the corner I came around.

The two girls who popped out from the laneway.

The young, sharply-dressed man who spoke to me.

Some of the shanty homes built on stilts above the old dumpsite.

Srealay emerges from her home with her son.

The final change in perspective Cambodia gifted me was meeting this man who'd had his legs blown off by a landmine. Read the flyer around his neck.

animal. "How old are you?" asked her equally cheeky, but slightly more shy friend, who wore a yellow singlet with a shiny Minnie Mouse design on the front. "I am 26," I said, pretending to be an old man holding his back and using a cane to walk. "You want to race?" I asked. "Three... two...one..." I said before running a couple of metres to show them what I meant. Two minutes later, I was bolting down the dirt road with ten to twenty kids chasing me.

My wife (who often travels with me and has seen me doing this a lot) would tell you that this is my happiest state. And I'd agree. Because whenever two souls meet, whether alone or in a group, there is a spark – a collision of energy. The problem is, fear or distrust often clouds or dampens that spark before we get a chance to see where it might lead us.

On this occasion that spark – which was more like a fire by this point – eventually led me down that cement laneway I'd originally started to head towards. With a small throng of children directing me, often pointing and yelling what I assume must have been "that is my house", I'd nearly forgotten about the burgeoning stench. "Shit!" I thought, as tens of younger children made their way through piles of rubbish – including needles, glass and used toilet paper – barefoot. Like their older siblings, these new and younger faces greeted me with a trusting curiosity, crowding around and hugging my legs tightly. 'Are they doing this so they can ask for money?' I wondered, but the request never came. Not even when the adults joined in, and began to fill in a few blanks I had about what I was looking at and who was living here.

"This is old rubbish dump, yes, but it is not used anymore, so we have made our home here now," said Srealay, one of the women who emerged from the rows of shanty huts to meet me. "We are some of us orphans, others are mistreated girls, or some are just having no schooling, so no good job, so this is where we can live," she says, in a calm, happy, even grateful way that was devoid of any bitterness. "So are you happy here?" I asked. "We must be, where else will we be happy?" laughs Srealay's friend Sompang, who butts in enthusiastically. "We are trying to make a better life for our kids, but we start from low down, because there was nothing for us as children, not much education or option for business, because the Khmer Rouge destroys everything," said Sompang.

"What are you doing?" asked a young, sharply dressed man with perfect hair. "I'm just hoping to find out what makes the people living here smile," I said, before being utterly mesmerised by his unexpected answer. "We may live on an old garbage dump, and many families also look after orphans too, so it is tough, but despite being very poor we believe in doing good, and sharing what we have. If there is a child with no parents, no human could just leave them, although some richer people do not like them, so we take them in and share our love with them. Smiling is simple if we give more than we take," he says. What you notice about those in poverty, and this is anywhere (except maybe in developed countries), is that most have this beautiful, simple perspective that can gift the rest of us so many specks of happiness.

Just this tiny interaction taught me to be thankful, worry less, love more, give more, fear less, and just stop thinking there is any distance or difference between me and anyone else. We are innately connected. Why else, or how else, did the existence of poverty in this world make me feel poorer? Why else had this dumpsite community taken it upon themselves to adopt orphans from disparate communities? Economically, it made no sense. More mouths to feed wasn't what any of these families needed. And yet, as Srealay said, "it was necessary for their happiness," because **when one suffers, all suffer**. This is the perspective that drives me. It's what informs my purpose, which is the alleviation of unnecessary suffering.

"Why not all suffering?" people often say. "Suffering will exist while ever love exists, while ever inequality exists, while ever death exists, while ever we exist," I'd typically respond. "What we must see is that love, death, and even inequality are innate and necessary parts of the human experience – they're everything!" I would say. "OK," most respond, before they rethink my statement. "Wait, why is inequality necessary?" the majority question. "To me, it's an inevitable by-product of diversity. And I can't imagine our happiest world being one where we're all clones. What makes our innate inequality a good thing is that it's what inspires the best in us. If we all had the same intelligence for instance, what would motivate us to learn or teach others. If we all had the same skin colour, if we all looked the same, what would be lost? Tolerance? Understanding? Beauty? Sex would definitely be strange. What if we were all born with the same resources, would we have ever bothered to explore the world? Would we have grown and learned to adapt as a species? How about if we all had the same level of health and lived for the same number of years, would we make the most of life? Would we have learned compassion? The point is, inequality, or at least the part caused by natural selection, is critical to our growth and happiness as a species. This doesn't, of course, mean we can't try to treat each other equally – but to wish away all the differences that cause inequality make for a bleak, boring reality."

By this time, most people's faces are staring blankly back at me. "Uh huh," most respond, as they mentally unpack my words. I know this perspective might not be a common one, but the happiest people and communities I've come across all tend to consciously or unconsciously do this – embrace their suffering and inequality. Most use it, or see it as an opportunity to learn, to grow and to better themselves and their family.

From a more Western viewpoint, acknowledging inequality and embracing suffering can help us to discover who we are, why we are, what we have to be grateful for, and who or where we should give our time and resources. These four critical elements to happiness are all aided by this mind-set, because recognising the darker elements of humanity lets us see life more fully. It lets us feel more whole.

This isn't only why I travelled to Cambodia and spoke to former sex slaves and people living on an abandoned garbage dump, but at the risk of never being let back in the country, it was also my motivation for visiting China – a place I'd long thought to be subtly and sophisticatedly oppressing 1.3 billion people.

Tiananmen what?

There were four things that happened in China that reaffirmed this perspective for different reasons. The first was that conversation (from Chapter 8) about there simply being too many people, which lead to an insatiable thirst and demand for competition, which had 'killed kindness'. The next was an incredible conversation that kept repeating itself as we journeyed in a giant triangle from Shanghai to Chengdu to Beijing and back to Shanghai (with a number of stops along the way). "People here in China, mostly the poor and middle classes, we know that there are certain families in this country who are being handed their wealth by our so-called socialist-communist government," said a well-spoken 22-year-old I met in Jiuzhai Valley National Park. "There are these rich kids we see on reality TV – we call them *fuerdai* (second generation rich) here – these privileged, pampered rich kids are mostly a product of their parent's elitism and this bizarre 'socialist market economy' we seem to have adopted – which I think is mostly about letting the eccentric millionaires feel more OK displaying their wealth. What regular young Chinese, who are aware of this – because we can hack or find our way around state sponsored websites to the truth – what we know is that there are people in this 'supposedly communist' country making a fortune off the broken backs and unhappiness of millions of factory workers. Most of whom were happier living as meager farmers, but were forced by the government to move to the cities to work on these production lines." What the girl I'll refer to as Chen La told me was that **if things don't change, there will be an uprising, sooner or later** (a year later, low and behold, the Umbrella Revolution began in Hong Kong).

The media and the internet, which Chinese autocrats have tried to control and block for decades, is slowly but surely exposing the unnecessary suffering and inequality caused by the Chinese Communist Party (CCP), and there's nothing they can do to stop it. In fact, the harder President Xi Jinping tries to curb the unrest, the more the masses are waking up to the truth. "It's not fair here," says Kim Lou (not her real name). "We are not blind. We see this. But if we speak out, if we say bad things about our government, we go missing, that is why you cannot publish my name. That is not happiness. How can we be happy when we are scared and mistreated? How can we be happy if no one will listen?"

When you read this, you should imagine 400 million young Chinese screaming it at you, because that is the reality. "We are not happy here," Kim Lou says. And it's not hard to see why. The wealth gap has widened alarmingly. The top 1% – particularly the junior one-percenters – are so out of touch with the optics of there being 'a super-elite class' in a socialist run state, that President Xi has gagged a lot of them. "In one infamous example, Wang Sicong – the son of Wang Jianlin, a real estate and entertainment magnate often considered China's richest man – posted a picture on social media of his pet dog wearing not one but two gold Apple watches," writes Time Magazine's Hannah Beech in her 2016 article titled *China Bans Rich Kids From TV So They Can't Embarrass Their Parents or the State*. "Xi's administration has tried to rein in fuerdai (rich kids), even as other members of China's gilded class complain that their reputations are being unfairly sullied by a few show-offs. Last year, more than 70 children of billionaires from Fujian province [alone] were

The smog in Shanghai was so bad you could barely see from one side of the river to the other.

Two friends disconnected by technology in front of the smog shroud city of Nanjing.

Beggars outside a church in Shanghai on Christmas Eve.

A husband begs with his wife who needs urgent medical treatment.

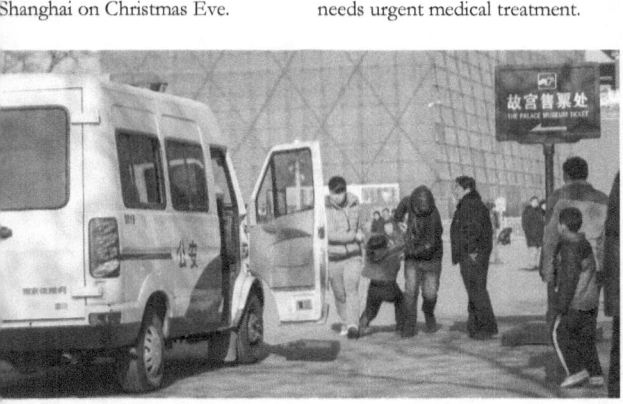

The woman being dragged into a police van by undercover police in Tiananmen Square.

A dancer resembling the China that the CCP is desperate to portray to the world.

'Fuerdai' at Song Dynasty Town theme park in Hangzhou.

A packed Shanghai shopping mall on Christmas Eve.

ordered to attend classes to promote their sense of patriotism and social responsibility, according to the *Beijing Youth Daily*," writes Beech.

Witnessing this dramatic and distasteful disparity in person was the third thing that added to my disparaging perspective of China. Don't get me wrong, the CCP have done a fabulous job of dragging roughly 850 million people out of financial poverty, but the gross inequality and slavish factory lifestyle that has come with it is dragging a dark cloud of unhappiness and distrust over the country. Nowhere was this more obvious than in Shanghai, on Christmas Day. Sash and I were heading back to our hostel from a church we'd attended when we came across a huge shopping precinct where scores of these fuerdai (rich kids) strolled from store to store with their arms bearing bags of Gucci, Versace and Ralph Lauren. The problem wasn't their fashion sense, it was the lines of beggars they bluntly ignored. Their entitled eyes literally never saw these people. Even outside a local church, which was just down the road from these exclusive shops, the burnt, broken and disfigured faces and bodies laying on the pavement might as well have been invisible. When we decided to stop and sit with a number of the beggars – rather than just throw money at them and feel that was enough – we were met with shock. Not only did rich locals scoff at us, but I remember one lady, who wore scars from acid being spilt on her in an industrial accident, looking at us like we were mad. It was as if we were the only people to have ever stopped and held her hand, or given her a hug.

A small but important aside: we actually had to attend a specific church that was only for international passport holders. We could not attend a local church and visa versa. This was not about language or belief, but control. The CCP is terrified of religious entities, because they could potentially mobilise and influence large groups of people, against the government. One of the more frightening and infamous examples of this, is what happened to Falun Gong practitioners. Attracted by Falun Gong's promise of spiritual cleansing and better health, it's followers couldn't understand why the government began labelling it an 'evil cult'. Upset by these defamatory statements in the media, around 10,000 Falun Gong members staged a protest in Beijing outside the headquarters of the ruling Communist Party in April 1999. Having grown to around 100 million followers by this stage, the CCP was obviously petrified their public smear campaign might backfire, so they upped the ante – officially banning the practice of Falun Gong and arresting practitioners who resisted. These political prisoners, and their families, were silenced. Most who were jailed have never been seen again. Then, something utterly unthinkable surfaced. In 2006, a Canadian report shone a light on a horrific allegation: that the Chinese Government was secretly harvesting organs of Falun Gong followers to supply the black market organ transplant industry. The claims are supported by substantial evidence, including the 2016 report *Bloody Harvest/The Slaughter: An Update* published by David Kilgour, David Matas and Ethan Gutmann. European, US, Canadian, Japanese and Australian parliaments have all heard and discussed the allegations, and in some cases laws are now being passed to ban people from these countries from travelling to China to get an off-book organ transplant. OK, maybe that wasn't such a small aside, but it shows the reason why locals were forced to attend local churches, where pastors and preachers were no doubt hand-selected by the CCP – who are the only god in China.

The final thing that threw me into a spiteful spin in China, was what happened in Tiananmen Square. It was sadly fascinating that tourist maps, local signage and even Google, wouldn't tell us where we could find this historic landmark. There were no tours, no guides sharing the history of what had happened there – and don't forget, this was where Mao Zedong proclaimed the founding of the People's Republic of China in 1949, so it was a place of great cultural significance. The reason Tiananmen Square has been wiped off the face of the (Chinese) earth, was of course due to the massacre of pro-democracy protesters in 1989. The incident, which took place on June 4, was the result of nearly a million Chinese, mostly young students, crowding into central Beijing to protest for greater democracy and call for the resignations of Chinese Communist Party leaders, who were deemed 'too repressive'. When the daily vigils, marching and chanting didn't stop, Chinese troops and security police stormed through Tiananmen Square, firing indiscriminately into the crowds of protesters. Reporters and Western diplomats on the scene estimated that at least 300, and perhaps thousands, of the protesters had been killed and as many as 10,000 were arrested.

What I personally saw take place in Tiananmen Square, twenty four years later, still haunts me. Standing there asking ourselves if this was 'the place' we wanted to see – the secret square we had to whisper about – Sash and I began to notice something strange unfolding. Out of nowhere, a van had entered into the square. There was a woman speaking aloud to passers by – a solo-protester who was angry about something. Minutes later, a number of plain clothed police who we thought were tourists walking through the square, grabbed her. Trying desperately to inform the undercover police as to why she was so upset, they flawlessly and systematically took her down. Onlookers seemed unsurprised as officers threw her non-resistant limp body to the floor, before carrying her toward the van and dumping her inside. Nervously capturing this entire thing on camera, I knew we needed to go, quickly. "If someone saw me photographing that, I could be the next one thrown into a van," I told Sash. For days I waited on edge, anticipating a knock at the door. Not because I'd done anything wrong, but because I'd captured the truth. It made me wonder: what was that woman saying? What warranted such immediate and brutal action? Had they not learnt anything from the internationally condemned massacre of 1989?

It might not come as a huge surprise, but China was, in my opinion, the unhappiest country I've visited. But, and again, that doesn't mean there weren't specks of happiness to be found. For instance, rather than get upset or lash out at the disgustingly rich who shunned the beggars in Shanghai (I was definitely angry enough to do it), Sash and I decided to use that energy and the money we'd planned to spend on each other for Christmas to take the homeless people we'd met out to lunch. More than the gift of food or the money we left them with, simply recognising these people as that – as people – was the most telling nugget of joy, because that is what led to the smiles and the hugs and the happiness we all soaked in. Coping with what I witnessed in Tiananmen Square was tough. I was fuming – that poor woman! But I knew there was no meddling with the Chinese government, especially not when you're a foreigner on their home turf. Not when they're willing to incarcerate anyone and everyone who disagrees with them – let alone an overseas journalist who is wanting to expose and protest on behalf of the silenced. As a journalist and someone who revels in truth, the only little bits of happiness I could salvage out of this was: one, seeing the sheer luck of being born in a country where free speech was a given; and two, the tiny voice and chance of justice I could give this woman (and others) by sharing her story with the world. Similarly, a few of the other more obvious specks that I sieved out of this experience related back to seeing the world through grateful eyes. Because, if you don't live in an overcrowded hyper-competitive country where 'kindness is weakness', be happy. Not living under a ruthless, oppressive, unequal regime is also something I have found lasting happiness in – because to me, that would be the worst kind of hell. And yet, as China is proof, this is a reality that billions cope with daily. But how? How do you turn those feelings of being powerless, sad, angry or trapped into something that can bring happiness? Under what lens can evil turn into good?

The subtle art of giving a f**k

One guy who has arguably nailed this is Jetsun Jamphel Ngawang Lobsang Yeshe Tenzin Gyatso, or as he's better known, His Holiness The Dalai Lama. He's turned his forced 60 year exile from Tibet (which is still under brutal and unlawful Chinese occupation) into an opportunity to talk about compassion, justice, love and human rights. In one of the most lens-altering interviews I've ever filmed (part of which you can view on thehappiest.com), the Dalai Lama and his friend Dr. Allen Wallace revealed why an informed, well-rounded perspective is critical to us finding our happiest state as individuals and a society.

Presented with a question about how he maintained such a happy outlook and if in-fact he ever got angry or sad, the Dalai Lama laughed. "I am normal human being, I think we all feel anger, otherwise I would appear in space, like an angel," he chuckles, mimicking the actions of an angel flying. Dr. Wallace, a leading Buddhist Scholar who has traveled extensively with the Dalai Lama, said he had often comforted his friend and had even held him weeping in his arms. Nodding along in recognition, the Dalai Lama then took the chance to explain that **all emotions, even anger, sadness and fear, can be a positive and lead to greater happiness if we approach them in the right way – with compassion.**

"I think sadness, with valid reasons, that's good [he laughs, as if acknowledging the peculiar message of his words]. That may bring enthusiasm to overcome that thing which is causing sadness," he says. "If sadness can bring that kind of enthusiasm and determination, then that sadness is good." There are a growing number of reality TV shows that feed off this exact formula – Biggest Loser, Married at First Sight, The Bachelor, Masterchef, Got Talent and so on – because when people overcome their sadness and challenges it stirs something in all of us.

When we see a mother or father who's shed 50kg able to run around with their kids again, when someone finds love after a shitty run with relationships or when that chef, singer, magician or dancer finally gets a chance to let themselves and their dreams shine, it is proof that sadness can motivate us, and we should not give up on anything – we just need to find a new, more enthusiastic way to view it.

When it comes to 'positive anger', His Holiness said this can be a powerful driving force in helping us to show compassion for those we care about enough to help them confront their problems. "When you have sincere concern for another's well-being and that being is going in the wrong direction, and out of a genuine sense of concern for that person – and the circumstances don't allow for any other alternative – sometimes you may need a little sort of harsh word or sometimes you may even need some sort of little harsh physical action in order to care," he explains. "In that short moment you need some sort of anger or ferocity necessary in order to carry the harsh word or harsh physical action. So that kind of anger is positive, because (it is) motivated by compassion."

The simple difference is: positive anger is about making the situation better, while negative anger is about making yourself feel better. One is selfish, the other, selfless.

Raised by an uneducated farming mother who was illiterate, the Dalai Lama, or Lhamo Döndrub as he was born, said his mother often taught him that understanding how our emotions affect us is important for our happiness. "There are many variety of emotions, fear can be positive or negative, desire can be positive or negative ... that is from a Buddhist viewpoint, you have to judge yourself, we cannot say all emotions are the same for every person or in every case." What we can all do however, says the Dalai Lama, is we can all learn how to limit the intensity of our 'negative' emotions and see a situation for what it really is – from every perspective.

"I think from a Buddhist view point most of the emotions which disturb our mind are based on or related with wrong perception," says the Nobel Peace Prize winner. "So I think simple way to explain this is that there's a gap – appearance and reality – so most of the emotions which increase disturbances, these emotions in most cases are spontaneous, so these emotions are based on appearances. On the level of appearances they are using most of these distracting emotions because they need some kind of independent, absolute kind of target or object." The (then) 76-year-old said that with anger, for example, people often feel they are a victim and need someone or something else to point the finger at. He said that reality is often overlooked in many situations where intense emotions arise – if a partner cheats for example, naturally the victim feels hurt and angry at their partner, when in reality chances are there was much more to it, and if we see past what appears black and white, there is an area of grey that can calm our emotions.

"When anger develops it needs some kind of target, something absolute and independent, so when that target is a little bit shaky then the intensity of anger also retreats a little bit, that's very clear. So if we have this target that is independent and absolute and we actually investigate and then answer, you will find – no," there is more to it, he says. So the grasping feeling that something "must be independent or absolute, is based on ignorance," says His Holiness.

Where I see this happening most often today, is on social media. People see a post they don't like or agree with, and tee off in a rage without thought, reflection or research. Take this conversation I posted via A Million Smiles Facebook page for instance, which was accompanied by a photo of the Italian guy I was chatting to.

> "It sometimes feels like depression is a luxury disease."
>
> "What do you mean?" (I asked)
>
> "Poor people seem to be born with a level of appreciation that allows them to find joy in the simple things. From working together as a family and community to find their next meal, to giving what little they have to those in even more need than themselves. I guess they just don't seem to dwell on problems like we do, which allows them to live in the now, and to me that's the key to avoiding depression."

The reason I'd decided to post this wasn't to offend. It wasn't for shock value. It was simply because this was a sentiment I'd heard over and over, from the East to the West, whenever I'd asked: "how do we stop the depression epidemic?" Initially, it seemed like this was a conversation worth bringing to the fore, as people commented saying: "True and wise!" "Well said." "Brilliant observation." "Great note." "Interesting perspective." "There is a lot of truth in this." Or even one person who'd tagged their friend saying, "Remember our convo on depression!" To which the friend replied, "Yeah, what is said above is very true. This is exactly what we spoke about too :)" Another girl who'd come from one of the 'poorer communities' in question, but who now lived in Australia, tagged a friend and wrote, "My not so politically correct answer, as above." Now, I'm not stupid, I knew not all would agree. I had anticipated some bringing up the hereditary nature of certain forms of depression, or that the reason it sometimes appears as if it is a 'luxury' disease is because doctors in developed countries are more aware of it – so it is diagnosed more often. I even thought some might discuss the potential injustice of poor people being left undiagnosed and untreated – and I dearly hoped some might get stuck into big pharmaceutical companies who seem (anecdotally) to be pushing GPs to overdiagnose and overprescribe. What I didn't anticipate to such a large degree was the vile hate that spewed from so many keyboard warriors toward this guy, and me.

"Bullshit." "What a load of nonsense!" "What a load of $#@*!!!!!" "You sir are an asshole." "How naive." "Such ignorance." "I am furious, this is an unbelievable statement, why was it ever posted." "A Million Smiles you must take this down, it's ignorant and offensive, and you must know why." "I'm now unfollowing this page – how offensive. Btw I was poor and I had absolutely nothing when I was depressed." "Can't believe you have posted this. Depression knows no socio-economic boundaries and to quote that it is a 'luxury' illness is damaging to those who are already fighting a very painful and lonely battle. Delete."

What people tend to do, as the Dalai Lama points out, is see the appearance of this post in black and white. They forget the reality, which is that he (or I) never labelled depression as a luxury disease. Rather he said "it *sometimes* feels like" it is – which is a thousand times softer and less absolute than what seemed to have entered into certain people's minds. What also seems to have been missed – because people tend to lose all focus and reason when angry – is that this guy was actually sharing his story and insight in the hope that it may help people with this disease – or stop people from becoming depressed in the first place. If memory serves me correctly, he actually worked in the counselling space, and had travelled the globe looking at how mental health was approached and treated in different communities. What he noticed, as you may have guessed, is that certain triggers that cause the chemical imbalance which is depression, were more prone in wealthy countries due to our lifestyles and expectations. Interestingly, and the Dalai Lama might chuckle at this, there is no right or wrong answer to this – it's all grey. One study will tell you 'people in poverty are twice as likely to be depressed', while another will say, 'wealthy countries have higher rates of depression'. What we must understand is that the truth (and happiness) remain hidden while ever we let our negative emotions control us.

That's why, as soon as I took my slightly annoyed, self-righteous, all-knowing ego out of it, I could see that this post needed to be taken down – not because what it said was wrong or ridiculously insensitive – but because it was causing undue pain and hate. The comment that broke me was actually by a woman named Clare, who wrote, "Honestly, I've had depression for years. It makes it sound like sufferers like me feel that it's something that can just be switched on and off. If there isn't enough hatred in this world already, they are adding some more into the mix!" To Clare and to anyone else who may have been offended by this story, I am sorry. I made a poor call in how to present a very necessary and interesting topic of conversation, which is "how do we stop the depression epidemic?"

My mistake, as it relates to perspective, was that I didn't employ a broad enough one. I saw only two sides of the coin. I didn't consider all the little grooves on the edge. Mostly, I failed to recognise the impact of that tiny itty-bitty little finger I'd pointed at some of those people who suffer depression, despite living in relative 'luxury'. I'd forgotten somehow that at the end of every finger there will inevitably be someone feeling unjustly attacked, no matter the intentions or reasoning behind it. Because an outstretched arm creates space between us. That's why negative anger – whether intentional or not – isolates us.

"Anger and hatred bring a sort of fear because anger develops a clear attitude where your self is distanced from others, so then there's distrust, suspicion, and that brings more fear and deep inside some unruly feeling," says the Dalai Lama.

In order to better equip ourselves with a compassionate, nurturing, forgiving mind, that doesn't so quickly turn to hate, anger or sadness, the Dalai Lama says we must learn to value warm-heartedness, just as we do intelligence.

"Generally people don't have adequate education about the value of warm-heartedness, so we do not pay attention about that, we consider that a religious matter. The intelligence side, the brain side, we rapidly develop, but the warm-heartedness stays dormant, and that is something we seriously need to think about." Because these qualities will give us a happier mental outlook, "a better perspective," he concludes.

To me, our reality is like a black and white sketch, while our perspective tells us how to colour it in. Without the right lens or filter, the reality of what I saw in Cambodia or China would be too much to cope with. There would be no light, no colour in my mind – just darkness – greys and blacks smudged angrily across the black and white image of my life. The thing about choosing to see and focus on the happiest bits life has to offer, is it equips you with a mind that can cope with the challenges this world seems destined to throw at us – because it lets you see hope, even when you're drowning in sadness, anger or fear. It's like the Dalai Lama says, a positive, well-rounded perspective lets us calm our emotions and avoid passing on the pain and suffering we may be feeling.

This isn't just the secret to us becoming our happiest as individuals, it's also how we put an end to the poverty, greed, division and war that prevents humanity from reaching its utopian potential. If we could all calmly, logically think about the moral responsibility each one of us holds in ensuring the happiest possible future for our children and this planet, I am convinced the world would change in an instant. What gets in the way is that age old foe – ego – because if I think I'm more important than you, then killing you, watching you suffer as a sex slave, watching you drown under rising seas as I profit from the sale of oil and coal, is acceptable. What lets our ego get away with this is the raw emotional reaction we have when confronted by those powerful fight or flight impulses it evokes. The sort of impulses that tell us death must have death (the mentality that drives war). The sort of impulses that tell us poverty is *their* fault, *not* ours. The sort of impulses that tell us it is unfair and wrong that I or my family should have to suffer the cost of going carbon neutral, when other countries continue to pollute. Ego tells us we're alone, disconnected; 'you're all that matters' it tells us, but I think most are coming to see that that's not the case. Not if happiness is what we seek.

Like it or not, just because we don't see things like Pai's brutal rape or that woman being abducted in China, it doesn't mean they're not happening, and thanks to our rapidly evolving awareness and interconnectivity via technology and travel, we are all feeling the unease and guilt of those who suffer in silence – because we're waking up to the fact that we're at best complicit, and at worst responsible. This is why **there will be no true form of global happiness while we turn a blind eye, while we let our mind have a 'too hard basket' where our empathy goes to die.** The alternative is to build a more positive brain that sieves out the crap and holds onto the good, because when we do this, nothing seems too difficult. The only decision becomes: which injustice do I chase? From a more optimistic viewpoint, we can see the meaning and opportunity that empathy brings us, because empathy's like that friend who knows what we should do even before we do – again – if happiness is the goal.

The other giant benefit of growing your perspective and training your mind to pan for the gold in life is you'll unquestionably become more grateful. If and when those who have enough (which is really anyone who can afford to buy this book) see that they have enough, there will be no need to war over land or resources, there will be no need to exploit the poor, no need to squabble over who should pay for the mistakes of our past in order to secure a better tomorrow.

The Tuvalu Connection

One place I definitely didn't expect to find people exemplifying this calm, rounded, positive perspective was Tuvalu. The tiny island nation is not only terribly poor and isolated, but it is also set to be the first country on Earth that will be wiped out as a result of the climate crisis. Within as little as 30-40 years, scientists expect the country to disappear under the sea, as the ice caps in Greenland and Antarctica melt into the ocean, causing a rise of up to 1.3 metres by 2100.

The climate crisis – which is being caused by deforestation, farming and the burning of fossil fuels – is the largest and most immediate threat to not only our happiest life, but any life. When I met Taafaki Semu, the nephew of Tuvalu Prime Minister Enele Sopoaga, I anticipated being met with hostility, anger and sadness. Australia was, after all, the biggest polluter per capita, and it was thanks to countries like mine, that he and his children would not be given the chance to live and die in their own country in the years to come. Instead of blasting me for my part

Two boys play in the ocean, which is never far away in Tuvalu.

Flying into Funafuti, the capital of Tuvalu. Supplied RNZ.

The people and country of Tuvalu.

Taafaki Semu.

Kids play on the main jetty. Something Sash and I often joined in.

A father and son.

A Tuvaluan child, whose future rests in our hands.

in his country's destruction, the 36-year-old offered me an unexpected insight and solution. Spending much of his life meeting with foreign dignitaries and showing them the undeniable proof and impact of global warming on his homeland, Taafaki says he'd come to see just one truth – **connection is the cure.**

"People need to be more connected. Like if people come and see our country, if they see the children, then maybe it will motivate them to find a solution to the seas rising," says Taafaki (in an interview you can view on thehappiest.com). "Connection is our only hope of happiness. But for bigger countries, their economy is more important. So they'll build more factories to keep their people getting their pay, rather than stop the factories, just because Tuvalu is sinking. The economy comes first," he says. The thing about the ocean and the climate crisis is that it connects us *all*, whether we like it or not. "The stakes are high for everybody," says Taafaki, "we will be the first, but who will be next, and then after that?" If the predictions of scientists advising the United Nations on global warming are correct, by 2070, the number of people living in the 136 biggest port cities who will be exposed to coastal flooding is projected to grow more than threefold, to around 150 million. According to a recent study prepared for the OECD (Organisation for Economic Cooperation and Development), the value of flood-exposed economic assets in these port cities – such as buildings, transport networks, utilities and other infrastructure – could grow even more dramatically than population exposure, reaching $35 trillion by the 2070s. That's approximately 9% of projected global gross domestic product.

"Bear in mind that the great port cities are often hubs of political power. They also include key financial and commercial centers in the United States and Europe, like New York, London and Rotterdam, as well as Asian centers like Tokyo, Osaka-Kobe, Shanghai and Bombay," writes journalist Michael Richardson in his Japan Times article *Facing a sea level rise*. "The OECD study found that the number of people in Tokyo at risk of coastal flooding by the 2070s would more than double, to just over 2.5 million, up from 1.1 million in 2005. This would rank Tokyo as the world's 19th most exposed port city. In terms of economic assets at risk from the flooding, Tokyo would be number 8 in the world in the 2070s after Miami, Guangzhou, New York-Newark, Calcutta, Shanghai, Bombay and Tianjin."

Witnessing the humble, connected, peaceful lifestyle of Tuvaluans, the solution seemed obvious. "The life in Tuvalu is very, very different compared to other countries of the world," says Taafaki. "Socialising is everything. Like if you feel bored at home, you can get on your bike and ride to your mate's place. He might be sleeping in a hammock on the beach or heading out to fish, it doesn't matter, he will accommodate you. Whatever you need, you can get from somebody, like if you are in need you can just say, 'Hey brother, can I have one or two fish?' and they will give it to you for free. That is freedom. That is the lifestyle in Tuvalu. **People really value doing good to one another, because these things have a value more than money** – they make us happy, they bring us peace that we will be OK, because we are not alone. It's as simple as that."

There's little doubt that if we all adopted the life and perspective of Taafaki and his countrymen, we'd see a happier world. Take, for instance, his response to my question: what's the best thing about this place? "Friendliness, the friendliness of the people. The freedom. The connection. The zero fear of crimes, you know?" 'No, I don't know,' I felt like saying, 'there's a lot of fear of crime in my country, despite of our relative wealth and equality.' "That is why we have happiness here," he continues, before showing a rare glimpse of the desperate sadness that's likely to infect this place in the coming decades. "But it will all be taken away by foreign countries if they continue polluting our earth. We're not asking ... we know you can't just stop everything overnight. We know that, but if people could see what we have in the past many years, they would know the climate is at a point of no return – *unless* we act now – but not many people visit us here, so we try to raise our voice for the cameras, to tell the world, 'Hello, we are here, we are happy, our children are happy, please don't take that away,'" he says. If we do ... if humanity does cause these people to flee their home, what will be lost? Knowledge? Beauty? Peace? Can we really be happy while others suffer?

This last question was one of the happiest specks I deduced from my time in Tuvalu. It's not an easy pill to swallow, but accepting that we are all connected, and therefore have a responsibility to protect and be kind to one another, is critical to achieving our happiest state as individuals and as a humanity. Without such a mind-set, we're doomed, said Prime Minister Sopoaga, at a dinner we attended at his private residence in January 2014. Some years later, I heard a speech he made to the UN that summed up the perspective Tuvalu left me with. "Of course we carry with us the hopes of our people, that we together shall act now, with urgency and high ambitions. We must stop greenhouse gas emissions that are causing global warming," said Prime Minister Sopoaga at COP23. "We must immediately shift the global economy to a renewable energy mix. This is an enormous task for me as leader of Tuvalu and it keeps me awake every night. No national leader in the history of humanity has ever faced this question – will we survive or will we disappear under the sea if no actions are done urgently. Again **I ask you all to think what it is like to be in my shoes."** And that's what perspective is: seeing things from other viewpoints. Whether it is the Prime Minister of a dying country, or the most powerful religious figure on Earth, there's something about climate change that's strangely connecting: "I can say to you 'now or never,'" said Pope Francis, at the same United Nations event. "Every year the problems are getting worse. We are at the limits. If I may use a strong word I would say that we are at the limits of suicide."

The reason I mention this second quote is that without the necessary reinforcements, the truth, or our perspective, can sometimes seem fragile or weak. That's not a bad thing, because seeing anything as all black or all white is inherently dangerous, as I've repeatedly said. So seeing some grey, some doubt, is a good thing, but so is grounding your perspective by searching out different views on the same topic – because that's what gives us the peace of mind to speak and act with confidence – which will make you happier. Writing a book like this, that's been one of the hardest things – defining my perspective – because there is never just one way to see things, and to be honest, the process of research, conversation, reflection and more research has seen me rethink a lot of what I thought I knew.

Wood you choose it?

Two of the human beings I've called on more than once for advice and their own perspective on things – because they're probably the happiest people I know – are Rob and Cheryl Wood. At 71 years apiece, their 14.2 decades (and counting) of being freakin' amazing human beings is something we should all hope to emulate – if happiness (and living a crazy, awesome life) is the end goal. Though, I do wonder, if someone read their story without such an introduction, would you choose it? Could you sacrifice owning a home for 63 years in order to pursue your passion? Would you be prepared to immerse yourself in warzones to help others? What if happiness came at the expense of ever having any disposable income? Could you cope with the lack of freedom or living without shiny things? What if I told you these sacrifices would let you find community, love, meaning and who you are? What if they guaranteed you'd find your happiest state? These were just a few of the questions that rattled through my head following a series of interviews and discussions I had with Rob and Cheryl in their Melbourne home and at Armagh, the Asia-Pacific headquarters of the organisation they work for – Initiatives of Change (IofC).

"Let's start from the start," I said. "Where did this uncanny life that you're both living begin?" As is so often the case, Rob's eyes jumped out of his face like a school-kid who desperately knew the answer, and wanted to share it. "Two turning-point experiences in my late teens changed my perspective completely," he says, with boisterous enthusiasm. "The first was in India, where I have had the good fortune to spend more than seven years of my life. Getting to know some of the slum dwellers in Mumbai was a high point of that experience. I had a friend who lived in a tiny shack and every time I visited, I had to crawl in through the doorway. His spirit of hospitality, even though he only ever had a cup of tea to offer, made me feel like I was the most important person in his world. It was then I realised that 'it's not what we have that matters, but who and how we are'. His simple acts of giving rearranged my mental furniture and helped me begin to focus more on my blessings and less on my rights."

The second incident occurred in a Paris cafe when Rob met a Vietnamese student who was struggling to deal with his country's bloody civil war. "I expressed my concern and asked if he'd mind answering a few questions I had about the Vietnam War," says Rob. "After answering these, he said, 'You know, it's hard to talk about these matters because I've got family on both sides and brothers fighting against each other. It really tears me apart when I think about that.'"

Seemingly out of nowhere, the young Vietnamese man then asked Rob the most surprising and telling question of his life: "what do you want to be?" Not quite understanding what this had to do with Vietnam, Rob told him he either wanted to become an international interpreter or a professor of languages with lots of letters after his name. The young man's response was brutal and honest. "Is that all you want to do with your life?" he said. "What do you mean, is that all, isn't that enough?" Rob replied. "That's going to take me long enough," he said. "At the very beginning you said you were concerned about my situation – are you really?" asserted the young man. "If you are, then what we need are people whose lives have an answer to the human problems of our country – the hate, selfishness and corruption that allows the war to continue. If we don't get solutions to those things, my family may not just be involved. Tomorrow they may die. Is that what you want?"

"His words went through me like a knife," said Rob. "And in that moment, I knew that although my head was concerned, my heart was in a very different place. My heart was focussed on a long list of 'my's' – my career, my marriage, my money, my plans and the list went on. What he did, was he challenged all that." A few days later, Rob made a decision that set him on an entirely different path. Nine months later, the then 19-year-old found himself in the middle of that 'concern' he'd had, as he set about building relationships of friendship and trust across South East Asia. "I felt I should do this in gratitude for the beautiful change I had experienced as a result of that young Vietnamese man asking me questions I didn't want to hear," says Rob.

Cheryl's path wasn't at all like Rob's. Rob's father, mother, grandfather and grandmother had all joined Initiatives of Change when George (Rob's father) came into contact with the organisation in high school in Scotland. Cheryl on the other hand, grew up in rural north-west Victoria, Australia, on a terribly isolated farm. "When I was 11 years old I went to a high school, which I've discovered later in life was outside the parameters of what a child can cope with comfortably. Recent research actually shows that if a child has to travel too far to go to school they become insecure. And I was probably no different," says Cheryl. "But not seeing kids outside of school, did teach me to look to other places for answers, and happiness. Walking through the back paddocks listening to the wind blow through the native Bull Oak trees at around 15, I came to see that **finding one's own path in life is about reaching deep within oneself and searching for some sort of divine source – that little voice that's just for us,**" she says.

Learning to focus on and trust that inner guide to her life (which is inherently linked to our perspective, heart, soul and conscience), Cheryl soon found herself graduating teachers' college and heading off to teach in another tiny farming town several hours from home. Secretly longing to head to Melbourne "to see what city life was like", Cheryl decided to disobey her mother's wish for her to remain in the country, and applied for a job in the big smoke. "Mum's never understood a lot of what I've done, but I knew if I didn't go, I'd never be able to live with myself. I'd gone through this sort of spiritual experience when I was 11 years old and my father's cousin brought me back this book from India that was about how people lived over there. It never left me – those images and that message of inequality – so I didn't just want to come and work in any old school in Melbourne, I applied in the most underdeveloped areas, to honour that responsibility I'd felt as an 11-year-old, to make a better deal for others less fortunate."

Well, Cheryl got her wish. Within weeks she was confronted by a raft of disadvantaged children from dysfunctional homes. "I didn't know what hit me," she refects. "One of my big wake up calls was when I thought we'd try to brighten up the classroom. I asked the kids to bring something nice to school the following day – like flowers or a painting. When just one girl managed to do this – and even she brought a solitary geranium she'd clearly picked on her way to school – it told me these kids really didn't have much, certainly not gardens, or nice things. From then on, I worked with the headmistress to give these kids broad experiences that might give them a chance to see things differently. We'd take them once a month to seemingly simple places like the airport, botanic gardens, Collingwood Animal Farm, and so on. One day I remember this little boy, who was in grade two, he laid eyes on the lawn in one of the parks we visited – I don't think he'd ever seen so much green grass. I just remember him yelling 'whoopi' as he rolled and played on the giant lawn. It was then that I saw the power of opening our minds to new worlds."

Whether it's green grass when all you've known is brown dust, or love when all you've seen is hate, Rob and Cheryl have dedicated their lives to broadening the perspectives of all people (including themselves) in order to mend the distrust, the ignorance and the greed that continues to tear us and this world apart. From performing in enormous stage shows that toured the world propagating peace in conflict areas, to delivering thousands of peace and people-building workshops in some of the most remote corners of the globe, this dynamic pair have seen and experienced a lot. Asking them how they've coped with the violence, the bloodshed and the hate they've been confronted by at times, they told me it was all about remembering why they were there.

"We are not the ones suffering – not like they are – we are there to serve," says Cheryl. "So when we forget the 'I' or the 'me', and focus on others, on listening to their pain, not on our own fear or sadness, then we tame that ego, and we come closer to seeing what the people we are there to assist see. The ego and the individual work against community, and therefore work against the conversations and peace we are often hoping to create. And that is what Initiatives of Change teaches, we must change ourselves before we can change the world. So if ego encourages greed and conflict, and that's what we're there to stop, then we must be without ego. We must focus on the other," says Cheryl, before Rob chimes in. "I think **often it's a choice between, what's in it for me and what's best for us**. They're our two options. And I've seen numerous examples of people choosing either way. Take those divers who went to Thailand and saved the lives of those soccer kids trapped in that cave. There was a huge element of risk in that. But still they chose to do it. They chose 'us' not 'me', and those children and their families will never forget that act of unselfish giving. The pain, or challenge the rescuers faced was nothing compared to the reward of seeing those kids safe. We see the difficulties we are confronted by through a similar lens – we're here to support these people to fix a problem – we're not here for 'me' so we must get rid of our ego's want to make it about us or our pain. When we can do that, we'll create a vision of the world as it ought to be," says Rob.

This notion of taking on the perspective of others is an intriguing one. **Seeing the world through another's eyes – their perspective – is undoubtedly the solution to all unnecessary suffering.** Conversely though, 'adopting' the perspective and values of others – which is something I see happening a lot – is undoubtedly at the core of so much unhappiness. That's because naturally we all have our own perspectives – there are (or should be) 7.68 billion ways to see the world – the problem is, we've been led to believe that some perspectives, some views, are better or more valid than others. Like the views of the rich and famous, who (whether they try to or not) propagate the myth that wealth and status equals happiness. I don't blame the 1% for doing this, their ego obviously demands that they protect their power and fortune – both of which rely on us valuing what they have – be it looks, lifestyle or fame. Where I start to see an issue is that due to these people having a louder voice than most (via TV, magazines, social media and paid advertising), what we're seeing is a sort of mono-perspective emerging. Knowingly or unknowingly, billions of people are adopting the thoughts and views of those with the loudest voice – in the hope that it will somehow give them what these people have. Be it Trump fans thinking racism and sexism will somehow make them the next business kingpin or president, or insecure women thinking botoxed lips and a fake ass will make them as popular and wealthy as the Kardashians – some monkey see, some monkey do.

While musicians, artists and athletes themselves often talk about and promote self-empowerment and chasing your dreams, there's normally some fat cat executive or business behind these stars who needs you to feel insecure and lost enough to blindly follow whatever their cash cow says. Take for instance Jennifer Lopez. J-Lo is an incredible talent with an even more amazing message that's all about making your own rules. She even goes so far as to say whether you have a little or a lot you shouldn't change – you should remain "Jenny from the block." What I wonder is, do these encouraging words about being yourself and being enough regardless of what you have, do they outweigh the endless product endorsements she does? The ones that tell us a Gucci dress, Louis Vuitton handbag and L'Oreal skincare is the answer to that hole in our soul. With nearly all big name celebrities essentially telling us to buy the same stuff – the same glamourous materialistic life, just differently branded – our natural diversity of perspectives is dying. This is why 41% of British kids just want to be 'rich' or 'famous', without specifying how or what vocation might get them there. It's as if we've taken the idea that 'happiness is a journey, not a destination' and we (or this Insta-famous glam-generation of megastars) has caused it to flip – and that's going to end in disaster. Because, as mathematician Samuel Arbesman deduced, just 0.0086% of people are famous, which tells me there's going to be at least 40.99% of those 41% of British kids who are disappointed with the life that confronts them.

What we need to ask ourselves honestly is how many of that 0.0086% of celebrities are happy anyway? According to Pat O'Brien, the much adored entertainment news anchor on 'The Insider', who routinely rubbed elbows with stars like Angelina Jolie and Kevin Costner, the answer is 10. Not 10%, but 10 people. "I can name, out of all of them, 10 really happy ones," said O'Brien in an interview with Oprah for her show *Oprah: Where Are They Now?* As O'Brien sees it, there are far more unhappy stars than happy, because, as he explains, their perspective is all off. "The thing about 'fame' is that we are people who love to be loved by strangers," O'Brien says. "We can't get enough... You want more, more, more. The only number you have is 'more.'" This insatiable thirst for adoration becomes a void in which many celebrities find themselves lost, battling unhappiness.

In private, O'Brien frequently turned to alcohol to help fill this void, drinking up to 14 bottles of wine a day, just to cope. Despite this, he never considered himself an alcoholic, and no one else did either. To the public, O'Brien was at the top of his game with nothing to complain about. The reality, he says, was much much darker – because his ego ruled.

"[I was] full of myself... A lot of people are like that," he says. "But, thank God I figured it out. I'm so grateful for all that." Now, O'Brien tells Oprah, "I wake up every morning ... and I look in the mirror, and I say, 'I want to be the person that I want to be today. Not who they want me to be,'" he says, pointing at the camera. "I work for that every day."

What saddens me most about this mono-perspective we're slowly adopting, is that through the shiny materialistic lens it feeds us, we fail to see or celebrate the pieces of happiness right in front of us – the people like Rob and Cheryl – who embody everything that is good about this world. When we spend our time – partly because the media force it down our throat – but when we spend our time looking up at those like J.Lo, who are worth $400 million, we become trapped in that "more more more" spiral that O'Brien explains. When, on the other hand, we search out stories about normal, real-life, everyday people who are humble, generous and ego-free, we give ourselves a chance of finding what they have – which is peace and happiness. Many of the happiest people are not out there asking you to 'like' or 'follow' them, but that's exactly why you should seek them out, because they're not wanting to change you, other than by encouraging you to be more you. Even Rob and Cheryl's perspective on their faith – Christianity – is utterly free of self interest.

"To me, I would say the message of Jesus is about two things. The first is death to ego or self," says Cheryl, before Rob intervenes. "But this is not just a message Jesus brought, it is something all faith traditions discuss. It's a decision we all face," concludes Rob, before Cheryl continues. "We're each a unique person, and so the second part to what

I was saying is that Jesus showed us that the best thing we can be is *who we are*. The trouble is in accepting that, because mum, dad, big business, everybody wants us to be something, but it's a cycle that starts with us, because **if we accept ourselves and accept others, then perhaps they might accept us and others.**"

"I think that leads into the other thing at the heart of Christian belief," says Rob "which is the notion of forgiveness. Because you know, to get to a point where we might all love one another, we must first forgive. This is what we see at the heart of all conflict, an unwillingness to let go of pain."

When the couple's most trusted advisor – God, or the universe – killed their only unborn child, "that was tough," says Cheryl. "I remember when we lost our baby, when I miscarried, I had the clearest question in my quiet time (meditation). 'Are you prepared not to have children for me?', I heard that little voice asking. 'No', I replied. I struggled for weeks, and it was a very testing time, I was 37 and we'd been married for two years, so everything screamed at me to have children, but here was the universe denying me that. Why? Had I done something wrong?" asks Cheryl rhetorically.

"Some time later, unable to escape the pain circling my head, I eventually said 'yes, I am willing to go without children,'" recalls Cheryl. "I couldn't tell Rob at this point, it was too raw. It took me some time to get past that hurdle," says Cheryl, as the emotion of her words display across her face. "When we lost our baby," Rob says, with a similar trepidation in his voice, "I was yearning to be a father and to do the things fathers do. It was deep within me, that desire to be a dad. But we were unsuccessful. It was hard."

"If we'd have continued to look at our situation in that way, we'd have been miserable," continues Rob. "Thankfully, lifting our eyes let us meet a lot of people who'd been going through a similar experience. It wasn't going to undo anything, but it was quite comforting to know we were not alone. Because you can feel quite separate and abandoned by life or the universe in that kind of situation. So we were lucky."

In true Rob and Cheryl fashion, the pair decided to use the time that not having a baby allowed them, to travel to Cambodia and work in the displaced peoples' camps on the Thai border. At the time, 1989, the camps were filled with people who'd fled the Khmer Rouge regime – which had just fallen. Working with an international team of volunteers to empower locals with knowledge on democracy, overcoming trauma and establishing peace, Rob says they were met by the most unlikely of god's messengers. "Running a session on forgiveness, there was a young boy who came up to us at the end of the session saying he'd chosen to forgive. Thirith (the name of the young boy) had lost his entire family, and people had told him to seek revenge, but he refused. He said, 'if I don't let go there will be nobody left'. Then, as any child might, he said 'without family or parents I am afraid... would you be my parents?', he asked us out of the blue," recalls Rob. "We looked at each other and said, 'well we have no children, so we're happy to accept your request.'"

Thirith was just the beginning. Rob and Cheryl have become parents, mentors and friends to countless orphans and young people in need of friendship, love and guidance. Their 'hiccup' of not being able to have children of their own became – after sieving through the pain of it – a reason to open their hearts, doors and wallets (offering what little money they had) to countless children in need. I know this because Sash and I have become part of the Wood family. Their love and friendship has actually been a major component of what's let me be my happiest self in recent years. Because if there were two voices we all ought to follow, it would be Rob and Cheryl's.

"Seeing what we have, we constantly feel lucky," says Cheryl. "We have given up certain things others might prioritise – like a house, a regular wage or creature comforts – but we are content with what we have, and we are happy with what this gratitude lets us do. Because wanting less lets us give who we are to the world," she says. "We've also managed to build this wonderful community on the back of needing others," says Rob. "We've been working (mostly voluntarily) with Initiatives of Change for most of our lives, and we lived at Armagh (which was IofC's headquarters as well as a communal home), in Melbourne, for 27 years, mostly because we had no money for our own place. But that's also given us these priceless connections with thousands of people who have enriched our lives."

Rob and Cheryl's ability to filter out the happy specks from the overwhelming pile of rubble that's confronted them, is what gives the couple the deeply contented and generous attitude that defines them. From an alcoholic Aboriginal man who Rob joined in sobriety as a sign of support, to the countless young and often troubled refugees that the couple have mentored into community leaders, the Woods have quite literally made a life out of transforming darkness into light.

"In 1976 we were invited to take one of our theatre productions to the Chiefs of the Treaty First Nations in southern Alberta in Canada, to try to build some kind of relationship between their people and white society," says Rob. "We spent months creating spaces and a means through which both parties could enter into dialogue. None of our work is ever particularly easy, peace and trust takes time, because there's years or decades or even centuries of hostility and suffering to overcome. What the Native Americans taught me was not to give up, because just as my young Vietnamese friend had said all those years ago, caring or good intentions aren't going to change anything, only taking and maintaining action could do that. The Native American perspective was this: your walk talks and your talk walks, and your walk talks more than your talk walks. In other words, it's doing and people seeing you doing that's most important."

Maybe this is why Rob and Cheryl tend to remind me of two elderly superheroes. The type that despite a nasty fall (Cheryl) or being fitted with a pacemaker (Rob), remain as active and committed as ever. They'll pretend they're slowing down, to keep people like Sash and I quiet, but in reality, the couple are still sitting on numerous boards, advisory groups and continue to facilitate one, two, three or even ten day long workshops, as well as coaching and collaborating with countless organisations, governments bodies and communities themselves. I suppose it's as Rob so often says, "If not me, who? If not now, when?"

The two biggest nuggets of joy that I've sieved out and embedded into my perspective since meeting these two are – One: Do! I know it's short, but sometimes it's just that simple. **If you want something, or if you want to see something, then *do* something about it.** Two: Integrity (and happiness) are the result of practicing as you preach (something these two do in their sleep). What I've come to notice about integrity is that it's the missing piece of the puzzle. It's what our leaders (and many of us) *most* lack. This is why we see such bitter division and lack of trust, because without integrity – doing what you say you will – how can anyone believe anyone? It's little wonder we're in the mess we are. Although, as Rob and Cheryl remind me, "the world might have its issues, but it's still in a better place than it's ever been."

Something I know people have said about me, and which some may think of such a blatantly optimistic statement or perspective, is "how naive; how can you say or think the world is doing just fine, look at the war, the poverty, the segregation and the inequality." What people presume, and often argue fiercely, is that I (or people like Rob and Cheryl) must be wearing some sort of willfully ignorant, rose-tinted glasses. The truth is – as you might have noticed from all the horrendous stories and experiences I've encountered – I'm not. I'm just not willing to hold onto all the shit most people are – not unless it's going to do me some good. Not unless the injustices inspire me to act. Not unless the inequality motivates me to donate to charity or volunteer or choose what's right. What we can't and mustn't do is let life's struggles overwhelm us. **"We can't let the hurt harden us,"** says Rob.

"I can remember sitting around our kitchen table and my parents saying to me, 'well we've got what we need for the next meal, but the one after that is a mystery'. So yeah, there were tough times where we had very little," recalls Rob. "When I was 13 or so, I can remember my mother going to the fish shop and asking for the broken off-cuts that were typically put aside for the local cats. One day I heard the fishmonger ask my mum, 'is this for your pets?' My mum said 'no', and then explained that this was what we live on. Mum never complained. She always let us feel as though we were the lucky ones. Even when I was struggling at high school in Scotland, because I had an Australian accent and was bullied mercilessly for it – to the extent that I had no friends – mum was there. I remember when I stormed in the house and threw my school bag down defiantly one day, mum asked me what was wrong. When I told her, she said she felt angry. But rather than blow up and call the school or parents, mum decided this could be a chance to help me. So we sat together and she said let's have some quiet time. Let's take a moment or two to think about what we can do to resolve this. During our silence a thought came to me. There was one other child in my class who was like me – isolated – so the next day I went and made a friend of him. Things were totally different from then on. Not only was I no longer alone, but my mind had undergone a giant change in perspective – I had seen the power of silence and the voice that it lets us hear."

This practice of *looking in* before *acting out* is something that has let both Rob and Cheryl face down some enormous difficulties. From Rob deciding not lash out at his best mate who stole away his first love, to Cheryl, who was forced to watch on as the man she hoped to marry ended up in the arms of another woman, the pair said the ability to stop and seek inner guidance, as difficult as it may be, is what will guarantee you find *your* path. "Because even when our heart screams at us to get angry, or sad, or vengeful, we all have the capacity to stop it," says Cheryl. "It's hard, I know. My ego still gets the better of me at times, even after 71 years, but if we can get to a point of silence, then we will normally find the truth, which in the case of Rob and I, was that we were not meant to marry those other people we'd fallen for – because we were meant to find one another. We both knew that immediately. It's just our ego couldn't see what the universe did, and it never will, not unless we're silent and willing to listen for long enough to hear it."

Spending enough time looking and listening to ourselves, or God, or the universe, or whatever that voice is that speaks to us when we're silent – doing that lets us see our happiest perspective with at least some clarity (which is as good as you're going to get). That's because when we're quiet – and void off disturbing emotions – our heart, mind, soul/conscience are given the chance to sync up. It's like connecting your phone, laptop and work computer via the cloud. Only through that process can we rid ourselves of the anxiety, worry and internal bickering that eats away at our peace and happiness. **"One cannot be happy unless what they see and say and do are in unison,"** concludes Rob, before Cheryl ends our conversation with one final observation. "Our heart speaks to us when we are silent, and that's what the world needs, people led by heart."

Having now heard more about it, I wonder, would you choose their life over yours? Will you now choose action over inaction? Could you sacrifice for fulfilment? What is your perspective telling you? Is it crying out for some silence? Some time to sync up? If you don't stop, how will you know where to start? Will you start? Does your worldview cloud your dreams? Or does it let you see the light that's forever hiding above the clouds? Just yesterday I heard someone say, "just when the caterpillar thought the world was over, it became a butterfly." Darkness, if we see it as such, is an opportunity, a chance to let your light shine – because no matter who you are, we all have a special light to share – some just choose to live in the comfort of their cocoon.

The difficulty with seeing or admitting there is hope, is that it means you see the solution, and if you see the solution, that little voice inside you is probably screaming at you to be part of it. The problem is, being part of it means sacrifice. And ego hates sacrifice. It doesn't want you

Cheryl and Rob in front of their first home, which they were able to buy with the money they inherited when their parents passed.

Mohammed Ali.

Imran.

Nemad.

Speaking to the Bangladeshi man.

The man who said he is treated like a dog.

A rare smile as the camel comes to pose for the photo.

The harsh conditions are felt by all.

The son of the owner of the farm.

Like their animals, these men are caged in a situation they can't escape.

to help others at your expense. It doesn't care if you've seen sex slaves, starving kids or an innocent woman being thrown in the back of a van – it cares only for you (the survival of your DNA). One of the crazier stories to have taught me the terror and also the joy that goes hand-in-hand with sacrifice, occurred during a trip to the Middle East.

I was already in the car when he told me, "I'm a member of the Taliban."

I can't disclose where I was for security reasons, but I can tell you what I was doing – I was searching for *Bedouin* people – nomadic Arabs who historically lived in the desert, herding and living off livestock. My first day trying to find these wandering tribes didn't exactly go to plan. I ended up having lunch in a rug shop with a dozen men who told me they'd never heard of anyone living in the desert. The following day, I travelled to a more rural town and commissioned a guide, Nemad, who told me I might be able to find some Bedouin at the local camel/sheep/goat market. Dropping me by the side of the road and pointing at some men he felt I should speak to, I was met by further disappointment. "No, we are not Bedouin people," said Mohammed Ali. "I am from Pakistan, and they are from Afghanistan, and he is from Oman [he pointed to various friends]." "But they do work for the Bedouin tribes sometimes," Nemad translated an Afghan man Imran as saying. Wait, what!? I thought. How do you work for a nomadic tribe? "We go to the desert now, to try to find you your Bedouin people," said Nemad, before I had a chance to ask.

Several hours later, we pulled up in the middle of nowhere and Nemad said, "OK, we are here." Where, I felt like asking. All I could see was sand. "Over there, you see the fence, and those small bits of white cloth, that is a Bedouin camp," he smiled, glad to have fulfilled his end of the bargain. Exiting the car, it was as if a giant, blisteringly hot hair dryer scorched my entire body. Trying to readjust my eyes and focus on the distant signs of life was difficult. Anything exposed to the fiery air was immediately sapped of moisture, including my eyeballs. I was actually terrified that the 60 plus degrees Celsius heat would fry my camera, so I shielded it in an old cloth Nemad handed me.

Trekking through the desert as sweat gushed from me, it was impossible to imagine anything could live out here, let alone humans. As we approached a man whose eyes peered through a slit in a white cloth covering his neck, face and head, you got the impression that no one was particularly comfortable living out here. "This man is not Bedouin. He is from Bangladesh," said Nemad. Strange, I thought. Was anyone in this place Bedouin? Venturing from tent to tent, camel pen to camel pen, speaking to whom ever we could find, the simple answer was no!!! Bizarre as it sounds, these 'farm hands' were paid to live out the harsh, unforgiving lifestyle of Bedouin people – living in the desert with little access to water and food, attending to animals and sleeping in shanty tents – while their masters (who used to be Bedouin people) lived in luxury, courtesy of their oil-rich government.

When a brand new white Land Cruiser came flying over the sand dunes surrounding the camp, I freaked out. Technically, we were trespassing and we were very obviously distracting the workers. We'd also discovered a number of awful truths that the Bedouin businessmen in the car wouldn't want getting out. "We are treated like a dog, not a human," said one of the Pakistani workers. "We are here semi-illegally, because these locall men take our passports, so we are forced to work out here. We cannot escape to the city. Sometimes they do not pay us properly too, so it is hard," said one of the Bangladeshi workers. Carefully caressing the egos of the businessman and his sons who emerged from the car, by interviewing them and taking their photo, I was able to discover two things: one, there wasn't much money in having these guys mimic the harsh Bedouin lifestyle, and two, like a lot of Arab men, these guys held a perspective that they were superior to these migrant men, which made it OK to treat them like dirt (or sand as the case may be).

Making my way back to where I was staying, which was an eight hour car and bus ride, I sat there wondering why these former Bedouin people were paying migrants to live as they used to? Clearly there were easier ways or places to farm goats, camels and sheep? Without a logical answer to explain any of this, and with a resounding rage building in me at the lack of empathy or perspective that people in this place had, I just needed to get to my accommodation and lie down.

Standing in the still-sweltering late-night air for more than 45 minutes desperately trying to hail a taxi – only to have people push in front of me every time one stopped – I eventually gave up and began walking. With no idea where I was or where I was going, I'd barely crossed the street when a man in an 'uber-like' car pulled up and asked me if I needed a lift. "Sure!" I said.

Jumping in the car, I'd barely told him the address of my hostel, when he began asking where I was from and where I was going. I told him I was from Australia and was heading to Afghanistan the following day (to see Hakim).

"I'm a member of the Taliban," he said, as if it were like telling me he was an accountant. My muscles tightened as I planned my escape. "What!!!" I replied, as my brain reeled. "It's OK," he said, "I'm no killer [he smiled]. All males in my village are forced to join the Taliban once they are 16. Actually, I am still forced to go back and train with them for one month every year. Otherwise they will kill my family."

"The worst thing is, my boys are getting older and soon they will have to join too. It is my greatest fear – that they will become killers. Because you know, as soon as that happens, you are killing yourself. Your soul slowly dies."

As I asked him how he planned to stop his boys from becoming killers, I had no idea what I was about to hear, and for fifteen minutes I sat there with my mouth wide open…

"One day while I was out in the garden, I heard some cries from beyond our property," he said. "They got louder and more frequent, so I began searching for the source, only to find, hidden away under a bush, a US soldier with a severe bullet wound to his leg. He was shaking with fear as he begged, 'I have a family, I have a family, please don't kill me, I have children.'"

"What could I do? If I didn't kill him, I risked my family and I being killed too," my driver continued. "As I stood there listening to him pleading for his life, I knew what I must do [he breathed deeply]. See, I had always taught my boys that what's right isn't always what's easy, and no matter what, no one can make you do anything you don't want to do, not even the Taliban. So, I looked around to see if anyone had been listening, and quickly lifted the man over my shoulder and took him to the spare room in our house, where my wife attended to his wounds to try and stop the bleeding."

"I knew I may be risking a lot, but I was no killer, and I knew I would be killing much more than this man if I pulled the trigger. I needed to save my family the heartache of being a household of murderers. I had seen what war and fighting had done to human beings for decades, and decided to play my part in creating the peace we all longed for. For years I had also been trying to teach my boys that there is an alternative to the hate and vengeance that fuels war. So, while the decision to save this man put us all in danger, I knew that a new reality could only be forged by those brave enough to lead a life of compassion, love and understanding."

"Despite our best efforts to stop the bleeding, the man was dying. He pleaded with us to take him to a nearby US base. 'I'm dead if you don't', he said. 'Please, for my family', he begged. Regardless of the risks, I knew my children needed to see how human beings could and should behave, so I called a friend who had a car, and prayed we could trust him with our secret. We got the soldier into the back and drove him to the base, but just as we were approaching I stopped the car. 'What will they think of me, a member of the Taliban arriving with a wounded US soldier? They'll kill me', I said, 'I can't go on.'"

"He told me I would be safe, that 'the military and my family would be forever grateful. Trust me', he said. The idea of trust was something that could solve so many of the problems we faced, for with it we might begin talking about the issues we all face, rather than trying to solve everything with violence. Ultimately, I told myself that I needed to believe in the world that I wanted and so 'trust' was a given."

"Some weeks later we received a letter that the man had survived and would be headed home shortly to see his family," said my driver. I was speechless. "Wow!" I replied. "And what did this experience teach you about happiness?" I asked. "I guess it just shows that no matter what, we must live life by those rules that make us happy, because if we don't, we can't very well expect others to," he concluded.

It's confronting to think all of this is up to you – your life, your mind and your perspective – but there is no escaping it. If you ain't happy it's up to you to change it. If you are happy, it's up to you to maintain it. People like Rob, Cheryl, Pai Somang or that man in the Middle East may impact us, but not if we don't let them. Similarly, the rich and famous may dictate what we see, but not if we don't adopt or believe in it. We decide what we let in and what we let slide right through. You decide how you wake up. How you see your privilege. How you see those with nothing. You dictate whether you see tragedy as a blessing or a curse. You choose how or who or what you believe. You choose your lens, your perspective. So… are you grateful for what you are? What you have? What about what you're not? Because if you're not a slave, if you're not a brothel owner, or a child living in Tuvalu, if you're not the one in five suffering depression or anxiety, if you're not born into crippling disadvantage, if you're not living in China or on a garbage dump, if you're not a rape, abuse or domestic violence victim, if you're not grieving for your murdered mum or living in a war zone, if you're not fighting cancer or weren't hit by a car, **be happy**. Because what all the perspectives shared in this book should tell you is that unless you answered yes to two or more of these, there's someone doing it as tough or tougher than you.

If you haven't picked up what I'm saying, it's this. Stop, take a breath. Literally do it…

OK. Now, ask yourself if you're living your life to impress others or to impress yourself. What was Sugathapala's approach, you might recall? Then, with the humble vigour of a wolf stalking its prey, pursue that most profound of questions: why you are here? Think Hakim, Gill, Bek or Passenger. Next, quit looking up at those few who have more, and take into account those billions with less. If you need help, re-read Nat, Tom or Padhmini's story. Once you've learned to appreciate what you have, it's time to become a givington – just like Gran. Opening your arms (and your wallet) is a sure fire way to build community – without having to survive on a diet of cow's blood, milk and cornmeal – like the Maasai. Culturally and politically, think about what your actions, your words and your vote means – what do they say about you – do they reflect your inner hero? If the answer is no – if you believe in Jesus but vote for Rome – then change. And the same goes for religion: if those one, two or ten thousand year old words and beliefs aren't making you a more compassionate, loving and connected human being – if they're not getting rid of your ego, but just adding to it – then change. If others don't like it – if they spew out hate or crucify you for your choices – then be that brave, bold soul that stops the cycle of suffering by letting go, forgiving and doing what's right, like Aly or Evelyn. This is how we forge the foundations necessary for love – of self, of others and of that crazy special person that's just for you.

Then, and maybe this is why I've left it for last, it's about reconstructing our mind to accommodate our happiest self and world. But again, none of this is possible if we don't first choose to 'wake up, wake up, wake up!'

A little bit of TLC

I wish to acknowledge the incredible contribution so many people have made in bringing this book to life. From my working-editor Andrew Tobin, who massaged my mind and helped me sieve through the myriad of stories you've just read (as well as those that were left out). To my sister Bek, who was my second-editor and the first person to read the entire thing, thank you for your honesty, abundant intellect and the debates we had over content. To my wife, who encouraged me when the words wouldn't come, or when all I wanted was to give up, your love is everything to me. To all my family and friends, but especially my parents, who supported and guided me in life, writing and all the other crazy dreams I've had, I am the happy person I am because of you, and no words can express the deep love I feel for you. Finally, to those thousands of 'strangers' I've met along my journey whose stories and insights have made this book possible, your faces and friendship will never leave me.

www.ingramcontent.com/pod-product-compliance
Lightning Source LLC
Chambersburg PA
CBHW020312010526
44107CB00054B/1811